Caroline Walker Bynum is Professor of Medieval History at the Institute for Advanced Study in Princeton, New Jersey. A past president of both the American Historical Association and the Medieval Academy of America, she was a MacArthur Fellow from 1986 to 1991. She is the author of several books, including *Metamorphosis and Identity, The Resurrection of the Body in Western Christianity, 200–1336, Fragmentation and Redemption: Essays on Gender and the Human Body in Medieval Religion, Holy Feast and Holy Fast: The Religious Significance of Food to Medieval Women,* and *Jesus as Mother: Studies in the Spirituality of the High Middle Ages* and is the editor, with Paul Freedman, of *Last Things: Death and the Apocalypse in the Middle Ages,* also published by the University of Pennsylvania Press.

Wonderful Blood

Theology and Practice in Late Medieval Northern Germany and Beyond

Caroline Walker Bynum

PENN

University of Pennsylvania Press
Philadelphia

Printed in the United States of America on acid-free paper

10 9 8 7 6 5 4 3 2 1

Published by
University of Pennsylvania Press
Philadelphia, Pennsylvania 19104-4112

Library of Congress Cataloging-in-Publication Data

Bynum, Caroline Walker.
Wonderful blood : theology and practice in late medieval northern Germany and beyond / Caroline Walker Bynum.
p. cm.
ISBN-13: 978-0-8122-3985-0 (alk. paper)
ISBN-10: 0-8122-3985-7 (alk. paper)
Includes bibliographical references and index.
1. Blood—Religious aspects—Christianity. 2. Blood—Symbolic aspects. 3. Sacrifice—Christianity. 4. Germany—Church history. 5. Germany—Religious life and customs.
BR115.B57 B96 2007
274.3'05—dc22 *2006051487*

In Memoriam:

Claudia Rattazzi Papka

May 28, 1966–March 23, 2000

Contents

Illustrations

Map

Tables

"We are reconciled to God through the death of his Son" [Rom. 5.10]. Where is this reconciliation, this remission of sin? . . . In this chalice, [Christ] says, "of the blood of the New Testament, which is poured out for you" [Matt. 26.28; Luke 22.20]. . . . We obtain it by the interceding death of the only Begotten and are justified by grace in the same blood. . . . Why, you ask me, by blood when he could have done it by word. I ask the same question. It is given to me only to know that it is so, not why it is so.

—*Bernard of Clairvaux,* Letter 190

[S]acrifice deals with the riddle of life and death, which are intimately linked and at the same time each other's absolute denial. The riddle cannot be resolved, it can only be reenacted.

—*J. C. Heesterman,* The Broken World of Sacrifice

Preface

This book uses a particular phenomenon in fifteenth-century northern Germany to enter into the religious world of the later Middle Ages without being primarily a study of that phenomenon. Moving from a specific pilgrimage site to competing cults in an obscure region of Europe, the account then turns to the controversies such cults engendered and the context of those controversies in certain basic patterns of late medieval piety and theology. This combination of specific and general owes something to its author's personal history but much as well to the historiographical moment. My decision to write about the blood obsession in late medieval Christianity in a way that moves from the local to the European, from specific sites and abstruse theological debates to themes that echo so widely as to seem obvious and banal, reflects a particular moment in the discipline of religious history.

When I first began to study what was then called "intellectual history" or "the history of Christian thought" in the late 1950s, the medieval master narrative was neo-Thomist, at least insofar as neo-Thomism still set the agenda for even those who reacted against it. It is hard to imagine now how heady was the excitement of American graduate students who discovered, in the work of M.-D. Chenu in the 1960s, a twelfth- and thirteenth-century "counterculture" of Waldensians, Dominicans, and Franciscans—a movement in which ideals of service, freedom, reform, and rejection of establishment values actually seemed to change the course of events (as we ourselves aspired to do). To study Christianity was now to study spirituality—lived religion—but religion shaped by ideas as well as by social forces. When Thomas Aquinas wrote "gratia non tollit naturam sed perficit," he described (so Chenu told us) not only an intellectual program for interpreting nature and scripture but also a religious concern for improving society that impregnated every aspect of human experience. We moved from studying theology to studying piety, from monastic orders to dissident groups and women mystics, without jettisoning a no doubt naïve confidence that we could ferret out mentalités, assumptions, that bound it all together. To study the past was to study people not ideas, but ideas still mattered; they could change the world.

As what came to be called simply "theory" triumphed in the 1980s and early 1990s, it became harder to see such broad patterns and structures. We learned to question terms such as "experience" and "meaning." Having only "texts," not the "intentions" or even the "voices" of the authors behind them, historians of religion began to focus on conventions of genre that constructed "author positions" or on the reception of texts, or they moved, as did many anthropologists, to studying themselves doing the studying. So-called master narratives crumbled. Nonetheless, even as everything came to be true only from a particular point of view or perspective, postcolonial and feminist historians moved increasingly to view things through, if not master narratives, at least master lenses, convinced that certain patterns of dominant and marginalized explained a wide diversity of human action. The resisting and the peripheral, like the monstrous and the grotesque, moved center stage. Whereas medievalists of the 1960s and early 1970s had loved the "long" twelfth century (they sometimes extended it to 1270) with its supposed optimism, corporatism, and interiority, historians of the later 1980s and 1990s turned with equal commitment to charting the failures and fragmentations of the fourteenth century and incidentally to reinterpreting, in a far darker vein, the twelfth. Just as the twelfth century of the 1960s seemed to call for a new master narrative, so the fourteenth century of the 1990s confirmed the hunch that the real view was from the margins, that the larger picture was one of parts not whole.

Why all this should lead me to the long fifteenth century (1370s to 1520s) I am not quite sure, but I am certain that it explains the shape of this book: its simultaneous commitment both to specificity of starting point and to broad sweep. For I am not able to jettison either a 1990s sense that there are only particular stories and voices nor my 1960s conviction that somehow, behind it all, lie common assumptions. The roots of such contradictory commitments are no doubt too deeply hidden for analysis (or, at the very least, an inappropriate subject for all but the most intrepid and self-absorbed scholar). But in the case of this book they are also to some extent empirically based. Once I began to think about the prevalence of blood in late medieval piety, I came quickly to see both that it was a common obsession (there *had* to be basic structures and assumptions behind patterns so widespread) and that what pilgrims were doing and poets were saying was a good deal more fraught, more convoluted, and more regionally specific than the secondary literature indicated. The standard descriptions of blood devotions—blood as eucharist, blood as love, blood as pollution—did not seem to capture the complexity of the texts, where so much was present in the interstices and silences or implied in obscure biblical allusions and echoes; the standard interpretations of blood pilgrimage—cult as escape valve for violent impulses or as instrument of clerical control—did not explain why such an odd collection of objects (bread, earth, wood, and so forth) came to be seen by clergy and laity alike as "blood." I could not, I found, discard my sense that I needed to study what people were doing in specific places and saying in specific texts, but I also could not escape my hunch that behind those battles, prayers, and practices some common assumptions lurked—assumptions that had something to do with the emphasis on blood as drops and globules, shed and separated bits, as well as with an insistence on the redness, liquidness, the being-alive-ness, of that which was poured forth in death.

The reasons why my study moves from local to European and encompasses both regional praxis and abstruse university debates are not purely personal, however, nor are they stimulated only by the data of my research. They rest in a conviction that much recent work on praxis, piety, and theology has, exactly because it has separated them from each other, either lapsed into mere description of their content and reception or tended to reduce them to social or economic mechanisms: tools of elites or instruments of popular resistance. But if we are to understand why themes such as bleeding become prominent at a particular moment in the history of a religion, we must (the point is an obvious one!) look at the whole of that religion: pious prayers and practices, local shrines, artistic commissions, theological debates, accounts of visions and miracles, ecclesiastical politics, and the context of all this in regional and national strife. Moreover, we must examine that whole for the basic, often implicit, human concerns that lie behind it. But we must also remain aware that such concerns, exactly because basic and implicit, will appear different from every particular vantage point. It is only by paying close attention to the radical oddness of specific practices and objects that we will avoid such generalizing and merely descriptive categories as "affective" or "expressionist" and penetrate instead to the anxieties and hopes evoked by specific cult sites and theological disputes. To give an example from what follows: we will not understand the spiritual theme of counting blood drops if we reduce it only to a late medieval enthusiasm for quantification in science, religion, and economic life, although the enthusiasm is a factor. The obsession with drops has something to do with the contested presence of bits of Christ in particular monasteries and pilgrimage sites, with the fierce debates of theologians about not just the devotional but also the ontological value of specific particles, and with the commissioning of individual Christ sculptures on which discrete globs or bloody bits stimulated a meditation that moved the adherent slowly into the interior of God. Nor will we understand the links between these phenomena, from economic, scientific, and artistic to devotional and theological, unless we recognize that a basic, yet historically contingent and specific, grappling with the riddle of life and death—that is, of change and survival—lies behind.

The book that follows begins with the cult of Wilsnack in the fifteenth century—a phenomenon well known to German medievalists but little studied in the Anglophone world—and then moves, in chronologically and geographically ever widening circles, through other blood cults in northern Germany, to theological disputes over the presence of blood, and finally to the broad themes of northern European devotion in the fourteenth and fifteenth centuries. I begin with Wilsnack not only because it was the most popular blood cult in late medieval Europe but also because it was unique among cult sites in generating theological tractates, devotional texts, and objects such as pilgrim badges in such great numbers. I move then to a detailed study of its regional context both because cult sites cannot be understood without attention to their individual characteristics and because the north of Germany has been neglected in favor of Bavaria in studies of pilgrimage and devotion. But before I turn, in Chapter 2, to my real starting point, I provide a general description of late medieval blood piety, a topic to which I return much later in the book. My purpose at the beginning is only to give a sense of what historians often tell us about blood in medieval Christianity and to indicate certain usual and seemingly obvious interpretive moves I am not going to make. Although I come, by Parts III and IV, to a spirituality and theology characteristic of much of fifteenth-century Europe, I try always to anchor what I discuss to particular characteristics of cults in Mecklenburg and Brandenburg and the disputes surrounding them, while probing for basic spiritual concerns and anxieties. For my purpose is not to explain the specific by the general nor to use the specific to illustrate the general, but rather to find, in discrete events and texts, deep human concerns that are historically particular as well.

This book is dedicated to the memory of Claudia Rattazzi Papka (May 28, 1966–March 23, 2000), student, colleague, and friend. More than anyone I have ever known, Claudia gave me hope that the things I value most about learning—clarity of prose, love of literature, integrity of scholarship, and dedication to giving past voices another chance—would continue into succeeding generations. It would therefore not be right to omit from a dedication to her those who carry her values and gifts into the future now that she cannot. Thus I include her mother Serena and her daughter Sophia in my dedication to her. I also express here my confidence that all my students will carry forward in their own work the clarity, passion, and integrity of mind and spirit Claudia embodied, and I offer them all my gratitude.

Some Notes on Usage

I have retained original spellings in Latin and vernacular quotations. All translations are my own unless otherwise indicated.

I have anglicized personal names, unless the Latin or German forms are so well known as to be expected. There is a certain amount of arbitrariness in such decisions, and no one (including the author who makes them) is ever completely satisfied with the results.

The map on p. 46 is intended only to show the modern locations (insofar as is possible) of places discussed in the text and is not intended to claim historicity for events attributed to those places. I have anglicized place names.

All English translations of the Bible are from the Douai translation. When medieval authors misquote or alter passages, I have not regularized their quotations.

Chapter 1

Introduction: A Frenzy for Blood

The Emergence of Blood Piety

Crucifixion is not a bloody death. As inhabitants of the ancient world knew well, the crucified die by suffocation.[1] However painful his execution, it is unlikely that Jesus of Nazareth died from blood loss. The synoptic gospels mention literal bleeding only in connection with Christ's sweating on the Mount of Olives (Luke 22.43–44),[2] and even this reference to bloody sweat is missing in some early manuscripts.[3] Only the gospel of John mentions the piercing of Jesus' side with a lance and the subsequent outflow of blood and water; and John makes it clear that the wound came only when Jesus was already dead (John 19.34).[4] The earliest association of Christ's death with bloodshed came through its assimilation to Hebrew ideas of covenant and Temple sacrifice (Heb. 7.27; 9; 10.10–12; I Pet. 1.2, 19; cf. Ex. 24.8).[5] The Last Supper and the martyrdom of Christ's followers were soon also assimilated to sacrifice.[6] But of the early accounts of a shared meal after the resurrection, two (Luke 24.35 and Acts 2.42) mention only bread. And despite Tertullian's famous claim that the blood of Christians is the seed from which faith grows, early martyr stories seem, as a number of scholars have noted, to occlude bloodshed and pain, stressing the repeated failure of attempts at execution and sometimes even substituting milkflow for blood in accounts of the final beheading.[7] Once monasticism (*martyrium sine cruore*, as Sulpicius Severus labeled it)[8] replaced martyrdom, the self-inflicted austerities of ascetics (fasting, social isolation, awkward prayer positions, etc.) were neither bloody in fact nor represented as attack on or penetration of the body. Although Jerome (d. 420) suggested that all Christ's blood was drained in the passion and referred to the column of flagellation "dyed with the blood [*cruore*] of the Lord," hence adumbrating the cult of blood relics,[9] it would be several hundred years before blood as object was revered in western Europe[10] and hundreds more before the bloodbath from an exsanguinated Christ moved to the center of European piety.

Yet by the later Middle Ages northern European devotional art and poetry seem awash in blood. The popular fourteenth-century Middle English treatise *A Talkyng of þe Loue of God* explained, in homey and erotic images inconceivable in patristic texts:

When in my soul with a perfect intention [*wiþ al hol muynde*] I see You so piteously hanging on the cross, Your body all covered with blood, Your limbs wrenched asunder . . . then I readily feel a marvelous taste of your precious love . . . which so fills my heart that it makes me think of all worldly woe sweet like honey, wheresoever I go. . . . Where is there any bliss, compared with the taste of Your love at Your own coming, when Your own mother, so fair of face, offers me Your own body on the cross. . . . Then the love begins to well up in my heart. . . . I leap at Him swiftly as a greyhound at a hart, quite beside myself, in loving manner, and fold in my arms the cross. . . . I suck the blood from his feet. . . . I embrace and I kiss, as if I was mad. I roll and suck I do not know how long. And when I am sated, I want yet more. Then I feel that blood in my imagination [*in þouȝt of my Mynde*] as it were bodily warm on my lips and the flesh on his feet in front and behind so soft and so sweet to kiss.[11]

With elaborate puns and conceits, devotional writers packed much biblical and theological learning into meditation on blood. Playing with the opposites "soft" and "hard," "stinking" and "sweet," "staining" and "cleansing," Richard Rolle (d. 1349), for example, prayed to rest "among the dead that lie stinking foully" yet are "softened in that sweet bath" that washes even while it "makes bloody my soul."[12] A well-known nineteenth-century manual of Carthusian devotions by Dom Cyprien-Marie Boutrais, compiled from late medieval material and often reprinted, provides many examples of fourteenth- and fifteenth-century meditations on blood, living and shed.[13] In a prayer for the fourth day of the month of the Sacred Heart, James of Jüterbog or Klusa (d. 1465), a Cistercian abbot who was later vicar of the Carthusians in Erfurt and an active contributor to the Wilsnack controversy of the 1450s, enumerates the reasons, both theological and devotional, for a wound inflicted after death:

. . . there was good reason for this Wound, for from the Side of Jesus the Sacraments receive their efficacy; and from the Side of Jesus, sleeping in death on the Cross, the Church was formed, as Eve had been formed from Adam's rib. . . . before his death Jesus knew that, after death, He would receive this Wound, and . . . this knowledge made Him suffer . . . keenly in anticipation. . . . Did not the thought alone of the sufferings of his Passion cause him such bitter grief in the Garden of Olives that He shed a sweat of blood?

. . . Let us look at His Side, pierced and open for us, and suddenly the fire of love will be kindled again in our soul. . . . Let us contemplate the Feet of Jesus, pierced with nails and bathed in blood. . . .

For this reason the Holy Ghost says to us in the Canticle: "Come, o my dove, into the clefts of the rock" [Cant. 1.13–14], come into the Wounds of Jesus Christ. . . .

Let us mark the threshold and the posts of the door with the Blood of the true Paschal Lamb, and the destroying Angel, seeing this Divine Blood, will not strike us.[14]

In a prayer attributed by Richstätter to James's contemporary Dionysius the Carthusian (d. 1471), blood becomes not only the birth, bath, refuge, and sacrifice offered by God for the soul but also one's very self, poured back into God:

Oh my Lord and my God, it gives me pain to have grieved thee. . . . give me the grace that my heart may be grasped by this and that I may spend the remainder of my life ruing my ingratitude. Why then can my love and my pain not pour out into thy most holy heart all the drops of my blood so that I may offer them up to you with my tears?[15]

By the late fourteenth century, devotions to the five wounds, to the side wound, and to the wounded heart were proliferating; the faithful were urged to count Christ's lesions and the number of blood drops he shed, using such numbers to calculate the prayers they owed for their own sins or those of their loved ones suffering in purgatory (see Plate 32).[16] A fifteenth-century devotion found in British Library Lansdowne MS 379, for example, urges Christians to say one hundred Pater Nosters for each of Christ's seven bleedings, one for each day of the week, and exhorts for Monday, on which the bloody sweat of the Mount of Olives is to be venerated,

thinke as yf thou woldest kenele / downe beside hym looking on his / blessed visage so fulle of hevy-ness / and begynne and say thy hundred / pater noster in the worsship of all / the dropes of bloode that he shedde / at this tyme whan he swette blood. . . . And thynk vtterly that yf all the paynes / and deseases of dethe and of other tormentes / that haue be or shalbe in Resonable crea / tures fro the tyme of Adam in to the / tyme of Antecryst yf alle the paynes / and deseases aforsaid were in oon creature / hit were but a poynte of payne or desease / in compareson of the payne and desease of / that our blessed lorde Ihesu Crist suffred in [his] precyous worthy body for oure loue.[17]

Nor was blood imagery only textual and literary; blood erupted in iconography and vision as well.[18] The so-called *imago pietatis* or Man of Sorrows, first represented as an apparently dead figure upright in his tomb peacefully displaying wounded hands and side, became increasingly a bold and living man, spouting cascades of blood.[19] In devotional images such as those of Mary (or God the Father or the entire Trinity) displaying the wounded body from the cross, as in narrative paintings of the flagellation or crucifixion, blood streamed ever more effusively, and wounds appeared all over Christ's body, often bubbling forth great bands or globules of blood that art historians frequently analogize to ribbons, bunches of grapes, or roses[20] (see frontispiece and Plates 11, 13–24). The visions that proliferated in Europe during the thirteenth to fifteenth centuries became increasingly bloody. Usually in the thirteenth century comforting appearances of a beautiful baby accompanied by sweet smells and sounds, by the fifteenth century they were often sinister and macabre.[21] Colette of Corbie (d. 1447), to whom Christ appeared as chopped meat on a platter, was warned that "the offenses people do against him . . . tear him into smaller pieces than the flesh cut up on this plate."[22] John Mirk in his *Festial* for preachers (ca. 1400) reported that a sick man who refused to confess cried out "I am damned" when Christ appeared, his wounds all red, and cast a great handful of blood from his side into the sinner's face.[23] Such intense visualizations of blood were also enacted in rituals and in bodies. Christ figures used in the liturgy to perform the events of Passion Week were sometimes outfitted with bladders of animal blood that could be punctured at appropriate moments to display Jesus' bleeding before the faithful;[24] cruets for eucharistic wine survive in the form of Christ images with spouts where the wounds occurred.[25] From the thirteenth century on, bands of flagellants roamed Europe, tearing out of their own flesh the suffering and joy of union with Christ. In the fifteenth century they were particularly active and particularly feared in Thuringia.[26] Among the Dominicans, self-beating or "taking the discipline" was a regular ascetic practice, and holy women in the later Middle Ages were admired for pious bleeding *in imitatio Christi*, both miraculous and self-induced.

Although in the thirteenth and fourteenth centuries eucharistic celebration focused increasingly on the elevation of the host, and ocular or spiritual communion (viewing) often substituted for sacramental reception (eating), frenzy for blood continually threatened to break out.[27] Mystics (especially women mystics) who were denied access to the cup at mass repeatedly experienced both the flooding of ecstasy through their limbs and the taste of the wafer in their mouths as blood.[28] Beatrice of Nazareth (d. 1268) was described by her hagiographer as inundated with Christ's blood when she received "the sacrament of the body of the Lord [*sacramentum dominici corporis*]":

> It seemed to her that all the blood which flowed from his wounds was poured into her soul, and that all the drops of that precious liquid were so sprinkled on it that it was wholly washed by these drops and most perfectly cleansed from all the dust of sin.[29]

Catherine of Siena (d. 1380) found blood in her mouth or spilling from it, although what she received was the host.[30] The priest John of Alverna (d. 1322), while celebrating, saw the crucified Christ bleeding into a chalice; when the apparition faded it was replaced by the form of bread.[31] A nun of Unterlinden, upon receiving the wafer,

> totally dissolved in the love of her beloved [and] suddenly, in a miraculous manner, perceived distinctly that the blood of our Lord Jesus Christ, whom she had received, flowed down like an impetuous rushing river through all parts of her body, reaching the most intimate parts of her soul.[32]

Complex though such perceptions of bread as blood may be, these particular eucharistic visions were not so much revelations to doubters, or rewards for those who never doubted, as substitutions of the withheld blood for the proffered bread.

The arguments of theologians and canonists that by concomitance both body and blood are present in each species often failed to convince the faithful. Demands for the chalice led to the distribution of various nonconsecrated cups (the ablutions cup, a chalice filled with wine that had been poured over blood relics, etc.) after or outside mass, perhaps without full disclosure as to what *sanguis Christi* they did nor did not contain.[33] Fifteenth-century dissident groups such as the Bohemian Hussites or Utraquists demanded access to the cup at mass. Not only did the lay chalice become their symbol of nationalist, anti-German, and anticlerical enthusiasm; those such as the Italian John of Capistrano who opposed the Hussite demand understood—as modern scholars sometimes have not—how central blood was to the claim.[34]

Pilgrimages proliferated to places (such as Wilsnack, Daroca, Walldürn) where hosts supposedly bled or chalices turned to blood; older cult sites that claimed relics of Christ's blood from the Holy Land (such as Bruges, Schwerin, and Weingarten) bloomed anew. So important was blood that the people and their priests labeled as *sanguis* an astonishing number of quite disparate forms of holy matter—bread, earth, wood, and cloth. In Hungary, for example, a supposed piece of the *sudarium* was revered as *sanguis Christi*.[35] Tales of wonder-working blood were sometimes attached to holy sites when the original events had been long forgotten.[36] A charge regularly leveled by theologians against such cults was that the faithful, in clamoring for them, misunderstood them as bloods superior to the blood of the eucharist; preachers and theologians who supported the cults argued that they only increased eucharistic fervor, being in fact a form of ocular communion. But whether they supported or combated the numerous blood pilgrimages of the fifteenth century, ecclesiastical authorities remarked on the prominence of blood in their advertisements and appeal.

Blood in the Fifteenth-Century North

This great welling up of blood piety was, at least in its most expressionist form, a northern European phenomenon. Two of its most sophisticated and fervent proponents were the Italian theologians Catherine of Siena and Catherine of Genoa (d. 1510), but a great swell of wound and blood poetry came from England, Germany, and the Low Countries as well. Moreover, the majority of blood pilgrimages and host miracles were German. Host-desecration libels were predominantly German, too, and anti-Jewish violence was worse in the north of Europe. The "brutal realism" and expressionism of northern art with its twisted bodies, bulging veins, and streams of gore is unmatched by the gentler suffering in images from the south.[37] Contemporaries themselves commented on this. For example, the secretary to a Roman cardinal who, in 1517, went with his employer north through Germany, France, and the Low Countries noticed a difference upon crossing the Alps. Not only were the representations of Christ dead between thieves larger than those to which he was accustomed, their impact was different. They were, he said, injured bodies, "fashioned to arouse not just devotion but terror as well." As Hans Belting has emphasized, the ubiquitous European image of the Man of Sorrows was more pitiful and corpselike in the south; in the north it was livelier and bloodier, demanding dialogue with the devout.[38]

Geographically, then, blood devotion was especially (although not by any means exclusively) northern.[39] Chronologically, as the above survey makes clear, it was characteristic of the fourteenth and fifteenth centuries.[40] The first anti-Jewish host-desecration libel was at Paris in 1290, and some fifteenth- and sixteenth-century accounts of bleeding hosts claim to tell stories from the thirteenth century.[41] But, as Peter Browe established long ago, host miracles changed from the thirteenth-century version, in which unusual phenomena (sometimes the figure of Christ himself, sometimes lights or sweet smells) appeared and then disappeared in the wafer, to a later fourteenth- and fifteenth-century version, in which the transformation lasts and is more and more frequently tortured flesh and blood.[42] Visionary experiences became more bloody, terrifying, and accusatory. Whereas the central liquids in thirteenth-century visions (even of wounds and hearts) are water, honey, and milk, the liquid in fourteenth- and fifteenth-century visions is blood, ever more copiously pooling or shed. Many of the iconographic themes associated with blood veneration are late fourteenth- and fifteenth-century creations: the dead or bleeding Man of Sorrows; the instruments of Christ's passion (*arma Christi*); the wounds of Christ or his separated body parts; the mass of St. Gregory; the figure of the dead Christ on his mother's lap (the pietà or Vesperbild), especially the version in which the body is covered with blood; crucifixions in which angels catch streams or drops, shed from all five of Christ's wounds (see Plates 2, 3, 5, 11, 13–25, 26–31). In the regions of Brandenburg and Mecklenburg I shall take as case studies, the construction of blood legends (whether miraculous appearances, host desecrations, or relic acquisitions) tends to occur in the later fourteenth or fifteenth centuries, regardless of whether an earlier historical event provides the kernel around which they were built. The great debates about the authenticity of blood relics and host miracles, as about the status of Christ's blood during the *triduum mortis* (the three days between Christ's crucifixion and resurrection) and hence about its appropriate veneration, occur in the later fourteenth and fifteenth centuries.

Certain developments in the European north that provided context and support for this blood obsession are specific to the long fifteenth century. Universities (and hence homegrown theological debate) came to Germany and eastern Europe only in the mid-fourteenth century; those especially involved in debates over the Wilsnack blood cult (Prague, Erfurt, and Leipzig) were founded only in the last quarter of the fourteenth or the early fifteenth century. Concern that pilgrimages, relics, and miracles might be fraudulent was triggered by reforming movements, such as the Franciscan Observants or the Bursfeld Benedictine reform, that spread widely in fifteenth-century Germany.[43] Regional and national tensions contributed as well. Suspicion of Wilsnack was stimulated from the beginning by Czech opposition to German pilgrimage sites. Representatives from Magdeburg to the Councils of Constance (1414–18) and Basel (1431–45) felt honor-bound to squelch rumors circulating there about dubious miracles at a site in their archdiocese. And two of the dissident or heretical groups about which theologians and pastors in the north of Germany worried were fifteenth-century movements in which blood played a prominent role: the cryptoflagellants of Thuringia and the Utraquists of Bohemia.[44]

I shall argue in what follows that blood debates and blood piety summed up peculiarly fifteenth-century anxieties. For behind debates over pilgrimage, relics, eucharist, miracles, and veneration, as behind a piety to which streams or drops of blood were central, lay two closely connected issues: the issue of holy matter, and the issue of access to God or, to put it another way, of God's absence and presence. How—if matter signifies change and change signifies decay—can God inhere in matter? Yet an incarnate God must so inhere. How—if Christ has gone away in resurrection and ascension—do Christians find him present here on earth? Yet without some presence, some access, there is no point to devotion.

These were issues raised not solely in blood piety. Questions about approach to God and matter's role in it, about Christ's simultaneous presence and absence, continued to be debated in the hundreds of pages penned by theologians on the eucharistic real presence, while new discussion emerged about the value of, respectively, access through eating (sacramental reception) and access through seeing (ocular or spiritual communion).[45] Popes repeatedly gave indulgences to objects questioned by university theologians and by their own legates. Reformers clashed again and again over relics and miracle stories; such clashes focused not merely on the dubious authenticity of specific objects but also on questions about the status of such supposed miracles as access to God.

Access became problematic in other ways. Visionary experiences proliferated in the fourteenth and fifteenth centuries as spiritual advisers taught ever more sophisticated techniques of meditation and visualization. To minds trained in meditation, the line between events of the mundane world and their deeper spiritual significance became thin; the visionary Margery Kempe (d. after 1438), for example, saw the flagellation of Christ when she observed a man or even a horse being beaten in the streets.[46] Confessors and spiritual directors encouraged such visualizing.[47] But visions, especially the visions of women, were ever more frequently tested, suspected of being demonic, or condemned as witchcraft or heresy.[48] Joan of Arc (d. 1431) was not the first charismatic woman to be adulated—or executed. Although the writings of female visionaries such as Mechtild of Magdeburg (d. 1282?) spread in the fifteenth century (especially in compilations made by male advisers and carefully arranged or excerpted to control extravagance of asceticism or devotion), the penning of new vision collections and convent chronicles by women that was such a distinctive literary activity in the fourteenth century disappeared by the mid-fifteenth.[49] Moreover, visual material—from the grand winged altarpieces of fifteenth-century northern Germany to tiny prayer cards, devotional pamphlets, and broadsides—proliferated. Indeed, iconography began in sophisticated ways to explore vision and visuality.[50] But theologians continued to warn that God was best approached without images, that material objects—whether relics and reliquaries, altarpieces and statues, or mental images mirroring the material world—were only signs pointing to a God beyond them. They all too easily became idols.[51] Images and imaginings—although more and more common—became more and more dangerous as well.

None of this is to say that skepticism, doubt, or anxiety per se was especially characteristic of the long fifteenth century. Given the nature of the evidence, it would be hard to know.[52] But it is to suggest that the blood piety and theology I explore here summed up some particularly fifteenth-century concerns in some particularly fifteenth-century ways.

Understanding the roots and significances of the religious obsession with blood can be achieved, then, only through attention to precisely where (geographically, chronologically, iconographically, and textually) blood bubbles up. I shall argue below that blood is the specific religious concern in a number of regional and philological contexts scholars have tended to study only apart from each other. But I shall also argue that interpretations of late medieval spirituality need to disaggregate phenomena often telescoped under terms such as "affective," "devotional," "expressionist," or "violent." Blood as theme links many things we have not usually linked, but we need to look at specific texts and contexts in order to understand what precisely it symbolizes or evokes.

Some Recent Approaches

As a general phenomenon, the blood piety of late medieval northern Europe is well known. For decades literary scholars have described themes of blood, wound, and heart in the religious poetry of late medieval England,[53] and recent interest in the body has brought in its wake much study of blood by historians of science and medicine as well as of art and devotion.[54] Students of anti-Semitism have examined blood libels;[55] scholarship on relic cult has explored blood relics;[56] surveys of eucharistic devotion have treated bleeding hosts, although more as *corpus* than as *sanguis*;[57] interpretive works on the humanism, individualism, interiority, and affectivity of late medieval spirituality have assimilated bleeding to suffering, whether sordid or sentimentalized;[58] feminist scholarship has connected blood obsession with increasing misogyny and fear of a polluting and female other;[59] emphasis on the expressionism and brutality of iconography has located blood in the context of public executions, torture, scapegoating, and persecution.[60] As in the texts and images, so in contemporary scholarship, blood bubbles up everywhere. Yet much of this work has assimilated blood piety to other topics without locating it in its immediate context of theology and praxis or paying close attention to what the texts, in their specificity of noun and verb, actually say. Blood piety becomes merely an aspect—and a secondary one at that—of a new emphasis on the transubstantiated host or the humanity of Christ. In its interiority, it supposedly foreshadows the Reformation rejection of externals and works, while its tendency to quantify and enumerate drops and wounds is seen as participating in exactly the mechanistic piety against which the reformers supposedly reacted.[61] Its violence is understood to reflect and construct the pogroms and persecutions in which a fourteenth- and fifteenth-century public delighted, to express a virulent misogyny in which female blood spilled from natural orifices is seen as polluting, and to project onto Jews a generalized fear of "the other" and a highly personal guilt at sin and unbelief.[62]

Three emphases in particular form the current scholarly context: the assumption (especially prominent among art historians and literary scholars) that blood signifies eucharist; the assumption (especially prominent among historians) that blood signifies violence; and the assumption (found especially in feminist work and in studies influenced by anthropology) that blood reflects structural dichotomies such as male/female, outside/inside, cultural/natural, purifying/polluting, good/bad. Each of these has obscured as much as illuminated the specific characteristics of fourteenth- and fifteenth-century Christianity.

The eucharist has been much emphasized in recent study of the religion of the later Middle Ages—the eucharist as corporate symbol, as instrument of clerical "management,"[63] as reflection of the much touted "visuality" of late medieval culture. And it is, of course, true that *corpus Christi* as feast and as holy object united and divided medieval society, expressed and constructed its corporate boundaries, and defined Jews and heretics as outsiders.[64] Moreover, the "desire to see the host" (as a famous study puts it) is an expression of the visual piety (*Schaufrömmigkeit)* of the fifteenth century.[65] Although many resisted the development, ocular communion (*Augenkommunion*) often replaced reception. The question of what one sees, of how one penetrates through the host to a God both present and absent, was an important theme of iconography as well as devotion.[66] And, as we shall see, important developments in eucharistic theology were drawn on in the controversies over, and the competition among, blood-relic cults and cults of the bleeding host.

But recent work on the eucharist has obscured much about blood piety, first, by its tendency to concentrate on the host (that is, on body), treating body and blood as symmetrical, and second, by treating all blood references, iconographical and textual, as eucharistic.[67] Even where eucharistic, however, references to blood have a very different valence from references to body. Body tends to signify community, inclusion, gathering in. Indeed even wound imagery in some sense evokes body more than blood; as the texts cited above demonstrate, wounds are access to home, community, refuge, safety.[68] Meditating on the crucifix, the twelfth-century devotional writer Aelred of Rievaulx stressed body as food and enclosure, but blood as that which exited, drop by drop by bloody drop.[69] More than a century later, the Dominican Gerhard of Cologne defended the blood relic of Weingarten in verbs that stressed not entry but outflow, as that which cleansed, fertilized, intoxicated: blood rained, dropped, gushed, poured.[70] When George Cartar, a thresher from Sawtry examined for heresy in 1525, saw a vision of the wafer with a rim or band around it to hold in the blood, he expressed graphically what lurks behind many a pious text: the profound asymmetry between, on the one hand, body as nourishment and container, unity and community, and on the other, blood as liquid and outflow, inebriation and washing, violation and reproach.[71]

A comparison of differing versions of that exceedingly complex iconographical motif of the Gregorymass (popular primarily in the fifteenth- and early sixteenth-century European north) makes the asymmetry clear.[72] In two north German paintings less than twenty-five years apart and exactly analogous in function (both are outer panels of winged altarpieces), the pope's vision of the Man of Sorrows involves the viewer in almost contradictory ways; the difference evokes visually what verb choice suggests in the texts. In the 1496 panel from Lübeck (see Plate 2), the pope raises high before the Man of Sorrows (depicted as a painted altarpiece rather than an apparition) a round white host, whose curves are echoed both above and below by the shoulders and buttocks of small naked figures (the poor souls in purgatory) lifted by angels toward heaven. Through Christ's body, subsumed in the host, the faithful rise to glory, as the viewer's eye is swept inexorably inward and upward, first toward host, then toward heaven.[73] In the 1473 version from St. Maria zur Wiese in Soest (see Plate 3), the Christ figure is less a painted panel than an animated figure who has just alighted before the pope.[74] The paten is empty; there is no host on the altar linen. Before an astonished Gregory, blood leaps from Christ's wounds into the chalice and thence not only from chalice to pope but also from chalice to graveyard, where the poor souls who receive it appear to rise from the dead under its saving power. The checkered floor (deliberately executed in careful perspective) carries the viewer's eyes not to pope or chalice but to the side wound itself; yet the sharp lines of blood then pull away not only from wound but even from chalice and toward the little angular figures in the churchyard. Our eyes move toward Christ and then away, toward the souls who need salvation. The movement is inward, then outward; the picture splinters to our right. Blood saves, but it spills out in order to do so. Whereas host incorporates and binds within, blood has a more complex valence, tying souls to the body from which it exits in a gushing stream.

Not only do the two Gregorymasses analyzed here reflect the differing significances and associations of body and blood; they are also not symmetrically eucharistic. Whereas the Lübeck painting is clearly a celebration—indeed it is the focal point of a fifteenth-century mass, the elevation of the host—the Soest panel is less clearly a mass. At Soest, the pope wears his tiara, which he would have doffed during the canon of the mass; there is no host on the paten (unless it is Christ himself).[75] The indulgence tablet hanging on the wall to our left is in this case illegible, but we know from many other examples that such tablets offered months and years off purgatory for specific numbers of Pater Nosters and Ave Marias said while gazing at Gregorymass depictions. Hence the blood featured here may offer salvation not through sacramental or ocular reception at all but through meditative participation via prayer in the vision of sacrifice Gregory saw. The Lübeck Gregorymass cannot be anything other than a mass; the Soest depiction may well be. Host is an unequivocal sign of eucharist; blood is not. This ambiguity underlines the second problem with current assumptions about blood devotion. Scholars tend to assume that blood references and allusions, wherever they occur, are eucharistic—a tendency that has led not only to a failure to understand the often heady competition between blood relics and miracle hosts but also to a misreading of late medieval devotional texts and iconography.

I give two examples. In a poem composed for the abbey of Fécamp just at the time Aelred was writing his meditation on the crucifix, pilgrims were urged to behold the relic of precious blood "not as you do in the sacrament" but as it flowed from the Savior's side.[76] A modern historian comments that this passage "demonstrates beyond a doubt that belief in the bodily relics of Christ was a form of eucharistic piety."[77] Almost the opposite seems, however, to have been the case. For the two devotions competed with as well as complemented each other, and the Fécamp poet, who says quite clearly "*not* this *but* this," evokes a blood not veiled by species but in its original form, vermillion and living (*en sa fourme proprement vermel*), as it broke forth from the cross to save the world.[78] A similarly skewed reading is sometimes given to the so-called "Fifteen Oes," a series of prayers on the passion, composed in Latin (the traditional attribution, no longer accepted, is to Bridget of Sweden [d. 1373]) and widely circulated in several Middle English versions in the fifteenth century. The prayers begin by evoking Christ's passion as the "sweetness" that "ransom[s] all mankind"; praise and pleading then tumble forth in verbs of drinking, washing, and drowning; Christ's wounds, even his bowels and bone marrow, are "holes" to hide the sinner from "the face of [God's] wrath"; blood is ink to inscribe Christ's wounds in the sinner's heart. At the climax, the fifteenth "O" exhorts and exults:

> Oh blessed Jesus, true and fully plenteous vine, remember your Passion and abundant shedding of blood. Your blood streamed copiously as if it had been pressed out of a ripe cluster of grapes. They pressed your blessed body on the press of the cross and gave us both blood and water to drink out of your body, pierced with the knight's spear so not one drop of blood or of water was left in it. At the end you hung like a bundle of myrrh . . . dried out. . . . Wound my heart so that my soul may be fed sweetly with the water of penance and with the tears of love both night and day. . . . Turn me wholly to you that my heart may always be a dwelling place for you.[79]

Although it is true that grapes and the winepress are traditional eucharistic images, the text speaks here of eating not the eucharist but penance; and it is important to note that, in many fifteenth-century devotions, the side wound is invoked either as the source of all seven sacraments or as the source of two non-eucharistic ones—penance (blood) and baptism (water).[80] Indeed, the legends introducing the "Fifteen Oes" in many exemplars focus on ransom and sacrifice, pain experienced, debts paid. Salvation in heaven and long life on earth are said to come from Pater Nosters and Ave Marias recited in sets elaborately calculated from the number of wounds in the Lord's body. Only if we come to the text assuming that blood is a symbol of eucharist can we interpret it as "assert[ing] that . . . the reader's heart is prepared for union with God" by "drinking sacramental wine, the blood from Jesus's body"—a drinking in fact unavailable to the laity for whom the prayers were composed.[81] Whatever the urging of communion and confession implicit in these lovely little texts, it is thoughtful visualization of the passion and repetition of simple prayers that move the faithful to participation in a blood-spilling that is both access and reproach. Like many other fifteenth-century prayers and practices, the "Fifteen Oes" are not primarily a eucharistic devotion.

As we shall see, controversy over eucharistic presence was indeed a major source of anxiety in fifteenth-century piety, but the tendency in recent scholarship to make eucharist the semiotics of the late Middle Ages[82] or to interpret all meditative practice as "spiritual communion" obscures much.[83] Medieval blood obsession drew on two distinct traditions: blood relics such as the one at Fécamp as well as eucharistic real presence. And as Aelred of Rievaulx, Gerhard of Cologne, and the "Fifteen Oes" suggest, behind these two very different modes of access to the saving blood of the lamb circled a plethora of images (washing, hiding, birthing, ransoming, suffering, punishing, living, dying) that lodged not communion or transubstantiated presence but sacrifice at the heart of hopes for salvation.[84]

Eucharist is only one of the themes into which late medieval piety has been subsumed. Since the (much misunderstood) work of Johann Huizinga, interpretation has also focused on the obsession of such piety with suffering, bleeding, dismemberment, and death.[85] As is well known, fifteenth-century devotional images featured pouring blood and severed body parts. Stories and paintings of the early martyrs became ever more popular and ever bloodier. So-called "speaking reliquaries" (*redende Reliquiare*) and crystal monstrances offered severed pieces of the saints for veneration, replacing the earlier house- or casket-shaped containers that more effectively masked precise contents. Depictions of Jesus' body on the cross or entombed became ever more corpse-like, even as the thieves crucified on either side took on the contorted shapes of criminals broken on the wheel in contemporary executions.[86] Images of the instruments that tortured Christ (the *arma Christi*) proliferated (see Plates 28 and 29). Christ's wounds were depicted as severed hands and feet, his body sometimes reduced to the side wound offered for veneration as a gaping and often erotically charged longitudinal slit.[87]

For such violence of depiction, recent scholarship suggests a social and political context in the violence—the expressionist violence—of the age. And it is true that the period was one of anti-Semitism and war, torture and public executions, incipient witch persecution and fear of "the other"—facts recently explored in a burst of what we might call violence studies.[88] Succeeding and growing out of the interest of the 1990s in the grotesque, the monstrous, and "the other," pain and cruelty seem to be the "in" topics and ready explanations of the early twenty-first century.[89]

It is not clear, however, that the period between the 1350s and the 1520s was more cruel or violent than other medieval centuries. War, social unrest, persecution, scapegoating, and enthusiasm for the public inflicting of pain were equally (if not, indeed, more) characteristic of later periods. Nor is it clear that the themes of dismemberment and blood in fifteenth-century piety are directly related to violence, either reflecting or deflecting it. As I have pointed out in another context, the motifs of dismemberment in fifteenth-century devotion are often about access or wholeness, not partition, and the openness or wholeness is the opposite not so much of violence as of corruption or decay.[90] The wound or wounds of Christ are more frequently hymned as doorway and access, refuge and consolation, than as violation; to penetrate is to open the way. Depictions of Christ's bleeding on the cross sometimes stress waves pouring forth but often focus visually on discrete red globes or drops; the blood is always fresh in crucifixion scenes, but it is as often bits dropping into chalices to feed and wash as it is torrents leaping onto the heads of sinners. Moreover, the body parts of Christ and the saints represented in devotional images and reliquaries are synecdoches for the whole person—indeed, for the glorified person. As Christ is present *integer* in every particle of the eucharist and every eucharistic celebration, so the saints are wholly present in every relic fragment. And that presence participates in glory and impassibility, as the gold and crystal material of reliquaries suggests.[91]

Scholars have perhaps been too quick to lump together themes of wound, heart, and blood, seeing in all such devotions a rather morbid fascination with violation and suffering. If we read carefully, however, we find that what flows from Christ's side in mystical visions, prayers, and hymns is often the sweetness of milk and honey, not blood.[92] The two German nuns usually credited with founding the devotion to the sacred heart—Gertrude the Great (d. 1301 or 1302) and Mechtild of Hackeborn (d. 1298)—write much of nourishing and cleansing liquid from the side of Christ, but it is almost never *sanguis* or *cruor*.[93] The nun Margaret Ebner, whose *Revelations* were probably edited by Henry of Nördlingen shortly after her death in 1351, speaks frequently of flowing, washing, and drinking, but what she experiences in visions is usually "milk," "water," or "sweetness," and it is allegory or metonym for mercy, grace, love, delight, fruition, or eternal life far more often than for either psychological or physical pain.[94] Study of the texts assembled by Richstätter in his classic work on the cult of the heart shows that blood, relatively seldom mentioned, not only violates and accuses, it also assuages and consoles.[95] Devotion to Christ's wounds, side, and heart is not, as is sometimes said, the source of blood devotion or closely related to it. The origin of devotion to Christ's side, to nursing from and achieving access through it, lies in the thirteenth century and is a sweeter, sunnier piety than the fourteenth- and fifteenth-century appeal to blood.

Moreover, as Anglophone scholarship has long emphasized, even blood devotion offers comfort as well as reproach. John Mirk's preacher might frighten his congregation with tales of Christ flinging bloodclots into their faces, but the pious laity who meditated along with the author of the *Talkyng* rolled erotically in a sweet nest of flesh and blood. On the continent, too, love balanced rage. A sister from the Dominican house of Katharinenthal received Christ's blood to assuage her struggle with unbelief, although Johannes Tauler, fierce preacher to nuns, warned in Christ's words: "The anger and cruelty of men almost destroys me, the sins of the earth drink my blood."[96] In a kaleidoscope of pain and glory, the blood of suffering and reproach shimmered into the blood of comfort and access and back again to reproach. Mechtild of Magdeburg saw the host change into "a bleeding lamb hanging from a red cross [*ein blůtig lamp, gehangen an einem roten crúze*]." But for the nun Diemut of Nuremberg Christ's real and horrible wounds were transformed in vision into a source of joy and triumph that revealed the entire Trinity.[97] In theological analyses such as those of Jan Hus (d. 1415) and John of Capistrano (d. 1456), blood devotion is associated at least as much with themes of wholeness and resurrection as with those of suffering and partition.[98]

It is true that devotional writers themselves sometimes registered unease with blood piety. Christina Ebner of Engelthal was reported to feel terror at a vision of the crucified, and the nun who recorded one of Gertrude's rare blood visions editorialized that blood is "in itself a detestable thing [*in se est abominabilis*]."[99] Discussions of the eucharist from the eleventh to the sixteenth century stressed that the real presence must be veiled to avoid *horror cruoris*; exposure to naked blood would terrorize the faithful.[100] Blood miracles were understood to express God's castigation of human failing at least as much as his revelation to or reward of faithful adherence. Death, a popular theme, was treated increasingly in a way that calls attention to processes of fragmentation and decay. But, as Valentin Groebner has trenchantly observed, severed limbs and spilled fluids are not per se brutal or shocking; it depends on the perspective of the viewer.[101] People attended executions with titillated enthusiasm and soaked up in their handkerchiefs the extruded blood of criminals as a kind of relic or talisman to ward off disease or disaster. None of the surviving literature that gives us insight into medieval reactions to body-part reliquaries, or to depictions of bodily fragments cast up for resurrection, suggests that people found these particular representations horrifying.[102] And theologians associated blood less with death than with victory over it. The cry of pilgrims was not "Blood of Christ appall me," nor "Blood of Christ comfort me," but "Blood of Christ save me." I do not think we can explain the fifteenth-century obsession with blood as a general fixation on cruelty, death, or guilt per se, or assume that blood signifies simply pollution, violence, or partition.

Nor is it enough to point out the opposite—to remark, as scholars have repeatedly done, that this piety balances cruelty with comfort as if the bloodshed is merely a sublimation of, or answer to, or denial of, a violent age. To argue thus is to read superficially. Much more is at stake, as we shall see, in the references to sprinkling and pouring, drops and streams, expiation and sacrifice. For there *is* a sense in which violation or desecration lies at the heart of blood piety. Those objects to which cult attaches—wafers, red fluids, bones, pieces of cloth or wood—are objects that have been violated, penetrated, or opened, as Christ was on the cross. The faithful who pray to, and through, the blood ask to be marked, consecrated, by that blood, shed from Christ the lamb. Blood is a sign of a desecration that makes holy; hence it sets apart, consecrates. In its characteristics of liquidity and separation—the way it remains shimmering and red in the shedding, yet pools in discrete drops apart from body—it symbolizes the presence and absence of the divine. But to understand this, as we shall do only after much further exploration, is not to see it merely as an escape valve for cruelty and greed, or a psychological substitute for reassurance and love.[103]

A third interpretation of the significance of blood has emerged in the recent literature of cultural studies and feminist literary criticism. At a conference held at Montpellier in 1997 (and published in 1999) on "le sang au moyen âge," several speakers tried to draw together the wealth of papers into a kind of structuralist analysis. Although not all the material presented fit the paradigm, many papers suggested that pure blood (the blood of Christ, the martyrs, and male military heroes) was blood shed from an artificial orifice as the result of a voluntary act. Impure blood, bad blood, polluting blood was blood eliminated naturally from a natural orifice.[104] Some recent anthropological work on sacrifice makes use of a similar contrast between sacrificial blood actively produced by ritual slaughtering and female reproductive blood (both menstrual and postpartum), often taboo in sacred spaces.[105] Drawing on such dichotomies, some feminist literary critics have seen medieval culture as equating good blood with male blood and bad, polluting blood with female blood. Hence the late medieval stereotyping of the male Jew as menstruating—a stereotype recently studied by several scholars—assimilates Jewish men to females, devaluing them by association with a natural, female, reproductive blood that was taboo in their own tradition.[106]

Some philologists and anthropologists have, however, understood inside blood (*sanguis*) as fertility, outside blood or bloodshed (*cruor*) as violence. In this reading (although it has not been that preferred by feminist criticism), *sanguis* might seem female and good (at least when inside) and *cruor* might seem male and problematic (at least in its military context). In any case, all recent work on blood attitudes, albeit often without theoretical underpinnings, tends to stress the power of blood as symbol to evoke elemental opposites such as life and death, fertility and violence, nurture and blight.[107]

It is of course true that Latin has two words for blood (*sanguis* and *cruor*), reflecting a general Indo-European pattern perhaps distantly echoed in the Middle English distinction (reflecting earlier Germanic tongues) between "blood" and the seldom used "gore" ("coagulated blood"; also "dirt" or "dung").[108] Medieval theorists themselves understood these two Latin terms to be structurally opposite. In an often cited passage, Isidore of Seville distinguished sweet, healthy, inside blood (*sanguis* = *suavis*) and corrupt, separated, outside blood (*cruor* = *corruptus*) as dichotomies.

> It is *sanguis* while it is in the body, but is called *cruor* when it has been poured out [*effusus*]. For *cruor* is named from that which, being shed, runs down [*effusus decurrit*] or from that which has spilled down by running [*vel ab eo quod currendo corruat*]. Others, however, interpret *cruor* as corrupt *sanguis* [*sanguinem corruptum*], which is spilled. Others say *sanguis* is so named because is it sweet [*suavis*]. But *sanguis* is not whole (that is, perfectly healthy [*integer*]) except in the young.[109]

When, however, medieval theorists and devotional writers use *sanguis* and *cruor*, things become far more complicated. For example, the encyclopedist Vincent of Beauvais (d. 1264) makes use of Isidore's dichotomies in such a way that initially the contrast seems even cruder. Following Galen's humoral theory, Vincent sees blood as the most positive of the humors.[110] "One says *sanguis* in Latin because it is *suavis*"; hence those in whom blood dominates are "delightful and charming [*dulces et blandi*]."[111] *Cruor* is called from the fact that, in running out, it corrupts, and, says Vincent (manifesting a fear of corruption we shall meet again in the pages ahead), it is also related explicitly to cruelty (*crudelitas*). Moving beyond etymology to natural philosophy, however, Vincent argues that inside blood can become stagnant and putrefy, necessitating bleeding to keep it pure and efficacious. Phlebotomy (purging from artificial orifices) is good, but what flows out is bad; moreover, demons are understood to use inside blood to act on the soul.[112] And in Vincent's piety, as in late medieval devotional texts generally, there is no consistently dichotomous use of *sanguis* and *cruor*. In a description of the flagellation he writes: "But the blows of the flails made the blood [*cruor*] flow on his back and a sweat of blood [*sanguis*] anointed the other parts of his body. So we can say that not only his hands and feet but also his side were sprinkled [*aspersa*] with blood [*sanguis*]." Even if *cruor* here has connotations of being torn out and *sanguis* of being emitted (as sweat), Vincent's point is less to contrast methods of egress than to underline that all Christ's bleedings are offered up in sacrifice. He continues:

> With great precision, John says [of the soldier with the lance] . . . "he opened," not "he struck" or "he wounded." By this he wanted to indicate that . . . the door of life was opened, from which came the sacraments of the church. . . . From this, it follows that there ran out without ceasing blood and water, blood in the remission of sins and water to sanctify, as in baptism.[113]

As Peggy McCracken has shown in a recent study of French vernacular literature, elegant readings can be constructed around the male/female, artificial/natural dichotomy if one limits the body of literature considered.[114] But the formulation artificial orifice = male = pure / natural exuding = female = impure does not work when one considers literature, theology, canon law, or piety as a whole. The male shedding of blood, heroic or salvific in one context, is contaminating in another. From the twelfth century on, clerics were forbidden to shed blood in execution or surgery,[115] and male fluids (especially semen) were in certain contexts technically polluting.[116] Despite occasional references in the encyclopedists to age-old menstrual taboos and misogynist stereotypes, menstrual and postpartum pollution is mentioned much less frequently in medical or philosophical texts than modern secondary literature suggests. To doctors, menstruation was seen as purging, and if menstrual blood was held in folklore to cloud mirrors and drive dogs mad, it could also ward off plagues of locusts and disease.[117] Theologians' emphasis on the origin of Christ's perfect body entirely in the pure menstrual blood of Mary (stressed, as we shall see, by John of Capistrano and in the Rome debate of 1462) surely disproves any simple equation of female or menstrual blood with impurity. The blood of birthing—female blood shed from natural orifices and in considerable pain—is often understood as good and fertile blood, in both fact and metaphor. James of Klusa's meditation on the birth of Ecclesia from Christ's side in the bloodshed of the cross, like Vincent of Beauvais's insistence that Christ's side was "opened" like a door (or a birth canal) rather than "pierced" as in wounding, is typical of many fourteenth- and fifteenth-century devotions that analogize saving with birthing, conflate natural and artificial bodily openings, and reverse supposed assumptions about natural female bleeding. Moreover, recent research understands postpartum ceremonies, both Christian and Jewish, as reintegration into a community once danger of death is past, not simply as cleansing from the contamination of postpartum bloodshed.[118] Although, as we shall see, blood is often gendered in both piety and theology, there is little evidence, in the wealth of blood practices or in theological treatments, of an assumption that female body or female blood is per se polluting.[119]

There is then something misleading about analyses that oppose natural to cultural (or artificial), female to male, even if they understand Christian symbolism to invert or sublimate or transcend such dichotomies. Anthropologists, historians, and theologians have long interpreted gospel precepts such as "many that are first shall be last," "the meek shall inherit the earth," "hath not God made foolish the wisdom of this world?" (Mark 10.31, Matt. 5.5, I Cor. 1.20, etc.) to invert worldly values and statuses;[120] hence they have associated such images of inversion with those who would rebel against or escape from this-worldly structures while those who would work within such structures supposedly preferred images that valued and instantiated bodily and social particularity.[121] According to such interpretation, images of Christ's blood as female bleeding might seem simply to reverse secular assumptions about blood, hence appealing especially to women and the poor or to those, such as friars and monks, who identified by renunciation with the disadvantaged of the world. But, as we have seen, secular assumptions were themselves not so clear cut: heroic romance and medical discourse, respectively, give rather different values to inside and outside blood. And meditations on Christ's saving blood, even when gendered, do not seem so much to reverse a different, secular, or folk discourse as to reverberate with a multitude of what we might call significances or "charges" carried by blood. However well (or badly) certain kinds of anthropological analysis may work for "body images," the complex blood rhetoric of medieval devotion, soteriology, and praxis does not seem to be a conflation, or alternately a reversal, of two structurally dichotomous "bloods."

The most useful anthropological insights seem rather to be those recent studies of sacrifice that understand ritual and belief as affixing to objects the multiple valences that make them "sacred" or "taboo." As Carlin Barton, Joan Branham, Heinrich von Staden, and J. C. Heesterman have argued, what religion—lived religion—does is to lift ordinary objects, in ways consonant with what they are *as objects*, into special significance that makes them conduits of power.[122] Hence, as Barton explains, the shedding of blood both in sacrifice and in execution was "taboo" to the ancient Romans not in the commonsense meaning of "forbidden" but in the technical sense of "set-apart" and "setting-apart." Or, as Branham and von Staden put it, pollutants cancel out other pollutants; they are simultaneously contaminating and effective against other contamination. The nature of the charge affixed lies in both the object, the stuff, the blood itself (its "natural symbol-ness," as anthropologist Mary Douglas would say) and in the historically particular traditions, practices, and theories that led to the act of affixing, the spilling of blood.[123] Such an approach suggests that rather than looking to perduring structures (such as natural/artificial) or parallel discourses (such as medicine, folklore, or romance) to explain blood piety we should look to what, at the moment in question, people did vis-à-vis blood and what they said, to blood as religious object and ritual act as well as blood in pious texts. The best clues to the obsession with blood in fifteenth-century religion will turn out, at the end of my story, to be the specific quarrels, frauds, and pilgrimages in which people engaged and the quite specific nouns and verbs with which they underlined its discrete particleness and living redness.

There are other current theories and approaches I could adduce here as background. Some of them—especially the analysis of blood devotion as instrument of clerical control or as projection of Christian scapegoating and guilt—will figure prominently in what lies ahead. But I have said enough already to suggest reasons for the odd combination of local and general in my exposition—a combination I attempted to justify historiographically in the preface above.

I begin with the bleeding hosts of Wilsnack, using a popular cult site in northern Germany as an entry into the theology, piety, and praxis of the later Middle Ages. Although the book that follows is not an exhaustive study of Wilsnack and its competing cults, I have nonetheless moved from the local to the European, proceeding from the little town in the Prignitz, through other blood sites in Brandenburg and Mecklenburg, to scholastic disputes over the presence of blood, and finally, returning where I began, to the broad themes of northern European devotion. Treating first the multiple valences of blood in specific settings and arguments, I turn then to the explicit and complex motifs of blood piety, only finally to attempt to ferret out the assumptions that seem to lie beneath cult, theology, and spirituality. When in the end I argue that there is something about blood as physical and physiological stuff—and hence as bodily symbol—that made it particularly appropriate to express the dilemmas and desires of fifteenth-century Christians, I hope it will be clear that what is at stake in such an interpretation is not an essentialist understanding of a perduring substance but rather the discovery, via medieval texts, acts, and objects, of some very specific medieval assumptions.

PART I

Cults in Northern Germany

Chapter 2
Wilsnack

When fifteenth-century theologians, preachers, and layfolk—whether aristocrats, villagers, or even condemned criminals—thought of the power in the blood, they probably thought first not of soteriological doctrine nor of the private devotion of monastic cell or bedroom, but of pilgrimage. The blood of Christ was something to which one traveled, drawn by stories of the miracles it worked, the adherents and revenues it garnered. For northern Europe, the goal of such pilgrimage was most often Wilsnack (now Bad Wilsnack) near Havelberg in the archdiocese of Magdeburg in northern Germany[1] (see map, p. 46). In my effort to explore the religious significance of blood in late medieval devotion and theology, it seems good to begin here at the very center of both blood enthusiasm and blood controversy. It seems good as well to begin with the details of the story.

The Events

If English-speaking medievalists have heard at all of Wilsnack, it is probably because it was one of several stops on the pilgrimage tour of the pious laywoman Margery Kempe.[2] Now a quiet market town, over which towers a fifteenth-century brick Gothic church (see Plate 4), Wilsnack in the Prignitz is a name unfamiliar to most modern Germans as well.[3] But it was, from the 1380s to the mid-sixteenth century, one of the most famous cult sites in Europe, surpassed in numbers of pilgrims only by Jerusalem, Rome, and Santiago de Compostela.[4] The site was singled out for special reproach, along with the not very distant town of Sternberg, in Martin Luther's diatribe against pilgrimage abuses in his *Open Letter to the Christian Nobility of the German Nation* of 1520.[5]

The cause of all the commotion was three miraculous hosts, supposedly discovered by the priest Johannes Kabuz (or Cabbucz) in the charred remains of the altar several days after the village was torched by a marauding knight in August 1383. Although the church had been burnt and the spot soaked with rain, Kabuz, alerted by a dream, found the hosts, dry and intact, on a dry corporal, and in the center of each was a drop of blood. According to the legend, probably written down in the early fifteenth century but not printed until 1520–21, various miracles happened almost at once involving candles that lit miraculously, miraculously refused to light, refused to be extinguished, or burned without being consumed.[6] Healings occurred; at least three of the earliest five were resurrections from the dead. When the bishop of Havelberg arrived to celebrate a mass in which he intended to (re)consecrate the hosts, fearing the people might be revering mere bread, the central host overflowed with blood, warding off the ritual abuse of double consecration. A papal indulgence, which (as was typical) does not mention any miracles, was issued a year later to promote the rebuilding of the church, and shortly thereafter the archbishop of Magdeburg with the bishops of Lebus, Brandenburg, and Havelberg gave an indulgence mentioning the hosts.[7] In 1395 the church was incorporated into the episcopal *mensa* of Havelberg. In 1396 the bishop, Johannes Wöpelitz, ordered a new division of revenues from the sale of pilgrim badges: henceforth a third went to episcopal buildings, a third to the cathedral chapter, and a third to the Wilsnack pilgrimage church.[8]

Both the pilgrimage and criticism of it flourished at once.[9] In 1403 archbishop Sbinko of Prague appointed a commission to look into it, after which he required the clergy of Bohemia to preach once a month against the pilgrimage.[10] Between 1405 and 1407 Jan Hus, a member of the commission, produced the first treatise against Wilsnack, which argued that, for theological reasons, the blood of Christ could not be left behind on earth.[11] In a more practical response, Conrad von Soltau, bishop of Verden, had the Wilsnack pilgrim badges ripped off the hats of those of his diocese returning from pilgrimage.[12] In 1412, a provincial synod at Magdeburg drew up ten articles to be answered by the bishop of Havelberg about Wilsnack that included, along with the suggestion that the former priest had admitted fabrication, the charge (article 4) that "there is nothing there and nothing similar to blood [*nullus ibidem habeatur nec quid simile cruori*]."[13] The indefatigable Heinrich Tocke, canon of Magdeburg, who spent much of his life combating Wilsnack, raised criticisms in the 1420s but was drawn aside into conciliar politics, while the archbishop of Magdeburg was preoccupied by the revolt of his city against him.[14]

The major campaign against Wilsnack took place between 1443 and 1453, the spokespersons on both sides being some of the most important German theologians of the fifteenth century, many of them connected with the University of Erfurt. Tocke, once court preacher to the Elector of Brandenburg, lost influence there when the Elector's son took over the Mark in 1437. But he visited Wilsnack in 1443 and, according to his famous "Synodalrede" of 1451, examined the miracle hosts in the presence of the provost and priest of the church, finding only spiderwebs. According to this later report, the provost, who had been in Wilsnack "more than a hundred times," said: "I see nothing red and I have never seen anything red."[15]

Tocke's attack (as adumbrated already in the synod of 1412) was two-pronged. Not only did he claim that nothing was visible on the supposed miracle hosts, either in 1443 or earlier. He claimed as well that Kabuz had previously confessed to fraud and requested absolution for it; and he quoted the theologian Christian of Hiddestorf, who allegedly reported that Kabuz had offered to stage a similar pilgrimage at Magdeburg "now that he had learned how to do it properly." Not surprisingly, others among the polemicists accused Christian (who was dead by the time the controversy peaked) of having lied, and Tocke of lying about Christian's assertions.[16]

In the midst of the charges and countercharges of the early 1440s, the new reforming archbishop of Magdeburg, Friedrich, count of Beichlingen, was won over to Tocke's side. The battle among ecclesiastical and secular authorities as well as university-trained theologians began in earnest. Meetings were scheduled, which the bishop of Havelberg boycotted. Charges were drawn up, the most important being the thirty articles and seven questions prepared by Tocke for the meeting at Ziesar, and the fourteen questions posed for the meeting at Burg, both in 1446. Late in the same fall, the faculty of Erfurt issued a learned theological opinion squarely against Wilsnack. The Franciscan Conventuals Matthias Döring and Johannes Kannemann wrote defenses of the blood, and the Elector sent Kannemann to Rome to press the cause for Wilsnack. Early in 1447 pope Eugene IV (enthusiastic supporter of miracle hosts elsewhere in Europe)[17] issued two bulls confirming the pilgrimage and requiring that a freshly consecrated host be placed alongside the miraculous ones offered for veneration.[18] Tocke, however, managed to persuade the papal legate Nicholas of Cusa, in Germany to preach the Jubilee indulgence and effect reform, to consider the matter at the provincial synod in Magdeburg in 1451.[19] Withdrawing a few days later to Halberstadt, Cusanus (whose Christology emphasized the fundamental in-dissolvability of the person of Christ) issued a categorical decree against such miracle hosts, without naming Wilsnack.[20]

We have heard from many reliable men and also have ourselves seen how the faithful stream to many places in the area of our legation to adore the precious blood of Christ our God that they believe is present in several transformed red hosts [*quem in nonnullis transformatis hostijs speciem rubedinis habere arbitrantur*]. And it is clearly attested by their words, with which they name this colored thing [*talem rubedinem*] the blood of Christ [*Christi cruorem*], that they thus believe and adore it, and the clergy in their greed for money not only permit this but even encourage it through the publicizing of miracles. . . . [But] it is pernicious . . . and we cannot permit it without damage to God, for our catholic faith teaches us that the glorified body of Christ has glorified blood completely un-seeable in glorified veins [*sanguinem glorificatum in venis glorificatis penitus inuisibilem*]. In order to remove every opportunity for the deception of simple folk, we therefore order that . . . the clergy . . . should no longer display or promulgate such miracles or allow pilgrim badges [*signa plumbea*] to be made of them, but these same transformed hosts should be consumed by the celebrating priest in communion rather than that the sacred eucharist given to us as a divine gift for spiritual refection should be permitted to disintegrate through the corruption of the species [*per specierum corruptionem desinere*].[21]

The decree was reissued at Mainz and Cologne with differences, among them the inclusion at Mainz of a reference to veneration of bloody cloths.[22] (The archdiocese of Mainz boasted not only the popular bleeding-host pilgrimage of Gottsbüren but also Walldürn, home of a miraculous corporal on which the bloody face of Christ supposedly appeared in drops of spilled eucharistic wine.)[23]

Neither the bishop of Havelberg nor the Elector had any intention of suppressing the Wilsnack pilgrimage.[24] Mutual excommunications of the prelates of Havelberg and Magdeburg followed. The archbishop of Magdeburg scheduled more discussions. The flamboyant Observant Franciscan preacher John of Capistrano (himself supposedly a miracle worker) was appealed to, with ambiguous results;[25] the Elector sent Kannemann once again to Rome. In 1453 Pope Nicholas V quashed all excommunications and supported the pilgrimage.

Learned theological discussion hostile to Wilsnack continued into the sixteenth century, but the cult flourished. A number of sources report a pilgrimage epidemic in 1475 in which people streamed to Wilsnack from as far away as Hungary, Austria, and France. The town councilors of Erfurt recommended closing the city for fear of being overrun by the hordes of travelers passing through.[26] According to chronicles from the Cologne and Erfurt areas, hundreds of children ran away from their parents and servants from their masters to flock to Wilsnack between the 1450s and the 1480s—a veritable "children's crusade."[27] The deacon of Havelberg, writing in 1558, remembered that, in his youth, crowds flocked to the church on the "day of the finding of the Holy Blood" and fell fainting when "the idol" was shown.[28] The pastoral theologian Johannes von Paltz (to whom I shall return) inveighed against the pilgrimage in 1503.[29]

The Reformation arrived in Brandenburg in 1539, but an evangelical pastor, Joachim Ellefeldt, was appointed to Wilsnack only in the early 1550s and found himself in conflict with the Catholic canons, who continued to display the miraculous blood at mass despite Ellefeldt's preaching against it from the pulpit.[30] On May 28, 1552, Ellefeldt, in the presence of another cleric and the local schoolmaster, opened the monstrance and burned the miraculous hosts, for which deed he was arrested and spent six months in prison, after which he was expelled from the Mark and disappears from history.[31] Stories of fraud at Wilsnack survived into the late nineteenth century, including the tale of the "sin scales" into which penitents supposedly put the price of their misdeeds while clever priests held down the basin from below with a stick; the scales and the supposed pot in which Ellefeldt burned the idol were displayed as a sort of Protestant relic of Catholic superstition.[32]

Historiography

Such is the story of Wilsnack—little known to scholars outside Germany but much studied in German historiography. All subsequent work has been based on the research of two Lutheran pastors, Matthaeus Ludecus (Lüdtke) in the later sixteenth century and Ernst Breest in the late nineteenth. (Even the collection of primary documents in Adolph Friedrich Riedel's *Codex diplomaticus* for Brandenburg is, for the most part, simply reprinted from Ludecus.) Hence the oldest retelling of the tale is a Protestant story of the failure of German reform in the fifteenth century, with Heinrich Tocke a kind of heroic reformer before the Reformation.[33] Nineteenth- and early twentieth-century Catholic versions too hint sadly at opportunities lost and tend to defend the supporters of Wilsnack as misguided representatives of a pastoral theology that saw even equivocal or fabricated pilgrimage as spiritually useful to the people.

Casting the story in a confessional mode was succeeded by a number of interpretations that understood the events as essentially political and economic—as conflict within the church for control, revenues, and influence (the archdiocese of Magdeburg against the episcopal see of Havelberg; secular clergy against friars; Franciscans versus Dominicans, Augustinians, and Carthusians; or Conventual versus Observant Franciscans) or as incidents in the larger struggle of the popes with the German princes. Although Hartmut Boockmann has shown that the various positions taken pro and con the pilgrimage did not line up in any predictable sense according to affiliation, antagonisms between ecclesiastical institutions and among orders did play a role.[34] There is, for example, no question that the ambition of the new universities in northeastern Europe contributed. (Prague, Erfurt, and Leipzig, all of which gave opinions, were all less than a hundred years old, and their theology faculties were eager to establish reputations.) Competition between secular and regular clergy, tensions over Observant reform within the Franciscan order, and nationalist aspirations contributed as well. Czech hostility against Germans surfaced, for example, in early attacks from Prague. Economic interests and matters of prestige were also in play. The bishop of Havelberg and the Electors of Brandenburg needed the benefits provided by a steady flow of visitors at a moment when their town, diocese, and region were experiencing economic depression, agrarian problems, and attendant political instability.[35] But ecclesiastics from Magdeburg were already, in the early days of the Council of Basel (1435), embarrassed by rumors that circulated there of quite improbable miracles at Wilsnack (withered limbs restored, staves turned into swords, resurrections of corpses). Their reputations as reformers were at stake. Moreover, it is certainly true, as Bruno Hennig established in 1906, that the framing event for the positions taken between 1447 and 1453 by popes and Electors was the Concordat of 1447, in which the Elector Friedrich II of Brandenburg and his brother, along with Emperor Friedrich III and the archbishop of Mainz, among others, performed obedience to the pope after they had for nine years kept studied neutrality in the conflict between the papacy and the Council of Basel. The papacy owed the Electors something, and the Electors wanted their pilgrimage.[36]

Recent treatments of Wilsnack have tended to situate the cult in the context of late medieval eucharistic devotion (often relating it tangentially to similar sites of supposed Jewish host desecration),[37] to connect it to the stunning increase of pilgrimage (and hence of popular piety, which is sometimes seen as retaining genuine folk elements),[38] or to understand it as part of the rise of visuality in late medieval and early modern devotion. This latter interpretation, especially popular with art historians, relates host pilgrimages to a trend in which sight replaces touch, as relic is replaced first by elevated host and then by miraculous image or by visions and dreams.[39] The prevailing historical interpretation—and the one found in the major English-language work on Wilsnack, a learned and influential article from 1988 by Charles Zika—is sociological and Foucauldian. In such interpretation, the complicated theological and pastoral moves of the clergy are seen as an effort to retain church control over popular devotion. Thus Zika, while maintaining that theological details matter, nonetheless reduces them to a complex strategy to replace relic veneration with pilgrimage to the holy sacrament (i.e. the newly consecrated host laid on since Eugene IV's bull and probably earlier), because consecrated hosts can be produced and displayed only by clerical power and under clerical control. "In dealing with the host," he says, "my approach is to regard it as an object which essentially derives meaning through its relationship to the clergy, those who have entrusted themselves with its management."[40] In microcosm then, scholarship on Wilsnack mirrors the course of early Reformation studies: from a religious and confessional emphasis, to a stress on political and social context, to an interest in levels of culture and in the role of power in their construction.

Recent Foucauldian interpretation is not unpersuasive. It is true that hostility to Wilsnack came increasingly to be hostility to disorderly pilgrimage or questionable relics, and that the addition of a consecrated host to the miraculous blood was an effort to divert devotion to the ordinary sacrament of the altar (although Tocke and the Erfurt theologians saw this itself as a hypocritical ploy to allow superstition to continue).[41] Moreover, both opposition to pilgrimage and diversion of attention from bleeding hosts to eucharist can, of course, be understood as the assertion of ecclesiastical control, the imposition of elite clerical values on popular ones, the triumph of host (with its hidden God) over tangible, seeable holy matter. But such analysis ignores the leitmotif of blood that runs throughout the story, tying together the most recondite of theological arguments with the supposedly disorderly religiosity the theologians combated. For even if the controversy was over control, why was blood the instrument that exercised or resisted it? Why did pilgrim enthusiasm focus on this particular form of presence, even as learned opposition to it became preoccupied with the metaphysical details of its nature and significance? We return where we began: why blood?

Blood at the Center

Examination of the Wilsnack material only highlights the enigma. For it is puzzling that blood became central. The earliest strand of legend seems, as Hartmut Kühne has argued, to have concerned the survival of holy matter through water and fire, and the first miracles concern inexhaustible and unruly candles.[42] By mid-century there seems to have been common agreement, at least among the clergy, that nothing red survived. The thirty articles of 1446, repeating the ten articles of 1412, assert: "The people venerate a blood there [*cruorem*] but we have no idea what it is [*nescimus quem*]; since there is in fact nothing there and nothing similar to blood [*nullus ibidem habeatur nec quid simile cruori*]."[43] The fourteen questions of the same year asked whether the insignia of Wilsnack with their three drops of blood could be worn, since "nothing true corresponds to them in fact [*nihil veritatis correspondeat in re*]."[44] (Tocke, however, never preached this to the people, and it is worth noting that his request to examine the hosts took place "after everyone had left the church.")[45] Theologians from Hus to Nicholas of Cusa argued: the blood of Christ *cannot* be there. Even the cult's defenders (mostly Benedictines and Franciscans) mounted only the uneasy argument that blood *might* be there (because it was present at other sites) but the real and impeccably proper goal of Wilsnack veneration was the ordinary sacrament of Christ's body and blood.

Yet what stands out in all this is the focus on blood. It was blood to which kings, clergy, and common people voyaged, blood that filled the hearts of penitents and the coffers of merchants, blood over which theologians fought, blood that inspired imitation and competition from churches and monasteries not only in the Mark Brandenburg but throughout northern Germany as well. Over and over again, the blood that "was not there" wrenched piety and argument into its purview and power. Indeed, for a hundred and fifty years, opponents as well as supporters admitted that blood was central to the pilgrimage. The opposition argued in 1412 and again in 1446: "Others cautiously assert that the sacrament, not blood, is revered there, but the common name of the place disproves this, for it is called *ad sacrum sanguinem*; and invocations run thus: *Adjuva me sacer sanguis* or *sacer sanguis me liberet*."[46] Eberhard Waltmann of Magdeburg charged in the early 1450s: "The common people are led into error, believing the bloodiness of transformed hosts [*sanguinolentas hostiarum transformatarum tincturas*] to be the natural blood of Christ [*sanguinem esse Christi naturalem*] and more efficacious than that in the chalice on the altar, and . . . not only simple people but also priests and devout religious."[47] It was bloody hosts that were depicted on the lead badges the bishop of Verden had ripped from pilgrim hats.[48] Three of the five earliest healing miracles were not mere healings but resurrections, the principle of *similia similibus* so common in miracle stories operating here as life restored by living blood. The feast of Corpus Christi was (irregularly—so opponents charged) celebrated as "the day of the holy blood" at Wilsnack.[49] The story of the host that poured blood to ward off the *iniuria* of double consecration may be an interpolation into the earliest version of the *Historia* but, whenever the story appears, it makes the centrality of *sacer sanguis* quite clear. Although the bleeding can be read as testimony that the hosts, because already consecrated, were clerically approved for veneration, it can also be interpreted as warding off an effort at clerical appropriation and thus confirming the miraculous and unmediated presence of living, flowing blood.[50] But whether read as supporting or opposing clerical control, the legend is one in which miraculous blood defends miraculous blood.

No matter how strident the Wilsnack opponents, nothing about their position suggests that claims about blood were incidental or trivial. When Heinrich Tocke, in his famous "Synodalrede" of 1451, went into extensive detail about his unmasking of a blood fraud at Wartenburg bei Wittenberg in 1429, the evidence hardly disproves the centrality of blood.[51] Rather it shows that blood was powerful enough to be worth faking and powerful enough to require powerful arguments against it. Tocke reported not only the complicated maneuvers necessary to extract the miracle host from the widowed wife of the duke, who had vowed to protect it, but also the carefully staged setting of the fraudulent miracle. Although the priest confessed—not under torture but under threat—to daubing his own blood on the host, Tocke clearly feared that such ploys, unless caught early, tended to succeed.

> How many would he and his followers have tricked, how many pious Christians would they have deprived of their worldly goods through this evil fraud, how many miracles would they have fabricated to the shame of the diocese! Praise be to God, who brought the truth to light so early, and to the archbishop, who did not allow such untruths to spread. Already we saw people with baskets to beg for the honor of holy blood. . . . Already people planned inns [to house the pilgrims] and surrounding towns hoped to be enriched through the flood of foreigners. The pilgrimage would have been great since it owed its origins not to a dream and vain imaginings but to the holy communion at Easter when many had already received and others stood at the altar in order to receive, while four ministers were there, of whom two held the chalice but the other two suddenly saw the bleeding host.[52]

Moreover, Tocke's own argument in opposition—that the supposedly miraculous bread appeared upon examination rotten, not red and living as originally claimed—is a crucial clue to the power of the blood (a point to which I shall return).[53]

Even chronicle accounts from the later fifteenth century, questionable in the reliability of their historical details but not as evidence of perception, make it clear that blood was the heart of the matter. The monk Cornel Zanfliet, for example, reported in his chronicle that Nicholas of Cusa "came to Wilsnack" where there were "three drops of blood" and established that they were either a fraud or had "vanished" long since.[54] Zanfliet's description was clearly derived from legend or pilgrim songs, not from Cusanus's decree, which concerned hosts. Long after, in 1552, it was "the blood" that the Protestant pastor Joachim Ellefeldt felt it necessary to destroy by fire. And the fact that he was incarcerated and then exiled for the act may suggest not only political maneuvering in the Mark Brandenburg but also some continuing sense of the holy matter as taboo even into a period that came to oppose and then ridicule it.

The larger context within which Tocke and others formulated their opposition to Wilsnack involved the religious significance of blood as well. The primary threat against which legates such as John of Capistrano and Nicholas of Cusa were sent to preach in northern Germany and further east was Hussitism. As we shall see, Jan Hus himself had objected to the Wilsnack wonder out of a deep concern to keep Christ's blood joined with his body in glory; the outcry in Bohemia for lay access to the communion cup originated with Jacobellus of Stříbro (Mies), not Hus, although Hus did hold communion in both kinds to have been the practice of the early church.[55] But by 1419, radical disciples of Hus (known as Utraquists) were demanding direct lay access to *sanguis Christi* in the chalice; the demand led to violent criticism of a church that had executed their hero and withheld the cup. Modern scholars of the Hussites have tended to see the movement as essentially an anticlericalism that evolved rapidly, in the community at Tábor, into social revolution. But at its core was the lay claim to Christ's blood.[56] Theologians at Erfurt in the 1440s and '50s feared that the Wilsnack cult encouraged other sorts of aberrant demands for access to blood, above all Hussite ideas.

Indeed, the theologians who participated in the Wilsnack controversy tended to lump various dissident threats together. At a meeting in Ziesar in 1446, for example, Tocke charged that the Wilsnack cult encouraged radical flagellants and Waldensian heretics to bypass the eucharist.[57] Thus it is important to note that such groups lie in the background to Wilsnack. In the 1390s, only a decade after the Wilsnack wonder, 450 Waldensians were tried in Stettin. There was a similar, although smaller, persecution of Waldensians and Hussites in Berlin in 1458.[58] Throughout the fifteenth century, fear of Hussites and Waldensians hovered behind clerical efforts to propagate Corpus Christi observance in Brandenburg and Pomerania.[59] Those theologians who supported the Wilsnack cult sometimes tried to use it as proof of orthodox eucharistic theology over against heretical claims to bypass eucharist and priests. James of Jüterbog and Johannes von Paltz, for example, claimed that God intended host miracles to refute heretics and Jews, who denied either that blood was present in the wafer by concomitance, or that blood was present at all.[60] But others feared that Wilsnack encouraged heretical claims to access without (or with only minimal) assistance of priests. And in nearby Thuringia the cryptoflagellant movement kept another sort of blood before the eyes of the faithful.[61]

Although there is less recent work on the cryptoflagellants than on the Utraquists, the line in modern scholarship has been the same. Interest has focused on their ecclesiology, anticlericalism, and their supposed apocalyptic or revolutionary ideas. But when we look at the documents that survive (and they must be used with caution for they come from hostile sources), it is clear that the claim for which the flagellants were persecuted throughout the fifteenth century was that redemption lay in blood—their own blood, shed in imitation of the bleeding of Christ. What exactly they taught about the consequences of self-flagellation is uncertain, but what the authorities feared was the idea that blood was a more immediate means of access to salvation than any sacrament of the church.

The sect of cryptoflagellants emerged in Thuringia and the southern Harz region after the last great flagellant upheaval of 1349–50 and seems to have received a program and some sort of organization from one Conrad Schmid. They were persecuted, along with beguines, beghards, and Waldensians (with whom they tended to be confused), in 1367–69 and again in 1446 in Nordhausen, in 1414 at Sangerhausen, in 1420 at Mühlhausen, at Stolberg in 1454 (the largest persecution), at Quedlinburg in 1461, and in 1481 at Schloss Hoym in the diocese of Halberstadt. The inquisitors in these cases were almost invariably theologians from the University of Erfurt. Lists of flagellant errors surviving from these interrogations include the claim that all sins, no matter how great, are removed by a single flagellation of the body [*sola corporis spontanea flagellacio*], done with contrition of the inner heart;[62] that, once the dispensation of flagellation begins, no one can enter the blessedness of heaven unless he wounds himself in flagellation until blood erupts;[63] that, under this same dispensation, all sacraments are replaced by the flagellation of one's own body done in memory of Christ's passion;[64] and that "one drop of blood [*una gutta sanguinis*] shed with the flail is worth more to God than rivers of the water of baptism . . . or pounds of the oil of extreme unction, which things are only uncleannesses."[65] Articles obtained from the heretics of Sonderhausen, tried in 1454, describe the members of the sect as beating themselves while they prayed prostrate on the ground with arms extended, saying:

Lord Father, Jesus Christ,
Since you are the only one
Who can forgive sin
Save us for a better life.
Have mercy on your children,
When we are in great sin.
For God's sake we pour out our blood
Which is good for [i.e., makes reparation for] sin.

[herre vater, Jhesu Crist,
sint dass du alleyne bist,
der dy sunde kan vorgeben,
frist uns uf eyn besser leben.
erbarme dich ober deyne kint,
wan wyr yn grossen sunden sint.
dorch got vorgyssen wyr unser blut,
dass ist vor dy sunde gut.][66]

The stress on salvation in a single drop and on blood offered up to God as reparation for sin finds echoes throughout fifteenth-century spirituality. Although cryptoflagellant claims are for the blood of ordinary human beings, not for *Blut Christi*, the drops that save are shed in imitation of Christ's own. It is easy to see why the Erfurt theologians, who worried about the miracle hosts of Wilsnack and Hussite frenzy for the chalice, also saw in flagellant blood a challenge to orthodox understandings of *sanguis Christi*.

Treatises *de Sanguine*

It is clear then that the cult at Wilsnack itself, and the competing dissident movements feared by its defenders and opponents alike, focused on blood. So did learned theological discussion. Although there was, in the mid-fifteenth century, increasing and sometimes vituperative debate concerning fraudulent miracles and inappropriate relic and host veneration (there is much abstruse discussion of *dulia* [reverence] and *latria* [worship] and which form of veneration is appropriate to what),[67] the issue at Wilsnack was never only fraud or proper host worship. Fifteenth-century scholastic material is full of *sermones*, *questiones*, *quodlibeta*, and *determinationes De sanguine Christi* (or sometimes *De cruoribus*, *Contra cruorem*, etc.).[68] The title is important. The discussion was about blood. While no university preacher or theologian argued that Christ's blood was palpably present in the Wilsnack wonder, two Leipzig-trained theologians from St. Giles in Braunschweig defended the earthly presence of *sanguis Christi* by analogy to their own relic. And right down into the sixteenth century we find lively and sophisticated debate concerning the status and effects of Christ's blood and our access to it—debate that involved basic Christological and soteriological (not to mention physiological) issues, such as the nature of Christ's body and ours, the integrity of resurrection, the absolute power of God, and the price of redemption.

I take as examples the *questio* and *tractatus De sanguine Christi* from 1406–7 by Jan Hus,[69] several texts from 1443 to 1455 (the height of the debate), and Johannes von Paltz's *Supplementum Coelifodiae*, written in 1503, a year and a half before Martin Luther joined Paltz's house of Augustinian hermits in Erfurt. In them, we see both what changed and what remained the same. Hus begins with the question whether Christ at his resurrection glorified all the blood that had flowed out of his body and argues for the premise (soteriological and christological) that "Christ as true God and true man died out of great love and, making himself obedient to the Father, poured out his blood for our sins and rose from the dead glorified in all things."[70] It follows therefore that

Christ, like all the saints, earned glorification for blood as well as body;[71] that at the moment of resurrection he reassembled and glorified his body and all its parts, as will happen for all Christians in the hour of death, since Christ is the firstfruits of all humankind;[72] that because the blood of Christ is immortal and cannot now suffer, it cannot appear outside his body; and that for Christians to revere anything that claims to be a particle of Christ, existing in time and place on earth, is a desecration of God, similar to revering the stuff of a creature (such as a horse's blood or something smeared on hosts by lying priests).[73] Hus dismisses with skepticism claims to possess the holy foreskin and ridicules as "unbelieving Jews" those who need visible signs.[74] He admits that God *de potentia absoluta* could cause Christ's blood, which is everywhere present in the sacrament, to be present and visible on earth while in glory but says we have no reason to think he has done so; and he argues that the blood sprinkled on bits of the true cross, the crown of thorns, and so forth, is only a red color left behind to trigger memory.[75]

And it is possible that the blood of Christ, which flowed out from his body in the circumcision, was substantially converted into something else according to form, or that the blood if drained out on the cross [*in cruce si exsiccatus*] and converted to vapor by the heat of the sun . . . reverted then by his power on the day of resurrection to its proper form and this was the same blood in number as in form. . . . Nor should the faithful fear that they will not receive again their bodies because wild animals have eaten them and drunk their blood. For in the resurrection all will be glorified. The voice of the saints does not cry out empty and in vain: Lord, vindicate our blood. The blood of Abel cries to the Lord from the earth [Gen. 4.10]. . . . And the Lord said to Cain: What have you done? The voice of your brother's blood cries to me. . . . So we wait happily for the glorification of our blood, even if it has been poured out for the dogs to drink in the name of our Lord Jesus Christ.[76]

The sense that spilled blood, blood poured out (*effusus*), pays a price and cries for restitution, and the sense that we *are* our blood, that blood is life, will recur in debate and sermons throughout the fifteenth century.

Against Wilsnack, Hus argues that the reported miracles are fraudulent; "that red thing [*illum rubeum, nescio quid*]" does no wonders.[77] It is the Creator of creation who should be revered; and if what is shown to the people is the sacrament, it is better to eat it than preserve it. Christ said: "take and eat, take and drink," not "take and preserve."[78] The true blood of Christ is the greatest wonder; it has destroyed the work of the devil; it is the price of salvation.[79]

Between Hus and Johannes von Paltz, much discussion focused on the credibility of the many reported Wilsnack miracles and on the abuses and greed of pilgrimage promoters. Much attention was also devoted to the general question of the proper disposition of transformed hosts—an issue Hus tended to ignore. Tocke's fourteen questions of 1446 opened by asking whether the sacrament that has in it any foreign element or transformation should be preserved and allowed to disappear slowly through age or should rather be consumed by a priest. The opinion of the Erfurt theology faculty in 1446 devotes more attention to this issue than to the remaining ones.[80] Although their treatment focuses on practical questions of what to do with transformed hosts, ontological issues are inevitably involved, since the theologians admit that species change may be miraculous as well as natural.[81] If the cause is supernatural, however, the agent may be the devil instead of God. Such a host should therefore be hidden not venerated, argue the Erfurt doctors, because even if miraculous, the blood is not Christ's in its own natural form. Christ's blood cannot now appear outside his body,[82] and even if he had left bits of inessential blood or "other humors" behind at his resurrection, it is not evident that they would appear on a host at Wilsnack nor even that God would preserve a momentary miracle beyond its natural course and keep such blood perpetually living and red.[83]

The defenses of Wilsnack penned by the Franciscans Kannemann and Döring at the height of the fray similarly range widely between matters of correct praxis and abstruse issues of soteriology and ontology. Franciscan support for Wilsnack is based, first, in arguments that pilgrimage is good for devotion and pacifies the region,[84] second, in the contention that the reverence offered at Wilsnack is really veneration of the sacrament, and, third, in recondite propositions that Christ could have left blood behind because glorified bodies need less blood than unglorified ones[85] or because not all human blood is crucial to core human nature (*veritas humanae naturae*).[86]

These defenses were based on earlier *determinationes* by two Leipzig-educated Benedictines, Johannes Witten and Hermann Bansleben from St. Giles in Braunschweig, who, in the course of defending their own very different *Blut Christi* (a relic brought from the Holy Land by Henry the Lion that had traveled somewhat circuitously from Lübeck to Cismar in Holstein and thence to Braunschweig), raised some basic issues concerning human identity.[87] Writing circa 1445, Witten argued for the presence of a true blood relic at St. Giles, citing the witness of powerful men present at the translation, the accompanying miracles, the analogy of the foreskin (the flesh of Christ left behind), and papal support via indulgences.[88] Bansleben, writing between 1448 and 1455, held that left-behind (separated) blood had not been part of the hypostatic union and hence was not to be venerated with *latria* (worship—the highest form of veneration).[89] It referred to Christ *signative*, not *entitative*; that is, it was a sign of Christ not an element of his wholeness. The identity of person (*homo*) is accounted for not by the presence of every bit of its matter but by "the same figural disposition"—that is, form. [*Esse hominis unum et naturale non consistit in ydemptitate materiali sed in ipsius debita dispositione figurali.*] Christ did not need to resume all his blood, for not all a person's nutritive blood (that is, the blood used in digestion over the course of a life) is necessary to his core (the "truth" [*veritas*] of his human nature).[90] Hence the blood at Braunschweig was *sanguis Christi*. Kannemann and Döring, and later Johannes Bremer, seized upon this to argue that, by analogy, there could be *sanguis Christi* at Wilsnack. Their opponents found it necessary right into the 1450s to refute the proposition that Christ's blood was left behind. At least among the schoolmen, neither the debates of the 1440s over transformed hosts, nor the bull of 1453 confirming the cult as essentially a eucharistic one, silenced discussion of the blood and the larger issues it posed: the price of salvation, the integrity of the human person in resurrection, and the possibility of "seeing" Christ (in the sacrament or outside).

Glossing the defenses provided by the Franciscans Kannemann and Döring, Eberhard Waltmann, a reforming Premonstratensian who had earlier been dean of the philosophy faculty at Erfurt, replied (probably in early 1451) that transformed hosts should be consumed by the priest, unless poisoned or disgusting, in which case they should be hidden among the relics.[91] But his primary concern was not with transformed hosts but with blood itself. The analogy of the foreskin should not be used, Waltmann said, because there are several in Christendom, and it is ridiculous to think God would have multiplied them.[92] To the ingenious argument that God might cause the blood on relics or on hosts to be present as accidents without substance (a sort of reverse transubstantiation in which the substance of Christ's blood lies in glory, leaving its accidents behind) or create a bloodlike matter on the altar by extracting blood color from substance, Waltmann replied that, whatever the *cruor* at Wilsnack is, it cannot be the natural remains of Christ (those shed on Golgotha).[93] To give to the faithful separated blood would be to offer the stuff of a dead body, a mere creature, and no creature should be revered. Even if the red color at Wilsnack is miraculous, it is not the *res* of the sacrament but only spots on it. To adore it is like adoring dirt or flyspecks on the host.

There *can* be miraculous transformations, argued Waltmann. God turned the host into a bloody finger in the presence of Gregory the Great when a woman doubted the real presence.[94] But such miracles are horrible [*horribilis*], because change done by God is horror-inducing. Like the blood plague in ancient Egypt, such wonders show God's wrath at sin or disbelief. St. Gregory did not rejoice at the transformed host but prayed that it be reconverted to its previous form. Why would God offer the faithful a dead creature? We have the living and glorified Christ.[95]

Writing in 1455, four years after Waltmann and two years after the promulgating of the decisive bull, the Franciscan Johannes Bremer took up the issue again in a *questio* called *magistralis*, a mark of honor seemingly awarded to no other text in the controversy. It is grouped in the surviving manuscripts with two more pastoral treatments from 1443, sermons on Hebrews 9, both with the incipit: "the blood of Christ cleanses the conscience."[96] In a complex and powerful analysis that draws on Bansleben and Bonaventure, Bremer's *questio magistralis* argues that Christ rose whole (*totus*, *integer*) if the term "blood" is applied categorematically (that is, to refer to something standing alone, to a substantive). In such use, it denotes Christ. One cannot say that Christ himself is partial or fragmented. But if used syncategorematically (that is, to refer to something not standing alone, a part), the term "blood of Christ" signifies an inessential part (e.g., a bit of blood not necessary to core human nature). So the term could be used of an inessential part that remained behind outside the hypostatic union and would not, in this usage, detract from Christ's *integritas*. Hence, true to the Franciscan tradition, Bremer allows for the possibility of bodily relics of Christ.

> There are, in the church militant, great and precious relics: the clothing of Christ, the cross, and other of his arms [*arma*—the instruments of the passion]. And there are, so the pious believe, major and more noble relics, that is, the flesh and blood of Christ reserved under their proper species [presumably the foreskin and blood relics]. And there are the greatest and most noble relics, in which it is necessary to believe for salvation—that is, the flesh and blood of Christ under the sacrament of the eucharist. The first are great, because they are Christ's *arma* and the instruments of our redemption, although separated. The second are greater, because they are something of the humanity of Christ and were joined to the divinity [*quia sunt aliquid humanitatis Christi et fuerunt divinitati coniunctae*].[97] The third are greatest and most precious because they are united in the *supposito divino* by the act of divinity [that is, they are Christ's humanity assumed by the Logos].[98]

The passage makes two things clear. First, there was a sort of cultural competition among kinds of blood: bodily relics, contact relics (such as the True Cross), and eucharist. Second, consensus was emerging that something "separated," "left behind," was problematic both as object of veneration and means of salvation. Yet Bremer, like Witten and Bansleben in the later 1440s and Waltmann in 1451, places the blood in the broader context of satisfaction and resurrection. Behind scholastic precisions concerning what is the "wholeness" of Christ and what is "necessary" for belief lie two fundamental convictions. First [conclusion 1], reparation cannot be made by the human creature alone [*Humana reparatio sub satisfactionis condignae modo et figura Nullatenus fieri potuit a sola creatura*]. Second [conclusion 3, corollaries 1 and 2], all that is of the perfection of humankind must rise to glory. Even the scars of the martyrs are glorified as a special ornament. Hence, although a few particles [*particulas*] might be left behind to jog memory and reverence [*pro memoria*], the copious redemption of the human species [*pro generis humani copiosa redemptione*] is by the blood of Christ poured out [*effusus*] and resumed [*reassumptus*]. Although it is not necessary that the resumption be total, *exitus* and *reditus* are basic. And it is blood that pours out and returns.[99]

Over the next fifty years, blood continued to draw the attention of both pilgrims and theologians. Critics of pilgrimage asked why people went.[100] Pilgrimages were, after all, more than chaotic; they were dangerous. Ecclesiastical authorities tried repeatedly to devise ways to keep the faithful from being swept away by "inordinate and violent impulses."[101] Their efforts at suppression are, however, testimony to the proliferation of blood cults in the second half of the fifteenth century. When Johannes von Paltz wrote his *Supplementum Coelifodiae* of 1503, a sort of handbook to prepare priests not only for preaching but also for the whole task of the cure of souls, he argued explicitly against Wilsnack.[102] But he allowed that some pilgrimages were true and laudable, and raised the question "why miracles of the blood of Christ are more numerous [*multiplicata*] than other miracles."[103] His assumption that the frequency of blood miracles is a well-known fact is as significant as the explanations he gives for it.

Following Johannes von Dorsten, who wrote in the 1470s, Paltz argues that such miracles are useful to reproach the negligence of priests, to counter infidelity, and to excite reverence toward the eucharist, which (says Paltz, quoting Giles of Rome) is "more doubted than other sacraments."[104] He refers to a miraculous showing of blood to a girl in Erfurt, who doubted that the *viaticum* could heal.[105] But the threat and allure of blood is now turned against outsiders as well. Blood miracles happen, says Paltz, to oppose the infidelity of the Jews, which was seen recently in Sternberg, when blood appeared on both host and cloth stabbed by Jews. And the Sternberg miracle, like an earlier one in Güstrow, was also directed against heretics—that is, Waldensians and Hussites—from the Mark Brandenburg to Bohemia; for "when blood flows from the host, our faith is confirmed, in which we believe not only the chalice but also the host to contain true blood."[106] The blood miracle is here analyzed as proving both the real presence and the doctrine of concomitance (that the whole Christ is present in each species of the sacrament); it thus refutes the demand of Bohemian Utraquists for the chalice. What is striking is that Paltz asserts categorically, following Johannes von Dorsten, that the *cruor* of such miracles is not blood from the body of Christ.[107] Christ as he is in the eucharist is not "tangible or passible or harm-able." Neither Jews nor heretics nor misguided Christians hurt God. God is immutable. But the blood is miraculous, created *de novo* by the Creator, because he can make something from nothing whenever he wants.

Paltz deals with a number of complicated questions about venerated blood. He treats the vexed issue of whether, as a creature, it can be honored with *latria* (worship) or *dulia* (reverence—a lower form of veneration suitable for the saints) and discusses various theories about its source—for example, the argument that Christ left behind nonessential blood (and could even have multiplied it as he did the loaves and fishes) and the theory that glorified bodies need less blood. Clearly such topics have not gone away in 1503. He concludes that such holy matter, as a miraculous thing produced by God for the confirming of truth, is to be honored with neither the *latria* owed to God nor the *dulia* offered to saints as rational creatures. But, as a sign of the "true blood of Christ poured out for us," it can be accorded both.[108]

These complex scholastic distinctions are not really the heart of Paltz's concern, however. As I pointed out above, he assumes that blood miracles, however accounted for, are frequent or numerous [*multiplicata*]. What interests him are the reasons. Exposing evil and confirming faith are only, as he puts it, the "special causes [*causae*]" of the blood. More important are the "general causes." ("Cause" here means "reason" or "significance.") They are three: to excite memory of the passion, to pay the price of salvation, and to accuse sinners.[109] Miraculous blood is thus only a special case of the blood of redemption. First, writes Paltz (quoting Lev. 17.11), blood is life, the friend of nature and rest of the soul. To pour it out is horrible [*horribilius fundere*]. Hence to have the blood is to have a memory of the passion of the Lord again and again at hand, for the passion is "vehemently imprinted" in the blood. Second, blood is the price [*pretium*] of our redemption. As Ambrose says, the precious blood of the immaculate lamb is paid to him to whom we were sold because of sin. In circumcision, the work of payment was done for individuals; but Christ's blood is the circumcision of all. We are all crucified at once in the death on the cross. Third, the blood cries out [*clamare*], for it was poured out, innocent [*innocens effusus est*]. The cause of this outpouring is sin, and we must not turn our backs lest we crucify Christ again, to our damnation. As the old covenant was confirmed by the blood of young bulls, so the new is confirmed by the blood of Christ. Paltz's concern (and I shall return to the point in Chapter 10 below) is not finally with devotional abuses or with the didactics of miracles but with the centrality of *cruor* as the price and confirmation of salvation. Behind the discussion of false and true pilgrimage or correct devotional practice lies a soteriology of sacrifice.

Larger Questions

The blood of Wilsnack was thus a major and a (literally) contested site in the fifteenth century. No modern historian doubts that the pilgrimage was a mass phenomenon.[110] The large pilgrim church, one of the most important late Gothic hall churches of northern Germany, itself attests to the pilgrimage's success (see Plate 4). The choir and crossing were perhaps finished by 1390; and the huge vaulted nave, built with only a third of the pilgrimage revenues, was completed in two bursts of building activity, one before 1412, the other between 1471 and 1500. (Adjustments were, however, made in the floor plan to shorten it and the planned tower was never added.)[111] By 1429 the aspiring city had dozens of inns, and Ludecus claims that the church soon became a *domus negotiationis* or *Kauffhaus* (sic)—a sort of souvenir shop for religious objects.[112] Although there is no way of confirming the estimates of some historians that as many as 100,000 people a year journeyed to Wilsnack, evidence attests that the pilgrims were a truly international lot. In the early years of the Council of Basel, attendees noted that a local church had a picture of one of the Wilsnack miracles.[113] Judicial proceedings from German, Flemish, and French cities sent offenders to Wilsnack as punishment and atonement. Wills have been found in Lübeck and Stralsund made by travelers before departing on a pilgrimage to Wilsnack from which they might not return or commissioning pilgrimages to be made in their stead after their deaths.[114] The Duke of Kleve went on pilgrimage to Wilsnack although there was a "holy blood" in his hometown; rituals in Augsburg, Constance, and other south German sites used blessings from Wilsnack, although they had local blood cults of their own.[115] Wilsnack pilgrim badges have been found all over Germany and in Denmark, Sweden, England, France, the Low Countries, Poland, Hungary, and Bohemia.[116] More than sixty bells with reliefs of the three bloody hosts of Wilsnack, cast between 1399 and 1522, have been discovered, not only in Germany but in Denmark as well.[117] Lübeck boasts a milestone giving the distance to Wilsnack.[118] Pilgrims wearing Wilsnack badges on their hats are represented in Books of Hours, woodcuts, and panel paintings.[119]

The extent of the polemic testifies as well to the power of the blood at Wilsnack. Already at the synod of Magdeburg in 1412, those involved in the controversy claimed, with exaggeration typical of medieval rhetoric, that more had been written about the alleged Wilsnack miracles than about Christ and the apostles.[120] Defenders and detractors alike later insisted (although we cannot prove it) that the Wilsnack wonder was discussed at the Councils of Constance and Basel.[121] Rome was repeatedly drawn in. Most of the theologians of northern Germany, and at least three university faculties (Prague, Erfurt, and Leipzig), replied to the lists of theses compiled for the various conferences. About twenty-five position papers pro and con are extant from the years around 1450 alone. Indeed over fifty *questiones* and *determinationes* concerning the Wilsnack blood are said to survive (a number of them copied many times), and they are found not only in north German libraries but as far away as Munich, Stuttgart, and Nuremberg as well.[122]

It should be clear from the way I have told the story that there is a larger geographical and chronological context to the phenomenon of the Wilsnack blood. Bremer and Paltz refer to cults at Erfurt, Güstrow, and Sternberg. Johannes von Dorsten, who opposed Wilsnack, supported veneration of the blood at Gotha; John of Capistrano, who waffled on Wilsnack, defended the host miracles of Brussels and Daroca in Spain, and argued with astonishing vitriol against Eberhard Waltmann that his denial of *latria* to the blood divided the divinity of Christ from his humanity.[123] The Carthusian James (Jacob) of Jüterbog (or Klusa), who attacked Wilsnack in his *Tractatus de superstitionibus* of 1452, worried that false miracles would encourage Jewish mocking of the host.[124] Tocke himself feared that the "false blood" would give encouragement to flagellants and Waldensians who denigrated the eucharist. Johannes von Paltz saw the blood at Sternberg as a useful warning against the infidelity of heretics and Jews. The odd theological precisions about left-behind blood from Golgotha (to which, in modern reasoning, the spots on wafers at Wilsnack—whether or not miraculous—are hardly analogous) draw in issues far removed from the question of the authenticity of the Wilsnack miracle. The streams of pilgrims who cried to the blood for salvation and the theologians who exhaustively explored the presence and absence at Wilsnack are part of a much larger blood obsession in the fifteenth century.

In order to understand the full complexity of this obsession, it is necessary to look, first, at blood cult in northern Germany in the later Middle Ages and then at certain abstruse debates over the soteriological significance of *sanguis Christi* that emerged far away in Spain, France, and Rome between the 1350s and 1460s. But already in the specific legends and miracle stories of Wilsnack, the learned texts and disputes over objects of veneration, and the pilgrim practices themselves, we begin to see that more lies behind blood obsession than the emphasis on suffering and violence, or on love, often lodged by scholars at the heart of late medieval piety. Theologians and villagers alike placed their convictions and their passionate disagreements in technical questions about blood as *integer* and *effusus* and in debates about where it might be found, when and whether it changed, and how long it lasted as living and red.

These are questions to which I shall return but only after I have broadened the geographical context a good deal. I turn then in Chapter 3 to the pilgrimage landscape of northern Germany both in the two centuries before Wilsnack and during the decades of its extraordinary success. Here we will see not only the competition offered by other bleeding-host sites to the little town in the Prignitz but also the claims of a very different kind of blood: the supposed bodily relics of the crucifixion. The fact that the same specific verbs and nouns, the same biblical allusions and physiological quandaries, cluster around this very different kind of blood suggests that behind issues of ecclesiastical discipline and control lay quite specific ontological and soteriological questions about the nature of the human person and about access to the presence of the divine.

Sites referred to in Chapters 2 and 3.

Chapter 3
Cults in Mecklenburg and the Mark Brandenburg

It may seem odd that the little village of Wilsnack in the Prignitz, an unimportant and unstable area of the German north, should have become the center of blood cult in fifteenth-century Europe. Insofar as blood pilgrimage is known today, sites in Catholic areas, such as those at Bruges, Deggendorf, or Weingarten, receive most of the attention—an attention that may distort our perception of the distribution of earlier cult.[1] Moreover, scholarship has long taught us to see blood pilgrimage as especially characteristic of southern or middle Germany. Enthusiasm for blood relics was concentrated, we are told, in Swabia, first during the Carolingian period and again in the thirteenth century, in response to an influx of eastern relics after the crusade of 1204.[2] Localized host miracles (those associated with a particular pilgrimage site) are said to have been more numerous in Germany than elsewhere in Europe (over one hundred German cases are known), reaching a high point in the early fourteenth century and again in the second half of the fifteenth, especially in south German lands. Enduring blood miracles (what Browe calls *Dauerwunder*—that is, miracles where the blood remained and was venerated rather than changing back into wine or bread) are thought to have replaced short-term apparitions in the fourteenth and fifteenth centuries and, especially when directed against Jews, to have involved gushing streams of blood.[3] It is also usually said that host miracles were more likely to involve anti-Jewish charges in south German lands, especially Bavaria and Austria. (Browe cites twenty-two southern as opposed to fourteen north German cases.)[4] These generalizations of mid-twentieth-century scholarship provide no hint that cult would arise and become successful in the 1380s in the backwater of the Prignitz.

Furthermore, pilgrimage was not easy to orchestrate, as Nicholas Vincent has recently shown in a study of Henry III's extensive and unsuccessful efforts to introduce the cult of the Westminster blood relic in thirteenth-century England. For successful pilgrimage, it was not enough to produce authenticating documents, arrange lavish processions and translations, garner ecclesial support, or secure indulgences.[5] A number of places in Germany that offered large indulgences for well-attested objects and engaged in extensive propaganda for them failed, as Westminster did, to induce or sustain pilgrimage.[6]

Nonetheless, despite the large difficulties faced by any new cult as well as what might seem disadvantages of specific location, Wilsnack became by far the most popular blood site in Europe—one that generated copycat, albeit largely unsuccessful, claims in the rest of northern Germany. In this chapter I wish to consider other blood cults in the lands around Wilsnack, both preceding and during the period of its popularity. I do so in order to accomplish four things. First, I want to explain Wilsnack's success by pointing out that blood objects were more prominent in north German lands than has previously been noticed. Although the vast amount of available research on Wilsnack has not made this rather obvious point, Wilsnack was prepared for in a way the failed Westminster cult, for example, was not.[7] Second, I want to explain the particular power of blood objects in northern Europe by considering the need for holy matter so prominent, yet so fraught with ambivalence, in fifteenth-century piety. In order to do this it is necessary to illustrate in some detail the variety of objects perceived as *sanguis Christi*. Despite the differing traditions behind them and the tendency of previous scholars to treat the types in isolation from each other, the various bloods of late medieval Germany—relics, contact relics, miracle hosts, desecrated wafers—were all material objects, called "blood," through which divine presence was mediated. Understanding this will, I shall claim, shed new light on the hideous anti-Jewish host-desecration libels characteristic of northern Germany in the late fifteenth century. Third, I want to make clear—at least as clear as the fragmentary evidence allows—the chronology of types of blood in the German north. The increasing association of blood with desecration revealed in this chronology supports my explanation of the growing tendency to associate eucharistic blood miracles with the Jews. Fourth, I want to tease out, where the documents allow us to do so, the common assumptions about blood's power and blood's behavior revealed in the words and actions of its adherents. We will not understand the drawing power of blood objects, and hence of the Wilsnack (and later the Sternberg) hosts as chief among them, unless we recognize that, for all the difference of relic and host, holy blood was understood to behave in quite specific ways. Although divided, it was whole in partition; hence its very division spread its power. Moreover, it made its fundamental appeal as something Christ both shed and offered up, left behind on earth and took away with him to heaven. Thus, in complex ways, it connected its adherents to the divine, yet accused those who provided it and even those whom it redeemed. The connection of cultic blood with desecration and accusation, as well as with manifestation and salvation, parallels with surprising precision the concerns of both learned theological discourse and popular devotion.

Once again I must treat a wealth of confusing detail, for it is only in the details of these cults that the specific concerns and anxieties of adherents become clear. But before I do so, some further words about the historiography and the evidence are necessary.

Historiography and the Problem of the Evidence

Any effort to place the cult at Wilsnack in a broader geographical context runs immediately into three almost insuperable obstacles. The first is the problem of evidence. Much of our material on European blood cults dates from long after the supposed founding events, whether relic inventions or host and corporal miracles. Indeed for Germany much of the evidence comes from chronicles and local histories of the sixteenth century. For the south, it is frequently a projection back of later pilgrimage propaganda; for the north, it often consists of Protestant accounts of Catholic "superstition," which may themselves overestimate the popularity of what they so stridently oppose.[8] Most of the original church records, miracle books, and broadsides from Mecklenburg and Brandenburg were destroyed in the horrendous devastation of the Thirty Years' War. Many scholars who have worked on blood veneration recently have therefore tended to focus on cultural construction or memory, but even this becomes risky when the date at which various legend motifs emerged is so imprecise.

The second problem, closely related to the first, is the nature of existing scholarship. For despite the fragmentary nature of what we can know, there are several quite brilliant early twentieth-century studies (above all, the work of Peter Browe in the 1920s and Romuald Bauerreiss in the 1930s but also the massive, learned, and never published doctoral dissertation of Johannes Heuser from 1948) that suggest general distributions and trends.[9] All subsequent work has relied on these, sometimes extrapolating to cruder generalizations. Hence certain patterns have become received wisdom—patterns that are, as Hartmut Kühne recently pointed out, more the outline of what we knew at a particular moment in German scholarship than the geography and chronology of the devotion of the Middle Ages. The elaborate charts of dates, locales, and types in Bauerreiss, Browe, and Heuser are often, as is inevitable given the fragmentary evidence, unreliable in their specific details;[10] the more we have learned about the individual cases, the less we are sure we know. And since Anglophone historians often do not make extensive use of German-language scholarship, the work of the Canadian Lionel Rothkrug, always fiercely intelligent but sometimes misleading, has introduced into English-language discussion a confident sense of distribution and percentages that German work has been overturning for decades.[11]

A third problem is related to the second. The existing scholarship has tended to divide blood cult into three (or four) watertight compartments: blood relics, eucharistic miracles (with anti-Jewish libels often treated completely independently), and bleeding images. Of the classic scholarly works, only Heuser relates the three.[12] Recent scholarship is, if anything, even more trapped in these categories. Blood relics have been studied as bodily relics of Christ (along with contact relics, such as thorns from the crown of thorns, bits of the true cross or the sponge and lance, or supposed body-part relics such as the holy foreskin) and subsumed generally into the history of medieval relic cult.[13] Bleeding hosts have been treated as eucharistic miracles and hence placed against the general background of eucharistic devotion.[14] Those blood miracles that supposedly resulted from Jewish host desecration have often been discussed apart from similar blood miracles and placed instead against the background of other anti-Jewish libels, such as ritual murder and well-poisoning, and the general growth of anti-Semitism.[15] Bleeding images—popular especially in the seventeenth and eighteenth centuries—have been understood in the context of a growing visuality in late medieval/early modern devotion with its attendant controversies over the iconic and over pilgrimage.[16]

In all this, there is nothing that explains why an obscure village in the Prignitz would—or could—emerge as the center of late medieval blood cult, both for Germany and beyond.[17] Indeed the general patterns proposed in mid-twentieth-century scholarship seem to suggest that blood was hardly important in north German lands at all. Yet for the past seventy-five years, local historians have been arguing that blood legends and blood cult were particularly prominent in middle and northern Germany, especially Brandenburg and Mecklenburg.[18] Moreover, distribution charts, even where accurate, tend to obscure chronology. Blood relics appeared in Saxony and the Hansa area later than in north Italy and Swabia, it is true.[19] Jewish persecutions reached Brandenburg and the Baltic Sea after the pogroms generated by the Rindfleisch and Armenleder movements (1298–1300 and 1336–38 respectively) and the Black Death (1348–49) in the south and thus tended to be judicial murder rather than spontaneous lynching. But by the fourteenth century, blood had arrived in the German north.

In order to understand the context of the Wilsnack blood, it thus seems

TABLE 1. BLOODHOST SITES, CATEGORIZED BY SUPPOSED FOUNDATION DATE

Date	*Place*	*Modern* Länder *(states)*
1191	Erfurt	(Thuringia)[20]
1210	Doberan[a]	(Mecklenburg)
1231	Wasserleben[a]/Halberstadt	(Sachsen-Anhalt)
1247	Beelitz[b]	(Brandenburg)
1249	Zehdenick[a]	(Brandenburg)
1287	Heiligengrabe[ab]	(Brandenburg)
1289	Jasmund-Bergen	(Pomerania [Mecklenburg-Vorpommern])
1290	Bernstein (Pelczyce)[a]	(Poland)
Before 1326	Nauen	(Brandenburg)
1326	Krakow am See[b]	(Mecklenburg)
1330–31	Gottsbüren	(Hesse)
1332	Güstrow[b]	(Mecklenburg)
1383	Wilsnack[c]	(Brandenburg)[21]
1399	Posen (Poznań)[b]	(Poland)[22]
1429	Wartenburg bei Wittenberg[c]	(Sachsen-Anhalt)[23]
1492	Sternberg[b]	(Mecklenburg)
1510	Berlin, Brandenburg, Stendal[b]	(Brandenburg)

[a]Cistercian; [b]supposed Jewish desecration; [c]suspected fraud

wise to turn not to what are sometimes thought to be general European patterns (about many of which we are now uncertain) but to the region itself and the wide variety of blood devotions in it.[24] But how do we handle the problem of the evidence?

If we take the approach of previous scholarship and categorize blood cults according to the alleged date of their foundation—that is, the date of the supposed host abuse or miracle, or the date of relic acquisition—the evidence for northern Germany and nearby areas would look something like Tables 1 and 2.[25]

Such tables, based on legends and charters usually composed long after the supposed miracles or donations, are, however, quite misleading. They sug-

TABLE 2. BLOOD RELICS, CATEGORIZED BY DATE OF SUPPOSED ACQUISITION

shortly after 1080	Einbeck	(Lower Saxony)
1222	Schwerin	(Mecklenburg)
1231	Marienfliess[a]	(Brandenburg)
1256	Cismar[b]	(Holstein)[26]
1283	Braunschweig[b]	(Lower Saxony)
1335	Mariengarten[a]	(Lower Saxony)[27]
?	Wienhausen[a]	(Lower Saxony)[28]

[a]Cistercian; [b]Benedictine

gest, for example, that anti-Jewish charges go back to the mid-thirteenth century, before Jews are known to have been in some of the towns in question. They give the erroneous impression that blood relics had little drawing power after the thirteenth century. They obscure the flurry of efforts to refigure and reconstruct blood cult in the years just before and after 1500. Most important, in a number of cases, they suggest the existence of cult and/or cult objects decades before there is any corroborating evidence for their presence.

Somewhat greater historical precision seems to be obtained if one studies the dates at which legends and documentary claims emerge. Much of our evidence for thirteenth- and fourteenth-century blood veneration then becomes evidence for sixteenth-century debate over reform, superstition, history, and culpability. What we study is memory and the construction of memory. The stories from Heiligengrabe, Zehdenick, and Beelitz, for example, jump forward from the thirteenth to the sixteenth century. The presence of blood at Marienfliess is redated to circa 1300, when the charter asserting its provenance was forged; and the relics of Cismar and Braunschweig are assigned now to the thirteenth century when their *Historia* was written, not to the lifetime of Henry the Lion, who supposedly acquired them from the Holy Land. The blood of Gottsbüren becomes in effect a subject for historians of nineteenth-century religious mentality.

But such discussion is almost as limited as that which simply charts foundation dates. For something predated and undergirded the legends. We have clear if incomplete evidence, for example, that something was revered at Beelitz and Heiligengrabe long before the anti-Semitic stories of the sixteenth century were crafted. The forged charter at Marienfliess provided a provenance for something. Just as older historiography was too trusting in its tendency to classify cases by their attributed date, so recent historians (quite understandably eager to dismiss the backward projection of fraudulent or anachronistic claims, especially anti-Jewish ones) have been too quick to ignore evidence that something was there—something people called sometimes *corpus Christi* but increasingly *Heilig-Blut*. The only way to make sense of any of this is to consider particular cases.

Blood Cult in Middle Germany and the Havelland

Some historians have suggested the blood pilgrimages of Gottsbüren (in Hesse), Wasserleben (in the Harz), and Einbeck (south of Hildesheim) as precursors of Wilsnack. Kurt Köster's 1961 article on Gottsbüren is titled "Gottsbüren, das hessische 'Wilsnack.'" All three sites are possible influences, although (as we shall see) Johannes Kabuz could have found inspiration closer to home. What is important about these examples is the fact that they are different kinds of blood with different histories. Yet what peeks through the little we are able to ascertain is a clear sense of a common drawing power behind the varied objects contemporaries felt they could call "blood."

About Einbeck in the Harz, we know only that the chapter was founded circa 1080 with a dedication to St. Alexander, that it was later said to have a blood relic, and that in the second half of the twelfth century the house had important political connections to Henry the Lion, with whom so many other blood relics became associated in legend. A major Gothic hall church with a chapel for the supposedly miracle-working blood was begun circa 1270. We have evidence of a donation to the holy blood chapel from 1306 and a document of 1489 from the bishop Julian of Ostia authorizing a procession of the holy blood. There is a Cranach blood altar from 1515.[29] In nineteenth-century accounts (typical in their confusion and conflation of bloods), the holy object is said to have been a relic given by the emperor Lothar III or Henry the Lion or a portion of the Wasserleben blood (a host or chalice miracle). Recent study asserts only that the pilgrimage, such as it was, was clearly tied to an important market at Einbeck.[30]

About Wasserleben more is known. A Cistercian cloister was founded there circa 1300 next to a blood chapel that was probably built shortly before; from the beginning the dedication was to the holy blood. The oldest document is an indulgence from 1288 for the showing of the blood. The oldest account of the finding legend is from fifteenth-century Braunschweig; it dates the host miracle to 1231. The longer Low German account of 1507 (clearly a polemic directed against Halberstadt) tells of a servant woman, Eringard, who hid the host in a cloth after receiving communion and laid it in a chest. After three days her master found it and, seeing her fear, took it to the priest, who opened it and found blood. The bishop of Halberstadt ordered it translated there but on the way the chalice containing it kept filling with blood (presumably to register protest at the move and a desire to return to the finding site). Only the cloth remained in Wasserleben, where more miracles were worked than in the rich city of Halberstadt.[31] The Halberstadt chronicle of Johannes Winningstadt reports, however, that the blood remained in Wasserleben and only the chalice went to Halberstadt, where it was walled up in a pillar of the church. A number of indulgences for the cult at Wasserleben are extant from the late thirteenth century and suggest that there was a major influx of pilgrims and gifts at Corpus-Christi-tide. We also have some evidence of wide-ranging efforts by the nuns to raise money for the chapel shortly after 1300.

Although there is no way to recover the earliest events, several things are clear about the Wasserleben/Halberstadt cult. First, there was pilgrimage at Wasserleben about a hundred years before Wilsnack, and it was to blood—either a bloody cloth, or a bleeding object, or a chalice of blood. And blood claims were still significant enough in the Halberstadt area a hundred years after Wilsnack to receive conflicting reinterpretations. Second, there was (at least according to later accounts) competition for control of the relic between the finding site and the diocesan authorities; and this competition was itself expressed by blood. Not only did the host bleed to protest the original violation of being improperly removed from the mouth of the communicant; a second bleeding miracle supposedly protested the translation to Halberstadt. Third and connected to this, there was disagreement (or at least differing perceptions) about whether to preserve the holy matter or wall it up in the church as canon law could be understood to demand. The theme of blood as result of, and protest against, violation is one we have met already at Wilsnack in Eberhard Waltmann's polemic; similarly, the concern for proper treatment of supposedly desecrated holy matter was a theme in Wilsnack discussions from Hus (circa 1406) to the 1450s.

Gottsbüren in Hesse in the north Reinhartswald has surely the most bizarre modern afterlife of any medieval blood site.[32] In 1837 the Protestant pastor of Hofgeismar, Carl Bernhard Nicolaus Falckenheiner, claimed that the *corpus Christi sanguineis guttis* allegedly found on lands in Gottsbüren owned by the Benedictine cloister of Lippoldsberg was a literal body, found undecayed and marked with blood drops, that was set out for credulous folk to see as the body of Christ.[33] Down into the twentieth century, the story was glossed as a fraud perpetrated by the abbess, who, in financial constraints, inflicted artificial stigmata on the body of a migrant working boy found dead in the house of a local smith and used it to stimulate a profitable pilgrimage.

We do not in fact know exactly what was found on the Gottsbüren holdings of the Benedictine cloister of Lippoldsberg (in the later Middle Ages the phrase *corpus Christi* clearly meant a host of some sort), just as we do not know what was found in the neighboring north Hessian town of Wolfhagen, where a chapel to the "glorious body of the Lord" was erected in 1332–37 but did not succeed in creating major pilgrimage.[34] We have, however, early documents attesting to fast growing cult at Gottsbüren and conflict over revenues. In June 1331 the archbishop of Mainz decreed that gifts collected up until then should be divided, with half to himself and half to Lippoldsberg, but henceforth two-thirds were to go to the cloister for maintaining pilgrims and building a pilgrimage church. In the same year, the parish priest sued for the revenues and was summoned to Trier, where he was sentenced to two days in prison for greed; his testimony speaks of the miracle as "new." An inscription on the Gothic hall church, which still stands, indicates it was begun in 1331. Evidence of the success of the cult is extensive. Pilgrim badges from Gottsbüren (a crucifix surrounded with the name) and the Gottsbüren sign stamped on bells have been found all over northern Germany, in the Low Countries, and in Scandinavia; tax lists and wills from north Germany, Sweden, and Flanders indicate that people made vows to go on the Gottsbüren pilgrimage and were judicially condemned to do so. The Lippoldsberg cloister, which moved to Gottsbüren, had increased to over a hundred nuns by 1343; it seems to have suffered problems in discipline owing to the hustle and bustle of care for pilgrims.[35] When the archbishop of Mainz ordered the nuns back to Lippoldsberg and moved the collegiate foundation from Hofgeismar to Gottsbüren in 1346, a fight over the revenues ensued. It is not clear how long the pilgrimage flourished. The Hessian princes still supported it in the late fifteenth century but a document of 1464 speaks with nostalgia of the olden times of glorious pilgrimage.[36]

Places as far afield as Gottsbüren may well have been known in Wilsnack. The Hessian pilgrimage was clearly a financial and religious success, with a far-flung reputation, thirty years before the host miracle of 1383. But the immediate context for the successful cult at Wilsnack is surely the circle of blood sites in the Havelland (Marienfliess, Heiligengrabe, and Nauen) and just beyond (Zehdenick to the east and Beelitz to the south). People in the Mark Brandenburg were used to petitioning the holy blood for assistance. Corpus Christi day was frequently called "holy blood day" in the Mark—a fact which helps to explain the concern of the experts from Erfurt that people might actually think the feast originated in Wilsnack.[37] The numerous Cistercian convents, established by margraves and local noble families (often against each other) to secure claims to contested borders, were accustomed to both financial and spiritual support from blood relics or bleeding hosts. And to the north in Mecklenburg lay another circle of holy bloods, several of them supposedly descended from each other and several, once again, Cistercian outposts of colonization.[38]

About Nauen and Beelitz, little is known. Records show that, at Nauen, in 1326, a chapel to the blessed sacrament was established by a wealthy burgher on the spot where the sacrament was supposedly found "in a miraculous way" under the ruins of the parish church after a fire—a parallel to Wilsnack sixty years later.[39] An extensive chronicle of a Jewish desecration at Beelitz was reported in the *Märkische Fürstenchronik* by the Protestant pastor Paul Creusing in the third quarter of the sixteenth century (Creusing deplored the cult as an idolatry that had been terminated by the Reformation) and was picked up a little later by Andreas Angelus in his *Annals* of the Mark, who dates the events to 1247.[40] But there is no evidence that the original object of veneration was in any way connected to Jews, who had not yet appeared in the Mark.[41] We do, however, have an indulgence given by Bishop Rutger of Brandenburg in 1247 which refers to a host abused by ignorant people and suggests that no perpetrator was subsequently discovered or punished. (Perhaps no effort was even made.) Indulgence letters from a few years later suggest at least a modest cult.

Although recent historians have mostly been interested in the fact that the sixteenth-century accounts of Beelitz are palpably false, the original document is itself a fascinating one. The bishop's interpretation of host miracles is, on the one hand, a sophisticated theology of presence in absence that parallels what theologians such as Cusanus would write 200 years later in the technical blood debates of the mid-fifteenth century. Bishop Rutger stresses that what Christ has left behind is a *pallium*; the term seems to mean literally "veil" rather than its more usual medieval denotation of a stole that conveys delegated ecclesiastical authority. It is important to Rutger that Christ remain hidden, and hidden means in some sense absent—that is, rapt away to heaven. The text begins with a striking reference to Christ "rising and ascending" in "suffering and death." On the other hand, the indulgence makes a virtue from sacrilege: host abuse becomes itself a sort of *felix culpa*. God may, in a special miracle, give visual undergirding to eucharistic theology and denounce those who attempt to use the consecrated wafer to conjure or defraud. But accusation is less important to Rutger than revelation. The perpetrators may never be uncovered, but the abuse committed by them brings a manifestation to the faithful. Ironically then, it is the abuse that assures ordinary Christians that the gone-away Christ is nonetheless present; it makes him palpable. It provides the stuff of pilgrimage.

> Rapt into heaven in a whirlwind, Elias relinquished the *pallium* to Elisha [4 Kings 2.11–15]. . . . Rising and ascending on high in the whirlwind of suffering and death, Christ left behind for his holy church his *pallium*, under which same *pallium* he visits it . . . in a feast to be eaten, under which *pallium* is given a visible sign of an invisible thing [*inuisibilis rei uisibile datum signum*], under which *pallium* is that ineffable sacrament of his body. But as in the field of that man Job there were . . . donkeys . . . so there are a number of sons of the church of simple mind . . . who do not yet believe that Jesus could veil his suffering . . . in the secrets of the sacraments and, doubting or astonished, they marvel that these things dwell under this *pallium*. So to those who err and cannot be protected from the simplicity of their error, God of his great clemency has revealed the flesh and blood [*carnem et sanguinem*] of the crucified and the strength of the Christian faith by confirming the sacrament. And it happens that, because the virtue of the sacrament is believed and the belief preached, some simple people, who are too daring, misuse the grace of the sacrament in sacrilegious, magical

or other kinds of criminal or unspeakable abuse [*quidam simplices nimis ausi trahunt ipsam sacramenti gratiam in abusum, in abusionem sacrilegam, sortilegam vel aliis modis nefariam et nefandam*]. Although the Lord hides or delays the vengeance for such things, he still reveals the truth of the faith to the innocent, just as we believe was made clear recently through the marvelous grace of God in the town of our diocese called Beelitz.[42]

It is important to note that a sense of abuse as beneficial, as making visibly present the departed Christ, is articulated long before any attribution of the abuse to Jews. It is also significant that the wonder at Beelitz, at first understood as a host miracle, was, by the third quarter of the fourteenth century, known as "holy blood."[43]

What is most striking about the Mark is the presence—a hundred years before Wilsnack—of three Cistercian women's houses with three clearly competing cults revering three very different kinds of blood: Marienfliess, Zehdenick, and Heiligengrabe[44] (see map, p. 46). In the early years of the fourteenth century (before the Wilsnack miracle) and again in the years around 1500 (when Sternberg to the north threatened to become a rival blood site), these houses competed with each other to attract blood pilgrims.

Cistercian nuns were established at Marienfliess in 1231 by a member of the Gans family, lords of Wittenberge in the Prignitz; at Zehdenick in 1250 by the Askanier family, who were margraves of Brandenburg; and at Heiligengrabe in circa 1287, also by the margraves. Women's monasteries, which remained under the visitation of local bishops and the financial control of local lords and provided prestigious homes for female members of privileged families, were a regular strategy used in border areas by small noble houses such as the Gans to resist princely presence and by lords such as the margraves of Brandenburg to assert it.[45] It is striking that in comparison to the more pacified southern areas of the Mark, where the houses are male, all the Cistercian houses founded in the northern part are women's houses. (The Premonstratensians, so prominent in the Havelland in the twelfth and earlier thirteenth centuries, had proved too powerful for comfort to the local nobility.) For all three of the nunneries in question the detailed blood legends are later constructions—in the case of Zehdenick and Heiligengrabe they date only from the sixteenth century—but in all three cases there were clearly efforts by 1300 to promote blood cult.

There is no direct evidence of blood cult from the early years of Marienfliess. We have, however, a charter dated to 1256, which asserts that emperor Otto IV received several drops of Christ's blood in Jerusalem and kept them in a secret place until one of his knights gave them to Johann Gans. Feeling that it was unworthy to keep such a thing in his residence, Gans founded a cloister at Marienfliess near Stepenitz and gave the precious object into the hands of the nuns. Historians have long agreed that the document (which is inaccurate in form and anachronistic in signatories) is a forgery of the years around 1300 and was intended to further a pilgrimage, probably in competition with Heiligengrabe to the south.[46] But the document itself demonstrates that neither such efforts nor suspicion of them was new, for it complains about lukewarm devotion and castigates contemporary arguments that the cause of holy objects is the greed of the clergy. It thus suggests that there was something there circa 1300 to which (fabricated?) claims could be attached; it also suggests both that debate about such cult objects was common and that they were successful enough to be thought the object of greedy motives. The fact that the margraves (presumably in a move against the house of Gans) gave a protection letter to Marienfliess in 1287, the year of the founding of Heiligengrabe, demonstrates that Marienfliess was worth competing over.

We are often told that blood relics were an older cult form, replaced by host miracles in the later Middle Ages. But there is nothing here to indicate that, at least in 1300, a blood relic lacked cachet over against newer forms of blood. Rather the evidence suggests that blood relics were politically, financially, and religiously desirable, and that Marienfliess's specific claim to blood was both plausible and contested in the late thirteenth century.

Exactly what the competing bloods of Zehdenick and Heiligengrabe were is not clear. Zehdenick appears as a town in 1217, and a Cistercian cloister was established there in circa 1250 at the advice of Hermann of Langele, confessor to the margraves; it received an indulgence in the 1280s.[47] A document of 1409 refers to the house as dedicated to the "holy cross," but around 1500 there was clearly a blood pilgrimage.[48] The pilgrim badge was a single host with three red spots, paralleling Wilsnack's three hosts, each with its single fleck. During the Reformation, the Protestant Visitors were concerned about the cult. They required that the cloister be closed and no mass said at Corpus Christi; and in 1541 they demanded that the nuns surrender "especially the container in which the holy blood was supposed to be, with which they had so long carried out idolatry." There is no record that the nuns surrendered such a vessel, however, or even that they possessed one, since none is listed in the inventory of 1536.[49] The legend of the host-finding, which obviously preserves an older but undatable tradition, is found in Angelus's *Annals* (1598). It begins: "In the year 1247, a woman in Zehdenick pressed a consecrated host in wax and buried it in the cellar in front of her beer cask so that the people would prefer to drink her beer."[50] After she heard a sermon (presumably against superstition) she felt compelled to confess, but the priest did not believe her. The people, however, dug in the cellar, where the earth began to bleed "in three or more" places;

carried to the church in vessels, it manifested its power by healing the sick. The gullibility of women, the association of the host with fertility and healing, the eruption of blood as both protest against misuse and revelation of sacral presence, the grubbing out of holy earth for distribution (a practice which apparently continued at Zehdenick),[51] and the appellation "blood" bestowed on holy stuff (here earth) that was clearly not in any simple sense blood—these are all motifs found in other host-desecration stories.

The legend of Heiligengrabe, as it has come down to us, is also a sixteenth-century construction.[52] The first documentary mention is of a "cloister near the village of Techow" in 1306; it is already referred to in documents as "Zum Heiligengrab" in 1317. The fundamental work by Johannes Simon (1928) proposed that the pilgrimage predated the cloister because the earliest blood chapel was located outside cloister grounds. Recent work has not agreed. Faensen's 1997 study argues that the cloister arose in 1287 as the result of cooperation between the bishop of Havelberg (who wanted a pilgrimage site in his diocese to compete with those of Beelitz and Zehdenick in the diocese of Brandenburg) and the Askanier margraves (in competition with the house of Gans). The legend of its founding took on a clearly anti-Semitic character only in the early sixteenth century when the abbess—in a frenzied effort to compete with other cult sites, to capitalize on the hatred of Jews unleashed by the Berlin trial of 1510, and to preserve old belief in the face of the encroaching Reformation—had a new blood chapel built and a series of fifteen panels depicting the host desecration painted and hung in the church. The panels, made in 1532, were based on earlier pamphlet material in Latin (1516) and German (1521); several examples of the German version are still extant. The abbess's ploy was not particularly successful, however; only modest offerings were reported on the occasion of the consecration of the chapel in 1512 when the miracle host was reinstalled. No significant pilgrimage developed.[53]

According to the sixteenth-century legend, a Jew who stole or acquired a host found his hands covered with blood and buried the holy object, ground into fragments, at a place of execution beneath a gallows. He later confessed and was himself broken on the wheel. Miracles and visions in which blood figured prominently induced the bishop of Havelberg, the margrave, the pastor at nearby Pritzwalk, and nuns from a neighboring house (Neuendorf in the Altmark) to establish a cloister on the site where the miraculous host fragments had been found, bleeding and reassembled. (A very odd moment in the story is the incident of the peasant who supposedly tricked the Jew into confessing by dressing up as a priest.) As is often the case with such legends, there is a clear division between the early and shorter section concerning the confession and execution of the Jew and the later, lengthier story of the host, so that the punishment of the perpetrator (a sort of prolegomenon) occurs before the discovery of the holy object and its subsequent adventures, which is the real subject of the pamphlet. A certain amount of theological ingenuity is spent in describing how the smaller of the two hosts, pulverized and hence taken up as red dust in a feather quill, is the undivided Godhead. The healing of a possessed woman is said to demonstrate that "without any doubt or fraud this was God [*unde ane allen twyuel unde bedroch de ware god*]," who is present "no less in the little pieces of bread than in the whole [*nicht weniger jn den brockessen dan yn deme gantzen*]."[54] The theme of wholeness in partition, of survival through corruption—here an exposition of the theological doctrine of concomitance often deployed against Hussites in the previous century—is one we have seen at Wilsnack and will see again.

Excavations in 1984–86 in order to install heating under the floor of the pilgrim chapel that stands opposite the church in Heiligengrabe revealed, in the middle of the rectangular nave of the first building on the site (which dates from the end of the thirteenth century), a holy grave: a brick vault, too small to contain a human body, over which lay a stone inscribed with the numerals 1287, the traditional date of the cloister's founding (see Plate 10). The little grave was found under a red (that is, blood-colored) plaster floor in which were stuck as if by accident several thirteenth-, fourteenth-, and fifteenth-century coins (evidence it was the site of pilgrim offerings); further excavation revealed the vault to be positioned over several severely mutilated bodies, suggesting that the chapel was indeed built on a place of death—whether of legal execution or lynching, of Jews or non-Jews, is unclear.

Recent scholarship (mostly local, archaeological, and antiquarian) disagrees about whether the little grave enclosed the miracle host of legend and/or its finding spot, or whether it was a replica of the Holy Sepulcher at Jerusalem of a sort known in German churches from the fourteenth and fifteenth centuries and used in the Easter week liturgy for the burial of the host during the *triduum*. We have a description from the middle of the seventeenth century that sounds very much as if there was at that point such a freestanding sculpture of the sepulcher of Christ in the western part of the chapel at Heiligengrabe, although the little vault that survives is clearly of a different type (and earlier date) than the holy graves we know at cloisters such as Eichstätt, Gernrode, and Wienhausen.[55] Bauerreiss and others have argued that Holy Sepulcher monuments and churches are very different in history and architectural form from host cult sites. Recently Faensen and Merback have argued that Heiligengrabe and other southern sites as well are cultic conflations of the two different devotions.[56] What seems clear is that cemeteries, execution sites, and pits or depressions in the earth were associated with both Holy Sepulcher churches and legends of host abuse (both Jewish and non-Jewish), reflecting the complicated connection many medieval people felt between blood-spilling as expiation and blood-spilling as retribution. Such ideas could make contact with the blood of criminals salvific, and execution sites (particularly sites of the lynchings of Jews and host abusers) places of reparation for the sins of all humankind. If one accepts Bauerreiss's argument that images tended to trigger or become folded into legends, one could understand the very presence of a place of gallows and wheel as suggesting the crucifixion of Christ in the host.[57] (And it is striking that the woodcuts of 1521 depict tortured figures—like the thieves crucified with Christ—flanking the Jew who buries the host.)[58] But, as several scholars have pointed out, the vault itself need not have been for either a Maundy Thursday host (buried liturgically during the *triduum*) or for a miracle host; it could have contained a relic from the Holy Land, such as earth, or could have covered the sacred space where a host had been found.

We will probably never know what was in the little vault at Heiligengrabe. Nonetheless, three things are clear. First, over the course of the fourteenth century, a blood cult developed there in competition with other cult sites in the neighborhood. Second, the Heiligengrabe blood was connected (either through the Easter liturgy, or through dedication of the cloister to the Holy Sepulcher, or through some conflation of cult objects) with the burial and resurrection of Christ. Paralleling the text of the Beelitz indulgence, themes of presence and absence (Christ gone away yet left behind) reverberate at Heiligengrabe in the actual architecture. Whatever the little tomb was, it—like a desecrated host—both did and did not contain Christ. Third, in the early sixteenth century, the nuns made efforts to build a pilgrimage around an anti-Jewish form of the founding legend that, while it presumably has no factual basis, echoes the all-too-real contemporary trials in Sternberg and a little later in Berlin.[59] At least some in the early sixteenth century, whatever they may have believed earlier legends to say, thought pilgrimage could be generated by holy matter, especially in the form of blood from a host allegedly desecrated by Jews. To all of these points I shall return.

North and West of Wilsnack

To the north of the Mark Brandenburg—in Mecklenburg, Lower Saxony, and Pomerania—blood relics were the most powerful form of blood presence in the later Middle Ages. There seem, however, to have been at least five cases of bleeding hosts in the two centuries before Wilsnack: Doberan, Jasmund, Bernstein, Krakow am See, and Güstrow. The latest two of these, Krakow am

See and Güstrow—at least as later reported—involved charges against the Jews. Doberan is the best known of the five, both because of the magnificent abbey church that still stands today and because of the elaborate (although thoroughly anachronistic) finding story, with its apparently folkloric elements.

Our oldest reference to the finding of a miracle host at the Cistercian house of Doberan (about five kilometers from the North Sea) is Ernst von Kirchberg's *Reimchronik* (from shortly before 1379). Kirchberg, like Albert Krantz in his *Vandalia* of 1519, refers to a great concourse of pilgrims and to miracles worked by the blood, but only in the past. Although Doberan is important to art historians for its surviving altarpieces and devotional objects, which suggest an active eucharistic cult with an iconographical emphasis on blood (we find, for example, the host mill, a Last Supper in which the sop is given to Judas, and the rare motif of Christ crucified by the virtues or *Tugend-kruzifixion*),[60] it is not clear how much pilgrimage was connected with the original miracle, dated by tradition to 1210.[61] A little shrine from 1320 may have displayed both the miracle host and a consecrated wafer, but documents and indulgences from circa 1400 refer only to setting out the eucharist for veneration.[62] As reported by Kirchberg, the legend concerned a shepherd, who hid the host in his staff. The host glowed, revealing itself to a woman who reported it to the village judge; bishop Brunward of Schwerin translated it to Cloister Doberan. The real flourishing of this story came, however, only in the anti-Catholic propaganda of the sixteenth century.

A miracle host story is also told of Jasmund on the island of Rügen in Pomerania (which belonged to the diocese of Roskilde), where a woman supposedly kept a host that turned into flesh and blood; it was allegedly translated by the bishop to nearby Bergen in 1289 for veneration.[63] Slightly better documentation exists for Bernstein (Pelczyce), south of Stettin/Szczecin in the Neumark, another of those houses of Cistercian nuns that became protectors of holy blood. On February 26, 1290, the archbishop of Magdeburg together with the bishops of Lübeck, Havelberg, and Brandenburg (dioceses that had—or would have—blood sites) gave an indulgence to all who made pilgrimage to the nuns at Bernstein, "where the body of Christ has miraculously changed into flesh and blood [*in carnem et sanguinem mirabiliter*] and done many marvelous things [*multa et crebra signorum miracula*]."[64] It is important to note that this indulgence makes no mention of desecration at all.

The same source that reports the story of the Doberan shepherd also reports supposed host abuses at Krakow am See and Güstrow. Kirchberg's *Reimchronik* attributes the host miracle at Krakow to 1325 and claims for it a large pilgrimage and rich offerings, from which the Elector set aside a part for the cathedral chapter of Güstrow. The revenues were apparently sufficient to finance a blood chapel, which was destroyed by lightning in 1503 and seemingly not rebuilt. According to Kirchberg, the Jews, who had tortured the host [*mit Mezirn Nadlen hartir, dy Hostien sy stachin, und mertirlich zu brachin, zu leist sy worfen sy uf dij Strahzen*], were discovered only after penitential fasts were prescribed throughout the area; they confessed under torture.[65] It is not possible to tell whether any of this happened or whether it is what people later thought ought to have happened. But just to the north, at Güstrow, there probably was, only a few years later, some sort of pogrom.[66]

A holy blood chapel was built in 1332 in Güstrow. It was allegedly built on the site of a destroyed synagogue. The desecration charge, reported by Kirchberg more than four decades later, was elaborated in a Latin broadside published in 1510 by Hermann Barckhusen, who in the same year issued a German pamphlet by Nicholas Marschalk on the blood libel of Sternberg.[67] Already in the fourteenth century, Kirchberg's account gives the familiar elements of the full host-crucifixion story: a Christian serving maid sells to the wife of a Jew named Eleazar a cloth containing a host, which bleeds greatly [*bluten sere*] when tortured and is then buried in the floor of the synagogue.[68] According to Kirchberg, a child is heard crying; the Latin account simply reports: *puncta et stilis et cultris ita vt mirificus sacer ille cruor copiose efflueret.*[69] A converted Jewess reveals the deed. After much fasting and ritual, the city authorities find a bleeding host in four pieces bound up in a cloth. As in other legends, blood announces both presence and violation; part remains alive and whole; clergy and people perform rituals of penitence and community affirmation.

The blood of Güstrow was still valuable a hundred and seventy-five years after the construction of its chapel. Following a fire in 1503, the site became a major point of conflict between the dukes of Mecklenburg, who were eager to establish a house of Observant Franciscans in Güstrow, and the cathedral chapter, who gave permission in 1509 for a cloister on the site of the rebuilt blood chapel only after securing their right "to bring the sacrament and the holy blood [*des heilige Sacrament und wunderbar heilig plut*], which were formerly kept in the holy blood chapel, to a suitable place in the cathedral for showing daily to the pious [*deme andechtigen volgk teglich weysen, auch ehren, wirdigen, loben allenthalben wie vormalen*]."[70] Those who had benefices to say the offices of the holy blood in the chapel retained the right to say them in the cathedral; the blood's costly possessions—its monstrance, cross, books, vessels large and small, the tablet on which its history was painted, and half of its chalices and vestments—went to the canons as well.[71] Whatever its sources, the Güstrow blood was alive and well—and profitable—in the first decade of the sixteenth century.

The nature of our evidence for these blood miracles from the far north is significant. If the original datings could be trusted, the stories from Doberan and Jasmund—like the anachronistic account concerning Zehdenick—would suggest that early host abuses were attributed to simple Christians (often women) and couched in less accusatory rhetoric, later ones attributed to Jews and brutally told. Doberan with its shepherd (attributed to 1210) and Zehdenick with its alewife (attributed to 1249) would predate—in both event and construction—the supposed abuses of Krakow am See (1326) and Güstrow (ca. 1332). Historians have documented a general pattern of change from Christian to Jewish perpetrators, accompanied by a growing paranoia of tone, in accounts from elsewhere in Germany, and trustworthy northern evidence corroborates such a change. The authentic indulgences from Beelitz and Bernstein either accuse misguided members from within the Christian community or simply register the miraculous as a positive event. Anti-Jewish libels, such as the sixteenth-century tale from Heiligengrabe, tend to be late and are unquestionably more accusatory, sinister, and brutal, whether or not the supposed trials occurred. Jews are said to be tortured and executed; serving maids, at least in these tales, are not.[72] But we must note that, for Mecklenburg, early versions of both sorts of legends appear in the same chronicle (Kirchberg's *Reimchronik* from the 1370s) and both sorts achieve their fullest retellings in sixteenth-century propaganda, long after the supposed events occurred. The Doberan shepherd, like the Zehdenick alewife, is in large part a construction of sixteenth-century anti-Catholic polemic. In Kirchberg then, we seem to catch an important moment at which blood stories are changing from host miracle to host abuse. But we have little reason to trust the details of either sort of account. The tale of the Doberan shepherd does not show what happened in 1210, nor does it show how people in the same period construed whatever it was that happened. Tales of superstitious serving women and peasants may retain earlier legends, but we can never know how long the roots of those legends are.

It was the area north of Wilsnack that would in the very late fifteenth century generate Wilsnack's most significant competition. But before the emergence of Sternberg, whose host-abuse libel is all too well documented in all its viciousness of construction, blood relics were probably more powerful than blood miracles both in generating pilgrimage and in expressing ecclesiastical politics.[73] Found in major towns such as Lübeck and Braunschweig, these relics attracted and sustained cult, consolidated alliances, inspired theologians to pen general defenses of holy blood, and were still renowned enough in the early years of the sixteenth century to draw fire from Martin Luther and his followers. Of particular importance were the relics of Cismar, Braunschweig, and Schwerin.

North of Lübeck, across a wide bay from Doberan, on a peninsula jutting into the Baltic Sea, stood the monastery of Cismar, to which the Benedictine monks of St. John's Lübeck (originally founded from St. Giles in Braunschweig almost two hundred kilometers to the south) moved in 1256 after the double house in Lübeck was closed by the bishop. The monks took with them a blood relic supposedly given by Henry the Lion to the bishop of Lübeck in 1177. Work began on the choir in 1260. In 1296 the count of Holstein and Schauenburg and his wife made a second big relic donation to Cismar, including a piece from the crown of thorns.[74] Meanwhile, in 1278, the house of St. Giles in Braunschweig (Cismar's mother house) was damaged by fire. In 1283, abbot Johannes V of Cismar sent a portion of the abbey's blood to Braunschweig to support the rebuilding. The movement of blood from a house in Lübeck (founded by Braunschweig) to Cismar, from whence a part of it returned to Braunschweig, makes clear the way in which transfer and division of relics undergirds relations of filiation and loyalty. This use of blood relics to consolidate relationships has parallels to the Swabian pattern of the tenth century that linked Mantua, Weingarten, and Weissenau in complex tales of the descent of one relic from another.[75]

The gift of 1283 is the context in which our source for the Cismar and Braunschweig stories was produced: the *Historia de duce Hinrico*, whose hero is not so much Henry the Lion as the holy blood of Braunschweig.[76] The *Historia*, composed by an anonymous monk of St. Giles shortly after 1283, tells of Henry's crusade to the Holy Land in 1177, during which he acquired a blood relic from the Greek emperor, which he subsequently divided between Count Gunzelin of Schwerin (this part of the story appears to be a fabrication based on the author's knowledge that Schwerin claimed a blood relic) and Bishop Henry of Lübeck. Much of this account is borrowed (although not the specific details of Henry's gift of the relic to St. John's Lübeck) from Arnold's *History of the Slavs* (completed ca. 1210). The anonymous author then gives what may be an eyewitness account of the festive installation of the blood at Braunschweig and reports its first miracles. He inserts documents from Bishop Volrad of Halberstadt in 1283 testifying to the authenticity of the relic and offering indulgences to those who venerate it.[77] A reference to the blood and water from Christ's side produced by the prick of Longinus's lance is probably meant to suggest Longinus as the relic's source.[78]

It was Braunschweig, almost two hundred years later, that produced two of the most sophisticated defenders of blood devotion: Johannes Witten and Hermann Bansleben. Reflecting a vigorous revival of cloistered life in fifteenth-century Lower Saxony and their university education at Leipzig, Witten and Bansleben defended blood relics generally, noting Benedictine cloisters as their special venue, and argued that the blood of Braunschweig was poured out at the time of the passion [*effuso tempore passionis*].[79] The arguments of their sermons and *determinationes* were adopted by Kannemann and Döring, and later by Johannes Bremer, at the height of the Wilsnack controversy to defend what did not to these protagonists seem a different kind of blood.

But not everyone in the years after Johannes Bremer's *questio magistralis* felt comfortable with the blood of Braunschweig and Cismar. Questions of authenticity as well as of theology continued. Despite the magnificence of the altar at Cismar, where a little door cut into the figure of the flagellated Christ probably opened on feast days for display of the blood in a silver reliquary, the bishop of Lübeck, Albert Krummendiek, had doubts. Perhaps they were exacerbated by representatives of the Bursfeld Benedictine reform, which seems to have reached Cismar in the second half of the fifteenth century.[80] In the document Krummendiek issued on July 20, 1467, he says that he began to question the wonderful blood preserved in the breast of a silver figure of the resurrected Christ because he could find no record of it in old or recent documents. Therefore in the library of the cloister, in the presence of the abbot and brothers, he opened the image and found inside only a piece of crumpled crimson silk. In order to avoid promoting error among the people, many of whom made pilgrimage from a great distance, he declared the veneration invalid and placed the little piece of silk with the rest of the relics.[81] The incident indicates that authenticity of provenance did matter by the later fifteenth century. The bishop investigated because he could not find documentation.[82] The fact that the reliquary contained crimson silk suggests that whoever filled it knew that redness also mattered. To be a convincing cult object, blood had to be authentic—that is, it had to be authenticated—and it had to appear fresh and living.

The history of the blood relic in Schwerin took a very different course, becoming implicated, as did the bloods at Heiligengrabe to the south and Sternberg to the north, in the polemic of the Reformation. When Count Henry I of Schwerin went on a crusade in 1219, he had already made donations for a chapel where the first count Gunzelin was buried. An indulgence for visiting the cathedral in 1220 mentions that "the sacrament of our Lord Jesus Christ" was "preserved there [*reconditum*]" and visited with much honor.[83] A document of 1222 then reports that Count Henry, on crusade across the sea, acquired the blood of the Lord in a jasper from the papal legate, Cardinal Pelagius [*ei dominicum sanguinem donaret in iaspide diligentissime conservatum*], on the condition that this incomparable treasure be kept in a conventual church [*in ecclesia conuentuali*] where the divine office would be celebrated without interruption.[84] So upon his return, Henry gave the blood to the church of Schwerin to be preserved in the chapel where his ancestor was buried, and bishop Brunward declared that henceforth Maundy Thursday and the feast of the ascension would be blood festivals, during which the priests of his diocese and their flocks should make pilgrimage to revere "the blood which Christ poured out for us on the cross [*quem in cruce pro nobis Christus effudit*]." In anticipation of substantial pilgrimage, provision was made to divide the revenues, with a third for building a cloister, a third for supporting the cathedral canons, and a third initially for buying books but afterward for maintaining the fabric of the cathedral.[85] The reputation of the blood spread, aided by word of the victory of its donor over the Danish king in 1223. Pilgrims and revenues poured in. Louis IX of France sent a thorn from the crown of thorns in 1260. In 1274, Count Gunzelin III established a daily service in the blood chapel and endowed a vicar of the blood. The cult may have faltered by the late fourteenth century, when the chapel was restored and redecorated, probably in an effort to revive it. When competition from the new blood at Sternberg (1492) further threatened the pilgrimage, the canons of Schwerin ensured that a third of the Sternberg revenues came to them and protected their own cult by acquiring a confirmation of old indulgences from pope Julius II in 1506. In 1533 the reformer Ägidius Faber, called in as pastor, attacked the "false blood and idolatry in the cathedral at Schwerin" in a tractate published at Wittenberg with a preface by Martin Luther. With his support, his friend Faustinus Labes (who had already made trouble in Güstrow) squared off against the blood at Sternberg. In November the Schwerin chapter complained to Duke Henry that Faber had denounced the holy blood, which had been brought to the church of Schwerin by the duke's forebears, and had made a polemical book with which he attacked and shamed the chapter [*hefft vpp dat hillige blodt, welcher von dusser lofftiken fursten vorfaren in der kerken Zwerin gebracht, eyn schandbock gemakett, dar inne he datt capitel personen der kerken ahngript myt schme unde schandtworden*].[86] The duke answered, in proper Lutheran style, that if they wished to refute Faber's book they must show that it contained something ungodly. Inventories of 1538–51 describe ex-votos hung around the Schwerin blood chapel and a little silver and gilt Christ figure with its arms lifted in the glory of resurrection and in the place of a heart a jasper filled with blood.[87] But shortly after 1540 the pilgrimage ceased.

The cults at Schwerin and Braunschweig suggest that, throughout the thirteenth and early fourteenth centuries, blood relics were felt to be powerful loci of contact with the divine. In the later fourteenth and even later fifteenth centuries, efforts to use them to compete with newer bloods were effective enough to trouble reformers. In general, however, as elsewhere in German lands, bleeding hosts tended to eclipse blood relics by the late fifteenth century, and such hosts were increasingly understood to be the result of Jewish abuse.

Anti-Jewish Libels Circa 1500: Sternberg and Berlin

Despite efforts by Schwerin in the fifteenth century to maintain its cult, the pilgrimage landscape of northern Europe was dominated by Wilsnack between 1383 and 1492. The occasional fraud failed to compete, and few new claims emerged; the church in the Prignitz eclipsed all rivals.[88] Soon after the Wilsnack pilgrimage peaked in 1475, however, the last of the successful blood cults of northern Germany emerged in the little town of Sternberg, about twenty-five kilometers northeast of Schwerin and southwest of Güstrow in the heart of Mecklenburg. Host-desecration charges in the neighborhood about a hundred and fifty years earlier (at Krakow am See and Güstrow) clearly were, as in fourteenth-century Bavaria and Austria, anti-Semitic fantasies; in the case of Güstrow, the anti-Jewish charges may have been projected back onto an actual pogrom.[89] But by the later fifteenth century, in Sternberg (1492) and Berlin (1510), stories of host crucifixion by Jews were elicited by torture in carefully regulated judicial procedures. As Heiko Oberman pointed out, the rise of legal process transformed legends and lynchings into evidence and judicial murder; the onset of "modernity" changed methods, not beliefs.[90]

The trial in Berlin has been extensively studied.[91] For this reason, I spend less time on it here, and also because—an important fact—it failed to produce cult. The series of events began in early 1510 in the little village of Knoblauch, where a tinker, one Paul Fromm, stole a monstrance from the church. Arrested half a year later in Bernau, he claimed to have consumed the hosts it contained, but then, under torture, changed his confession and reported that he had sold one of them to the Jew Salomon of Spandau. Brought to Berlin and tortured, Salomon confessed to having mishandled the host, which miraculously sprang into three pieces. Portions of the martyred host were then supposedly distributed to Jews in the towns of Brandenburg and Stendal for further abuse. At least a hundred Jews were rounded up from various places in the Mark for questioning; several were accused of ritual murder. After a three-day trial in Berlin, thirty-nine were burnt and two beheaded. Paul Fromm was torn apart with red-hot irons.

Widespread publicity followed: six pamphlets describing the events appeared in 1510 alone. Deliberate efforts were made both to spread fear and persecution throughout the region and to foster pilgrimage. The bishop of Brandenburg had several objects associated with the desecration translated to

Berlin (the wafer, a table top, and a blood-soaked paint chip.)[92] Moreover, the model provided by the events at Berlin, Brandenburg, Spandau, and Stendal clearly contributed to contemporary efforts to refigure other blood cults in the region, such as that at Heiligengrabe, as anti-Jewish libels. But no pilgrimage emerged in the Mark. Like the abbess's legends and panel paintings at Heiligengrabe, the bishop's publicity failed. Twenty years earlier, however, in the backwater of Sternberg, where the pastor and secular authorities worked harder for cult, a highly successful pilgrimage emerged—one which was attacked, along with Wilsnack, in Luther's *Open Letter to the Christian Nobility of the German Nation* of 1520 and later, in the 1530s, by Faber and Labes.[93]

At the core of the Sternberg pilgrimage were consecrated hosts allegedly provided to the Jews by a priest, Peter Däne, in order to redeem a pawned cooking pot. (According to one account the pot actually belonged to his concubine.) Those hosts were supposedly stuck with knives or nails until blood flowed from them and then, when they could not be sunk in water, were buried on the grounds of the former court of the duke. Revealed finally to the local clergy, they were found, blood-spotted, and worked miracles. Sixty-five Jews were tortured and confessed to the host desecration. Twenty-seven were executed by burning in a place still known as the Judenberg, on the edge of which was, in modern times, the cemetery of the Jewish community. The priest was burned a year later in Rostock. The remaining Jews were expelled from Mecklenburg, where they are not found again until the second half of the seventeenth century.[94] The burning of Däne gave the duke of Pomerania an occasion to expel the Jews from his lands as well.[95] Comparison to the economically more lively and prosperous Brandenburg, where Jewish money and trade were needed, is instructive. After the expulsion of the Jews there in 1510—consequent upon the Berlin trial—Jewish merchants and bankers soon returned, first as itinerants, then as inhabitants.[96]

We have extensive documentation of the events at Sternberg: both a protocol of the first examination of witnesses and a second testimony, the *Urgicht* (Confession) of 20 October 1492, which was clearly extracted under torture.[97] The torture was apparently attended by both dukes. The evidence was disseminated by that new technique of modernity—printing—in an effort both to spread anti-Jewish propaganda and to advertise cult. A single-sheet broadside, probably produced in Magdeburg soon after the executions and taken directly from the *Urgicht*, was circulated widely, as were longer versions in both Latin and High and Low German. A wooden tablet reproducing the original *Urgicht* was erected in the Rathaus. Already in 1493 a world chronicle produced in Nuremberg reported the events in Sternberg. The humanist Nicholas Marschalk, doctor of both laws and member of the council of the duke of

Mecklenburg, penned a full description of the events under the title *Mons stellarum* (printed in 1510 in German, 1512 and 1522 in Latin). Although critical of what he saw as the accretion of folk material around the account, Marschalk did not doubt that the desecrated hosts flowed with the blood of Christ.[98]

The ensuing cult at Sternberg grew steadily. Miracles were reported, both healings and resurrections; important pilgrims, including Danish royalty and a Spanish princess, came. By March 1494 the bishop of Schwerin had established a division of the pilgrim revenues: a third to the pastor at Sternberg, a third to the bishop of Schwerin, and a third to the cathedral chapter of Schwerin (with some provision for the neighboring chapter at Rostock). Initially all the revenues were to go to Sternberg for building the blood chapel, which was completed by 1496. Six priests were delegated to pray the Hours of Christ's passion and a seventh to show to the faithful twice daily the martyred, wonder-working hosts. In a competition for revenues that is reflected in the legend itself (the host supposedly resisted a move from court to church), the duke built a chapel on the finding site, where, before 1500, more miracles were worked; finally, against the opposition of both the bishop of Schwerin and the pastor at Sternberg, he managed to extract a portion of the pilgrim income to finance a cloister of Augustinian hermits on the site in 1510. The cloister was supported by two of the major Augustinians of the early sixteenth century, Johannes von Paltz and Johannes von Staupitz.

In the baptismal chapel of the parish church at Sternberg we still find today a large table top, heavily scored with knives, on which is written "Dit is de tafele dar de Joden dat hillige sacrament up gesteken und gemartelt hebt tom sterneberge im Jar 1492," and a badly eroded wooden relief of the burning of the Jews[99] (see Plate 8). Mortared into the wall of what was once the main portal of the church is a stone that bears large prints of two bare feet—supposedly marks left by the wife of the Jew Eleazar when she tried unsuccessfully to cast the abused host into a nearby creek (see Plate 9). In the early sixteenth century not only the stone and tabletop were displayed but also the awls or nails with which the host was pierced and the iron pot the priest allegedly tried to redeem by providing hosts to the Jews.[100] The objects in which the crime was supposedly inscribed, the hosts themselves, were, in the early sixteenth century, kept in a tall painted and gilded tabernacle in the parish church; gorgeous ex-votos hung around it, including a little silver model of the city of Kolberg.

Things changed quickly with the coming of the Reformation. The Evangelical preacher Faustinus Labes attacked the Sternberg hosts as "devils," and Luther, after his attack of 1520, wrote to the prior of the Augustinian cloister in Sternberg in 1524: "I rejoice that you have stopped this superstition."[101]

Within fifteen years, the pilgrimage disappeared. Gifts for maintaining the eternal light before the shrine dried up. A Protestant Visitation in 1535 "forgot to ask" about the miraculous hosts.[102]

Historians have tended to treat the events at Sternberg, like those in Brandenburg and Berlin twenty years later, as political and economic in inspiration. Nineteenth-century Protestant scholars argued that the fraud was probably engineered by clergy, in particular the provost of Schwerin, Johannes Goldenboge (also a member of the chapter in Rostock and soon pastor in Sternberg), who managed to acquire a third of the revenues. More recently historians (questioning why the ecclesiastical authorities in Schwerin would create a competing cult in Sternberg, however much they might have tried to control events once unleashed there) have interpreted the trials in Sternberg and Berlin as a move of the estates (cities and local nobility) against the princes (dukes or margraves). Such persecutions would have led, they argue, to loss of Jewish tax income for the princes, whereas both cities and local nobility would have benefited from the dissolution of debts and the confiscation of Jewish property. It is hard, however, to find any consistent pattern of political motivation. For example, the Jews of Braunschweig, implicated by the Brandenburg Jews under torture, were freed by the town council after swearing their innocence. No confession was forced, despite the fact that the Elector of Brandenburg urged persecution. Although required to leave the city, the Jews returned a year and a half later—a course of events which suggests both that the city found them useful as creditors and that the Electors of Brandenburg feared economic competition from moneylenders in Braunschweig.[103]

Nonetheless, it is obvious that there was political jockeying and rank anti-Judaism behind all these events, even if the moves were highly inconsistent. The Jew Josel von Rosheim noted in his commonplace book a report from 1539 that the tinker Paul Fromm had confessed before his execution that his charges against the Jews were false. But when the confessor reported this to his bishop, Hieronymus of Brandenburg, the bishop refused to let the priest bring the matter to the attention of the Elector.[104] There is evidence that, a few years earlier, the Cologne Dominicans, together with the converted Jew Pfefferkorn, used the desecration story from Brandenburg-Berlin-Spandau-Stendal to persuade the emperor to issue a new mandate against Jewish writing.[105]

Behind the Jew-hating, greed, and in some cases naked hypocrisy, there was clearly a religious element as well. What the Jews supposedly produced was blood. More than simply proof of their guilt, it was also a manifestation of the divine to a Christian folk grown tired and cynical.[106] In the very year of the anti-Jewish libel in Sternberg, a synod in Schwerin warned that people tended to ignore the sacrament because it was too familiar.[107] Eucharistic devotion needed stirring up with a little outrage. Throughout the fifteenth century, as we have seen, authorities both in the Mark Brandenburg and farther north in Mecklenburg and Pomerania had worried about competition from Waldensians, cryptoflagellants, and Hussites, who were thought to undermine the eucharist by doubting the sacramental power of priests and demanding a very different sort of blood.[108] From Bernstein and Wilsnack to Sternberg, blood miracles were understood to demonstrate not only the presence of God in the sacrament but also the presence of blood in the bread/body. Thus James of Jüterbog could argue in the 1450s that the miracles Jews induced God to perform accused more than Jews. Jews provided evidence against heretics as well as against themselves.[109] Johannes von Paltz echoed the argument in 1503. Indeed Paltz seems to suggest that the primary point of the blood at Sternberg, like that of Güstrow before it, is the confuting of heretical theology.

> The fourth reason [for the appearance of the blood] is because the infidelity of the Jews must be resisted, as it appeared recently in Sternberg, where they attacked two hosts bought from a certain priest. . . . And the fifth is to warn against heresy. And for this reason I think the miracle was done in Sternberg. For many Waldensian heretics, who are known as *foveani*, have come from Bohemia to the Mark. And they hold the sacrament of the eucharist to be only blessed bread and wine as *lagana* [unleavened bread] is blessed at Passover and do not believe that the body and blood of Christ are contained there. Therefore lest they infect the whole land from the Mark,[110] I believe the divine clemency appeared in this miracle at Sternberg as earlier happened in Güstrow. . . . And the sixth reason is to confute the errors of the Bohemians. For when the blood flows from the host, our faith is confirmed against their errors, since we believe that true blood is contained not only in the chalice but also in the host.[111]

In such arguments, Jews are seen to be useful for making manifest a blood that excites devotion, precipitates pilgrimage, and defends the faith against all unbelievers.

The behavior of blood is described in these texts as people believed blood was wont to behave. Dividing, it remained forever whole; and its distribution created filiation and community. In the trial accounts from Sternberg and Berlin, the Jews are repeatedly accused of dividing the host (which of course remains unsinkable, unburnable, unharmed, and whole) and sending pieces to their compatriots. The motif is not only a literalizing of Christian fears of conspiracy and a tactic by which charges (and confiscations of property) can be spread from town to town. It is also an exact parallel to stories of the blood relics of Braunschweig and Schwerin found in the *Historia* of Henry the Lion. Whether taken (allegedly) by the Jew Salomon from Brandenburg to Stendal or (allegedly) by Henry the Lion and his followers to Lübeck and then to Cismar and Braunschweig, the sharing of blood creates relationship. From the time of the indulgences issued for Schwerin (1222), Beelitz (1247), and Bernstein (1290), the same themes echo again and again. Blood—even when produced by hideous sacrilege—makes visible an invisible God.[112] The red and living stream manifests both presence and violation. Never divided even when ground into dust, the holy matter works miracles of restoration and resurrection, creates networks, and carries its supposed wholeness with it.

The Fate of Cults in the Sixteenth-Century North

In the north of Germany, blood cult was regularly destroyed by Protestant reformers in the mid-sixteenth century. What is striking, however, is how much it still mattered—so much so indeed that much of our evidence about it comes from these reformers, who may have exaggerated the significance of the "idols" they inveighed against. The blood at Güstrow was profitable enough in 1509 to be the subject of a major financial dispute between the canons and the Franciscans and important enough still in the early 1530s for Faustinus Labes to attack, as he did at Sternberg. It was the Protestant Visitors at Zehdenick who insisted that the nuns surrender a miracle host they must still be venerating. It is not clear that the nuns even knew any longer where the "idol" was. At Wilsnack, Ellefeldt spent six months in prison for burning an object Tocke had declared a hundred years before (but never to the people) to be spiderwebs and mold. The humanist Nicholas Marschalk, writing in 1510 to demonstrate (probably inaccurately) that it was the dukes of Mecklenburg who led in the persecution of Jews at Sternberg, charged the bishop and local clergy with disbelief because they suggested consuming rather than preserving the miraculous blood-flecked hosts (a procedure for which there was considerable support in canon law).[113] In the late sixteenth century, the Protestant theologian Cyriakus Spangenberg could still report, with considerable ire, that the clergy and town council of Hettstett in the Harz elevated in procession a host desecrated in a church robbery.[114]

In the transitional years of the early sixteenth century, the themes we have seen in fifteenth-century blood cult thus continued in two very different ways. First, blood continued to play a central role in soteriology. Second, what we might call blood's contact relics survived.

In the 1440s and 1450s, theologians had already differed over whether the blood at Wilsnack was idol or sacral presence. The debate continued into the 1530s, now involving Sternberg, Güstrow, and Schwerin as well. Can Christ's blood be left behind, or does divine wholeness require that Christ *totus et integer* be before the throne of God in heaven?[115] Despite such debate, however, polemic in the opening decades of the sixteenth century makes it clear that there was no ultimate difference in soteriology between the reformers and those who resisted them, as there had been none a hundred years before between the Benedictines of Braunschweig and the reforming canons of Magdeburg. Whether visible or invisible, the blood is what saves; and salvation lies in its shedding. Johannes von Paltz claimed in 1503 that blood miracles were more numerous than other miracles because they are "signs of the true blood of Christ poured out for us freely in his passion."[116] Ägidius Faber wrote in 1533:

> The pope smears this blood [at Schwerin] with his indulgences and shows . . . that he and all his adherents are babies under the skin and not concerned with the salvation of souls. . . . And the devil . . . thinks: I want to build a flea market at Schwerin and offer there a colored thing as Christ's blood, which the pope can confirm with his indulgences, so that ordinary, simple, uneducated people are led away from worship.[117]

The blood from desecrated hosts and images might be a simple miracle [*ein blos mirakel*], said Faber, referring to Sternberg and Güstrow. But it had never flowed from the body of Christ. For it had never been in Christ's body but was only a creature, something new brought to the exterior of Christ's body and blood [*creatur ausserhalben des leibs vnd bluts Christj auff ein newes da hin gebracht*]. The veneration owed to God should never be shown to anything created. "Damned is the person who seeks help, comfort, and holiness in creatures."[118] The true blood of Christ is "strong enough in its nature to stand against sin, hell, death, the world and the devil."[119] Eberhard Waltmann of Magdeburg had voiced a not dissimilar opinion in his treatise of 1451. Although reformers such as Luther and Labes attacked miracle hosts and relics, the role of *Blut Christi* in salvation was, if anything, even more central in Reformation theology than it had been to preachers and propagandists a hundred years before, whatever their particular view of the Wilsnack hosts.[120]

It is also important to note that, for all the coming of the Reformation, objects that had been in contact with bleeding or abused hosts survived.[121] The wood of the gallows under which the Jew supposedly buried the host was said to have been built into the roof of the church at Heiligengrabe.[122] The tabletop, nails, and cooking pot reputedly associated with the Sternberg abuse were displayed not only as historical evidence of the events of 1492 but also as the instruments through which Christ had appeared; the tabletop survives to this day. A blood-encrusted paint chip (supposedly carved from a tabletop by one of the Jewish desecrators), along with a table and knife implicated in the trial of 1510, was taken to Berlin,[123] and the table was still being exhibited, albeit as a wonder in the sense of rarity or marvel, in 1675.[124] At Wilsnack, where the faithful had earlier revered miraculous candles and the corporal on which the miracle hosts had lain,[125] the chains and handcuffs of released prisoners were still displayed as ex-votos in 1586, as was one of the swords reputedly transformed from a pilgrim's staff by miracle.[126] The scales in which the pious supposedly paid off their sins were preserved and displayed into the late nineteenth century as proof of Catholic superstition.[127] In the sixteenth century, such objects may have retained for many of the faithful a sense of the sacrality of the hosts reputedly tortured and/or revered there.

Holy Matter and the Jews

In the wealth of detail I have given above, several broad patterns are clear. First, the success of places as different as Schwerin, Wilsnack, and Sternberg suggests the basic drawing power of blood. The specificity of cult sites was, of course, important. There is evidence that different bloods were thought to have different efficacies. As I noted above, pilgrims came to the Wilsnack blood from Kleve and Augsburg, which had bloods of their own. Theologians worried that the faithful might prefer one sort of blood to another or be lured into voyaging from blood to blood for quite particular experiences and cures. For all the confusion modern scholars feel about the provenance of certain bloods, such as those of Wienhausen or Rothenburg ob der Tauber, shrine keepers and ecclesiastical authorities preserved and even, as we have seen, fabricated evidence (for example at Marienfliess) to document the specific nature and background of their cult objects. The repeated disputes over and assertions of authenticity, like the doubts which led to the occasional deaccessioning (as, for example, at Cismar), suggest how much both the history and the theological justification of specific sites mattered by the late fifteenth century. Not all bloods were the same. But behind the details of individual cults lay a general power: the power in the blood.

Second, it is clear that, whatever the problems with our evidence (and they are considerable), the Wilsnack cult was prepared for by repeated blood claims. Authentic indulgences indicate that something called blood was shown for veneration at Beelitz, Wasserleben, Bernstein, Cismar, Braunschweig, Schwerin, Marienfliess, Krakow am See, and Güstrow in the hundred years before Wilsnack. Gottsbüren had a lively pilgrimage at least fifty years before, and in the Mark Brandenburg itself, the three Cistercian convents of Zehdenick, Marienfliess, and Heiligengrabe offered competing blood cults (with very different kinds of holy objects) in the years around 1300. There were plenty of examples to inspire Johannes Kabuz, just as the success of his enterprise encouraged subsequent efforts at Zehdenick and Sternberg, Heiligengrabe, and Berlin.

Third, the type of cult changed. Although blood relics such as that of Schwerin, and host miracles such as that at Zehdenick, continued to seem threatening to Protestant reformers well into the sixteenth century, the source and power of blood cult came increasingly to lie in claims of Jewish abuse.[128] The first real competition to Wilsnack came from the anti-Jewish libel at Sternberg. And even before Wilsnack's success, a chronicler in the 1370s attributed the bloods of Krakow am See and Güstrow to Jewish desecration. However unreliable the early stories of serving girls, shepherds, and the travels of Henry the Lion may be, authentic documents indicate that the earliest bloods in the north of Germany were, on the one hand, blood relics in the cities of Schwerin and Lübeck, and, on the other hand, putative miracles at obscure places such as Beelitz and Wasserleben in which something changed into blood. Most of our earliest evidence of host cult suggests that something happened to induce a manifestation of blood, but the early indulgences (for example, from Nauen, Beelitz, and Bernstein) stress what is revered more than the act of abuse. God acted; blood appeared. Traces of this focus last even into the anti-Jewish libels, which sometimes stress the miraculous manifestation of Christ at least as much as Jewish guilt.[129] But the later the constructed account (even where the perpetrator is said to be from within the Christian community, as in the anachronistic stories of Erfurt, Zehdenick, and Doberan), the more stress there is on an act of desecration as generator of blood.

We are often told that eucharist replaced relic in late medieval piety, as the visual replaced the tactile.[130] Seeing the host is supposed to have eclipsed earlier rites of touching relics; appearances of the Virgin are said to have substituted for journeys to relic sites, drinking the wash water of holy people, or collecting dust from tombs. But the changes in fifteenth-century blood cult do not support quite this way of putting it. The rise of eucharistic pilgrimage and the complicated discussion it elicited were not in any simple sense a substitution of the see-able for the touchable. This is so for three reasons. First, both relic and host were increasingly displayed for veneration from a distance; at blood sites such as Wilsnack or Schwerin, it is not at all clear what the pilgrims were actually able to see. Insofar as there is a move in the fourteenth and fifteenth centuries toward miraculous "action at a distance"—that is, toward healings and revelations that occur before a visit of thanksgiving to the saint who effects them rather than after touching a holy object—this trend characterizes shrines of all types.[131] Second, for all the discussion of spiritual communion (reception by meditation before the host), those who theorized both host miracles and the "ordinary" eucharist increasingly stressed seeing *through* or looking *beyond* at least as much as contact *with* the visible. The "seeing" stressed in the fifteenth century was, in many ways, a not-seeing, just as the touching was a *noli me tangere*.[132] Third and most important, what we find in north German blood cult is not a replacement of relic by eucharist but rather a move from blood relic to miracle host. And both were material objects, designated as sacred by something that had happened to them. The move from relic to host miracle to abused host was the replacement of one kind of sacred matter by another. Understanding this enables us to see, on the one hand, why northern areas were so eager for blood objects and, on the other, why Jewish abuse became the supposed source of host cult. It also gives us an entry into the themes of desecration and revelation that, as we shall come to understand, mark not only pilgrimage and praxis but university discourse and devotional writing as well.

In order to explain why a particular form of holy matter, blood, became so important in German areas, a few obvious reminders are necessary.

Holy matter had long been central to medieval piety. At the heart of Christianity lay, after all, the conviction that Jesus' incarnation—the coming of the divine into matter—was the pivot of salvation.[133] From the late third century, relics—pieces of the bodies of the martyrs or bits of stuff (earth, cloth, etc.) in contact with those bodies—had been venerated by the Christian faithful as especially powerful witnesses to and contact with God's presence. Translated into altars, they established sacrality.[134] Despite the insistence on Christ's bodily resurrection and on Mary's assumption into heaven, we find, as early as the fourth century, claims to contact relics—even bodily relics—for Christ and Mary as well: the nails of the crucifixion, the crown of thorns, the cross of Calvary, Mary's mantle, Christ's baby teeth, and so forth.[135] Moreover, from the early Middle Ages through the disputes of the fourteenth and fifteenth centuries, an increasing emphasis on eucharistic "real presence" tended to make the consecrated bread and wine into a kind of holy matter, as Hubertus Lutterbach, Peter Dinzelbacher, and G. J. C. Snoek have argued.[136] Not only was it treated, liturgically and devotionally, as a relic (buried in altars, used as an amulet against disasters, etc.); it was Christ literally present in the eucharistic elements, and surrounding objects such as altar linen could absorb its power as the wood and earth of holy graves absorbed the presence of the saints.

I shall return below to the complexities of eucharistic theology, but what is relevant to the discussion here is the particular problem the acquisition of holy matter posed for all of Germany—and especially for the German north—in the later Middle Ages. The great martyrs of the early church had died in the Mediterranean basin hundreds of years before. Relics of the saints were thus scarce in the north of Europe and difficult to acquire.[137] Even the enormously valuable contact relics of Christ—bits of the true cross or the crown of thorns—were available only at great expense and chiefly through increasingly difficult crusade to the Holy Land. Moreover, as we shall see in the next chapter, neither theologians and spiritual advisers nor the ordinary faithful were entirely comfortable with the subsuming of eucharist into relic. However much it might be holy matter, eucharist was both more and less than relic. It was Christ, but it looked like bread and wine.[138] Whereas Mary's mantle was Mary's mantle and St. Margaret's foot her foot, eucharist was God; but it was God veiled.

In a context then in which holy matter was needed—to attract pilgrims, to excite devotion, to make places sacred, even to bolster regional competition—blood might seem to trump other forms of presence.[139] Relics of Christ's blood could be understood to outclass all other relics, as the bishop of Norwich preached in thirteenth-century London.[140] They were Christ, whereas St. Margaret's foot was only St. Margaret. Although it referred to the power of God, the foot was not God himself. But *Blut Christi* was the blood of Christ. Not merely a contact object, which had touched Jesus, it was his body, still living and red.[141]

Bodily relics of Christ were, however, as difficult and expensive to obtain as his contact relics (shroud, thorns, and so forth). As the cases of Cismar and Marienfliess suggest, their provenance could be suspicious and difficult to substantiate. In miraculous bleeding hosts, the same immediacy of presence could be found. In them, inner and outer conformed as they did not in the "ordinary" eucharist; blood spots made the veiled God visible as well as present. And their appearance depended not on lengthy crusade or complex financial and political negotiation but on the action of God. Hence eucharistic miracles became a major source of supply for that special form of holy matter in which God was manifest—that is, for God visible in blood.

But, even in eucharistic miracles, the appearance of blood seemed in fact to depend on more than God's will. Blood did not appear randomly. Holy matter needed some sort of dramatic event—whether abuse or another kind of threat or crisis—in order to make manifest the divine. Although blood appeared only on holy objects—wafers,[142] altar linen, chalices, devotional images such as crucifixes, and so forth—it appeared when someone behaved improperly (or worse) toward such objects. As it does when human bodies are struck or pierced or opened, blood leaped from holy objects that were in some way harmed, whether by superstition, unbelief, ritual mistakes, or direct abuse. It was the appearance of such blood that affixed a charge to the object—that, in a sense, "consecrated" it exactly in its mutation or desecration. The charge or spark was what stimulated pilgrimage.

Blood relics were, of course, by their very nature associated with violation or penetration, especially where legend tied them to Longinus and the lance prick. And there is no question that devotional writing tended, as we shall see, to stress the connection between blood and attacks on Christ—a connection that sometimes, as in the case of the holy lance of Nuremberg, helped to enhance enthusiasm.[143] But it was difficult to retain over hundreds of years the association of blood relics with the killing of Christ. A more immediate link to violation helped. Relics needed to be associated with military victory, as was the blood of Schwerin, or to triumph over disaster. The blood relic at Braunschweig, for example, arrived from Cismar to support rebuilding after the church had burned. It was, I suggest, not only the festive installation—of which we have accounts—that made the relic effective in miracle working but also its association with reemergence after fire, paralleling the hosts of Nauen and Wilsnack, which were also signs of survival through and rebirth from ashes.

Abuses of the host or chalice, even where naïve or inadvertent, were similarly charged events. Something happened to holy matter that was protested, and triumphed over, by the matter itself. Thus fire, flood, or pillage (as in the Wilsnack case), robberies of churches (as in the Heiligengrabe story), ritual mistakes of the clergy (as in the Erfurt story), or mistaken devotion that resulted in guilty secretion of hosts outside the sanctuary (as in the legends from Zehdenick and Doberan) were understood as acts that led to a self-marking of the eucharistic elements in reaction. The marking—the more dramatic the better—was a trigger of community response that would be expressed in a dramatic translation of the holy matter into church or monastery. It is significant that, even after the coming of the Reformation, we find a late sixteenth-century case (Hettstett) where a damaged host was venerated by the clergy and faithful, almost exactly as had occurred earlier when a different eucharistic theology prevailed.[144]

Desecration was a particularly intense and vivid mode of marking holy matter, of forcing it to make visible its sacrality. Abuse stabbed significance out of the wafer—made its dangerous holiness suddenly manifest. Although scholarship since Peter Browe has treated eucharistic appearances as if there were a continuity between the typical thirteenth-century transformation that appears and disappears and the later *Dauerwunder* or enduring transformations, there is in fact a significant disconnect between them.[145] Visions and apparitions were sometimes responses to ritual mistakes or skepticism, although they were often rewards for devotion; but they did not provide matter—stuff—for veneration in the same way as *Dauerwunder*, which were in general markings of holy matter in acts of abuse or desecration.

Moreover, in the course of the fifteenth century, the marking or desecration in question became a serious accusation. Although we are not sure how far back the stories go, the shepherd at Doberan and the alewife at Zehdenick are hardly sinister figures. At Beelitz, as we have seen, the earliest reference (Rutger of Brandenburg's indulgence of 1247) suggests that no perpetrator of host abuse was ever found. Although evidence of skepticism and superstition, the misuse of a wafer was, to bishop Rutger, far less important than the revelation of God it occasioned.[146] But by the end of the fifteenth century, even for Christians, desecration was a capital offense, as Peter Däne and Paul Fromm discovered. It was still a valuable source of access to the divine (and to pilgrim revenues) but it was increasingly accusatory; hence the community found it safer, and less disruptive, to project it onto outsiders. It is significant that the early reference from Beelitz seems to understand whatever was done to the host as a *felix culpa*, an inducement to the appearance of God and an occasion for his providence and pedagogy. The account from the 1570s simply blames the Jews. In the host-desecration libels at Sternberg and Berlin, as in the recasting of earlier stories at Güstrow and Heiligengrabe, a feared and despised alien became the source of a holy matter provided in other accounts by the superstitions of Christian women (as at Zehdenick or Wasserleben/Halberstadt) or the ritual mistakes of clerics (as at Erfurt or Walldürn).[147] By the fifteenth century, desire for miraculous matter and hatred of the Jews collaborated, each supporting the other. Thus, if holy matter was necessary, Jewish desecration might seem increasingly necessary as well.

Historians have long blamed host-desecration libels on the growing anti-Semitism of late medieval Germany. In a broad sense this is unquestionably so.[148] Gavin Langmuir has, moreover, attributed host libels to the doubts Christians themselves felt about eucharistic real presence.[149] According to this argument, Christians doubted transubstantiation and projected their guilt about doubting it onto the Jews. Such an interpretation is, in a general sense, convincing as well. There is certainly evidence of Christian doubt about various understandings of real presence. The dissident movements prominent in northern Germany—Waldensians, Hussites, and cryptoflagellants—were all perceived by contemporaries as in some sense doubting eucharistic real presence. And many of the earliest visions of blood in the host (especially those from the thirteenth century) were supposedly given in response to skepticism. Johannes von Paltz quoted Albert the Great as saying the eucharist is "more doubted than the other sacraments," and, as we have seen, Paltz was not alone in maintaining that the major point of blood miracles was to excite correct eucharistic reverence and teach correct eucharistic theology.[150] Moreover, a Parisian case from 1493, in which a priest attacked host and chalice as "lies," asserts that the cause of the priest's doubts was Jewish influence.[151] But when Christians worried about Jewish unbelief, they worried about more than the eucharist. Johannes Witten, defender of the Wilsnack hosts, argued that blood relics refuted not Jewish denial of real presence but Jewish denial of the passion of Christ.[152] What I am suggesting here is that the history of blood cult in Germany argues for a specific interpretation of host-desecration libels in addition to general causes such as anti-Semitism or the projection of religious doubt.

The way in which anti-Jewish host-desecration libels were constructed suggests that the point of the stories was not merely hatred of Jews and greed for Jewish property, which any sort of libel could have unleashed.[153] Nor was it merely Christian guilt about eucharistic doubt and uncertainty. Such doubt was certainly present but it was probably less widespread than its opposite: a sort of religious materialism—a frenzied conviction that the divine tended to erupt into matter. What both the specific language of the accusatory accounts and the chronology of sites suggest is that Christians needed Jews to produce miraculous blood.[154] Anti-Jewish legends, such as the one fabricated under the direction of the abbess of Heiligengrabe, tend to divide into two parts, treating the anti-Jewish charges as prolegomenon to the real story, which is that of the blood manifestation and the miracles it works.[155] Some anti-Jewish accounts (for example, one from Güstrow in 1510) are titled not "the abuse of . . ." but "the miracle of . . ."; and one of the early Sternberg broadsides begins simply: "Let all Christians know that a great miracle happened in the land of Mecklenburg in the city of Sternberg. . . ."[156] Even the early broadsides from Brandenburg are titled "a marvelous history." Although deliberately formulated to spread vilification and foment persecution, what they stress is the sacrality of the sacrament and its marvelous self-revelation.[157] The texts construct their narrative to culminate not in a verdict of Jewish guilt (of which they were, of course, completely convinced) but in the wonderful blood of God made visible in matter by Jewish desecration.[158]

I shall need to say a good deal more about all this before I finish. For as we have seen (and shall see again in the next chapter), many university theologians felt serious and telling doubts about both the forms of holy matter I have discussed: blood relics and bleeding hosts. The story I have to unfold is by no means simply one of northern Europe's need for an accessible form of holy matter in the absence of the other types, or of the role of anti-Judaism in that need. Wilsnack and Sternberg reveal to us a crucial aspect of the long fifteenth century not only because they were, in their day, major blood cults and prepared for by earlier blood enthusiasm, but also because they raised for the learned of Europe basic soteriological questions. In this chapter I have treated the manifestation of blood in holy matter as a practical and devotional problem, but it was a theological problem as well. It is to the theology that I turn in the next two chapters.

PART II

Blood Disputes in Fifteenth-Century Europe and Their Background

Chapter 4

Debates About Eucharistic Transformations and Blood Relics

At sites in Brandenburg and Mecklenburg in the fourteenth and fifteenth centuries, as we have seen, different types of blood were revered. These bloods competed for revenues, pilgrims, and political influence. The lords of Gans and the Askanier margraves of Brandenburg maneuvered against each other through the nunneries of Marienfliess and Zehdenick, each with its different blood. The abbess of Heiligengrabe tried to divert pilgrims from Wilsnack and Sternberg by building a new chapel and redeploying its blood legend. The canons of Schwerin engineered a share of Sternberg revenues when the Sternberg host threatened to eclipse their own relic. Moreover, the bloods had quite individual traditions and claims. Christians in northern Germany, as elsewhere, defended their particular cults with miracle stories, propaganda, and assertions of historical authenticity.

Yet those such as Bansleben, Döring, or Paltz who supported the very different bloods of Schwerin, Sternberg, and Wilsnack, like those such as Heinrich Tocke and Faustinus Labes who attacked them, tended to conflate the bloods. One argument did for all. However much they might compete on the practical level for revenues and attendance, the bloods tended on the theoretical level to spring to each other's defense. The charge "there is nothing there" was used against the Cismar relic and the Wilsnack hosts; the defense "Christ could have left blood behind on earth" was used to support the Wilsnack blood and the Braunschweig relic.[1] In order to understand how such different sites evoked such similar polemics, it is necessary to look at some very recondite theological argument in the centuries before and after 1383. For the Wilsnack controversy of the 1440s and 1450s is part of a European-wide debate. Not only do the views expressed there draw on discussions that were over two hundred years old; they also adumbrate positions that would be taken a decade later in the disputation staged in Rome before Pope Pius II himself. It is to such European debate that I now turn, placing the cults of Mecklenburg and Brandenburg in a wider and more theological setting.

Three lines of theological argument in particular fed into discussions of *sanguis Christi* in the 1440s, '50s, and '60s: debates about eucharistic visions and transformed hosts, debates about the theoretical possibility of bodily relics of Christ, and debates about the status during the *triduum* of the blood shed on Calvary. I begin with debates about the eucharist. In surveying them, I treat, first, the complex positions taken by theologians from Aquinas to such mid-fifteenth-century figures as Capistrano, Tocke, and Gabriel Biel and, second, the practical problems raised for prelates, preachers, and confessors by the demand of the pious for two very different forms of holy matter—the eucharistic chalice and miraculous hosts. Behind all the details hovers the paradox of presence and absence. For whatever the doubts raised by Hussite and Waldensian preachers about exactly how Christ was present in the eucharist, whatever the disagreements of theologians about the meaning of "transubstantiation" (and, contrary to what we are often told, there was no established definition of it in late medieval theological discourse),[2] behavior and pronouncement suggest not cynicism or skepticism about presence but eagerness for encounter.[3] Pilgrims voted with their feet, theologians with their tractates. The very fact that educated and uneducated alike argued about how Christ, although at God's right hand in heaven, was also present on the altar—whether or not visible, whether or not enduring, whether or not substance—testifies to the strength of their desire that something be there. But the present something had to be absent and in glory as well. Those who asserted its miraculous ever-living redness, like those who asserted its invisibility, agreed at a deeper level: mere presence was not enough. There had to be ascension too. If Christ had not gone away, there was no connection to the power beyond.[4]

The paradox of presence and absence also undergirds European-wide debates about bodily relics and about the *triduum mortis*, as we shall see. But I begin with discussions of eucharistic visions and transformed hosts because this is how the issue arose at Wilsnack, and it was with Wilsnack that I started my story many pages ago.

Visions and Transformations

The first sustained discussion of eucharistic visions arose in the wake of a wave of such events that emerged after the eucharistic debates of the late eleventh century.[5] What were theologians to make of the supposed appearances of Christ as a baby or a finger or bloody flesh, documented by such respected figures as Guitmond of Aversa and Peter Damian in the eleventh century, Herbert of Clairvaux in the twelfth, or Thomas of Cantimpré and Caesarius of

Heisterbach in the first half of the thirteenth?[6] And as such stories came increasingly to involve not private and transitory visions but *Dauerwunder*—transformed hosts flecked or pouring with blood, or chalices that lasted blood-filled—practical as well as theoretical questions were raised. What were such things? What should a priest do when they occurred? Along with the wave of appearances and visions went a profound distrust of them.

For all the popularity of visions and the visual, theologians in the later Middle Ages often expressed doubts about seeing. According to accepted theory, which went back to Augustine, there were three sorts of vision: corporeal (by which one saw the things of the exterior world), spiritual (by which one saw inwardly but used mental images that were like bodily ones), and intellectual (by which one saw the highest, imageless truth).[7] Hence there was suspicion of both devotional images and visions among spiritual directors. Theologians stressed that the highest form of encounter was without images, that devotional objects and church furnishings were only simulacra, and that even relics were to be revered because of the saint whose worship they inspired (however much the pious simply conflated relic and saint).[8] We find indeed some hesitation before images and visions even among those visionaries, especially but not exclusively women, whose understanding of their own union with Christ was not only expressed in increasingly graphic and somatic language but also manifested in bodily phenomena such as levitation, stigmata, and mystical pregnancy.[9]

It is true that, in certain ways, the visual replaced the tactile.[10] Both laypeople and members of religious orders felt increased reluctance about a sacramental reception that would, because it placed God objectively in their mouths, damn them if any element of their spiritual intention or preparation was flawed. The faithful were urged to encounter with eyes where encounter with lips was dangerous and rare, to "eat" by "seeing." By the thirteenth century, we find stories of people attending mass only for the moment of elevation, racing from church to church to see as many consecrations as possible, and shouting at the priest to hold the host up higher.[11] An account even survives of guild members bringing charges against a priest for assigning them places in church from which they could not see the elevated host.[12] But preachers and spiritual directors often described such seeing as with the inner rather than with the outer eye; "spiritual communion" was more than—sometimes indeed contradictory to—ocular communion. Christ could be received outside mass, outside church, even outside any stimulus except a whispering deep in the heart. Hence eucharistic presence was both object and absence; it became profoundly inner—unencompassable, untouchable, unseeable.[13]

Moreover, there was, by the thirteenth century, a long theological tradition that treated the eucharist explicitly as unseen. As far back as the controversies of the eleventh century, major figures such as Alger of Liège, Lanfranc, and Guitmond of Aversa argued that veiling of presence was necessary in order to support faith.[14] If one simply saw the flesh and blood, belief would not be necessary; the New Testament sacrifice would then be in no way superior to the Old.[15] Veiling was also necessary in order to discourage obscure heresies such as stercoranism (which supposedly saw Christ as polluted by digestion and excretion) and to protect against *horror cruoris*. As Roger Bacon wrote, the sacrament "is veiled . . . [because] the human heart could not endure to masticate and devour raw and living flesh and to drink fresh blood."[16] Or, as Thomas Aquinas put it: the veiling comes so that nothing horrible happens in the eucharist.[17]

According to a number of theorists, even a vision of Christ's body on the altar was not a seeing of Christ. Theologians (especially Dominicans) from Thomas Aquinas to Nicholas of Cusa explained that when a pious individual saw the sacrament as "a small particle of flesh or at times . . . a small child," no change took place in the accidents of the sacrament. Rather, as Thomas put it, the change was in the beholder "whose eyes [were] . . . affected as if they outwardly saw flesh, or blood, or a child." The substance was Christ; the accidents were those of bread and wine, given the appearance of Christ by God in a special miracle. In other words, the viewer does not, in a eucharistic vision, see "what is really there" but sees something at two removes so to speak rather than one, because he sees neither the unseeable substance nor the seeable accidents but an appearance substituted by God for the accidents in order to indicate the unseeable substance beneath.[18] The same is true even when a number of the faithful claim to see such things simultaneously, and the flesh or blood or child appears to perdure. Because "done to represent the truth," such moments are not deceptions, but if preserved in pyxes or monstrances, such objects cannot be Christ; for it would be "wicked," says Aquinas, to think Christ's freedom could be abrogated by incarceration. Thomas even argued that the blessed in heaven see the *corpus Christi* under the sacrament only by intellectual vision, since it has no accidents and thus cannot impress a "similitude" on the air to be taken by "intromission" into the eye as is done in corporeal vision.[19]

Behind Thomas's concern that the *corpus* remain unseeable lies his explicit concern that it remain immutable. If the substance of the bread changes into the substance of Christ there is change in the bread, he argues, but not in God. "It is not unsuitable for bread to change but it is unsuitable for Christ to change."[20] Hence Thomas held, as a technical position, "transubstantiation" (change of the bread into Christ) rather than "annihilation" (the replacement of the bread's substance by Christ's)—although several thirteenth- and fourteenth-century theologians thought the latter position more philosophically cogent. God makes the bread go over into *corpus Christi*, which remains as it is, experiencing not even the *mutatio* of change of place. Any eruption of Christ into visibility would be taking on new accidents—and hence changing—from one moment to the next. Nonetheless, says Thomas, there should still be reverence and devotion in response to miracle hosts, since the accidents God provides in miracle are *similia* to the accidents of the true body of Christ and are induced there by divine virtue for our instruction.[21]

Not all theologians agreed with Thomas. In the twelfth century, some, such as Gerhoh of Reichersberg, seem to have assumed that Christ chose simply to reveal himself in eucharistic appearances.[22] An indulgence letter of pope Innocent VIII in 1487 spoke of the corporal miracle of the Spanish monastery of Maria del Zebrero as if it revealed Christ's real blood: "Suddenly in the aforesaid chalice true blood miraculously appeared visible to bodily eyes and part of it flowed from the aforesaid chalice onto the linens which were on the altar, and this same blood remained visible and today is on view reserved as a relic, like the blood of a man or a goat recently spilled, although it appears coagulated [*coagulatus*—that is, not dried]."[23] As late as the fifteenth century, Gabriel Biel refused to decide whether Christ was really present or not in visions and miracle hosts.

In general, Franciscans were more sympathetic to host miracles than Dominicans. Duns Scotus thought Christ appeared *sensibiliter* in order to confirm faith and be adored, but only in cases where many saw the apparition. Scotus's reasons were more devotional than theological ("lest faith be confirmed by phantasms or the community commit idolatry"), as were those of Peter Auriol (d. 1322), who thought Christ was really present when the vision was a comfort but not when it was a threat. Moreover, the majority even of later Franciscans agreed with Thomas.[24] When the Augustinian Johannes von Paltz defended the miracle of Sternberg in the early sixteenth century, following a long tradition of such defenses, he argued that the blood, ever devotionally useful, proved the real presence, but it was not God. Christ as he is in the eucharist is not seeable or tangible or passible.

Despite differences in attitude toward specific miracle claims, theologians increasingly stressed *corpus* and *sanguis Christi* as unseen. Jean Gerson (d. 1429) wrote: "It is not what our bodily eyes see but what the eyes of our heart see that is our God." Gabriel Biel (d. 1495), who refused to decide on miracle hosts, used the distinction between substance and accidents to argue that communion with the eyes reached only the accidents of bread, whereas those who eat consume species and the *vere contentum* as well.[25] It was such arguments that provided the theoretical underpinnings of Nicholas of Cusa's opposition to the hosts of Wilsnack: "[Such things are] pernicious . . . for our catholic faith teaches us that the glorified body of Christ has glorified blood completely un-seeable in glorified veins. . . . [W]e therefore order that . . . the clergy . . . should no longer display or promulgate such miracles. . . ."[26] Some theologians even argued that the *continuation* of the accidents of bread and wine was what signaled sacramental presence after consecration; hence Christ was present only in the whole and undecayed accidents; he disappeared when they were altered. A stark repudiation of the assumptions of popular practice, such argument made it logically impossible for Christ to be present in any completely altered host, any chalice filled entirely with blood. Ironically, in such formulation, unseeability guaranteed presence![27]

The Practical Issue of Transformed Hosts

By the fifteenth century, then, university theologians tended to insist that supposed eruptions of blood on matter were, at the very least, to be regarded with suspicion. Many argued that, even if miraculous, they were not truly *sanguis Christi*. But some theologians defended some forms of host transformation; popes gave indulgences for miracle hosts; pilgrimages continued. The enthusiasm for Wilsnack, if anything, increased. The issue of eucharistic transformation was therefore not merely a problem of theory. There were practical considerations as well. What should be done with hosts and chalices that appeared, either to one person or to many, to be transformed?

As the work of Peter Browe and Wolfgang Brückner has made clear, theologians developed a somewhat shaky consensus (seen, for example, in Eberhard Waltmann's "De adoratione et contra cruorem") that was at odds with usual practice. Aquinas argued that "the use of the sacrament should be appropriate to the matter of the sacrament." That is, if it appears to someone to be flesh, it should not be consumed by that person but by another to whom it has not appeared thus; if it appears to a group to be transformed and bloody, it should be placed among the relics, and the celebrant should consecrate another host. Aquinas admitted, however, that some thought that spiritual communion—that is, reception by the eyes only—should suffice under these latter circumstances. And some of his contemporaries (for example, Alexander of Hales) argued for this, suggesting that a second consecration would be to celebrate another mass—which was nowhere required.[28]

Although, as Browe points out, a number of missals leave the issue undecided, diocesan synods seem increasingly to have espoused the Thomistic position. A Spanish manual for priests from 1333 requires that a priest must consume a host if only he sees something miraculous within it; if all see the miracle, the priest must pray for its reconversion and consume it if it reverts. In late fifteenth-century Würzburg, a tractate on "the perils of the eucharist" maintained, drawing on diocesan regulations: "It is a *periculum* to the host if the figure of flesh or a child or any other thing appears in it." Such an appearance is a miracle for the viewer, but for the sacrament, there is "no change." The priest should therefore consume such a host immediately if an individual claim is made; if, however, many people profess to see it, the priest should repeat the consecration with new hosts, and the transformed one should be hidden from view so that every opportunity for a crowd to gather is avoided.[29] The condemnation of the Wilsnack hosts by Erfurt theologians in 1446, like Waltmann's attack five years later, drew on exactly these considerations. Kabuz should have consumed the hosts at once eighty years before, they claimed. At the very least, he should have prayed for reconversion as did Gregory the Great when confronted with a finger in the chalice.[30] Even if it *is* a miracle, the eruption of blood is a threat, not a comfort. Blood shows God's wrath at sin or disbelief. Unless diseased or poisoned, miracle hosts should be consumed by the celebrant.

Bloody or stained corporals and transformed or spoiled hosts were indeed sometimes placed with relics. As G. J. C. Snoek has recently shown, hosts had been used in the consecration of churches as a kind of relic for hundreds of years.[31] As early as the ninth century, an English synod required the host to be placed next to relics in the *sepulchrum* of the altar; and the eucharist alone sufficed if no relics were available. Thus, as Heuser points out, the altar was literally as well as symbolically the "grave of Christ."[32] By the thirteenth century, canonists began to feel some hesitation about such use of the host as substitute relic but urged the burying of soiled altar linen, or odd or transformed hosts, in the altar *sepulchrum*. Such ritually correct disposal of damaged hosts, corporals, or eucharistic vessels could be the occasion years later of supposed blood miracles, when someone found a chalice or cloth in the altar with the inscription *sanguis Christi*.[33] What was buried and later retrieved might have been a putative miracle but it might also have been merely a cloth on which wine was spilled or a deformed wafer labeled *corpus* or *sanguis Christi* before it was deposited in the altar and later misunderstood as miraculous presence. In any case, it does not appear that the injunctions of university professors or diocesan administrators about disposal were ordinarily followed. As we see repeatedly in the miracle stories from Mecklenburg and Brandenburg, the usual response to a transformed host or blood flow was to translate the holy object and consult the bishop—often in that order rather than the reverse. The learned Nicholas Marschalk, to make a polemical point, accused the clergy of Sternberg of unbelief because they considered consuming the miracle host found in the duke's courtyard. The duchess who protected the fraudulent host of Wartenburg bei Wittenberg from episcopal examination felt she was supporting piety against irreligion.

Although not every miracle of host or corporal or chalice produced cult, it seems that it was rare for clergy to simply consume miraculous blood or deposit it in altars. What then was to be done with such holy matter when cult emerged? In the absence of theological consensus about whether Christ was present in transformed wine or hosts or, if present, how long he (or some miraculous matter produced by God for the occasion) might linger there, only a ritual or administrative solution was possible. That solution was to place a consecrated host alongside the putative miracle to assure that, whatever was present, the faithful had something worth traveling to.

Such a solution was, of course, something of a theological fudge. At Wilsnack, some hard-liners such as Tocke saw it as rank hypocrisy.[34] If—as preachers had been pointing out ever since 1412—the only point of the pilgrimage was the eucharist, that was present for every pilgrim in the church back home. Nonetheless, the solution of associating transformed hosts with the "ordinary" eucharist obtained already in the fourteenth century. In 1338 the bishop of Passau ordered a supposed miracle host in Pulkau (almost certainly a fraud) to be overlaid with a consecrated host.[35] The Council of Basel may have ordered a freshly consecrated host to be displayed at Wilsnack—at least opponents of the Wilsnack blood later claimed so—and this was certainly required in 1447, and again in 1453, as a condition of Nicholas V's confirming of the cult.[36] In 1480 Sixtus IV, who took an interest in blood piety, required such overlaying in the case of a cult in north Tirol. We should note, however, that almost as quickly as cults were tamed into eucharistic veneration of a more ordinary sort, new and extraordinary bloods, such as those at Sternberg or Brandenburg-Berlin-Stendal, tended to emerge.

Concomitance and the Cup

The host miracles so offensive to the Erfurt faculty became bloodier, both more tactile and more visual, in the two centuries before 1446. Increasingly, hosts that appeared red, spongy, or flesh-like, in whole or in part, were preempted by bloody cloths, overflowing chalices, and wafers that poured blood. Yet chalice miracles (such as the brimming cup at Halberstadt) were always a minority of eucharistic miracles. The primary form of blood wonder in the fourteenth and fifteenth centuries was the eruption of blood from the (mishandled or desecrated) wafer. Thus we might say that, for the most part, it was bread, not wine, that turned into blood.

Such asymmetry of miracle may seem odd. And indeed it appears even odder in light of certain emphases in eucharistic devotion to which I shall come in Chapter 7 below. For, as we shall see, theologians and spiritual writers stressed the symbolic importance of the dual nature of the eucharist. In it, wine/blood represents soul, bread/body represents body; wine/blood represents Christ's passion, bread/body his incarnation. Hence it might seem that, in a piety for which the sacrifice of the cross became increasingly central and the psychosomatic unity of person was stressed, chalice miracles would outweigh miracle hosts. In order to understand why miraculous outbursts of blood were nonetheless usually in wafer not chalice, we need to understand another aspect of eucharist practice.

The status of the chalice had long been unclear. Already in the twelfth century, it sometimes contained merely a drop of the precious blood mixed with unconsecrated wine (the so-called lay chalice). In the thirteenth century, the people were sometimes offered simply a cup of unconsecrated wine for cleansing the mouth after communion,[37] and over the course of the century, consecrated wine was gradually withdrawn from the laity, eventually even from cloistered nuns. The interchange of the various chalices often went unnoticed by the faithful, and theologians argued over whether they should be taught that they received the body and blood in the wafer and mere wine in the chalice, or whether the cup of the laity indeed held the blood of the Lord.[38] Aquinas and many theologians after him justified withholding the cup entirely by pointing out that the priest receives both species; as Berthold of Regensburg (d. 1272) explained, the communicating priest "nourishes us all," for he is the mouth and we are the body.[39] Increasingly, the withdrawal was defended by the doctrine of concomitance.

Concomitance theory had been elaborated already in the eucharistic debates of the eleventh century to refute arguments that Christ was ripped or shredded when the wafer was eaten.[40] According to this theory, only the eucharistic accidents are touched by teeth or digestion; *corpus* and *sanguis Christi* are present in substance, unreachable by any of the human senses. Thus, no matter how divided, Christ is whole in the eucharist. Concomitance explains, moreover, how Christ can be *integer et totus* in many masses, completely present in every place and moment, every particle. When, over the course of the thirteenth century, the cup was withdrawn from the laity, concomitance seemed (at least to the satisfaction of erudite theologians) to be the answer to the frenzied desire of communicants for *Blut Christi. Totus Christus*, blood as well as body, was present in every particle of the host. Host miracles were hence often seen by such theologians either as support for concomitance theory or as accusation of those who refused to accept it. Johannes von Paltz argued thus in 1503 when he proposed that one of the purposes of the Sternberg blood was "to confute . . . the errors" of those who refused to accept that "true blood is contained not only in the chalice but also in the host."[41] The early sixteenth-century version of the Heiligengrabe story took the occasion of a supposed Jewish host desecration to provide a little theological disquisition on concomitance. Broadsides concerning the host libel of 1510 in the towns of the Mark Brandenburg used a perverse form of the doctrine to charge that Jews took Christ from community to community through little particles of host.[42]

Appearances of blood were more, however, than refutations of heresy or undergirdings of anti-Jewish libels. They were also direct results of eucharistic craving. Already in the thirteenth century, eucharistic fervor was, with many of the faithful, intense. As the power of priests was increasingly elaborated and the notion of eating and drinking God seemed more and more audacious, some of the devout found that their hunger merely intensified, seasoned by awe. The deathbeds of pious people became the setting for bitter struggle between priest and recipient over how often the holy food could be taken.[43] Religious superiors, bishops, and canon lawyers legislated against reception during ecstasy, in an effort to control the waves of frenzy for the eucharist that shook religious houses. It was danger of spillage when the devout grabbed for the salvific blood that was the most frequent reason given for the denial of the cup.

Yet withdrawal of the cup only increased the people's sense of its power. Desire kept pace with—and circumvented—prohibition. As I illustrated in Chapter 1, some of the cloistered, denied access to the cup at mass, received it in vision. Others (for example, Beatrice of Nazareth and Catherine of Siena) experienced the proffered wafer as the withheld blood, gushing into their mouths or over their bodies. What the clergy denied them, they simply obtained in another way. Miracles of blood erupting from wafers were thus not only illustrations of concomitance to teach those who mistakenly insisted on Christ's blood in the cup; they were also a means of immediate access to that blood.

Morover, it was not just visionaries and mystical women who craved *Blut Christi*. Ordinary laypeople too cried out for the withheld chalice. In fifteenth-century Bohemia, the demand for the eucharist in both species (*sub utraque specie*) gave its name to a group of the followers of Jan Hus, the Utraquists, also known as Calixtines (from cup or *calix*).[44] At the Council of Constance in 1415 and again at Basel in 1432, the doctrine of concomitance was used to brand as heresy the Hussite demand for the chalice: heretics supposedly failed to understand that blood was present in consecrated bread.[45] Yet the demand for the chalice continued. Blood in body was not enough. However much some radical Hussites later objected to technical ideas of transubstantiation, preferring to emphasize the spiritual and moral effects of a communion that pointed to Christ in glory, they clung to the chalice as access to the power in the blood.[46]

Modern historians have usually glossed Hussite Utraquism as rebellion, with strong social overtones, against clerical domination; and the history of Hussitism in the first quarter of the fifteenth century, leading as it did to radical claims of social equality, supports this interpretation. Embracing an ecclesiology in which laity were the equal of priests and the model of the primitive church was held up against recent innovation and corruption, Utraquists moved to demand not only the lay chalice but also frequent reception, even infant communion. In the radical Hussite community at Tábor, eschatological or chiliastic elements led finally to a kind of communism and a spiritual understanding of eucharist: the faithful could become Christ's body by simply espousing Christ. Nonetheless, interpretations of Hussitism that stress primarily its nationalism and anticlericalism tend to be guided by sixteenth-century questions, to see fifteenth-century Bohemia as foreshadowing the Reformation.[47] Looked at from a late fourteenth- or early fifteenth-century perspective, what is striking is the way in which demand for direct access to *Blut Christi* became central, not only to those such as Jacobellus of Stříbro, who led the movement in the days after Hus's execution at the Council of Constance, but also to those figures, such as John of Capistrano, who were enlisted by the papacy to counter it. A hundred years after Hus, devotional writers such as Paltz, who held out miracle hosts as proof of concomitance against Waldensian and Hussite heretics, were still responding to the clamor for blood; after all, what these miracles offered the faithful was visible redness, separate drops—not only the wafer but that which separated itself from it, not only body as container but also blood spilled out.

This discussion of the Hussites leads me naturally back to Jan Hus and his tractate *de sanguine*. Hus was not, as many historians have pointed out, a Hussite. Indeed his own very high blood theology stressed Christ in glory, and it was Jacobellus of Stříbro, not Hus, who initiated the campaign for the lay chalice in Bohemia. But we do find in Hus's treatment of the Wilsnack blood several of the strands of fifteenth-century theorizing I consider in this chapter.

Hus objected to the Wilsnack miracle blood not only because he thought the clergy used it to abuse the trust of the people but also because he thought the blood of Christ must be with Christ's body in glory so that ultimate meaning, the promise of human redemption and resurrection, would reside in wholeness, not in fragments and division. In a sense, then, Hus's objection to the blood of Wilsnack in 1406–7 involved his own version of the doctrine of concomitance. Not concerned with access to the cup (although he did assert that the faithful received both species in the early church), Hus was nonetheless passionate about the power in the blood.[48] He wanted to keep blood joined with the body in communion and in resurrection, not left behind as a mere particle of matter on earth.[49] Although he was accused at the Council of Constance of adhering to Wycliffe's doctrine of "remanence" (the dual presence of bread and body, wine and blood), what Hus, like Nicholas of Cusa, stressed was the invisible and indivisible presence of Christ in the sacrament. Only the species of bread and wine are broken and drunk. Christ's body and blood are untouchable and impassible. Thus, *totus et integer*, the invisible Christ can be present both on the altar and in glory, whole in every place and moment; but he is no creature, no spot of stuff shut up in crystal or bloodchest to suffer decay. The salvific blood is Christ ever risen and alive.

Hus's treatise not only deploys against miracle hosts a number of arguments drawn from long-standing debates over the eucharist. It also offers us an entry into the second line of theological discussion implicated in fifteenth-century blood controversy. For despite the fact that Hus was part of a commission to evaluate claims concerning bleeding hosts, he drew on another set of arguments, quite different from the eucharistic ones I treated above. I turn now to this second set of arguments, which concerned relics of Christ's blood. After outlining them, I shall return to Hus's treatise to show how the discussion of blood relics complemented that of visions and hosts and how the same basic concern with presence and absence throbbed beneath both. However different relic and eucharist, the essential ontological question remained: could Christ's blood, now pleading before the throne of God in heaven, appear red and living on earth? If so, how? If not, why not?

The Debate over Blood Relics: Background

Ever since Braulio of Saragossa in the seventh century, relic cult had led theologians to debate whether all of Christ's blood rose at the resurrection.[50] Asked about supposed blood relics venerated not locally but in the east, Braulio replied with a focus more soteriological than physiological or ontological. Whether or not bits of Christ's blood were left on earth (and Braulio uses

Augustine to argue that superfluous blood need not rise), two things are clear: first, that faith should be placed in the blood of the eucharist, which is surely Christ's; second, that we receive our blood back in resurrection for, as Luke 21.18 promises, "not a hair of your head shall perish."[51] Although Braulio sees already, as had Augustine, the relevance of medical theory to resurrection (he indeed makes an argument that fluids lost in miscarriage need not rise in either parent), his concern is wholeness and identity—to ensure that we, like Christ, rise both perfect and ourselves.[52]

Writing in the early twelfth century, Guibert of Nogent displayed the same fundamental concern. Guibert categorically denied the possibility of any bodily relics of Christ. If any part is left behind (for example the tooth relic at Soissons, which was the focus of Guibert's animosity), how can Christ be whole in resurrection? And if Christ does not rise whole, how shall the faithful hope for their own wholeness in the promised resurrection at the end of time?[53] Although Guibert, like Braulio, wants to privilege the eucharist over other forms of presence, such as relics, it is the avoidance of decay and fragmentation that above all else seems to animate his theology of relic and resurrection.[54] The blood and water from Christ's side were not absorbed by earth or stone because they would face decay there.[55] Indeed any particle of Christ that remains behind—even the hardness of tooth or bone—is thereby "excluded from incorruption" and must eventually perish, if not before, then at the fire that will come with the end of the world.[56] Yet God will not give his holy one "to see corruption (Ps. 15.10)."[57]

> If by the mouth of the Doctor of the Gentiles, in whom Christ speaks, we are promised that he "will reform the body of our lowness, made like to the body of his glory [Phil. 3.21]," how will he raise the despicableness of human corruption [*corruptionis humanae despicabilitatem*] to conformity to his glory [*ad suae claritatis . . . conformitatem*] if he left behind a part of his body [*partem corporis sui*] in useless condescension and without any rational cause and showed himself powerless to take up again something that was of himself [*ad id resumendum quod sui fuit*]? [58]

A stark fear of the bodily division and decay he finds imaged in body parts seems to lurk behind Guibert's strident opposition to relics. To Guibert, Christ's promise to humankind is a promise of survival and identity grounded in material continuity.[59]

Although Guibert and Braulio differed about whether to admit the possibility of blood left behind, they agreed in preferring eucharistic presence to relics. Still focusing on body rather than blood, and basing themselves both in Luke 21.18 and in Augustine's lengthy discussion of the resurrected body as parallel to a broken or melted statue reconstituted by a creator God, they took the crucial issue to be wholeness (that is, the nature of the model of resurrection held out to humans) rather than access (that is, direct encounter with the blood that saves). About a hundred years later, Pope Innocent III, who took up in passing the question of Christ's bodily relics, seemed to agree with Guibert that everything must rise; not a single hair can be omitted from glory.[60] But Innocent also muddied the issue by employing a new technical phrase—*veritas humanae naturae*—and arguing that incorruptibility was especially the goal of an essential material core of the body. The blood that will not perish is the blood of this core. Then, having adumbrated two rather different arguments against blood relics, Innocent (guided by the practical need to take into account extant relics in Rome) refused to decide.

> And it can be asked whether Christ, rising from the dead, took back that blood which he poured out on the cross. For if a hair of your head shall not perish (Luke 21.18), how much more will that blood not perish which was of the truth of [human] nature? [But] what is to be said of . . . the foreskin . . . believed [to be] preserved in the Lateran basilica? . . . It is better to commit such questions entirely to God than to define rash and overconfident answers.[61]

When we turn to the thirteenth century, we find no such hesitation. Eucharist and resurrection remained contexts within which bodily relics were discussed, but rash and confident answers now were given, based on a very different sort of physiological and philosophical analysis. And the focus was squarely on blood. Indeed two of the most important thirteenth-century discussions—those of Grosseteste and Gerhard of Cologne—were defenses of specific relics: the bloods of Westminster and Weingarten.

Grosseteste, Bonaventure, and Aquinas on Blood Relics and Identity

Robert Grosseteste's short tract "De sanguine Christi" was perhaps commissioned by Henry III himself to answer doubts that were apparently widely raised about the blood relic Henry acquired under the seals of the patriarch of Jerusalem and various prelates of the Holy Land and had delivered with considerable pomp to the cathedral of Westminster in 1247.[62] The treatise was copied by Matthew Paris into the *Additamenta* to his *Chronica majora* and was perhaps, as Nicholas Vincent argues, fairly well known after mid-century. As Vincent has pointed out, the treatise is too polished to have been delivered as a sermon in the form in which we now have it. But it is possible that Grosseteste attended the ceremony and gave arguments similar to those later recorded in the tract.[63] Toward the end of "De sanguine," Grosseteste indeed makes the same argument Matthew Paris, in the *Chronica majora*, attributes to the bishop of Norwich on the occasion of the translation. The bishop's sermon underlined both the very practical use of relics in political promotion and competition and the special soteriological significance of this particular relic, blood.

> Of all things held sacred by mortals, the most sacred is the blood of Christ, for it is the price of the world [*pretium mundi*] and its shedding is the salvation of the human race [*ejus effusio salus generis humani*]. . . . The holy cross is a most holy thing; but it is holy on account of the sprinkling [*aspersionem*] of the more holy blood upon it, and not the blood holy on account of the cross. . . . And we [Matthew Paris] believe him [the bishop] to have said these things so that England should rejoice and be glorified no less in the possession of this treasure than does France in having obtained the holy cross, which the king of France . . . loves and venerates more than gold and jewels.[64]

Matthew Paris makes clear, however, that doubts persisted after the bishop's sermon.

> After talking among themselves, some of those sitting round grunted in doubt and posed the question: "how could the Lord have left blood behind on earth when he rose with full integrity [*plene et integraliter*] on the third day after the passion?" which question the bishop of Lincoln at once discussed [*determinabatur*], just as we have written it down in the appendices of this book.[65]

Grosseteste's arguments, which have recently been studied by Mark Daniel Holtz and Nicholas Vincent, were in part historical.[66] They were also theological and physiological and, as such, seem to have entered into the general thirteenth- and fourteenth-century discussion of blood, although only one manuscript of the tractate is known to have survived.[67] Not fully consistent in its physiological reasoning, the treatise is nonetheless important for introducing new medical precision into the discussion. In the first part, Grosseteste lists four sources of Christ's blood—reddened water from washing, blood from punctures and scourgings (mixed with other fluids), blood (pure and unmixed) from hands and feet, and blood from the side or heart itself—to which he adds a fifth liquid, the bloody water from Christ's side; he then suggests that Joseph of Arimathea kept some of the blood as "a treasure and a medicine." He makes clear, however, neither which blood Joseph kept nor which blood is present at Westminster. In the second part of this treatise, Grosseteste turns to the objection raised by the grumblers and argues that the blood left behind is only superfluous, nutritional blood, that generated from food and of the sort lost in nosebleeds or other effusions, not the consubstantial blood of core human nature (the *veritas humanae naturae*)—that blood called by physicians "the friend of nature" and by Moses "the seat of the soul."[68] "Of this [consubstantial] blood we have as it happens [*forte*] none on earth," says Grosseteste, although he adds: "I say *forte* because God can do anything."[69]

Grosseteste's first argument thus seems to privilege the pure blood of hands, feet, and heart (and perhaps suggests that Henry's relic is of such blood), whereas the second argument seems to make relic blood only nutritional blood and therefore secondary or "superfluous"—an odd defense of the Westminster treasure.[70] But the inconsistency suggests that, for all the innovation of the physiological discussion, the source of the blood is not, to Grosseteste, the point. The point (as it was to Guibert of Nogent and will be to Jan Hus, both of whom rejected relics) is the wholeness promised to humankind in the resurrection. What was left behind must be other than the *veritas humanae naturae*, so we can have confidence that we ourselves will rise whole at the end of time, "without mutilation or deformity." It is important then that Grosseteste ends with a discussion of the wounds of Christ, which, like the blood, both are and are not signs of mutability. The basic question is: what constitutes perfection? What Grosseteste stresses here is that Christ appeared glorified yet tangible and visible (Luke 24), entering "through closed doors" but "demonstrably and palpably wounded"—in other words, ghostly (immutable and whole) yet bodily (mutable and injured).[71]

The theological treatment of both blood and wounds comes at the end of the treatise and is very short.[72] The few phrases focus on the wounds as proof offered to unbelief, as somehow pointing beyond earth to glory. Grosseteste thus seems to be trying to find a naturalistic way of saying that blood is in some sense both present in relic and resurrected, just as he sees Christ both marked by crucifixion and perfect in heaven. Moreover Grosseteste not only emphasizes the paradox in the gospel account itself of present and absent, spirit and flesh, glorified and wounded; he also stresses that it was at Christ's "own will and pleasure" that he appeared thus. Hence behind the logical inconsistency that results from Grosseteste's enthusiasm for the latest physiological theory lies a devotional consistency—a sense that the testimony of Christ's blood is an act of God's power and Christ's will. Christ *chose* to appear scarred as a reminder that the divine wholeness chooses to be fragmented for the salvation of humankind. If he left particles of his blood behind on earth, it was as a sign of our wholeness to come.

As context, it is important to remember that Grosseteste argued, in his *De cessatione legalium*, that Christ died by divine power, not by loss of blood.[73] The piercing of his hands and feet would not have caused enough bleeding to result in death in three hours, and Christ's loud cry on the cross showed that he was still fully alive. Hence he *chose* for soul to be separated from body. The pouring of blood when his side was opened after death was a miracle (like his rosy wounds in resurrection); dead bodies do not pour blood.[74] What saves is, to Grosseteste, the death itself—of which the blood is a reminder, also willed by God. Both Grosseteste's somewhat tortuous medical arguments and his sense that blood relics are important less as physiological fragments than as signs of the simultaneity of life and death will appear in later Franciscan discussions of *sanguis Christi.*

Neither Bonaventure nor Thomas Aquinas wrote treatises *de sanguine Christi*, nor did they treat blood relics at length. But, however briefly expressed, their opinions reflect the new physiological interest we find in Grosseteste. Bonaventure's Sentence commentary (written about the time of Grosseteste's little treatise) seems merely to suggest that divine power (*divina dispensatio*) could have permitted relics of foreskin and blood to survive on earth.[75] He also suggests that certain bodily fluids or "humidities" flowing outside the veins might be excluded from resurrection.[76] He holds, however, that blood is part of the truth of human nature, which is informed by soul and assumed hypostatically by the Word (i.e., itself directly united with the Logos). Not everything assumed by Christ is assumed for eternity. Using the patristic principle known as *Quod assumpsit . . . nunquam dimisit* ("The Word of God never laid down what he assumed in assuming our nature"), Bonaventure nonetheless excludes certain "co-assumed" human qualities, such as the capacity to suffer (passibility). But it is not clear that he thought (as later commentators held) that blood itself was ever excluded from essential human nature or the hypostatic union.[77] Unless Christ's blood rises with him, the wine in the chalice could not become blood, argues Bonaventure.[78] Moreover, although Christ's blood poured out in sacrifice is the price of our reconciliation with God, Bonaventure emphasizes (as does Grosseteste) that Christ *chose* the form of our redemption. Although his divinity was forever impassible, he wished to shed not merely drops but waves of blood [*non exivit gutta, sed effluxit sanguinis unda*], choosing an immensity of physical and mental pain.[79] Hence for all the oddness of the discussion of Christ's bodily fluids, Bonaventure's asides about blood relics are part of a larger sense that the resurrection of every particle is less important than the promise that humankind will be perfect morally as well as physically in its redemption, a promise sealed in blood.[80]

Aquinas took up blood relics in two places: a quodlibetal question of 1271 and the third part of the *Summa theologiae* (from before the end of 1273).[81] In the *Summa* he argued simply:

All the blood which flowed from Christ's body, belonging as it does to the integrity of human nature,[82] rose again with His body; and the same reason holds good for all the particles which belong to the truth and integrity of human nature. But the blood preserved as relics in some churches did not flow from Christ's side, but is said to have flowed from some maltreated image of Christ. [83]

In the quodlibet, however, Thomas was drawn into the (to our eyes) odd physiological reasoning popular in his day; perhaps, as Vincent has suggested, he knew of it from Grosseteste.[84] Arguing from the maxim *Quod assumpsit*, Aquinas posed the problem thus:

What is assumed . . . is never laid down, but the Word of God assumed in our nature not only body but also blood. Therefore his blood was never laid down and returns to him in resurrection. But, to the contrary, the blood of Christ is said to be preserved in several churches up to today.

To this, the reply is that in resurrection, both Christ's and ours, all that is of the truth of human nature [*de veritate naturae humanae*] is restored but not those things that are not of the truth of human nature. And about this—that is, what is of the truth of human nature—there are different learned opinions, according to one of which not all nutritive blood [*sanguis nutrimentalis*]—that is, blood generated from food—pertains to the truth of human nature. Since therefore Christ ate and drank before the passion, nothing prohibits there having been in him some nutritive blood that would not pertain to the truth of human nature and would not have to return to his body in resurrection.[85]

Aquinas, however, rejects the argument that nutritive blood might remain behind, first, because Christ suffered at the age of human perfection (and presumably the blood he shed was therefore essential, not superfluous); second, because the blood in which Christ suffered should, like that of the martyrs, have special glory in resurrection; and third, because the blood shed at the passion was that which saves the whole human race by virtue of its union with divinity (Thomas quotes Heb. 13.12).[86] Although the logic is a bit elliptical, the argument seems to be that Christ's perfect body could have included nothing truly superfluous and that what flowed from it as the price of human redemption had to be essential to core human nature, which was always united to the Logos. Thus Thomas concludes, in phrasing less clear than that of the later *Summa*: "The blood of Christ that is displayed in certain churches, however, is said to have flowed miraculously from a certain image of Christ that had been struck or else otherwise from the body of Christ [*vel etiam alias ex corpore christi*]." The *alias* is particularly unclear.[87]

The key technical term in all this discussion, *veritas humanae naturae*, has recently been exhaustively studied by Philip Lyndon Reynolds, who argues that twelfth- and thirteenth-century debates were about change itself.[88] Exploring a passage from Peter Lombard's Sentences (II.30, cc. 14–15), theologians asked whether a material core (the *veritas*) handed down in generation multiplied of itself in the process of growth or whether food was really changed into (assimilated by) the human body in the process of digestion. The passage that generated all the fuss read:

> A boy who dies immediately after being born will be resurrected in that stature that he would have had if he had lived to the age of thirty, impeded by no defect of body. From whence therefore would that substance [*substantia*], which was small in birth, be so big in resurrection, unless of itself in itself it multiplied? From which it appears that even if he had lived, the substance would not have come from another source but it would have augmented itself, just as the rib [of Adam] from which woman was made and as the loaves of the gospel story [were multiplied].[89]

Glossing this, many thirteenth-century theologians argued that some essential core of the human body persisted, to which food was not properly speaking assimilated. Therefore growth was a kind of miracle ("of itself in itself . . . multiplied"). Aquinas held, following Aristotle, that there was real assimilation.[90] The individual persists formally (as does a city with different citizens, or a river with different water), while material components come and go. Such a solution would seem to suggest that numerical identity (being the same person or object over time) resides in form; if the pattern (the city or river) is the same, any matter can flow in and out. It would follow logically—as Durandus of St. Pourçain (d. 1383) would later conclude—that the resurrected body could contain any matter animated by its own form and hence that stuff could be left behind. Most thirteenth-century theologians seem to have held, however, that material continuity was necessary for identity. They argued that in the process of digestion and growth food was incorporated into the *veritas humanae naturae* but that some distinction continued through life between true (or essential) and untrue (or superfluous) bodily parts (such as fingernails and sputum). The *veritas* (or true core) had to persist in order for the being to be human, and that core, although not of course all the matter that had been present in it during a lifetime, would return materially the same in resurrection. In agreement with most of his contemporaries, Thomas held that the soul would recover in resurrection the same body (matter) it animated on earth, although not all (every particle of) the same matter.

This position could have justified blood relics in two senses. It could have supported relics of humors or inessential blood, as it did in the rather different use Bonaventure made of such technical points. Or, in a logical extrapolation from it (that no one in fact made in the thirteenth century), Thomas could have held that any matter informed by the soul (form) was the body of the person whose soul informed it; bits could be left out. (Although one must note that, technically speaking, such left-behind stuff, no longer informed by the form of the person, would not be that person's body.)[91] In fact, Thomas held that continuity of matter was necessary for continuity of body and that all essential matter must be resumed. (Because of Christ's perfection, all his blood was essential.) Both Christ's body and ours resume the same physical stuff in resurrection.

As I have argued elsewhere, the popularity of saints' cult generally may have provided some of the pressure on Thomas toward his somewhat philosophically incoherent insistence on the survival of material bits in resurrection. The bones of the saints were not really "theirs" unless exactly those bones rose at the end of time.[92] Although historians have tended to ignore the fact, popular piety unquestionably shaped Thomas's philosophy. But his philosophy also shaped his understanding of cult. His theory of formal identity through unicity of form—that is, that the soul is the one substantial form of the human person—undergirds his opposition to blood relics of the resurrected Christ. Orthodox opinion had long held that, in the *triduum*, Christ's body and soul were divided from each other, although each continued united to the Logos (the divinity). Since during this period there was, according to Thomas, no form of the body strictly speaking—for the person has only one substantial form, the soul—the parts and particles were the body of Christ only by union with the Logos.[93] Such philosophical analysis bolstered Aquinas's conviction that all bits (or at least all true bits) poured out in crucifixion remained united to the Word and rose on Easter Sunday. None (or at least no essential part, such as salvific blood) could be left behind. It seems clear then that complex philosophical positions lie behind the physiological discussions of blood relics, but also that philosophy alone would not have determined the conclusions. An insistence on the immutability of God and the salvific power of blood also drives Aquinas's insistence that no fragment be left behind.[94]

Thomas's concern, like Bonaventure's, is not finally with the particles but with larger issues of devotion and perfection. In the *Summa*, the question that touches on blood relics (ST 3, q. 54, art. 3) occurs between one on the nature of Christ's glorified body (q. 54, art. 2) and one on the resurrection of Christ's scars (q. 54, art. 4). The Christ treated here is the paradoxical Christ of Luke 24, who passes through closed doors yet eats fish and has touchable wounds. Thus, just as in Grosseteste, the immediate context is, first, an emphasis on the glorified body as both ghostly and palpable, but in every way incorruptible (for it is "unseemly" that corruption touch Christ), and, second, an affirmation that Christ's scars "will always remain on his body."

Art. 3, Reply Obj. 2: As Augustine says . . . "perchance . . . some keener critic will . . . say: . . . why not . . . phlegm? . . . But whatever anyone may add [to the body that Christ reassumes], let him take heed not to add corruption [*corruptionem*] . . . because Divine power is equal to taking away such qualities as it wills from the visible and tractable body, while allowing others to remain, so that there be no defilement—i.e. of corruption—though the features be there . . ." [*ut absit labes, scilicet corruptionis, adsit effigies* . . .].

Art. 4, Reply Obj. 1: The scars that remained . . . belong neither to corruption nor defect, but to the greater increase of glory [*non pertinent ad corruptionem vel defectum, sed ad maiorem cumulum gloriae* . . .].

Art. 4, Reply Obj. 2: Although those openings are a certain dissolution of continuity, still the greater beauty of glory compensates for all this, so that the body is not less integral but more perfect [*non sit minus integrum sed magis perfectum*].[95]

The Savior must be human and in history, palpable and broken, marked by the experience of death, and eternally sacrificed for human sin. Yet he must be simultaneously and eternally glorious and whole (*integer*), immutable, incorruptible, untouchable God. Like his wounded and perfect body, his blood must be forever spilled and forever in glory.

Thomas, like Grosseteste and Bonaventure, actually, in a sense, defends existing cult by positing bleeding images as a source for blood relics. (He is usually understood to have had the miraculously bleeding cross of Beirut in mind.)[96] His position on veneration (which will be quoted repeatedly in fifteenth-century disputes) is, however, a complicated one.[97] Aquinas both gives some objective value to holy matter (the true cross and the bodies of the saints) and yet holds that "reverence is due only to the rational creature."[98] He seems to say that holy images are honored only for that to which they refer but that bodily relics are venerated both because of that to which they point (the saints in heaven) and also as temples of the Holy Spirit that the saints will reassume at the end of time.[99] Apropos the true cross, he argues that it can be worshiped with the same *latria* owed to Christ, since it is both image—that is, like Christ in "representing the figure of Christ extended upon it"—and physical stuff touched by the physical stuff of Christ—that is, unlike but "in contact with the limbs of Christ and . . . saturated with his blood." Aquinas draws on Damascene's idea that image is adored only because of exemplar—because of that of which it is the image.[100] The insensible, the nonrational, the inanimate cannot be adored. But in his discussion of the true cross a stronger sense of holy matter—powerful not because of likeness but because of contact—peeps through. This sense may have informed his willingness to accept some sort of blood relics, if only effluvial ones (that is, those pouring or oozing from images).

Aquinas's argument is finally, however, based in the salvific power of the blood. If blood poured out by martyrs is glorified, how much more that of Christ, which saves the world (Heb. 13.12)? Assumed in incarnation and spilled on the cross, *sanguis Christi* can redeem only if it is never separated from the Godhead. Hence the cross can be adored because it was in contact with Christ, but the redeeming blood itself cannot have been left behind; the body of Christ rises *integer* and perfect and must necessarily take back all the blood that saves humankind.

Gerhard of Cologne

Thomas and Bonaventure (like Grosseteste) raise issues that range far beyond the physiological and cultic ones that provide the immediate context for their discussions of blood relics. Those issues returned in the fourteenth century with Duns Scotus, Francis de Mayronis (Meyronnes), and the debate over the *triduum mortis*, to which I shall return.[101] But first I devote a few words to the other thirteenth-century treatise *de sanguine Christi*, whose Dominican author rejected not only Thomas's position but also the obsessive and medicalized discussion of physiology and identity that formed a dominant strand in blood theology right down into the 1460s.

Gerhard of Cologne's *Tractatus de sacratissimo sanguine domini* was composed in 1280 at the request of abbot Hermann of Weingarten to defend the monastery's blood relic against skepticism, both theological and historical.[102] Much of Gerhard's defense lies in his account of the relic's descent from Longinus, via Mantua, to its present home at Weingarten (near Ravensburg, just north of Lake Constance); his case also rests on the fact of cult and popular enthusiasm for it. Gerhard is, in this treatise, something of a populist. Subtle arguments about *subtilitas* and wholeness are all very well for theologians, he says, but Christ is a doctor who appeals directly to ordinary hearts—that is, to the sort of folk who make pilgrimage to Weingarten.

Forced to deal with the physiological arguments he almost certainly learned by studying with Albert the Great at Cologne and reading Aquinas, Gerhard maintains against his teachers that resurrection can be total and integral even if particles are left behind and suggests in one passage that there are bits such as fingernails and spittle that Christ could have shed without damaging his integrity.[103] It does not detract from Christ's perfection if an angel gave the holy foreskin to Charlemagne at Aachen. Moreover, says Gerhard, caricaturing literalist arguments, if all Christ's blood had to rise, where did that shed in the circumcision wait in the thirty years between circumcision and resurrection? Gerhard's basic ontological argument, however, is that physiological nitpickers, "followers of Aristotle, Pythagoras and Hippocrates," are "pseudophilosophers," who miss the simple point that blood relics are miracles.[104] The flow of water and blood from Christ's side after death was miraculous; dead bodies don't bleed. Hence by a similar miracle God makes Christ's blood present both on earth and in heaven. For

> just as he could make his subtle and glorified body touchable and visible to his disciples, so he could not do without one and the same blood in heaven and yet left it behind as a comfort for his believers here on earth. Cannot one and the same all-powerful Savior in one and the same moment be changed into the sacrament in the hands of a thousand priests, really here present and undivided, and yet not be absent there [in heaven]?[105]

Gerhard thus uses the theory of concomitance worked out to justify the *integritas* of Christ in resurrection and eucharist to defend the bilocation of *sanguis Christi*. If all Christ is in every particle, then (argues Gerhard) Christ's blood can be totally in heaven and yet present both in eucharist and in relic. If Christ's body after the resurrection was so glorified and subtle that it could go through doors and yet was touchable by Thomas the Doubter, so his blood can be glorified (almost immaterial) in heaven and yet palpable drops (seeable, touchable, and even drinkable) here on earth.

Placing his argument in the context of the same gospel account referred to by Grosseteste and Aquinas, Gerhard indeed suggests (in an argument to which both earlier and later theorists would vigorously object) that relic is superior to eucharist. Pilgrims to the Weingarten blood are like Doubting Thomas, "who came to belief later than the others and had to touch the scars," but they are more than Thomas, for he felt only wounds whereas they "see the blood itself, rose-colored and shining red." Lukewarm Christians have ignored the many other signs left behind by Christ: the Testaments, the Jews themselves (spared by the church to serve as an eternal reminder of Christ's suffering), the sacrament of the altar, and the contact relics that took his life (cross, nails, lance, and thorns). So Christ, "who knew all beforehand," has left his blood itself that those sleeping "may come again to love" through "the sight of blood drops before their eyes."[106] It is important to Gerhard that the relic is still living blood—visibly shining and red. In a flood of images, he apostrophizes it as dew, seed, and fertility; cleansing water, quencher of thirst, and intoxication; a spark or flashpoint (*scintilla*), from which a frenzy of guilt, love, and longing can be ignited. It is suffering, torture, and bloodshed—a sacrifice offered for salvation yet an indictment of those who made such sacrifice necessary. Hence it is accusation as well as violation. It accuses the Jews, who (in Gerhard's view) killed Christ, but it also charges the Christians of Gerhard's own day with being the "new Jews," who kill Christ again by their lethargy and neglect.

Braulio, Guibert, Innocent III, Grosseteste, Bonaventure, Thomas, and Gerhard of Cologne can all be seen as addressing the authenticity of blood relics, and as responding "yes" or "no" to the question whether Christ did or could leave particles of himself behind on earth.[107] They all explicitly indicate that the most immediate theological context of the issue is the doctrine of the general resurrection, and they all make some use of physiological theory in an effort to determine what constitutes the *veritas* or core of human nature with which humankind will rise at the end of time in imitation of the resurrection of Christ himself. Yet by the late thirteenth century, the focus is increasingly on blood. Whereas Braulio, Guibert, and Innocent III dealt with *sanguis Christi* primarily as part of a general discussion of the bodily relics of Christ, the defenses of Grosseteste and Gerhard were commissioned by supporters of existing or potential blood cults. And larger issues of praxis, of spirituality, of theology and ontology circled round. Whether the blood at stake was from abused images (such as the cross of Beirut), or from some nonessential yet tangible bit of the crucified, or from Christ's heart opened by the lance on Calvary, theorists tended to stress not only its historical or physical provenance but also the action of divine power in establishing and maintaining its presence. It is surely significant that Grosseteste, Thomas, and Gerhard differ so emphatically in their conclusions about the possibility and provenance of blood relics, yet not only do all three place the issue in exactly the same exegetical and theological context, they also agree in concluding that, paradoxically, blood is both present and absent. As discussions from Braulio to Gerhard make clear, actual relic cult pressured theologians to an increased attention to the soteriological significance of blood. But, as the discussions also make clear, a devotional and pastoral need for the power in the blood—a power both accusatory and reconciling—drove cult.

Discussions of Blood Relics in the Fifteenth Century

When Jan Hus in the early fifteenth century produced both a technical *questio* and a treatise *de sanguine Christi*, he had the Wilsnack blood particularly in mind. And one of his most insistent charges was that ordinary people were misled by such false miracles to believe that Christ's blood even in the sacrament of the altar is visible. Thus the visible, "that red thing," is substituted for the invisible, faith in general is devalued, and some are led to doubt whether the divine can be present unless visible and touchable.[108] Such concerns are clearly informed by two hundred years or more of a learned debate over transformed hosts. But the bulk of Hus's very sophisticated argumentation is drawn from debates over blood relics, not hosts; the theological and exegetical context, from specific references to Luke 21.18 and 24 to general discussion of exactly which parts return in resurrection, is that within which Grosseteste, Aquinas, and Gerhard of Cologne set their discussions of blood and *veritas humanae naturae*. Acknowledging that (as Gerhard argued) God could have willed his glorified body to be both in heaven and on earth "according to its natural substance," Hus nonetheless concludes that God has not done so, because he will not give his holy one to see corruption (Ps. 15.10).[109] All of the blood shed from Christ's body received the gift of glory, for Christ could not have been the "firstfruits" of resurrection unless he had been completely recomposed into harmony [*armonia*] of body at the very moment of his rising.[110] Even if something red somehow authentically appears (and the Wilsnack blood—the "fetid blood of a dead horse"—is not such an authentic appearance), it is only a memorial, not blood itself.[111] Nonetheless, to Hus, the true blood of Christ, present invisibly in eucharist and in heaven, is so precious that any drop was a sufficient price (*pretium*) for our salvation.[112]

Hus's treatise makes it very clear that, by the fifteenth century, theological arguments concerning bleeding hosts and those concerning blood relics have fused into the question whether there can be *Blut Christi* on earth. The question in this form returned in 1448 at La Rochelle (in the diocese of Saintes), where the Franciscans had long presented a particle of the blood of Christ to the faithful for veneration.[113] As the theological faculty at Paris put it: "discord and dissension" arose there concerning "the matter of the blood of Christ shed for the redemption of the human race," some asserting that Christ did not reassume all his blood [*totum sanguinem suum*] in the resurrection, and others asserting the opposite.[114] In response, the faculty at Paris established a commission of five professors of theology to look into the question, and they concluded unanimously that "it is not repugnant to the piety of the faithful to believe that something of Christ's blood poured out at the time of the passion [*quod aliquid de Sanguine Christi effuso tempore Passionis*] remained on earth."[115] In spite of this decision, however, the bishop of Saintes, Guy de la Roche, forbade the Franciscans to present the relic for public veneration. The Franciscans brought the matter to Nicholas V (who was to intervene a few years later in the Wilsnack controversy). Speaking of the long tradition of the blood of La Rochelle, "on account of which a great multitude of people were accustomed to congregate," Nicholas commanded Guy to "allow the Christian faithful accustomed to gather there to persevere in their pious devotion, since this is not contrary to the truth of the faith and supports piety. . . ."[116] In his decree, Nicholas pronounced this conclusion after a reference to the icon of Beirut, which, "cruelly struck by the impious Jews, shed much blood"—blood that was sent to many parts of the world and, adored by the faithful, did not cease to work miracles.[117] Thus Nicholas seemed to take the position Thomas had articulated almost two hundred years earlier—that is, that the blood venerated in churches, while useful in stimulating popular devotion, was a miraculous flow from images, not a portion of the physical body of Christ. At least according to Reformation polemic, however, the Franciscans at La Rochelle continued to advertise their relic as the blood of Christ collected by Nicodemus at the time of the crucifixion.[118] And Nicholas Vincent has recently discovered that they obtained letters from Pius II in July 1461 repeating the Paris judgment of 1448 that it was "in no way contrary to faith to affirm that our redeemer left behind on earth as a memorial of his passion some portion of his blood."[119]

Historians have usually claimed that, with Nicholas V, the discussion shifts from the nature of putative blood relics to the problem of what conduces to piety.[120] And there is no question that Nicholas saw the disputes about transformed hosts and blood relics at Wilsnack and La Rochelle, respectively, as issues of praxis. Papal response to questions of cult and miracle (such as, for example, stigmata and miraculous fasting) tended in general to be theologically minimalist—that is, to focus on what was spiritually useful to the faithful, not on doctrinal pronouncement. But whatever the considerations behind papal decisions, it does not seem correct to argue that the basic issues of the mid- to late fifteenth century, either to university theologians or even to devotional writers and pilgrims, were issues of practice. Exactly the decade of the controversy at La Rochelle saw—at Wilsnack and at Rome—strident debate over soteriology and ontology.

By the 1440s and 1450s, a third strand had become woven into discussion of relics and transformed hosts: the question of the status of Christ's blood during the *triduum mortis*. This debate shows very clearly that fifteenth-century controversy over the presence or absence of blood was not just debate over proper eucharistic piety or the authenticity and veneration of relics. Rather it was, on the one hand, a matter of the relation of the body and blood of Christ to each other and to his person, and on the other hand, a question of how Christians gain access to the *sanguis Christi* that saves. If we look carefully at the details of this very complicated and abstruse debate and at some of the less polemical theological discussion that led up to it, we see two things.

First, blood has become an increasingly contested and increasingly important object of cult and devotion. Second, the status of blood, both as integral to (*integer*) and as separated from (*effusus*) Christ is central to the theology of the fifteenth century. I turn in the next chapter to the *triduum mortis* debate and its background.

Chapter 5
Christ's Blood in the Triduum Mortis

By the middle years of the fifteenth century, holy blood was crucial in the religious life of northern Europe. In Bohemia, Hussites clamored for blood in the chalice. In Thuringia, cryptoflagellants saw in it a sacrament higher than other sacraments. In the Mark Brandenburg and Mecklenburg, churches and cloisters such as Schwerin and Zehdenick vied for pilgrims and donations to it. At Wilsnack, people journeyed from afar for a glimpse of it. In Prague, Erfurt, Barcelona, and Paris, theologians debated what it was and how it should be made available to the faithful. Politics in every sense of the word—the politics of towns, regions, and nations, of monasteries, cult sites, dioceses, universities, and orders—were involved. If the details of all those treatises *de sanguine* penned concerning Wilsnack, Westminster, Weingarten, and La Rochelle are hard to grasp, it is nonetheless easy to see what people were fighting over. If Christ's blood saved, it mattered whether it was "really there" on host or in reliquary.

In turning to the controversy at Rome in 1462–64, I come to the place where the issues are hardest to understand. The debate was over the question of whether Christ's blood was joined to his divinity during the three days between his crucifixion and his resurrection. For most modern readers, it is hard to see why this mattered. Hence there has been a tendency on the part of historians to focus on what is to many of them the only easily recognizable element: the competition between the orders involved.

The competition between Dominicans and Franciscans is certainly one thread we can follow through the maze of blood debates from the thirteenth century on. As we have already seen, there were differences on questions of eucharistic visions, transformed hosts, and blood relics between Dominicans, who followed Albertus Magnus and Thomas Aquinas, and Franciscans (often joined by Benedictines), who followed Bonaventure and Duns Scotus. These differences continued in the controversy over Wilsnack and that over the *triduum mortis*. Although there were always a few theologians (such as the Dominican Gerhard of Cologne and the Franciscan John of Capistrano) who did not follow the school line, a general Dominican-Franciscan split is clear.[1]

Dominicans tended to what we might call a "higher" blood theology, one in which the accessibility of the blood of Christ in either eucharistic vision or relic was problematic and the blood was adored precisely in its distance and glory. Like Cusanus in his decree at Halberstadt, they argued for unseeability. In contrast, Franciscans, exactly in their stress on the humanity (indeed the body and the bodily death) of Christ, made the blood more earthly and more accessible here below—that is, theologically "lower" but present, not glorified but a promise of glory.[2] Like Döring and Kannemann in their treatises concerning Wilsnack, they defended blood relics and bleeding hosts as access to the divine, but they demoted Christ's blood ontologically, so to speak, by denying that the bloodshed of the crucifixion was united with the Logos while Christ lay in the tomb.

To focus on the politics of the orders is, however, to miss something deeper. This is so for two reasons. First, as we shall see, the two groups were not really so far apart. As often happens in lengthy controversies, the sides moved closer to each other over the course of decades. This was possible because behind both positions, even where they were genuinely different theologically and devotionally, lay an emphasis on sacrifice as crucial for salvation. Second and connected to this, these abstruse texts help us to probe more deeply into what was at stake in the fifteenth-century blood obsession. The technicality that seems initially so disconcerting is in fact revealing. For behind the detailed discussion of Christ's physiology or of eucharistic accidents and substance lie the same concerns we shall see when I come to the themes of blood piety. The choice of adjective and verb, and the Scriptural passages repeated again and again, are clues. What the texts speak of is blood *effusus* and *vivens*, sacrificial blood, shed blood, blood that purifies, washes, and pays a price, blood that is poured out, sprinkled on, offered up. None of this language is imprecise or casually employed. Just as I did not give all those details of cults in Mecklenburg and Brandenburg simply to put historical material on the table, so I do not spend time on the *triduum mortis* discussion only in order to provide information about a moment in fifteenth-century theological debate. Rather it is my contention that we can see, in the specific details of theological controversy as in those of cult development and propaganda, the basic religious assumptions of the age.

Mayronis and the Barcelona Controversy of 1350–51

Although much in earlier theological debate prepared the way for it, the status of Christ's blood as a component of his humanity seems to have first emerged as a controversial issue in Barcelona in 1350,[3] when the Franciscan Francis Baiuli preached during Lent to the clergy and people [*clero et populo in vulgari*] in the church of his convent that the blood poured out in the passion became separated from the divinity of Christ at his death and was therefore not to be adored as the blood of the Son of God. (He also asserted that if Christ had died as an old man, he would not have failed in his mission.[4]) Brought to trial by the Dominican inquisitor, a certain Pontius (about whom nothing else is known), Baiuli retracted his statement but imperfectly, saying that the question of the blood of Christ still needed to be explored.[5] Pontius then preached against Baiuli's opinion. Several Franciscans who took notes during the sermon charged Pontius in turn before the vicar of the bishop of Barcelona with ten errors. The surviving manuscript record of these events tells us that, at this point, messengers returned from Rome with two bulls, one of which replaced Pontius with the Dominican Nicholas Roselli as inquisitor; the other ordered Roselli to proceed against Baiuli's second opinon as heresy. (The Franciscans had agreed to retraction of the opinion about Christ's age.) No papal documents survive, although we have three letters from Cardinal John of Moulins to Roselli that purport to express the pope's opinion.[6] Francis Baiuli was then questioned about twenty-seven articles, the first twenty-four of which related to his preaching about the separated blood.[7] Roselli was especially anxious to ascertain whether ordinary people had been taught the Franciscan position on the blood of Christ. After the interrogation, Roselli called together a council, in which no Franciscans were present; it required Baiuli to recant in a notarized document and also to revoke his earlier statements publicly in the vernacular in the city of Barcelona.

The learned study by Michelle Garceau of MS Add 22795, which is our only full record of these events, argues that what was key in the controversy was Baiuli's preaching *in vulgari*—that is, his attempt to share the technicalities of theology with ordinary Christians, thus creating a "public sphere." And it is unquestionably true that Roselli's questioning of Baiuli focused on who said what to whom, just as it is true that Baiuli showed considerable bravery in not implicating his fellow Franciscans. (He mentioned only Francis de Mayronis as a precursor, and Mayronis was safely deceased.) But it is also clear that the specific content of the teaching was at stake. After all, Baiuli was initially charged with two errors, yet the second (concerning the age at which Christ completed his mission) did not arouse either the ire of his inquisitors, who devoted only three of twenty-seven questions to it, nor the defense and counterattack of his own brothers. The Franciscans quietly agreed that Baiuli should drop his speculations about the life cycle of Christ, but on the blood they fought back, charging ten errors against the inquisitor who opposed them. What was—depending on point of view—either threatening or worth defending was not just any vernacular preaching but vernacular preaching about blood.

The disagreement between Franciscans and Dominicans in 1351 over whether *sanguis Christi* was separated from the body of Christ during the period between crucifixion and resurrection was in part propelled, as M.-D. Chenu and others have pointed out, by philosophical differences between the two groups over how to account for person.[8] To followers of Thomas (as I explained in Chapter 4), the human person qua person was accounted for by one substantial form (the soul); hence blood, like flesh and bones, was directly informed by rational soul. After death, Christ's body, having been separated from soul, was no longer technically a human body. It preserved its identity as his body only by the direct relation of its essential elements to the Logos. The blood of salvation—which had to be understood as Christ's essential blood exactly because it saved the world—was thus worthy of adoration because of its indivisibility from the Word. To Franciscans, who espoused the doctrine of the plurality of forms, body was accounted for qua body by a *forma corporeitatis*. Hence, during life, Christ's blood was co-assumed by the Logos only as part of body. Although Christ's body continued united to the Logos after death, not all elements included under body by virtue of the *forma corporeitatis* were in death necessarily connected to the Logos.[9] What saved in the pouring out of blood was not so much the physiological element itself as the suffering and death it signaled.

The position for which Francis Baiuli was condemned had, as he admitted, been elaborated by Francis de Mayronis (Meyronnes) (d. ca. 1328). And, as Nicholas Vincent has argued, Mayronis was known to Clement VI from debates in Paris in 1320–21.[10] Hence, despite the vagaries of document survival, it is quite believable that Clement took a strong position in the Barcelona controversy.[11] In any case, a glance back at Mayronis shows how positions had developed between 1300 and the controversy of 1350–51.[12]

Drawing on Scotus's understanding that the body possesses, in addition to the soul, a *forma corporeitatis* that determines the body to be an organic body ready to receive life from the soul, Mayronis expounded—in his Sentence commentary and in later sermons—the doctrine of four separations in the death of Christ.[13] First, Christ's soul and body were separated from each other (as is true in any death). Second, soul and body were separated from "any third entity"—that is, from humanity—because Christ was not a man (a living person constituted of soul and body) in the *triduum*.[14] Third, divinity was separated from humanity, although not from separated soul and body. Fourth, blood was separated from body when it poured out from the side.

Thus blood was separated from the divinity, because separated from body; body, however, remained joined to divinity. Through the traditional doctrine of the "communication of idioms," we can say God is in the tomb (with the body) and God is in hell (with the soul), but we cannot say God was shed on the cross or lay scattered on the earth.[15] Consequent upon the four separations were four *conjunctiones* or reunions: first of soul with body (resulting in humanity), second of divinity with the humanity that results from the first *conjunctio*, third of blood with body, and fourth of blood with divinity.[16] From this Mayronis concluded, first, that not all the blood of Christ remained on earth but some particles could remain because the glorified body "perhaps needs less blood";[17] second, that such blood, if discovered in relics, should be revered less than the blood of the eucharist because eucharistic blood was blood reunited with the divinity after the *triduum*; third, that the principle *Quod assumpsit* (which he attributes to Anselm) was to be understood as relating to the principal parts of humanity (soul and body), not blood;[18] and fourth, that the resurrection is, after the incarnation, the greatest mystery, because in each mystery, God was made man. (Christ not having been man in the *triduum*, he was made man again in the resurrection.)[19] Mayronis's argument thus defends the possibility of bodily relics only by diminishing their ontological status and places the devotional emphasis less on blood as saving matter than on bloodshed as a sign of the humiliation of death. These ideas and the condemnation in 1351 of a position extrapolated from them make it clear that already in the second half of the fourteenth century both devotion and theology focused increasingly on questions concerning Christ's blood: whether it remained on earth; how it was joined to body, soul, and divinity; how its various manifestations (eucharist, bodily relics, miraculous apparitions, images) should be ranked; and when and whether it could be venerated.

John of Capistrano on the Precious Blood

Controversy flared again in 1462 in Rome itself. It was stimulated in general by the Wilsnack debates of the 1440s and '50s over miracle hosts and the La Rochelle conflict of 1448 over blood relics, and in specific by the preaching on Easter Sunday in Brescia of James of the March (d. 1476), who revived Franciscan ideas on the *triduum mortis* from 1350–51. Positions taken on both sides in the ensuing controversy were sophisticated and complex, and extensive original documentation survives. Indeed the fullest surviving record of the events of 1350–51 exists because it was copied into a dossier prepared in 1463 for "certain religious men" to study as background to the debate over the *triduum mortis*.[20]

The best introduction to the issues at stake is a treatise *de Christi sanguine pretioso* penned by the charismatic Observant Franciscan John of Capistrano twenty years earlier, in 1440–42—the first treatise *de sanguine* that was neither a defense of, nor an attack on, blood relics or miracle hosts but rather a theological monograph on the saving blood of the Lord.[21] A Franciscan who defended Thomas's position on blood relics over against the Franciscan tradition represented by Mayronis, yet (unlike Thomas, who was suspicious of eucharistic visions) a passionate enthusiast of blood hosts and anti-Jewish host-desecration libels, John is an anomaly.[22] Moreover, his treatise, which exists in only five manuscripts (these may be his own earlier and later recensions),[23] had as such no influence, although he used some of its arguments in his controversy ten years later with Eberhard Waltmann over veneration of the Wilsnack blood—arguments which then became more widely known and discussed.[24] I cite the treatise here to show what broad and basic theological issues circled around the salvific blood of Christ by the mid-fifteenth century. As the text makes abundantly clear, Capistrano's fundamental concern was not, as is sometimes said, devotional and practical but ontological; the central topic is the necessity of *sanguis Christi* to Christ's core humanity and the immutable union of this with the Logos.

John frames his treatise as an exploration, in the form of a disputation, of the question: *An Christi sanguis necessarius ad esse hominis, post mortem Christi, fuerit separatus a divinitate?* He begins by summarizing and rejecting Mayronis's doctrine of the separation of the humanity from the divinity and of the blood from the divinity, arguing that the blood is united "immediately" to the Logos on account of "its innocence and our utility." As Augustine and Peter Lombard both argue (in the words of Ps. 29.10): "What profit [*utilitas*] is there in my blood if I descend into the pit [*descendo in corruptionem*]?" As Bonaventure holds, God has guaranteed (in the words of Ps. 15.10) that he will not "give his holy one to see corruption [*videre corruptionem*]."[25] Complex arguments follow but behind them hovers, as these passages from the Psalms suggest, both a horror at decay—mutability (moral and physical)—and a conviction that there is in the blood the profit of redemption but only if that blood remains immutable God. It cannot be separated from the Logos even in the piercing and spilling of crucifixion. Although treating physiological issues, Capistrano's fundamental arguments are from theology, not from physiology.

Following (and extrapolating from) Thomas's Quodlibet 5.5–6, which he quotes at the end of his treatise verbatim, Capistrano gives a series of proofs of blood's *utilitas* and *innocentia*. This usefulness and innocence are based, according to Capistrano's first set of propositions, in the integrity, immutability, incorruptibility, and glory of God. The argument seems to be that God has promised salvation by *sanguis Christi*, but *sanguis Christi* could not save if it were not fully, completely, indivisibly, incorruptibly, eternally, omnipresently, and gloriously God. Moreover there could be no moral justification for Christ's blood, which was sinless, ever to be separated from divinity. Because it is without sin, it cannot be cast away. Indeed if the blood were separated from divinity, both church and the sacraments of eucharist and baptism/penance, which were born in and of that blood, would not bring salvation. It is true that the blood shed from Christ's side came after death and was therefore not experienced by his body as pain. (Belief that the lance prick came after Christ's death had been required by the Council of Vienne in 1311–12.) Nonetheless this bloodshed was a penal purging of the sins of the world, because the spilling of blood (*effusio sanguinis*) signifies a penalty (*poenalitatem*) in the common law. *Sanguis Christi* saves only if it is shed innocent and yet never separated from immutable divinity.[26]

Connected to these ontological and soteriological arguments are a number of subsidiary and more physiological ones about the nature of body and blood. Capistrano argues that there can be no humanity without blood, for the human being cannot live without blood. Blood is not simply a secondary element assumed by Christ only via body. It is integral to human nature. And John uses Scotellus (Peter of Aquila) against Scotus to argue that Christ was a man at least *materialiter* (although not *formaliter*) during the *triduum*.[27] He, however, uses Scotus to argue that the body in the *triduum*, fully a body and subject to Aristotle's laws of generation and corruption, would have decayed, were it not for a second (Scotus's term was "new") miracle imposed by God.[28] Capistrano goes to great lengths to explain that Christ's original body was formed entirely from Mary's pure blood—a blood completely adequate to provide a material body without the admixture of male semen. Indeed this body was pure exactly because of the lack of such admixture. (It is worth noting—given recent assumptions in scholarly literature about female blood as polluting—that uterine blood is here conceptualized as entirely pure when free of the contamination of sexual intercourse. Impurity is based in sexual activity, not gender.[29]) Again and again one is struck by Capistrano's determination to make Christ's human body real—really conceived and born, really undergoing generation and corruption, really suffering and bleeding, really dying—and yet to argue that the bloodshed of salvation can in fact save only if it "does not see corruption." As he insists repeatedly: *Putrefactio enim nihil nobis valuisset.*[30]

Although John's treatise is usually described as Thomist, it in fact draws on several strands of earlier soteriology and Christology. The stress on Christ's body as physically human—not only capable of suffering but also in need of a special miracle to prevent its decay—is clearly a legacy of the emphases of John's fellow Franciscans, Grosseteste, Bonaventure, and Scotus, as is the acceptance of host miracles.[31] But Capistrano does draw explicitly on Dominican and Thomist positions (as do Hus, Tocke, Cusanus, and Waltmann) not only in his rejection of blood relics but also in his insistence on the glory and immutability of *sanguis Christi*—that is, on its distance from, and difference from, sinful humanity.

Charged by the papacy with a mission against the Hussites and reputed to be himself a miraculous healer, John was passionately concerned to defend miracles of host, image, and corporal. In his *De Christi sanguine*, he mentions the bleeding image at Piscaria;[32] the putative corporal miracles at Bolsena/ Orvieto and Trani;[33] the blood at Daroca, which allegedly repelled Muslim attack; and the miracle host at Brussels, which he saw and authenticated on a legation to the Low Countries.[34] A decade later, during the Wilsnack affair, Capistrano initially warned the curia against the supposed blood hosts as questionable. But he then changed course and directed a vitriolic attack (that seemed an oblique defense of the cult) toward Eberhard Waltmann's theory of veneration. Waltmann had argued against *adoratio* of pictures and relics, asserting that veneration can be given only to rational creatures and worship (*latria*) only to God. Questioning whether hosts ever mutated in species, he had argued that, if something extrinsic were added to a host (such as red color), it would be mere created matter and could not be adored. Capistrano responded in fury, calling Waltmann's theory of *adoratio* blasphemy (not to mention contrary to Thomas) and defending veneration of miracle hosts if their miracles were certain.[35] In the *De Christi sanguine*, Capistrano even interpreted the problematic *alias* in Thomas's Quodlibet 5 to mean "other things from the consecrated body of Christ" and used it to support miracles of bloody corporals.[36] Thus, for all his "high" blood theology, Capistrano differed from most Thomists in formulating complex explanations that allowed *Blut Christi* to be present in some sense on earth, if not in relic at least on miracle hosts and corporals. But he joined with Waltmann in one response to miraculous hosts. Waltmann, although he tended to doubt transformation claims, argued that eruptions of blood, if they appeared, were accusations of sin. To Capistrano, blood miracles, once authenticated, are signs of God, pointing to Christ's sacrifice. But Capistrano also associates them with vengeance, claiming that the blood at Daroca incited Christian troops to violence "as blood excites elephants."[37]

My treatment of Capistrano here is not in any way intended to cover up the anti-Semitism of his defense of putative blood miracles such as that at

Brussels (supposedly resulting from a Jewish desecration in 1369–70). John was an enthusiastic advocate of anti-Jewish charges.[38] Nor is it meant to obscure what may well have been an element of self-promotion in his general support for miracles. Eager to spread the reputation of his miracle-working patron and hero, San Bernardino of Siena, John was not averse to letting some of the charisma rub off on himself. But it is important to note that, whatever his focus elsewhere, his treatise *de Christi sanguine pretioso* was written outside any immediately polemical context.[39] Its basic topic was soteriology. Capistrano's intention was to underline both that the Son of God really died a physical death, suffering the generation and corruption the flesh is heir to, and yet that the blood he shed to effect salvation never lost—could never lose—the physical and moral purity, the wholeness and incorruptibility, it promised humankind in resurrection. In Capistrano's account, the blood is Christ, characterized by the paradoxes of incarnation and resurrection; it is descending yet ever in glory, absent and present, shed yet never separated from God.

Many of John of Capistrano's arguments from 1440–42, like many of the Wilsnack arguments of the 1450s, return in the *triduum mortis* dispute of 1462–64, but in the latter dispute Franciscans (in line with their fellow friars at La Rochelle and in the Mark Brandenburg, and in contrast to Capistrano) defend blood relics.[40] The controversy was not, however, about either blood relics or miracle hosts, except somewhat incidentally. Like John's treatise *de Christi sanguine*, it was about the relation of Christ's sacrificial blood to the hypostatic union (that is, the union of humanity and divinity in the person of Christ), and ultimately about how to conceptualize the saving event of the crucifixion. In this controversy, it is the Dominicans not the Franciscans who give voice to John of Capistrano's paradoxical stress on *sanguis Christi* as both living and spilled. It is the Franciscans, however, who confront, in both their theology and their piety, the raw fact that the salvific blood-spilling was the death of Christ.

The *Triduum Mortis* Debate of 1462–64

The *triduum mortis* dispute began when James of the March revived the Franciscan teaching of 1350–51 that the blood shed in the passion was separated from the Logos and hence should not be adored.[41] The Dominican inquisitor general of Lombardy, James of Brescia, commanded James of the March to recant; but he preached again, citing Mayronis, Richard of Middleton, and others; sides were rapidly taken. The question having been referred to him, Pius II imposed silence on both orders and summoned them to send representatives to the curia for a debate, which finally (after several postponements) took place on Christmas day and the two days following in 1462. A number of treatises were written by both sides in the context of the debate and in the two decades afterward. On August 1, 1464, in the bull *Ineffabilis summi providentia*, Pius II (who tells us that he was favorable to the Dominican arguments but feared to offend the Franciscans, whose support he needed for a crusade against the Turks) simply declared the issues uncertain and forbade each side to charge the other with heresy in holding that the precious blood either was or was not separated from the Logos in the *triduum*.[42] Treatises on the issue continued to be written down into the seventeenth century, and Benedict XIV (inconclusively) reviewed the controversy again in the 1740s in considering the canonization of James of the March.[43]

We have a lengthy description of the debate of 1462 in book XI of the commentaries of Pius II, who was pope from 1458 to 1464. Known for three centuries in a mutilated text and under the mistaken attribution to one John Gobel (Gobellinus), an intimate of Pius II and his copyist, the work was restored to the pope as author by painstaking nineteenth-century scholarship, which culminated in the discovery of the original manuscript.[44] Pius's account favors the Dominican position (which receives much lengthier treatment) but nonetheless sets out the theological issues remarkably clearly (it is striking how close they are to those raised in the treatises of Capistrano and the Wilsnack theologians) and with a vivid sense of their devotional implications. Vain and ambitious though Pius II may have been, he had a sense of the grandeur and theatricality of the Christianity of his day, orchestrating the entry of St. Andrew's head into Rome in 1461 to stir up crusading enthusiasm[45] and reporting a Corpus Christi procession only a few months before the Christmas debate with admiration for the extreme realism of its depiction of the suffering Christ.[46] However pro-Dominican his summaries, he makes it clear that the central issue was one of fundamental soteriology not relic cult, and that each side strove to express in its full theological and devotional implications the fact that the death on the cross was the price of redemption. As Pius II saw it, Franciscans and Dominicans having agreed that the blood of Christ was united with his divinity before it was shed (as Christ said in Matt. 26.28) and after it was reabsorbed in resurrection (as Christians recognize in the celebration of every mass), the question concerned only the *triduum*; and the Franciscans, having conceded union before and after, were harder pressed to prove separation.[47]

As recounted by Pius, the Dominican argument (put forward by Gabriel of Barcelona, James of Brescia, and Vercellin of Vercelli) was physiological, philosophical, theological, and finally what we might even call sociological.

Basing themselves in the principle *Quod assumpsit*, they argued that Christ took his body from the Virgin's holy blood in the womb; hence *sanguis Christi* was present from the beginning, for there is no life without blood.

> They said that the Son of God, coequal with the eternal Father and the Holy Ghost, when he was incarnated and made man [*humanatus est*] to redeem the human race, was not united to the flesh previously existing with identity of its own, but while dwelling in the womb of the Holy and Immaculate Virgin He had His own person put on from the ever holy blood of the Virgin flesh animated with reason and intelligence [*non praesubsistenti secundum se ipsam carni vnitum fuisse sed inhabitantem in vtero sanctae Virginis incircumscriptae in sui ipsius hypostasi ex castis semper Virginis sanguinibus carnem animatum anima rationali et intellectuali substituisse ac nostrae massae primitias assumpsisse*]. . . . God, who was by nature perfect, became perfect man and in the very instant of union, when the Word was made flesh, blood was present. For there was present flesh (and living flesh), which philosophers say cannot exist without blood; and there is no doubt that the Son of God, when he was made man, took on at one and the same time flesh, blood, bones, sinews, skin and all other things that belong to man.[48]

The account is clearly calculated to reject a Scotist understanding, according to which blood is assumed under or via a bodily form (and hence secondary), while at the same time it underlines the completeness and complete bodiliness of Christ's body (formed like all bodies from the blood of the womb). Later in the debate, as recounted by Pius, the Dominicans explicitly reject the idea that Christ's humanity might be analyzed in such a way that certain parts could be put down and reassumed; anything truly superfluous was, they argue, never assumed in the first place.[49] (If a tiny bit of the foreskin remains in the Lateran collection, divinity was not united with it, and that bit was never necessary for perfect form.[50]) Moreover, human beings cannot live without blood, even for an instant, because the body begins in vital blood. It is from menstrual blood (*ex sanguine menstruo*) that all structures of the body are generated.[51]

The fact that blood does not feel or fall sick does not prove that it is not alive. The Dominican controversialists point out that bones and brain have no sense of touch and yet live. One speaks commonly of sick blood as "dead blood." The death of blood is its corruption (*mors sanguinis corruptio eius est*).[52] It is important to note that the contrast used here is between Christ's living blood, which is *always* living, and inessential blood, which shows that it is not essential by the fact that it corrupts. The basic structural contrast is life versus decay/death, not inside blood versus outside blood. Christ's essential physiological blood is understood to be both inside and outside, both alive and shed (separated). What it opposes, and defeats, is corruption and death.[53]

The Dominican argument turns rapidly from such physiological and philosophical considerations, however, and becomes a theology of the atonement: the blood is the price (*pretium*) of salvation.[54] It redeems by making restitution owed to God; it cleanses guilt; it gives life; it confirms the gospels. The crucial text is Hebrews (9.13–14 and 22), and again and again sacrifice is emphasized, a new sacrifice replacing the old. If the unclean blood of goats and bulls sanctifies the flesh, the spotless blood of Christ purges the spirit. The obsessively repeated verbs are "sprinkle" and "shed." But, at the soteriological level as at the physiological, the blood must be both shed and divine.

Saving blood must of course be outside blood, the Dominicans argue. "Only after it had been shed [*sparsus*] did blood have the power of purification and absolution."[55] But it cannot be the price of salvation if it ceases to be the blood of God, for then God would be offered a cheap restitution, one less than himself. Thus it must continue not only alive but also joined to divinity. Moreover, the guiltless blood of Christ could not be punished by a separation only sin would deserve. Although the Dominicans admit the Franciscan objection that God might have decreed salvation in another way, they argue that he chose for all eternity that the price of redemption would be his own blood; hence we should not speculate that it might have been different. "A bloody, grievous, and horrible death was chosen that greater love might be shown [*vt charitas maior ostenderetur*]."[56] Only blood both shed and divine can pay the price, cleanse the guilt, demonstrate the love, and arouse our loving response.

Once the central soteriological point is made, the Dominican argument returns to a more physiological one but now with devotional and even sociological overtones.

> For what love, what piety, what humanity could endure that the blood, but now cherished in the bosom of divinity and held united with the Word and one person with it, should without cause, without guilt be abandoned, rejected, insulted? We cannot think this of God whom we proclaim to be good and just. . . . "It is my blood," kings say, "Do not touch it [*Meus est sanguis . . . noli tangere*]." As far back as man's memory can reach noble families honor their own blood in men and women of the direct and collateral lines and to remote degrees and desire that it shall be kept unstained. . . . But why do we speak of illustrious men? Plebians and rustics ignorant of letters and of laws, with no guide for their lives but nature, when their line is injured, say "Our blood has been injured," and if it is a question of a wound or death they say, "They have shed our blood," and do not hesitate to risk blood for blood. It is a common practice with all men to gather up [*colligere*] the blood of a kinsman from the ground and lay it in the tomb. . . .
>
> And shall we say that a gracious and merciful God scorned his own and left it lying on the ground because at His bidding it had left the body?[57]

God would not have given his own blood, understood now as Son and Heir, unto the disrepute of real scattering.

In an even more starkly physiological and literalist turn, the Dominicans then argue that normal blood, if poured out, corrupts. And corruption is not only decay, it is pollution. Hence if the shed blood were separated from divinity, it would lie polluted (*pollutum*) on the ground in contradiction to the two phrases from the Psalms used by Capistrano repeatedly to the same effect: Psalm 15.10 and Psalm 29.10. Blood that goes down into the pit profits us nothing; if Christ's shed blood—the price of redemption—suffers decay, this violates not only God's promise to keep his holy one from corruption but also the salvation won for humankind in the shedding.[58]

To all this, the Franciscans Francesco della Rovere (later Sixtus IV), William of Vaurouillon, and Lorenzo Roverella (bishop of Ferrara) replied with arguments first physiological, then theological. After asserting that the status of the blood during the *triduum* is mysterious, since there is no scriptural account, the Franciscans argued that Christ's blood before the shedding was united to the Logos through body by a kind of concomitance. Blood is not necessary to the *veritas* of human nature because the embryo is conceived in the womb, and indeed ensouled there, before the blood enters it, for blood is generated from the liver. Thus for a brief moment there is life without blood.[59] Blood is moreover (according to Innocent III and Albert the Great) a humor; therefore, say the Franciscans, it is not alive.[60] If it were, it would not corrupt when spilled. But it does corrupt, as we know from existing blood relics (demonstrably dried and brown) at the Lateran, Mantua, and Venice.[61] (It is important to note that any Franciscan defense of blood relics involved in this polemic is one which demotes them ontologically to inessential parts of Christ's body and diminishes them visually by denying the redness and liquidity so stressed in pilgrim propaganda.) Accusing the Dominicans of an excessively literalist understanding of *Quod assumpsit*, the Franciscans assert that the body joined to Logos in incarnation, death, resurrection, and ascension is an essential body, not the extraneous bits of effluvia (snot, sweat, or humors such as blood) Dominican theory would hold to be included.

When they come to theology, the Franciscans' basic argument is once again against Dominican literalism. What is important is what Christ accomplishes. Redemption is a price paid, the washing away of sin, but blood is a synecdoche for the death of Christ.

> And the Master of the Sentences [Peter Lombard] understands that the blood by which Peter in the Epistle asserts that we were redeemed signifies the death of our Lord, for he says, "For he reconciled us to the Trinity through his death, as Peter says 'not with corruptible things like gold and silver etc.,' interpreting here 'precious blood' as death, which may be called precious because through it Christ paid the price [*per eam Christus soluit pretium*]." . . . On this principle everything that is said about the blood

of Jesus is to be taken as referring to His death or His life. And we must not think that his blood was the price of mankind since that which has no life would have been an unworthy price for that which has [*quia indignum fuisset pretium pro animato anima carens*]. . . . The human race could have been redeemed without blood if the Son of God had laid down his life for us without shedding it [*Potuisset & genus humanum sine sanguine redemi, si filius Dei retento sanguine, pro nobis animam posuisset*].[62]

Putting aside abstruse considerations about the celebration of mass during the *triduum* (which, they assert, is nowhere recorded), the Franciscans argue that divinity would in any case have been present because of blood that remained in the body; moreover, the phrase "blood of the Lord" can be used during the *triduum* as a reference to the humiliation and confusion of Christ. Indeed the separation of spilled blood from the divinity casts no contempt on the Godhead of Christ but makes his death "more glorious in proportion as it was more humiliating."[63] The stress is on the pain and desolation of the crucifixion. Francesco della Rovere, stating the Franciscan case a few years later in his treatise *de sanguine Christi*, used the passages from Hebrews that had been crucial to the Dominican position but argued that the blood of Old Testament animal sacrifice prefigured not the blood but the death of the New Testament.[64]

Behind the differing physiological theories displayed here thus lie differences of theological and devotional emphasis. To Dominicans, the blood itself—shed yet living—is the price of salvation. To Franciscans blood is a sign of the death of Christ; it is the death that pays the price for human sin. But the controversialists on both sides agree on two things. First, a price must be paid. Second, our hope lies in a fundamental paradox. It is in the separation/death of Christ's blood/Christ that our wholeness/life rests. Whereas the Franciscans assert that, paradoxically, life is made possible by death, the Dominicans assert that, paradoxically, wholeness lies in separation.

Some Arguments Attributed to Nicholas of Cusa

Further light is cast on the issues of 1462–63 in a set of fourteen questions and five arguments convincingly attributed by Rudolf Haubst to Nicholas of Cusa and dated to the months just after the December debate when Cusanus was in Rome. Tying the Wilsnack controversy to these later issues, the texts echo vividly not only the resurrection theology within which Hus had located the question of *sanguis Christi* fifty years earlier but also Cusanus's concern in the Halberstadt decree of 1451 to keep the salvific blood *in* Christ's person and invisible in glory, not on display in monstrances.[65]

Although closer to the Dominicans than to the Franciscans, Cusanus's argument is not fully Thomistic. In a complex theological move that almost makes Christ's humanity a Platonic idea subsisting through death into resurrection, Cusanus turns away from Thomas (and late medieval consensus) to embrace the older position of Peter Lombard and Hugh of St. Victor that Christ continued to be a man (*homo*) during the *triduum*.[66] Despite the separation of body from soul in death, Christ's humanity subsisted and was never separated from his divinity, argues Cusa; nor was his blood divided from his humanity. Stressing price paid and blood spilled less than either Franciscans or Dominicans, Cusa expounds a theory of Christ's human nature as a conduit (*manuductio*)—a fullness of being that lifts us all into God. Nonetheless, it is crucial to his entire theological program to emphasize both the reality of Christ's death and the freedom of his essential humanity (and ours) from mortality.[67] We were created capable of not-dying, argues Nicholas. Christ restores this capability by triumphing over death, catching our mortal humanity up into his, which is immortal, perfect, indivisible, and full. Not concerned with the fate of particular particles or relics, Cusa's argument that neither Christ's blood nor his humanity was ever separated from divinity is at heart a worried concern to keep Christ ontologically whole.[68] If the principle *Quod assumpsit* does not obtain, argues Cusa, then division—breakage—enters into God.

In a dense discussion, not all of whose details I can consider here, he concludes:

> That which rises was never separated from the person rising. . . . For we are certain that the smallest sparrow does not perish nor a hair of our heads [Luke 12.6–7 and 21.18]. . . . For we know that nothing perishes in death and that after death [even] those remain who are sent into Gehenna. . . . Therefore Christ, who is perfect God and man in the glory of the Father . . . is . . . soul, body, flesh [and blood], never separated. . . . For a man who was decapitated rises with his head, and because of this it is true that the head, although separated from the remaining body, never ceased to be his head. . . . Therefore the blood of Christ, which is now in Christ, never ceased to be his blood through separation from his person. . . . Gregory Nazianzus . . . affirmed rightly that the drops in Christ are the "blood of God" and of the Only Begotten according to the person of which it is the blood.
>
> . . . And Christ, when he said: "this is the chalice of my blood, which is shed for you," expressed clearly that what was in the chalice and what was shed was his blood. But what was in the chalice was united to divinity, and [this was] so for what was poured out. The effect of this pouring is expressed in the words "for remission of sins" [Matt. 26.28]. And this effect requires that the union remains. Those who say that the blood was in the chalice and was poured out, first united then separated, do not understand that the hypostatic union is substantial, not accidental. . . . [N]or does spatial separation of body and blood ever separate Christ from soul or Christ from glory . . . ,

although the senses that see them separated do not reach the glory. But good faith and intellect see them in glory . . . , just as in the sacrament of the altar the body under the species of bread and the blood under the species of wine are seen to be in the glory of Christ, because this body is believed to be the body of Christ and this blood his blood, although senses do not however see this.[69]

It is worth noting that, even in this abstract treatment, Cusanus does make reference to practical issues. (He clearly has in mind the relic of St. Peter's head when he refers to separated heads.) But what is important for my exposition here is the way in which these questions and proofs reiterate the issues of the 1450s and '60s. Like the Franciscans in Rome (and Grosseteste and Scotus before them), Cusanus is concerned that Christ's body, and hence his bodily death, remain real and not phantasmal. Like the Thomists, he is determined to emphasize both body and blood as glorified. Like the theologians at Wilsnack, he is concerned with the threat to eucharist he finds implicit in notions of separated blood. Like Hus, he sees implications for resurrection doctrine. More clearly than all, he is obsessed with the idea that any separation of blood from humanity, or of humanity from divinity, undercuts a salvation effected only by that which is both *effusus* and *indivisibilis*.

Patterns in Dominican and Franciscan Theology

In closing I return to the figures in the 1462 debate itself, for there too we can see a tension between "poured out" and "indivisible," yet an effort to embed salvation in the paradoxical assertion of both.

There were real differences between Franciscans and Dominicans in this debate. To Dominicans, blood was of the *veritas humanae naturae*; to Franciscans it was not. To Dominicans, blood was in itself alive; to Franciscans it was not. Dominicans, moreover, located salvation in the shedding and sprinkling of blood, a New Testament sacrifice replacing the animal sacrifice of the Jews; Franciscans held this to be too literal, claiming "all that is said about blood has reference to the life and death of Christ," and insisting (with Augustine) that salvation resides in Christ's obedience to God's will although "he had given no cause for death."[70] The differences were thus in physiological theories of the human person (what constitutes the *veritas humanae naturae*) and in exegetical stance (how to interpret passages from Hebrews, the Psalms, and John's Gospel understood as referring to the blood of Calvary). But the two sides came closer to each other than scholars usually admit on matters both of praxis and of soteriology. Despite their accusations against each other, neither group either denied categorically the existence of bodily relics of Christ's blood or accorded them worship as the living God. Dominicans preferred to think that no blood from Calvary had been left behind but allowed that, if it had been, it was of "some superfluous part of nutrimental blood."[71] Franciscans were more favorable to the idea that inessential bits might be on earth but by the time of the Rome debate they held such blood relics to be dead matter—dried, even corrupted [*incineratus atque corruptus*]. Both groups conceded that the Lateran might possess a trivial bit of the foreskin.

In theology, Dominicans and Franciscans agreed in seeing the death on Golgotha as a salvific sacrifice. The Epistle to the Hebrews was a key text, whether blood was read as Christ himself or as a sign of his lonely, bloody, and humiliating death. Whether in the Dominican stress on blood as divine, ever lifted up in glory, or the Franciscan stress on blood as laid down, a sign of obedience unto death, *sanguis Christi* was shed. Moreover, the devotional implications seem not so distant from each other. Dominicans fear that separating blood from the Logos will undercut the saving power of the sacrifice: if blood is separated from the Godhead, how can it pay the price owed by humankind, a price utterly beyond anything damaged humanity can offer? Franciscans fear that denying separation during the *triduum* will undercut the fact of Christ's sacrifice: if the blood is forever alive, forever part of the *veritas* assumed by the Logos, how is the death on the cross a real event, the blood really shed, the price really paid? Whether the stress is on the death or on the blood, on the separation or on the glory, neither group denies that the event of Calvary gains salvation for humankind by paying the price of an innocent life or that the starkness of that event elicits from humanity a response of guilt and love.

Modern scholars have found these positions confusing, so much so that they have sometimes misunderstood them entirely, assuming the Dominican position to be more favorable to relics.[72] And whatever the theology suggested, there were of course some quite practical reasons for the particular polemical positions taken in the fifteenth century. The support Benedictines and Franciscans gave to blood relics was in many cases based in actual possession.[73] Often founded in the two great periods of relic influx into Europe (the Carolingian era and the thirteenth century), when patrons wished to parade their international connections, Benedictine and Franciscan houses (such as those at Braunschweig and La Rochelle) tended to possess blood relics. Even the occasional Dominican was favorable to blood relics when his house claimed them.[74] And there were Franciscans (such as John of Capistrano) who supported blood miracles but feared relics as competition to eucharistic piety. It is clear that the existence of relic or host cult exerted pressure toward certain theological positions. But the differing attitudes toward blood relics and miracle hosts went deeper than the competing claims and situations of particular houses. As I said above, they lay in part in differences between Scotists and Thomists on the nature of the human person and on physiology. But neither historical circumstances nor physiological theory seem entirely to determine the value placed on blood. The differences were devotional as well.

The Dominicans, with their high blood theology, were suspicious of earthly manifestations of the living God—whether in bodily relics (subject to decay) or in eucharistic wonders and apparitions. Even if the result of miraculous transformation, spots on the host were susceptible to disappearance or corruption; they could indeed be understood as *being* decay—fungus or flyspecks—the result of natural processes of growth and dissolution. Hence, to Dominicans, bits of earthly matter did not visibly reveal the blood paid and now in glory. Franciscans, on the other hand, with their stress on the event of Christ's death, could theorize eucharistic wonders or bodily relics as revelations of God's substance in the wafer, as miracles created by God, or as remnants—inessential but real—of the body cared for long ago by Mary Magdalene, Longinus, or Joseph of Arimathea. If the blood pointed to the death on the cross, its presence was of utmost utility in arousing and sustaining devotion. Visible manifestations were important because they pointed beyond.

In view of these differing emphases, it is perhaps not surprising that both orders manifest intense blood devotions but of a somewhat different kind. Actual blood-spilling—self-flagellation, known as "taking the discipline"—was a particularly Dominican practice. To Dominicans, blood was alive; in shedding his blood a person shed himself. Flagellation was thus a particularly intense form of *imitatio crucis* and self-offering.[75] But there is nonetheless, to Dominicans, a great divide between Christ's blood in glory and any blood on earth.

To Franciscans, in contrast, blood is a sign of the death that saves. Thus it is not difficult to understand why it was Franciscans whose adherents included so many stigmatics.[76] Francis was the model, of course; and much of the popularity of this particular paramystical phenomenon was owing simply to his reputation as *alter Christus*. But it is not insignificant that stigmata are marks of the passion remaining on the body—scars (although often open scars)—that point to the event of the Savior's death. To Franciscans, blood relics, miracle hosts, and stigmatics were not so much literally the blood of sacrifice itself as visible marks in—or bits of—matter, reminding Christians of the bodily death in which salvation lay.[77]

Historians of theology usually assert that over the course of the next two hundred years the Franciscans "won" devotionally on the issue of blood relics:

at least the possibility of such relics was defended by the papacy. Dominicans, on the other hand, "won" on physiology and theology: blood came to be understood as essential to core humanity, and bloodshed itself was accepted as the means of salvation.[78] My analysis above suggests that already in the 1450s and 1460s the positions, however divergent on physiology and exegesis, were not really, in theology and praxis, so far apart. Both traditions gave some credence to blood relics, while reducing their ontological claims. Both traditions stressed the sacrifice of the cross, whether as pouring blood or as humiliating and lonely death. And in both orders blood practices—albeit of different kinds—reached new intensity in the fifteenth century. Thus, despite their strident, polemical differences, the prominence of blood in both traditions is clear. Whether they displayed a high or a low blood theology, a suspicion of visible presence or an enthusiasm for the miraculous, fifteenth-century friars and theologians, both at Wilsnack and at Rome, focused on blood.

Conclusion

In the fourteenth and fifteenth centuries, Wilsnack was not only the central blood site in Europe but also the most contested. Although relics at La Rochelle, Cismar, and Braunschweig, like hosts at Pulkau and Brussels, were debated, none evoked the wealth either of enthusiasm or of attack that the Wilsnack hosts elicited. None involved figures as prominent as those (for example, Jan Hus, Matthias Döring, Nicholas of Cusa, John of Capistrano, or Johannes Bremer) who were drawn into the Wilsnack debate, or generated anything approaching the number of theological treatises. It is for this reason that I began my book with the *Wilsnackerstreit*.

Nonetheless, as the *triduum mortis* debate makes clear, *sanguis Christi* generated intense theological dispute in the 1450s and 1460s quite apart from the claims of various sites. Emerging from its earlier context in general discussions of relics, visions, and miracles, the blood of Christ per se became by the fifteenth century a standard subject of theological investigation. Physiological and philosophical considerations of *veritas humanae naturae*, around since the twelfth century, focused increasingly on blood. Blood came to such prominence among eucharistic miracles that even host wonders were denominated *Blut Christi*. Although occasional claims to the foreskin or teeth of Christ circulated, only blood relics (among supposed bodily relics of Christ) drew theoretical attention. Subtle and erudite theorists such as Johannes Bremer and Nicholas of Cusa formulated basic positions in metaphysics (such as the nature of formal identity) and Christology (such as the nature of the body Christ took from Mary) in their writings on blood.

Professors, ecclesiastical authorities, and polemicists debated pious practice, to be sure. Some of the effort to suppress Wilsnack, Zehdenick, Sternberg, Wartenberg bei Wittenberg, and so forth stemmed from concern about superstition, clerical greed, or fraud. But the scores of *questiones* penned about the status and necessity of Christ's blood on earth were not simply broadsides in debates over relics and miracles. The treatises *de sanguine* of Cusanus and Capistrano addressed, as we have seen, fundamental issues of ontology and soteriology quite apart from questions concerning cults.

As I explained in Chapter 1, recent scholarship has tended to treat the fifteenth-century obsession with blood either as an aspect of eucharistic piety or as a reflection of an increasingly voyeuristic devotion to violence, wounds, and suffering.[79] But cults such as Schwerin, Doberan, Zehdenick, and Sternberg and debates such as those over the *triduum mortis* or the blood of La Rochelle were not simply reflections of a general devotion to Christ's body, either eucharistic or crucified. We will understand them in their specificity only if we pay careful attention to what the texts actually say. The many cases considered in Chapters 2 to 5, like the spiritual literature introduced in Chapter 1, suggest certain questions. Why were verbs of spilling and pouring so central in blood preaching and theology? Why was resurrection—not only Christ's but also that of all humankind—so often the context for discussion of Christ's blood? Why do accounts of blood relics and miracle hosts display such concern with corruption and decay on the one hand, bodily integrity and perfection on the other? Why, theologically, did it matter whether blood was alive or how exactly it was part of *humanitas*? Why do monastic blood liturgies, miracle stories, and pilgrim hymns assert so insistently the redness and liquidity of a blood that shrine attendants knew was dried and brown behind its crystal? Only careful attention to the specific language of miracle stories and theological *questiones* and to their broader context in the texts and objects of fifteenth-century piety will suggest why blood—both living and spilled, *sanguis* and *cruor*—was so crucial in the fifteenth century.

It is to the basic assumptions behind texts and cult that I turn in the next three chapters.

Plate 1. Crucifixion, woodcut, Germany, probably Ulm, ca. 1480. The large, round, red blood drops that spill down Christ's body and hang from his hands here are typical of German woodcuts of the fifteenth century in the attention they call to blood as both living and shed. (Graphische Sammlung, Staatsgalerie, Stuttgart.)

Plate 2. Mass of St. Gregory, outer wing of the Altar of the Corpus Christi Fraternity, Lübeck. Attributed to Wilm Dedeke, 1496. The altar is from the workshop of Henning van der Heide. In this version of the popular motif of the Gregorymass, the focus is on Christ's body. The pope raises high before the Man of Sorrows (depicted as a painted altarpiece rather than an apparition) a round white host whose curves are echoed both above and below by the small naked figures, representing souls, lifted by angels. Through Christ's body, subsumed in the host, the faithful rise to glory, as the viewer's eye is carried inward to the center of the painting and then upward to heaven. (Copyright © Museen für Kunst und Kulturgeschichte der Hansestadt Lübeck.)

Plate 3. Mass of St. Gregory, a panel from an outer wing of the Altar of St. Anne and the Holy Kinship, from the church of St. Maria zur Wiese in Soest, 1473. In this Gregorymass, where the focus is on blood, the movement within the image is more complicated than in the version seen in Plate 2. The Christ figure is not a painted panel but an animated figure who has just alighted before the pope. The checkered floor carries the viewer's eyes to the side wound itself, yet the streams of blood then pull away from wound and chalice toward the little figures in the churchyard, who represent souls. Blood saves, but it spills out in order to do so. The plaque on the wall (illegible in the original) represents an indulgence. (Foto Marburg/Art Resource, NY.)

Plate 4. The imposing pilgrimage church at Wilsnack, dedicated to St. Nicholas, fifteenth century. (Verlag Schnell & Steiner/Thomas Helms, Hamburg.)

Plate 5. Bloodchest in the church of St. Nicholas, Wilsnack, fifteenth century. On the chest in which the supposed bleeding hosts of Wilsnack were kept, we find depicted the classic eucharistic miracle of the Gregorymass, which tends, in its northern European version, to show a live and bleeding Christ on the altar before a praying or celebrating pope. The particular form of the Gregorymass depicted here stresses the pomp and power of the clergy. The figure of Christ is squeezed far to the left and is quite small; most of the picture space is devoted to the clerical procession approaching the altar. Above the Gregorymass are two angels bearing a monstrance, presumably that holding the Wilsnack miracle, which was displayed with a newly consecrated host. The partly damaged inscription, which reads "adoratio salutis est istud … mirabile in oculis meis," suggests that what is important is less the scene depicted than the wonder that lies inside the doors. (Sächsische Landesbibliothek Staats- und Universitätsbibliothek Dresden/Abt. Deutsche Fotothek.)

Plate 6. On the inside left door of the Bloodchest at Wilsnack, the triune God reigns in a so-called "Throne of Grace" (a figure of the Father holding the crucified Son surmounted by the dove of the Holy Spirit). (Simone Ahrend.)

Plate 7. On the inside right door of the Wilsnack Bloodchest, facing the "Throne of Grace," Christ is jeered at in a brutal rendition of the "Ecce Homo." His body is covered with bright drips and clots of blood. The faces of the persecutors are caricatures of what contemporaries thought to be Jewish facial structures. (Simone Ahrend.)

Plate 8. A large table top, heavily scored with knives, on which is written "Dit is de tafele dar de Joden dat hillige sacrament up gesteken und gemartelt hebt tom sterneberge im Jar 1492." The table top is displayed today in the baptismal chapel of the parish church at Sternberg along with a badly eroded wooden relief of the execution of the Jews by burning. The chapel serves now as a memorial to the Jews murdered in 1492 and by the Third Reich. A large menorah stands opposite the table top, and a plaque beneath the wooden relief, titled "the Sternberg Pogrom against the Jews," states that murder took place in 1492 on the occasion of "a supposed host desecration" and declares the chapel a "reminder" of 1492 and of the Holocaust. (Photograph by the author.)

Plate 9. A large stone with prints of two bare feet, mortared into the wall of what was once the main portal of the church at Sternberg. The prints, on the edges of which chisel marks are clearly visible, were held by local tradition to be marks left by the wife of the Jew Eleazar when she tried unsuccessfully to cast an abused host into a nearby creek. Unable to cast away the host, she supposedly sank into the stone. (Photograph by the author.)

Plate 10. A small brick vault discovered during excavations in 1984-86 in the pilgrim chapel that stands opposite the church in Heiligengrabe. The vault is inscribed 1287, the traditional date of the cloister's founding; several thirteenth-, fourteenth-, and fifteenth-century coins found stuck in the red plaster over it provide evidence that it was the site of pilgrim offerings. Further excavation has shown that the chapel was built over a place of death—whether of legal execution or of lynchings is unclear. Scholars have suggested that the vault was built either to enclose a blood miracle or to provide a replica of the Holy Sepulcher at Jerusalem. (Photograph by the author.)

Plate 11. Catherine of Siena flagellating herself before the crucifix. Paris, Bibliothèque nationale, MS All. 34, fol. 4v. The German translation of Catherine's Life, known as "Der geistliche Rosengarten," was widely disseminated in fifteenth-century Germany as a work of spiritual edification for women. The crucifix depicted here, like Catherine herself, is covered with vibrant splashes of blood that fly into or hang in the air in both drips and streams. (Bibliothèque nationale de France.)

Plate 12. Detail from a French *Moralized Bible,* circa 1240, MS Bodl. 270b, fol. 6r. The image draws an explicit parallel between the little figure of Ecclesia slipping out from Christ's side (below) and the emergence of Eve from Adam sleeping in the Garden of Eden (above). Whereas Genesis 2.21-23 depicts the latter event as formation from a rib, medieval iconography imagines both events as separation directly from a male body—a kind of male birthing—although the rib is still depicted. (Bodleian Library, University of Oxford.)

Plate 13. Meister Francke, Thomas Altar, ca. 1424. Hamburg Kunsthalle, Inv. 490-98, Hamburg, Germany. In fifteenth-century art from all over Europe, but especially from the north, emphasis was laid on the blood of Christ as alive, even when the body was clearly depicted as dead. In this image of Christ laid in the grave, his wounds are still running with fresh blood. (Bildarchiv Preussischer Kulturbesitz/Art Resource, NY.)

Plate 14. The so-called Kaufmann crucifixion, Bohemia, ca. 1340. Gemäldegalerie, Staatliche Museen zu Berlin. This famous and widely imitated image shows Christ's blood (and that of the crucified thieves) flowing freely in both streams and discrete droplets at the very moment when the centurion remarks on Christ's death (Matt. 27.54; Mark 15.39). The way in which the red and living drops from Christ's right hand spray toward the grotesquely twisted head of the good thief makes it appear as if the tear-shaped red bits are falling into his open mouth. The unrepentant thief turns away from the saving drops. (Bildarchiv Preussischer Kulturbesitz/ Art Resource, NY.)

Plate 15. Fritzlar pietà, probably before 1350. Not only do Christ's hands and side drip in large star-shaped or petal-like rosettes, but his arms and legs as well are covered with little bunches of bright red drops, whose roundness and fullness are emphasized. In its medieval form, this pietà actually had blood drops of papier mâché affixed to the body. The large, concave side wound may have held a reliquary monstrance. (Landesamt für Denkmalpflege Hessen.)

Plate 16. Large pietà from Marienstern, ca. 1360-70. The blood drops, arranged in groups of three, are scattered over Christ's whole body and emphasized by high relief. (Kloster Marienstern, Panschwitz-Kuckau.)

Plate 17. Anröchte pietà, Soest, ca. 1380–90. The blood drops that descend from Christ's side wound here are so large as to be more like icicles than petals or drops. Whatever analogies the shapes suggest, however, the visual impact is above all to stress the multiplicity of what extrudes—the separateness of the units of what is poured out. (Westfälisches Landesmuseum für Kunst und Kulturgeschichte, Münster/Rudolf Wakonigg.)

Plate 18. Altar of the Resurrection from Arnstadt, central panel. Thuringia, ca. 1430. Gemäldegalerie, Staatliche Museen zu Berlin. A rising Christ, crowned with a kind of tiara, displays five neat rosettes as wounds. These wounds are not so much healed as turned into bright flowers or jewels. The blood, although not dripping and liquid, is nonetheless still vibrant and red. (Bildarchiv Preussischer Kulturbesitz/Art Resource, NY.)

Plate 19. Johann Koerbecke, Marienfelder Altar, panel, ca. 1457. Gemäldegalerie, Staatliche Museen zu Berlin. A fresh globule of blood, ready to drop, hangs from Christ's arm just as the centurion speaks the words on his banderole that signal that Christ is dead: "Truly this was the Son of God" (Matt. 27.54; Mark 15.39). (Bildarchiv Preussischer Kulturbesitz/Art Resource, NY.)

Plates 20 and 21 (detail). Christ on the cross, probably Bohemian, about 1430. Gemäldegalerie, Staatliche Museen zu Berlin. If one looks closely, one can make out tiny angels, scratched into the gold background, who catch the tear-shaped drops swinging from Christ's hands and arms. The size and significance of the drops is emphasized by the fact that the chalices held by the little angels are only just big enough for a single drop. It is also important to note that the still-dripping side wound is a sort of blood rosette. (Jiří Fajt, Leipzig.)

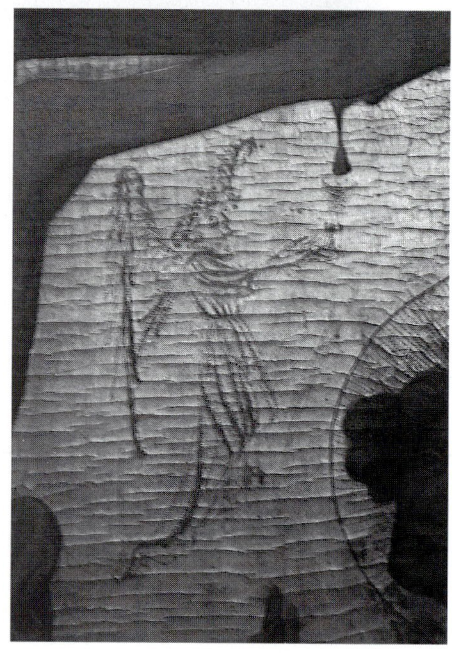

Plate 22. Hans Multscher, Landsberger Altar, ca. 1437, resurrection panel. Gemäldegalerie, Staatliche Museen zu Berlin. The narrative sequence of this altar, which depicts the events of Holy Week, stresses the freshness of the blood throughout. In the resurrection panel, the wounds look a little like rosettes, but blood still flows from them. A long stream runs down from the wounds, especially from the feet, and ends with a round, red globe. (Bildarchiv Preussischer Kulturbesitz/Art Resource, NY.)

Plate 23. A Dominican nun receives the blood-covered Christ in her arms. Miniature pasted onto a flyleaf in a Book of Hours from the cloister of SS. Margaret and Agnes in Strasbourg, second half of the fifteenth century. Bibliothèque du Grand Séminaire Strasbourg MS 755, fol. 1r. (Bibliothèque du Grand Séminaire Strasbourg.)

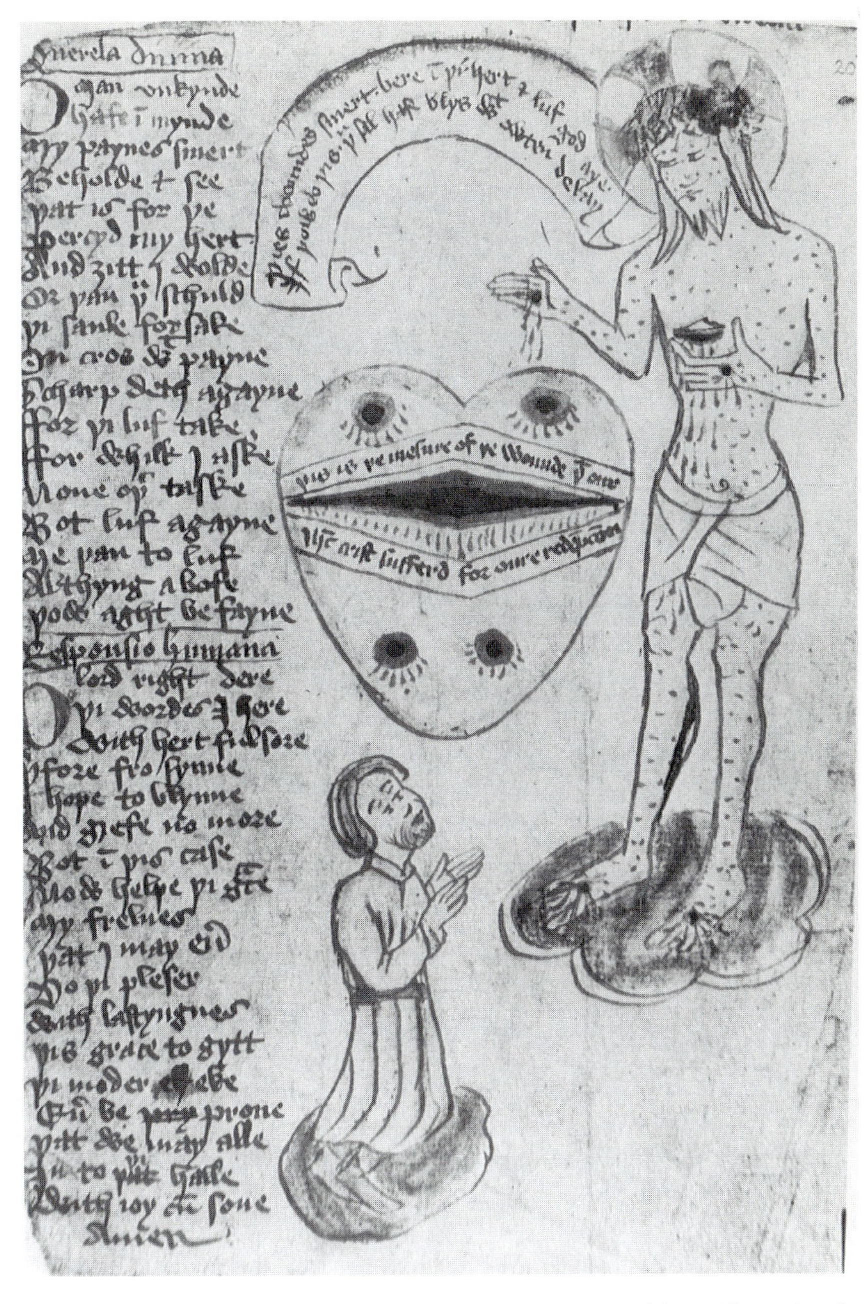

Plate 24. Carthusian Miscellany, British Library MS Add. 37049, fol. 20r. Illustrating the idea that *sanguis Christi* not only offers salvation but also cries out in accusation, this miniature shows the bleeding Man of Sorrows, who offers his heart to a little lay figure kneeling below and complains, "O man unkynde, hafe in mynde, my paynes smert. Beholde and see, that is for the, percyd my hert. . . ." On the heart, which bears all five wounds and is thus a synecdoche for the whole Christ, the side wound is arranged horizontally as if it were a mouth speaking reproach. (British Library.)

Plate 25. Christ Suffering Under the Sins of Mankind, Mass of Saint Gregory, and Saints, wall painting, ca. 1400. St. Georg bei Räzüns (Graubünden), Switzerland. Images of laypeople crucifying Christ by profaning the Sabbath, cursing, or blaspheming are found on the walls of churches in fifteenth-century England and Germany. In graphic reproach, the tools or mouths of working people are linked by little ropes of red to the torn and bleeding body of Christ. Thus we see that the depiction of blood as stream or ribbon, which sometimes represents access or bond, can also signify accusation. In this wall painting, the Christ who appears in the Gregorymass is not bloody, but the thin red lines on the adjoining Christ figure point like arrows to the perpetrators of sin. The instruments of everyday toil, when misused, are analogized to the *arma Christi*, which appear on the right surrounding the Man of Sorrows. (Drawing by R. Berliner, *Münchner Jahrbuch der Bildenden Kunst* 3rd ser. 6 [1955], fig. 18.)

Plate 26. Lucas Cranach the Elder, Schneeberg altarpiece, inside right panel, first open state. St. Wolfgangskirche, Schneeberg, 1539. The sixteenth century saw no lessening of emphasis on salvation by blood. In this panel from an altar on whose iconography Luther advised, we see John the Baptist in a red robe of triumph standing with Adam below the figure of Christ crucified and pointing to the red blood that flows from the side wound onto the chest of Adam. Below the cross stands the sacrificial lamb. The inscription reads: "Behold the Lamb of God who takes away the sins of the world (John 1.29)." (Constantin Beyer, Weimar.)

Plate 27. Jacob Lucius, Luther and Hus Distributing Communion to the Saxon Princes, ca. 1550, woodcut. Kupferstichkabinett, Staatliche Museen zu Berlin. The association of Christ's sacrificial blood with both baptism and eucharist continued in Protestant theology. Here Martin Luther and Jan Hus are shown offering the Lord's Supper in both species under an altar on which a huge grape vine curls around a chalice or font, over which hangs the crucified Christ. (Bildarchiv Preussischer Kulturbesitz/Art Resource, NY).

Plate 28. Workshop of the Master of the Augustine Altar, Mass of St. Gregory with Saints Catherine, Thomas Aquinas, Francis, and Vincent Ferrer, panel, ca. 1490. Around the vision of Christ as the Man of Sorrows appear the *arma Christi*, the instruments of his torture. As is true in Plate 31 as well, it is not clear who inside the picture sees either the figure on the cross or the surrounding objects. (Germanisches Nationalmuseum, Nuremberg.)

Plate 29. *Arma Christi* with Five Wounds, Buxheim Altar, panel, ca. 1500, Ulm. In this depiction of Christ's Five Wounds, surrounded by the instruments that tortured him, the Savior's body disappears entirely, to be replaced by bleeding fragments. (Ulmer Museum, Ulm.)

Plate 30. Crucifixion of Christ by the Virtues, Doberan, retable, central panel, ca. 1300. The rare motif of Christ crucified by the virtues (the so-called *Tugendkruzifixion*) is found in two sites associated specifically with blood cult: Wienhausen and Doberan. In such images, the bleeding and death of the Savior are executed by the spear and nails of little figures clearly labeled *Caritas*, *Humilitas*, and so forth. Although the *arma* that tortured Christ are frequently understood to accuse sinners, in this iconography they are represented as the tools of transformative love. (Jutta Brüdern, Braunschweig.)

Plate 31. Master of the Holy Kinship, Mass of St. Gregory, panel, ca. 1500. Cologne, Wallraf-Richartz-Museum. This version of the Gregorymass is an example of a late medieval image that explores the relation between kinds of seeing and kinds of depicting. The artist manipulates the space of the altar so that the Man of Sorrows and the instruments of Christ's passion appear as a dramatically rendered retable, bracketed in architectural elements, with the sarcophagus forming a sort of predella and bottom frame. It seems that no one is looking at the retable-vision. The picture might be simply a picture of mass before an elegantly appointed altar. Yet the status of the altarpiece as altarpiece is challenged not only by Christ's cloak, which breaks across onto the altar table, but also by the hand of the servant bearing the basin for Pilate. The depiction clearly raises the questions: Who sees? What do they see? (Rheinisches Bildarchiv, Cologne.)

Plate 32. Descent from the Cross, German (Bavaria?), colored woodcut in a manuscript miscellany, mid-fifteenth century, put together at the abbey of Tegernsee. Bayerische Staatsbibliothek, MS Clm 20122, fol. 88. In this image of the deposition from the cross, which was glued into the prayer collection opposite a poem on Christ's wounds, gigantic blood drops are applied to Christ's body in thick red paint. An early reader has written directly on the woodcut in the space below Christ's arms: "It is read that Christ received 5,440 [corrected to 5,460] wounds for our redemption. Whoever therefore completes each day of the year fifteen Pater Nosters and the same number of Ave Marias should know that he has uttered one Pater Noster and one angelic greeting for each wound." (Bayerische Staatsbibliothek, Munich.)

PART III

The Assumptions of Blood Piety

Chapter 6
A Concern for Immutability

Having devoted several chapters to presenting individual cult sites and texts in sufficient detail to reveal something of both their specificity and their complexity, I now switch strategies. In the next six chapters, I move analytically, not chronologically or geographically. My purpose is to spell out the basic assumptions that undergird blood piety, praxis, and learned theological discourse.

Three points of introduction are necessary. First, I shall keep as much as possible to the northern European context, since Italian spirituality was rather different in tone. As students of devotional poetry such as Douglas Gray and specialists in northern art such as James Marrow have clearly shown, there is a particular brutality and bloodiness in northern depictions of the passion.[1] Although some well-known blood cults (for example, Piscaria and Bolsena/Orvieto) were Italian and Italy is probably the origin of the famous motif of the bleeding Man of Sorrows, Italian art and piety are less expressionist than those of the north, and southern treatments of blood were more symbolic.[2] In attempting to situate theological debate and cult practice against the background of piety, it has therefore seemed to me appropriate, even necessary, to use northern material.[3] It is important to remember, however, that blood cults drew an international clientele. Moreover, as we saw in Chapter 5, debates over the soteriological meaning of *sanguis Christi* disregarded the boundaries of geography and language. So although I shall try to draw my examples of devotional literature and art especially from England, Germany, and the Low Countries, some of what I will ultimately need to take into account is European wide and centuries old.

Second, I include in what follows praxis, piety, and theoretical discussion (or scholastic theology). Like many recent scholars, I reject a dichotomy of popular and learned religion. The word "theology" as I use it refers not just to the *quodlibeta* and *questiones* of university theologians but also to the writings of contemplatives and visionaries, both within and outside the cloister, to sermons and manuals of religious practice, and to the prayers, broadsides, and devotional images used by Christians, both orthodox and dissident. Theology is the exploration and expression of religious convictions—that is, convictions concerning God and God's relationship to nature and humankind.[4] Rejecting a learned/popular, or clerical/lay, or Latin/vernacular distinction is not, for me, so much a theoretical position as a result of scholarly study.[5] What I am asserting throughout this book is that certain basic assumptions undergird both religious behavior and statements about it (whether of university professors, ecclesiastical authorities, devotional writers, pilgrims, or dissidents). There are indeed, as we shall see, profound dichotomies in fifteenth-century religious attitudes toward blood but they are radical oppositions *within* cultic practice, folktales, popular devotions, and theoretical discourse, respectively, not divisions between various of these genres or their authors and adherents.[6]

Third, the approach I take here provides an argument against understanding blood cult and controversy about it as primarily a matter of politics or—what amounts to the same thing—power. As I have stated above, to interpret the events at Wilsnack or Sternberg as a struggle for control over religious practice (and hence over community boundaries) against those such as Jews, Hussites, flagellants, or ordinary pilgrims who were perceived as threatening group identity is not wrong. But it is incomplete.[7] Because it ignores the blood—stuff as well as symbol—at the heart of the controversy, it misses certain very practical, human issues at stake. For to see the issues as soteriological and ontological is to affirm, not deny, that they were practical—that is, that they touched that inner place (psychological or spiritual) where people worry about the nature of the world around them and the reasons for death and life.

If we consider the bloods of late medieval northern Germany in their cultic, devotional, and theological context, we find several basic themes running all the way from what we can learn about the behavior of actual pilgrims (at Wilsnack and elsewhere) to the abstruse deliberations of Erfurt, Leipzig, Paris, and Prague professors. These themes are echoed generally in the preaching and devotional texts of the fifteenth-century north and in the iconography of its religious art. This dense web of blood symbolism may perhaps be summarized by saying that, in it, blood is life and death, continuity and separation, immutability and violation. It is both a protest against change and a breaching or pouring forth. It is spilled out and lifted up. Both sides of these paradoxes need extensive glossing, and I devote the remainder of this book to doing so. I turn in this chapter to the concern with immutability that runs through the events at north German cult sites all the way from what we can glimpse of actual village praxis to the most abstruse of theoretical debates. For, however counterintuitive it may seem, the eruption of blood was a miracle announcing the indestructibility of God.

The Immutability Theme at Wilsnack

As Hartmut Kühne has argued, the motif of the earliest events and miracles at Wilsnack, as far as we can tell, is survival through fire and water. What made the Wilsnack hosts miraculous was the fact that they were found *integer* after fire and rain—not burnt, not wet, not dispersed, not rotten, but whole, perfect, unchanged. They resisted decay, as do those funny candles in the early miracle accounts that burn without using up any wax. Kühne sees these elements as folk motifs in competition with learned eucharistic ones. He also argues that the story of blood flow confirming the original consecration of the hosts is an interpolation from elite clerical culture into older folk beliefs concerning fertility and survival.[8] Yet the blood story can itself be seen as reflecting anticlerical resistance. It opposes episcopal reappropriation. Although the bleeding can be read as testimony that the hosts, because already consecrated, were clerically approved for veneration, it can also be interpreted as a proof of a sacral presence that defeats the bishop's attempt to seize control. And the early healing miracles (which include a woman who survives drowning and a canon whose body triumphs over water and fire) are also quite astonishing resurrection miracles whose basic motif is life given by a bread that shows itself alive. The eruption of blood on wafer in the midst of ashes (and we have no reason to doubt that blood on the hosts was an early element in the story) was both an astonishing transformation and, like the roundness and dryness, a sign of immutability, because the blood was red and living, not the dark decaying matter of death. The sacred emerged from fire and destruction alive—that is, whole and undecayed.

The theme of immutability is not simply a folk element but rather is found at all cultural levels in the Wilsnack story. Polemicists and propagandists, like excited villagers and pilgrims, assumed that the holy is that which resists the ordinary change of decay. The ecclesiastical authorities were not only concerned to divert popular enthusiasm to the host they consecrated and hence controlled; they were also concerned (they say it repeatedly) that the people not revere corruptible matter, decayed stuff like the blood of horses or the spots left by flies. After all, Tocke's basic charge was that the host *cannot* be miraculous because it has changed. There is nothing red there; it appears to be spiderwebs and mold. The ultimate quarrel of the Wilsnack opponents with the blood wonder was suspicion that, whatever was there originally, living blood—even if miraculous—did not, could not, remain unchanged. James of Jüterbog (or Klusa), who attempted (in convoluted and somewhat vapid argument) to suggest that both sides in the *Wilsnackerstreit* might be right, took the fact that the hosts had changed as evidence against their miraculous status.[9]

The insistence by controversialists in the Wilsnack case, as in other cases, that miraculous blood must be liquid and red is a clue to the fact that deep assumptions about the nature of matter, body, and presence are at stake.[10]

The Transformed-Hosts Debate: A Deeper Issue

As we saw in Chapter 4, much of the debate of the 1440s that circled around the cult at Wilsnack was about transformed hosts. University theologians disagreed about whether blood spots on wafers were revelations of eucharistic substance, special miracles performed by God to reflect it, or disturbing illusions. In the analysis I gave above, I situated these arguments against a long tradition of debate over visions and visuality, presence and absence. But there was an even more fundamental issue. Although scholars have not usually put it this way, the debate was about change and immutability.[11]

It seems to have been important to theorists from the eleventh to the sixteenth century (and a tremendous amount of ink was spilled over this) to maintain that change in the eucharistic species was not change in Christ. Such fear of change lay behind the outraged charges of "stercoranism" (from *stercus* [feces]) made against theologians who stressed the real presence to the point of worrying about what happens when the eucharist is digested in human entrails. (Although it is difficult to find anyone who thought God could be literally chewed, corrupted, or excreted, it is significant that charging an opponent with thinking so was an effective polemical tool.)[12] In a similar effort to avoid the threat of mutability, a number of theologians struggled to gloss transubstantiation as involving no change. It was not a change of God's substance. Nor was it even a radical change in the substance of bread. Hence many university theologians rejected so-called annihilation theory—the idea that bread's substance ceased to be and was replaced by God's—although some observed that either it or the theory of consubstantiation made more philosophical sense. But God would not, they argued, annihilate any substance, even bread's. Transubstantiation could only be the going over of bread into God.[13] As Innocent III stressed already in the early thirteenth century:

> Although that which was bread is the body of Christ, the body of Christ is not however something that was bread, since that which was bread is now totally other than it was; but the body of Christ is in every way that which it was. . . . [Hence the eucharist is not parallel to the Incarnation.] For the Word remaining what it was is made flesh when it assumes flesh; it does not go over into flesh; but the bread ceases to be what it was and thus becomes flesh because it goes over into flesh rather than assumes flesh.[14]

In other words, to Innocent, the bread becomes the eternal "is" that is God.

Fifty years later, Albertus Magnus struggled with how the immutable, which gives and receives nothing, can experience even the change of something into itself. "The whole substance of bread becomes the whole substance of Christ," writes Albert, so that body "necessarily remains the same but becomes present where transubstantiation occurs."[15] Later still, Scotus, Ockham, and Biel found themselves troubled to explain how the conversion of bread into Christ leaves God completely without *mutatio*. Indeed theologians tended to maintain that consecration did not involve God in "coming down"; rather the bread and wine went up. Even change of location was apparently injurious to God. We become Christ in the eucharist, he does not become us.[16] Adelheid Langmann wrote: "We eat God not so that he changes into us but so that we change into him."[17] At the moment of consecration, it is the eucharistic elements that change place, ascending to join Christ where he resides with the angels in heaven. In answer to the riddle "Where is earth higher than heaven?" Christina Ebner of Engelthal replied: "Where God's body is transubstantiated."[18]

As we saw in Chapter 4, many theorists, following Aquinas, maintained that eucharistic visions involved no change in the host itself. Rather, as Thomas put it, the change was in the beholder, whose eyes were affected as if they outwardly saw flesh, or blood, or a child.[19] Not all theologians agreed. Franciscans, following Scotus, held (at least in the fourteenth century) that Christ might appear *sensibiliter* in cases where many saw the vision or host wonder.[20] But Thomas's position tended to win out in the fifteenth century and, according to it, the faithful did not see Christ in such miracles. The substance was unseeable; and if the seeable accidents (bread and wine) were replaced by other accidents (something red and flowing), these were only appearances substituted by God to indicate the unseeable divine substance underneath. Because God cannot change, his substance is not changed but changed into; moreover, his accidents cannot suddenly appear. Behind Thomas's concern that Christ's body and blood remain unseeable lay an explicit concern that they remain immutable. "It is not unsuitable for the bread to change but it is unsuitable for Christ to change."[21] This position is echoed in Cusanus's decree of 1451: ". . . the glorified body of Christ has glorified blood completely un-seeable in glorified veins. . . . [Hence, miracle hosts] should be consumed by the celebrating priest in communion rather than . . . permitted to disintegrate through the corruption of the species [*per specierum corruptionem desinere*]."[22]

When Eberhard Waltmann asserted that revering spots on a blood host was revering mere dead matter, not a revelation of the presence of Christ, he seemed to go one step beyond Thomas and suggest that corruptible matter cannot manifest the divine. And indeed there was precedent for this opinion. In the later thirteenth or early fourteenth century, a follower of Alexander of Hales seems to have assumed that changes in the host were the work of the devil or of human falsification when the species was later found dry or black with decay. The truth of the sacrament could never be demonstrated through something simulated or fabricated, or through something similar to the blood of animals, he argued. Only if the miracle persisted uncorrupted could it be said to be from God, for the body of Christ is *incorruptibile et incomputribile.*[23] Albert the Great even went so far as to argue that it was the continuation of the accidents after consecration that signaled the *presence* of Christ. Only total immutability (even of the veiling appearance) guaranteed presence. Once the wine and wafer looked different (because, for example, of spoilage or spillage), they ceased to be even the invisible real presence.[24]

The concern of popes and other ecclesiastical authorities to lay a newly consecrated host over the reputedly miraculous one was thus not only an effort to divert the attention of the people to the ordinary sacrament of the altar and away from miracles. It was also an effort to display for veneration something intact and undecayed.[25] Although Tocke and the other opponents of Wilsnack saw it as hypocrisy, it was an attempt to deal with the same problem Tocke raised: if it changes, the miracle host cannot be God. The repeated concern to keep pilgrims from realizing that the host had changed suggests that to theologians as well as shrine attendants, immutability of matter supported sacrality. In this connection, it is worth noting that the 1510 account of the Berlin-Brandenburg-Stendal host-desecration libel of the same year reports that a particle of the abused host, taken to Berlin, "worked miracles and then turned into bread again, crumbled, and slowly vanished [*do wunderzeichen gescheen, und das Prot thut sich auff, velt und löst sich melich abe*]." It seems important in this account for the miraculous stuff to revert to bread—that is, to be the bleeding body of Christ no longer—before it crumbles and vanishes. When it works miracles, it is Christ—that is, unchangeable. Only once it is not Christ—that is, once it becomes bread again—can it change. Propaganda written for the populace here echoes learned theology in its concern that the body and blood of God in the eucharist not suffer decay.[26]

Indeed it was this concern that led to controversy both about whether miracle hosts should be renewed and about the theological implications of doing so. As Manfred Eder has shown, such discussions continued down into the twentieth century. At Deggendorf (in lower Bavaria), for example, the supposedly miraculous host was clearly replaced a number of times over its long history and yet was offered to the faithful for veneration as more than an ordinary host. The pilgrimage was discontinued only in 1992, more for reasons of its anti-Semitic overtones than because of contradictions inherent in the veneration of supposedly unchanged and bleeding hosts.[27]

Immutability in Debates over Blood Relics and Treatises *de Sanguine*

The concern for immutability, for resisting not just corruption (negative change) but any sort of transformation, is also a central motif in debates over blood relics from the time of Guibert of Nogent on. As we have seen, the biblical context of such discussions is Psalms 15.10 and 29.10 (". . . nor wilt thou give thy holy one to see corruption"; "What profit is there in my blood, whilst I go down to corruption?"), Luke 21.18 ("But a hair of your head shall not perish"), and the gospel accounts of a resurrected Christ whose body was both ghostly and physical. (It passed through doors and warned the Magdalene against touching, yet ate and drank with the disciples and offered its wounds to Thomas the Doubter for probing.) The basic theme is the warding off of change through a Christ human yet incorrupt—a Christ whose blood was of profit because it did not go down into the pit, whose graspable body was beyond the physiological processes of generation and corruption. Guibert went so far as to assert that the blood and water from Christ's side did not sink into earth or stone, because they would there be subject to decay; and he argued that even the hard remains of bone and teeth—remains that might be seen as decay-resistant, as they were often thought to be in the reliquaries of saints—could not be left on earth. Even such hard bits perish eventually, wrote Guibert—if not earlier, then in the fire at the end of time. Hence any part of Christ left behind might be contaminated by the "despicableness of human corruption" and no such thing can touch Christ. It is as if, to Guibert, any change is corruption, and any separation of part from whole is powerlessness. The threat is not only to divinity but also to the power of the divine to save humankind from the same horror of change.[28]

A similar obsession with change underlies John of Capistrano's treatise *de Christi sanguine pretioso*, but in John's hands it is less an almost psychological horror at decay than an explicitly theological concern for the immutability of God. He writes:

> The fourth argument [that the blood of Christ is immediately united with the divinity] is because of the immutability of God [*ratione immutabilitatis Dei*]. As Thomas [Aquinas] argued . . . the body of Christ in death was not separated from the divinity. And this argument should be accepted . . . because, since he [God] is immutable, everything which is perfectly joined to him exhibits immutability that it may

adhere to him immutably. Thus I argue: the blood of Christ, in the body of Christ, is joined to the immutability of God. Therefore the immutable God offers immutability to the aforesaid blood as to the soul and the body so that the immutability of God adheres to the aforesaid blood as to the soul and the body.
1.) . . . And this is confirmed by blessed Gregory who says . . . the whole God is everywhere and he alone is perfect and immutable. For everything that changes . . . is not able to remain. . . . But to God it truly is [of his nature] never to be dissimilar [to what he is]. Whence it was said to Moses: "I am Who am". . . .
2.) And blessed Severinus [i.e. Boethius] said of God: remaining fixed, he gave movement to all things [*stabilisque manens, dat cuncta moveri*]. . . . Therefore this immutable [*stabilis*] and unchangeable [*incommutabilis*] God steadfastly and immutably united human nature to himself and not without blood. Thus the blood of Christ was not separated from him in the moment of death.[29]

The blood shed in the sacrifice of the cross *is* Christ, to Capistrano, and must participate fully in the absolute integrity, incorruptibility, and glory of the Godhead. Hence *sanguis Christi* must be living and entirely free from any contamination—even the contamination that might have come from sexual intercourse had Mary not conceived as a virgin.[30] Capistrano argues (as had Scotus) that Christ's body and his separated blood were in the *triduum* protected from the ordinary process of corruption that sets in after death by a second miracle (beyond the first miracle of the incarnation) imposed by God explicitly to hold back fragmentation and decay.[31] For all his Franciscan determination to arouse devotional response through graphic encounter with the suffering and death of Jesus, Capistrano repeats almost as a mantra the need for *sanguis Christi* to avoid *putrefactio* and *disiunctio*.[32] Moreover, even Mayronis, who argued for the separation of blood from *corpus* and Logos during the *triduum* and hypothesized that unimportant fragments of the blood might be left behind after Christ's resurrection, held in one of his sermons that blood separated from body in the passion was preserved from corruption by divine grace.[33]

Nicholas of Cusa's fourteen questions and five proofs concerning blood and resurrection can also be seen as expressing a determination to avoid introducing any change or division into the Godhead, or even into *humanitas* (ours as well as Christ's).[34] Cusa's discussion, apparently penned just after the debates of December 1462 in Rome, does not deal with blood relics and never treats directly the question of whether all Christ's bits return when he rises. Nonetheless, as Rudolf Haubst has demonstrated, Christ's un-destroyability is crucial. Although Cusanus's earliest preaching apparently agreed with the late medieval consensus that Christ was not a man during the *triduum*, by the time of his great works, the *Learned Ignorance* (1439–40) and the *Vision of God* (1453), Cusa had come to hold that the division of Christ's body from his soul in death did not essentially affect the union of his humanity with divinity.[35]

Death brought only a dissolution of the "truth of human nature" on the level of accidents of time and place; some idea (here almost a Platonic Idea) of *homo* perdured exactly because body and soul both perdured in the Word. Thus when Nicholas argues in his proofs concerning the resurrection, first, that at resurrection all will be restored that ever belonged to person and, second, that what rises was never separated from person, he is not just defending the union of Christ's blood with his divinity during the *triduum*. What he really wants to stress is that Christ's *humanitas* was not destroyed, even when soul and body were separated, and that his body (veins, blood, etc.) was always glorified, no matter how hidden the glory. Some "formal union" was lost in death; Christ really died. Cusanus repeatedly refers to the necessity that blood be shed for the remission of sin. But in order for that death to save all humanity, it is necessary that Christ never be separated from humanity.[36] Cusanus's preoccupation with both the un-destroyability of Christ's *humanitas* and with the absolute perdurance of the hypostatic union is based in his brilliantly original argument that Christ's humanness is a *manuductio*, a leading back of all creation to God. But behind it seems to lurk a fear of change or division as metaphysical destruction—a fear, that is, that separation of the elements body and soul might damage or cancel the human nature they together constitute. Thus the separation of death (division of body and soul) that Christ puts on must be denied at a higher level (humanity is not separated from divinity) even while it briefly reigns. Division, *corruptio*, is the threat; union, wholeness, the answer. On an ontological rather than a psychological level, Cusanus agrees with his less gifted theological predecessor, Guibert of Nogent.

Behind Nicholas's abstract arguments concerning the *triduum mortis*, as in those of the Franciscans and Dominicans who battled at Rome, we see the question of corruption and continuity that Christ's relics raised in a more practical way. Early defenders of blood relics seem to have tried to insist that they were red and liquid. An indulgence granted for the blood of Weingarten in 1279 by bishop Rudolph of Constance asserts that the blood was still miraculously preserved from corruption.[37] Gerhard of Cologne defends it as a more immediate encounter with salvation than the eucharist because in it the faithful see Christ "rose-colored and shining red."[38] Whatever reservations theologians may have admitted in university chambers, pilgrims to and protectors of blood-relic cults claimed to encounter living blood. Indeed the increasing use of crystal reliquaries for blood relics may have been intended to allow the faithful to see the liquid state of the blood—that is, to identify it as blood. At Weissenau a legend stressed the blood as seeable, and warned that those who could not see it in the reliquary would die within a year.[39] When the blood of Hailes in Gloucestershire, England, was questioned in 1538, claims differed about exactly how it was fraudulent. Was it duck's blood, colored gum, birdlime, or dyed honey? But the discussions all make it clear that the relic appeared to be red liquid.[40] The crimson satin discovered in the monstrance at Cismar in the later fifteenth century was intended to bring vivid redness before the eyes of the faithful.[41] Stories were even occasionally told of blood relics that proved themselves alive by liquefying or dividing and reuniting.[42]

When, by the mid-fifteenth century, Franciscan theologians began to defend blood relics only as brown and dried, this defense of material that had clearly been touched by change entailed the admission that it was only an inessential, superfluous, or nutritive fluid. Paradoxically, the argument that the particles *were* Christ's came to depend on the fact that they were corruptible. Christ could not by definition have left anything essential and incorruptible behind without jeopardizing the perfection of the Godhead; the fact that they are dry and corrupt thus proves the particles in the monstrance to be left-behind blood. Any blood relic that appears living must be the subject of a special miracle such as liquefaction. Franciscan arguments at Rome in the 1460s were not propaganda for blood relics but defenses of Christ's sacrificial death against what Franciscans saw as a literalizing fixation on only a portion of his humanity. In a sense then, they came close to agreeing, in their basic premise, with Dominican arguments that supposed relics of left-behind blood or foreskin could not be Christ because they corrupt.[43] By the later fifteenth century, polemical discussions of Christ's bodily relics, like those of host wonders, reflect a determination to preserve holy matter entirely from any *mutatio*, so much so that such matter is ontologically demoted to an inessential part of Christ or the imposition of something merely bloodlike on hosts the moment there is any suggestion of change.

The association of Christ's blood with a life that triumphs over *mutatio* and *disiunctio*—over change, fragmentation, and dissolution—explains why discussions of resurrection and the scars of Christ are so often the context for blood theology and piety. To figures such as Guibert, Grosseteste, Aquinas, Gerhard, Hus, Mayronis, Capistrano, and the theologians of the Wilsnack and Rome debates, the blood poured out on Calvary is the pledge of resurrection—a pledge fulfilled at Easter and at the Last Judgment. What God restores to Christians through the death on the cross is moral and physical salvation—a return to wholeness at the end of life and the end of time. However much theologians disagreed during four hundred years of debate about apparitions on hosts, bits of inessential blood, or the status of separated blood during the *triduum*, none doubted that the *sanguis Christi* that effected salvation was now in glory, or that Christ's resurrection from death was a victory for all humankind over fragmentation, separation, mutability, and decay. The urgency of debates over the status of blood rested in the fear that if any corruption or separation persisted for Christ it might presage incomplete wholeness and glory for the faithful. And not only was resurrection the context within which blood theology was repeatedly discussed, the scars of Christ and the wounds of the martyrs also frame the discussion (as, for example, in both Aquinas and Grosseteste). The conviction of the theologians that the scars of the crucified (and of the saints) persist in heaven is a conviction that the saving event of the cross is both a real death and a triumph over the bodily dissolution that is what death really means.[44] If the scars were simply erased, it would be as if the death, the separation, the *pretium*, were never paid. But those scars must be healed—or at least flowing with living blood—in order to signal that what that death achieves is life. The scars, like the blood but in a simpler sense, both assert and cancel death. Although historians have neglected the theological context of blood piety in favor of its context in debates over superstition, clerical control, reform, and pilgrimage, it is exactly the theological context that helps us see why it was so difficult and so important for preachers and adherents alike to formulate exactly how *Blut Christi* could be both shed and ever living. If Christ's blood were not in some sense alive and whole, neither would we be at the end of time. The promise of salvation *was* the promise of *integritas* and *immutabilitas*.

Understanding the ways in which an obsession with immutability underlies fifteenth-century blood theology helps us to grasp why the defenders of Wilsnack felt that one sort of blood relic supported another (no matter how much the cults might compete). It seems odd to us that blood relics (supposedly derived from Golgotha) and miracle hosts were so often assimilated in debate, and that learned men seriously offered as a defense of red spots on a wafer in north Germany the argument that Christ could have left blood behind when he rose in Jerusalem. Even if there were separated blood, how (as the Erfurt theologians asked in 1446) would it get onto the miraculous hosts?[45] But the issue was not simply the bilocation or multilocation of blood across time and place. One could after all argue that God can do anything *de potentia absoluta* or even that Christ's glorified body could, by concomitance, be everywhere. Gerhard of Cologne argued this in the thirteenth century.[46] The issue was immutability. How could anything of the God-man be left behind? If he shed particles, he was changed. Both kinds of blood—miracle hosts and relics—presented the same problem. The same argument then could justify or refute the presence of any sort of left-behind, separated, or visible blood. But it had to deal with the theological necessity: Christ must be unchangeable and whole.

What fifteenth-century theologians were really debating when they debated the possibility of blood relics and miracle hosts was the nature of identity.[47] Could something remain the same—wholly and identically itself—without the persistence of every material particle? Would a substance that corrupted or separated be "the same thing" if reassembled?[48] What constituted identity of person? It is ironic, as H. Herbst pointed out long ago, that certain of the Franciscan arguments for numerical identity without persistence of every material particle come closer to the Thomistic philosophical positions of the thirteenth century than did some later followers of Thomas such as Cusanus, Capistrano, the Erfurt theologians, and the Dominicans at Rome.[49] Whereas these latter thinkers assert that all Christ's blood must be in glory in order to guarantee his wholeness and ours, defenders of the Wilsnack and Braunschweig bloods such as Bremer and Bansleben argue that blood miracles and relics negate neither Christ's integrity nor our hope of resurrection. For wholeness lies not in the sum of material particles but in the form of the body (*dispositio figuralis*) and that perdures even if nutritive blood is left behind unglorified. In other words, whereas Hus and Capistrano follow Aquinas's pronouncement in the *Summa theologiae* that all Christ's blood returned to glory in resurrection, Bremer and Bansleben follow the logic of Aquinas's understanding of change and identity.[50] If substantial form (not matter) accounts for identity, then Christ's blood could be Christ's blood without the preservation of every material particle. As Bansleben argued in defending blood cult, separated blood is *sanguis Christi signative* not *entitative*. It is not so much bits of Christ left behind as it is signs pointing to glory. Dominicans and Franciscans differed about how blood related to body and person, but for each position, wholeness and immutability were central to salvation.

Throughout the Wilsnack controversy, from Hus to Bansleben, Bremer, and Paltz, the implications of blood cult for resurrection theology recurred as an issue. Those theorists who supported, like those who attacked, various sorts of separated blood agreed at some basic level: the blood that saves is the blood that is with Christ. Hence, to defenders and opponents alike, separated blood was, paradoxically, a sign of the overcoming of separation—a sign of resurrection, of return, of the gathering of all into glory. Its very status as outside, shed, left-behind blood raised the question of what constitutes the identity of the person who rises; if it was not to threaten the integrity of Christ and the promise of salvation it had to point beyond itself to the true *Blut Christi*, the risen blood that pleads for sinners not on earth but in heaven.

Wholeness and Immutability in Story and Cult

The assumption that salvation is immutability and wholeness is not, however, merely a theme of learned debate. It echoes in the propaganda that supports blood pilgrimage. For example, in the indulgence of 1247 offered to those who visit Beelitz, the bishop refers to the miracle of the abused host as a revelation for simple folk of the hidden Christ now ascended to heaven—a Christ who left behind in the eucharist a visible pledge of the invisible that these same simple people seem unable to grasp in its ordinary form. The blood on the host is clearly glossed as a sign of the immutable, un-seeable blood in glory.[51]

Indeed a concern with attaining changelessness runs throughout fifteenth-century piety. The Wilsnack legend is far from the only story in the later Middle Ages in which resistance to division and corruption is a sign of the holy. Such stories were penned by learned authors of canonization briefs as well as by collectors of *exempla* for the edification and entertainment of the populace. As is well known, martyrologies for liturgical use, collections of hagiography made to provide ready material for preachers, and vernacular saints' lives read aloud or sung for courtly or bourgeois listeners stress the triumph of holy bodies over repeated efforts to dismember them.[52] It is exactly the prominence, in martyr stories, of the theme of victory over partition that accounts for the fact that so much late medieval hagiography returns to these early stories rather than concentrating on more modern saints (who had fewer opportunities to defeat literal fragmentation and corruption). Moreover, the incorruptibility of a corpse came increasingly to be seen as a sign of sanctity;[53] by the end of the Middle Ages, incorruption of the cadaver was almost a requirement for female saints.[54] In a bizarre parallel to bleeding hosts and blood relics, we even find cases where the blood shed by stigmatics was thought not to corrupt.[55]

Claims to miraculous immutability circled around the various forms of *corpus* and *sanguis Christi* as well—incorruption heaped on incorruption. Raoul Glaber, Conrad of Eberbach, and Salimbene told stories of eucharistic bread buried in altars that survived hundreds of years without decay; Rupert of Deutz and Rudolf of Schlettstadt reported hosts and blood relics that came unscathed through fire.[56] In the early fourteenth-century French poem that recounts the invention of the blood relic at Fécamp, the "blood" is really a pipe that refuses to burn and remains red and sweet-tasting when broken open.[57] For many of the cult sites in Brandenburg and Mecklenburg I discussed in Chapter 3, the holy object's claim to sacrality was supported by, or based in, resistance to decay and destruction. At Nauen as at Wilsnack, the host survived through fire. At Berlin-Brandenburg-Stendal, at Sternberg and Heiligengrabe, and slightly further afield at Bamberg and Posen, it allegedly resisted burning, drowning, and fragmentation. At Zehdenick and Güstrow (at least according to legend), it triumphed over burial.[58] When forced by politics and circumstance to accept the miracle hosts of Andechs, Nicholas of Cusa based his approval on their incorruptibility, avoiding any reference to blood spots.[59] In these cases, the miracle lies in changelessness, in resistance to the natural processes of decay and fragmentation.

At first glance it might seem as if blood miracles fit only awkwardly into such basic assumptions of sacred immutability. As Kühne has suggested, surviving through fire and water is a different sort of motif from the eruption of blood. Stories of hosts and bodies resisting change might thus seem to preclude the appearance of something newly visible as a sign of the sacred. How can change signal non-change? Spots on bread appear after all to modern eyes to be simply the product of decay or contamination.

Some fifteenth-century theorists offered, as we have seen, similar arguments. (Tocke and others make much of finding the contents of the Wilsnack monstrance to be only spiderwebs and mold.) But in the Wilsnack and Heiligengrabe stories as they come down to us, the appearance of blood and the resistance to assault go together. The Wilsnack hosts bleed to assert their sacrality, warding off attempts at reconsecration. The crumbled wafer at Heiligengrabe bleeds to announce that it is whole in every particle. To the pilgrims, blood clearly manifested continuity and immutability, the presence of the ever-living Christ. And that is exactly, of course, what university theologians claimed too in attempting to sublimate pilgrimage enthusiasm into worship of Christ's immutable, glorified, and unseeable blood that pleads eternally before God's throne in heaven. Both in praxis and in learned discourse, then, blood was a sign of the living Christ, the Christ who perdures, who never dies. Whether on the surface of the host (as it was to the pilgrims) or hidden within the host's substance (as it was to many of the theorists), whether a vestige of Christ's own crucified body (as some pilgrims believed) or a sign of Christ in heaven (as shrine attendants and ecclesiastical authorities often asserted), the red and liquid blood was the immutable God. Because rosy and living, blood resists the physical decay of mold and the metaphysical decay of sin—that is, the death of matter and spirit.

In a sense then blood makes apparent the continuity, the potential for survival, within corruptible matter. Its sudden eruption into visibility is a change that sublimates and transcends change. Poured out in death, it nonetheless lives and brings life. On the lead badges at Wilsnack and in the songs of pilgrims, it is alive and red. Travelers to Boxmeer in the Low Countries sang:

Come people from far away
And fall at the feet of the Lord
You see here at Boxmeer
Still the drops of his blood.

[Komt menschen wyt en veer
En valt dyn Her te voet
Gy siet hier se Boxmeer
Nog droppels van zyn bloet][60]

An old French flagellant song appealed to Christ's red and living wounds (*tes cinq rouges playes*) for rescue from sudden death.[61] The monks at Weingarten, in a liturgy of great beauty, hymned the blood that resided in their cloister and in heaven as liquid drops, bright and red.[62]

Hail, saving Blood, taken from the living spring [*de vivo . . . fonte*], cleansing us and making us fruitful for the good [*nos emundans et ad bonum nos fecundans*]. O new wine of the true Vine, quenching the power of our thirst. Drop full of sweetness, make us worthy for the honor of heaven.[63]

To adherents, the blood is always in the present tense. In its fluid redness, it resists *mutatio* and manifests the life that endures behind physical change.

And not only resists. It protests *mutatio* as well. The miracle corporals of Bolsena and Walldürn cried out against ritual abuse; paralleling at least one version of the Erfurt blood miracle, they were protests against the uncleanness or spilling of eucharistic vessels.[64] A crucial motif in host-desecration stories was, as we have seen, the inability of the Jews to destroy the host. It cannot be drowned; it cannot be burned; it cannot be dismembered. The hosts supposedly desecrated at Sternberg, at Berlin-Brandenburg-Stendal, and at Heiligengrabe stream forth blood as if they are living bodies, crying for vengeance but proving that God cannot perish. The published account of the fact-finding commission concerning the events of 1510 in the Brandenburg area, for example, stresses that the Jew Salomon "pierced and stabbed [the host] many times but could not harm it [*mehrmals gehawen, gestochen, jedoch nit verwundern mögen*]." The host then divided itself into three pieces as if at the consecration [*der heylig fronleichnam Christi wunderbarlich in drey tayl . . . getaylt*], and the cracks were marked with blood. After sending two of the fragments to his friends, Salomon struck the remaining piece again and again; blood drops flowed out, but the same particle, "drowned, burnt, and in other ways persecuted," could not be "destroyed" [*Den selben Partikel hat er wollen vernutzen, jns wasser werffen, verprennen, und in mancherlay weysz umbringen. Jst jme aber alles onmöglich gewest.*] As the language makes clear, division and bleeding are not destruction but rather proof of life, of indestructibility. Although separated, the particles remain each fully alive and indeed, when distributed throughout the Mark, spread the presence of Christ and the guilt of the Jews.[65] Desecrated hosts were thus, in their changed changelessness, both proof of the presence of the divine (Christ is alive in them) and protest (even advertisement) against the attempted *mutatio* of violation (Christ's blood cries out). In such stories, we come close both to the folk motif of indestructibility Kühne has discussed and to the ancient lives of the martyrs (which themselves, of course, drew partly on folk motifs) in which hero or heroine remains alive through repeated burning, drowning, and dismemberment.[66] The account of the host desecration at Heiligengrabe, constructed in the early sixteenth century, joins motifs of miraculous indestructibility with learned theology when it argues that the bits of host buried under the gallows bled in demonstration that Christ is whole, fully present in every particle.

Devotional Images

Fifteenth-century blood chests and monstrances reflect the association of blood with victory over mutability and fragmentation. As art historians have long pointed out, the enormously popular devotional image of the Man of Sorrows (*Schmerzensmann* or *imago pietatis)*, from whose side (in some versions) blood poured, was often upright in the tomb—risen as well as suffering. This suffering Christ offers wounds and/or blood, but he is not writhing in torture; his is not a figure of expressionist agony but of tranquil yet immediate and vivid presence. Unlike narrative scenes of the flagellation or *Ecce homo* or the crucifixion itself, this devotional image (like all devotional images) telescopes many moments of the gospel story and many responses.[67] The Man of Sorrows brings before our eyes the incomparable sorrow of the death offered, but it echoes as well, in its representation of manifestly living blood (or, where bleeding is absent, in its upright, "resurrected" pose), the hope gained by that death.[68] It is significant then that the *Schmerzensmann* is the devotional figure most often associated with blood cult.[69] On the blood chest at Wilsnack, Christ appears thus, alive and bleeding in his sarcophagus (see Plate 5). On the inside doors of the same chest, he seems to be jeered at by Jewish figures in a brutal rendition of the *Ecce homo* on the one side but, on the other, reigns as the triune God in a so-called Throne of Grace (a figure of the Father holding the crucified Son surmounted by the dove of the Holy Spirit) (see Plates 6 and 7). The panels that bracket the place where the miracle host itself was preserved thus evoke both the horror of Christ's suffering and the victory gained, separating into two visual moments the multiple significances that coinhere in the figure of the Man of Sorrows.[70]

Moreover, the *sanguis Christi* in reliquaries is often associated with resurrection. The reliquary monstrance for the blood relic at Schwerin was (as we know from an inventory of 1542) a silver Christ with the blood in a jasper in his breast, his arms raised as a sign of the resurrection.[71] The reliquary at Cismar was also a figure of the Savior, which was apparently displayed on feast days through a little door cut in the altarpiece so that the *Salvator* figure replaced a Christ of the flagellation. In the famous Riemenschneider altar at Rothenburg ob der Tauber, the blood (which is perhaps a conflation of a blood relic and a bloody corporal miracle) is surmounted by a resurrected Christ showing his wounds.[72] The title-page woodcut in the gruesome 1521 German version of the Heiligengrabe foundation legend shows the triumphant Christ rising from his tomb.[73]

Conclusion

Although it is not always understood in the same way, the theme of immutability reverberates in the Wilsnack texts through the entire fifteenth century. Jan Hus asked in 1406–7: if Christ is not whole in heaven, how shall we be whole when we rise? Nicholas of Cusa asserted in 1451: Christ's blood is glorified and invisible in invisible veins. Johannes von Paltz argued in 1503 (following Johannes von Dorsten): God does not himself appear and disappear although he may, for devotional purposes, create something—even something bloodlike—*de novo*.[74]

It is in this last passage that we see the theme of immutability put most succinctly. Although Paltz supported blood relics and argued for the usefulness of the miracle host of Sternberg, he nonetheless asserted: the blood that is there cannot be Christ's blood, for the living Christ cannot be harmed again. An essential portion cut off from Christ cannot remain behind, detracted from the fullness of glory. Salvation rests in the triumph of Christ over death and mutation—in the change to changelessness.

And yet, to Paltz, blood also symbolizes the ultimate change of death itself, the horror of blood poured out. Whether on miracle host or in reliquary, blood makes visible not only the suffering but even the dying of Christ. What is hidden in the mass or in history erupts into visibility, and it is visible as drops, as something separated or shed. As we have seen, the blood controversies of the fifteenth century were exactly about blood as bits, about whether particles can be left behind. Shedding, partition, fragmentation was threatening. It had to be overcome by glory. But the blood miracles Paltz and others supported as reminders and as special creations were manifestations of a separation they also denied. There is thus a paradox at the heart of blood piety.

Blood is not only a symbol of triumph over death and decay; it is also a sign that the immutable changes, the whole divides, and that exactly that change is necessary for salvation. I must thus turn now to other contradictions within blood piety. For the eruption of blood, whether in miracle or text, manifests not only the *immutabilitas* of God but also his mutation and division.

Chapter 7

Living Blood Poured Out

An attempt to ferret out the assumptions behind the fourteenth- and fifteenth-century preoccupation with blood in theology, piety, and praxis reveals immediately that *immutabilitas* is only half the story. Indeed, as I suggested at the end of Chapter 6, *immutabilitas* itself is not merely changelessness and impassibility. Even in its resistance to and sublimation of mutation, *Blut Christi* is seen as living, throbbing, and red, not merely unchanging and stable. Overlying and expressing the paradox of Christ, changing yet immutable, is the paradox of blood that is living and in continuity with body as well as shed and separated from body.

A glance at the iconography of Christ's death will serve to introduce this paradox both because the paradox can be seen so starkly in art and because it has been so little remarked upon. Depictions of the crucifixion, which proliferated throughout northern Europe, make clear the emphasis on blood alive in death. Even in representations that focus—as many fifteenth-century ones do—on events occurring after the death of Christ, the blood is usually depicted as liquid and red. Those that privilege the centurion's cry as he points to the dead Christ tend nonetheless to depict blood as distinctly alive. When Christ rises after three days, his wounds are often shown flowing with fresh, red blood.

Indeed, northern crucifixions generally show *sanguis Christi* as liquid and flowing, not coagulated or drying. Blood is depicted either as falling in a rain of fresh drops or as gushing out in streams; the two types (drops and streams) are often found in the same image. The first sort of blood hangs pendulant from hands, feet, and side. In many crucifixions where angels hold up chalices to catch the globules or swinging drops, for example, those drops do not even reach the chalice but hang poised midway, so fresh they have not yet broken free of the open wounds. Johann Koerbecke's Marienfelder Altar from circa 1457, now in Berlin, shows a fresh little globule, just ready to drop, as the centurion speaks the words on his banderole: "Truly this was the Son of God [Matt. 27.54; Mark 15.39]" (see Plate 19).[1] If one looks closely at a small panel painting probably from Bohemia circa 1430, also now in Berlin, one can make out tiny angels, scratched into the gold background, who catch the tear-shaped drops swinging from Christ's hands and arms (see Plates 20 and 21).[2]

In the second sort of depiction (waves, or streams, or even great smears of red), the blood spurts in a vibrant cascade, usually to fall onto Longinus or pour into a eucharistic vessel. The famous Kaufmann crucifixion from circa 1340 shows Christ's blood flowing freely in both streams and discrete droplets at the moment when the lance prick and the centurion's words clearly attest the Savior's death (see Plate 14).[3] A fifteenth-century illuminated manuscript of a German translation of Catherine of Siena's life, widely disseminated as a work of spiritual edification for women, shows the crucifix covered with large smears of red that fly into or hang in the air like globules or splashes (see Plate 11).[4] Moreover, in numerous depictions of the resurrection, Christ's wounds still display uncoagulated blood. In contrast to many sixteenth-century images, and many southern European ones, that show a body with drying, or healed, or even luminescent scars, fourteenth- and fifteenth-century northern representations often depict the risen Christ with blood running from feet and hands to pool in fresh, red circles below. For example, the Landsberger Altar by Hans Multscher, circa 1437, stresses the freshness of the blood throughout its narrative sequence. In the resurrection panel, the wounds look a little like rosettes but a long stream runs down, especially from the feet, and ends with a discrete, round, red globe (see Plate 22). Northern depictions of the Last Judgment also sometimes show Christ with freshly bleeding wounds.[5]

In images and piety, this connected, continuous, and ever-living blood is also its opposite. Whole and alive, it is also divided and changed. A sign of death, it breaks away from body, which it breaches and transgresses. In contrast to body—symbol, since the patristic period, of ingathering and community—blood erupts across boundaries.[6] Whereas body encloses, blood separates from. In the process, it violates, although its release can also cure and cleanse.[7] Whether cleansing or threatening, however, shed blood is a body part. It breaks away from body. We do well to remember that the blood in question in fifteenth-century theological disputations and at cult sites was globules, particles, or fragments. What polemicists debated at Braunschweig, Wilsnack, or Marienfliess was *particulae*. It was bits in reliquaries (derived—that is, divided from—other bloods) or spots on hosts. What friars fought over at Rome was whether the *drops* of blood shed at the crucifixion remained united to divinity.

Once again the parallel to art is instructive. Just as the faithful enumerated, in many popular devotions, the number of blood drops Christ shed during the passion (see Plate 32), so sculptors and painters carved or depicted, in thick layers of paint, bulbous pellets extruding from wounds on images such as the Man of Sorrows. In the Landsberger altar, for example, Christ's wounds are rosettes of glowing blood, the droplets arranged as if in high relief (Plate 22). A number of late medieval *pietàs* show the body of Christ covered with discrete red globs (carved or painted on the figure, or sometimes enhanced with papier-mâché) that insist on their nature as separate particles (see frontispiece and Plates 15–17).[8]

Both the paradox of blood drops as separated continuity and the theme of blood as living need further exploration. I turn to these themes in the next two chapters. In this chapter, I focus on the complex implications and connotations of the fifteenth-century insistence that blood—although shed in death—is enlivening and alive.[9] Once again, I use material that ranges from the legends and propaganda of northern cult sites to the themes of devotional and university theology, arguing that the same basic assumptions underlie them all.[10] Because I am, in this chapter, dealing with one side of a paradox, the full significance of many of the texts I look at here will be clear only at the end of Chapter 8. But I hope that even this partial discussion will indicate how much more complicated themes of blood devotion are than the explanation usually given. Although blood is an important element in late medieval devotion to Christ's humanity, it signifies more than suffering love.

Blood as Fertility

The assumption that blood liberates and enlivens runs through a wide range of fifteenth-century material. I turn to Wilsnack for my first examples. In the theology connected with the Wilsnack controversy, all the way from Jan Hus to Johannes von Paltz, the link of blood to resurrection is stressed over and over again. Whether controversialists argued that all Christ's blood must rise to glory as a promise of our eventual wholeness or held that spots left behind on wafers were a visible pledge of this promise, blood was understood to signify life. The early miracles collected in the Wilsnack *Historia inventionis* were stories in which what blood effected was literally a return to life; blood's first healing miracles were earthly resurrections. For criminals sentenced to travel to Wilsnack in order to expiate their crimes, blood liberated and brought life in a specific and technical sense. Once the sentence was performed, the penitent could be reintegrated into the social community; he regained social life.

Moreover, as we have seen in other stories from Brandenburg and Mecklenburg, fertility was assumed to be both consequence and connotation of blood. Shepherds, serving girls, and alewives who allegedly stole the host for conjuring hoped for fertility—the increase of flocks or beer or love.[11] The liturgies of blood cult and defenses of blood relics throb with vegetal images of engendering, flowering, and sprouting. Both feeding and washing are associated with this fertilizing power of blood. Its liquid redness washes away dirt and sin; it intoxicates with sweetness. Gerhard of Cologne, for example, apostrophized Weingarten, in phrases that evoke the eucharist but probably refer more directly to a ritual in which wine poured over the blood relic was offered for drinking:

> You, the true vineyard [Weingarten], surpassing all others, [are] where the health-bringing wine out of the side of the Lord makes believers intoxicated with the wonderful drunkenness of which the Psalmist speaks. . . . You, fertile and fecund vineyard, [are] planted by God. . . . So that you are made fertile, God has let his mild rain flow out of the highest clouds, his flesh, which never bore sin. But so that you may become drunk with the juice of the grape, the same Christ has poured out his totally pure blood from the winecellar of his flesh; and the Lord wanted this intoxicating wine, this fructifying rain, this soul-cleansing water to be drunk and stored up in his most glorious vineyard [Weingarten].[12]

As Mark Daniel Holtz has shown, Weingarten's liturgy is shot through with images of fertility and fructification.[13] Blood quenches thirst, cleanses, and makes fecund [*emundans et . . . fecundans*]. "In the midst of the Lord's little breast, a wellspring flowed," sang the monks, "throwing wide the gate of paradise. . . ."[14]

From folk tradition to scientific discourse, we find the same understanding of blood as life bringer—fertilizing, healing, feeding. In medical recipes, as in the story of Longinus that circulated in later medieval Europe, blood vivifies and restores; it cures leprosy, blindness, and epilepsy as well as sin.[15] An early fourteenth-century Low German meditation on the passion, for example, rings changes on the theme of blood as curative when it describes Longinus wiping his eyes with hands stained in Christ's blood and crying: "His holy blood has made my blindness see and his dead heart, which I wanted to kill, has made my dead heart alive and healthy."[16]

Secular literature from the Middle Ages is full of stories of people seeking blood (especially that of children or virgins) to cure mortal illness or quench hemorrhages.[17] A number of examples survive of charms in which blood, or (on the principle of *similia similibus*) red objects such as threads or silk, are used against abnormal blood flow. In such practices we see a fundamental ambivalence located exactly in the assumption that blood carries life. Its loss (outflow) is loss of life, but only it is powerful enough therefore to stop such outflow. It is blood that stanches wounds and brings again the life and fertility it also threatens. Implicit in the ritual murder libels against Jews was the assumption that, in stealing blood, Jews were stealing life in order to gain life.[18] In a warped and graphic story from the early modern period, we have evidence that a Christian woman did try to sell blood (obtained from a soldier who had been bled in a medical procedure) to local Jews, and there seem to have been fourteenth-century cases as well.[19]

Folk traditions were behind such stories, of course, as they were behind the stories of objects that liquefied or bled to demonstrate sacrality—stories to which I shall return. Biblical tradition and classical medical teaching underlay them as well. Scholastic theologians from Grosseteste and Aquinas to Johannes von Paltz cited Leviticus 17.11 ("the life of the flesh is in the blood") and quoted "doctors [*phisicos*]" to describe blood as "the friend of nature and the seat of the soul."[20] I turn now to the complex ways in which blood was understood to be not only fertilizing and healing but actually the locus of life or spirit or self. But first, an aside.

Blood as Social Survival

There is one sense in which "blood" is used in modern parlance that is surprisingly infrequent in late medieval devotion: blood as the life of future generations, as social survival, as lineage or family continuity. The fact that blood as kinship or descent is relatively rare in such texts is significant and lends support to recent arguments that older scholarship overemphasized lineage in the later Middle Ages.[21] Nonetheless, I have found a few references that do suggest that possessing common blood—*con-sanguinitas*—is sometimes implicit in notions of being the child of God or of sharing community. In *Piers Plowman*, passus XVIII, for example, sharing blood means kinship.[22] Moreover, the cry of blood for vengeance is often analogized to the blood of Abel crying out against Cain; such usage also suggests a sense of blood as kin-group.[23] Baldric of Bourgueil in his *Historia Jerosolimitana* refers to avenging attacks on Christ's holy places as an avenging of blood relatives.[24] And in Pius II's summary of Dominican arguments that Christ's blood never left the hypostatic union, we find a clear sense that a person's blood is his kin. The fact that Pius's disputants here appeal to common usage suggests that passing references to sharing blood did sometimes carry overtones of belonging to a descent- or kin-group (although not an exclusively patrilineal one).

> "It is my blood," kings say, "Do not touch it." As far back as man's memory can reach noble families honor their own blood in men and women of the direct and collateral lines. . . . Plebians and rustics ignorant of letter and of laws . . . say, "Our blood has

been injured" . . . and do not hesitate to risk blood for blood. It is a common practice with all men to gather up the blood of a kinsman from the ground and lay it in the tomb.[25]

Blood here expresses a continuity of family and family honor; it requires vengeance if violated. There is the same sense of blood as family implicit in warnings, such as Catherine of Siena's, that Christians as "sons of God" should act to defend their father when human sins shed his blood.[26]

But in all these passages, blood signifies primarily the individual, not group identity or continuity and certainly not lineage. To the Dominicans (as recorded by Pius II), the blood of a kinsman, gathered up to be laid in the tomb, is understood to be (or at least to be united with) the person. It is exactly this understanding that supports the Dominican argument that even separated *sanguis Christi is* Christ. To Catherine of Siena, the son who sees his father's blood shed and feels impelled to avenge it recognizes himself as the enemy: "Let us act as does a true son who sees his father's blood shed. A hatred grows within him for the enemy . . . [and the enemy is] we who commit sin. . . ." The point, to Catherine, is not blood as family but blood as self-accusation.

Blood as Engendering and Gendered

As Pius's larger discussion of the debates over *sanguis Christi* makes clear, blood as lineage or collateral relationship is not a very important symbol or image in devotional or academic discourse. A very different philosophical and scientific understanding of blood as descent or continuity is, however, crucial. According to medieval theories of physiology the fetus is formed from maternal uterine blood, animated by the blood or seed of the father, and is fed by blood, both in the womb and from the breast. (All bodily fluids are some form of blood in medieval medical theory.)[27] Hence in a startling sense, the blood from which the individual is constituted is gendered female; the body *is* the mother's blood. As we have seen, John of Capistrano argued for the high ontological status of *sanguis Christi* by stressing the formation of Christ's body entirely from the pure menstrual blood of his mother's womb.[28] This sense of Christ's body as formed from—as *being*—Mary's blood had theological ramifications for Christology and Mariology (especially the doctrine of the Immaculate Conception). It also spilled over into devotion. In a striking phrase from a decree of Abbot Berthold of Weingarten concerning the Saturday mass in honor of the Virgin, Christ's body and the stuff of Mary's womb are so completely assimilated that Christ's body almost becomes blood—his mother's blood! The *pretium* of redemption (we should note here the technical soteriological language) is the uterine blood Mary offers. And this gushing forth from a female body is not just future promise but also medicinal cure.

> Therefore, we are bound to . . . [honor her] who, providing to the whole world the price [*pretium*] of human redemption and pouring forth from her virginal womb for the Christian faithful the universal cure [*ex virginali vtero refundens medicinam*], granted us a pledge of hope and a bodily token in his worshipful blood.[29]

The technical idea, drawn from physiological theory, that the fetus is formed from female blood became a common image of salvation in late medieval spirituality. Christ's receiving of us into his heart, which should be matched by our reception of him into ours, was understood less as *re*-ceiving than as *con*-ceiving. Hence the adult Christ was imaged sometimes as a female, sometimes as a pregnant male. Not only extravagant mystical visions but also simple prayers were quite graphic in their descriptions both of Christ pregnant with souls and of souls pregnant with Christ.[30] For example, a sermon on the incarnation attributed by Pfeiffer and Richstätter to an unknown preacher of the thirteenth or fourteenth century elaborates on this theme of God as mother with specific reference to conception and to blood:

> With what love he bore us in himself, with deeper love than a mother ever bore her child, for she bears the child under her heart while the father bears us in his heart, as the son shows us. For he let his heart be pierced with a spear so that we might see the burning love the father feels for his children. How? Because the blood of every man is cold when it stands in death, but his was hot and flowing.[31]

The metaphor not only makes the bearing of souls in God a kind of (male) pregnancy; it also seems to imagine the blood of the side wound not as the coagulating ooze of a dead body but as birthing blood, living and red.

Medieval hymns and sermons had long stressed that all birth is in blood. As early as the eighth century, Bede, in commenting on the Song of Songs, drew a parallel between the incarnation and the resurrection/ascension, arguing that Christ came into the world *de sanguine* (i.e., from his mother's womb) and left also in the blood of the cross.[32] By the fourteenth and fifteenth centuries, not only is Christ understood to be born and born anew in blood; he himself gives birth. The blood of the passion is the blood of birthing. Hence the fertile, separated blood from Christ's side is female blood. As we saw, for example, in the passage from James of Jüterbog (Klusa) quoted in Chapter 1, devotional texts regularly analogized the opening of Christ's side by Longinus to giving birth: ". . . from the side of Jesus the sacraments receive their efficacy . . . and the church was formed. . . ." Thus they stressed, as did Vincent of Beauvais, that the side was opened like a doorway (as in a natural process), not stabbed or violated.[33] In one of the most graphic and extensive uses of the image,[34] the Carthusian prioress Marguerite of Oingt (d. 1310) conflated Christ's bloody sweat with the crucifixion and imagined the blood, bursting from ruptured veins, as drops or globules, falling one by one.

> My sweet Lord, I gave up for you my father and my mother and my brothers and all the wealth of the world. . . . Nor do I have father or mother besides you. . . . For are you not my mother and more than my mother? The mother who bore me labored in delivering me for one day or one night but you, my sweet and lovely Lord, labored for me for more than thirty years. Ah, my sweet and lovely Lord, with what love you labored for me. . . . But when the time approached for you to be delivered, your labor pains were so great that your holy sweat was like great drops of blood that came out from your body and fell on the earth. . . . Ah! Sweet Lord Jesus Christ, who ever saw a mother suffer such a birth! For when the hour of your delivery came you were placed on the hard bed of the cross . . . and your nerves and all your veins were broken. And truly it is no surprise that your veins burst when in one day you gave birth to the whole world.[35]

The *Showings* of the English recluse Julian of Norwich (d. after 1413) illustrate the point as well.[36] Although not explicitly gendered female, the living blood of glorious suffering that Julian sees poured out from the cross in her initial vision is clearly related to the famous insight into the motherhood of God to which she came after long meditation. Since, to Julian, God's motherhood is a taking on of our physical humanity, a kind of *creation* of us, as a mother gives herself to the fetus she bears, the blood Christ sheds in saving us is clearly analogous to the blood a woman sheds in childbirth.[37] It is significant, however, that in Julian's visionary experience, the gushing out (or birthing) *precedes* the nestling within (conception). For the conception is also a re-conception. Julian, to whose soteriology of representation I shall return below, embeds an understanding of the blood of the cross in a larger sense of all humanity (both Adam and Christ) resting in the womb of a mother God.[38]

To give a final example from iconography: the birthing theme receives dramatic, typological expression in the explicit parallel drawn between the little figure of Ecclesia peeping out from Christ's side and the emergence of Eve from Adam sleeping in the Garden of Eden (see Plate 12). Scripture depicts the latter event as formation from a rib, with God as actor (Gen. 2.21–23); medieval iconography, however, imagines both events as birthing. In late medieval depictions of the crucifixion, the figure of Ecclesia not only receives blood from Christ's side in what is clearly an image of feeding, hence of eucharist;

she also emerges from the wound in Christ's side, taking her very being from him. For Church, we must remember, is not only born *from* Christ's body; she also *is* Christ's body.

Thus much more is involved in the association of blood with conception and birthing in these texts than simply the idea that giving birth is a bleeding during which new life emerges. Birthing is not merely suffering in order to release another being. For the new life that is born is flesh formed from the mother's blood; her blood literally continues in—*is*—the child's body. And the blood in that body is its life. Hence blood is more than that which washes away sin, softens hard hearts, or suffers for others; it is more than a force which fertilizes or heals. As the Weingarten liturgy implied, the blood Mary gives to the world *is* the body of Christ. As Pius II suggested, those who gather up the blood of kinsmen see themselves as gathering up the person. Or, as iconography made explicit, birthing in blood is creation, or re-creation, as in the forming of Eve or the creation of Ecclesia. We will not be able to understand late medieval soteriology unless we take this way of speaking seriously.

Such imagery does not imply the divinization of the soul. The implication is not that faithful Christians are emanations from God, or that they are absorbed or re-absorbed in, or become, him. Nonetheless there is a startling sense of shared *humanitas* here. For if Christ is born in and *of* Mary's blood, he is not only fully human but also, quite literally, a part of her body. And if we are reborn in and *of* his blood, then we, as reborn, receive a part of—indeed are remade from—that blood, and he, as re-conceived in our wombs, takes a part of us into himself. The images suggest a radical incorporation of all humanity in Christ to which I shall return in Chapter 9.

Blood as *Sedes Animae*

A second aspect of physiological theory is as important in medieval devotion as the idea that the fetus is formed from uterine blood. This is the topos of blood as the "seat of the soul."

There were, of course, a number of different medical theories available in the Middle Ages about the physical location of soul. In his *Tractatus de Christi sanguine pretioso*, John of Capistrano, who locates soul in blood, admits that some say it is in the heart (*in corde*), some argue it is in the brain (*in cerebro*).[39] There were also, as we have seen, a number of theories put forward by scholastic theologians about the relationship of blood to body. To mid-fifteenth-century Franciscans, blood was joined to self only via body's form (the *forma corporeitatis*). Franciscans did not think blood is self or even that blood is per se assumed by the Word in the incarnation.[40] Even to Thomists, there was no implication that soul was literally in the blood.[41] All core aspects of body were informed immediately by soul, which indeed made them the person's body. Without the *veritas humanae naturae*, including blood, the person would not be the person. But soul or spirit, as nonmaterial, could not have a physical location. It had to be present throughout body—whole in every part, by a kind of concomitance.[42] Nonetheless a good deal of devotional and preaching language from the High Middle Ages implies that blood carries life or is the seat of life.[43] Thomas, Bonaventure, Grosseteste, and Biel all quote Leviticus 17.11: *anima carnis in sanguine est.*

As carrier of soul or life, blood was equated, allegorically or symbolically, with spirit. Thus throughout technical theological discourse as well as devotional writing, the body/blood contrast was used explicitly to symbolize the opposition body/soul.[44] Gabriel Biel wrote in his commentary on the mass (partly citing Alexander of Hales):

> Therefore in the receiving of the body of Christ under the species of bread is signified the union [*coniunctio*] of members of the body of Christ with its head achieved by the incarnation. In the receiving of the blood under the species of wine is signified our redemption through the spilling of Christ's blood [*per sanguinis Christi effusionem*]. Hence in one sacrament is signified the incarnation and the passion. . . . Since, however, as the Gloss says, . . . [our redemption is] whole [*totus*] under the species of bread, whole under the species of wine, why is the sacrament not given in one rather than two [kinds]? In order that Christ show his whole human nature, that is, that he assumed body and soul that both might be redeemed. For the bread refers to the body, wine to the soul, because wine represents blood in which is the seat of the soul [*sedes animae*]. Thus this sacrament is celebrated in two species that the taking up of soul and body in Christ and the freeing of both in us may be signified.[45]

Aquinas, basing himself on Albertus Magnus, held that blood is the seat of life and, indeed, of the whole body *in potentia*. "The blood of Christ, or his own corporeal life which is in the blood, is the price of our salvation."[46] Johannes von Paltz wrote, citing Leviticus explicitly: "The memory of the blood stamps [in us] the memory of the passion. For blood is the friend of nature and the seat of the soul. Hence, as in Leviticus 17, it is horrible to shed it."[47] The phrase "friend of nature," which we also find in Grosseteste, perhaps goes back to Aristotle and, along with the quotation "seat of the soul" from the Hebrew Scriptures, seems to be something of a commonplace in medieval discussions.[48]

For example, when the Carthusian Peter Dorlandus (d. 1507), in his popular devotional treatise, the *Viola animae*, explained how Mary understood the blood of Christ's flagellation, he used a reference to physiology (which was an echo of Leviticus as well) to bolster both affective piety and soteriological theory. We are, says Dorlandus, like the man who went down from Jerusalem to Jericho and fell among thieves, who left him half dead. That man is Adam—that is, all humanity—with whom Christ, in his compassion, identifies, clothing us and binding up our injuries. Dorlandus then departs from the parable text to explain that Christ is not only the Good Samaritan but also the wounded man.[49]

He wished to be wounded that he might repair our wound and poured out his blood that he might by grace revive to life those only half alive. For just as the life of all ensouled creatures is in the blood, so the life of the just person comes through the blood of Christ, which he therefore in compassionate generosity pours out from his body so that you can drink it with your mouth and slake your thirst from it in your heart.[50]

Not only the drink of the eucharist and a metaphor for interior encounter and comfort, blood is here quite literally a transfusion: a gift of life itself.

A curious entry in one of the Sister-Books from early fourteenth-century Germany also seems to imply that blood carries life (or soul or self). A certain Adelheid, a widow, was troubled by the fact that she was not a virgin. After several years, in which she cried night and day,

an angel came and said to her: "Cheer up, God will answer your prayers as far as is possible." And he led her into the air. There were also other angels who had a wine press. And they laid her on it and pressed her so hard that she imagined not a drop of blood was left in her body. And they said to her: "We have pressed out of you all the blood that sinned in you; and we shall pour virginal blood into you, and you will become as similar to virgins as is possible. But you cannot become a virgin again." And when she came to again, she lay in a pool of blood.[51]

The image of the wine press, prominent in the art of the period as a eucharistic theme, is here transferred from Christ to a nun, whose blood-soul-life is squeezed out and replaced in order to alleviate her individual anxiety and guilt and alter (as far as is possible) her status. The close association of blood with sexuality and reproduction is clear, as if the sexual act marks the blood in some way forever after; but the blood is more than sexual and social or marital status; it is more even than the bearer of ethical status, that is, purity or impurity. It is as if the body is only a mold into which blood as animating force or soul or self is poured. To exchange the blood is almost (although not quite) to change the self.[52]

As a final example, I take something very different: a political execution from the later fourteenth century. It occurred in the south of Europe, an area where the piety was, in some ways, quite different from that in the northern lands on which my book is primarily based. Nonetheless the incident is a famous one—almost always cited in discussions of blood devotion although seldom with attention to the details of its heroine's own report—and blood was in certain ways its author's signature theme. It would be almost perverse not to mention it here.

The details are well known. In 1375, one Niccolò di Toldo, a political prisoner, asked the holy woman Catherine of Siena to accompany him to his execution. Standing by the scaffold, she received his head in her arms and was covered with his red, sweet-smelling blood. The incident is often cited as evidence of the almost thaumaturgic power of blood, especially the blood of criminals, in the later Middle Ages or as an example of the expressionist violence of urban life and piety. What is not usually noticed is Catherine's own understanding of exactly what happened. Whether Catherine literally saw a vision when the head fell or articulated her understanding of the significance as something "seen," what she tells us is that the young Perugian's blood was lifted into Christ's side and incorporated into Christ's blood.

His head was resting on my breast. I sensed an intense joy, a fragrance of his blood. . . . [And] when he had received the sign I said: "Down for the wedding, my dear brother, for soon you will be in everlasting life." He knelt down very meekly; I placed his neck [on the block] and bent down and reminded him of the blood of the Lamb. His mouth said nothing but "Gesù!" and "Caterina!" and as he said this, I received his head into my hands, saying, "I will!" with my eyes fixed on the divine Goodness.

Then was seen the God-Man as one sees the brilliance of the sun. [His side] was open and received [Niccolò's] blood into his own blood. . . . Once he had been so received by God . . . , the Son . . . gave him the gift of sharing in the tormented love with which he himself had accepted *his* painful death . . . for the welfare of the human race. . . .

Now that he was hidden away where he belonged, my soul rested in peace and quiet in . . . a fragrance of blood . . . ![53]

The theme of our blood shut up in Christ's is a common one in Catherine. She wrote to her confessor and biographer, Raymond of Capua, in what is for her a typical salutation:

I, Caterina, . . . send you my greetings in the precious blood of God's Son. I long to see you engulfed and drowned in the sweet blood . . . , which is permeated with the fire of his blazing charity. . . . I am saying that unless you are drowned in the blood you will not attain the little virtue of true humility. . . . [S]hut yourself up in the open side of God's Son. . . . There the dear bride [the soul] rests in the bed of fire and blood.[54]

But in the description of Niccolò's execution that follows this salutation, blood is more than the bed in which we rest, a purging fire, inebriating drink, and billowing flood. Niccolò's blood *is* Niccolò, and *sanguis Christi is* Christ.

Indeed in another, explicitly Christological passage that perhaps foreshadows arguments her Dominican successors will make in Rome a century later, Catherine almost equates Christ's blood with his humanity.[55] "There is no way our appetite can be satisfied . . . except with his blood. . . . Only the blood can satisfy our hunger, because the blood has been mixed and kneaded with the eternal Godhead [*che 'l sangue è intriso e impastato con la Deità eterna*], a nature infinitely greater than we."[56] What joins divinity in the incarnation is here not *humanitas* but *sanguis*. Moreover, this *sanguis* is not merely a synecdoche for body or humanity, joined with God in incarnation. It is Christ, present and absent, left behind as well as gone ahead to glory.

> . . . the lance was thrust into his side. Longinus was the instrument of this, when he opened Christ's heart. When this cask was emptied of physical life through the separation of soul from body, his blood was *placed at hand* [*messo a mano*]. . . . So up, dearest daughters! . . . with anguished sorrow . . . let us enter the open storehouse of the side of Christ crucified, where we will find the blood. (my emphasis)[57]

For Catherine then, it is not just that blood stands as *pars pro toto* but that it is uniquely appropriate to do so. There is something about Christ's blood itself that bilocates—that is both "at hand" and in Christ's side, both alive in God and yet spilled forth. Hence the blood that departs and remains at hand is also the blood that leads back into God. It is a ribbon that connects as well as drops poured out.

This quality of blood as continuing alive while in separation made it especially apt as a soteriological image. Red and pulsating while poured out and left behind, blood could signal both Christ dying and Christ alive, both Christ present on earth (that is, shed—so to speak, *cruor*) and Christ gone to glory (that is, alive—so to speak, *sanguis*). We find this paradoxical sense of continuity in discontinuity expressed in a curious motif of late medieval piety: the devotion to Christ's complete exsanguination in the crucifixion. I turn now to this theme because it makes clear not only the obsession with life in the midst of separation but also the awareness of some devotional writers that such an image ran counter to ordinary physiology. Thus they used both, on the one hand, the similarity between normal blood and Christ's blood and, on the other, the radical difference in the behavior of *sanguis Christi* at the lance prick to make a soteriological point.

Continuity in Discontinuity: The Exsanguination of Christ

As early as the thirteenth century, the *Life* of Beatrice of Nazareth spoke of the holy woman resting "deliciously" in Christ's blood. In a passage I considered above in a different context, we now note, nestled in the midst of an extravagantly somatic piety, a technical soteriological reference—*pretium*—and those telltale verbs *fundere* and *spargere*, with their echoes of the sacrifices of Exodus and Leviticus. What we notice most, however, is the repetition of "all."

> At another time when Beatrice had . . . received from the priest's hand . . . the price [*precium*] of our redemption . . . it seemed to her that *all* the blood which flowed from his wounds was poured into her soul [*omnis sanguis qui ex eius vvlneribus emanauit, ipsius in anima funderetur*] and that *all* the drops of that precious liquid were so sprinkled in it [*omnesque gutte tam preciosi liquoris spargerentur in illa*] that it was wholly washed by these drops and most perfectly cleansed from . . . sin.[58]

The stress on Christ's complete exsanguination continued in piety over the two hundred years after Beatrice. Ludolf the Carthusian (d. 1378) and others of his order, which was known for its early devotion to the Sacred Heart, wrote again and again of Christ's blood and water, shed to the last drop in the repeated bleedings of the passion story. The association in Carthusian prayers is usually with the sacraments of penance and baptism; hence blood is life-giving, expiating, cleansing.[59] The great fifteenth-century theologian and preacher Gabriel Biel stressed that the last drops of blood, which remained in Christ's body after the flagellation and the nails, were taken from him with the lance.[60] Although an often quoted phrase (supposedly from Bernard of Clairvaux but not actually found there) asserted that one drop of Christ's blood was enough to save the entire world, Bernard himself stressed that Christ poured forth not drops but waves of blood; and to the devout what became increasingly important was the large number of drops shed.[61] I shall return in Chapter 8 to the stress on drops and the devotional practice of counting them. At this point it is sufficient to note the emphasis on the complete emptying of Christ's veins and/or heart on the cross.

For all the stress on the emptying of Christ, however, the blood that flowed was understood to be alive. Thus both sides of the paradox were accorded flamboyant exaggeration. From a dead body (and devotion followed Scripture in stressing that Christ was dead when Longinus came with his lance), all the blood was extruded as if it and its body continued alive.[62] The paradox was one that raised physiological as well as theological questions. Medieval theologians and preachers knew full well that dead bodies do not normally bleed.[63] And in order to avoid Docetism, Christ's body had to be fully and really body. Something special (beyond the fact of the incarnation) was therefore required to explain the behavior of its blood. Hence theologians found it necessary to argue that the gushing forth of water and blood in "living" streams at the opening of Christ's breast was done by special or second miracle. The polemicist Gerhard of Cologne, for example, held that Christ's side blood had to have been shed miraculously because blood in dead bodies becomes coagulated and stagnant (*stringitur et stagnatur*).[64]

Some devotional writers reflect such physiological curiosity as well. For example, David of Augsburg (d. 1272), perhaps the first mystical writer in German, said that the heart of the crucified Christ continued to glow beyond death to warm his holy blood. But David's concern is finally less with the physiology than with the spirituality; he wishes not to deny either the death or the physicality of Christ but to assert the ever-living quality of blood, heart, and love.

> . . . and that it flowed from a glowing heart . . . was for us a living witness. For if the body there had been cold and dead, the blood could not have flowed; it would have stood and coagulated as is usual in nature [*gestanden und solte unvlüzzic sîn gewesen von natûre*] as one sees it with the dead. But this did not happen to you [Christ]. And through this it is given to us to understand how the love's glow of your heart was so strong that a sweet stream ran down from your wounded side.[65]

Mechtild of Magdeburg too acknowledges the physiological difficulty but attributes the blood flow to grace and divinity. In her *Flowing Light of the Godhead*, the figure of "soul" ponders: "I am confused. How can someone dead still bleed?" But the Lord answers:

> "My body was then in a human manner dead [*menschlich tot*] when my heart's blood flowed with a beam of the Godhead through my side. The blood issued forth by grace, just as did the milk that I drank from my virginal mother. My divinity was present in all members of my body while I was dead, just as it was before and afterward [i.e., in the resurrection]. After its long sadness, my soul rested the while in my Godhead. And a spiritual image of my humanity [*ein geistlich bilde miner menscheit*] has always existed without a beginning suspended in my eternal Godhead."[66]

Skirting the physiological issue, the monk of Evesham claimed to see, in a vision of the crucifix, "blood flowing from the side of the image on the cross, as it does from the veins of a living man when he is cut for blood-letting."[67]

Robert Grosseteste (d. 1253) indeed used Christ's flowing blood as proof that his choice of death operated up to the very moment of his expiration on the cross. Christ died not as other men die but young and vigorous, shouting and alive. Thus we know, said Grosseteste, that Christ's death was voluntary even at the end.[68] A young and healthy man would not have died by bleeding from such small wounds. Christ did not bleed to death but rather chose for his soul to be separated from his body for our salvation. But after death, by a special miracle, he deliberately poured out for us the blood from his heart, a living gift.[69] Like later Franciscans, Grosseteste puts the emphasis on Christ's death rather than on bloodshed per se. But whether or not Christ dies by bleeding, it is by Christ's bleeding that, to Grosseteste, we live.

Blood as Alive

In some of the discussion of Christ's exsanguination, the pouring out at the lance prick is understood as a miracle. Physiological theory is drawn upon to support this; and the difference between ordinary blood, which coagulates, and Christ's, which does not, is stressed. But there is also a sense in which theology, devotion, and practice in the fifteenth century simply assume that blood itself—*sedes animae*—is alive. Some kind of traditional idea, found in many Indo-European cultures, that blood is life seems to fuse with the idea that *Blut Christi* is miraculous; it is sometimes impossible (and unimportant) to try to sort out whether the life of *sanguis Christi* is the life carried by all blood or the result of a special act of God. What is striking is the pervasive sense that blood is alive.

Indeed, the conviction that *Blut Christi* lives in separation is found at all cultural levels in the fifteenth century, from university disputation to folk- and miracle-story. For example, because the Dominicans at Rome in 1462 assumed that blood is life, they argued that only sick blood can be called dead. It is decay of blood extruded outside the body, and not the extrusion itself, that is called the death of blood. Living blood is both within and outside (or spilled); the basic dichotomy is not inside versus outside blood but living (which includes inside and outside) blood versus blood that is sick or dead—that is, decaying or decayed.[70] However much the Franciscans disagreed with this in certain technical ways, their emphasis on *sanguis Christi* as poured out in waves tended to assume that salvific blood was flowing and red.[71]

Moreover, the sense that blood is itself vivifying and alive probably undergirds the stories of holy blood that liquefies or spontaneously divides. At Schwerin, the story was told that the blood relic divided into three parts and worked miracles every Friday at the hour of Christ's death.[72] Ecclesiastical authorities and hagiographers were sometimes willing to accept such claims as miracles. Clement V, in a bull granting an indulgence to the blood procession in Bruges, cited the liquefaction and boiling up of the holy blood there every

Friday between 1303 and 1309 from morning until the ninth hour.[73] Contact relics of Christ were also thought to show living blood. For example, we are told that when Jane Mary of Maillé (d. 1414) had a relic of the true cross cut in two, blood flowed out.[74]

In devotional theology, the assumption that blood is alive is even clearer. However wide the range of description in late medieval affective piety, however diverse the devotional responses to the humanity of Christ, the chosen adjectives for blood (in contrast to those for wounds, body, heart, etc.) are "red," "fresh," "hot," "liquid," and above all "living." There is something quite particular to blood that is emphasized in this array of characteristics. In closing this chapter, I cite a few devotional texts in order to underline the point.

For example, in words attributed to an early fourteenth-century Dominican preacher to nuns, Conrad of Esslingen, the stress on hot, bubbling redness evokes the physical appearance of blood from a fresh wound.

> His holy blood is hot, it flows, it is red [*es ist heis, es ist flússig, es ist rot*] . . . through its heat [*hitze*] it burns off the rust of the soul. [Even he who has confessed and repented] continues to suffer the pains of the sinner, but the flow of the blood washes him, . . . the color of the blood restores him [*das weschet aber die flússe des blůtes . . . die farwe sines blůtes wider verwetet*] and renews the divine image that is impressed on the soul.[75]

However devotionally complex the references to *imago Dei* within the soul or to the rust of sin, the blood described here is not merely a metaphor for rubbing off, or stamping in, or making clean. What it evokes is Christ himself, glowing, throbbing, living, before the eyes of the soul. A more paradoxical evocation of the bloodflow of the crucifixion, the middle English *Prickynge of Love*, similarly exhorts:

> Open . . . with full faith the mouth of thy heart and let this blood drop into the marrow of thy soul, for know thee well that Christ's blood is yet as hot and as fresh [*als hot . . . als fresch*] as it was when he died on Good Friday and shall be so in holy church unto the day of doom.[76]

In this passage, *sanguis Christi* not only remains alive and fresh at the moment of the crucifixion; it is hot and liquid at the end of time, fusing past and future, death and resurrection, Christ here and Christ in glory.[77]

In all this, what is stressed is the immediacy and physicality of *sanguis Christi*. Warm and alive itself, it warms and liquefies the blood of sinners who have grown cold, hard, dried, and dead in selfishness and alienation.[78] It restores life to the *imago Dei* within the self, as liquid warmth softens hard wax. But it goes farther. It fuses with—becomes—the blood of the self. A simple Low German prayer for efficacy in preaching asks:

O sweetest heart of Jesus Christ, may the powerful and living flood of thy precious saving blood, out of thy torn veins, out of thy holy wounds, and out of thy broken, compassionate heart, stream through the veins of thy preacher for the salvation of the people so that it may announce to them everywhere the glowing and fiery word of God.[79]

Once again what is stressed is heat, flow, physical life. The blood that rushes through the preacher is the living Christ.

A little treatise on the passion of the Lord, attributed in the sole surviving manuscript (from about 1500–1510) to Dionysius the Carthusian (d. 1471) and probably authentic,[80] sums up the multiple senses of living blood I have attempted to uncouple and explicate here. It combines physiological, theological, exegetical, and devotional discourses, all put very simply and concisely. For this reason—and because Dionysius actually accompanied Nicholas of Cusa on his legation through Brandenburg and hence brings us back again to the locale of the Wilsnack host—it is worth quoting him in some detail.[81] Meditating on the lance prick, Dionysius stresses, as did Grosseteste, Christ's *choice* to shed blood—a choice made in order to show love. He emphasizes, as did Ludolf, his fellow Carthusian, and Gabriel Biel, that Christ shed *all* his blood and that such exsanguination was miraculous, because blood naturally coagulates a short time after the body's death.[82] He explains, as did Vincent of Beauvais following Augustine, that John carefully selected the verb "open," not "stab," because Christ's side is the door of salvation, opened as a gift not penetrated in violation; and, like Marguerite of Oingt, he underlines the parallel to birth—of Eve from Adam and of Church (and her sacraments) from Christ. He also stresses that such shedding (and the verb is repeatedly *effluere* or *effundere*) is a reproach to all who injure Christ, but especially to the eternally condemned Jews. Dionysius writes:

[The soldier with clouded eyes] took the lance and pierced [Christ's] heart. . . . But whether he did this of good intention, that is compassion, that he might die more quickly, or of evil, wanting to be part of his death, is not known. . . . Commonly the learned believe that he did it of a good and simple heart. . . . When the blood reached his hands he touched his eyes and immediately received his sight. . . . And thus, according to Chrysostom, there were two miracles relating to Christ's dead body, first, that at the touch of that noble liquid the blind soldier received his sight, and, second, that blood and water came out from a dead body [*de corpore mortuo*], which was done miraculously and contrary to nature, because naturally blood coagulates in a dead body so that it is not able to flow out naturally [*quod factum fuit miraculose et contra naturam, quia naturaliter in quolibet corpore mortuo sanguis coagulatur, ut naturaliter fluere non possit*]. And there was a watery element . . . for the body of Christ was composed of four elements. . . . Thus Christ had a true human body not a celestial or fantastical one as the heretics say. . . . For a fantastical body does not give forth blood and water. And he chose to pour out this blood from his dead body [*de corpore suo mortuo effluere voluit*] so that he might show the full and perfect love which he had for the redemption of the human race; hence he wished to retain no blood within his body [*nullum sanguinem in corpore suo retinere vellet*] but to pour it all out for our reconciliation [*sed totum pro nostra reconciliatione effundere*]. And note that Augustine says that John says that the soldier "opened" [*aperuit*] the side of Christ; he does not say "struck" or "wounded" [*percussit vel vulneravit*]. For truly a door, like a window, is opened, and thus the soldier opened for us the spiritual door through which the sacraments of the church flow, without which no one enters into true life. And just as from the side of Adam in his first sleep in paradise Eve was formed, so from the side of the second Adam was formed the church. Thus it is said that the sacraments came out, without which no one enters into life . . . redemption and ablution, that is, eucharist and baptism. . . . The opening of this side was prefigured in Genesis 6 when Noah at God's command made a window in the side of the ark. . . . Thus they saw him who was pierced [Zach. 12.10] and the Jews will see this in a future judgment, for the scars of Christ's five wounds are preserved in his body not only to certify his resurrection but also to convict at the last judgment those guilty of the sin of his death.[83]

Hence, to Dionysius, the blood of Christ's side is willed yet miraculous, liberating yet accusatory. I shall return in Chapter 8 to the elements of accusation and anti-Semitism. But what I wish to stress here are the multiple significances Dionysius gives to the fact that the blood is flowing and alive.

Noting the extravagantly physical emphasis devotional writing places on heat, redness, and liquidity (in explicit contrast to brownness or dryness) helps us to understand why it was so important to shrine attendants that blood relics and host miracles be fresh, shining, and red if they were claimed actually to be *Blut Christi*. The decay or change of miracle hosts or relics was not only a contradiction of the immutability of the God they revealed; it was also a contradiction of blood's essential characteristic: life. Hence, as we have seen, the brownness and dryness of holy matter could, paradoxically, be used by opponents such as Tocke to argue it was not *sanguis Christi* and by defenders such as the late fifteenth-century Franciscans to suggest it was blood but only inessential blood, not part of Christ's core human nature.

The vividly physical descriptions of devotional writing also help us to understand the sacramental overtones of blood piety so emphasized in recent scholarship. As many historians have noticed, descriptions of Christ's blood are not only evocations of his suffering love. In their emphasis on washing and inebriation, they are also references to baptism, penance, and eucharist.[84] Such references are very frequent in the fifteenth century; devotional writers often assert that all the sacraments flow from Christ's wounded side.[85] But the analysis I have given above helps us to see that the characteristic liquidness and redness of blood does more than facilitate its use as a symbol of cleansing, feeding, marking (or dyeing), and quenching thirst. The characteristics have a deeper meaning. They convey a sense that *sanguis Christi* is the true continuing—because living—presence of Christ here on earth. Whatever happens in the crucifixion to accomplish salvation (and there are other aspects of soteriology we have yet to consider), the event is not simply a death if the blood of Christ remains alive. In medieval medical theory, blood is the fluid from which all other body fluids are formed; it is the only body part that is in any sense capable of retaining life while separated from body. Hence blood is uniquely appropriate to represent life in and through death, Christ both gone to glory and present on earth. It images a power that can descend or fall away from, and yet remain in continuity with. Hence blood is not merely a reminder of the pain and humiliation of Christ's death. Nor is it only a metaphor that evokes the material stuff of the sacrament, whether water or wine. What blood means, to Mechtild of Magdeburg and David of Augsburg, as to the pilgrims at Wilsnack and Schwerin, is the power or life within it—a life that, to the fifteenth-century devout, is Christ himself.

Chapter 8
Blood as Separated and Shed

However much ecclesiastical authorities struggled with the fact that both blood relics and miracle hosts faded into cobwebs and dust, the tropes of fifteenth-century devotion stressed blood as alive—roseate, wet, and hot. But blood was also torn from, separated, poured out, shed. To Aquinas, blood was thus the special image of the passion [*sanguis specialius est imago dominicae passionis*].[1] As he put it:

> [The separate presence of the whole Christ under each species] is not without purpose. For . . . this serves to represent Christ's Passion, in which the blood was separate from the body; hence in the form for the consecration of the blood mention is made of its shedding.[2]

Or, as Gabriel Biel said, commenting on the mass: "In the sacrament is signified the blood of Christ as it is poured out as the price of our redemption [*ut effusus in precium nostre redemptionis*]."[3] But "blood cannot be separated without the wounding of the body."[4] In other words, blood is not only *sanguis*—inside blood, the stuff of life—it is also *cruor*—outside blood, blood *shed*. The verb associated with blood in the texts more than any other is *fundere, effundere*. Thus blood is not only life, continuation *of*; it is also death, separation *from*. It is time for me to turn to the other side of this paradox.

The Stress on Separation

We find an emphasis on blood as separation—a separation that is nonetheless also a vehicle of return—in both the cult of blood relics and in eucharistic theology. For example, the preface, *Sacrosancte dominice*, to the earliest texts (ca. 1200) concerning the blood relics of Mantua and Weingarten, makes clear that Christ's blood on earth is a part left behind that signifies the wholeness of resurrection [*resurrexionis et totius corporis Christi glorificationis*].

> For he, who could accomplish such an overturning of nature that, without any human commixture, he was born a man of a pure [*intacta*] virgin, was also able in the glory

of resurrection, having granted a part of this blood to those who love him [*suis dilectoribus huius cruoris parte indulta*], to take up his true body again [*verum . . . corpus resumere*] without injury to nature. . . .[5]

Or, as Gerhard of Cologne wrote some eighty years later in defense of the Weingarten relic: Christ rose entire, yet left behind his blood on earth to inflame us with his suffering.[6]

It was not only in German areas that the liturgy and polemic associated with blood relics stressed separation. The second of two French texts celebrating the blood relic at Fécamp stresses that it was not hidden under the species of bread as the sacrament is, but bright red just as when Christ shed it for our sake [*en sa fourme proprement, Vermel comment il le sengna*]. It was not necessary then, argues the poem, that all the blood rise with Jesus, for he wished to leave some for us, so that (in the words of Ephesians 2.13) those who are "afar off" may be made "nigh" by the blood of Christ.[7] Because poured out, separated, left behind, yet alive and red, the blood is a part that communicates to us the wholeness of heaven. According to such argument, relics are superior to eucharist exactly because the fact of presence in separation, of blood *shed*, is manifest not hidden.

Moreover, fourteenth- and fifteenth-century eucharistic theology agreed with Aquinas in emphasizing that it is blood more than body (host) that signifies the passion. This is because it is separated as well as united with body, shed as well as living. In his analysis of concomitance, for example, Thomas of Strasbourg (d. 1357) stressed that one Christ is present in the consecrated wafer and wine but adds: "[The fact of two species signifies] that, in the passion of Christ, his blood is separated from his body by effusion."[8] Following Aquinas, who emphasized that the cutting and killing of animals in sacrifice is an image of Christ's suffering and death,[9] Herveus Natalis (d. 1323) argued that the passion is signified more by blood than by body "and especially by blood poured out as from a wound [*maxime in sanguine effuso, in quo intelligitur vulneratio*]."[10] Gabriel Biel explained that the eucharist signifies both the incarnation and the passion. The incarnation (the joining of divine with human and of Christ with his church) is expressed especially in body under the species of bread; "the sacrament of the blood under the liquid species of wine," however, expresses "our redemption in the pouring out of blood."[11] As I pointed out above, the bread of the eucharist had, ever since the patristic period, been a symbol of gathering into one, of incorporation. Many grains of wheat make one bread. But in eucharistic poetry and commentary from the twelfth century on, the wine, which had earlier been an image of incorporation too (many grapes make one wine) became increasingly a symbol of separation, rupture, and violation.[12]

Blood as Drops

In all this, the attention to blood not just as streams but also as drops is so striking as to need exploration. What was at stake in the debates over blood relics—and sometimes over what appeared on bleeding hosts as well—was after all the status of bits, that is, discrete drops or globules, left behind. Cult therefore induced consideration of *sanguis Christi* as *guttae*. But long before the fierce fourteenth- and fifteenth-century theological debates over flecks on hosts or stuff in monstrances, indeed even before thirteenth-century defenses of relics such as Gerhard of Cologne's, devotion to Christ's blood as drops was widespread in the piety of those who preferred private devotion to pilgrimage. A stress on blood drops runs throughout several of the texts analyzed in Chapter 1 and in the preoccupation with Christ's complete exsanguination discussed in Chapter 7.[13]

Explicit reference to drinking discrete drops of Christ's blood appeared quite early in the development of devotion to the humanity and passion of Jesus. In circa 1060, the reformer Peter Damian, contemplating alone in his cell, saw Christ "pierced with nails, hanging on the cross" and wrote, in what may be the first example of such visionary drinking: "with my mouth I eagerly tried to catch the dripping blood."[14] In the late twelfth century, an English monk from Evesham abbey was found as if lifeless on Good Friday with "the balls of his eyes and his nose wet with blood." Once recovered, the monk recounted to his brothers a vision of the cross.

> While I was kneeling before the image and was kissing it on the mouth and eyes, I felt some drops falling gently on my forehead. When I removed my fingers, I discovered from their color that it was blood. I also saw blood flowing from the side of the image on the cross, as it does from the veins of a living man when he is cut for blood-letting. I do not know how many drops I caught in my hand as they fell. With the blood I devoutly anointed my eyes, ears and nostrils. Afterward—if I sinned in this I do not know—in my zeal I swallowed one drop of it, but the rest, which I caught in my hand, I was determined to keep.[15]

The monk of Evesham's desire to take *sanguis Christi* literally and experientially between his lips finds parallels that are only slightly more metaphorical in those meditations on Christ's flagellation in which the devout are told to imagine the spurting blood falling into their mouths.[16] In the passage from Peter Dorlandus quoted in Chapter 7, Mary explains that the blood of the scourging is made available to the faithful to drink with mouths and hearts.[17] Nor should we forget the stress in flagellant spirituality on blood drops as washing and absolving those on whom they fall.[18]

Alongside the well-known affectivity Dorlandus describes, late medieval religion was, as is also well known, obsessed with quantification. The obsession reflects an enthusiasm for counting and measuring found throughout the society,[19] and some of the excitement about enumerating wounds, drops, and prayers is clearly owing to the general late medieval determination to quantify everything—virtues, merits, and credits toward salvation (see Plate 32). This mentality is reflected in a well-known story used by late medieval preachers that not only underlines the soteriological significance of Christ's blood but also considers it as a discrete unit of payment: a dying monk, seeing in a vision devils and angels weighing his deeds, begs for one drop of *sanguis Christi* to be added to the scales on the side of his virtues in order to effect his salvation.[20] In a more theological version of the same sense of soteriological bookkeeping, a bull of Clement VI in 1343 repeats the platitude long attributed to Bernard of Clairvaux that one drop of Christ's blood was enough to save the world.[21]

More is involved, however, than an enthusiasm for quantity and quantification. There is no stress on counting up credits or merits in the theology of the late fourteenth-century devotional writer Julian of Norwich, but the same sense of Christ's blood as discrete, round bits is found in her own description of her vision of the crucifixion:

> The great drops of blood fell from beneath the crown like pellets, looking as if they came from the veins, and as they issued they were a brownish red, for the blood was very thick, and as they spread they turned bright red. . . . The copiousness resembles the drops of water which fall from the eaves of a house after a great shower of rain, falling so thick that no human ingenuity can count them. And in their roundness as they spread over the forehead they were like herring's scales.
>
> At the time three things occurred to me: The drops were round like pellets as the blood issued, they were round like a herring's scales as they spread, they were like raindrops off a house's eaves, so many that they could not be counted. This vision was living and vivid and hideous and fearful and sweet and lovely. . . .[22]

It is worth noting not only that the droplike quality of the blood was striking to Julian herself ("round like pellets as they issued . . . round as they spread . . .") but also that it appeared to change from brownish—that is, the color of drying or dead blood—to a vibrant red. Thus Julian underlines the paradox of "issued" yet "living," which she explicitly glosses with other paradoxes: vivid and hideous, fearful and sweet.

As I pointed out at the opening of Chapter 7, devotional objects from the fourteenth and fifteenth centuries also underline drops. In a number of statues that survive from Germany (both the Rhineland and areas farther east), Christ lies across the lap of his grieving mother and displays his wounds in a presentation that gives special emphasis to the blood as large, round pellets (see frontispiece and Plates 15–17).[23] In some of these pietàs (for example those from Fritzlar, Wetzlar, Leubus, and Marienstern), not only does the hand wound drip in large star-shaped or petal-like rosettes but the arms and legs as well are covered with little bunches of bright red drops, whose roundness and fullness are emphasized in high relief carving (see Plates 15 and 16).[24] The Fritzlar pietà, in its medieval form, actually had blood drops of papier-mâché affixed to the body. In panel paintings too, the droplike quality of blood is stressed. The Arnstadt resurrection altar from Thuringia (ca. 1430), for example, shows a rising Christ, crowned with a kind of tiara, who displays five neat rosettes as wounds (Plate 18).[25] Even in depictions that (unlike the Rhineland pietàs) are not especially expressionistic or violent, and in which the wounds do not appear to be rosettes or bunches of droplets, fifteenth-century painters sometimes stress the droplike character of blood, which hangs in encapsulated, pendular red globes from Christ's hands or feet and is suspended above, not falling into, a receiving chalice held by angels (see Plates 19 and 20).[26] In the Bohemian crucifixion of circa 1430 (Plates 20 and 21), the size and shape of the descending drop are emphasized by the fact that it hovers over a tiny chalice whose lip is only just big enough to receive it.

Art historians have usually taken such blood drops (especially when they occur in clusters) to represent grapes (and hence the eucharist) or flowers (hence possibly the Virgin as "Hortus conclusus," or the rosary).[27] In the case of several pietàs, the visual parallel to flowers, which also appear on the socle or the Virgin's mantle, is clearly intended.[28] But one must be careful about extrapolation from the visual to the textual or doctrinal.[29] The pietà from Anröchte near Soest, for example, has blood drops descending from the side wound that are so large as to be more like icicles than petals or grapes (Plate 17), yet art historians continue to describe such wounds as eucharistic.[30] Whatever analogies the shapes suggest, however, the visual impact is above all to stress the multiplicity of what extrudes—the separateness of the units of what is poured out. The clusters on the Röttgen, Fritzlar, Anröchte, Marienstern, and Wetzlar pietàs, whether the elements are rounded or oblong, make vivid both the size and the discreteness of those elements.

There are, it is true, late medieval paintings where Christ's blood is drawn as red ribbons and some very late sculptures in which blood is actually represented with red wires.[31] In such depictions, blood is sometimes a band joining adherent and savior. For example, in the Soest Gregorymass I discussed in Chapter 1, the streams of blood—although they break away from the Christ figure to the poor souls rising in the churchyard—nonetheless seem visually to bring life from Christ to the faithful (see Plate 3). In some depictions, the red line of blood is, as we shall see, an arrow of accusation. But depictions, such as the Röttgen pietà, that show blood as drops tend to underline its separateness from the body that spills it forth. The clusters of pellets descending from gaping wounds seem to image not so much an opening into, as a spilling out of, body.

Some of these treatments of *sanguis Christi* as drops, or spilled, relate to a piety of purgatory in which merits are accumulated. The faithful amassed benefits for themselves or others as they used the number of drops Christ shed to count off prayers owed. Other blood-drop meditations express experiential devotion to Christ's suffering humanity, penetrated, tortured, and killed. But something deeper is at stake, I think, than simply blood as an image of merits or a locus of affective response. What is important is, on the one hand, the separateness of blood—the discontinuity of the pellets from the body out of which they drop—and, on the other, the fact that the disconnected drops continue, as Julian of Norwich said, alive and red.[32] Blood was the only part or bit of the ever-living Christ that was, according to Scriptural accounts and patristic theology, separated from him.[33] Although later piety sometimes treated the holy foreskin as a similar left-behind body part, this devotion was far rarer. And even devotion to the foreskin, as an aspect of devotion to the circumcision, was in a sense a blood devotion.[34] In any case, no matter how much controversialists might fight over the authenticity of blood relics or the fate of blood shed in the *triduum*, blood was the only aspect of Christ that could claim both to be cut off from him and to continue his presence. Hence blood imaged and evoked a Christ left-behind. As such, it offered comfort or contact. Yet it was also a result of violence against Christ. It breached his body. Thus it was accusation and reproach.[35] Washwater that cleansed the faithful, blood was also a stain that fell upon them, coloring or marking them as guilty. In order to explain the complexity of blood-drop images as found even in quite simple, vernacular piety, I turn for a moment to a text I mentioned in Chapter 1, the *Revelation of the Hundred Pater Nosters.*

The *Revelation of the Hundred Pater Nosters*

Because the *Hundred Pater Nosters* comes to us accompanied by the little story of a husbandman whose ox was cured by the accompanying prayer, the meditation probably expresses themes that were actually accessible to pious laypeople in the fifteenth century. A number of these themes are important for my purposes. First, the meditations, although ostensibly a devotion to the seven bleedings of Christ (intended to parallel the seven days of the week), make repeated reference to the blood as drops. The text begins: "Worsship not only of oon or two dropes but more in the worsship of / euery drope of alle his blessed blode / must needs be of excellent vartu & / able to purchace not only thees / v specialle graces aforsaid but also / more grace and more mercy than euer / heart may thynke or tonge telle."[36] A second emphasis found in this particular quotation is important as well. The meditation is not merely an exhortation to experiential participation in the sufferings of Christ; there is a soteriology of ransom here. Christ's blood pays a price for us—purchases—our salvation. Or as the text later puts it: it is "the goulde that / he payed for thyn Raenson when / thou were lost and endited and condemned / as a theffe to perpetuelle prison. . . ."[37] Notwithstanding the stress on payment and punishment, however, the text is a classic example of affective piety. The adherent is to peer into Christ's bloody face, lie down with his whipped body, and "yf thou cannot Remembre / the angwyssche of hys payne take / and pynche thy self by the finger / or som other place of thy body And / so by the felyng of thyn owen lytell payne thou shalt be better Remembred / of hys grete. . . ."[38] Look at your hands, exhorts the author, and think how it would hurt to be crucified; then remember that you deserve it and he does not. As Bernard said, Christ would never have died for you except that he loved you better than he loved himself.[39]

Alongside traditional soteriological references to ransoms and debts, on the one hand, and examples of love, on the other, we also find a concern with the details of Christ's physiology that we have come to recognize as characteristic of the fifteenth century. Even in this simple little text, we find references to "the philosopher's" theories of the humors to explain that salvific blood is not superfluous, nutritive blood but the blood of what the university theologians called *veritas humanae naturae.* A propos the bloody sweat of the garden, the author writes:

> Remembre what the / [p]hilosofre saieth, he saieth that the mater / [of] [t]he swettyng commyth properly of the / [superf]luite of humours in euery body But / [in] [ou]re lordes body might neuere be eny / [superfl]uite, Therfore hys swettyng was / [more] of bloode than of water, and Remembre / [how] mervellous a payne and how grievous and / [ang]oyssche he had inwarde in his saule / that swette outewardes in his body bothe / bloode and water.[40]

The blood that falls on the sinner, pays his ransom, and enflames his love is thus Christ's essential blood. It must be his core, nothing superfluous. It must all be shed. Repeatedly the meditation exhorts: "say thy hundred pater nosters in the worsship of all the dropes of bloode . . ." But despite the emphasis on the pouring forth of all Christ's blood, his bleeding dry, there is a distinct sense here that part is whole. It is enough to worship a part. Discussing the circumcision (the first bleeding of the seven), the author advises: "[keep] thy mynde euere asmoche as thu mayst ou that blessed Childe or on dyuerse / [part]es of hys fayre body or on hys / [pre]cyous bloode." The blood, like other body parts, stands here *pars pro toto*, as it does even more explicitly in the meditation on the flagellation, where the believer is urged to think that, when "a parte" of the blood falls on his face or clothes at the strokes of the scourge, he should begin his hundred Pater Nosters in "worsship of all the dropes of bloode that he shedde. . . ."[41] No matter how simple the images, it is clearly crucial, in this sort of piety, that the blood *is* Christ (his essential, not superfluous, life and physicality), and that *all* of it is *shed* (that is, separated). It is also crucial that *any part is* the whole; what falls on the believer is all of Christ poured out. Like the blood relics and host miracles many people, both learned and unlearned, rejected, the blood of devotion stands for whatever it is that Christ, although gone away in resurrection, nonetheless leaves behind here on earth.

This leads me to my final point about the *Revelation of the Hundred Pater Nosters*. Despite the love it engenders and the presence it provides, the separated blood is bloodshed. At the end of his evocation of the side wound, the author explains: "forgete / not that yf thou have Right thou / shuldest be endyted for thys good / lorde dethe / For thou art the cause of hys dethe."[42] At the same period, both across the Channel and in England, we find evidence of quite extravagant and guilty identification with the sufferings of Christ.[43] No matter how much blood imagery may carry the sense of a presence that remains behind to comfort or provide access, what the image of blood as drops or particles conveys most forcefully is accusation and reproach.

Accusation and Reproach

As the *Hundred Pater Nosters* makes clear, the blood piety of the fifteenth century never forgets the horror of bloodshed. Blood poured out is killing as well as birthing. In this context, it is important to remember that the basic blood taboo of late medieval canon law is the interdiction of clerical blood spilling. Clergy were forbidden to practice forms of medicine such as surgery or leeching in which blood was let. Church courts were prohibited from direct participation in any form of evidence-gathering or execution that spilled blood; hence cases involving torture and execution were "relaxed to the secular arm."[44] Although there are in the writings of canonists and encyclopedists vestiges of menstrual taboos, the basic blood pollution necessitating reconsecration of sacred space was the blood of male violence.[45] Churches offered sanctuary to those who were pursued by enemies in feud or warfare or even legal processes and had to be purified when contaminated by violent blood.[46]

Medieval literature, both secular and religious, is full of stories of blood as accusation. Church walls were said to erupt in blood when sanctuary was violated.[47] Relics bled to protest division as well as to assert sacrality.[48] Moreover, it was widely believed that the corpse of a murdered man or woman would bleed in the presence of its murderer. Alain Boureau has argued that some of the urgency of disputes at Paris and Oxford in the late thirteenth century over the nature of body stemmed from the story that the bones of Thomas of Cantilupe bled to accuse archbishop Peckham of having denied him justice. In a quodlibet of 1283, Roger Marston tried to argue that such "cruentation" might be the natural result of the soul's experience of cruelty, which affected the body.[49]

Against this background, it is easy to understand why *Blut Christi*, separated blood, was conceptualized as blood shed against, as well as for. It accused as well as liberated. Already in the later thirteenth century, Mechtild of Magdeburg asserted that the wounds of Christ will bleed until there is no more human sin—that is, they will bleed, accusing sinners, until Judgment Day itself. Margaret of Cortona agreed.[50] More and more frequently in the fourteenth and fifteenth centuries, blood named the perpetrator. As Hus put it, blood cries out. A miniature and the accompanying dialogue in the well-known fifteenth-century Carthusian Miscellany, Brit. Lib. Add. MS 37049, illustrates the theme. It shows the bleeding Man of Sorrows, who offers his heart to a little lay figure kneeling below and complains: "O man unkynde, hafe in mynde, my paynes smert. Beholde and see, that is for the, percyd my hert. . . ."[51] (see Plate 24). In both Germany and England, images of laypeople crucifying Christ by profaning the Sabbath, cursing, or blaspheming (the iconographic motif known as the *Feiertagschristus* or "Christ crucified by the sins of the world") are found on the walls of churches in the fifteenth century. In graphic reproach, the tools or mouths of working people are linked by little ropes of red to the torn and bleeding body of Christ[52] (see Plate 25). As I suggested above, even the depiction of blood as stream or ribbon, which sometimes represents access or bond, evokes accusation here: the thin red line points like an arrow to the perpetrator of sin.[53]

Indeed we can see a tendency to move from love to blame if we look at the figure of Longinus, the soldier who lanced Christ's side with a spear. Over the course of the fourteenth and fifteenth centuries, the image changed. Understood in the early Middle Ages as a penitent sinner who knelt to ask forgiveness and was healed under the cross by Christ's blood, Longinus later came to be seen as the facilitator of redemption who opened Christ's side so that the saving blood might descend. In his exposition on the passion of the Lord, Dionysius the Carthusian (or his follower) could still observe that we do not know whether Longinus acted from compassion to end Christ's suffering or out of evil, "wanting to be part of his death." But Dionysius thinks his motives were good. Whatever these motives, however, Longinus came in many fifteenth-century interpretations to stand for accused humankind.[54] Although in the *felix culpa* of the lance prick he spilled saving blood, Longinus represented the human sins that attack Christ.

Thus the lance and indeed the entire *arma Christi* (the arms or instruments of Christ's passion) came to have new meaning. Frequently represented in art and meditated upon in sermons and devotional poetry, these *arma*—the nails, thorns, flail, lance, sponge, and so forth—carried a broad range of meanings, to some of which I shall return[55] (see Plates 28 and 29). What is important for my purposes here is to understand that they were not simply a means of evoking compassion at Christ's suffering or gratitude for the salvation it offered. By the later Middle Ages, they were major inducers of guilt as well, for they were to be meditated upon as the weapons ordinary human beings daily wield against God. As such they became accusatory as well as salvific and were sometimes described not only as our attack on God but also as God's attack on humankind. In the later thirteenth century, the author of the immensely popular *Golden Legend* argued that the *arma* show Christ's mercy and justify his anger, for they remind us that not all people are willing to accept his sacrifice. The author of the *Speculum humanae salvationis* thundered in the fourteenth century: "All Christ's weapons are aimed against sinners."[56] We are the Christ killers. The enemy is us! Internalizing such guilt, the Carthusian John of Torralba (d. 1578) wrote, in a prayer to be offered before confession, "I have crucified you," and pled for one drop of the saving blood to fall on each sinner's suffering soul.[57]

Increasingly this guilt was projected outward onto Jews, dissidents, and heretics. As early as the eighth century, the wounds of Christ had been given multiple significances. Bede enumerated these. The wounds were proof of Christ's death, intercession to God the Father, demonstration of love, reproach to the evil and the damned, and a trophy of victory.[58] By the thirteenth century, texts regularly expanded the fourth category, that of reproach, to target the Jews. A German sermon explained that the purpose of the wounds was to demonstrate at the Last Judgment the guilt of the Jews.[59] Bonaventure wrote, in a paean of praise to Christ's blood:

Consider therefore how great was the impiety of the Jews, who thirsted for the innocent blood of the one who loved them so much that he wished to pour out his blood for them, and how great was the devotion of Christ, who so pitied the impious that he poured out his blood for those who wished to shed his blood.[60]

The Provençal mystic Marguerite of Oingt, in a different enumeration of Christ's wounds, wrote that Jesus held a book for teaching in which the white letters told his life, the silver ones detailed his blood poured out for us, the black described "the blows and slaps and filthy things the Jews threw in his face and on his noble body . . . [until it] looked like a leper's."[61] In a Dürer woodcut of 1510, the *Schmerzensmann* accuses all Christians, with the overtones of anti-Semitism we find in Paltz's blood theology as well:

I bear these cruel wounds for thee, O man!
And I heal thy frailty with my blood.
. . . .
But thou dost not thank me. With thy sins thou often tearest open my wounds.
I am still lashed for thy misdeeds.
Have done now.
I once suffered great torment from the Jews.
Now, friend, let peace be between us.[62]

In most stories of host desecration, as we have seen, bleeding is protest and accusation. Whether abused by the "superstitious" as charm or amulet, ritually misused or spilled by careless priests, tossed away by robbers, doubted by the simple or the skeptical, or supposedly deliberately attacked by unbelievers, heretics, or Jews, the mistreated object bleeds in protest. In the sixteenth-century account of the Wasserleben-Halberstadt blood, for example, the initial bleeding protests the female communicant's removal of the consecrated host from her mouth at communion; a subsequent bleeding protests the translation to Halberstadt. A parallel story from Bergen in Holland tells of hosts that survived a great flood in a pyx but turned to a heap of bloody stuff when they were not properly revered.[63] Parallel to the Wilsnack legend, the Bergen hosts bleed both to vindicate their claim to miraculous triumph over water and to accuse those who fail to believe that claim.

As Peter Browe has established, early eucharistic miracles tended to be temporary revelations of Christ, usually without blood; such temporary visions were often blessings or rewards for devotion. But enduring host transformations (*Dauerwunder*) were either instruction or, increasingly in the fourteenth and fifteenth centuries, punishment or accusation.[64] After the first Jewish host-desecration charge at Paris in 1290, such *Dauerwunder* became more and more frequently tales of the pouring out of blood. Even where not directed against Jews or heretics, *Dauerwunder* were often understood to accuse. Eberhard Waltmann and the Erfurt theologians who opposed the Wilsnack miracle hosts argued that blood miracles, even where genuine, are signs of God's wrath not his favor. Blood was proof that the divine was present and that evil had been done to it. It accused the perpetrator and called for the community to avenge the desecration and expiate the sin. In his controversy with Waltmann, John of Capistrano praised the blood miracle of Daroca for inciting to war "as blood incites elephants."[65] The blood that saves is also a blood that calls for revenge.[66]

The paradox of simultaneous accusation and redemption was, as confessors and preachers knew full well, not simply theological and devotional but pastoral. The pouring out so emphasized in sermons and in popular poetry and prose, violates the glory and impassibility of Christ's resurrection. The charge that sin daily crucifies Jesus—thundered repeatedly from pulpits—implies something exegetically and theologically quite dubious: it implies that Christ is daily killed anew. And however useful such assertions might be homiletically to bring Christians into the congregation and the confessional, they patently contradict Hebrews 9.28: "So also Christ was offered *once* to exhaust the sins of many. The second time he shall appear without sin to them that expect him unto salvation [emphasis added]."

The challenge of Hebrews 9.28 was a problem with which theologians struggled. After the enormous amount of ink spilled over transubstantiation, the eucharistic issue most often discussed between the thirteenth century and the Council of Trent was the conflict between a victim offered in every mass and one offered once for all on Calvary.[67] Moreover, as the examples cited just above suggest, the faithful and their priests oscillated between confidence in the blood poured out once and guilt induced by its constant pouring in response to sin. They were caught between the immutability of glory already achieved and the price eternally being paid (for which humankind was eternally responsible).

Why then this stress on life forever poured out? After all, as a priest pointed out to Margery Kempe, in an effort to quell her guilt and grief: "Lady, Jesus died a long time ago."[68] Techniques of distancing were possible. Yet late medieval Christians, dissident as well as orthodox, increasingly exaggerated the bloody elements of a gospel story in which blood was not especially prominent. Why did they lodge what Gertrude the Great and Johannes von Paltz called an abominable thing—a symbol of murder and destruction—at the heart of redemption? In other words, we return to the question: why blood?

In answering this question, I take two steps. First, in the next section, I summarize the point to which we have come in understanding blood as symbol. In this analysis, I draw extensively on the discussion of theological debates in Part II above, as well as on the analysis of blood piety in Part III and the description of pilgrimage and cult in Part I. Thus the section below serves as a summary of my argument so far. In my final section, I suggest that there is a deeper question we still need to explore.

Blood as Symbol

For the past hundred years, scholars have tended to see affective devotion to the passion of Christ—that is, emotional identification with his physical and spiritual suffering and with that of his mother Mary—as the central characteristic of late medieval religiosity. Embedded within it, they have found a paradox of comfort and reproach. In a sense, what I have done in Chapters 6, 7, and 8 is deepen this paradox, arguing that blood was central in late medieval devotion exactly because it represented more than simply love and guilt. As piety became, from the twelfth century on, increasingly affective and experiential and much of the most creative grappling with basic religious issues was done in sermons, vision literature, meditations, and prayers, the deployment of images and symbols became an important locus—perhaps *the* important locus—of theology. The particular language used in fifteenth-century cult, learned discourse, and devotion expressed something quite specific about the saving action of Christ when it underlined the separated discreteness of a part that was nonetheless whole, the bubbling, roseate, and organic life of an immutable deity, the complete exsanguination of a Christ whose tiniest particle would in itself save the world. In order to explain how blood as symbol encapsulated and gave expression to the basic religious assumptions of the later Middle Ages, I reprise some material touched on above.

Change was a basic theme of scholastic theologians. It resounds in their repetitious debates over the exact form of eucharistic presence: transubstantiation? consubstantiation? annihilation? It is the basic philosophical problem dealt with in their complex theories of how embodied identity might survive or return in resurrection.[69] Matter and body—although (and also because) redeemed—were highly problematic. Anxiety about the threat of *mutatio* echoes behind the contradictory instructions of spiritual directors that the faithful should visualize the details of Christ's suffering yet hold suspect any special favors he might grant in visions. More than an expression of misogyny (although it was that), late medieval literature on the discerning of spirits expressed a deep suspicion of exactly the bodily experience it also valued. Identifying (as the faithful were exhorted to do) with the passion of an incarnate Christ might seem to trap both Christ and the faithful in a matter that was by definition mutable, passible, forever *in potentia*.[70] The same privileging and denying of change undergirds the almost schizoid attempts of ecclesiastical authorities and theorists simultaneously to authenticate relics, uncover relic fraud, and deny that divine presence can inhere in matter. Increasingly authorities and the ordinary devout both insisted and doubted that objects manifest God. The ambivalence was acted out in devotions and pilgrimages to relics and hosts that were held to erupt in blood to express divine presence (that is, to change) and yet had to remain liquid and red (that is, unchanged) if their sacrality was to endure.

As the learned theologians Bernard, Aquinas, Bansleben, and Bremer, as well as innumerable popular devotions, all made clear, God cannot change. Yet his universe is afflicted by change—the physical corruption of decay and the moral corruption of sin—and, as much recent interpretation stresses, the fourteenth and fifteenth centuries were profoundly concerned with both. A vast penitential system, whose rules stretched into the next world via purgatory, was constructed to expiate and alleviate moral *corruptio*.[71] A new concern not only with dying but also with the significance, physical as well as moral, of the decay of the corpse was reflected in such well-known artifacts as Dances of Death and *transi* tombs, as well as in practices such as partible burial.[72] In such a context, the canceling of decay and restoration of changelessness (virtue, immortality, perfection) was a fundamental soteriological challenge. Blood—understood as separated yet alive—was an earthly image of change (matter, body, decay, death) that has been redeemed.

We find a particularly clear example of these complicated symbolic valences in the same Gertrude whose hagiographer quoted her outraged cry: blood is abominable. In another passage in the *Legatus*, the hagiographer reports that Gertrude received a vision in which Jesus plunged a host into the heart of God and withdrew it "rosy red, as though it were stained red with blood [*roseam . . . velut sanguine rubricatam*]." Gertrude was deeply troubled, because "red symbolizes suffering [*passionem*]" and God the Father can never be marked red with any trace of suffering. But she received no answer to the confusion into which her vision threw her. A little later, however, she saw the Lord descending by a scarlet ladder and remembered Wisdom 6.20: "incorruption bringeth near to God." The passage, which associates blood with both access and incorruption (moral and physical), suggests a desperate need for something separated from God (a *red* something, present here below and linked to human mutability) that nonetheless lifts the seeking Christian into the wholeness and oneness of the divine.[73]

Blood served to express this paradox of separation that provides access—detestable breaching that is a ladder to God—because of what it was understood to be as physical and physiological fact.[74] Bloodshed was dying and violation; it was also source, origin, and birth. *Sanguis* and *cruor*, blood was ambiguous because profoundly bipolar. Each term had both positive and negative connotations in the fifteenth century: the shedding of *cruor* could be heroic, health-bringing, criminal, or polluting; *sanguis* could be congested and unhealthy, or the very stuff of life itself. Although there are certainly gendered aspects to medieval understandings of blood, there was nonetheless, behind any male/female dichotomies, the deeper paradox: blood—all blood—signified life and death.

When it was separated, shed, blood could disappear, dissipate, decay. It flowed out in pain and violence; its presence threatened and polluted. Viscous and clinging, blood dirtied. It symbolized loss, filth, and destruction. Clerics were forbidden to shed it. Corpses might bleed to accuse their murderers. Yet, as fluid, blood cleansed. Phlebotomy—leeching or "bleeding"—was a basic medical procedure to cure disease and bring the body into balance.[75] Menstrual blood could cloud mirrors but it also averted locusts. The blood of virgins, of executed criminals, and of martyrs had talismanic qualities. Moreover blood had life even in separation. As Pius II reported Dominican theologians to argue, blood is kinship and heirs—not merely lineage but, more broadly, relationship.[76] The blood of Cain that cried out for revenge, like the blood of heroes demanding burial, was the heritage and continuity of family and clan. Indeed, as Catherine of Siena, Marguerite of Oingt, Julian of Norwich, and John of Capistrano all, in their various ways, asserted, blood is not only the occasion and stuff of life, it is life itself. Birthing blood is blood joyous in pain: it torments and separates, yet enables life and survival. In medieval physiological theory, the human child *is* in some sense the mother's blood, formed from the bloody stuff in her womb. Semen, which carries animating force, is processed blood too. Blood poured out is then a risk of death, but it is also future generations. Hence blood symbolizes both the destruction and the continuation of the personal and the social self. Natural blood is the ultimate synecdoche: the human part that *is* the human and the social whole.

Piety and theology picked up the synecdoche. What throbbed under the cry "Blood of Christ, save me!" was the sense—explicitly articulated by Gerhard of Cologne—that each particle was the whole of Christ. Even when poured out in acts of breaching and violence, blood was a means of access and continuity. Spilled at the prick of the lance, *sanguis Christi* was nonetheless the living Christ. We have seen, in both the Wilsnack and the Rome debates, how much it mattered to the theorists to get this exactly right. Some took "blood" to refer to all its particles and others to its essence or *veritas*; but all insisted that saving blood was in some sense both shed and alive. All affirmed *Blut*

Christi to be with God now in glory yet present on earth in every mass. Left behind and ascended with Christ, cut off yet liquid and red, blood imaged the presence of the living Christ who had gone away, the absent presence that was at the heart of fifteenth-century Christianity.

Yet Christ had died, as humans die. Guibert of Nogent, Francis de Mayronis, Peter Dorlandus, and John of Capistrano knew what every pilgrim knew as well: the basic *mutatio*, the ultimate *putrefactio*, is death itself. In all fifteenth-century theological formulations, Christ's blood is separated from his body in the passion (and to some theologians it is sundered from his humanity and divinity as well). There is real partition, violation, loss. As Catherine of Siena put it: the blood is placed at hand *by its separation*. Or as Pius II reported the Dominicans to argue at Rome: ". . . only after it had been shed did blood have the power of . . . absolution."[77] It is insofar as it is poured *out*, mutable, cut off, that Christ's blood represents, incorporates, ours. Blood is then an earthly image of change that has been redeemed, of part that, though whole, is also and forever part. As theologians emphasized and artists depicted, Christ's scars were not erased. To some poets, such as Mechtild of Magdeburg, and some artists, such as Hans Multscher, they were not even healed but continued bloody and hot to the end of time. Mutable *immutabilitas* remained, written on the body of God.[78] Hence blood—with all the complexity the fifteenth century invested in it—seemed to work better than any other material symbol to express the paradox inherent in the need to reconcile mutable and immutable through the mutation and separation of the immutable itself.[79] As John of Capistrano asserted, it was necessary for salvation that "the immutable and unchangeable God steadfastly and immutably united human nature to himself and not without blood."[80]

The Deeper Paradox: Sacrifice

Something is missing, however, in putting the issue this way. For blood, living and shed, is not only, in fourteenth- and fifteenth-century theology, a symbol of the paradoxes of immutability and decay, presence and absence, matter and immortality. What Dionysius the Carthusian and James of Klusa invoke in their blood devotions is something they can offer and receive, something that spills onto them, marks them, lifts them up. They want not just to find meaning in the blood; they want to do something with it. Indeed, as is well known, late medieval piety was characterized by a frenzy for agency. All those devotions to numbers of drops, all those indulgences collected, were (as later Protestant polemicists asserted) frantic efforts to act in the interest of one's own salvation. Behind the paradoxes of divided wholeness and spilled life found in texts such as Dionysius's or James's lie not only an ontology but also a theory of access to God. Indeed, the specific nature of the paradoxes reveals the theory. The ubiquitous references to *effundere* and *spargere*, to Leviticus and Hebrews, are clues. Perhaps because the language seems so traditional, scholars have ignored it. But if we pay attention, a soteriological theory—often unmentioned, largely untheorized, and immensely consequential—is reflected everywhere in the texts I have cited above. It is the theory of sacrifice. The wonderful blood of the lamb—shed, sprinkled on the altar, and lifted to God—is the instrument of salvation.

To look back at a few examples. When Beatrice of Nazareth's biographer describes her as receiving blood along with the consecrated wafer, it is called the "price" of redemption, "sprinkled" as "drops" in her heart.[81] When Catherine of Siena herself writes of blood as the humanity of Christ kneaded into the Godhead, she begins by saying: "'[Christ], you gave us life. By bearing our iniquities with patience, you punished them in your own body on the wood of the cross [*le ponesti in sul legno della croce sopra el corpo tuo*]!' In his blood, . . . he created us anew to grace [*ci creò a Grazia*]. His blood . . . clothed us again in grace."[82] And Catherine repeatedly glosses blood as sacrifice.

> . . . this gentle Word [Christ] is like the eagle . . . [who] looks into the sun of the Father's eternal will, and there sees his creatures' sin and rebellion. . . . In his obedience he chooses to fulfill in us the Father's truth, to restore grace in us, deliver us from servitude to the devil (which gives eternal death), and lead us back to serve our Creator. . . . So he flies up with his prey to the heights of his most holy cross, and there he eats it in indescribable and anguished desire. In his own person he punishes our sins [*e sopra sè punisce le nostre iniquitadi*] by suffering physically, and with his will he makes satisfaction [*satisfacendo*] by his hatred and contempt for sin. With the power of the divine nature that is in him he offers the sacrifice of his blood to his Father [*porse il sacrificio del sangue suo al padre*], and his sacrifice is accepted.[83]

German devotional writers of the fourteenth century sounded the theme as well. For example, Margaret Ebner of Engelthal prayed thus at the elevation of the host, joining herself to the priest's offering, which itself is joined to Christ's.

> I say, when the priest holds Him [Christ] in his hands . . . "I greet you, Lord of the whole world, only Word of the Father in heaven, only true sacrifice and only living flesh and only totally divine and truly human one. . . ." And at the lifting up of the chalice: "I thank you . . . that you have changed bread and wine into your Holy Body and Blood, that you . . . have deigned . . . to be offered to your Father by the priest to your eternal honor to console, help and sanctify us. . . . Now offer Yourself today, oh

Lord, for all the evil we have done against you and for all the good we have failed to do."[84]

Mechtild of Magdeburg, in pondering the living blood that flowed from Christ's side after death, asked why her Lord suffered such distress. Christ answered that his earlier suffering did not "satisfy my Father [*minem vatter genuͤgete also nit*]."

For all the poverty, all the toil, and all the suffering and humiliation are a knocking at the gate of heaven up to the time when my heart's blood poured onto this earth [*an die stunde, das min herzeblůt uf dise erden gos*]. Only then was heaven opened.[85]

Even in the prayers of the cryptoflagellants of Thuringia, the blood of ordinary Christians is not so much ascetic self-discipline as reparation; it is "good for"—that is, it counts for—salvation. Such devotion to blood is not merely a response to heightened descriptions of agony or proffered evidence of passionate love. Blood "satisfies," but only when "poured out" upon altar or earth. As Catherine says, salvation requires *il sacrificio del sangue.*[86]

The texts of Engelthal achieved only limited circulation, and by the time Mechtild's gorgeous devotional writing began to circulate widely, it had become anonymous and often fragmentary.[87] But Catherine's blood piety was influential and imitated in the German north. Moreover, sacrificial theology hardly needed to be propagated, or argued for. References to sacrifice, with their overtones of empathetic yet guilt-ridden participation in the suffering and death of Christ, are ubiquitous in late medieval devotion. A fifteenth-century poem in Middle English, "Wofully araide," found in a number of manuscripts, can serve as an example of the immense popularity of such sacrificial images. Christ speaks to the sinner:

Thus nakid am I nailid, O man, for thi sake.
I love the, thenne love me. Why slepist thu? Awake!
Remember my tender hert-rote for the brake,
With paynes my vaines constrayned to crake.
    This was I defasid,
    Thus was my flesh rasid,
    And I to deth chasid.
Like a lambe led unto sacrefise,
Slayne I was in most cruell wise. . . .[88]

Peter Dorlandus's popular dialogue, the *Viola animae*, makes the Old Testament parallels even clearer, connecting Exodus 24.6–8 with Hebrews 9. We know, writes Dorlandus, how Moses sprinkled the vessels of the sanctuary with blood [*vasa sanctuarij sanguine respersit*], because it is written in the law that all things are cleansed in blood and without the spilling of blood there is no remission of sin [*omnia in sanguine mundant et sine sanguinis effusione non sit remissio*]. And we know too how the priests once a year entered the Holy of Holies with blood. So, reasoning mystically, we understand easily that this shows why the Savior of humankind chose to pour out his blood on the cross [*sanguinem suum voluerit in cruce diffundere*].

For this blood mitigated the ancient wrath of the Father, brought peace to the angels, opened heaven, emptied hell, destroyed the devil, and wiped out all the sins of the world. . . . Thus in this we drink the waters and slake our thirst in joy at the fountain of the wounds of the Savior, for not in foreign blood [*non in sanguine alieno*] but through his own [*per proprium sanguinem*], he himself entered the Holy of Holies, mercifully sprinkling the vessels of the sanctuary [*vasa sanctuarij clementer aspergens*]—that is, cleansing again [*repurgans*] the souls of the elect with his blood.[89]

Remarks such as these, repeated in devotional texts and sermons, echo the statements of scholastic theologians such as Aquinas, Capistrano, or Paltz, who saw *sanguis Christi* as the price of redemption, the circumcision of all Christians, and the confirmation of a new covenant, paralleling the old one established by the blood of bulls and doves. Aquinas, for example, affirms that the passion is "a sacrifice properly so called" "done to appease God," and draws an analogy between "the altar of holocausts constructed of timbers" (Exod. 27) and the wood of the cross.[90] Capistrano, in arguing for the inseparability of Christ's blood during the *triduum mortis*, saw blood as that in which Christ's purity lies, because it is by blood that things are consecrated to God.

[We dispute here] concerning blood. Therefore we must insist on the definition of this word *sanctum*, when [the psalmist] says: "Nor will you give your holy one to see corruption." . . . *sanctus*, that is pure or incorrupt [*castus sive incorruptus*], religious, whole [*integer*], clean [*purus*], ordained, separated from the desires of earth and the body; but according to the etymology of the term, *sanctus* is in the strict sense [*proprie*] that which is anointed with blood [*sanguine unctus*]; for the ancients consecrated all things with blood [*omnis sanguine consecrabant*].[91]

At that basic level at which medieval exegetes understood etymology to reveal the very structure of things, "*sa-nctus*" equals "*sanguine unctus*." "Holy" *means* "anointed" or marked "with blood."

Whether expressed in the difficult arguments of Capistrano and Cusanus or Mechtild's lyrical verses, such theology assumes blood to be more than an image of comfort or a reproach to sin, more than a making present of the sorrows and suffering of Jesus, more than a symbol of eucharist or penance. Blood accomplishes the work of salvation, and it does so, in these passages, not by being born of Mary or by ascending into heaven, but by being shed and sprinkled. "And almost all things, according to the law, are cleansed with blood; and without shedding of blood there is no remission [Heb. 9.22]." Blood is no mere synecdoche for Christ or incarnation.[92] It works objectively; something happens in the moment of its spilling. Blood changes the history of humankind and reorders the ontological and moral economy of the universe; and it does this by coming out of a dead body in living drops—drops that in some way change or consecrate those for whom and on whom they fall. As Innocent IV put it in 1247–48 in a statement of belief for missionaries he sent to the Great Khan:

> God . . . sent from the lofty throne of heaven down to the lowly region of the world His only-begotten Son . . . clothed in the garb of human flesh. . . . The Creator of that creature became visible, clothed in our flesh . . . in order that, having become visible, He might call back to Himself, the Invisible, those pursuing after visible things. . . . He deigned to suffer death by the torture of the cruel cross, that, by a penal end to His present life, He might make an end of the penalty of eternal death, which the succeeding generations had incurred by the transgression of their first parent. . . . He therefore offered Himself as a victim for the redemption of mankind and, overthrowing the enemy of its salvation, He snatched it from the shame of servitude to the glory of liberty, and unbarred for it the gate of the heavenly fatherland. . . .[93]

The statement from which I have just quoted is quite a complicated theory of redemption. Christ's role is by no means limited to that of sacrificial victim. Nor is it obvious here—or in any of the other passages I quoted above—exactly how the spilling of blood effects salvation, or how Christians, for all their frenzy for agency, actually participate in the moment of sacrifice. I shall come back to this below. But perhaps I have said enough to suggest that, in fifteenth-century theology and devotion, sacrifice is no mere vestige of patristic exegesis, no simple echo of an earlier soteriology. The many references to Exodus, Leviticus, and Hebrews, the repetitions of the verbs "poured" and "sprinkled," the insistence that only hot, red, liquid blood saves—these verbal clues suggest that the blood mystics drank with the lips of their hearts and pilgrims strove to see in smoke-filled churches, like the blood theologians fought over in university disputations, was the sacrificial blood of the lamb.

Behind the paradox of blood as comfort and reproach, access and accusation, waves and drops, living and separated, was the paradox of sacrifice: life lies in killing, redemption in the shedding of blood. It is to blood as sacrifice that I turn in the fourth and final part of this book.

PART IV

Sacrifice and Soteriology

Chapter 9
Late Medieval Soteriology

Behind the paradoxical valences of blood as symbol so prominent in fifteenth-century Christianity lay a sense of blood as sacrifice that went back to the Hebrew Scriptures and the New Testament, especially Exodus, Leviticus, and the Epistle to the Hebrews. It is, however, often unclear exactly what theory of redemption is assumed in references to *sacrificium* or *pretium*, *effusio* or *guttae*, *stimulus amoris* or *hostia*. For all its centrality to cult and devotion, the nature of Christ's saving act on the cross was never defined in theological debate or papal pronouncement.[1] The little statement of belief from Innocent IV quoted in the previous chapter is, for example, far from transparent soteriology. Christ defeats the enemy, offers himself up to torture as a victim, and pays the penalty incurred by Adam for all of humankind; he also provides an example, offers sweetness, and teaches an interior spirituality turned away from the things of the world. But what is it exactly that the crucifixion, or its reenactment in the mass (if it is a reenactment), accomplishes? And why by blood?

Answering this question is more difficult than might first appear. The natural tendency of modern scholars in studying theological questions is to turn to the learned theology of the past for explanations. But much of the treatment of redemption or atonement in fifteenth-century disputations is, as we have seen, implicit or indirect. Professors of theology assumed both the eucharist and the crucifixion to be "sacrifice" *pro nobis* but did not theorize the concept. In the *questiones* of figures such as Capistrano, Cusanus, and Bremer, even when these *questiones* are not polemical, blood tends to come up most intensely either in technical questions of Christology and eucharist (the nature of Christ's body in the *triduum*, human identity, or transubstantiation) or in practical debates over what the faithful should be told about cult. For all the assertions that blood saves, it is hard to reach behind these highly technical discussions to the basic soteriology. A soteriology is there. Bansleben and Witten, like Capistrano and Paltz, refer repeatedly, if in passing, to a blood that saves. As had been true since the days of the Church Fathers, particular verbs occur again and again—*fundere*, *effundere*, *spargere*—and they have specific theological connotations. If, however, we wish to ferret out the assumptions about blood in the fifteenth century, we must look beyond the narrow focus of university theology. We must also, as I suggested in Chapters 6 to 8, look to piety. But in piety too, the soteriology is implicit. Thus we must pay attention in it, as in formal, scholastic theology, to the verbs and adjectives chosen, the biblical passages quoted, and the silences, echoes, and missed connections that almost slip past us. We will not find fifteenth-century popes and professors, or spiritual writers, visionaries, and pilgrims, giving a technical or sophisticated definition of sacrifice (and indeed their avoidance of doing so is itself important). But if we probe for the basic assumptions behind all those echoes of sacrifice that reverberate through blood cult, blood devotion, and theological disputes, we reach three conclusions. First, a complex theory of sacrifice is present. Second, the fourteenth and fifteenth centuries saw hints of doubt about it that would be eclipsed for awhile in the dogmatism and definitions of the sixteenth century. Third, ideas of sacrifice created for the faithful certain problems in achieving exactly the contact with Christ they craved.

In order to understand all this, some background is necessary. I turn first, in this chapter, to what we are usually told about medieval theories of redemption and atonement; then, in Chapters 10 and 11, I turn to themes of sacrifice themselves. Although this chapter will survey some of what modern scholars have argued about medieval soteriology, my point is not to provide a general history. Rather I intend, first, to show that the usual textbook account ignores the importance of sacrifice, substituting a few theological formulations in two very great twelfth-century thinkers for the richer (if less clear and explicit) soteriological discourse of the later Middle Ages. Second, I want to illustrate the context of certain often-ignored and quite specific connotations of blood in the theological debates, spiritual writing, and pious practice I treated in the first three parts of this book. For even where writers and pilgrims did not relate blood directly to sacrifice, it had soteriological overtones we have yet to explore.[2]

Salvation as Satisfaction and Response: The Conventional Account

It is often said that late medieval theology oscillated in theories of salvation between the satisfaction theory of Anselm of Canterbury (d. 1109) and the exemplarism of Peter Abelard, both of which emerged in the years around 1100.[3] Anselm's *Cur Deus Homo* jettisoned, we are told, the older idea that Christ saved humankind by tricking the devil or ransoming man from his power and argued instead that Christ satisfies and redeems the debt man owes to God because of human disobedience. In accord with the early scholastic search for the "necessary reasons" of things, Anselm argued that payment for sin must be made, since a simple declaration of absolution would unjustly equate justice and mercy; hence salvation must come via a God-man—that is, a union of Christ (who, being God, *can* pay the debt of sin, although he does not owe it) with humanity (who cannot pay but must).[4] In many recent interpretations of Anselm, the heart of this argument is understood to lie in the idea that Christ is a "substitute" for us in "satisfying" God; he undergoes the punishment we deserve, makes the payment we owe, expiates and atones for our guilt. Abelard (d. 1142), on the other hand, in his famous commentary on Romans, is understood to have rejected the idea that bloodshed could rectify disorder in the universe. If God wished to forgive, he would simply do so; therefore Christ's death on the cross provides not expiation but rather a pattern for Christians to imitate and a spiritual awakening of, a stimulus to, love.[5]

Modern theological writing and historical scholarship have often tried to justify one theory or the other but usually favor Abelard. Such scholarship also, however, tends to insist that Anselmian satisfaction was increasingly understood as a theory that Christ substitutes not only for our debt but also for the punishment we must endure (something Anselm nowhere said). Moreover, it argues that substitution theory, often in the form of "penal substitution" (substitution for punishment), dominated late medieval theology and culminated in the sixteenth century in both Protestant and Catholic formulations (however vastly different their implications) that Christ's death on the cross is both satisfaction and sacrifice. In this account, Anselm—at least as later understood—becomes the villain; and Abelard's understanding of redemption is regretted as the great medieval missed opportunity. Returning to the ideas of René Girard popular in the 1980s, this interpretation sees the period from 1100 to 1600 as a culture of persecution, scapegoating, and terrorism to which such soteriology significantly contributed.[6]

This received wisdom about medieval soteriology is misleading in several respects. First, as some commentators have recently remarked,[7] Anselmian and Abelardian understandings of Christ's work of redemption were far closer to each other than such a simplified survey suggests. Anselm and the great critic of Abelard, Bernard of Clairvaux, both speak at length of the impact of Christ's example on the hearts of Christians. Indeed, Abelard's position, although usually labeled exemplarism, is better understood as a theory of response, for his argument in the Romans commentary stresses less example and *imitatio* than the idea that Christ's self-immolation for us is a stimulus that compels the response of repentance and love. Both Anselm and Bernard in fact agree with

Abelard that empathetic participation in Christ's suffering arouses humankind to a love that is the first step toward return and reconciliation.

It is ironic that the clearest theoretical statement of this conception of redemption comes from Bernard, who attacked Abelard as "Pelagian." In the opening chapters of his *Steps of Humility and Pride*, Bernard explores Hebrews 5.8 ("He learned obedience by the things which he suffered") and explains that Christ as Wisdom could not learn but that he "appeared to learn" in order to give us an example.[8] More, however, than an echo of Abelard's idea that Christ enkindles our love by providing an example of the man who dies for his neighbor, Bernard's exegesis is embedded in an exploration of the individual's return to God, which he expresses as the restoration of *similitudo* (likeness) to the *imago* in which we were created (Gen. 1.26). Bernard explores the process of return, the repairing of similitude, in a number of texts, which have significant variations. Some versions involve love of neighbor in the process; others do not. But the general argument is that the human person, lost in narcissism (sin), is turned from self-love to love of God through the intermediate step of encounter with the suffering Christ. The recognition that Christ's suffering is at least as terrible as ours and that it is offered *pro nobis* wrenches us from self to other and moves us into a process of return that outlasts life itself and carries us to union. Although Bernard clearly assumes (as did Abelard) that grace is necessary for such empathetic reorientation, what Christ offers here is a suffering self that inflames co-suffering (*com-passio*) in us. For Bernard, we are able to return to similitude, to co-suffer, because we are created in the image of God, just as, for the great devotional theologian of the fourteenth century, Julian of Norwich, we experience ecstasy in the blood because of our "godly will," which is never separated from God.[9] Optimism about the human person is thus embedded in medieval redemption theology along with obsessive guilt and heightened attention to pain.[10] The blood that must be offered to make reparation is a blood that turns us on to love. And it turns us on because we are turn-on-able—we are, as medieval theologians said, *capax Dei*, God-capable.

Just as ideas of satisfaction are woven into ideas of response, so response is predicated on the idea of something offered. Abelard never intended his commentary on Romans to be a complete soteriology. But even there, he speaks of Christ's love providing justification—that is, offering something objective that repairs the chasm opened in the universe by sin. Like Bernard and Anselm, Abelard sees both the cross and the mass as satisfaction. Describing Christ as model and friend, but also blood price, purchase, and redemption, he wrote to his discarded lover, Heloise, in rhetoric couched to produce guilt as well as love:

[Christ] bought you not with his wealth but with himself. He bought and redeemed you with his own blood. . . . The Creator of the world himself became the price for you. . . . He is the true friend who desires yourself . . . who said when he was about to die for you: "There is no greater love than this, that a man should lay down his life for his friends" [John 15.13].

It was he who truly loved you, not I. . . . You say I suffered for you, and perhaps that is true, but it was to bring you not salvation but sorrow. But he suffered truly for your salvation, on your behalf of his own free will, and by his suffering he cures all sickness. . . .[11]

There are, in other words, subjective and objective elements in the theories of both Anselm and Abelard.[12] Indeed, to all later medieval theologians, Christ's suffering on the cross both induces response and effects ontological repair. It wrenches the hearts of humans toward empathy and healing and provides a totally undeserved and God-given bridge across the breach torn in the cosmos by Adam's disobedience in the garden of Eden. Hence it is quite wrong to see two redemption theories warring for precedence in the later Middle Ages. What I am calling Abelardian response and what is generally labeled Anselmian satisfaction together constitute (along with vestiges of earlier positions) an explicit theory of redemption in the later Middle Ages and the sixteenth century. Peter Lombard's *Sentences* expresses well the standard and multifacted medieval theory of the atonement. Lombard retained the early medieval idea that Christ on the cross defeats the devil. He maintained (without using the word itself) that satisfaction is due for sin and is paid by Christ, and he clearly, unlike Anselm, saw such satisfaction as substitute punishment. He also argued for redemption as the enkindling of love.

But how are we loosed from sin through his death? . . . Because by his death, as the Apostle says (Rom. 5.8), the love of God is commended toward us, that is, a special and praiseworthy love of God toward us appears, in that he gives his Son over unto death for our sins. And a pledge of such great love having been shown to us, we are moved and kindled to the love of God who did such a great thing for us; and by this we are justified—that is, loosed from sin, we are made just. Therefore the death of Christ justifies us, since through it love is excited in our hearts.[13]

A careful reading of Thomas Aquinas shows there also a complex theory where response and satisfaction interweave.[14] Modern accounts often claim that Aquinas shifts the soteriological focus to an insistence that satisfaction is not necessitated by the structure of the universe (as Anselm is understood to argue) but rather willed by a God who becomes, in fourteenth- and fifteenth-century theology, increasingly understood as absolute will or power. This is so, but it is a less dramatic shift than is sometimes claimed. The idea that God chose blood satisfaction as his means when he might have chosen other ways is implicit in earlier theology. Long before Aquinas, theorists such as Bernard of Clairvaux understood Christ's death as "appropriate [*conveniens*]" (Aquinas's word), not imperative; God might have done things another way.[15] And, as we have seen, Franciscans and those associated with them (such as Grosseteste) came increasingly to stress that Christ's death on the cross was freely willed because of love.[16] What is important for my purposes here is that Bernard and Abelard, Grosseteste and Aquinas, like later thinkers such as Wycliffe, Gerson, Cusanus, Dionysius the Carthusian, and Gabriel Biel, hold that the blood of the cross is both satisfaction and the enkindling of love.[17] There are not then two redemption theories (Abelardian and Anselmian) in the Middle Ages but one.

It is true that, within this theory, one strand—which was built upon at the Council of Trent—figures redemption as a kind of exchange and expresses it in almost quantitative terms. Christ is seen as offering to God in man's stead and on man's behalf an uncoerced and sinless obedience which so far outweighs human debt that the additional merits earned suffice for whatever recompense humans will ever need to make for their sins. But even at the level of university-trained theologians, satisfaction and exchange are still part of a theology in which the cross is also the object of *compassio* and *imitatio*. As such, it is not just a pattern to be built into the life of the Christian but also a suffering and self-giving presence in which the individual is enclosed and thereby lifted to heaven.[18] In discussing the "appropriateness" of the passion, Aquinas asked why God chose to save by violence, which is surely (as Aristotle said) "a severance or lapse [*excisio, seu casus*]" of nature. Among the many answers he gives, the first is that God chose to save by death and blood so that man might know how much God loves him and be "stirred to love" in return.[19] Hence even in university discourse, Christ's death not only restores the balance of the universe so that sinners can draw upon it for redemption; it is also a vast well of blood in which the Christian encounters and becomes one with love.

Sermons, prayers, and vision accounts also interweave themes of response with themes of satisfaction. In much of the literature I quoted in Chapter 1, the theme of response and imitation is prominent. The sudden outburst of stigmata and other paramystical phenomena in the thirteenth century—an outburst that continued right into the sixteenth—makes clear that Christ's passion was sometimes received and imitated quite literally in contemplatives and visionaries. Some bodies (especially female bodies) poured blood just as Christ's was thought to have done on the cross or under the flail or crown of thorns. But such piety expressed expiation and satisfaction too. The monk of Evesham, whose revelation of blood drinking I discussed in Chapter 8, saw a vision in which the bleeding and pain of Christ's crucifixion were shared by the blessed in heaven. Inducement of ecstasy, blood was also (wrote the chronicler who recounted the vision) vanquisher of the devil, reproach to sinners, and a payment that lifts humankind from "their infernal prison-house" to "the choir of angels."[20] Despite the highly experiential and somatic quality of much vernacular piety, themes of satisfaction are seldom absent. Indeed Margery Kempe, and others like her, wept so loudly exactly because Christ suffered *for* human sin.[21] Fixated, it is true, on Christ's quite physical body, Margery nonetheless saw that body not only as experience to be imitated but also as offering to be made. The author of the fifteenth-century *Talkyng of þe Loue of God*, whose highly erotic description of suckling and rolling in Christ's blood I quoted in Chapter 1, saw blood not only as "love-token" but also as "the price of my soul [*prys of my soule*]," ". . . rich, precious blood, which bought the whole world [*Riche precious blod that al þe world bouȝte*]."[22]

An example from iconography makes the same point. The complex theme of the *arma Christi*, immensely popular in the fifteenth century, shows the interweaving of soteriological concepts (see Plates 28 and 29). We have already seen how the *arma*—"arms" in the sense both of weapons and of insignia, "coats of arms"—were shields defending sinners against the devil's assault and yet offensive weapons, accusing humans for the death of God. They were graphic depictions of victory won, weapons wielded, payment made—sign of an objective change in the universe that offers to Christians a defense behind which salvation lies. As such, they seem to have evoked (as we saw above) not only gratitude but also a guilt-inspired determination to root out the cause of that payment, whether in Jews and heretics or in the believer's own heart. But the *arma* were more than weapons wielded against God by humans and hence against humans by God. They evoked more than payment made, with all the spiraling guilt and repression implicit in such awareness. They were also the tools of transformative love. We find them represented thus in the odd theme of Christ crucified by the virtues (the so-called *Tugendkruzifixion*)—a rare motif that is, however, found in two sites associated specifically with blood cult: Wienhausen and Doberan. In such images, the bleeding and death of the Savior are executed by the spears of little figures clearly labeled *Caritas*, *Humilitas*, and so forth (see Plate 30). In the Wienhausen image, Christ leans from the cross to embrace *Caritas*, who embraces him in return and puts her weapon into his side to release the living blood that saves. The *arma* of God's auto-sacrifice are literally here the instruments of love.[23]

Salvation as Participation

Thus it is clear that Anselmian and Abelardian elements are interwoven in late medieval thought, both in scholastic theories and in devotional theology. It is inaccurate to dichotomize them. But the artificial separating of satisfaction and response is not the most worrisome of the mistakes in the received account. Missing also is a sense of what historians of theology sometimes call "participation" or "representation"—the idea that Christ quite literally incorporates all humankind in his death and resurrection.[24] For in late medieval theology and devotion, what is offered on the cross and in the mass is not merely, or even primarily, a substitute for payment owed. It is true that Christ pays—and dies—in the stead of humanity and on its behalf. As Abelard said, "The Creator of the world himself became the price for you. . . ."[25] But the substitution at the heart of redemption is also a substitution in which the individual is subsumed into—*is*—species; part *is* whole. What is offered to God in the death of Christ is not merely one man as a substitute for many but all humanity subsumed in Christ. Despite the individualism of a piety that increasingly stressed interior responsibility and private prayer, this subsuming joined Christians into a wider community. In the sacrifice of the cross, Christ was understood to represent all humankind because he incorporates humanity, lifting its distress and guilt into God.

The notion had roots in earlier ideas. Its most obvious source was Paul: "For as by the disobedience of one man many were made sinners; so also by the obedience of one many shall be made just" (Rom. 5.19). Although some modern theologians argue that the idea of the incorporation of all in Adam is based in false science, the idea is not a physiological or genetic one.[26] It is rather philosophical, or legal, or perhaps even literary.[27] Insofar as it is a notion of the representing of a group or body by its head, it has origins in corporate images (both biblical and antique) for society—images much explored in late medieval political theory and canon law.[28] Insofar as it is the idea that an individual instance is explained ontologically—that is, accounted for in its nature—by an exemplar, its roots are Platonic. Both these ideas—that is, that the head *is* the body and that the instance *is* (has being) because it participates in the exemplar—are in a sense conceptions of representation, that is, of how one stands for many. (They are also distant ancestors of Bernard's notion of the *imago* that must return to *similitudo*.)[29] Even more central to the notion of representation as we find it in late medieval understandings of redemption is, however, what we might call the habit of concomitance or synecdoche—the tendency to think that part *is* whole.

As we have seen, concomitance was worked out in the eleventh century in the context of eucharistic debate to explain how Christ is totally present in every celebration of the mass and every particle of the fragmented host. It was later used to justify withholding the cup from the laity and to explain how Christ's blood could be simultaneously preserved on earth in reliquaries and joined with his glorified body in heaven. Beyond such technical argumentation, the tendency to see whole in part, part as whole, became the characteristic response to the saints, who were understood to be fully present in their every bodily fragment (this was the great period of relic division and distribution) and yet fully present before the throne of God in heaven. The bodies of kings and cardinals, similarly divided and distributed, were understood to be *pars pro toto* as well.[30]

This late medieval habit of understanding part to be whole, instance to be *in* exemplar, made it possible to think not only of humans subsumed in the *humanitas* of Christ but also of relatives, neighbors, even heretics as subsumed into one's own suffering in a union that was more participation than substitution. It is a problematic assumption—one Aquinas himself questioned when he argued that a person can substitute for his or her neighbor's punishment but not for that neighbor's contrition.[31] Even pious women such as Hadewijch and Catherine of Genoa, who stressed experiential union with Christ's death, were not sure how far they could spread their own participatory suffering to others. Nonetheless, this notion of representation is at the heart of late medieval theology.[32] Sometimes it does seem to be a version of substitution or satisfaction. Christ's sacrifice on the cross is understood to substitute for earlier and incomplete sacrifices. His life pays in our stead and on our behalf; in some formulations, it suffers our punishment as well. Moreover the suffering of the saints not only substitutes for our penalties in purgatory but can also be offered up in a kind of exchange for the evil deeds of heretics, Jews, blaspheming artisans, thieving servant girls, etc., who supposedly crucify Christ.[33] Even the radical self-denial of ordinary Christians—the bodies whipped in flagellant processions, starved in convents, or torn apart on the scaffold—can be offered in the place of payment and punishment.

Often, however, such substitution is not so much exchange or replacement of one by another as representation in a synecdochal sense. We are all wrapped in the flayed skin of Christ, poured out with his blood, lifted to God as he is lifted up.[34] The holy women Alice of Schaerbeke and Catherine of Genoa not only offered their pain *for* others; they felt that, through it, they were caught up with others into the salvific pain of God.[35] As Abelard and Anselm, Bernard, Catherine of Siena, Gabriel Biel, and Julian of Norwich all said, we are selves that can be turned on by evidence of God's self-sacrificing love for us because we see ourselves in the suffering servant. Indeed not only do we see ourselves there; we have our existence in (that is, are incorporated in, are ontologically accounted for by) his *humanitas*. And, as all are incorporated in Christ, so all can be incorporated in each. The individual can see herself as all humankind. Thus there are hints (although only hints) of universalism, especially in the form this piety takes with late medieval women. Hadewijch wanted her sufferings to remove souls from hell itself, although she admitted that the request was "wrong." Adelheid Langmann arrogated to herself a kind of priestly function, not only placing herself in a long line of powerful intercessors such as Abraham, Moses, and Esther but also explicitly locating the salvation of the entire world in the union of herself with God in her own heart.[36]

Such ideas of participation were frequently expressed in blood imagery. As we saw in Chapter 7, blood often stands for self or life in late medieval piety. The idea of blood as *sedes animae* makes blood a special kind of synecdoche—a body part that not only stands for body but also stands for soul or person. Giving blood tends to mean giving or sharing self. Suffering *for* someone else means not so much replacing them as being together with them in a way which increases the value of their experience or lessens its pain. For example, Catherine of Genoa (d. 1510), the great theorist of purgatory, assumed that her own suffering was part of a vast pool in which it fused with the expiation owed by her neighbors and the death agonies of Christ. Imagining that her own blood/life/self might in some way inform or even become the truth of *humanitas*, she wrote: "If by taking my blood and giving it to humankind to drink, I could make known to it this truth [about love], I would give all my blood for love of humanity. I cannot endure the thought that humankind, created for the good that I see and know, should lose it. . . ."[37] However audacious it may seem, there is something here beyond penal substitution. The pain/blood/self women offer to God yearns to subsume and incorporate the pain of others and to become the pain/blood/life of Christ himself.[38]

Julian of Norwich

The fullest articulation in the Middle Ages of a theology of participation, with strong overtones of universalism, is the Long Text of Julian of Norwich's *Showings*, especially her famous parable of the servant. As Julian explains, she struggled for years to understand the meaning of her vision of a servant who, flying to do the will of his Lord, fell into a ditch in his eagerness but was, in the end, rewarded by the Lord because of his suffering. How (wonders Julian) can failure and pain lead to God's reassurance that "all will be well"? The answer to which Julian finally came was that the servant was not only Adam but also Christ—an answer she understood not didactically (as an allegory deciphered or a doctrine illustrated) but experientially. Just as she had, at age thirty, experienced in acute illness a oneness with the agony of Christ's love for humankind, so she now saw that all humanity was forever represented, subsumed, and incorporated in the pain and glory of Christ.

The lord is God the Father, the servant is the Son, Jesus Christ, the Holy Spirit is the equal love which is in them both. When Adam fell, God's Son fell; because of the true union which was made in heaven, God's Son could not be separated from Adam, for by Adam, I understand all mankind. Adam fell from life to death, into the valley of this wretched world, and after that into hell. God's Son fell with Adam, into the valley of the womb of the maiden who was the fairest daughter of Adam, and that was to excuse Adam from blame in heaven and on earth. . . . For in all this our good Lord showed his own Son and Adam as only one man.

And so has our good Lord Jesus taken upon him all our blame; and therefore our Father may not, does not wish to assign more blame to us than to his own beloved Son Jesus Christ.

. . . His rushing away was the divinity, and his running was the humanity; for the divinity rushed from the Father into the maiden's womb, falling to accept our nature, and in this falling he took great hurt. The hurt he took was our flesh, in which at once he experienced mortal pains. . . . And . . . he could never with almighty power rise from the time that he fell into the maiden's womb until his body was slain and dead, and he yielded his soul into the Father's hand, with all mankind for whom he had been sent. . . .

And [on Easter morn] . . . our foul mortal flesh, which God's Son took upon him, which was Adam's old tunic, tight-fitting, threadbare and short, was then made lovely by our saviour, new, white and bright and forever clean, wide and ample. . . .

. . . Now the Son does not stand before the Father as a servant . . . but richly clothed in joyful amplitude, with a rich and precious crown upon his head. For it was revealed that we are his crown, which crown is the Father's joy, the Son's honour, the Holy Spirit's delight, and endless marvellous bliss to all who are in heaven.[39]

To Julian, Adam incorporates all humankind. Thus Christ, as the second Adam, redeems all that is human—redeems, that is, the "substance" of human-ness (what it by definition is) and its "sensuality" (its fallen state).[40] Moreover, redeemed *humanitas* is not only what the human is but also all human participants in it. The Son who stands as a new Adam before the Father wears our mortal flesh as a clean garment and upon his head a crown that is us.

Given this understanding, Julian struggled against what she understood to be the church's requirement that some remain in hell.[41] For if *pars* is *totum*, and *totum* includes all *partes*, how can any particle be left behind? As Julian wrote: "because of the true union [*ryght onyng*] which was made in heaven,

God's Son could not be separated from Adam, for by Adam, I understand all humankind [*alle man*]. . . . For our good Lord showed his own Son and Adam as only one man [*in alle this oure good lorde shewed his owne son and Adam but one man*]." Julian saw herself not merely enkindled by, but also incorporated in, this "one man," this unity of "his own Son and Adam." Hence she not only, as Kate Greenspan suggests, claims a universal voice within the personal; she *is* one with all Christians, caught up in the "one man" that is also Christ. This is a universalism that not only empowers the individual voice (male or female); it also sees all humankind incorporated in the God-man, and it places the individual in unity with, and responsible for, all her fellows.

> . . . we are all one in love. . . . If I pay special attention to myself, I am nothing at all; but in general I am . . . in the unity of love with all my fellow Christians. For it is in this unity that the life of all men consists who will be saved. . . . For in mankind which will be saved is comprehended all [*in mankynd that shall be savyd is comprehendyd alle*], that is to say all that is made and the maker of all. For God is in man and in God is all. And he who loves thus loves all.[42]

One hears in this passage Julian's compromise with the doctrine of damnation, when she says Christ is the life of "all men who will be saved," although the logic of her theology suggests that it should read simply "all." Julian accepts what holy church teaches her she must accept. My point here is not, however, to underline the limits of fourteenth-century inclusiveness,[43] but to illustrate how far her understanding of incorporation or representation took her toward universalism. It is also important to note that we find traces of it elsewhere in fourteenth- and fifteenth-century piety, again in the context of a radical understanding of representation or participation. Peter Dorlandus's image of Christ himself as not only the good Samaritan but also the wounded man makes exactly the same theological point, if less explicitly. What Dorlandus suggests is not only that humankind is healed by God's love, ministering to it in its misery, but also that wounded humankind is caught up in Christ.[44]

Thus, for all the guilt-tripping and scapegoating implicit in the late medieval obsession with human responsibility for the death of Christ, there were, at least in theologians such as Julian, optimistic and universalist implications in the understanding that Christ's death is representative. If it is *humanitas* that suffers, if *pars* is really *totum*, then *all* are in the suffering body lifted to God and *all* are in every self that joins with, that performs, the *humanitas* of Christ. Hierarchy and difference can be subsumed into oneness. Moreover, to Julian as to Catherine of Siena and Catherine of Genoa, incorporation in Christ—an incorporation of all Christians (perhaps all humankind)—is an incorporation in blood. And we have seen above why blood—*sedes animae*, living yet part—is an especially appropriate image of such synecdoche.

Julian's "First Showing" makes clear that blood was her pivotal experience. It was in a moment of visionary fusion with Jesus' bleeding that she died and returned to life.

> And when I was thirty and a half years old, God sent me a bodily sickness in which I lay for three days and three nights, and on the third night I received all the rites of Holy Church and did not expect to live. . . . So I lasted until day, and by then my body was dead from the middle downwards, as it felt to me. Then I was helped to sit upright and supported, so that my heart might be more free to be at God's will, and so that I could think of him whilst my life would last. My curate was sent for to be present at my end; and before he came my eyes were fixed upwards and I could not speak. He set the cross before my face, and said: I have brought the image of your saviour; look at it and take comfort from it. . . . After this my sight began to fail. . . . Everything around the cross was ugly and terrifying to me, as if it were occupied by a great crowd of devils.
>
> . . . And suddenly at that moment all pain was taken from me, and I was sound. . . .
>
> And at this, suddenly I saw the red blood flowing down from under his crown, hot and flowing freely and copiously, a living stream, just as it was at the time when the crown of thorns was pressed on his blessed head. . . .
>
> And in the same revelation, suddenly the Trinity filled my heart full of the greatest joy. . . . And I said: Blessed be the Lord! . . . and I was greatly astonished by this wonder and marvel, that he who is so to be revered and feared would be so familiar with a sinful creature living in this wretched flesh.
>
> . . . [And] I saw that [our Lord] is to us everything which is good. . . .[45]

As we see from this passage, blood is to Julian neither substitute for debt owed nor sacrifice offered up. It is enkindling, but it is more than proffered example or arousal. Flowing blood is the locus of life and joy. As Julian says explicitly, love is the answer.[46] Blood is love.

Perhaps this understanding is related to the gendered implications of her conception of blood discussed in Chapter 6. To Julian, the blood poured out of a mother God has overtones of uterine and birthing blood, although it is significant that Julian sees Christians as nestled into a God "out of whom [they] shall never come."[47] Conception, or re-conception, in God comes, so to speak, after birthing. Although blood flows in the "First Showing," the flow is less a spilling forth than a vibrant pooling that indicates its freshness. For all Julian's emphasis on blood as drops or pellets, the blood is not so much blood shed as blood that gives life. In a sense, then, to Julian, the self never departs from God.[48]

Hence, in Julian's theology, evil—especially moral evil—never seems fully real; it is never fully accounted for. Her Adam is Christ; and the fall is more the experience of being lost or separated than an act of deliberate evil. The sense of *pars* as forever *pars*, of blood as shed, that is so prominent in most late medieval devotional or learned theology is, in Julian, almost eclipsed by wholeness. Blood to Julian does not signify sacrifice.

Theology such as Julian's or Hadewijch's was, in its universalist implications, dangerous, radical, and exceedingly rare. Even Catherine of Siena, who combined a strong sense of *humanitas* participating in Christ with an equally strong sense of sacrifice, was unpopular among some in her own city; and her spirituality was extravagantly reinterpreted soon after her death in reports by male supporters.[49] Ideas perceived as universalist were persecuted where articulated to the laity, and even where kept within convent or anchorhold, they had little influence.[50] Thus, in a sense, Julian is the exception that proves the rule. The understanding of incorporation in Christ that was widespread in the fifteenth century was not her idea of love, in which pain turns to glory, nor yet her idea of a union in which all are lifted to a God from whom they, in some sense, never depart. Julian's contemporaries were, as I have demonstrated throughout this book, far more likely to see themselves liberated by, because implicated in, a blood spilled out in sacrifice.

Conclusion

This discussion may seem to take us far away from cults in the north of Germany. My point, however, has been twofold. First, I wanted to provide some context for those references to payment and substitution, example and arousal, incorporation and participation, that cluster around *sanguis Christi* in theology, devotion, and cult. Not only are all these ideas in fact caught up in blood references; blood seemed to medieval writers, because of its particular characteristic as living and shed, an especially appropriate image for satisfaction, response, and participation. In the passages I have discussed throughout this book, blood is repeatedly characterized as *pretium* and *exemplum*. Those who felt themselves accused of murdering Christ were accused by blood, as Judas, Pontius Pilate, and Cain had been; it is blood that "cries out," exacting a blood price.[51] The example that arouses the faithful to experiential participation in the suffering of Jesus is more vivid because seen (whether in meditation or in vision) in bright red waves. Moreover, the life (the blood) of the pious person is often said to be incorporated in the life of Jesus, entering through his side, melting into his heart. To Catherine of Siena, Niccolò di Toldo's redemption *was* the incorporation of his blood into the blood of his Lord. However implicit or understated the concepts may be, the various strands of fifteenth-century soteriology were woven into and expressed by metaphors of blood.

Second, I wanted to underline how partial are the existing textbook accounts of medieval ideas of redemption, even if we expand the traditional understanding of satisfaction to include representation or participation. I needed to call attention to this because traditional accounts of late medieval soteriology can never fully explain why theology, devotion, and practice fixated on blood. The conventional story of redemption theory as satisfaction and response does help to explain and contextualize the medieval emphasis on Christ's suffering and death. Death and execution had for centuries been understood as retribution, payment, and satisfaction; suffering could be conceptualized as trigger of response. Both suffering and death could be taken to prove that Christ shares our humanness; and given assumptions about instances and exemplars, such sharing could be seen as an incorporation of individuals in the God-man. Blood was, moreover, a particularly apt image for retribution and satisfaction, for arousal, and for the synecdoche implied in incorporation. But nothing in these theories necessitates that the death be a bloody one. What necessitates blood is exactly what is missing in the traditional account: sacrifice. Unless we recognize that the act at the heart of atonement and redemption was understood to be the slaying of the lamb of God on the altar of the cross, we will not understand the emphasis on blood.[52] I turn finally to sacrifice in my next chapter.

Chapter 10
Sacrificial Theology

References to sacrifice in later theology and piety frequently cite what patristic authors extrapolated from New Testament ideas—ideas which themselves constructed a theology of sacrifice by adding what were understood as Old Testament foreshadowings to the gospel narratives of the crucifixion. Without some understanding of these earlier concepts of sacrifice, it is not possible to grasp the multiple contradictions implicit in medieval references nor the ways in which blood both as symbol and as pilgrimage goal encapsulated these contradictions.

The Biblical and Patristic Background

Scholars have spilled vast amounts of ink on sacrifice in the Hebrew Scriptures and New Testament, and I cannot attempt to summarize those debates fully here. But a number of points seem clear about the several kinds of sacrifice we find in Exodus and Leviticus, and later echoed in the Prophets and Psalms. First, although not all are blood sacrifices, blood is crucial to most of them;[1] and it is central to the ritual that the blood be poured out and sprinkled fresh upon the altar, a sprinkling that is clearly understood to mark and cleanse. Second, not only is the animal killed and given to God, but a portion (in some cases all) is also destroyed by fire; and the sweet odor of that fire has something to do with the presence of God.[2] Third, the blood which is poured out is taboo—that is, made sacred or highly charged. Not only is it not to be eaten (Lev. 3.17; 17.10–11); it is explicitly connected to general blood prohibitions and hence to a sense of female, sexually related blood (that is, menstrual and postpartum) as polluting.[3] Yet, as a charged or taboo substance, blood also creates sacrality. Sprinkled on the faithful, it marks and cleanses them. Moreover, it is the bloodshed of circumcision that effects God's covenant with his people (Gen. 17). Fourth, a meal is not always an element, but where it is (as in peace offerings) it too creates community.[4]

However much scholars may disagree about fine points of interpretation, there are, in these rituals, elements of propitiation—that is, of doing something to make up for sin, if not exactly to appease God—and elements of recognizing God's power. Whether or not the sacrifice is a gift of life to life or a return of life to that from whence it comes, there seems to be an element of what Nahmanides's later commentary suggests: an acknowledgment that all power is God's.[5] Killing and destruction are central to sacrifice, but, as Jonathan Klawans and J. C. Heesterman have pointed out, the ritual is not violent, nor (pace René Girard) does it appear to be concerned with violence.[6] Indeed, in its detailed rules for what is destroyed, sacrifice is the opposite of violence: the sacrificer and priest mimic, in reverse, God's act of creation, disassembling in careful order what God has made and hence enacting a tribute to his power.[7]

These aspects of Hebrew sacrifice were taken over in New Testament language both for crucifixion and for eucharist, despite the fact that crucifixion was not a death by bleeding.[8] The gospel accounts of the Last Supper in Matthew 26.26–29, Mark 14.22–25, and Luke 22.15–20 all connect the breaking of bread and sharing of the cup to sacrificial elements such as remission of sins (blood shed *pro nobis*) and creation of community. I Corinthians 10.16–21 and 11.23–29 explicitly identify eucharist with sacrifice. Philippians 4.18 glosses what Paul has received from his fellow preacher as "an odour of sweetness, an acceptable sacrifice, pleasing to God." Many passages in the Epistles speak explicitly of the death on Calvary as a sacrifice: for example, I Peter 1.18–19 ("Knowing that you were not redeemed with corruptible things . . . But with the precious blood of Christ, as of a lamb unspotted and undefiled . . .")[9] and Ephesians 5.2 ("And walk in love, as Christ also hath loved us and hath delivered himself for us, an oblation and a sacrifice to God for an odour of sweetness"). The fullest exposition is the non-Pauline Epistle to the Hebrews (9.6–28):

> . . . into the first tabernacle the priests indeed always entered, accomplishing the offices of sacrifices.
> But, into the second, the high priest alone, once a year; not without blood. . . .
> . . . .
> But Christ, being come a high priest of the good things to come, by a greater and more perfect tabernacle, not made with hands . . .
> Neither by the blood of goats or of calves, but by his own blood, entered once into the Holies, having obtained eternal redemption.
> For if the blood of goats and of oxen and the ashes of an heifer, being sprinkled, sanctify such as are defiled, to the cleansing of the flesh;
> How much more shall the blood of Christ, who by the Holy Spirit offered himself unspotted unto God, cleanse our conscience from dead works . . . ?
> And therefore he is the mediator of the new testament; that by means of his death for

the redemption of those transgressions which were under the former testament, they that are called may receive the promise of eternal inheritance.

. . . .

For when every commandment of the law had been read by Moses to all the people, he took the blood of calves and goats, with water and scarlet wool and hyssop; and sprinkled both the book itself and all the people;

Saying: This is the blood of the testament. . . .

. . . .

And almost all things, according to the law, are cleansed with blood; and without shedding of blood there is no remission.

. . . .

So also Christ was offered once to exhaust the sins of many.

Themes of washing are especially prominent in the Apocalypse (1.5: he "who hath loved us . . . washed us from our sins in his own blood"; 5.12: "worthy is the lamb that was slain . . ."), and in this text also a connection is made between Christ's blood/death and that of the early martyrs, whose robes are washed and made white "in the blood of the Lamb" (Apoc. 7.14).

The significance of these echoes, metaphors, allusions, and definitions is immensely complex and has been endlessly debated, but certain points are clear. The Last Supper and the execution on Golgotha are not described as literal sacrifices. Neither Pilate nor the Roman soldiers nor the Jews are understood as sacrificers; and if Christ is seen as the priest offering his blood on Calvary or at the Last Supper, he is not in these texts perceived as destroying the bread and wine or himself, or as returning life to God. Something, however, is given to or done for God (Phil. 4.18 and Eph. 5.2); there is explicit reference to Christ as the paschal lamb; much stress is laid, at least in Hebrews, on the power of blood, which is said to be "shed" for remission, "sprinkled" to cleanse, and "offered" in oblation.

Many modern scholars who theorize sacrifice see it as a form of gift and understand gift in the basic sense proposed by Henri Hubert and Marcel Mauss as an exchange that establishes a mutual obligation. As Marcel Hénaff has, however, pointed out, the element of reciprocity involved in gift-giving is not the same in all cultures. It can range from a generalized reciprocity to a tight legal sense of debt or obligation.[10] There are elements of reciprocity in Hebrew sacrifice, of course; sacrifice restores a mutual relationship with God after some earlier disequilibrium, either sin or some sort of disorder. The New Testament understandings of Christ's death as sacrifice seem mostly to envision the gift element as Christ's gift of himself—that is, of salvation—to humankind. But there is also, in the earliest texts, a sense of something due to God. Both reparation and creation of covenant (a bond of reciprocity) are central in the words of institution for the cup at Last Supper: "This is my blood of the new covenant, which is shed for many for the remission of sins." Clearly sacrifice is not here primarily what it comes to denote in modern parlance: surrendering or renouncing (that is, giving something up).[11]

In the New Testament texts, blood is the key. But, as Rohling has pointed out, it often serves as a synecdoche for the fact of Jesus' death.[12] Its actual spilling is little emphasized. Moreover, it has, in these passages, little to do with the experience of suffering. What is important is that something is done, and that act bestows a gift (that is, brings salvation), redeems (that is, buys back or expiates), purifies, washes, and sanctifies (that is, makes holy), and creates a new community (that is, establishes a mutual obligation) both among those who participate in or are marked by the blood, and between them and God.

Patristic writers elaborated these New Testament themes to make blood a central element in their theories of redemption.[13] Already by the early third century, Tertullian stressed the bloodiness of Christ's death more than the gospels had done, connecting *sanguis Christi* to martyrdom as well as to eucharist and baptism. To Tertullian, the spilling of blood was crucial to salvation, but what he emphasized above all were the positive effects of bloodshed: cleansing, sealing, freeing, protecting, restoring, vivifying, inebriating, reinstating, redeeming. By the late fourth century, language of price (*pretium*) and even ransom became more prominent, alongside language of offering and gift (*oblatio*); an element of necessity seemed to enter in; accusation of those who incur the debt (sinful humanity) became more prominent too. The death on the cross was sometimes imaged as a business transaction. Not only does a gift bind giver and recipient in mutual obligation (God to man and man to God); Christ is now seen as a merchant who gives good money for our redemption. "*Emptor Christus est, pretium sanguis, possessio orbis terrarum.*"[14]

It is not possible here to survey the history of sacrifice images over the first millennium of Christian history. What is important for my purposes is to note that there are already present in patristic texts several themes that reverberate through late medieval devotional theology in far more experiential language. First, the stress on blood as living and blood as separated runs incessantly through patristic discussion. In Augustine, for example, blood is over and over again described as *incorruptibilis, sacer*; Christ's blood is explicitly understood as alive and lifegiving. But Augustine, like Ambrose, Chrysostom, and Jerome, also stresses that *sanguis Christi* was separated from Christ's body during the passion. It is, in the eucharist, a second species, becoming present by a second consecration, and hence signifies death and division.[15] Second, overlying the dichotomy of living and spilled is a dichotomy of offered up and poured out: on the one hand, the blood shed is something the offerer gives to God (freely lifted up in worship or love, and hence carrying the offerer upward); on the other hand, the slaying is a destruction that stands for punishment undergone or payment made (that is, something taken from the offerer because owed). Third, the problem of once for all yet daily has already reared its head. In a passage often quoted in later discussions of the eucharist, Gregory the Great attempted to explain how the sacrifice of Christ's body and blood could be both completed for all eternity and yet offered in every celebration of the mass.[16] In doing so, he stressed division and pouring out as well as eternal presence.

Therefore we ought to despise with all our minds the present world, which we see to be already finished, and offer daily to God the sacrifice of tears [*lacrymarum sacrificia*], the offerings [*hostias*] of his body and blood. For this is the victim [*victima*] that can uniquely save the soul from eternal extinction, that reenacts [*reparat*] in mystery for us the death of the only begotten, who risen from the dead dies no more . . . [Rom. 6.9] . . . [and] living in himself immortally and incorruptibly [*immortaliter atque incorruptibiliter vivens*], is nonetheless sacrificed for us anew in the mystery of the sacred oblation [*pro nobis iterum in hoc mysterio sacrae oblationis immolatur*]. His body is consumed there, his flesh is divided for the salvation of the people, and his blood is poured out not into the hands of the infidels but into the mouths of the faithful. Let us therefore consider what a sacrifice [*sacrificium*] this is for us that, for our absolution, always imitates the passion of the only begotten Son. For who among the faithful can doubt that in the hour of this immolation, at the word of the priest, the heavens are opened, . . . choirs of angels are present, . . . earth is joined to heaven, and things visible and things invisible are made one.[17]

Living eternally and incorruptibly, Christ is nonetheless sacrificed again repeatedly for us (*iterum*).

In patristic discussion, two things are striking. First, no real definition of sacrifice is given. Sacrifice is used as an analogy to explain the saving action of crucifixion and eucharist, but it is itself not theorized. Second, elements not fully elaborated in the New Testament texts come to the fore exactly in the paradox of living separation of which late medieval devotion will make so much. There is an increasing sense here of life (often expressed as *pretium* but clearly something more) given not merely to humankind but also to God. Thus blood, which is both life and death, expresses that which continues and separates. Unless his blood spills, separates from his divided body, Christ has nothing to give (to God or to humankind); gift and giver must be conceptually distinct. Even if there is no explicit element of physical destruction of the body of the sacrificial victim, killing (*cruor*) is necessary. The blood of Christ is the death of Christ. But Christ also has nothing to give unless his blood (*sanguis*) is life. Unless his blood lives, red and vibrant like the blood of heifers that foreshadows it (Lev.), it cannot mark and make sacred those it touches and acknowledge the life that comes from God. As a verb, sacrifice is killing and offering; as a noun, sacrifice is death and (demonstration of, making present of, lifting up of) life.

Hence, although these texts do not theorize sacrifice, there is implicit in their repeated use of *effundere* (pour out) and *praebere* (bring, offer) an aspect of sacrifice modern interpreters have underlined.[18] J. C. Heesterman puts it this way: sacrifice "presents the *aporia* of a gift that must be destroyed in order to be a gift."[19] Patristic texts affirm the same paradox but with the emphasis reversed: in order to be an effective sacrifice the slaughtered victim must remain alive. In the fifth-century martyrdom account of St. Andrew—a text often cited in the eucharistic controversies of the eleventh and twelfth centuries—the saint supposedly justified his refusal to sacrifice to the Roman gods by saying:

> To God all powerful . . . I sacrifice every day, not incense, nor the flesh of bulls, nor the blood of goats, but a spotless lamb which I sacrifice daily on the altar of the cross [*immaculatum agnum cotidie in altare crucis sacrifico*]. And after the whole believing populace has eaten and drunk the blood, the lamb thus sacrificed remains whole and alive [*integer perseuerat et uiuus*]. He is truly sacrificed and his flesh truly eaten and his blood truly drunk, yet he remains no less whole, spotless and living [*cum uere sacrificatus sit . . . et uere sanguis eius sit bibitus, tamen ut dixi integer permanet et immaculatus et uiuus*].[20]

The lamb, daily killed and eaten, remains (*perseuerat*) whole and alive (*integer et uiuus*). Only God makes this possible. In both passion and eucharist, there is then the further aporia of a sacrifice of God by God.[21]

Destruction and Oblation

These patristic ideas reverberated in learned theology down into the sixteenth century, in discussions of both atonement and eucharist. Already in the eucharistic controversies of the eleventh and twelfth centuries, certain shifts of emphasis become apparent. For example, when Alger of Liège in his *De sacramentis* asserts "it is not that Christ in the mass is newly put to death but that he does on the altar what he did on the cross," we see both increased anxiety about the contradiction of Hebrews 9.28 (once for all, yet daily) and a sense of sacrifice as an act with objective results—as a "something done."[22] Although over the next four hundred years sacrifice remained without a fully developed theory, the spilling of blood and Christ's experience of suffering were increasingly emphasized, even in scholastic theology. Yet worry about exactly this bleeding and killing, connected to articulated anxiety about any *mutatio* in the body of Christ, seems to have led by the fifteenth century to discussions of sacrifice that strain to avoid the death at its heart. Late medieval discussions not only enhance elements of bleeding and suffering; they also avoid them by telescoping *sacrificium* into *oblatio*.

If we look for a moment at what Thomas Aquinas and other thirteenth-century theologians say about both atonement and eucharist as sacrifice, we get a sense of the emerging of new concerns within a continuity of patristic citation. The only definition as such available to medieval theologians was Isidore of Seville's etymological one: "sacrifice is called from *sacrum factum* [made sacred]," which might have reduced it to a simple gift or even a blessing, but also permitted a distinction between something "made sacred" and something simply "offered."[23] To this Aquinas added a broader understanding from Augustine:

> I answer that: a sacrifice properly so called is something done [*aliquid factum*] for that honor which is properly owed [*debitum*] to God in order to appease him [*ad eum placandum*]: and hence it is that Augustine says: 'A true sacrifice is by good work done in order that we may cling to God in holy fellowship. . . .' . . . and this voluntary enduring of the passion was most acceptable to God [*maxime acceptum*], as coming from love. Therefore it is manifest that Christ's passion was a true sacrifice.[24]

Although these definitions are too broad for his purposes, Aquinas uses them to lay greater stress than his predecessors had done on expiation and appeasement (a sense of price paid is repeated and central to his discussion) and on Christ's suffering (which was, he argues, greater than all other human pain—psychological and physical).[25] Christ's free yet obedient choice to suffer and die, to be the *hostia*, is crucial, so that God himself (not the perpetrators) is priest and sacrificer as well as victim.[26] A stress then on willing and loving combines with a sense of objective act (*aliquid fit*). As Thomas's teacher, Albertus Magnus, said: the blood poured out *has the result*—is the *doing*—of salvation (*sanguis . . . effusus effectus habet redemptionis*).[27] The sacrifice is offered not to the devil but to God. Not only satisfaction, it is cleansing and reconciliation as well.[28] But, as Albert's contemporary Alexander of Hales put it, quoting Hebrews 9.22: an act is necessary and that act is bloodshed. The fathers of the Old Testament retained the chirograph or certificate of debt—that is, the inability to see God—even after repenting; for the death of Christ had not yet freed them. *Sine sanguinis effusione non fit remissio*.[29]

To Aquinas then, sacrifice cannot be simply any gift made to God, as he understands Augustine to suggest.[30] Sacrifice is pouring blood—blood which purifies the earth in its spilling, blood which redeems life because it is life (as Leviticus says).[31] It is superior to Old Testament sacrifice because it is human, not animal, flesh; it is fit for immolation because it is mortal and passible (i.e., changeable). Aquinas is even willing to go so far as to include in sacrifice an element of destruction, however uncomfortable some of his contemporaries are with such formulations. The "something done" not only consecrates the victim, makes it sacred, sets it apart (as the liturgist John Beleth would also argue).[32] In sacrifice *stricto sensu*, something is broken or destroyed. When discussing Old Testament sacrifice, Aquinas says:

> . . . the term *oblatio* is common to all things offered for Divine worship, so that if a thing be offered to be destroyed in worship of God, as though it were being made into something holy, it is both an oblation and a sacrifice [*ita quod si aliquid exhibeatur in cultum divinum quasi in aliquod sacrum quod inde fieri debeat, consumendum, et oblatio est et sacrificium*]. Wherefore it is written [Exod. 29.18]: "Thou shalt offer the whole ram . . .".[33]

Although Aquinas does not build on this sense of something consumed or destroyed when considering the mass as sacrifice, stressing rather the benefits of spiritual nourishment and reconciliation gained, he nonetheless sees the mass as image or representation of the true blood sacrifice of Christ on the altar of the cross.[34]

> . . . as Chrysostom says in a sermon on the passion: "He suffered upon a high rood . . . in order that the nature of the air might be purified: and the earth felt a like benefit, for it was cleansed by the flowing of blood from his side. . . ."[35]

> And this [the passion] is a most perfect sacrifice. First of all, since being flesh of human nature, it is fittingly offered for men, and is partaken of by them under the sacrament. Second, because being passible and mortal, it was fit for immolation. Third, because, being sinless, it had virtue to cleanse from sins. Fourth, because, being the offerer's own flesh, it was acceptable to God on account of His charity in offering up his own flesh.[36]

Other thirteenth-century theologians also struggle to take account of an element of destruction they recognize in sacrifice. Baldwin of Canterbury understands Old Testament sacrifice as destroying or putting to death;[37] Robert Paululus considers whether the destruction of bread and wine in transubstantiation mirrors sacrificial destruction but then pulls back from seeing even the species as destroyed.[38] None of these theologians is comfortable with importing into either the mass or the passion the idea that destruction could touch Christ. We have seen in Chapters 4, 5, and 6 how constantly their theology rang changes on the other note: ". . . nor wilt thou give thy holy one to see corruption [Ps. 15.10]." Yet some sense of a victim breached, killed, even destroyed, lurks behind the idea of Christ as *hostia* whose spilled blood consecrates him and those on whom it falls, making both something special, something sacred, something set apart to God.

Useful for expressing the centrality of the passion and its representation in the mass, such implications were deeply disturbing, as we can see in Paululus's gesture toward and hasty withdrawal from the idea of destruction. Late medieval discussion of the eucharistic real presence shows quite clearly how troubling to many was the idea that any mutation (even change of location or temporary eruption into visibility) could touch God. How much more offensive then was the attribution of slaughter to God—either as slaughterer or as slain. Hence some theologians moved to stress the mass as blood "spread out" and "offered up" rather than "spilled."[39] The more the mass was theorized as a sacrifice in which real body and blood were present, the more important it seemed to hold that, although the blood might be present, the killing was not daily performed anew.[40] From the thirteenth to the sixteenth century, two contradictory pressures grouped around ideas of mass and passion as sacrifice. On the one hand, both devotional theology and university discourse moved increasingly to stress *sanguis Christi* as drops, bloodshed, as something "poured out"; on the other, theologians struggled to keep the sacrifice of the mass "bloodless"—an image of crucifixion in which the blood is offered up but not spilled anew. The more blood became price, expiation, accusation, empathetic experience of the pains of God, metonym for death, the more troubling became the idea that sacrifice is an *aliquid factum*. The more clearly the act seemed killing or pouring out, the more stress was laid on a broader Augustinian sense of oblation rather than on act. For example, Albert the Great argued:

> [One can ask] whether Christ is immolated in every sacrifice? . . . Or one can ask it thus: why is it called *immolatio* or *sacrificium*? To which one should say that Christ is truly immolated every day when sacrifice is offered to God the Father. For immolation is said to be the act of oblation with regard to the thing offered [*ex parte rei oblatae*] and the same act is said to be a sacrifice with regard to the result [*ex parte effectus*]. Since with regard to the thing offered the oblation remains forever something lifted up for us that ought to be offered [*oblata et offerenda*], we therefore immolate and sacrifice forever. But this is not, however, true of the crucifixion; for it is said to be not the act of the thing offered but rather a wicked act of the Jews or a suffering caused by them [*actum iniquum Judaeorum vel passionem, prout est ab eis illata*]; thus however it was not repeated and therefore is not the same.
>
> . . . Our immolation is however not only a representation [*repraesentatio*] but a true immolation—that is, the offering of a truly sacrificed thing by the hands of priests.

Hence there are two things referred to—that is, the object killed and the oblation [*rem occisam et oblationem*]—because immolation, properly so called, is the offering of something killed to the worship of God [*quia immolatio proprie est oblatio occisi ad cultum Dei*]. And thus the oblation is not only a representation but also a true act of offering. But it is not an act of killing and crucifying.[41]

This formulation tends both to telescope sacrifice into offering and to separate sacrifice from killing. But awareness of the killing of Christ remains: what is offered is a *rem occisam*.

Gabriel Biel, who saw the doubleness of the eucharistic species (bread and wine) as signifying the doubleness of incarnation (bread) and passion (wine), stressed that redemption lay in the pouring out of blood. Thus he gave a greater soteriological significance to blood than to body. But he then tamed the stress on "pouring forth," by giving blood its own double-ness—comfort as well as appeasement. "Blood" signified, he said, pouring out or ransom paid; but the phrase Christ actually used, "chalice of the blood," signified refection as well.[42] Jean Gerson, despite a sense of blood as expiation (*placatio* and *impetratio*), moved away from any stress on sacrifice as destruction. Although he proposed to define it as "an oblation made to God in recognition of his sovereignty [*oblatio facta Deo in recognitionem supremi dominii sui*]," he did not by this mean so much to signify God's power over the life of sinful humankind, symbolized by the destruction of the matter offered up, as to suggest the superiority of the New Testament over the Old.[43] David, Solomon, and those under the old law offered bulls and lambs without number to the Lord, he said. But for Christians there is "a new law, a new flock, a new sacrifice and a new testament, not of bulls but of the blood of Christ [*non vitulorum sed Christi sanguine confirmatum*]." Lifting from their eyes the veil that was rent at the time of the passion and turning inward to the law of the spirit, they can now find all sacrifices, holocausts, and offerings made new in the Lord's body and blood, which is lamb and dove, manna of the desert, bread of heaven, and promise of paradise.[44] As historian Marius Lépin has chronicled in exhaustive detail, scholastic theology struggled to shift the passion as represented in the mass away from the *mutatio* and *occisio* that lay at the root of sacrifice and toward a notion of giving or offering up—to move, in Aquinas's terms, from *sacrificium* to *oblatio*.[45]

The same complex sense of *sanguis Christi* as spilled and offered up (destruction and oblation) reverberates in iconography and devotional writing as well. The valences of such visual and verbal images are extremely complex because, on the one hand, piety gave greater and greater emphasis to the death on the cross as death—excruciating death—with all the guilt-tripping of

Christians that implied; yet it tended, on the other hand, as did university theology, to subsume that sacrifice into gift—either the gift of Christ to the faithful or an offering of the faithful to God. "He suffered and died for you," thundered preachers from pulpits. Christians accused themselves of this in their hearts. "Slayne [he] was in most cruell wise. . . ."[46] Yet for all the need to identify emotionally and spiritually with Christ's suffering, the meaning of *sacrificium* in devotional literature is often *oblatio*, something lifted up. For example, in an odd reversal of what learned theology would seem to teach even about oblation, Mechtild of Hackeborn (d. 1298), one of Gertrude's sister nuns at Helfta, received a revelation in which she saw Mary offering "the blood of the divine heart" in a golden pyx as a sacrifice to her son. Here, sacrifice means gift, and the divine heart-blood offered to Christ by Mary signifies the love or mercy of *divinitas* granted to humans because of Christ.[47] In a prayer attributed to Dionysius the Carthusian, the faithful soul desires to offer up its own blood drops to Christ as a sign of its regret for ingratitude. Like the blood Catherine of Genoa wished to offer for all humankind, the individual's own blood in this prayer can be an oblation because it is parallel to (even subsumed in) Christ's.[48] When Adelheid Langmann and Christina Ebner wrote of the ascent of the eucharistic elements to heaven, they not only indicated the quite technical theological idea that Christ cannot change location (i.e., does not descend into the chalice) but also reflected the importance of eucharist as offering, the lifting up of Christ's blood.[49]

The iconographical motif of the Gregorymass I discussed in Chapter 1 also clearly reflects understandings of blood as offering, especially in those versions where the pope appears actually to celebrate mass. Although the versions that stress wafer, or body, tend more simply to depict offering up (as, for example, in the Dedeke panel from Lübeck, Plate 2), those in which the blood spills outward (as, for example in the panel painting from Soest, Plate 3) also make it clear that the blood is an oblation. What is offered up in devotional literature and art, then, is not the killing but the blood. The death of Christ, like his suffering, is supposed to arouse the Christian to guilt and love. But where *sacrificium* is discussed or depicted, it tends to mean the blood or the lamb that is offered, not the act of killing.

Yet there was always the fact of the death of Christ. The "something done" could not be completely refigured into giving, or giving back. No matter how alive the blood, Christ died. As William of Auvergne pointed out: in the case of an animal, the slaughterer can kill or spare it at will. So we are between the hands of God, who can have mercy or put us to death for our sins. Sacrifice is humankind's recognition that we deserve to die, that Christ dies in our stead.[50] Exactly the *mutatio* that should never challenge or threaten the immutability of God was not only enacted on a *hostia* offered to him but also done to God himself if Christ was truly sacrificed. All the efforts to avoid dying and destruction in explicit references to *sacrificium*, like the increased stress on Christ's willing of his own death in an act of love, are not a discarding of the concept of bloody sacrifice so much as a struggling with its enigmatic power. Although university theologians gave little attention to sacrifice as an explicit topic, they regularly alluded to it, as did devotional writers and artists, in their calls to guilt and love. Moreover, when *sanguis Christi* became a topic of dispute, what was debated was exactly the question of what it meant for the blood to be poured out (whether during the *triduum mortis* or in blood relics and miracles), and how far the faithful could touch and be touched by it in its separated, left-behind state. If we pay attention to what the texts say, it is the riddle of sacrifice (a breached victim offered to an immutable God, a destruction that nonetheless restores life) that lies behind all those *determinationes de sanguine Christi*, behind the visions and meditations of devotional theology, behind those frenzied pilgrimages to the living blood. The texts speak repeatedly of sacrifice. It was the act that restored the world, and it meant a victim offered in blood.

Sacrifice in Blood Cult and Controversy

If we return to the immediate context of Wilsnack and the writings of Johannes Witten, Hermann Bansleben, and Johannes Bremer, the centrality of sacrifice to blood cult becomes clear. As I pointed out in Chapter 2, a number of compilations of Wilsnack material exist in libraries throughout Germany.[51] Even the incipits of the texts in these collections show that the Scriptural passages at the heart of blood discussion were exactly those that had always been the central texts in a Christian theology of sacrifice. At their heart is blood, spilled (*effusus*) and sprinkled (*aspersus*). For example, Hermann Bansleben's sermon *de sanguine relicto*, included in several of these manuscript collections, treats Isaiah 63.3 (*Aspersus est sanguis . . .*), a complicated reference to those trampled in the winepress whose blood is splashed on the garments of him who comes in vengeance and redemption, dyeing them red. It is the passage from which derives the iconographic image of Christ crushed under the beam of the winepress and pouring blood.[52] Johannes Witten begins his *determinatio . . . de sanguine Christi relicto* with Matthew 26.28: "For this is my blood of the new testament . . . shed [*effundetur*] for many unto remission of sins."[53]

Even in Bremer's *questio magistralis* of 1455, what is key is less the ontological status of separated blood, which Bremer as a Franciscan defends, than the fact of blood poured out (*effusus*) and resumed (*reassumptus*). Although, as we saw in Chapter 2, Bremer devoted sophisticated analysis to the question of how Christ could be *totus* when *particulae* are left behind, much of his emphasis is on the salvific effect of blood shedding, even as he is careful to stress that the spilling (*exitus*) is effective because the blood also joins with Christ in glory (*reditus*). Bremer penned more, however, in the context of the *Wilsnackerstreit*, than the *questio magistralis*. He also wrote two more pastoral treatments of blood, the sermons of 1443. The fact that these were collected in several of the Wilsnack anthologies demonstrates the centrality of sacrificial theology to the controversy.

Both Bremer's sermons treat Hebrews 9.13–14, the crucial New Testament sacrifice text:

> For if the blood of bulls and of goats and the ashes of an heifer, being sprinkled, sanctify such as are defiled, to the cleansing of the flesh,
> How much more shall the blood of Christ, who by the Holy Ghost offered himself unspotted unto God, cleanse our conscience from dead works, to serve the living God?

In both sermons, the sacrificial echoes are clear. The basic theme of the first is blood poured out to feed, heal, and above all to purify (*mundare, emundare*). Christ's blood is said to be hot and nourishing, like the milk of Mary's breast;[54] it is a price paid,[55] a red and cleansing wave. Bremer repeats the conventional idea that one drop is enough for our salvation but stresses that blood poured from the side wound even after Christ's death.[56] The second sermon too is dominated by traditional sacrifice theology, glossed with a typically fifteenth-century physiological interest. Humankind cannot make satisfaction; hence Christ must be wounded in every part and blood must flow in healing, fructifying, and cleansing waves. Hebrews 9 is repeatedly cited alongside rather technical references to blood as curative and liberating, even as defensive and avenging.[57] For all the assumption that Christ's blood is a price paid, the dominant motion of the blood is outward, not upward; it is, in these sermons, less *oblatio* than *effusio*. The major verb is *emundare*, but *sine effusione non fit remissio* is cited again and again. Salvation is the sprinkling and inundating of humankind with blood, shed from the lamb of God.

Fifty years later, Johannes von Paltz returned to the paradigm of Old Testament sacrifice in his discussion of the "general causes" (that is, the basic reasons) for the passion of Christ. Christ's sacrifice is the new sprinkling of blood, because the voice of our sin cries out as the blood of Abel cried (Gen. 4.10); it is the offering of life, for the seat of life is in the blood (Lev. 17.11). Christ is the lamb without defect (I Pet. 1.19)—the immaculate animal required in Hebrew sacrifice.[58] Even Nicholas of Cusa, in whose soteriology the lifting up of humanity into God through Christ is more central than any sense of sacrifice offered or price paid, nonetheless assumes that *guttae sanguinis mundum totum reformantes.*[59] Formed from the virgin blood of Mary and risen glorified on Easter morning, *sanguis Christi* is, as he decreed at Halberstadt, "invisible in glorified veins," not seeable in miracles or monstrances.[60] But Cusanus's focus in his "Quod resurgit . . ." is on blood far more than on body, and his insistence that Christ's blood never ceases to be blood and yet never ceases to be joined to the Only-Begotten Word, is owing not only to the disputes of the 1450s and '60s into which he was drawn but also to the theological premise those disputes assumed. *Fusus* (the word is Cusanus's) *sanguis Christi* reconciles and reforms the world.[61]

At the heart then of the fifteenth-century discussion of the blood of Christ were those passages from Hebrews and I Peter in which the death on the cross subsumes and replaces, as well as cancels, the Old Testament shedding and sprinkling of the blood of bulls and heifers. Such references had a long history of association with the cult of Christ's blood.

Our earliest text connected with blood cult—the *De pretioso sanguine* from between 923 and 950 that recounts the translation of the Reichenau blood relic—opens with sixteen lines of hexameter that praise the blood of the "tender lambkin shed from his snow white flesh" for our salvation [*quem nivea agnellus fudisti carne tenellus*].[62]

> He was once prefigured in that lamb as by a type, so that just as that lamb freed the people once chosen by God from the destruction of the devastating angel by the sprinkling of its blood, so too might this true lamb redeem us from the assault of the foe by the flow of the blood which he shed, of which the Apostle says, "For Christ our pasch is sacrificed."[63]

The earliest Latin text (late twelfth century) concerning the blood relic at Fécamp, which contains an account both of the invention in 990 and of the translation of part of the relic to Norwich in 1171, refers to the "crimson blood of that most gentle lamb, who cleansed the bond of the old crime with his blood."[64] Matthew Paris reports that the bishop of Norwich described the Westminster blood relic as *pretium mundi.*[65] On the Cismar altarpiece, whether the central panel showed the bleeding Christ of the flagellation or was replaced on feast days by a silver figure of the resurrected that contained *Blut Christi*, believers saw, above it all on the very pinnacle, the sacrificial lamb of God.[66]

The theme of sacrifice was also central in the blood debates of mid-fifteenth-century Rome. In a nonpolemical context, John of Capistrano wrote that the new covenant is born with the blood of the Son just as the old was begun in the blood of animals. It is, John argues, exactly in the blood spilled forth that the promise of incorruption (Ps. 15.10) lies.[67] The blood that saves is salvific *because* it is the blood of sacrifice. When Pius II summarized the argument of the Dominicans concerning blood shed during the *triduum*, his description makes it clear that the blood in question is sacrificial blood.

> And Peter in the Epistle says, "You were not redeemed with corruptible things, as gold and silver . . . but with the precious blood of Christ, as of a lamb unspotted and undefiled [I Pet. 1.18–19]"; and he is speaking of the shed blood under the figure of a spotless lamb, which in the Old Testament was the symbol of the Savior, and one whose blood was shed. The shed blood of Christ would not have been a fit price if it had been abandoned by divinity. And Paul writes to the Hebrews, "For if the blood of goats and of bulls and the ashes of an heifer, being sprinkled, sanctify such as are defiled, to the cleansing of the flesh; how much more shall the blood of Christ, who by the Holy Ghost offered Himself unspotted unto God, cleanse your conscience from dead works, to serve the living God [Heb. 9.13–14]?" He compares the blood of Christ to the blood of goats and bulls, shed blood to shed blood, and prefers that of Christ. . . .
>
> . . . only after it had been shed did blood have the power of purification and absolution. For with this they used to smear the doorposts and altars and unless this were done the high priest dared not enter the holy of holies. The symbol must agree with the thing symbolized [*coaptanda est figurato figura*] and we must conclude with the Apostle that Christ's blood outside his body is of more efficacy than the blood of those animals. . . . [T]he authority of John Chrysostom on John is cited. . . . "This blood when shed washed clean all the world. . . ."
>
> . . . it is the opinion of all learned men that the blood of Christ as the price of our redemption was offered not to the Devil, as some have foolishly thought, but to God the Father and the Trinity itself. . . .[68]

It was crucial to this Dominican polemic that *sanguis Christi* be shed or separated: ". . . only after it had been shed did blood have the power of purification and absolution." It was also crucial that the blood was still Christ: "the shed blood . . . would not have been a fit price if it had been abandoned by divinity." To these Dominican theologians then, the paradox of the crucifixion—death brings life—is mirrored in blood. A symbol must "agree with" what is symbolized. The characteristics of *cruor*, which can pour out yet remain (at least for a little while) red and living, are appropriate representations of Christ the *hostia* who both remains with God and yet spills onto humankind. But the blood of sacrifice is, in these arguments, more than a symbol of continuity in discontinuity. It is an act—a "something done." It is paid to the Creator and smeared on humanity to reconnect it to God. In such arguments, the concept of blood sacrifice provides more than technical arguments for a particular position on the nature of Christ's body during the *triduum*. It summarizes soteriology.

As we saw in Chapter 5, Franciscans took a different position on blood in the *triduum*. To Franciscans, the "blood of the Lord," when used of crucifixion and *triduum mortis*, referred to the humiliation and death of Christ. Francesco della Rovere, stating the Franciscan case in his *De sanguine Christi* of 1467, used the same passages from Hebrews cited by the Dominicans, but he used them to argue that the blood of Old Testament sacrifice prefigured the death rather than the blood of Calvary.[69] Franciscans did not, however, reject the concept of Christ's passion as sacrifice. A death was necessary; whether bloody or not, something had to be done for humankind's salvation. Nor was the paradox of living separation absent from their piety. Indeed their support for blood relics as genuinely left behind, if inessential, particles of *sanguis Christi* involved a complex sense of the way in which part mirrored, and directed devotion toward, whole; blood laid down referred finally to another blood, one that never departed from glory. In the Wilsnack controversy of the 1440s, it was Franciscans and Benedictines who not only supported pilgrimage to the miraculous blood in the Prignitz but also argued for the possibility that some real, physical portion of Christ, left behind or miraculously appearing, might provide special access to God.[70]

Sacrifice in fifteenth-century theology and piety was thus no mere vestige of patristic discussion. In it were interwoven the various elements of soteriology I tried to disentangle in Chapter 9: price paid, example given, the incorporation of all humankind in Christ the God-man. But sacrifice expressed something deeper and more difficult. If what redeems is an act, an *aliquid factum*, then destruction and immutability, death and life, come together. The very blood flow, the dying, the killing, somehow consecrate and set apart both victim and those in whose name the sacrifice is made. What was at stake in mid-fifteenth-century debates over hosts, relics, and *triduum mortis*, whether at Wilsnack or at Rome, was how Christians gained access to the paradox at the heart of soteriology. Not only the faithful who clamored for *Blut Christi* and the authorities who rewarded its veneration with indulgences, but also those theologians who argued against its visible presence, were struggling to understand this paradox. As the debates themselves suggest, however, it was a paradox that continually threatened to slip from their comprehension.

I shall return in Chapter 11 to some of the ways in which piety and theology in the fifteenth century began, however tentatively, to explore the deep contradictions and incongruities in sacrificial theology. But before I do, a final point about the continuity of the tradition must be made.

The Sixteenth Century

Sacrificial theology did not disappear in the sixteenth century. If anything, the emphasis on sacrifice became stronger and more fully articulated as various elements of soteriology and Christology were vigorously debated and their premises made clear. Although Protestants and Catholics came to differ over how the benefits of Christ's sacrifice were made available to the faithful or whether the Lord's Supper was itself a sacrifice, they did not differ over the centrality of blood sacrifice, understood as such, for redemption.

I take first a sixteenth-century Catholic example: the English ecclesiastic and opponent of Henry VIII, John Fisher, who was executed in 1535. Fisher wrote that as often as God's creatures receive his sacraments, "so oft it is to be byleued they are sprencled with the droppes of the same moost holy blode. whose vertue perseth vnto the soule, and maketh it clene from al synne."[71] Although Protestant contemporaries would not have agreed with Fisher's idea that all sacraments are sacrifices, they did not dissent from his assumption that the holocaust of the old law foreshadows the new or from the association of sacrifice with cleansing.

> . . . as saynt Poule sayth he offred hymselfe of very grete and feruent charyte vnto his fader almygthy god as a sacrefyce of swete odour. No man may doubte of this that by the aspercyon of blode of beestes before the Incarnacyon was sygnefyed and represented the effusyon of the blode of Cryst for our redempcyon.[72]

> For as the vnreasonable beest was slayne for clensynge of synnes, and the blode of it shedde vpon the awter, so cryst Ihesu the lambe vndefyled, moost innocent beest was put to dethe vpon a crosse and all his blode shedde for the remyssyon of synners.[73]

Blood, to Fisher, is accusation and threat as well as consolation.[74] Christ's blood pays the "ransoum," reconciles, and comforts. Atonement (that is, redemption) means at-one-ment with God.[75] Neither Abelard nor Anselm, neither Bernard, Aquinas, Scotus, nor Biel, neither Cusanus nor Bremer, Döring nor Heinrich Tocke, would have disagreed with Fisher when he said:

> Sinne so deadly wounded and blotted the soule of man, that with out shedding of the most precious bloud of our saviour Christ Iesu, no lyfe could be restored vuto sinners, nor the soules might be washed from the fowle abhominable corruption of sinne.[76]

Nor was the centrality of sacrifice merely a Catholic trope. When the reformers Ägidius Faber and Faustinus Labes attacked the relic of Schwerin and the Sternberg hosts as papistical superstitions, they opposed to such colored nonsense the true blood of Christ, poured forth in sacrifice, "strong enough in its nature to stand against sin, hell, death, the world and the devil."[77] Luther himself said:

> the sprinkling of which St Peter is speaking (and which is signified by this sprinkling [baptism]) is none other than preaching [cf. I Pet. 1.1–2]. . . . The tongue of the preacher or Christian is the aspergillum. He dips it into the rosy red blood of Christ [*tunckt er in des Herrn Christi rosenfarb blut*] and sprinkles the people with it [*besprenget damit das volck*], that is, he preaches to them the gospel, which declares that Christ has purchased the forgiveness of sins with his precious blood, that he has poured out [*vergossen*] his blood on the cross for the whole world, and that he who believes this has been sprinkled with this blood.[78]

The shift of the sacrificial sprinkling image from eucharist to preaching is, of course, in line with the Protestant emphasis on the Word, but the connection of blood-sprinkling to baptism is typically late medieval. And the understanding of sacrifice is exactly that of Hebrews 9.

All over north Germany in the first half of the sixteenth century, Protestant woodcuts and altarpieces depicted the blood of the crucified, splashing on the heads of Christians to bring salvation.[79] For example, on one of the wings of the Schneeberg altar—the earliest and most complete of the Protestant Cranach altars, about whose iconography Luther himself advised—we find John the Baptist in a red robe of triumph standing with Adam below the crucified figure of Christ pointing to the red blood that flows from the side wound onto Adam's chest (see Plate 26).[80] The dove of the spirit springs from Christ's side along with the blood. Below the cross stands the sacrificial lamb bearing a banner of victory, and the inscription reads: "Behold the Lamb of God who takes away the sins of the world (John 1.29)."[81]

A woodcut of circa 1550 (Plate 27) provides another example of the continuation in Protestant theology of the association of Christ's sacrificial blood with both baptism and eucharist. Here Martin Luther and Jan Hus are shown offering the Lord's Supper in both species under an altar on which a huge grapevine curls around a chalice or font. The crucified Christ hangs over the basin, pouring out for the faithful his washing and feeding blood.[82]

I shall not carry the story I tell in this book beyond the very early sixteenth century. That century would see, as is well known, intense and explicit theological debate over how the price Christ paid in the death of the cross, the example he offered, and the victory he won were appropriated by or attributed to Christians. What was scrutinized was how the death of Christ justifies or redeems, and whether the faithful can contribute to, or in some way earn, this salvation. Whether the mass was a sacrifice also received fierce theological attention: did it repeat the moment of Calvary, manifest its eternal presence, or remind believers of its significance?[83] Moreover, as we have seen, questions about earthly or literal manifestations of saving *Blut Christi* were also debated, not only between Catholics and Protestants but among them as well. Even in Catholic areas, where blood pilgrimages continued and popes forbade polemicists to deny the religious usefulness of relics and miracle hosts, the attention of the faithful tended, by the late sixteenth century, to shift to bleeding statues and places where visions allegedly occurred. The point I wish to underline here, however, is that—for all the vitriolic polemic and the sophisticated religious controversy between and among Catholics and Protestants—Christians did not disagree that the crucifixion was a blood sacrifice.[84] Neither the paradox of oblation made possible by destruction nor the even deeper paradox of the sacrifice of God to and by God was explored. The question "why by blood?" was not asked.

In my penultimate chapter I turn to certain ways in which a few religious writers of the fourteenth and fifteenth centuries began to ask that question.

Chapter 11
The Aporia of Sacrifice

The blood piety so characteristic of the fifteenth century caused anxiety, both on the part of the faithful, who often sensed blood as accusation, and on the part of their spiritual advisers, who not only urged them toward empathy and guilt but were frequently chagrined as well by the immediacy with which these sentiments were felt. Contemporaries noticed that their devotions were bloody and that blood was horrible. Pious women mystics sometimes found the passion frightening.[1] University theologians stressed repeatedly that, despite occasional host or chalice miracles, God chose to veil the real presence in the eucharist so that the faithful would not be offended by *horror cruoris*. (It is significant that the standard phrase targets blood, not flesh, as the potential offense.)[2] Confessors attempted to rein in an extravagantly somatic spirituality that imitated the cross in paramystical experiences or self-inflicted suffering. For all the popularity of flagellant processions in certain regions, they were outlawed in others.

What I wish to explore in this chapter is more than the anxiety such intense piety generated, although the anxiety is important as background. I wish to consider the problems raised by a theology of sacrifice. The problems, like the theology itself, are more implicit than explicit. But I want to argue that we find, in the fourteenth and fifteenth centuries, a questioning of blood alongside the frenzy for it. First, I explore hints in the texts themselves of devotional and theological discontent with placing blood at the center of salvation. We have already met some of these in the Franciscan side of the debate at Rome considered in Chapter 5. Second, I point out ways in which the understanding of sacrifice as inherited from biblical and patristic sources did not map entirely comfortably onto either the gospel story or theological ideas elaborated around it. One obvious consequence was that the idea of God as victim could be both guilt-inducing and difficult to integrate into piety. A no less real but less obvious consequence was that the faithful could feel bypassed in the circle of sacrificer-sacrifice-recipient, as they also did in the clerical action of withdrawing the cup. Finally, I return to the questions of cult and holy matter I raised so many pages ago. For understanding the way in which the concept of sacrifice informed ideas of blood relics and miracle hosts only sharpens our awareness of the paradox of immutable matter/mutable divine that undergirds blood pilgrimage as well as blood piety.

Questioning Blood: The *Meditations on the Life of Christ*

Already in the twelfth century, Bernard of Clairvaux had asked the question I cite as epigraph to this volume: why blood?

> "We are reconciled to God by the death of his Son" [Rom. 5.10]. Where is this reconciliation, this remission of sin? . . . In this chalice, [Christ] says, "of the blood of the New Testament, which is poured out for you" [Matt. 26.28; Luke 22.20]. . . . We obtain it by the interceding death of the only Begotten and are justified by grace in the same blood. . . . Why, you ask me, by blood when he could have done it by word. I ask the same question. It is given to me only to know that it is so, not why it is so.[3]

By the later Middle Ages, a few thinkers, mostly Franciscans, repeated the question. It seems to express a discomfort with sacrifice. We should not over-interpret the discomfort. It occurs in the context of a stress on the necessity for obedience—Christ's in acceding to God's demand that he be the victim and ours in acceding to his choice in doing it this way. It is moreover embedded in the extravagant voluntarism of late medieval theology, which stressed, as the other side of obedience, the utterly free nature of God's will in organizing everything, including our salvation, entirely as he chose.[4] The point is ultimately that God cannot be bound by the rules of logic or necessity nor by our paltry human questions and anxieties. In the passage I quote above, Bernard is not really asking "why?" His question is included in an attack on Abelard for heresy.[5] He is actually advocating acceptance where divine reasons surpass human understanding, and ridiculing those who prefer their own questions to God's teaching.[6] Similarly, when Gertrude the Great and Mechtild of Magdeburg express discomfort with blood and ask repeatedly why Christ must suffer such distress, they are not rejecting what they see as the theological given that Jesus' death is the pivot of salvation but rather underlining his love.[7] Aquinas and Grosseteste, who stress Christ's choice to die at the moment he renders up his soul, are not undercutting the centrality of sacrifice when they suggest it could have been done another way. What they are emphasizing is the paradox of lodging life in bloodshed, and hence the power and incomprehensibility of God.

Nonetheless, whatever resolutions to their queries these authors reach and whatever purposes they intend to serve by raising them, the questioning is there. I turn for an extended example to one of the most influential texts of the later Middle Ages: the fourteenth-century Franciscan *Meditations on the Life of Christ* (sometimes known as the pseudo-Bonaventure), written for Franciscan nuns and widely propagated in vernacular translations to readers throughout Europe.[8]

If one reads again with fresh eyes this often-discussed manual for meditation, one notices something curious in the description of the passion. The text is, of course, experiential and calculated to bring the reader to identification with the suffering of Christ and Mary. Those sufferings are described in excruciating detail, both physiological and psychological. All this is quite familiar to scholars of the later Middle Ages. But two usually unnoticed points need to be made. First, blood is not very prominent in the *Meditations*. There is pain, ripping and tearing, humiliation and unbearable shame, but very little bloodshed. As it did in traditional accounts of the crucifixion in the patristic period, blood occurs mostly where it occurs in the Gospels—on the Mount of Olives (in the bloody sweat) and at the lance prick, when the side is opened. (There is also mention of blood in the context of the flagellation and nailing, with explicit reference to relics of the supposedly blood-spattered column and cross revered in European churches.)[9] As both the spirituality of Grosseteste and the arguments of Franciscan theologians in the Rome debate might lead us to expect, the text stresses death more than blood but couples blood, insofar as it is spiritually important, to actual relics. A second, less expected point also needs to be made. Blood references are the places where the account becomes theological in a technical sense, not merely experiential. It is blood that raises the basic soteriological question, and to that question, sacrifice is clearly the answer. Thus the point of blood in the pseudo-Bonaventuran text is not so much to impel the adherent to immerse herself in an experience of suffering as to call attention to, and indeed raise questions about, the rationale of a particular organization of salvation.

Sweating out his blood, Christ asks that the cup pass away, and God answers: "My most beloved Son knows that the redemption of humankind [*humani generis redempcio*], which we so desire, cannot be accomplished properly without the shedding of his blood [*sine sui sanguinis effusione*]; consequently if he wishes the salvation of souls he must die for them."[10] The reply is not only an illustration of the psychological suffering of Jesus and of his humble obedience; it is also a soteriological statement of the necessity for sacrifice. Jesus accepts, as he also accepts God's subsequent (hideously anti-Semitic) proposal that the Jews must become killers so that others may see.[11] The echoes of Hebrews 9.22 are clear: no remission without bloodshed.

Later in the text, Mary returns to the question. Understanding full well both the culture of sacrifice and the theological importance of the freedom of God, she issues her challenge. Why sacrifice? He could have done it another way.

. . . most merciful Father, I recommend to you my most beloved son. You will not treat him cruelly, for you are good to everyone. . . . . is my son Jesus to die? . . . . just Father, if you wish the redemption of humankind, I implore you to effect it in another way, for all things are possible to you.[12]

Bound to the cross as sacrificial animal, "most gentle lamb," Christ gives the answer:

Behold, I am here, my Father. For love and salvation of humankind you wished me humbled as far as the cross. It pleases me; I accept; and I offer myself to you for those whom you gave to me, wishing them to be my brothers. Therefore, Father, accept, and for love of me be pleased to wipe away and remove all old stains from them: I offer myself to you for them, Father [*pro eis enim me offero tibi*].[13]

Mary accepts. But in her prayer below the cross that God lessen Christ's suffering, a slight reservation (or is it helplessness?) seems to undergird her obedience: "Father and eternal God, It pleases you that my son should be crucified: it is not the time to ask him back from you."[14] It is hard not to be reminded that, as Barbara Newman has pointed out, another mother also protests for the first time in the later Middle Ages. It is only in fifteenth-century drama that Sarah, Isaac's mother, appears in the Abraham story to ask: why my son? why this way?[15]

With the aid of Bernard of Clairvaux and other earlier texts, which he quotes liberally, the author of the *Meditations* tries to make sense of the atonement. Both the theory of Christ as satisfaction—the price of salvation—and the theory of Christ as example appear prominently.

For if I [sinful humankind] could repay you [God] . . . with heaven and earth and all their beauty, surely I would not reach the measure of my *debt* at all [*ad mensuram debiti, nullatenus attingere possem*]. That I give back what I owe and what I can pay of my debt to you, O Lord, is by your favor. [*Vt autem et adipsum quod et debeo, et possibile mihi est, retribuam, tui muneris est, Domine.*] [Attributed by the author to Bernard but actually pseudo-Anselm, Meditation 9.] (my emphasis)[16]

From his own side he [Christ] drew forth the *price* of satisfaction [*pretium satisfactionis*] that appeased the Father. . . . Truly plentiful, for not a drop but a wide wave of blood [*non gutta, sed unda sanguinis largiter*] flowed from the five parts of his body. [Quoted from Bernard.] (my emphasis)[17]

The emptying of Christ was not simple or moderate: He emptied himself as far as the flesh, as death, as the cross. Who could properly weigh the humility . . . ? But someone says: "Could the creator not repair his work without such difficulty?" He could, but he preferred to do it with his sufferings . . . . Indeed he assumed many wearying things so that he might *hold man*, his debtor, *in great love*, and that the difficulty of the redemption might *move* him to acts of gratitude. . . . [Quoted from Bernard.] (my emphasis)[18]

Behind the repeated references to *pretium* and *exemplum* (Anselmian satisfaction and Abelardian exemplarism, as the textbooks would have it) is the "most gentle lamb" of the cross. The price paid is drawn from the side wound; redemption is complete "emptying." As in Christ's words to Mary quoted above, sacrifice is crucial: it is blood spilled that washes away the sins of humankind and creates community. In these particular passages then, there is more at stake than urging the pious to enter empathetically into Christ's suffering and Mary's. Blood raises the question "why?"

The *Meditations on the Life of Christ* is a text of devotional theology, and it was a vastly popular one. It offered an account of, and reaction to, the passion that readers from the fourteenth to the sixteenth century wanted to hear. Hence it is significant that the only soteriological rather than simply experiential discussion it includes is triggered by and firmly associated with blood. It is also significant that the discussion is an exposition of sacrifice, one in which Bernard's question remains present and only ambiguously answered: "Could the creator not repair his work without such difficulty?"

The same question hovered around the edges of the fifteenth-century debate concerning the status of left-behind blood. As we have seen, the Franciscans at Rome were concerned not so much to defend the possibility of blood relics and host miracles as to stress the humiliation of Christ's death. To say that Christ's shed blood was without divinity during the *triduum* cast "no ignominy or contempt . . . on the divinity of the Savior, whose death became more glorious in proportion as it was more humiliating."[19] But in the course of argument, the Franciscan interlocutors raised the possibility that "the human race could have been redeemed without blood if the Son of God had laid down his life for us without shedding it." It was not a new theological consideration. Aquinas himself had mentioned it but in the context of emphasizing Christ's obedience and God's love.[20] Here, in the context of countering a Dominican emphasis on the glory of blood, the Franciscan position went so far as to suggest that God might have effected a bloodless salvation. In replying to this point, the Dominicans indeed went further, admitting that Christ could have saved humanity without dying, although they asserted that God did not choose to do it thus.[21]

The Franciscan argument was not, however, a direct and explicit questioning of sacrifice. For the Franciscan effort was to stress the wholeness of the offered Christ—body and soul as well as blood. And, as the Dominicans argued in rebuttal, the Franciscans knew well that "Christ did not die without shedding blood nor give up His life without bloodshed." "A bloody, grievous, and horrible death was chosen that greater love might be shown, and so the ancient transgression was blotted out according to the predictions of the prophets."[22] Whether or not blood took central place as the metonym for and symbol of death, sacrifice remained.

In comparison to the popular and accessible *Meditations,* the abstruse arguments about Christ's blood during the *triduum* that engaged the papal court in the mid-fifteenth century were so complex and obscure that many who attended did not understand them and scholars have been confused ever since.[23] Yet behind both the *Meditations* and the Rome texts hovers an uncomfortable sense that the choice of sacrifice by God is in some way arbitrary and inexplicable. He could have done it another way. Ultimately the will of God—which became increasingly central in late medieval theology—was the only explanation for the lodging of blood sacrifice at the heart of redemption.

Avoiding Sacrifice

In addition to texts that articulate questions about sacrifice (whatever the purpose of the articulation), there are a wide range of texts from the fourteenth and fifteenth centuries that avoid or attenuate sacrifice, although retaining the term. They do this in several ways, either by denying explicitly that sacrifice is killing, or by telescoping sacrifice into oblation so that the Old Testament sense of the destruction of the offering is eclipsed, or by glossing sacrifice simply as a gift of love or grace or life from Christ to humanity. In these moves, the act necessary for blood flow is strangely occluded, despite the fixation, characteristic of the period, on the death agonies of Christ as arousal and proof of love. Where a vivid sense survives that Christ died on the cross—and indeed, as we have seen, this emphasis grew more and more strident—the texts are careful to call this death killing (by Jews, infidels, heretics, blasphemers, ordinary wayward Christians, or even the devout), not sacrifice.

As we have seen, late medieval theology pulled back from exactly the element of destruction it understood to be implicit in sacrifice. Indeed devotional emphasis on the side wound (a blow delivered after death, according to John 19.34) tended to dissociate blood—even spilled blood—from killing. Writers as different as Vincent of Beauvais and Dionysius the Carthusian, for example, using an argument that went back to Augustine, stressed that Christ was not pierced on the cross but opened like a doorway or a birth canal. Vincent wrote: "With great precision, John says [of the soldier with the lance] . . . 'he opened,' not 'he struck' or 'he wounded.' By this he wanted to indicate that . . . the door of life was opened. . . ."[24] In this interpretation, the lance prick is neither an act of killing nor an act of violence. The voluntarism of late medieval theology also contributed to a certain attenuation of the idea of sacrifice as an act of killing, an act "done to." Humankind owed a price but the blood Christ shed to pay it was shed in utter freedom. To theologians such as Grosseteste or Dionysius, the cry on Golgotha at the moment of Christ's expiring was a statement of choice. In devotional literature such as the *Prickynge of Love*, the stress on Christ's ability to pour forth living blood even after death occasionally seems to obscure not only the killing and violation but even the fact of dying such experiential piety was also intent on emphasizing.[25]

In eucharistic discussion, some theologians simply tried to keep the killing invisible. Although they sometimes asserted the superiority of New Testament sacrifice over Old by claiming a human victim to be more effective than animal ones, they also claimed, as did Alger of Liège, that Christ's offering up of himself in the mass replaces and improves upon the sacrifices of the old covenant exactly because the bloody offering is unseen. Some argued that Christians are superior because they offer bread and wine not animal flesh. Despite the torture that *mola* in its meaning of millstone might have suggested, John Beleth related *immolatio* (sacrifice) etymologically to grain or flour (*mola, . . . far vel ador*) sprinkled on the altar.[26]

As we have seen, scholastic theologians struggled to avoid the suggestion that sacrifice was repeated in the mass, although it was present there. Albert the Great argued, somewhat convolutedly, that the eucharist is an oblation forever, because it is forever lifted up. But the killing is a wicked act of the Jews that is not repeated. The act of crucifying is not sacrifice, although both the dead Christ and the offering up [*rem occisam et oblationem*] are. In other words, as a noun, sacrifice is both *oblatio* and *res occisa* (or *hostia*); but as a verb, it is only *offerre*. Indeed Robert Paululus argued that what God gives humankind is a *donum* (gift); what we offer him is only *munus* (service), because it is given from inferior to superior. We call it a sacrifice only insofar as we offer (*offerimus*) a memorial of Christ's passion by lifting up a little portion withdrawn from our daily sustenance.[27] In such analysis, not only is the act of Christ's death not sacrifice; anything humans can offer is not really a sacrifice. When devotional writers such as Dionysius the Carthusian ask plaintively "what can I offer him?" or express hesitation in phrases such as "would that I could offer . . . ," we should not ignore their nagging sense that they cannot make true sacrifice or that even the oblation of the mass does not include them in it.[28]

References to Christ as sacrificial animal, such as Mechtild of Magdeburg's evocation of Jesus as bloody lamb on a bloody cross, continue, of course, to be very frequent.[29] But, like scholastic discourse, devotional writing often obscures or softens the full Levitical sense of sacrifice. The implications of gift exchange are undercut by stressing Christ's gift to humankind more than humanity's offering to Christ.[30] For all the stress on mass as *oblatio* or on offering prayer for one's fellow human beings, gift language in devotional theology tends increasingly to refer to Christ's washing, flowing onto, sprinkling, and warming his human lovers; the direction of the gift is from Christ to sinner. The agency is God's. In a typical pious expression, Adelheid Langmann said: "When he [Christ] died out of love, his side was pierced, and water and blood flowed from it. This he gives as a gift to all those who love him."[31] It is striking that Adelheid says "when Christ died," not "when Christ was killed"; that the death appears to be chosen by the one dying ("died out of love"); that no agent is given for the piercing ("his side was pierced"); and that the blood and water are simply a gift Christ chooses to give.

The text known as "The Little Book of Love" (from the later fourteenth century and sometimes attributed to Suso) puts it in similar language:

> *O sapiencia eterna*, oh eternal wisdom. . . . For the sake of your precious blood, open my heart. . . . Lay all my understanding in your wounds and my wisdom in your scars [*Lege alle min kunst an din wunden und min wisheit an din wundtmal*], so that I may henceforth draw closer to your death in you alone, true book of love, and absent myself from all earthly things [*und dinem tode zů neme und allen zergangklichen dingen ab neme*]. So now may I be not I but you in me [*ich nút ich, sunder . . . dir in mir . . .*], and may I thus remain bound forever in you by the bond of your love.[32]

This piety is not passive or quietist.[33] The author struggles to draw himself to Christ, to absent himself from the world, and to lie in Jesus' wounds. But the blood is the gift of Jesus. For the sake of his own blood (that is, himself), Jesus draws his lover upward, opens his heart, and binds him in the blood forever. It is Christ's blood offered to himself that brings salvation.

Although late medieval Christians, especially pious women such as Julian of Norwich and Catherine of Genoa, had a strong sense of offering up their suffering for others, this understanding of *oblatio* involves the idea of representation or incorporation I explored in Chapter 9. It is by the subsuming of their suffering into that of Christ—and indeed by the subsuming of their fellow Christians (*evyn cristen*) into themselves—that the offering is made. If we look at the seemingly simple little prayer of Margaret Ebner, "I greet you, Lord

. . . only true sacrifice. . . . And I thank you . . . that you . . . have deigned . . . to be offered to your Father by the priest . . . ," we note that the sacrifice with which Margaret wishes to join, although ostensibly made by the priest, is actually made by Christ to Christ. "Now offer Yourself today, oh Lord, for all the evil we have done against you and for all the good we have failed to do."[34]

The *Tochter Syon*, a thirteenth-century text that was popular in fourteenth- and fifteenth-century Germany in both its Latin and its German versions, reflects the same sense that the ultimate actor is God. In a scene that echoes the iconography of the *Tugendkruzifixion*, the virtues are described as hunting the King of Glory and wounding him with their darts of love. The point of the hunt is to bring four drops of blood down into the individual soul. Described as the infusion of grace, the knowledge of God, the yearning for heaven, and the transformation of joy, the drops are said to be sprinkled on the faithful. Thus the language of sprinkling, so often associated with Levitical sacrifice, is here a free gift from Christ. The act of making the gift accessible—the opening of the Christ (and here it is wounding, not killing)—is done by love itself.[35]

Moreover, sacrifice in devotional texts sometimes comes to take on the attenuated meaning it has in modern discourse although not in scriptural. Whereas in Scripture the act of sacrificing clearly entails reciprocity or gift-exchange, "sacrifice" when done by humans begins to mean the act of renouncing or giving something up.[36] For example, Anna von Munzingen, author of the Adelhausen nuns' book (from the second decade of the fourteenth century), reports that when a sister named Metze Tuschelin prayed to be spared the office of prioress, she heard a voice saying:

> Go back to the chapter room and receive obedience. For you shall know that I prefer your obedience. It weighs more before my eyes than Abraham's obedience, for he sacrificed what was outside him while you sacrifice what is inside: that is, your own will [*der oppferte dz vsser im wz. So oppferet di dz in dir ist dz ist din eiigener will*].[37]

Abraham's proposed blood sacrifice of Isaac, usually understood as a foreshadowing of eucharist and atonement, becomes here a kind of practice or work, a mere external observance; the nun's will is, in some sense, her self, and its renunciation is her service of God. In this context then sacrifice is a surrender to God, not a gift rendered to God in return for, or recognition of, what he has given us. Understood against the long tradition of Benedictine stress on utter obedience, there are here overtones of total abnegation of self.[38] Thus there is a sense in which what is offered—Metze's will—is destroyed in the offering. But Metze's sacrifice is not a gift exchange either initiated from God to humankind or offered from humankind to God. Despite the reference to

Abraham's blood sacrifice, there is no sprinkling or pouring, no bond created, and nothing for which shed blood is metonym. The point is a valuing of inner response over outer practice. Sacrifice is giving up the activities of a choir nun to take on, in obedience, a less desired role; it is giving up outer ritual or practice in order to direct one's intentionality toward Christ.

Metze Tuschelin's understanding of *sacrificium* as denying individual preference, Suso's idea of blood as a bond of love, Adelheid Langmann's conception of it as a gift poured into the heart of the visionary, Albert the Great's argument that sacrifice is oblation and victim but not killing—these concepts are very different from those in Leviticus or Hebrews, where the destruction of life is a rendering up of that life to God in an act that is expiation, purgation, and union. Whether consciously or not, devotional writers and theologians were, by the fourteenth century, beginning to avoid some of the most obvious associations of Levitical and New Testament *sacrificium* while enhancing others. If something about sacrifice expressed what they needed to say soteriologically, it troubled and perplexed them as well.

In a sense the reason for this is obvious. The Middle Ages was not a culture of actual sacrifice. Neither humans nor animals were killed and offered to God. Even the bread and wine of the eucharist were not so much destroyed or set apart as shared. Hence the template overlaid on crucifixion and eucharist by the Epistle to the Hebrews did not really fit.

Religious writers in the Middle Ages had quite a sophisticated knowledge of that template. They quoted Isidore repeatedly: sacrifice is named from *facere sacrum*; it is an act—a something done (*aliquid factum*). They were aware of the element of destruction in the act. As Thomas Aquinas put it, unless something is destroyed in the ritual moment, a sacrifice is only an offering like other offerings.[39] Or, as Capistrano said: Christ *is* the sacrifice because he is anointed with blood (*sanguine unctus*). A moment of cutting and spilling and marking is necessary.[40] Exactly these aspects made the image of blood sacrifice useful for pastors and theologians who wanted to present the doctrine of transubstantiation or graphically to evoke the need for human repentance. Important elements of Old Testament sacrifice—the creation of covenant (i.e. community), the evoking of the presence of God in the ritual moment, the sense of blood both poured out and lifted up—were usefully echoed in descriptions of passion, atonement, and communion. Blood—exactly in its paradoxical quality of separated-ness yet remaining-alive-ness—was an especially appropriate symbol of gift of self. But as a model, sacrifice was also a problem in three related senses.

First, the sacrality affixed to the victim in Levitical sacrifice through the act of killing and offering up was an act that needed to be repeated. The taboo quality of the object or objects made sacred by the sprinkling of blood abated with time. Second, the sacrificial victim was, paradoxically, destroyed yet given as a gift to God, source of all power, order, and creation. Third, sacrificer, victim, and recipient were distinct. The one who slaughtered and/or offered up the victim was not, of course, the victim itself, nor was he the recipient of the offering, although he benefited from the reciprocity created by the act. None of these characteristics fitted closely the New Testament sense of *sanguis Christi* as the gift of life to Christ's followers once and forever. For all their invoking of Hebrews 9 and their ubiquitous references to the blood of the lamb, for all their sense of being caught up ("represented") in a bloody death that somehow gave back to God something loving or something owed, medieval Christians found it difficult to see, in the details of the death on the cross, the Old Testament sacrifice it supposedly subsumed in superseding.

Hence fifteenth-century theologians and devotional writers skirted and bypassed some aspects of the sacrifice they so frequently evoked. They tended to obscure the destruction, the killing, behind references to offering up (*oblatio*); they tried, as Albert did, to separate the victim and the act that provided it; they worried about how a sacrifice done once and for all could be daily reenacted (and about their own guilt if it were); they strained to argue that eucharistic blood was poured out (in some sort of eternally existing pool) rather than spilled anew; they stressed blood as symbol of free gift and spoke of love or God himself as the one who wounded God. Both, on the one hand, the consecrating moment at the heart of the ritual and the element of destruction they knew it to entail, and, on the other hand, the subsuming of victim and celebrant into recipient posed difficulties. I turn to an exploration of each of these problems.

Who Sacrifices? Including/Excluding Christians and Blaming Jews

The idea of Christ as sacrificial lamb raised two very different problems vis-à-vis the performer of sacrifice. First, those who had done the act and made the victim—that is, killed—had to be seen as doing evil, not sacrificing. But according to the historical account medieval Christians accepted, these figures—Romans and above all Jews—came in such a theory perilously close to performing the ritual, to doing or effecting good. Second, if omnipotent and immutable God is sacrificed (changed, violated, killed), such an act can be performed only by God. How then is the ordinary Christian to be included in the act; how is he or she to make, or even offer up, the sacrifice?

As we have seen, a few thinkers such as Julian of Norwich and Peter Dorlandus developed notions of incorporation or participation that explained how all Christians (or even all humankind) are caught up in the Christ who dies on the cross. Much devotional literature expressed at least implicitly a sense of being enclosed or wrapped in (that is, incorporated in) this Christ.[41] But if that victim offers himself to make all things well (or even to give assurance that they are so), Christians must be incorporated in the act of offering too. They must be sacrificers.

Christians were, of course, told that they were represented in the priest, who not only consumed the blood in their stead but also was co-sacrificer with Christ.[42] This assurance was undercut, however, by the simultaneous insistence that the priest only lifted up the victim. Even the Christian celebrant was at most a kind of co-offerer of a sacrifice actually made by Christ himself as priest, victim, and recipient. In the mass, blood is not spilled anew, argued the theologians; the priest merely offers, on behalf of Christendom, a pool spread out for all eternity—a pool both separated and whole, shed and living. Such attenuation of the idea that Christians sacrifice through the priest is reflected in an unusual iconographic motif that appears in Paris in the fourteenth century: the depiction of Christ in priestly garb elevating the host after consecration. The motif is often interpreted to represent the idea that the priest celebrates *in persona Christi*; hence it is said to enhance the power and dignity of the clergy. But the visual effect of the image is rather different. What this motif does visually is *replace* the priest with Christ, making it clear that the eucharistic sacrifice is one in which God is victim, celebrant, and recipient. Hence all the action is God's.[43]

Such a notion of Christ as agent, act, and receiver, on the one hand, created anxiety about how Christians are included in the ritual act. But on the other, it helped to separate those who executed Christ on Golgotha from any participation in an act of sacrifice. The other side of the dilemma of "who sacrifices?" was exactly this need to distinguish clearly between the sacrifice of Christ and the killing of Christ.

As we have seen, scholastic theologians such as Albert and devotional writers such as the author of *Tochter Syon* strained to separate what I am calling the circle of sacrifice (sacrificer-victim-recipient) from the act of killing. This is especially clear in charges against the Jews. Indeed, for all the accusatory elements packed into the elaborate descriptions of Christ's suffering so characteristic of late medieval devotion, his killing was never understood as a sacrifice by Jews or Romans. It is striking that, despite their efforts to see supposed Jewish outrages against consecrated wafers as reenactments of the crucifixion, Christians never described these acts as sacrifices, although contemporary Jewish accounts were quick to affix the label "sacrifice" to Christian slaughtering of Jews.[44] What Christians understood Jews and ignorant Christians to do was to "torture" or "martyr" Christ.

I take a few examples from texts considered in Chapter 3. The 1510 account of the host desecration at Güstrow says the host was "pierced with sharp instruments and knives, tortured, and thrown into the fire [*puncta et stilis et cultris . . . cruciata in ignemque crudeliter proiecta*]."[45] The reports of the 1510 libel at Brandenburg speak of the Jews giving the host over to torture (*zeu Martern*).[46] The late sixteenth-century account of the event at Beelitz calls it an outrage by Jews; the earlier evidence speaks of simple people subjecting the host to abuse [*trahunt in abusum*].[47] Accounts of the events at Sternberg refer to them as "miracles" or as "ill-treatments (*mysehandelinge*)."[48]

In other parts of Europe too, Jewish host abuse was regularly described as torture. Indeed since the point was to stress that the figure in the host is the living Christ, host-abuse libels usually did not speak of killing but rather of violating. The chronicler John of Winterthur reported that a Christian servant ran out of the house of Jews, crying "the body of Christ is being horribly tortured."[49] The inquest of 1402 in the supposed host abuse at Brussels in 1370 refers to the Jews as "piercing" the host (*contemptuose et ignominiose crudeliter transfixerunt*); an independent document refers to the sacrament as having been stolen and "punished" [*de Sacramento punito et furtive accepto*].[50] A charge that comes closer to the suggestion that Jews kill Christ anew in such abuses is the sermon of one Giordano of Rivalto (1304), who argued that Jews "recrucify Christ in their hearts and souls," although he also described abuses of both hosts and devotional images as "doing cruel things."[51] Ritual murder charges, which tended to assimilate killing Christian children to killing Christ, sometimes made use of imagery with strong sacrificial overtones. For example, Thomas of Cantimpré, in his *Book of the Bees*, related a ritual murder charge to a Jewish world conspiracy and claimed that Jews need blood each year because they have taken on the guilt of Pilate (Matt. 27.25) but misunderstand it as requiring a blood offering. Thus Jews themselves spill blood rather than understanding that Christ's blood daily (!) spilled for them could cleanse them of their sins. Thomas's account comes close to making ritual murder a sort of perverted sacrifice, but it does not use the word; and it clearly charges Jews with misunderstanding sacrifice as necessarily repeatable rather than "once for all."[52]

To point out the careful way in which the language of Christian preaching, devotion, and scholastic theology tended to dissociate sacrifice from killing, and killing from torture, is not to obscure the anti-Judaism of such devotion. Christians did obsessively insist that Jews had killed Christ on Calvary. Indeed the author of the *Meditations on the Life of Christ* puts into Jesus' mouth the extraordinarily offensive idea that Jews became killers so Christians might see truth.[53] But even the changes Christian writers rang on this theme tended to emphasize Christ's torture more than his death, partly because the devotional use to which the motif was often put was a stress on Christ's enduring (and hence ever-living) love. Bonaventure wrote, as we have seen, "Consider therefore how great was the impiety of the Jews, who thirsted for the innocent blood of the one who loved them so much that he wished to pour out his blood for them. . . ." [54] The specific language employed blames the blood-thirsty Jews yet keeps the sacrificial action with Christ; it is he who "pours out" the blood, and he does this because he "wishes" to, not because anyone kills him.

Even Christian reproaches against themselves as the "new Jews" were accusations of killing not sacrificing God.[55] Once again the language carefully separates the actions: the verb for what sin does is "kill" or "harm." In one of those telling etymologies medieval writers loved, Caesarius of Heisterbach said that cross (*crux*) derived from *cruciare* (to torture or put on the rack) and connected this to the fact that "we Christians" daily martyr Christ.[56] Echoing the distinction Albert drew apropos the eucharist, Aquinas put it succinctly: what Christ undergoes is sacrifice, what the persecutors inflict is execution. Christ willed to sustain death *propria voluntate*; this was the sacrifice. What was done to him by his persecutors was not sacrifice but sin.[57] The well-known Dürer woodcut of the early sixteenth century charged the Jews with having tortured Christ: "I once suffered great torment from the Jews." It accused Christians of doing such evil today: "thou often tearest open my wounds."[58] Neither evil is called sacrifice.

It is true that Christians stereotyped Jews as especially associated with blood. Stories were told of male Jews menstruating, and the curse of Matthew 27.25 was understood to lie on them.[59] Ritual murder accusations came increasingly to focus on blood.[60] Connections between blood miracles and Jewish abuse sprang readily to fifteenth-century minds even when the miracle legend had nothing to do with Jews. At Wilsnack, one of the inside wings of the chest where the miraculous blood was stored depicts an "Ecce Homo" in which the faces of the persecutors are caricatures of Jewish facial structures (see Plate 7).[61] Eberhard Waltmann, in his polemic with Capistrano in the 1450s, used the association of Jews with bloody signs in the Old Testament to argue that blood is an indication of the wrath of God.[62] As we saw in the case of the supposed desecrations in the towns of Brandenburg in the early sixteenth century, accusations of ritual bloodletting and murder became conflated with stories of host abuse. Such accusations would have a long and virulent history in Europe after host libels waned.[63] But it was clearly important for Christian polemicists to dissociate Jews from sacrifice, just as they dissociated sacrifice from killing.

It is not clear how much the writers who described the alleged host abuses of northern Germany knew about actual Jewish practice, although by the late fifteenth century there were clearly Jewish communities in Brandenburg and Mecklenburg.[64] Christian intellectuals at least knew that Jews did not any longer practice Temple sacrifice and managed to twist this fact itself into a libel. As early as the twelfth century, Aelred of Rievaulx had remarked that the Jews could no longer hope to find the Messiah in their midst because they had lost sacrifice.[65] Peter the Venerable suggested that Christians have a monopoly on genuine sacrifice but somehow suggested as well that the Jews continue to make offerings, which are continually rejected by God.

> You [O Lord] clearly distinguish between us and the Jews or pagans. . . . You reject the Jews like the hateful Cain . . . and you do not light a fire on their offerings. Yet you do desire the hosts of the Christian people, just like the offerings of Abel; you approve of its sacrifice, like the holocaust of Elijah. . . .[66]

For all their association of Jews with blood and of blood with killing as well as sacrifice, Christians felt a need to claim precedence. In an odd turn of supersessionist illogic, they denied to Jews the sacrifice they had inherited from them, lauding Christian substitution of human sacrifice (Christ) for animal yet claiming superiority in offering up a blood that could not be seen.

Ironically, however, awareness of the element of killing or destruction they knew to lodge at the heart of sacrifice became self-accusation and exclusion. Christians used anti-Jewish libels to blame not only Jews but also themselves. According to a pilgrim song from Passau in 1477, the blood that flows from desecrated hosts not only accuses Jewish abusers but also provides an example to Christians of what their own sins inflict.[67] Thus there was a vicious circle of projection of guilt: self-blame stimulated blame of others, which in turn exacerbated blame of self.[68] But it seems likely that the projection was more complicated as well. Indeed it may have reflected profound ambivalence about sacrifice itself. The fact that scholastic theologians argued that eucharist is superior to Jewish ritual both because it is bread, not flesh, and because it is human sacrifice, not animal, suggests a certain discomfort with the whole notion, as does all that theoretical maneuvering to make expiration in the midst of execution an act of choice. The development I discussed in Chapter 3, whereby the role of providing holy blood for veneration was transferred from misguided or negligent Christians to malevolent Jews, also suggests a growing unease with acts that generate the eruption of blood, however much the blood itself is seen as divine presence. Moreover, guilt about the element of destruction involved in sacrifice may have contributed to Christians' own sense of exclusion from the sacrificial circle. As killing and sacrifice were ever more sharply distinguished, Christians had to see themselves to be, like Jews, killers not sacrificers.

Fifteenth-century piety was characterized by a frenzy for encountering divine presence, and by a certain frenzy as well for accumulating merit and tokens of it (in indulgence letters, pilgrim badges, and so forth). This is well known. The other side of this frantic, questing piety, however, and one of the reasons for it, was, I would argue, the centrality and ambiguity of the concept of sacrifice. For Christians increasingly accorded themselves only a passive role in exactly the redemptive—that is, the sacrificial—aspect of the death of Christ. Insofar as they were responsible for providing (that is, killing) the victim, that was not sacrifice. Moreover, it was a deed profoundly to be repented of. Insofar as things were put right with God by oblation, Christians could only lift up a victim (Christ) through a priest, who was himself only a placeholder for Christ. Christians stood on the sidelines, redeemed by a victim who slaughtered and offered himself. Neither priest, provider of the sacrificial lamb, nor victim, they participated in the saving act only when blood fell on them. Even Julian of Norwich, for all her theology of representation, came to understand participation in Christ only through a deathbed vision of Jesus' blood pouring down. It was in sprinkling and washing (words which reverberate again and again in fifteenth-century hymn, story, and prayer) that the faithful were touched by salvation. Although they could do many things to seek contact with Christ—offering up chains of prayers, paying for masses, purchasing quantities of indulgences—they could do nothing active to provide salvific blood unless, like the cryptoflagellants of Thuringia, they not only took up the flail but also equated their own blood with Christ's. The oxymoron of a sacrifice in which there is only one party—of God by God for God—was present implicitly in the New Testament itself. But it emerged more clearly in medieval discussions of eucharist as sacrifice and was reflected more stridently in those popular meditations that asked "why blood?" Perhaps then the frenzy for some sort of palpable contact with *Blut Christi*, in cup or vision, monstrance or miracle, was not, as some historians have argued, doubt about presence or guilt over such doubt but rather a desire to participate in the saving stuff of sacrifice in the only way left if one could be neither gift nor giver—by being washed in (that is, marked by) the blood of the lamb.[69]

Sacrifice and the Marking of Matter

There was a second contradiction in fifteenth-century understandings of redemption as blood sacrifice that underlay the frenzy for *Blut Christi*. This is what we might call the problem of repeatability.

Sacrifice is an act, a moment, an event; as Isidore and Aquinas said, it is something done (*aliquid factum*). Levitical sacrifice was intended to be repeated as often as covenant needed to be renewed, or sin expiated, or reverence shown. But if Christian sacrifice is of the God-man, how can God the unchangeable and omnipotent be repeatedly sacrificed? The Christian passion and mass were supposed to supersede Jewish Temple sacrifice exactly in their quality of once for all eternity. Yet if Christian sacrifice is once for all, how are the sanctifying effects forever maintained in a temporal world? If Christ is not sacrificed anew on the altar, how do Christians plug into, or keep afresh, a moment of erupting holiness that is anything but momentary? Although the Council of Trent lies beyond the chronological boundaries of my story, it is worth noting that the Fathers of the Council struggled with the question of whether the crucifixion could be reenacted in the mass and, if it were not, how Christians then participated in its salvific effects. After fierce debate, which makes it clear that something important was at stake, they were able to give only a very general and imprecise answer.[70]

The problem of the repeatability of sacrifice—or, to put it another way, of sacrifice as moment or act—was reflected in fifteenth-century blood cult more specifically, however. For the objects of such cult—whether relics or hosts—were understood as revelations or vestiges of Christ's sacrifice. Although the superstitious shepherds, ignorant serving maids, negligent clergy, and unbelieving Jews to whom such abuses were attributed were not said to "make sacrifice," the blood that erupted on wafers or in chalices as a result of their acts was understood to be a manifestation of or participation in Christ's sacrifice. The relics from Calvary revered in churches were said to be *particulae* (whether essential or inessential) of blood poured upon the earth *pro nobis*. Thus the blood that was, or that marked, holy matter was sacrificial blood. If it appeared and disappeared, it raised exactly the question also raised by the sacrifice of the mass: how could it be momentary yet eternal? But blood hosts and relics raised this question more graphically, for they raised it by how they were observed to behave.

As I argued at the end of Chapter 3, the power of objects such as the bloods of Braunschweig, Heiligengrabe, Wilsnack, and Sternberg was understood by many as an eruption of the divine. Whether relic translation, or miraculous survival through disaster, or desecration, it was an event—an act—that ignited or stimulated attention to their sacrality. Contemporaries were intensely aware of this quality of blood miracles—that is, their immediacy and horror. Eberhard Waltmann saw them as signals of God's wrath exactly because of their disruptive and disturbing quality, while his opponent Capistrano underlined (and applauded) their capacity, being violent themselves, to incite violence.[71]

Yet events fade; their manifestations in objects attenuate. The miracle at Daroca, which (according to Capistrano) incited to war "as blood incites elephants to violence," did not continue to wage military campaigns. For all the romantic tales of shepherds and alewives that accompanied them, cults such as Doberan and Zehdenick faded long before reformers emerged to attack them. Blood relics sometimes needed to liquefy anew in order to regain their charge or drawing power. Thus all the cults I considered in Chapter 3 faced a problem that went beyond the inevitable swings of fashion and financial support. The problem was theoretical as well as practical. Authorities, from shrine keepers to theologians, were confronted with a basic ontological quandary when holy objects (charged with power at a moment of desecration, translation, or revelation) faded or decayed. And the quandary was heightened because the objects were understood as Christ—not Christ reigning but Christ sacrificed, that is, Christ at the moment of crucifixion. What made the object Christ or the manifestation of Christ was exactly the eruption of—or its appearance as—that changeable stuff, blood. But *sacrificium Christi* was once for all. If that once-for-all sacrifice was repeated in miracles of bleeding hosts and host abuses—was, in other words, instantiated in holy matter—the problem of matter and the problem of sacrifice converged and fused. Matter, by definition mutable, was expected to preserve and convey the immutability of God. By definition different at every moment, it was expected miraculously to retain forever the consecration or marking of the event of Christ's bloodshed. And that event itself was, also by definition, one historical moment in the long sweep of salvation history.

Against this background, it is easy to see why sophisticated and unsophisticated Christians alike worried about changes in miracle hosts and decay in blood relics. Scholastic theologians had after all debated since the eleventh century how long the transubstantiated bread and wine lasted *as Christ* in the eucharist; newer debates about whether all portions of Christ's shed blood were eternally joined to the hypostatic union circled around the same issue. Some ecclesiastical leaders solved the problem of change and repeatability by substituting new hosts when supposedly miraculous ones decayed; some created red effects (with ribbons or doctored liquids) behind crystals said to hold *Blut Christi*; some, either devoutly or fraudulently, attributed to the foolish or the evil occasions for new manifestations of Christ's sacrificial death when old ones lost their drawing power. Such acts were all in a sense efforts to keep the charge affixed to the object alive, to sustain the manifestation, to make the moment of sacrifice perdure.

Those who responded to claims of relic or miracle with suppression were usually manifesting a similar sense of the problem of sacrifice. When Eberhard Waltmann stressed Pope Gregory's prayer that the bloody finger revert to eucharistic elements and be consumed, he was arguing not that God never appears in holy matter but that the charge, the moment, does not last. As Aquinas said: to think otherwise would be to incarcerate Christ.[72] James of Jüterbog displayed a similar understanding when he argued, in his rather rambling and inconclusive discussion of the Wilsnack affair from the 1450s, that the decay—that is, the disappearance—of the hosts spoke against authenticity. If the miracle were from God, argued James, the hosts would have been preserved and there would be no need to lay new hosts upon them.[73] Even in the early sixteenth-century host-desecration libel in Brandenburg, the authors of the broadside advertising the scandal insisted that the blood on the miracle host in Berlin had disappeared *before* the host crumbled.[74] It seemed obvious to them that it could not crumble if it were God.

Yet bread crumbles. The problem remained.

Behind all the debates over when the eucharistic elements ceased to be the real transubstantiated presence of Christ, when the bloody hosts obscenely "consecrated" in supposed Jewish or Christian abuse ceased to reveal God, whether any bits Christ shed on Golgotha could survive on earth, lay the problem of how matter could manifest the divine. But without an eruption in matter, a moment, a something dramatically done, there *was* no consecration, no affixing of sacrality. Theologians and faithful alike craved the moment of sacrifice as the palpable intersection of God and matter; but exactly because the intersection was with and in matter, repetition was required. Yet the divine is not repeatable. There were reasons on every level—theological, devotional, logical, psychological, and material—why perduring sacrifice seemed an oxymoron.

I have studiously avoided in this book an approach that sees the fifteenth century primarily as prelude to its successor, and I shall not lapse here into the enterprise of spotting Reformation or Catholic/Counter-Reformation forerunners. It is, however, worth underlining that the holy matter so vehemently attacked by early Protestants such as Ellefeldt and Faber continued to exert its attraction well into the sixteenth century in Protestant areas, and that in deploring it and ferreting it out, reformers may have given it new visibility and viability.[75] But whatever became of bleeding hosts or tabletops, monstrances or devotional images, the concept of bloody sacrifice that lay behind such material manifestations of the divine clearly attained new prominence in the sixteenth century in both Catholic and Protestant regions. Although Catholics affirmed the mass to be offered as sacrifice whereas Protestants denied this, what is far more striking is a renewed and strident theological articulation, in both traditions, of Calvary as sacrifice.[76] This articulation seems, for a time, to have eclipsed the nuanced ambivalence of some fourteenth- and fifteenth-century discussions. In the north of Germany, on which I have focused, altars depicted and hymns declaimed the power in the blood anew.[77] The aporia of the sacrificial circle (the gift exchange of Christ with himself) was only strengthened by the Protestant move to attribute everything to the grace of God.[78] In certain ways then, the devotional world I have studied in this book had disappeared in Mecklenburg and the Mark Brandenburg by 1552, when Ellefeldt burned the Wilsnack hosts. But at a deeper level, the horror and wonder of the blood endured, and it was the blood of sacrifice.

Chapter 12

Conclusion: Why Blood?

There were many bloods of Christ in the north of Germany in the long fifteenth century. Tales of bleeding hosts led parish churches such as Wilsnack and Sternberg to become pilgrimage goals, vying with older sites such as Braunschweig and Schwerin that claimed to possess vials of *sanguis Christi* from the Holy Land. The holy blood that lured pilgrims was authenticated by a wide variety of texts and events—by documents detailing donations from powerful figures such as Henry the Lion or the Askanier margraves of Brandenburg; by miraculous healings and resurrections collected at places of fire and flood, of ritual abuse, or of supposed deliberate desecrations; by legal proceedings that included depositions elicited under torture; and by episcopal and papal pronouncements that authorized veneration, sometimes after considerable dispute.

The functions of these many bloods were many as well. They drew pilgrims, swelled church coffers, established boundaries, and accused dissidents and outsiders. It is no accident that a number of the Cistercian convents founded by political authorities in the border areas of Mecklenburg and Brandenburg were endowed, either by gift or by local miracle, with blood. Dukes, margraves, and counts were eager to endow women's houses because they were more easily controlled than men's; blood gave the house cachet, appeal as a pilgrim site, and an aura of sacrality that inhibited attack (or indeed sometimes itself went on the offensive).[1] In the controversy over Wilsnack, polemicists explicitly debated whether the vast flood of pilgrims stimulated or undermined local peacekeeping and prosperity.[2]

There is no doubt that blood relics and miracle hosts were both instruments of clerical control and elements of religious and social resistance.[3] Authorities in Brandenburg and Mecklenburg throughout the fourteenth and fifteenth centuries used Corpus Christi processions and veneration to oppose Waldensians, flagellants, and Hussites, whom they tended to lump together in their references to heresy. Tocke in 1446 mentioned flagellants and Waldensians by name as the errors encouraged by the false blood, and an old history of the church at Stolberg in Thuringia refers to a persecution of "Hussites" when what is meant is probably cryptoflagellants.[4] Nonetheless it was Hussite or Utraquist propaganda that was feared above all. In Bohemia, anticlericalism and popular political resistance fused around the demand for the chalice.[5] The importance of blood in fifteenth-century reform and rebellion as a symbol of, and inducement to, breaching—or breaking away from, or rejecting—the larger community cannot be overstated.

Moreover, objection to host cult was often an effort to rein in the enthusiasm for special effects that aroused elites (secular and religious) as well as ordinary Christians. When opponents such as Hus and Tocke objected to bleeding hosts, they wished to return pilgrims to their local parishes and to the (hidden) blood of the eucharist. But special effects were useful as well. Popes, cardinals, and bishops issued indulgences for blood sites. Neither Tocke nor Cusanus was finally successful in getting Rome to quash the Wilsnack pilgrimage. To be sure, indulgences were issued in part in order to facilitate local church construction through pilgrim revenues; but the prelates also acted to increase eucharistic devotion, assuring a focus on clerically controlled hosts by insisting that newly consecrated wafers be displayed alongside miraculous ones. As we have seen, scholastic theologians fought over whether blood relics were theologically possible, and some, following a Dominican line, rejected eucharistic miracles as well, working out elaborate protocols for dealing with such things by burying them in altars or forcing their immediate consumption. But increasingly over the course of the fifteenth century, ecclesiastical authorities came to accept that the diverse bloods of pilgrimage sites could enhance piety and serve as vestiges (even if inessential, "nutritive" blood) or manifestations (even if only special miracles, not the real presence) of Christ. Indeed the desire for such vestiges and manifestations clearly undergirded the anti-Judaism of host-desecration libels, elevating the Jews to major providers of holy matter for pilgrimage once it became too dangerous to give the role to ill-educated clergy, greedy church custodians, servant girls, or thieves. Desecrations were now capital offenses, too abhorrent and disruptive to attribute to simple ignorance or mistakes within the Christian community. A need for holy blood as well as for Jewish property drove the tales, propagated by elites as well as ordinary Christians, of Christ martyred anew, spilling his blood to consecrate new sites and launch new reproaches against communities where such things could happen.

The desire for access to God through holy matter was, of course, complicated and ambiguous by the fifteenth century. Something was there in reliquary or monstrance; but to the throngs of pilgrims who clamored for *sanguis Christi*, it was as much veiled as seeable. Blood relics were paraded in elaborate monstrances that obscured as well as displayed their contents; miracle hosts were seen mostly from afar. Although historians are right to stress the visual dimension of late medieval piety, they have often underestimated the ambivalence it aroused and the complexity of its role. Criticism of the visual came from two directions, so to speak. Some wanted to return from seeing to more tactile encounter; others wanted to penetrate beyond the seen to an invisible reality. Indeed the two critiques tended to combine in the fifteenth-century stress on sacramental reception. By mid-century, preachers and spiritual advisers such as Biel found it necessary to urge again and again that the faithful communicate with lips as well as eyes, that they receive the eucharist as well as meditate upon it. Some theologians and pastors clearly thought that the enthusiasm for ocular or spiritual communion instead of reception at the altar had gotten out of hand. Adoration of host or relics could be displacement, even a kind of idolatry. The conflict of Waltmann and Capistrano over *latria* and *dulia* was really a conflict about the nature of access to the holy.

I have explored at length above the general suspicion felt by many theologians not only of claims that holy matter erupted into visibility in liquefying relics or bloody hosts but also of eucharistic visions, even private ones. Many spiritual directors in the fifteenth century agreed with Jean Gerson that the visionary experience of Christ was dangerous and immature or with Nicholas of Cusa that Christ's blood is "completely un-seeable in glorified veins." The same spiritual directors who encouraged visualizing meditation also tried to curtail visionary experiences.[6] Even the iconography of visions became more self-referential—became, that is, an exploration of itself as a means of depiction.[7] Yet palpable and visible images—scenes, figures, and stories, painted or carved on wood, glass, or stone—were the basic means of access to the holy for the ordinary faithful. As Herbert Kessler and Thomas Lentes have recently underlined, devotional images called attention to their own materiality.[8] Theologians insisted that they were not to be themselves revered but only reverenced as indicators, or signs, pointing to a God beyond. And dissidents attacked them as idols, foreshadowing the iconoclasm that would emerge in some branches of the sixteenth-century Reformation.[9] But their materiality itself was quasi-sacramental; it was access to the divine.[10]

Moreover the blood relics and miracle hosts at the center of blood cult raised issues of materiality in another sense. They were held, at least by some of their supporters, not only to manifest or provide access to, but also to *be*, Christ. Vestiges of the body crucified on Golgotha or that body not only transubstantiated but actually visible in matter, *Blut Christi* seemed to make the radical claim that matter could be God. Blood miracles and blood relics lodged the divine in bodily bits or in visibly transformed and/or violated bread—that is, not just in matter but in matter at a moment of fragmentation, desecration, or change. Thus *Blut Christi* raised some of the questions about part and whole, corruption and salvation, that were raised in what has long been understood by scholars to be the fifteenth-century obsession with death and corruption. That fetishizing of fragmentation and decay was not so much a morbid fixation on dying as an effort to transcend it by giving it moral significance. Wall decorations and inscriptions made from human bones gave new emphasis to their discreteness as particles; devotional literature, hagiography, and auto-hagiography, such as Catherine of Genoa's own writings, concentrated in excruciating detail on death scenes; treatises on the "signs of death" gave new attention to the physiological processes of dying; so-called *transi* tombs (which depicted the decaying corpse under the richly robed, elite dead) warned that death lurked in the midst of life.[11] These motifs were efforts to make physical corruption useful as an image of moral *corruptio* and hence an inducement to its opposite, conversion. But they were more. Reliquaries displayed pieces of bone in gold and crystal settings that denied their evident fragmentation and friability. Devotional images of the five wounds pictured Christ's hands, feet, and heart as severed body parts (Plate 29), although Scripture clearly asserted that the body on the cross was unbroken. Paintings of the risen Christ, even of Christ in majesty, showed his blood still flowing, liquid, and red (Plate 22). Such images located access to the eternal in change and dissolution itself.

An analogous sense of the ambiguity of seeing and of materiality lurks behind blood debates, from Barcelona in 1350–51 to the Rome debate of the 1460s. Repeatedly the learned argued for what we might call "invisible revelation" or encounter through a specific holy matter that was nonetheless in its essence unseen. Ecclesiastical authorities often did this while skirting the deeper issues involved. Popes repeatedly required a consecrated host to be displayed beside supposed miracle hosts and silenced debate over blood relics, asserting that belief in them was not heretical but refusing to pronounce on their source. Diocesan synods came increasingly to legislate, as had Nicholas of Cusa, that miracle hosts such as those at Sternberg and Wilsnack, or corporals supposedly stained with blood from overflowing chalices (such as the one at Walldürn), should be walled up with other relics, not displayed to the faithful for cult. It is clear, however, that the injunctions of church authorities, like the doubts of university theologians, were mostly ignored. Host miracles became increasingly bloody, more tactile and visual, in the fourteenth and fifteenth centuries. Denied access to the cup at communion, the laity clamored for other means of access to the blood and were little inclined to acquiesce in having it hidden in altars or consumed by celebrants. When Heinrich Tocke arrived to investigate the alleged fraud at Wartenburg bei Wittenberg in 1429, he found the supposed miracle host protected by the duchess. Nicholas Marschalk maintained that efforts by the clergy to consume the Sternberg hosts were impious. Authorities who displayed blood relics for veneration tried—through the manner of their presentation—to make them appear alive and red even in partition. Yet from Guibert of Nogent to John of Capistrano, those who rejected the possibility of such relics, like those who supported them, repeated almost as a mantra the words of Psalm 15.10: "nor wilt thou give thy holy one to see corruption." Thus it is clear that Wilsnack, Braunschweig, Schwerin, and later Sternberg kept a particular kind of holy matter, *sanguis Christi*, before the religious consciousness of Europe; but they did so at a time when many devotional writers and theologians were stressing, ever more vehemently, the importance of inner response and the dangers of seeing, of bodily experience, and of materiality. The *Wilsnackerstreit* prepared for later controversies not only because it raised issues of superstition and fraud but also because it epitomized a deep fifteenth-century ambivalence about the nature of divine presence that would erupt in a sixteenth-century obsession with the nature of eucharistic presence and a tendency, even in Catholic areas, to turn from relic cult to other foci of pilgrimage and ways of intersecting with the divine. The fourteenth- and fifteenth-century cults I have explored were sites where the very possibility of access to God through specific, sacralized matter was contested and explored.

This is the story I have told in the first two parts of this book. And I have underlined repeatedly the ways in which historians ever since the nineteenth century have interpreted the control of piety as the fundamental issue. Until the 1950s, interpretation focused on the failure of reform, seeing figures such as Tocke and Cusanus as attempting, perhaps prematurely, to combat a superstitious, even fraudulent, enthusiasm for miracle and turn misguided pilgrims toward inner response to Christ's presence. More recent work, building (not always consciously) on earlier descriptions of conflicts such as Wilsnack in the 1440s or Rome in the 1460s as essentially debates over practical issues, has seen the basic question as ecclesiological or political: who controls access to the divine and how? Although historians gave up several decades ago the idea that late medieval piety was empty, desiccated, or mechanical, they have sometimes—even when focusing on the religious eagerness of the faithful *as religious*—tended to reduce fifteenth-century Christianity to its practices: its busy buying of indulgences, endowing of masses, journeying to shrines, and commissioning of devotional objects.

I have argued, however, that the issue of access to a God both hidden and revealed was not primarily a disciplinary one; it was soteriological and ontological. At its heart lay the question of how the unchangeable omnipotent could meet humanity (by definition changeable in both its physical and moral nature), and the deeper question raised by the conviction that salvation came through the bloody death of the God-man who *was* that meeting point. How can the eternal reside in time and matter? How can that which is separated and cut off be whole and continuing? How can violation—and later miracles that mirror it—represent grace and love? How can death bring life? Such contradictions had lurked at the heart of Christianity from its inception, of course, but the debates and struggles studied above make it clear that they had never been so acute as they were in the later fourteenth and fifteenth centuries. The more pilgrims flocked to sites of holy matter, the more some theologians questioned what was present there. The more devotional writers stressed experiential encounter with suffering body, visualized as present to the corporeal eyes, the more they warned the faithful to turn from externals to inner response. The more ecclesiastical authorities stressed the way the faithful could draw upon the merits earned, and the satisfaction made, by Christ's sacrifice, the more the bloodshed seemed to accuse exactly the Christians it redeemed. The more preachers urged the faithful to see death and decay as images of sin, even warnings of the torture and fragmentation awaiting them in hell, the more they lodged salvation in another death: the death of Christ. Presence and absence, agency and exclusion, corruption and salvation, were complicated as never before. Clearly there was something about blood as symbol, blood as object, and blood as doctrine that encapsulated these complexities, anxieties, and contradictions for the long fifteenth century. In the third and fourth parts of this book I have tried to explore how it did so.

I shall not attempt to recapitulate here the paradoxical images of blood as drops and waves, separation and life, that I have found in fourteenth- and fifteenth-century iconography and piety; I have discussed this at length in Chapters 7 and 8. Nor shall I attempt to summarize the complex ways in which blood sacrifice—a momentary marking or sacralizing of matter that was understood to perdure eternally—lay behind devotion and pilgrimage, undergirding both persecution of others and blame of self. I have explored this in Chapters 10 and 11. Moreover, paradox—the simultaneous assertion of opposites—cannot, by definition, be summarized. All one can do is sort out, seriatim, elements that the symbols and practices themselves affirm simultaneously. Like riddle (as anthropologist J. C. Heesterman describes it), paradox cannot be explained by elimination of one of its poles, solved by reduction to something else, or even accurately set forth in discursive exposition.[12] For paradox is not contradiction but denial of it by the simultaneous assertion of opposites. And paradox was at the heart of fifteenth-century Christianity.

The life-giving death of a God-man was central to soteriology from the earliest layer of New Testament writings. And the overlaying of this fundamental teaching with the template of Levitical sacrifice, in the Epistle to the Hebrews, only deepened the paradox. To the aporia of Old Testament sacrifice (that is, the destruction of the gift in order to give it), Christians added the further aporias of, on the one hand, a gift exchange in which there is only one party and, on the other, the eternal performance of a historical (that is, temporal) violation that cannot be repeated. I have suggested that, by the fifteenth century, awareness of the ways in which Levitical sacrifice did not fit with central Christian doctrine lurked around the edges of piety. Medieval Christianity was not a religion of actual sacrifice; and the intricate metaphorical and symbolic uses to which the idea of sacrifice had been put since the patristic period began, very tentatively and occasionally, to give way both to ideas of sacrifice as simple renunciation and to efforts to occlude the killing at its center. But the paradoxical assertion that life lies in, is made present by, is given by, death was never rejected. Blood encapsulated, represented, asserted, enacted it—blood shed and living, drops and flow, moment and eternity, violation and salvation.[13]

Not all religions give meaning by such stark, simultaneous assertion of life and death as does medieval Christianity.[14] Hindu understandings of karma and Australian aboriginal ideas of the Dreaming give significance to individual lives and account for the problem of death and corruption (physical and moral) in other ways. This is not the place to muse about the nature of religion or of Christianity. But it is important to point out that, in contrast to earlier periods, Christian theology and praxis in the fourteenth- and fifteenth-century West saw a more acute sense of paradox, reflected in the new emphasis on crucifixion (more than resurrection or incarnation) as the moment of salvation. We find this sense of paradox not only in the often noticed devotional emphasis on reproach and love but also in the aporias of blood sacrifice and the insistence in piety and theology on that oxymoron, holy matter.

My argument thus explains religion by and through religion, culture by and through culture. Yet it attempts to penetrate beyond the explicit terms of theological debate, the articulated clichés of piety, and the observable movements of people to hidden and underlying assumptions. Because the assumptions are hidden and underlying, they manifest themselves as much in silence and resistance, in questions partially avoided or arguments left incomplete, as in papal pronouncements, ducal decrees, or the recommendations of university faculties. The fear of corruption I speak of above is reflected as much in the structure of reliquaries and the repeated citing of Psalms 15.10 and 29.10 as in explicit regulations about the replacement of miraculous wafers or the Christological writings of Cusanus and Capistrano. We can count the number of treatises that remain from the *Wilsnackerstreit* and summarize their arguments; but the power of blood as epitome of the paradox of Christianity is evidenced just as tellingly in the fact of Utraquist rebellion, in the cryptoflagellant practice of literal blood shedding, or in those German woodcuts where it is vibrant drops of exaggerated size and roundness that provide a means of calculating what the Christian owes to God (see Plate 32).

This observation about method brings me full circle to the personal and historiographical remarks with which I began so many pages ago. I have touched on many approaches in passing: gender analysis, functionalism, arguments from social control, readings that highlight scapegoating and anti-Semitism, anthropological interpretation in which cultural symbols mirror or reverse social structure, and the explanation of ritual as sublimated societal violence or psychological anxiety. All, to some extent, contribute to understanding the events and ideas I have explored, and at various places I have pointed out how, while remarking on their limitations as well.[15] But I suggest in closing that what we need to do also is to turn such analysis on its head. Rather than trying to explain the paradoxical grappling with life and death by something else (social control, war, fear of the other, and so forth), we should begin with the particular formulations of that paradox in the fifteenth century—that is, with the basic religious concerns implicit in religion. We can then ask how they help us to understand society. Without proposing to substitute a religious determinism for any other, I nonetheless suggest that struggling to take seriously the paradoxes of late medieval religion will pose for us new questions about family, society, and politics. If, for example, we observe that blood in fifteenth-century devotion seldom meant family or descent, we may learn something about the importance (or lack thereof) of lineage in the period. If we accept that the saving stream from the side of Christ was conceptualized at least by some devotional writers more as the flow of birthing than as the flow of wounding, we will begin to see that dichotomies of gender were used, reversed, and transcended in more fluid ways than we have hitherto imagined. If we see that accurate knowledge of human physiology led theologians to posit a special miracle to keep Christ's heart and blood alive after death, we understand not only an odd theological implication of the doctrine of the incarnation but also the widespread medical curiosity characteristic of the fifteenth century. If we really notice the fixation on drops and bits so prevalent in devotional poetry and in the iconography of Christ's body, as well as the significance given to parts as whole in burial practices and blood cult, we begin to develop an analysis of medieval notions of fragmentation and violence, identity and representation, that may have implications for the politics of the period as well as the theology. I could press such examples further, but these are matters for other books.

To look for underlying religious assumptions is not to deny chronology or specificity. Blood cult changed between 1300 and 1500. One kind of holy matter (bleeding hosts) tended to replace another (blood relics); anti-Semitic charges received legal underpinning; the troubling, left-behind bits of Christ came increasingly to be interpreted as inessential body, although theorizing the death on Golgotha as blood sacrifice did not abate. But the change is not a simple one from tactile to visual, from relic to eucharist, from popular devotion to learned attack upon it, from exterior practice to inner response. Nor is the fifteenth century merely a pause, of importance primarily for devotion and praxis, before the creative storm of sixteenth-century theology. If we look squarely at the controversies and cults of the 1440s–60s, rather than at what we know is coming with Luther or the Council of Trent, we see a struggle not so much over reform of practice as over how to understand the soteriological significance of a central given of Christianity: the death of Christ.

Why blood? In one sense, the source of such piety lay in far-off, patristic ideas, newly energized in late medieval preaching and devotion—a process that began long before 1400. More proximately, the origin lay in the multiple needs of local communities, in the furious battles over what sort of sacrality should or could be present where, and in the theological conundra posed by proliferating claims to experience a divine that was both incarnate in matter and largely unseen. Blood was unique among cult objects and symbols. Despite the occasional claims of monasteries or beguinages to possess Christ's foreskin or milk teeth, blood particles were the only pieces of Christ himself widely believed to have been left behind on earth, living and red. Unlike Christ's holy name or true cross or even his face in the *sudarium*, *Blut Christi* was a symbol—and a soteriological statement—that (at least according to some accounts) rested in a physical bit of Christ, a bit both left behind and gone away. Moreover, given fifteenth-century physiological assumptions, blood was the stuff of—and life of—the body, yet its spilling was violation and dying; blood came forth in both death and progeny; it leaped onto those it saved and those it accused; it was continuity and rupture, presence and absence. Hence both as natural symbol and as cult object, blood encapsulated and evoked the aspirations and anxieties of fifteenth-century Christianity as no other object or symbol could.

There can be no single explanation—such as violence or social structure, political infighting or a new sense of the visual—for so complex a set of phenomena as the theological, devotional, and practical obsessions with blood in late medieval northern Europe. But a recognition of how widespread the paradoxes of blood devotion were in the long fifteenth century begins a needed process of restoring to this little-studied period of religious history a character of its own. Rather than interpreting blood as merely one among many objects in a struggle for control or one among many themes in an extravagantly emotional religiosity, we should see in blood the central symbol and central cult object of late medieval devotion—and perhaps the central problem as well.

Abbreviations

AASS. Bollandus, J. and G. Henschenius. *Acta sanctorum . . . editio novissima.* Ed. J. Carnandet et al. Paris: Palmé, etc., 1863– . Not all the volumes in this series are in their third edition, but the series as a whole is the third edition.

Aquinas, ScG. Aquinas, Thomas. *Summa contra Gentiles.* In *S. Thomae Aquinatis opera omnia.* Ed. Robert Busa. 7 vols. Stuttgart-Bad Cannstatt: Frommann-Holzboog, 1980. Vol. 2.

Aquinas, Sentence Commentary. Aquinas, Thomas. *In quattuor libros Sententiarum.* In *S. Thomae Aquinatis opera omnia.* Ed. Robert Busa. 7 vols. Stuttgart-Bad Cannstatt: Frommann-Holzboog, 1980. Vol. 1.

Aquinas, ST. Aquinas, Thomas. *Summa theologiae.* In *S. Thomae Aquinatis opera omnia.* Ed. Robert Busa. 7 vols. Stuttgart-Bad Cannstatt: Frommann-Holzboog, 1980. Vol. 2.

Bonaventure, Sentence Commentary. Bonaventure. *Commentaria in quatuor libros sententiarum.* In *Opera omnia.* Ed. Collegium S. Bonventurae. 11 vols. in 10. Quaracchi: Collegium S. Bonaventurae, 1882–1902. Vol. 4.

Breest, *Das Wilsnacker Wunderblut* (1888). Breest, Ernst. *Das Wilsnacker Wunderblut.* Für die Feste und Freunde des Gustav-Adolf-Vereins 77. Barmen: Hugo Klein, 1888.

Breest, *Wunderblut* (1881). Breest, Ernst. *Das Wunderblut von Wilsnack (1383–1552): Quellenmässige Darstellungen seiner Geschichte.* Märkische Forschungen 16 (1881): 131–301.

Capistrano, *De sanguine.* Capistrano, John of. *Tractatus de Christi sanguine pretioso.* Ed. in Natale da Terrinca, *La devozione al Preziosissimo Sangue di nostro Signore Gesú Cristo: Studio storico teologico a proposito di un trattato inedito di S. Giovanni da Capestrano.* Rome: Pia Unione del Preziosissimo Sangue, 1969, pp. 1*–29*, and in Natale Cocci, "Il sangue di Cristo in San Giovanni da Capestrano," *Sangue e antropologia* 3: 1342–87.

CCCM. Corpus christianorum: Continuatio medievalis. Turnhout: Brepols, 1966– .

CCSL. Corpus christianorum: Series latina. Turnhout: Brepols, 1953– .

CSEL. Corpus scriptorum ecclesiasticorum latinorum. Vienna: Tempsky, etc., 1866– .

Denzinger. Denzinger, H. and Adolf Schönmetzer, eds. *Enchiridion symbolorum definitionum et declarationum de rebus fidei et morum*. 36th ed. Freiburg: Herder, 1976.

DHGE. *Dictionnaire d'histoire et de géographie ecclésiastiques*. Ed. A. Baudrillart et al. 27 vols. Paris: Letouzey et Ané, 1912–2000.

DMA. *Dictionary of the Middle Ages*. Ed. Joseph R. Strayer. 13 vols. and supplement. New York: Scribner's, 1982–2004.

DS. *Dictionnaire de spiritualité, ascétique et mystique, doctrine et histoire*. Ed. M. Viller et al. 17 vols. Paris: Beauchesne, 1932–95.

DTC. *Dictionnaire de théologie catholique*. Ed. A. Vacant et al. 15 vols. and tables générales. Paris: Letouzy et Ané, 1909–50.

EETS. Early English Text Society. London: Paul, Trench, Trübner, and Oxford: Oxford University Press, 1864–1955; continued Oxford: Oxford University Press, 1955– .

Festschrift zur 900-Jahr-Feier. *Festschrift zur 900-Jahr-Feier des Klosters: 1056–1956*. Ed. Gebhard Spahr. Weingarten: Weingarten Abtei, 1956.

"Hundred Pater Nosters." Ed. in Francis Wormald, "The Revelation of the Hundred Pater Nosters: A Fifteenth-Century Meditation." *Laudate* 14 (1936): 165–82.

LTK. *Lexikon für Theologie und Kirche*. 2nd ed. Ed. Josef Höfer and Karl Rahner. 11 vols. Freiburg: Herder, 1957–67.

Mayronis, Sentence Commentary. Mayronis, Franciscus de. *In Libros Sententiarum, Quodlibeta, Tractatus Formalitatum, De Primo Principio, Terminorum Theologicalium Declarationes, De Univocatione*. Venice, 1520; reprint Frankfurt: Minerva, 1966.

MGH. Monumenta Germaniae historica. Hannover: Hahn, etc., 1826– .

900 Jahre Heilig-Blut-Verehrung. *900 Jahre Heilig-Blut-Verehrung in Weingarten 1094–1994: Festschrift zum Heilig-Blut-Jubiläum am 12. März 1994*. Ed. Norbert Kruse and Hans Ulrich Rudolf. 3 vols. Sigmaringen: J. Thorbecke, 1994.

Pius II, *Commentarii*. *Pii secvndi pontificis max. commentarii rervm memorabilivm, qvae temporibvs svis contigervnt, a r.d. ioanne gobellino . . . compositi. . . .* Frankfurt: Aubriana, 1614.

PG. *Patrologiae cursus completus: series graeca*. Ed. J.-P. Migne. 162 vols. Paris: Migne, 1857–66.

PL. *Patrologiae cursus completus: series latina*. Ed. J.-P. Migne. 221 vols. Paris: Migne, 1844–64.

RDK. *Reallexikon zur deutschen Kunstgeschichte*. Ed. Otto Schmitt et al. 10 vols. to date. Stuttgart: Alfred Druckenmüller, 1937– .

RGG. *Die Religion in Geschichte und Gegenwart: Handwörterbuch für Theo-*

logie und Religionswissenschaft. 2nd ed. 7 vols. Tübingen: Mohr [Siebeck], 1957–65.

Riedel, *Codex dipl. Brandenb.* Riedel, Adolph Friedrich, ed. *Codex diplomaticus Brandenburgensis: Sammlung der Urkunden, Chroniken und sonstigen Quellenschriften für die Geschichte der Mark Brandenburg und ihrer Regenten.* 41 vols. in 32. Berlin: Morin, 1838–69. First Section = A.

Le sang au moyen âge. *Le sang au moyen âge: Actes du quatrième colloque international de Montpellier, Université de Paul Valéry (27–29 novembre 1997).* Ed. Marcel Faure. Cahiers du C.R.I.S.I.M.A. 4. Montpellier: Université Paul Valéry, 1999.

SC. Sources chrétiennes. Paris: Éditions du Cerf, 1941– .

TRE. *Theologische Realenzyklopädie.* Ed. Gerhard Krauss, Gerhard Müller, et al. 36 vols. Berlin: de Gruyter, 1977–2004.

Verfasserlexikon. *Die deutsche Literatur des Mittelalters: Verfasserlexikon.* 2nd ed. Ed. Kurt Ruh et al. 10 vols. Berlin: de Gruyter, 1978–99.

Notes

Chapter 1. Introduction: A Frenzy for Blood

1. On this point, see Rohling, *The Blood of Christ*, pp. xvii–xxxii and passim; Roux, *Le sang*, pp. 181–84, 285–304; Hirsh, *Boundaries of Faith*, p. 93.

2. References to blood as metaphor for guilt are of course prominent: see Matt. 27.4, 24–25.

3. Rohling, *The Blood of Christ*, p. xxv.

4. In the early fourteenth century, Ubertino da Casale argued, in response to Peter Olivi's speculation that Christ might have died after the spear wound, that the incident of the wounding was inserted before Christ's death in several manuscripts of the Gospel of Matthew, one of which he had seen as corrected by Jerome. Modern scholars have supported the claim of a variant. See Burkitt, "Ubertino da Casale," pp. 186–88, and Burr, *The Spiritual Franciscans*, pp. 154–55.

5. See Klawans, "Interpreting the Last Supper," pp. 1–17. Rohling, *The Blood of Christ*, p. 71, points out that in patristic texts "in the hundreds of times that this blood is spoken of, apart from the doctrine of the Eucharist, it is scarcely ever mentioned without some reference, expressed or implicit, to its shedding, either as 'to be shed,' as 'being shed,' or as 'having been shed.' "

6. I Cor. 11.23–27; John 6.53–56; Rom. 12.1. The best accounts of attitudes toward the blood of Christ in the patristic period are Rohling, *The Blood of Christ*, and Daley, " 'He Himself Is Our Peace.' "

7. See Roux, *Le sang*, pp. 181–82, and Perrot, "Du sang au lait." I have also profited from an unpublished lecture given by Bruno Reudenbach in Frankfurt in May 2003: "Märtyrer, Heilige und das *Corpus Christi*: Darstellungsformen von Zerteilung und Verklärung." Tertullian did not in fact make the statement with which he is almost universally credited: "The blood of the martyrs is the seed of the church." The misquotation goes back to the index of the PL. (I owe this point to Susan Kramer.) The correct quotation is from Tertullian, *Apologeticum* 50. 13, in *Tertvlliani opera*, vol. 1, p. 171. The allusion to blood as seed was common in antiquity; see, for example, Augustine, *Enarrationes in Psalmos*, sermon 1, pt 5 on Ps. 58.3, in *Sancti Avgvstini opera*, pt 10.2, p. 732. See also Salisbury, *The Blood of the Martyrs*, p. 1.

8. Sulpicius Severus, Epistula 2, in *Svlpicii Severi opera*, p. 144.

9. Rohling, *The Blood of Christ*, p. 42 n. 114.

10. Ibid. Holy blood was supposedly discovered at Mantua in 804 in Charlemagne's presence. Its fate is unknown, but another vial, found in the mid-eleventh century, became the center of an important cult and was later claimed to be the source of the famous relic at the German cloister of Weingarten near Ravensburg. See Chapter 3 n. 19.

11. *A Talkyng of þe Loue of God*, p. 61; Middle English p. 60. The passage comes from the third part, *Þe Wohunge*, written for a nun (or possibly a recluse) although adapted in the *Talkyng* for a male reader; see p. xxxi.

12. "Meditations on the Passion," in *English Writings of Richard Rolle*, pp. 23–27. "I have appetyte to peyne, to beseke my Lorde a drope of hys reed blod to make blody my soule, a drope of þat watur to waschyn it with" (p. 23). "I wolde among þe dede, þat lyn styngynge fouly, lay me flat on þe grounde, and neþerere ʒyf I myʒte, þe vertu and þe grace to kepe of þi blood. Þennes wyl I not ryse, ne non gate flytte, tyl I be with þi precyous blood bycome al reed, tyl I be markyd þerewith os on of þine owne, and my soule softyd in þat swete bath. So may it falle, gloryouse Lord, þat myn herd harte may opene þerewith, þat is now hard os ston, bycomen al-nesche and quyckenen in þi felyng. . . . Whe, Lord, a drope of þi blood to droppe on my soule in mynde of þi passyon may hele al my sore, souple and softe in þi grace þat is so harde, and so dyen whan þi wylle is. I wot wel myn herte, gloryouse Lord, is not worthy come to þe þat þou þereinne lyʒte" (p. 26). And see Tixier, "Richard Rolle," p. 381.

13. *Ancient Devotions . . . by Carthusian Monks*. The earliest version of part of this work, by a nun of Dijon in 1694 (only one copy of which is extant), was reprinted in a third edition in 1886 by Boutrais (an expert on Lanspergius), who added to it a series of "elevations to the Sacred Heart" culled from late medieval devotion; see pp. v–viii. In cases where I have not been able to locate the originals of these devotions, I cite the 1895 English version.

14. *Ancient Devotions . . . by Carthusian Monks*, pp. 17–19. Richstätter, *Die Herz-Jesu-Verehrung*, p. 146, cites what seems to be the same passage from James and gives a reference to B. Hermes, *Der Kartäuser Landsberger und die Andacht zum göttlichen Herzen Jesu, aus dem Französischen des Dom Boutrais* (Mainz, 1880), p. 45, which I have not been able to consult. On James, also known as "of Cracow," "of Paradies," and "the Carthusian," see Mertens, "Jacques de Paradiso," in DS, vol. 8, cols. 52–55; idem, "Jakob von Paradies," in *Verfasserlexikon*, cols. 478–87; Meier, *Die Werke des . . . Jakob von Jüterbog*, which (according to Mertens) has some inaccuracies; and Ziesak, "'Multa habeo vobis dicere,'" pp. 228–29.

15. Richstätter, *Die Herz-Jesu-Verehrung*, p. 150, citing an unpublished manuscript.

16. See Breeze, "The Number of Christ's Wounds"; Areford, "The Passion Measured"; Raynaud, *Images et pouvoirs*, pp. 23–38 and plates 1–16; and Lentes, "Gezählte Frömmigkeit." The number of wounds was often calculated as 5,460, 5,475, 5,490, or 6,666. Typical formulae calculated 28,430 or 547,500 drops of blood; see Peter Schmidt, article on entry 47, in Parshall et al., *Origins of European Printmaking*, pp. 181–82 and 187. Rhodes, "The Body of Christ," p. 389, refers to a "detailing tendency" in fifteenth-century piety. Gray, *Themes and Images*, p. 133, speaks of a "grotesquely statistical turn." Biel, *Canonis misse expositio*, lectio 53, vol. 2, pp. 329–30, gives the traditional numbers 5475 and 6666 for the wounds and adds that, whatever the number, "certum est quod totus sanguis effluxerat." For the details in the caption to Plate 32, see Schmidt in *Origins of European Printmaking*, pp. 181–82.

17. "Hundred Pater Nosters," p. 174. I am grateful to Marlene Hennessy for calling my attention to this text.

18. See, for example, the early fourteenth-century Rhenish devotional drawing of St. Bernard and a nun at the foot of the cross, reproduced in Hamburger, *Nuns as*

Artists, fig. 1 and plate 1. The fact that the nun's hands are over the gushing flood may suggest that the adherent is still at some distance from immersion-union, but it may also suggest that access to the Christ of blood and suffering is through touch, grasping, physical encounter. There is, in this period, a strong devotional emphasis on touching as well as seeing the precious blood—an emphasis found especially in the references (both visual and textual) to Thomas putting his hand into Christ's side and touching his heart; see Appuhn, "Sankt Thomas," and idem, "Der Auferstandene und das Heilige Blut," pp. 90–94. For the misreading involved in late medieval understandings of the Doubting Thomas story, see Most, *Doubting Thomas*.

19. On the Man of Sorrows, see Schrade, "Beiträge zur Erklärung"; Bauerreiss, "Der 'gregorianische' Schmerzensmann"; idem, *Pie Jesu*; Eisler, "The Golden Christ of Cortona," pp. 107–18, 233–46; Belting, *Image*; and Ridderbos, "The Man of Sorrows."

20. Dinzelbacher, "Das Blut Christi," pp. 421–22. And see Chapter 8 at nn. 23–31.

21. Browe, *Die eucharistischen Wunder*.

22. Bynum, *Holy Feast*, p. 67.

23. John Mirk, *Mirk's Festial*, Homily 20: "De dominica prima quadragesime," pp. 90–92, cited in Duffy, *Stripping*, p. 247, n. 38. The *topos* was apparently a fairly common one. See Tubach, *Index exemplorum*, no. 2960, for the story in the fourteenth-century *Gesta Romanorum*.

24. Scribner, "Popular Piety and Modes of Visual Perception," p. 456.

25. Dinzelbacher, "Das Blut Christi," pp. 421–22.

26. For general accounts, see Alberigo, "Flagellants," and Largier, *Lob der Peitsche*. Appearing in Italy around 1260, the movement became very popular in Germany and Belgium immediately after the Black Death in the mid-fourteenth century. There were regional revivals in eastern Germany in the 1360s and in Thuringia in the 1370s and later; on the cryptoflagellants of fifteenth-century Thuringia, see Chapter 2 at nn. 61–66.

27. On the rise of spiritual communion, see Dumoutet, *Le désir de voir l'hostie*; Browe, *Die Verehrung der Eucharistie*; Baix and Lambot, *La dévotion à la eucharistie*; Torsy, "Eucharistische Frömmigkeit"; Caspers, "*Meum summum desiderium*"; and idem, "The Western Church."

28. See Bynum, *Holy Feast*; Grégoire, "Sang"; Rubin, *Corpus Christi*, especially chaps. 2 and 5; and Dinzelbacher, "Das Blut Christi," pp. 415–34. Dinzelbacher maintains that the substitution of blood for communion wine in visions was fairly infrequent, p. 425.

29. *The Life of Beatrice of Nazareth*, chap. 12, pp. 276–79; on the complexities of the text, see Pedersen, "The In-Carnation of Beatrice of Nazareth's Theology."

30. Bynum, *Holy Feast*, p. 177; on Catherine's blood mysticism generally, see ibid., pp. 174–79, and Gerl-Falkovitz, "'Die Braut auf dem Bett'."

31. Bynum, *Holy Feast*, p. 399 n. 49.

32. "Les 'Vitae Sororum' d'Unterlinden," pp. 352–53; discussed in Langer, *Mystische Erfahrung*, p. 135, and Hamburger, *Visual and the Visionary*, p. 413.

33. On concomitance, see Megivern, *Concomitance*. As Megivern points out, the old argument that the doctrine of concomitance was developed to justify the withdrawal of the cup is untenable. The roots of the idea are in early medieval efforts to refute the notion that receiving communion divides Christ into pieces. On the ablutions cup, see Bynum, *Holy Feast*, p. 56. On drinking wine poured over blood relics—a

custom we know was practiced at Weingarten—see Jensch, "Die Weingartener Heilig-Blut- und Stiftertradition"; Nagel, "Das Heilige Blut Christi"; and Rudolf, "Heilig-Blut-Brauchtum im Überblick."

34. Kaminsky, *Hussite Revolution*, esp. pp. 97–140, and Šmahel, *Die Hussitische Revolution*, especially vol. 1, pp. 479–652. It is striking that both of these basic and excellent works, whose focus is primarily on political history, leave virtually unremarked the fact that the demand for the cup is a demand for Christ's blood.

35. The site is Garamszentbenedek. See Tüskés and Knapp, "Die Verehrung des Heiligen Blutes in Ungarn," pp. 179–80.

36. For examples, see Chapter 3.

37. See, for example, Marrow, *Passion Iconography*, and Merback, *The Thief, the Cross, and the Wheel.* The phrase "réalisme brutal" to characterize the difference of northern iconography from southern comes from Rigaux, "Autour de la dispute *De Sanguine Christi*," p. 402. On the greater anti-Jewish violence in the north, see M. Cohen, "Anti-Jewish Violence," esp. pp. 107 and 125.

38. Groebner, *Defaced*, p. 89; Belting, *Image*, pp. 32–33.

39. See Chapter 6 n. 3. I do not intend to make an argument for northern particularism here, but only to be careful about evidence, since I have not studied Italy in any detail. Historians have tended to see north-south differences. But I would be the first to admit that some of what I discuss below, especially in Chapters 5, 7, and 8, shows similarities. See Chapter 7 nn. 38 and 48 and Chapter 12 n. 13 for Italian examples.

40. Scholars generally agree that, until the fourteenth century, body was more important than blood. Roux, *Le sang*, p. 302, however, calls the thirteenth "le siècle du sang du Christ." Mâle, *L'art religieux*, p. 87, gives the standard interpretation: "Dès le commencement du XIVe siècle, la passion devint la grande preoccupation des âmes."

41. On 1290, see Rubin, *Gentile Tales*, pp. 40–47, and Einbinder, *Beautiful Death*, pp. 155–79. On the unreliable nature of most of these early attributions, see Chapter 3.

42. Browe, *Die eucharistischen Wunder.*

43. See Chapter 2 at n. 34 and Chapter 3 n. 80.

44. See above n. 26 and Chapter 2 nn. 61–66, and Chapter 4 at nn. 44–49.

45. Caspers, "*Meum summum desiderium*"; idem, "The Western Church."

46. *The Book of Margery Kempe*, ed. Meech and Allen, p. 69.

47. Newman, "What Did It Mean to Say 'I Saw'?" and Carruthers, *The Craft of Thought.*

48. Elliott, *Proving Women*; eadem, "Seeing Double"; Caciola, *Discerning Spirits*, esp. pp. 309–19; Voaden, *God's Words, Women's Voices*; and Hamburger, "Seeing and Believing," esp. pp. 48–52.

49. Peters, "Vita religiosa und spirituelles Erleben"; G. Lewis, *By Women, for Women*; Bürkle, *Literatur im Kloster*; Garber, *Feminine Figurae*; and Poor, *Mechthild of Magdeburg.*

50. On the importance of ocularity in the later Middle Ages, see Scribner, "Vom Sakralbild zur sinnlichen Schau." Basic is still Mayer, "Die heilbringende Schau." For intelligent caveats about this recent emphasis, see Binski, "The English Parish Church," pp. 13–14. For iconography exploring itself as representation, see Bynum, "Seeing and Seeing Beyond."

51. For the ambivalence of late medieval attitudes toward images, see Hamburger, *Visual and the Visionary*; Camille, *The Gothic Idol*; and Chapter 12 nn. 7, 8.

52. A point made by Swanson, *Religion and Devotion*, pp. 329–40.

53. In addition to works already cited, see Gray, "Five Wounds"; idem, *Themes and Images*, pp. 51–54; Bennett, *Poetry of the Passion*, pp. 43–45; Haug and Wachinger, eds., *Die Passion Christi*; Scribner and Johnson, eds., *Popular Religion in Germany*; Gy, "La passion du Christ"; Pollard and Boenig, *Mysticism and Spirituality in Medieval England*; Bartlett and Bestul, eds., *Cultures of Piety*.

54. For example, *Le sang au moyen âge*; Bradburne, ed., *Blood: Art, Power, Politics and Pathology*; and Bildhauer, "Blood," pp. 45–47.

55. Browe, "Die Hostienschändungen"; Rothkrug, "Popular Religion and Holy Shrines," esp. pp. 27–28; Lotter, "Innocens Virgo et Martyr"; Langmuir, "Tortures"; and works cited in Chapter 11 nn. 59–68.

56. Heuser, "'Heilig-Blut'"; Vincent, *The Holy Blood*; and Holtz, "Cults." On parallels between blood relics and eucharist, see Snoek, *Medieval Piety from Relics to the Eucharist*, and Dinzelbacher, "Die 'Realpräsenz' der Heiligen." See also Kolb, *Vom Heiligen Blut*, which is unreliable in some of its details but gives an overview from a Catholic perspective.

57. Browe, *Die eucharistischen Wunder*; Rubin, *Corpus Christi*; and Bynum, "The Blood of Christ."

58. This would be true of a number of the works cited in n. 53 above. On the origins of the devotion to Christ's humanity in the twelfth century, see now Fulton, *From Judgment to Passion*.

59. McCracken, *The Curse of Eve*; Elliott, *Fallen Bodies*.

60. Merback, *The Thief, the Cross and the Wheel*; Groebner, *Defaced*.

61. For an elegant exposition of the traditional interpretation of the Reformation as a turn from a medieval sense that outer mirrors inner to a piety in which there is disjunction between them, see Lentes, "'Andacht' und 'Gebärde'."

62. Langmuir, "Tortures," and Bynum, "A Matter of Matter."

63. Zika, "Hosts, Processions and Pilgrimages." Remarking on another kind of blood, Roberts, "The Relic of the Holy Blood," p. 137, says "Relics were politics."

64. Rubin, *Corpus Christi*; James, "Ritual, Drama and Social Body."

65. Dumoutet, *Le désir de voir l'hostie*, and see n. 27 above.

66. Bynum, "Seeing and Seeing Beyond."

67. There has also been a tendency, which one can see in an excellent survey article by Thomas Head on relics, to view relic cult, tactility, and local saints as replaced, in the later Middle Ages, by eucharist, visuality, and devotion to the universal figures Christ and Mary. See Head, "Relics," esp. p. 299. I shall argue at the end of Chapter 3 that bleeding-host cults were in many ways a kind of veneration of holy matter and therefore, as Snoek has argued in *Medieval Piety from Relics to the Eucharist*, parallel to relics; hence the development is more complicated than it first appears.

68. I have elaborated this argument in Bynum, *Holy Feast*, chap. 2; "Blood of Christ"; and "Das Blut und die Körper Christi." For an example of the eucharistic elements as symbols of the pious gathered into one church, see Rupert of Deutz, *Commentaria in Joannem*, bk 6, sect. 206, PL 169, cols. 468–69 and 483D–484A.

69. Aelred of Rievaulx, *De institutione inclusarum*, chap. 31, p. 671; and see Dutton, "Eat, Drink, and Be Merry," p. 9.

70. Gerhard's *Tractatus* is edited and translated into German (somewhat freely) by Berg, "Der Traktat des Gerhard von Köln." And see Bynum, "Blood of Christ," pp. 699–704.

71. Peacock, "Extracts from Lincoln Episcopal Visitations," pp. 251–53, and see Rubin, *Corpus Christi*, pp. 344–45.

72. For bibliography on the Gregorymass, see Bynum, "Seeing and Seeing Beyond"; Meier, "Die Gregorsmesse im Bildprogramm"; Marti, "Der Papst in der Klausur"; and Lentes, "So weit das Auge reicht." I have not been able to obtain Thomas Lentes and Andreas Gormas, eds., *Bild der Erscheinung: die Gregorsmesse im Mittelalter* (Berlin: Reimer), announced for 2004 but not yet in print. A collaborative project on the Gregorsmesse is underway at the University of Münster; for information see www.uni-muenster.de/kultbild.

73. Mass of St. Gregory, attributed to Wilm Dedeke, in St. Annen-Museum, Lübeck; see Heise and Vogeler, *Die Altäre des St. Annen-Museums*, pp. 67–73.

74. Mass of St. Gregory, Wing of the St. Anne Altar, Wiesenkirche, Soest; see Schiller, *Ikonographie*, vol. 2, plate 806.

75. It seems that, from at least the twelfth century on, the pope would have removed his tiara (as bishops today remove the mitre) during the canon of the mass. See Braun, *Die liturgische Gewandung*, pp. 485–87, and on the tiara as a form of mitre, see Ladner, "Der Ursprung." This suggests that the Soest depiction is not (or not solely) of the moment of consecration.

76. "Non pas comment u Sacrement / Mès en sa fourme proprement / Vermel comment il le sengna / Quant pour nous mort soufrir dengna," ed. in Kajava, *Études sur deux poèmes français*, p. 95.

77. Sumption, *Pilgrimage*, p. 48. The competition is all the more interesting in light of that fact that the cult at Fécamp appears to have originated in a eucharistic miracle that was later re-figured as a blood relic; see Vincent, *Holy Blood*, pp. 57–58.

78. Dinzelbacher, "Das Blut Christi," p. 430 n. 202, quotes the parallel opinion of priest and religious at Wilsnack that their blood relic is more efficacious (*efficacius*) than consecrated wine.

79. "The Fifteen Oes," p. 117.

80. See *Ancient Devotions . . . by Carthusian Monks*, esp. pp. 1–4, 17–28, 47–48, 61–62, 185; and homily 54 of the Carthusian prior John Justus of Landsberg or Lanspergius (d. 1539), in *D. Joannis Justi Lanspergii opera omnia*, vol. 3, *Opera minora*: "In passionem agonemque Christi Jesu salvatoris nostri homiliae quinquaginta sex," p. 117: "Quomodo autem hic amor ostendi posset melius, nisi quod non solum corpus, verumetiam cor lancea vulnerari permisit? Carnale igitur vulnus, spirituale ostendit. Ex sanguine et aqua quae de latere Christi fluxerunt, efficaciam habent Ecclesiae Sacramenta, potissimum Baptismus et Poenitentia, quibus Deo renascimur." In the quotation from Vincent of Beauvais discussed in n. 113 below, the sacraments that spill from the door opened in Christ's side are "blood in the remission of sins [that is, penance] and water to sanctify, as in baptism." Even in dissident spirituality, blood is understood to represent or bypass more than eucharist. The cryptoflagellants of Thuringia, for example, were accused of preferring the blood they tore from their bodies to the water of baptism or the oil of unction. See Chapter 2 n. 65.

81. "Fifteen Oes," p. 109. Krug's overall analysis is balanced and suggests other themes as well.

82. For example, Gallagher and Greenblatt, *Practicing New Historicism*.

83. For an interpretation that takes all encounter with Christ as a kind of spiritual communion, see Caspers, "*Meum summum desiderium*"; idem, "The Western Church";

and Oliver, "Image et dévotion." See also Schrade, "Beiträge zur Erklärung"; Eisler, "The Golden Christ of Cortona"; and Belting, *Image*, esp. pp. 75–80, who see the Man of Sorrows as basically a eucharistic image. In my opinion, little is gained simply by declaring everything in fifteenth-century piety to be eucharistic, as this line of argument tends to do, much as I admire the reaction against earlier condemnations of late medieval piety as mechanistic. Not all of the emphasis on suffering and blame in prayers or in iconography is preparation for spiritual communion. As Douglas Gray pointed out long ago, the theme of reproach takes on a life of its own. See Gray, "Five Wounds."

84. It is important to note that very few blood altars relate relics or bleeding hosts to the Last Supper iconographically. For the few that do, see Welzel, *Abendmahlsaltäre*, pp. 24, 26, 116–31. Such depictions of the Last Supper are usually of the moment of Judas' betrayal, *not* of the consecration—a fact that links such blood to the theme of accusation I treat in Chapter 8.

85. Huizinga, *Autumn of the Middle Ages*. For a recent interpretation that sees blood cult as "a collective *passio*—all but an epidemic of morbidity, a murky disease of the soul," "vampiric," and "convulsive, obsessive, almost maniacal," see Camporesi, *Juice of Life*, pp. 54, 59.

86. Merback, *The Thief, the Cross, and the Wheel.*

87. Gougaud, *Dévotions et pratiques ascétiques*, pp. 74–128; Schiller, *Iconography*, trans. Seligman, vol. 2, pp. 184–98; F. Lewis, "The Wound in Christ's Side"; and Lochrie, "Mystical Acts, Queer Tendencies."

88. For just a few recent examples, see Raynaud, *La violence au moyen âge*; Puppi, *Torment in Art*; Viljamaa, Timonen, and Krötzel, eds., *Crudelitas: The Politics of Cruelty*; Groebner, "Der verletzte Körper"; Baraz, *Medieval Cruelty*; Meyerson, Thiery, and Falk, eds., *"A Great Effusion of Blood"?*; and Manuel and Herberichs, eds., *Gewalt im Mittelalter.*

89. Note the recent revival of interest in (and criticism of) the theories of René Girard from the 1970s; Hamerton-Kelly, ed., *Violent Origins*; Dumouchel, ed., *Violence and Truth*; Wallace and Smith, eds., *Curing Violence*; and Merback, "Reverberations of Guilt and Violence." For an interpretation of the later Middle Ages as a culture of guilt, see Delumeau, *Sin and Fear.*

90. Bynum, "Violent Imagery." Klawans, "Pure Violence," p. 147, makes an interesting distinction between blood and death, on the one hand, and violence, on the other, arguing that sacrifice in the Hebrew Scriptures is bloody and deadly but not violent.

91. Hahn, "The Voices of the Saints"; Legner, *Reliquien*, esp. pp. 134–99 and 256–316; and Bynum, *Resurrection*, pp. 208–14.

92. Grégoire, "Sang," and Barnay, "Le coeur de la Vierge Marie."

93. In Gertrude the Great's *Legatus*, there is a vivid sense of blood as purifying, especially in bk 2, which she wrote herself (see chaps. 3 and 4). But far more frequently what flows from Christ's side is water, honey, heat, light, etc. (see bk 2, chaps. 4, 6, 7, 19, and bk 3, chaps. 9 and 74). In bk 3, chap. 26, for example, the hagiographer reports that "the Lord who, though he dwells in the highest heaven, loves to impart his grace generously to the humble, seemed to send down a sort of golden drinking straw [*fistulam*] from his heart, which was hanging over that soul like a lamp. . . . Through this tube he caused to flow into her in a wonderful way the flood of everything she could

desire." *Legatus, Oeuvres spirituelles*, vol. 3, p. 124. The Saxon convent of Helfta was a major center of spiritual writing in Germany in the later thirteenth century.

94. Margaret Ebner, *Offenbarungen*, pp. 11, 18, 48, 69, 76, 77–78, 87–88, 99–101, 165–66; for translation, see Margaret Ebner, *Major Works*, trans. Schmidt and Hindsley, pp. 91, 94, 112, 122, 126, 127, 132–33, 139–40, and 177–78. Although Margaret imagined Christ's bitter pain, and Mary's, at the circumcision (*Offenbarungen*, p. 100; trans. Schmidt and Hindsley, pp. 139–40), she seldom mentions blood. Far more typical are visions such as that of John "drinking and suckling from the sweet breast of Christ" (*Offenbarungen*, p. 79; trans. Schmidt and Hindsley, p. 125) or of "the Godhead [from which] flows down mercy, Christ's humanity [from which] flows goodness, the Holy Spirit [from which] flows love" (*Offenbarungen*, p. 74; trans. Schmidt and Hindsley, p. 122). For another example of piety in which wounds are sweetness and joy and blood is drink and bath, while suffering is minimized, see William Billyng's *Five Wounds of Christ* (probably early fifteenth century), discussed in Gray, "Five Wounds," pp. 164–65.

95. Richstätter, *Die Herz-Jesu-Verehrung*. Duffy, *Stripping*, and Gray, "Five Wounds," make the same point.

96. Richstätter, *Die Herz-Jesu-Verehung*, pp. 115 and 107 respectively.

97. *"Das fliessende Licht der Gottheit"*, ed. Neumann, bk 2, chap. 4, vol. 1, pp. 43–44; trans. Tobin, *The Flowing Light of the Godhead*, p. 75. And see Hindsley, *Mystics of Engelthal*, p. 159, for Diemut. For Julian of Norwich's similar vision, see Chapter 9 at n. 45.

98. On Hus and Capistrano, see Chapters 2 and 5. The point of devotional writing about the passion was often to stress Christ's modesty and patience more than his suffering. See, for example, the *Compendium theologicae veritatis*, bk 4, chap. 19, a moralizing text on Christ's five bleedings, by Hugh Ripelin of Strasbourg (circa 1260), printed by Speer in Haug and Wachinger, *Die Passion Christi*, pp. 72–73. Holtz, in "Cults," p. xiii, wisely argues against equating the cult of blood relics with devotion to suffering or to the humanity of Christ.

99. Hindsley, *Mystics of Engelthal*, pp. 159–60, and Gertrude, *Legatus*, bk 3, chap. 30, *Oeuvres spirituelles*, vol. 3, p. 142. See also Swanson, "Passion and Practice," p. 11, and Merback, *The Thief, the Cross, and the Wheel*, p. 102.

100. Dutton, "Eat, Drink, and Be Merry," pp. 9–10.

101. Groebner, *Defaced*, pp. 31–32 and passim.

102. See Bynum and Gerson, eds., *Body-Part Reliquaries*. Guibert of Nogent's discussion of relics and resurrection is, however, counter-evidence to what I argue here; see Chapter 4 at nn. 60–63.

103. Although much current scholarship sees blood piety as experiential and affective rather than theological, my approach is to take seriously the complex soteriological positions implicit—and often explicit—in it. On treating piety as theology, see Chapter 6 n. 4.

104. *Le sang au moyen âge*. For interpretation in which the dichotomy is male blood-solid-shed-symbolic/female blood-liquid-circulating-actual or literal, see Holtorf, "My Blood for Thee," p. 21.

105. Branham, "Blood in Flux."

106. Trachtenberg, *The Devil and the Jews*, p. 149; Kruger, "The Bodies of the Jews," p. 303; Biller, "Views of Jews from Paris"; Rubin, *Gentile Tales*, p. 73; Johnson,

"The Myth of Jewish Male Menses"; Resnick, "Medieval Roots"; and McCracken, *Curse of Eve*, pp. 102–4.

107. For example, A. Closs, "Blut," LTK, vol. 2, cols. 537–38; Schumann, "Blut: religionsgeschichtlich," RGG, vol. 1, cols. 1154–56; Kasper, "Der bleibende Gehalt"; Roux, *Le sang*, p. 11; and Bildhauer, "Blood."

108. Dumézil, "Le sang," pp. 401–4. German has, however, no such distinction. *Das Blut* is simply *das Blut*.

109. Isidore, *Etymologiarvm . . . libri*, ed. Lindsay, bk 11, chap. 1, paras. 122–23, vol. 1, p. 17; also in PL 82, col. 412A–B. And see Rohling, *The Blood of Christ*, p. 93 n. 45.

110. *Vincentius Speculum*, Doctrinale, bk 13, chap. 17, vol. 2, col. 1179, cited in Tarayre, "Le sang dans le *Speculum majus*," p. 344.

111. *Vincentius Speculum*, Naturale, bk 28, chap. 27, vol. 1, col. 2010; cited in Tarayre, "Le sang," p. 345. Vincent takes the etymology from Isidore.

112. *Vincentius Speculum*, Naturale, bk 26, chap. 68, vol. 1, col. 1880; cited in Tarayre, "Le sang," pp. 347 and 349. On phlebotomy, see Conticelli, "Sanguis suavis."

113. *Vincentius Speculum*, Historiale, bk 7, chap. 42, vol. 4, p. 236, bk 7, chap. 46, p. 237 respectively; cited in Tarayre, "Le sang," p. 352. On the sacrificial overtones of *aspersa*, see Chapters 10 and 11. The contrast between "opening" and "striking" comes from Augustine; see Chapter 7 at n. 82.

114. McCracken, *Curse of Eve*, who focuses on vernacular romances. I find many of McCracken's readings of romance literature persuasive but think she has overestimated the role of blood pollution in other medieval texts. Although she cites Miramon, she does not really take into account the complexity his work introduces into the topic of attitudes toward menstruation, blood, etc. See Miramon, "La fin d'un tabou?" and idem, "Déconstruction et reconstruction du tabou." Not only does his work cast into question some of her generalizations about female blood, it also suggests that male blood (shed in violence) and other male fluids (such as semen) are polluting in complex ways she does not take into account. I have not in my book attempted to consider secular literature.

115. Tarayre, "Le sang," p. 355. And see Chapter 8 n. 44.

116. As Miramon clearly shows, it was the intentionality behind the shedding of fluids that, at least in canon law, determined whether or not they polluted a sacred space, hence necessitating reconsecration.

117. In ancient sources, menstrual blood (like other pollutants) blights but also cures and brings fertility. Branham, "Blood in Flux," pp. 63–64, and von Staden, "Women and Dirt," p. 16. In the Middle Ages too, natural female bleeding was both contaminating and fertilizing. See, for example, that extremely negative, and often misinterpreted, discussion of the human body, Innocent III's *On Human Misery*. Although Innocent understands menstrual blood to be impure (*detestabilis et immundus*) and women poisonous, he also sees female blood as nourishing the fetus in utero. Innocent's entire discussion of the body (both male and female) as a bag of dung must be placed against the background of that medieval deploring and abhorring of change as putrefaction that I discuss in Chapters 4 and 6. See Innocent III, *De miseria humanae conditionis . . .* , p. 11. On menstruation as a physiological process, medieval medical and theological discussion was, in general, ambivalent. Necessary for reproduction, menstruation was also related to the pain of childbirth and the sin of the fall. Hence theologians were divided about whether the Virgin Mary menstruated; see Wood, "The

Doctors' Dilemma," and L'Hermite-Leclercq, "Le lait et le sang de la Vierge," who disagrees with some aspects of Wood's interpretation. On menstruation as a mark of fallenness, see Blamires, "Beneath the Pulpit," p. 149.

118. See Wilson, "The Ceremony of Childbirth"; Cressy, "Purification, Thanksgiving and the Churching of Women"; Karant-Nunn, *Reformation of Ritual*, pp. 72–90; Larrington, "The Candlemas Vision"; and Baumgarten, *Mothers and Children*, pp. 92–118.

119. Both McCracken, *Curse of Eve*, pp. 40–43, and Jay, *Throughout Your Generations*, pp. 112–27, argue that sacrifice itself is gendered male because performed only by fathers. As Jay acknowledges, only Christ (as both priest and victim) really performs sacrifice in medieval literature and devotion; but in her analysis of the parallels between social and ritual organization, the conception of eucharist as sacrifice underlines the religious domination of the male priesthood and hence the social forms of patrilinearity and male descent. See Chapter 7 n. 21 and Chapter 10 n. 7.

120. For such Biblical inversion, see Bynum, *Jesus as Mother*, p. 127. Douglas, *Natural Symbols* is the *locus classicus* of this sort of anthropological analysis.

121. For example, Baschet, "Âme et corps."

122. Barton, "Emotional Economy of Sacrifice"; Branham, "Blood in Flux"; Heesterman, *Broken World*; and von Staden, "Women and Dirt." Enormously useful to my thinking about sacrifice have been Hénaff, *Le prix*, and Klawans, "Pure Violence."

123. Douglas, *Natural Symbols*. Medieval authors themselves explored the connection of the physical object and its religious significance. Robert of Melun (d. 1167), for example, argued that God can change anything into anything but in fact he converts bread to flesh and wine to blood because wine has more "similitude" with blood; see Jorissen, *Die Entfaltung*, pp. 27–28.

Chapter 2. Wilsnack

1. The chapter that follows makes no pretense to being an exhaustive study of Wilsnack. As many scholars have commented, it would take years to locate, sort through, and read the surviving manuscript material relating to theological controversies concerning it—a task no one has attempted since Breest in the nineteenth century—and even Ziesak's recent effort to catalogue this material is incomplete. I have consulted Ludecus's sixteenth-century account, on which much later work (including Riedel's *Codex diplomaticus Brandenburgensis*) is based, and the major manuscript compilations on Wilsnack in the Herzog August Bibliothek in Wolfenbüttel.

2. *The Book of Margery Kempe*, ed. Meech and Allen, bk 2, chaps. 4 and 5, pp. 232–35.

3. On the church, see Krüger, *Die Nikolauskirche*; Lichte, *Die Inszenierung einer Wallfahrt*, pp. 25–38 (which has been harshly reviewed); and Cremer, *Die St. Nikolaus- und Heiligblut-Kirche*, who revises previous accounts of the building and argues that the present church was erected in two phases, 1396–1412 and 1471–1500. Rejecting the older theory that Lüneburg was the model for brick Gothic churches in the area roughly between the Weser and the Elbe (and hence for Wilsnack), Cremer argues for the church at Verden and the systematization of church organization in the diocese as the most important model and influence.

4. For claims that it was, in its day, the largest pilgrimage in Christendom, see Hennig, "Kurfürst Friedrich II," p. 102; and Meier, "Wilsnack als Spiegel," p. 59. Browe, however, speaking of expiatory pilgrimages to which criminals were condemned ("Verwandlungswunder," p. 154), says Santiago and Rocamadour (which were not blood pilgrimages) were ten times as popular as Wilsnack.

5. Luther, "An den christlichen Adel deutscher Nation," *Luthers Werke*, ed. Clemen, vol. 1, p. 402. For the general account of Wilsnack that follows, I have used Breest, *Wunderblut* (1881); idem, *Das Wilsnacker Wunderblut* (1888); Hennig, "Kurfürst Friedrich II"; Cors, *Chronik*; Browe, *Die eucharistischen Wunder*, pp. 166–71; Löffler, "Mittelalterliche Hostienwunder," pp. 9–11 and 20–22; Meier, "Wilsnack als Spiegel"; Gandert, "Das Heilige Blut von Wilsnack und seine Pilgerzeichen"; Fliege, "Nikolaus von Kues"; Boockmann, "Der Streit um das Wilsnacker Blut"; Zika, "Hosts, Processions and Pilgrimages"; Lichte, *Die Inszenierung einer Wallfahrt*; Buchholz and Gralow, *Zur Geschichte der Wilsnacker Wallfahrt*; Cremer, *Die St. Nikolaus- und Heiligblut-Kirche*, vol. 1, pp. 45–47, 75–129, 140–44, 151–210, and 320–24; Kühne, "'Ich ging durch Feuer und Wasser . . .'"; and Watanabe, "The German Church." As Kühne comments ("'Ich ging durch Feuer und Wasser . . .'," pp. 50–51), it is still very difficult, despite the vast amount of modern scholarship, to know exactly what happened at Wilsnack. By the time the pastor Matthaeus Ludecus wrote in the 1580s (with polemical intent), the miracle book was no longer extant and its fate was unknown. See Ludecus, *Historia von der erfindung* (1586), Vorrede, [p. 23]. (I have used the copy of Ludecus in the Rare Books Collection at Princeton; it is neither paginated nor foliated.)

6. The *Historia inventionis et ostensionis vivifici Sacramenti in Wilsnack* (Lübeck: Stephan Arnd, 1520) was published a year later in a somewhat shortened Low German translation (Rostock: Ludevicus Dietz). Both texts are found in Ludecus, *Historia von der erfindung*, numbers 1 and 2. The German text, "Van der Vyndinge vnnde Wunderwercken des hilligen Sacramentes to der Wilssnagk," is also found in Riedel, *Codex dipl. Brandenb.*, A 2 (1842), pp. 121–25. Tocke claimed to have seen a copy of the *Historia* when he visited Wilsnack; Breest, *Wunderblut* (1881), p. 137. On the text of the *Historia* and on problems in dating the original events, see the excellent discussion by Kühne, "'Ich ging durch Feuer und Wasser . . .'," pp. 55–56 and passim. The Latin version gives August 24 as the date of the discovery of the miracle hosts and August 31 as the date of the first candle miracles. Paul Heitz has published an early sixteenth-century broadside with fifteen woodcuts telling the Wilsnack story in *Das Wunderblut zu Wilsnack: niederdeutscher Einblattdruck*. The woodcuts begin with a depiction of the fire.

7. For the papal indulgence, see Riedel, *Codex dipl. Brandenb.*, A 2, doc. 2, p. 140; for the archepiscopal and episcopal indulgence of 1384, see ibid., doc. 3, pp. 140–41. The bishops offer forty days of indulgence for visiting not just "locum Vuilsnak" but also "corpus Dominicum ibidem" and forty days for each circumambulation of the church where "dominus noster Jesus Christus in sui corporis sacramentalis veritate sic dignatus est operari, quod in tribus hostijs per Rectorem dictae Ecclesiae consecratis, et ante incentionem in Ecclesia retentis, et post concremationem dictae Ecclesiae super altare in corporali in parte concremato, octauo die concremationis super altare miraculose inuentis, in qualibet hostia appareat gutta sanguinis manifesti" (p. 141). An indulgence of 1388 (ibid., doc. 4, pp. 141–42) once again does not mention the hosts,

but an indulgence from the bishop of Schwerin in 1391 (ibid., doc. 6, pp. 142–43) refers to the "gutta sanguinis" and attendant miracles.

8. See Riedel, *Codex dipl. Brandenb.*, A 2, doc. 1, p. 139, for Boniface IX's decree incorporating the church into the *mensa* of Havelberg. (Riedel attributes it incorrectly to Boniface VIII and dates it to 1300; but in the bull itself the pope refers to his predecessor Urban VI.) See ibid., pp. 143–44 (cited from Ludecus) for the bishop's order concerning division of revenues.

9. Already in the 1430s, representatives from Magdeburg attending the Council of Basel supposedly saw a depiction of a Wilsnack miracle in a local chapel; see Breest, *Das Wilsnacker Wunderblut* (1888), p. 26; Tocke, "Synodalrede," p. 178; and Boockmann, "Der Streit," p. 390.

10. See Breest, *Wunderblut* (1881), pp. 162–65, and *Das Wilsnacker Wunderblut* (1888), pp. 17–19. John of Wünschelburg's criticism of Wilsnack was erroneously dated by Ludecus and Riedel to 1400; see Cremer, *Die St. Nikolaus- und Heiligblut-Kirche*, vol. 1, p. 99 n. 101. According to Ludecus, John reported a fraud in which the priest smeared his own blood on a host. See Ludecus, *Historia von der erfindung*, introduction to number 5, and Riedel, *Codex dipl. Brandenb.*, A 2, p. 128. On John, see Herrmann, "*Veniet aquila.*" John's *De falsis signis et miraculis libri duo*, which Herrmann thought lost, exists in U Basel O III 40, fols. 1r–24v. I owe this information to Robert Lerner.

11. Hus, "Questio de sangwine Christi," and "Tractatus," pp. 3–37.

12. According to Tocke, in his Synodalrede of 1451. See Breest, *Wunderblut* (1881), p. 163 n. 3, and Tocke, "Synodalrede," p. 178. This would have occurred some time before 1407, when Conrad died. See Lichte, *Die Inszenierung einer Wallfahrt*, p. 14, and Tönsing, *Johannes Malkaw*, pp. 408–9.

13. Breest, *Wunderblut* (1881), pp. 175–77 and app. 1, p. 296, and *Das Wilsnacker Wunderblut* (1888), pp. 20–25.

14. On Tocke, see Hölzel, "Toke, Heinrich." Lehmann, in "Aus dem Rapularius," discusses an extant, alphabetically organized commonplace book partly by Tocke, the "Rapularius," now available in *Der Wolfenbütteler "Rapularius"*, ed. Hölzel-Ruggiu. The contents show his extensive concern with "superstition" and church practice.

15. Tocke, "Synodalrede," p. 178. Tocke remarks that he is not surprised that those who were with him saw nothing, since he himself saw nothing. But he emphasizes that the provost, born in the neighborhood and often present at Wilsnack, claims he has never seen anything. I use Breest's German translation of Tocke's *Sermo synodalis oder Tractatus contra cruorem*, from the only extant manuscript, Dessau StB Cod. BB 3944, fols. 261ra–271vd; see Ziesak, "'Multa habeo vobis dicere . . .'," p. 242. Extensive excerpts are also printed in Meier, "Christianus de Hiddestorf," pp. 52–57, who treats the question of Christian's reportage of the priest's admission of fraud.

16. Meier, "Christianus de Hiddestorf," p. 53, quotes Tocke (*Sermo synodalis*, Tractate 1, art. 3, chap. 1): "Facto verbo de concursu Wilsnacensi ait dictus magister Christianus: Cum ergo, inquit, essem lector Magdeburgensis, venit ad conventum nostrum ille plebanus de dicto loco Wilsnack, qui se tres hostias maculosas asseruit invenisse. Petiit sibi dari audientiam coram senioribus et iunioribus conventus, quibus congregatis dixit: 'Video, Patres, vos multis indigere, quia ecclesiam frangitis et meliorem proposuistis. Scitis, quam famosus est in Wilsnack concursus per me procuratus. Si meis acquieveritis consiliis, vobis concursum ordinabo maiorem quam sit in Wilsnack. Ego enim cum ibi agerem non ita bene novi modum, quemadmodum nunc

excogitavi.' Fratres autem timentes Deum responderunt se taliter pecunias non quaesituros, et verecundus abscessit."

17. On Eugene, see Rubin, *Gentile Tales*, pp. 163 and 187. The pope is said to have sent a miraculous host as a gift to Duke Philip of Burgundy in the 1440s; see Vincent, *Holy Blood*, p. 122 n. 16, also p. 138 n. 5. On the ecclesiastical politics of all this, see Zika, "Hosts, Processions and Pilgrimages." For the dating of Eugene's bulls, see Fliege, "Nikolaus von Kues," pp. 63–65. (Zika uses the old date of 1446, from Riedel and Breest.)

18. Riedel, *Codex dipl. Brandenb.*, A 2, docs. 13–14, pp. 149–52; see also Sullivan, "Nicolas of Cusa," p. 403 n. 101. Eugene's decree was confirmed by Nicholas V; see Riedel, *Codex dipl. Brandenb.*, A 2, doc. 15, pp. 151–52.

19. On Cusanus, see Vansteenberghe, *Le cardinal Nicolas de Cues*; Sullivan, "Nicolas of Cusa"; Meuthen, *Nikolaus von Kues*; and idem, "Die deutsche Legationsreise," pp. 421–99.

20. There is debate about whether Cusanus was at Wilsnack between June 22 and 24. The older opinion was that he was not. Meuthen and (following him) Watanabe think he was. See Meuthen, "Das Itinerar der deutschen Legationsreise," Meuthen and Hallauer, eds., *Acta Cusana*, vol. 1, fasc. 3(a), pp. 944–46, numbers 1401–3; and Watanabe, "German Church," p. 219.

21. See Riedel, *Codex dipl. Brandenb.*, A 2, doc. 17, pp. 152–56, for the archbishop of Magdeburg's reissue of Cusanus's decree. And see Binterim, *Pragmatische Geschichte*, vol. 7, pp. 257, 278, 474, 486, 541, 548. See also Browe, "Verwandlungswunder," pp. 156–57 nn. 60, 61. Note the emphasis on corruption of species, to which I return in Chapter 6. For Cusanus's views concerning the blood of Christ and the hypostatic union, see Haubst, *Die Christologie des Nikolaus von Kues*, pp. 276–304. Haubst discusses a set of christological questions (Cod. Cus. 40, fols. 144r–146v), which he attributes to Cusanus and places in the context not of the Wilsnack controversy but of the 1462–63 debates in Rome (pp. 7–8 and 298–99). There is, however, an echo of the Halberstadt decree in questions 12–14 (ed. Haubst, in ibid., pp. 318–19), where Cusanus cites Gregory Nazianzus to the effect that "a few drops renew the world" (q. 13: *guttae sanguinis paucae mundum totum reformantes*) and argues that "the blood assumed with Christ's body is in indivisible and in-dissolvable union with his person" (q. 14: *in unionem personae Christi indivisibilem et infinibilem*). This is the blood that rises glorified in Christ's resurrection (q. 12); and this is what the faithful believe to be "truly the blood in the consecrated chalice" (q. 14: *in calice consecrato veraciter sanguinem illum esse*). Cusanus does not treat directly the question of whether all blood poured out in the crucifixion returns in the resurrection.

22. Binterim, *Pragmatische Geschichte*, pp. 473–74 and 486. Nicholas of Cusa's decree against miracle hosts must be placed in the context of his general opposition to frequent display of the eucharist, which reflects a desire to keep the holy hidden. At the end of decree, Cusanus ordered the removal of certain statues that were detracting from veneration of the sacrament of Christ on the altar, commenting that the pious are unfortunately particularly drawn to visible images: "propter figuram visibilem in suis adorationibus vulgus ipsum specialius recurrit . . ."; Riedel, *Codex dipl. Brandenb.*, A 2, p. 155; Binterim, *Pragmatische Geschichte*, p. 473; and Sullivan, "Nicolas of Cusa," pp. 399–400.

23. Gottsbüren was the site of an extensive bleeding-host pilgrimage dating from

1331. See Chapter 3 at nn. 33–36. On Walldürn, see Kolb, *Vom Heiligen Blut*, pp. 163–67, and Heuser, "'Heilig-Blut'," p. 17.

24. Theological and papal support for such hosts continued. Nicholas of Cusa himself approved the miraculous hosts of Andechs in 1451, presumably in order to avoid offending the duke, who was friendly to reform. In 1446, the cardinal bishop Peter of Augsburg supported the miracle host of Benningen-Memmingen, somewhat ambiguously, not as the body of Christ but as a "holy thing." The inquisitor Heinrich Krämer or Institoris defended the miracle-working (and supposedly miraculously preserved) host of Augsburg in 1496. See Brackmann, *Die Entstehung der Andechser Wallfahrt*, p. 22; Heuser, "'Heilig-Blut'," pp. 77–79; and Zika, "Hosts, Processions and Pilgrimages," pp. 27–30.

25. Breest, *Wunderblut* (1881), pp. 243, 255–74, and Riedel, *Codex dipl. Brandenb.*, A 2, doc. 26, pp. 164–65 (misdated). Capistrano wrote initially to someone in the Curia warning that the supposed miracle at Wilsnack was questionable. Then in 1452, after he sent a letter which used the Wilsnack blood on its seal, he engaged in a fierce polemic with Eberhard Waltmann, provost of Magdeburg, on the proper adoration owed to the blood of Christ, in which he accused Waltmann of not understanding Thomas and supported two Italian sites of supposed miracle hosts. See Capistrano, "Epistola responsialis ad Everhardum Waltmann . . . Veram in vtroque sententiam . . . ," Wolfenbüttel H.A.B. Cod. Guelf. 550 Helmst. fols. 198r–209v. Ten years earlier, Capistrano had written a treatise on the blood of Christ in which he defended the Thomistic position on blood relics (that is, that Christ resumed all his blood in the resurrection) and argued that the blood of Christ remained united to the Word hypostatically in the *triduum mortis* as in life. But he defended several host miracles in this same treatise. No one seems to have noticed that Capistrano lifted a number of paragraphs from his earlier treatise into his attack on Waltmann, including a verbatim quotation of Thomas's Quodlibet 5 and a lengthy description of the miracle of Daroca and the blood libel of Brussels, which Capistrano claimed to have authenticated on a legation to the Low Countries. Cod. Guelf 550 Helmst., fols. 204r–207r, repeat verbatim Capistrano's *De sanguine*, articles 13.B–16. See Chapter 5 at nn. 21–39.

26. Heuser, "'Heilig-Blut'," p. 106. And on the pilgrimage see Gandert, "Das Heilige Blut," pp. 74–80; and Cremer, *Die St. Nikolaus- und Heiligblut-Kirche*, vol. 1, pp. 151–210.

27. Browe, "Verwandlungswunder," p. 160.

28. "Auff den tag S. Bartholomei Apostoli, ist *maximus concursus* der grosseste zulauff wie sonsten durchs gantze Jar auff ein mal nicht gesehen dahin gewesen, zu welcher zeit die Leute aus allen ortern in solcher grossen anzal dahin Kirchfarten gangen sind, das die in vnd ausserhalb der Kirchen, welche beide orter doch in jrer *Circumferente* vnd vmbkreis zimlich weit, wie es noch augenscheinlich ist, begriffen sind, nicht platzes noch raumes gnug haben können. Sonderlich aber ist in der Kirchen vnter dem Ampte der Messen, fürnemlich wenn der Abgott aus seiner behaltnus hat getragen werden sollen, ein solch gross vnmessig gedrenge von den Wallenden Leuten, Menlichs vnd Weiblichs Geschlechts nach dem vermeinten heiligen Blute gesehen worden, das offtmals jrer etliche in schwere onmacht plötzlich gefallen sind, die man mit geweiheten Wasser, dessen in der Kirchen allenthalben viel vorhanden war, vnd anderen eilenden mitteln wiederumb hat ausskülen und erfrischen müssen." Ludecus, *Historia von der erfindung*, Vorrede, [pp. 16–17].

29. Johannes von Paltz, *Supplementum Coelifodinae*, pp. 390–413.

30. Cremer, *Die St. Nikolaus- und Heiligblut-Kirche*, vol. 1, pp. 187–88. According to Breest, Ellefeldt managed to suppress public showing of the blood after 1551; see Breest, *Das Wilsnacker Wunderblut* (1888), p. 49.

31. Ellefeldt was arrested by the Kurfürst at the instigation of Domchapter. See Cors, *Chronik*, pp. 25–26, and Breest, *Wunderblut* (1881), pp. 282–95.

32. On the sin scales, see Ludecus, *Historia von der erfindung*, Vorrede, [p. 18]. For another kind of object in the sixteenth-century sanctuary, note the chains left behind as ex-votos by freed prisoners; see ibid., [p. 24]. Breest, who was pastor at Wilsnack, describes three platters as they were displayed in the church in 1888. Two were possibly plates for scales. One was a baptismal basin and not, as claimed, the kettle in which Ellefeldt destroyed the hosts. See *Wunderblut* (1881), p. 150. See also Schäfer, "Märkische Fronleichnamsverehrung," p. 105.

33. Boockmann, "Der Streit," can be seen as a sophisticated version of this argument, his basic question being why reform did not come a century earlier. He sees new media such as print, and the new willingness of the sixteenth century to include the people in theological discourse, as the telling differences. The recent article by Watanabe, "The German Church," adopts the traditional interpretation.

34. Boockmann, "Der Streit." Most but by no means all of the supporters were Franciscan Conventuals; Benedictines and Carthusians also supported Wilsnack and blood piety generally. It is worth noting that some of the most sophisticated work on the theological issues has been done by the twentieth-century Franciscan Ludger Meier, writing in part to defend Kannemann, Bremer, and other Franciscans; see Meier, "Der Erfurter . . . Johannes Bremer," and idem, "Christianus de Hiddestorf."

35. For the roots of pilgrimage in the economic problems of fifteenth-century north German parishes and dioceses, see Escher, "Brandenburgische Wallfahrten," p. 128.

36. Hennig, "Kurfürst Friedrich II." See also Escher, "Brandenburgische Wallfahrten," pp. 133–34.

37. Browe, *Die eucharistischen Wunder*; idem, "Verwandlungswunder"; Brückner, "Liturgie und Legende"; and Merback, "Channels of Grace." According to Heuser ("'Heilig-Blut'," p. 79), the basic interpretation that such cults are a fallout from eucharistic controversy goes back to the 1908 work of A. Schönbach. A large amount of literature connects host cult to anti-Jewish host-desecration libels. See, for example, Browe, "Die Hostienschändungen"; Rubin, *Gentile Tales*; Langmuir, "Tortures."

38. Kühne, "'Ich ging durch Feuer und Wasser'."

39. For the interpretation (which has been influential but not generally accepted) that such cult goes back to devotional images, see Bauerreiss, *Pie Jesu*. For the emphasis on hosts replacing relics, see Merback, "Channels of Grace." For the general argument that seeing visions (that is, visuality) tended to replace traveling to relics (that is, tactility), see Sigal, *L'homme et le miracle*, and Soergel, *Wondrous in His Saints*, pp. 20–30.

40. Zika, "Hosts, Processions and Pilgrimages," p. 26. This is basically also the interpretation of Lichte, *Die Inszenierung einer Wallfahrt*.

41. See below n. 46. Seeing the mid-century controversy as essentially about praxis is not in fact a new interpretation. Zika's formulation in terms of power is, of course, new, but his account of what was at issue to contemporaries is drawn from Breest and other Protestant historiography that emphasizes reform.

42. See above at n. 6. On veneration of the supposedly miraculous candles as relics, see article six of the articles presented to the bishop of Havelberg in 1412 and article nine of the articles sent by Tocke and Heinrich Zolter in the name of the archbishop of Magdeburg in 1446; Breest, *Wunderblut* (1881), apps. 1 and 2, pp. 297, 298.

43. Breest, *Wunderblut* (1881), app. 1, art. 4, p. 296, repeated almost verbatim in the articles of 1446, app. 2, art. 4, p. 298. Riedel, *Codex dipl. Brandenb.*, A 2, doc. 26, pp. 164–65, gives a document (misdated) of John of Capistrano in which he expresses confidence in whatever the papal deputies decide, says he does not know whether the claim is true or false, but reports that many say the blood has disappeared because nothing now appears to those viewing [*cruorem illum . . . ita esse annihilatum, vt iam nihil appareat conspicientibus*].

44. Breest, *Wunderblut* (1881), app. 3, q. 3 of Tocke's fourteen questions sent to the Erfurt faculty, p. 301.

45. See Hennig, "Kurfürst Friedrich II," p. 80.

46. Art. 5 of the 1412 articles; repeated in art. 7 of the 1446 articles; Breest, *Wunderblut* (1881), apps. 1 and 2, pp. 296, 298. The charge goes on to say (with slight variations of wording): "Etiam quod non necesse est ad illum locum propter sacramentum recurrere, cum ubique in ecclesiis reperiatur" (pp. 296, 298). Tocke makes the same point in the Synodalrede of 1451; "Synodalrede," pp. 168, 176.

47. Eberhard Waltmann, "De adoratione et contra cruorem," art. 1, Wolfenbüttel H.A.B. Cod. Guelf. 630b Helmst. fol. 14r. The text (misidentified as an otherwise unknown *Gutachten* of the Erfurt faculty from 1452) is transcribed from Marburg UB Hs. 58, fols. 303ra–309ra, by Damerau, *Das Gutachten der theologischen Fakultät Erfurt 1452*, p. 14. According to Ziesak, "'Multa habeo vobis dicere . . .'," pp. 244–45, there are many mistakes in Damerau's transcription of the Marburg MS; the version I used in 630b Helmst. gave, for whatever reason, much better readings. Waltmann's "De adoratione" is also found in Wolfenbüttel H.A.B. Cod. Guelf. 153 Helmst., fols. 280r–286r, misidentified in Ziesak, "'Multa habeo vobis dicere . . .'," p. 228, as a treatise by James (Jacob) of Jüterbog or Klusa, the Carthusian. On Waltmann, see Backmund, *Monasticon Praemonstratense*, pt 2, pp. 278, 304.

48. See above n. 12. In his "De adoratione et contra cruorem," art. 4, q. 3, Eberhard Waltmann replies to the argument that the badges are only signs by saying: "But if we pay attention to what the badges are intended to signify, we see that those who buy badges in Wilsnack seek a really existing blood [*cruorem actu existentem*], which they revere as existing [*quem ut existentem colunt*]" (Wolfenbüttel H.A.B. Cod. Guelf. 630b Helmst., fol. 22r). It is not certain that pilgrim badges were painted to show blood drops on the hosts, but I interpret the evidence, including Waltmann's words and Ludecus's sixteenth-century description, to suggest this; see nn. 116–19 below.

49. This suggested (or so opponents charged) that the feast itself "took its origin [*ortum habuisse*] from Wilsnack." See question 12 of the 14 questions sent by Tocke to the Erfurt faculty in 1446, app. 3, Breest, *Wunderblut* (1881), p. 301. And see Schäfer, "Märkische Fronleichnamsverehrung," p. 100, for this practice at other places in the Mark.

50. For the argument that it is an interpolation, see Kühne, "'Ich ging durch Feuer und Wasser . . .'." The fact that several later texts mention as an argument against the hosts the fact that they have been reconsecrated (Damerau, *Das Gutachten der . . . Erfurt*, pp. 62–63) may support Kühne's argument that the incident in which

bleeding miraculously opposes reconsecration is in fact an interpolation. Rather than being mistaken about the facts, these discussants may have been right about the reconsecration.

51. Tocke, "Synodalrede," pp. 175–76. Such frauds had been known for at least a hundred years before Wilsnack. For the host at Klosterneuberg (1298), generally agreed to have been a fraud, see Browe, "Verwandlungswunder," p. 162; idem, "Die Hostienschändungen," p. 190; and Heuser, "'Heilig-Blut'," p. 75. Hus in "Tractatus," sect. 14, p. 34, accuses blood miracles of leading the faithful to believe that "sangwinem visibilem quem dyabolus vel dyaboli sacerdos procurauit" is "verum sangwinem Domini," as people have believed in frauds in Krakow, Bononja, and elsewhere. In such places, says Hus, "cruorem presbiteri, quem de digito emisit in hostiam, tamquam verum Christi sangwinem adorauerunt."

52. Tocke, "Synodalrede," p. 175. I translate from Breest's German translation.

53. Both opponents and defenders agreed that lasting redness counted. Tocke reported that the priest seized in the supposed Wartenburg fraud claimed "goat's blood lasts long." Tocke, "Synodalrede," p. 175. This was understood as a slanderous reference to Wilsnack; it also suggests that perduring redness was necessary to a miracle claim. Some modern theorists of sacrifice suggest that the power of sacrificed objects lasts only as long as they keep and manifest the sacrality affixed to them in the violent act of sacrifice; see Barton, "An Emotional Economy of Sacrifice."

54. Binterim, *Pragmatische Geschichte*, pp. 546–47. There is debate about whether Cusanus was ever at Wilsnack. See n. 20 above.

55. Scholarship has tended to find in Hus's ideas the seeds of both his own decision to submit to church authority and Jacobellus's defiance of the church; Kaminsky, *Hussite Revolution*, pp. 5–6, and Šmahel, *Die Hussitische Revolution*, vol. 1, passim, especially pp. 487–510, 555, 651–54. On Hus's attitude toward the lay chalice, see Hilsch, *Johannes Hus*, p. 254, and Werner, *Jan Hus*, pp. 99–104.

56. See Chapter 4 nn. 46–50.

57. Kurze, *Quellen*, pp. 38, 286.

58. Kurze, *Quellen*, passim; Lichte, *Die Inszenierung einer Wallfahrt*, pp. 40–43.

59. In 1441, the bishop of Brandenburg permitted the city of Bernau to remember its liberation from the Hussites with a Corpus Christi procession; see Lichte, *Die Inszenierung einer Wallfahrt*, pp. 40–43.

60. See Chapter 3 nn. 109, 111.

61. See Hoyer, "Die thüringische Kryptoflagellantenbewegung," and Reifferscheid, *Neun Texte*, pp. 32–36 (on Sangerhausen) and pp. 37–40 (on Sonderhausen). I am grateful to Robert Lerner for suggesting that I explore the cryptoflagellants.

62. Reifferscheid, *Neun Texte* (articles confessed by the heretics of Sangerhausen before Henry Schonfeld, Dominican and theologian), p. 34, art. 23.

63. Ibid., p. 34, art. 28.

64. Ibid., p. 34, art. 30.

65. Reifferscheid, *Neun Texte* (articles held by heretics taken and burned in Sonderhausen), p. 38, art. 12.

66. Ibid., p. 37, art. 2.

67. In, for example, the polemical exchange between Eberhard Waltmann and John of Capistrano; see n. 25 above.

68. In the many collections of Wilsnack polemic still in manuscript not only are

the *determinationes* almost invariably called *De sanguine Christi*; the scholastic *questiones* and *quodlibeta* are sometimes accompanied by sermons on the major Old and New Testament texts specifically concerned with salvation by blood: Hebrews, Isaiah, Leviticus, I Peter. See Meier, "Der Erfurter . . . Johannes Bremer"; and Ziesak, "'Multa habeo vobis dicere . . .'."

69. Hus, "Questio de sangwine Christi," and "Tractatus," fasc. 3, pp. 3–37. Hus's work was widely accepted and circulated. It reached Magdeburg via Erfurt (which was in close contact with Prague) and was influential in the formulation of the articles of 1412; see ibid., p. II, and Breest, *Wunderblut* (1881), p. 173. There are summaries of Hus's treatise in Breest, *Wunderblut* (1881), pp. 164–74, and Holtz, "Cults," pp. 261–90. On Hus generally, see Hilsch, *Johannes Hus*. The older work by Spinka, *John Hus*, is still useful.

70. Hus, "Questio," pp. 3–4.

71. Hus, "Questio," p. 4: "Conclusio 1a."

72. Hus, "Questio," pp. 6–7.

73. Hus, "Questio," pp. 7–8. Hus goes on in the "Tractatus" (pp. 9–11) to argue at length against the idea that contact relics such as the *sudarium* or thorns from the crown of thorns could have on them the blood of Christ.

74. Hus, "Tractatus," pp. 20–22. Hus then asserts that Christians consume in the eucharist a *Christus absconditus* who is really body and blood. But only Jews and infidels wish to see with bodily eyes, as they also wished to see the divinity hanging on the cross.

75. Hus, "Tractatus," reply to objs. 1, 4, and 5, pp. 9–10, 13–15. The reply to objection 1 is complicated. Hus argues that one can say *participaliter* but not *nominaliter* that the relics were once stained with blood (if the relics are authentic); the redness might remain apart from the substance of blood, as accidents remain in the eucharist when substance is replaced. But if the relics are authentic and if there is redness, it is only a memorial, not the blood itself: "Si nominaliter, tunc antecedens argumenti est falsum, quia nec paniculus, nec tunica, nec sudarium habent in se sangwinem tinctum vel aspersum, sed habent rubedinem sangwinis Christi in memoriam derelictam (supposito, quod tunica, sudarium . . . et sic de aliis habeantur)." The implication is clearly that the relics might not be authentic. Hus also devotes a good deal of attention to questioning the claims of miracles at Wilsnack; "Tractatus," pp. 26–36. For more on Hus's concern with identity, see Chapter 4 n. 109.

76. Hus, "Tractatus," pp. 16–17. Hus's emphasis on the resurrection of the body makes it clear that the issue to him is primarily soteriological, not devotional.

77. Ibid., p. 26.

78. Ibid., sect. 14, pp. 35–36.

79. Hus, "Questio," p. 5. See also "Tractatus," p. 25: "melius est pro fidei merito nobis Christum et eius sangwinem esse absconsum, nam alias tolleretur meritum"; p. 28: "Vbi habes, quod sangwis Christi maximum est miraculum, quia per totum mundum vicit leonem, i.e. dyabolum."

80. "Super dubiis" (the *Gutachten* of 1446), Wolfenbüttel H.A.B. Cod. Guelf. 152 Helmst., fols. 160vb–164va. Qq. 1–2, which treat this issue, are the longest section of the discussion and are found on fols. 160vb–162rb. The fourteen questions are printed in Breest, *Wunderblut* (1881), app. 3, pp. 300–301; for an account of the events, see ibid., pp. 197–255.

81. "Super dubiis," q. 2, fols. 161rb–162rb. For the theologians' concern with avoiding decay, worms, and contamination, see especially q. 1, fols. 160vb–161rb. They point out repeatedly that if hosts are allowed to age they acquire foulness and worms (*putrefactio et vermes*), and argue that changes in the species of a host can be owing either to miracle or to natural change such as worms or dust. Such analysis suggests that naturalistic explanations of red spots on wafers (the sort of explanation for miracle hosts popular with nineteenth- and early twentieth-century historians) were far from impossible in the fifteenth century. See Chapter 3 n. 17.

82. "Super dubiis," q. 2, fol. 161vb: "Et cum corpus Christi modo sit inpassibile et inmortalis verissime sentiendum est quod sanguis Christi extra corpus suum nulli apparet."

83. Ibid., fols. 161vb–162ra. A summary of the argument of the *Gutachten* is given by Breest, *Wunderblut* (1881), pp. 220–23.

84. See Chapter 12 n. 2. Supporters of the blood were not limited to Benedictines and Franciscans. The Carthusian Werner Rolevinck from Westphalia, for example, also supported the Wilsnack hosts because they excited piety; see Heuser, "'Heilig-Blut'," p. 78 n. 21b.

85. Oliger, "Johannes Kannemann," pp. 46–47.

86. See Bansleben, "Questio de sanguine relicto in hoc monasterio," conclusion 3, corollary 2, Wolfenbüttel H.A.B. Cod. 19.6. Aug. 2°, fols. 87v–89r, quoted passage at fol. 88v; also in Herbst, "Literarisches Leben," p. 161 (with slight differences). "Non resumptus est a Christo omnis suus sanguis nutrimentalis quia non omnis talis secundum doctores est de veritate vite humanalis." On the centrality of the question of the *veritas humanae naturae* in late medieval soteriology, see generally Bynum, *Resurrection*, pp. 133–35, 213, 262, and Reynolds, *Food and the Body*.

87. On Hermann Bansleben and Johannes Witten of Braunschweig, see Herbst, "Literarisches Leben," pp. 131–89, and Hellfaier, "Die Historia de duce Hinrico," pp. 378–80. On Kannemann, Döring, and Bremer, see Breest, *Wunderblut* (1881), pp. 198–231; Albert, *Matthias Döring*, pp. 62–72; Oliger, "Johannes Kannemann"; Meier, "Der Erfurter . . . Johannes Bremer"; and Kleineidam, *Universitas Studii Erffordensis*, vol. 1, pp. 145–53. The Braunschweig relic was also defended by Johannes Schorkopp (d. 1509), canon of St. Blaise in Braunschweig; see Ziesak, "'Multa habeo vobis dicere . . .'," pp. 213 and 239, and Meier, "Der Erfurter . . . Johannes Bremer," p. 1253. Schorkopp's "Questio de sanguine Christi," Wolfenbüttel H.A.B. Cod. 19.6. Aug. 2°, fols. 46r–54v, argues that not all Christ's blood is reassumed at the resurrection but "tantum quantum sufficiebat ad gloriosi corporis perfectionem et decorem" (fol. 54v).

88. "Determinatio de sanguine Christi relicto," Wolfenbüttel H.A.B. Cod. 19.6. Aug. 2°, fols. 89r–90r, quoted passage at fol. 89v: "Quemadmodum autem caro Christi mansit in terris propter fidem confirmandam . . . sic etiam Christus quasdam particulas sui sacri sanguinis in terris miserat ut per illas sue passionis veritatem ostendatur." There are anti-Semitic overtones in Witten, who argues that the particles of Christ left behind refute the Jews, who argue against Christ's passion; Herbst, "Literarisches Leben," p. 159 n. 12.

89. See Chapter 5 for this argument made by the Franciscans in the Rome dispute of 1462.

90. Bansleben, "Questio," conclusion 1, in Herbst, "Literarisches Leben," p. 160, and see above n. 86.

91. Waltmann's "De adoratione et contra cruorem," art. 4, qq. 1–2, Wolfenbüttel H.A.B. Cod. Guelf. 630b Helmst., fols. 20v–21v. Waltmann is replying to Tocke's questions. The "De adoratione" has been misidentified by R. Damerau as an otherwise unknown *Gutachten* of the Erfurt faculty from 1452; see above n. 47. For Damerau's transcription from Marburg UB Hs. 58, fols. 303ra–309ra, see Damerau, *Das Gutachten der . . . Erfurt*, pp. 24–27.

92. Waltmann, "De adoratione," art. 1, fol. 14r–v.

93. Ibid., arts. 1–2, fols. 14r–17v, and art. 4, q. 11, fol. 23r–v. For example, art. 1, fol. 14v, argues against the positions of those such as Kannemann and Döring: "Dicunt etiam quidam quod color sanguinolentus post domini resurrexionem in corona spinea, statua crucis, peplo beate virginis et lancea steterat sicud accidentia sacramenti altaris sine subiecto. Alii quod virtute divina materia crocea consimilis materie cruoris in quam transformationem sanguis fuisset conversus sit substrata colori sanguinolento. Auctor tocius nature in hac novit veritatem. Pia fides tamen quid tucius est teneat. Sed sine sic sit sive non. Non est credendum vocatum cruorem in Wilsnack esse Christi naturalem derelictum. Sed de sanguine miraculose aliquid esse repertum sepe legimus tam in hostiis transformatis quam circa hostias transformatas." (The version Damerau gives from the Marburg manuscript makes no sense.) Art. 2, fol. 15r, discussing *latria*, which is properly owed only to God, argues: "Sic in hoc non sacramentum cui cruor vincitur sed cruorem principaliter intentum populus colit et adorat predicta tria [that is, creation, re-creation, and remuneration] attribuendo. Quid aliud ex premissis concludi poterit nisi . . . populum omnes partes latrie exibere pure creature intentione principali. Immo creature inanimate cui nec dulia debetur."

94. Waltmann, "De adoratione," art. 2, fols. 14v–17v, esp. fols. 15v–16r, where Waltmann argues that the supposed wonder deserves no more or less veneration than the consecrated host placed with it and suggests that, even if it is a miracle, it shows wrath, not favor. "Nec unquam fecit aliquid miraculum quia pura creatura est. Omnes qui sic eum coluerunt et coluerint ydolatriam commiserunt et committunt. Non enim plus sanctus estimandus quamvis hostie consecrata adiacens ab extrinseco nisi quantum si ex miraculo factum est magis ostendit iram dei ut patuit in conversione sacramenti in digitum sanguinolentum in manibus beati gregorii pape, ut canit historia quam forte faceret alterius colore tinctura."

95. Waltmann, "De adoratione," art. 2, *tertio subiungitur*, fol. 16r. Waltmann argues that transformed hosts should be placed among the relics not offered for veneration: ". . . dum transformatio fuerit adeo horribilis quam hostia in cibum conservata. . . ." He adds: "Non enim gaudebat beatus gregorius de hostie transformatione. Ideoque orabat pro conversione in pristinam formam." See also art. 3, fols. 17v–20v, especially fol. 18v, where he argues that if Gregory could see such things now he would not rejoice "in cruenta carne" but rather weep. Blood miracles are a sign of the devil or of God's anger at sin. Waltmann returns to the point later in the article, fol. 19r: "Nam si vere miraculose hostie fuissent transformate pocius exinde dei iram debebant timere quam de dei speciali gratia gaudere. Quia taliter sanguis miraculosus in Egypto in hostia per judeos perforata et in cypho virginis cuiusdam scaturitus [?] in quo aqua dicitur conversa in sanguinem erat peccati principale signum." The general argument (against the seen and for the invisible) is close to Hus's (see nn. 74–75) and Cusanus's (above n. 21). While these positions certainly suggest that visibility and visuality were major issues in the mid-fifteenth century, they do not suggest that the basic trend was, in any simple sense, toward the visual.

96. Extensive excerpts from Bremer's "Questio" are transcribed by Meier, "Der Erfurter . . . Johannes Bremer," pp. 1255–61, from Stadtbibliothek Braunschweig MS 48, fols. 194c–218b. On the connections between the two sermons and the "Questio," see Meier, p. 1249. Union Theological Seminary, New York, Cod. 13, fols. 165r–184v, gives the title as "questio notabilis." In Wolfenbüttel H.A.B. Cod. 19.6. Aug.2°, fols. 69v–84r, both incipit and explicit give "magistralis questio."

97. Note that Bremer says "*are* of the humanity" and "*were* joined." He would seem to be arguing here the traditional Franciscan position that the blood of Christ's body had been assumed by the Logos in the womb but that shed blood was not united with the Logos during the *triduum* and hence a bit of it could remain behind.

98. Meier, "Der Erfurter . . . Johannes Bremer," p. 1262, from Braunschweig MS 48, fol. 209d.

99. Meier, pp. 1259–60, from Braunschweig MS 48, fols. 204–9. Like Bansleben's, Bremer's position is complicated; both oppose Aquinas's contention that all Christ's blood rose but use Thomistic ideas of identity to argue this.

100. For the controversy between Johannes von Dorsten and Ulrich Rissbach over the Wilsnack pilgrimage of 1475, see Ziesak, "'Multa habeo vobis dicere . . .'," pp. 213, 232–33, 238. Portions of Dorsten's "De cursu simplicium ad sacrum cruorem in Wilsnack asservatum" are found in Paltz, *Supplementum Coelifodinae*, and in Wattenbach, "Beiträge zur Geschichte der Mark Brandenburg," pp. 605–7. Breest gives a summary of Dorsten's arguments in *Wunderblut* (1881), p. 253. For Johannes von Dorsten's influence on Paltz, see Hamm, *Frömmigkeitstheologie*, pp. 60–67, 309–13.

101. Paltz, *Supplementum Coelifodinae*, p. 401. Paltz gives six remedies against such impulses, the first and most important of which is *poenitere de peccatis suis*. For two chronicle accounts that stress the frenzy of the pilgrimage in the 1470s and 1480s, see Zika, "Hosts, Processions and Pilgrimages," p. 58 nn. 110–11.

102. Paltz, *Supplementum Coelifodinae*, pp. 390–96. He charges that pilgrimages to Wilsnack, like those in the Rhineland, are flawed both when they are compulsory and when they are impulsive; their participants are drawn to blasphemy, lying, and ribaldry. He describes pilgrim behavior that we would call hysteria.

103. Paltz, *Supplementum Coelifodinae*, p. 405.

104. Ibid. See Giles of Rome, "Theoremata de corpore Christi," prop. 23, fol. 14v. In Giles's analysis of eucharistic visions, body is more important than blood. By the fifteenth century, things have changed.

105. For more on the miracle to which Dorsten and Paltz here refer, see Paltz, *Supplementum Coelifodinae*, p. 405 n. 16, and Chapter 3 n. 22.

106. Paltz, *Supplementum Coelifodinae*, p. 407: "Cum enim ex hostia sanguis fluxerit, confirmatur fides nostra, qua credimus non solum in calice sed etiam in hostia verum contineri sanguinem, contra errorem ipsorum [Bohemorum]." Paltz's position here supports the argument of Gavin Langmuir that Jews (and heretics) were useful to express and deal with Christians' own anxiety about unbelief. For more on this see Chapter 3 at n. 149.

107. Paltz, *Supplementum Coelifodinae*, pp. 405–6. The fact that Paltz is quoting Johannes von Dorsten here means that we have evidence about the 1470s as well as the early sixteenth century.

108. Ibid., pp. 409–13. In other words, as signs, the true cross, the lance, etc., can receive *latria*, but the *latria* is for the God they signify. Paltz here quotes from an otherwise unknown *determinatio* of Johannes von Dorsten; see ibid., p. 408 n. 19.

109. Ibid., p. 407, following Dorsten.

110. On pilgrimage in the Mark Brandenburg generally, see Escher, "Brandenburgische Wallfahrten."

111. Krüger, *Die Nikolauskirche zu Wilsnack*, p. 9. See also Cremer, *Die St. Nikolaus- und Heiligblut-Kirche*, and n. 3 above.

112. Ludecus, *Historia von der erfindung*, Vorrede, [p. 17].

113. See n. 9 above.

114. Buchholz and Gralow, *Zur Geschichte der Wilsnacker Wallfahrt*, pp. 8, 12.

115. Heuser, "'Heilig-Blut'," pp. 38–39; see also pp. 106–7.

116. See Buchholz and Gralow, *Zur Geschichte der Wilsnacker Wallfahrt*, pp. 22 and 25, and Gandert, "Das Heilige Blut von Wilsnack und seine Pilgerzeichen," pp. 81–90 and plates 2–4. The oldest, and most widely disseminated, form of the badge seems to have been three hosts superimposed on a triangle. The later form (of which no old examples survive) shows two kneeling figures under a gable holding up a monstrance; it probably originates in the first half of the fifteenth century. See Gandert, plates 4 and 6.

117. Ludecus, *Historia von der erfindung*, Vorrede, [p. 19] describes the badges thus: "Wenn nu die Bligrimen jre gelübde geleistet, die opfferungen verrichtet vnnd widerumb anheims rheisen wollen, sind jnen sonderliche zeichen von Bleij gegossen, gleich einer hostien mit dreyen rot geferbten flecken, wie Blutstropffen, zugerichtet, zum gezeugnis, das sie die heilige stedte besucht hetten, mitgeteilet worden. Welche zeichen die Wallbrüder vorn an jre hüte gehefftet vnd damit erleubnis zu wandern erlangt haben."

The earliest surviving badges show various figures (Christ crucified, Christ risen, and Christ at the column of the flagellation) in the center of the hosts. On the milestone referred to in n. 118 below, there are simple crosses in the center of the hosts. I interpret Ludecus's description of the hosts as "prepared [*zugerichtet*] like a host with three red-colored spots like blood drops" to suggest that blood drops were painted on them. Ludecus also says that the badges were both cast and prepared [*gegossen und zugerichtet*] in the churchyard of the cathedral, suggesting two steps in the process of manufacture. On Waltmann's objections to the badges as indicating real blood on the hosts, see n. 48.

118. Gandert, "Das Heilige Blut von Wilsnack und seine Pilgerzeichen," plate 1.

119. Buchholz and Gralow, *Zur Geschichte der Wilsnacker Wallfahrt*, pp. 26–31. For another example, see the St. Katherine Church in Brandenburg, which has an altar dedicated to St. Hedwig of Silesia with a retable from about 1480 (restored 1972–75). On the upper left side wing, St. Hedwig gives food and drink to pilgrims, three of whom wear the triform pilgrim badge of Wilsnack on their hats. See Dehio, *Handbuch . . . , Brandenburg*, p. 134; *Die Kunstdenkmäler der Provinz Brandenburg*, vol. 3, pt 3: *Stadt und Dom Brandenburg*, p. 66; and—for a description and indistinct reproduction of the wings—Wochnik, *Brandenburg: St. Katharinenkirche*, pp. 16–17.

120. See app. 1, in Breest, *Wunderblut* (1881), p. 296; also Schannat and Hartzheim, eds., *Concilia Germaniae*, vol. 5, p. 35; and Browe, "Verwandlungswunder," p. 157 n. 63.

121. Ludecus claimed this; Breest found no direct evidence but considered it likely; idem, *Wunderblut* (1881), pp. 178, 186.

122. It has become conventional to say "more than 150"; see Boockmann, "Der

Streit um das Wilsnacker Blut," p. 395, and Zika, "Hosts, Processions and Pilgrimages," p. 50 n. 78, basing themselves on Meier, "Wilsnack als Spiegel." But 150 may be an exaggeration. Ziesak, "'Multa habeo vobis dicere . . . '," lists about 50 different titles, although she does not claim to have found everything.

123. See above nn. 25, 43.

124. Damerau, *Das Gutachten der . . . Erfurt*, pp. 66–72, discusses James's text as found in MS 58, UB Marburg, fols. 3rI–25rI, and give excerpts from his opinion on Wilsnack found on fols. 34v–36v. James argues that the supposed miracles of Wilsnack—to which he joins the miracles of John of Capistrano as similar frauds—encourage the Jews to ridicule Christianity. Claiming to be answering Jewish charges, James explains how certain supposed cures can have natural causes, and argues that the cowardice of clergy who will not speak out against superstition leads many of the faithful to conclude that all saints and martyrs are invented (fol. 36rI; cited Damerau, p. 70). Damerau also prints (p. 31) a short anonymous text from MS 58, UB Marburg, fol. 309rII, which argues against the Wilsnack hosts as "illicita et mala" and gives as the sixth argument (of eight) against them that "confortat hereticos, presertim eos, qui detrahunt sacramento eukaristie ut Waldenses." On the problems with Damerau's transcriptions, see n. 47 above.

Chapter 3. Cults in Mecklenburg and the Mark Brandenburg

1. Kolb, *Vom Heiligen Blut*, surveys blood cult from a present-day perspective. Recent large studies of blood cult are Eder, *"Die Deggendorfer Gnad"*, and the Festschriften devoted to the Weingarten cult: *Festschrift zur 900-Jahr-Feier* and *900 Jahre Heilig-Blut-Verehrung*.

2. For lists of blood relics, see Holtz, "Cults," pp. viii–xii; Vincent, *Holy Blood*, pp. 51–53; Bynum, "The Blood of Christ"; Barbier de Montault, *Oeuvres complètes*, vol. 7: *Rome*, pt 5.2, pp. 524–37; Nagel, "Das Heilige Blut Christi," pp. 197–98; Sumption, *Pilgrimage*, pp. 44–49 and 312; and the works cited in these studies. On the chronology, see Heuser, "'Heilig-Blut'," p. 179. For the circle of blood-relic sites in Swabia, particularly in the area around Lake Constance, see Kolb, *Vom Heiligen Blut*, p. 38.

3. Anti-Jewish miracles are a minority, although a large minority, of the bleeding-host cases; see Browe, *Die eucharistischen Wunder*; idem, "Verwandlungswunder"; and Heuser, "'Heilig-Blut'." For a useful overview that concentrates on the south of Germany, see Rubin, "Imagining the Jew." Of anti-Jewish libels, the charge that Jews desecrated images was the oldest, going back to the early Middle Ages; see Browe, "Die Hostienschändungen," and Lotter, "Innocens Virgo et Martyr." Charges of ritual murder appear apparently first in England in 1147–57 but soon after in Germany. Recent scholars such as Yuval, Lotter, and McCulloh, for different reasons, doubt England's priority. See Lotter, "Innocens Virgo et Martyr"; McCulloh, "Jewish Ritual Murder"; Stacey, "From Ritual Crucifixion"; and Yuval, "'They tell lies'." The host-desecration story appears first in France in 1290 and soon after in Germany; see Chapter 1 n. 41. Host-desecration charges then seem to be mostly (not entirely) limited to Germany and Austria. It is worth noting that the Paris, Brussels, and Posen/Poznań cases have generated a vast literature, and that Brussels was an important pilgrimage site into the nineteenth century. On Brussels, see the classic studies by Lefèvre, "La valeur histori-

que" and "Le miracle eucharistique." For a brief survey of anti-Jewish persecutions with emphasis on the particularly lethal nature of host-desecration charges, see Langmuir, "At the Frontiers of Faith," pp. 151–52. (I do not agree with Langmuir's description of these persecutions as "not religious," although the question of characterization seems to me largely a semantic matter.)

4. See above n. 3. Host-desecration charges were a more common anti-Jewish libel than ritual murder charges in German lands in the fourteenth to sixteenth centuries, but accusations of ritual murder, which came to include cannibalism, steadily increased. (Israel Yuval says there were about ninety in Europe before 1600.) See Yuval, "'They tell lies'," p. 88. Charges of well-poisoning were relatively rare.

5. Vincent, *Holy Blood*. Vincent concentrates his efforts at explanation on three factors: the shaky provenance of the blood relic, the competition from eucharistic devotion, and the inadequate political skills of the English king. These are plausible explanations. A comparison with German cases suggests that part of the explanation for the failure of Westminster also lies in the fact that there was (despite the success of Hailes, which Vincent discusses) no strong tradition of blood cult in England. The Havelland in northern Germany had no such problem.

6. See the examples of Heiligengrabe and Berlin-Brandenburg-Stendal discussed below. For political explanations of German blood cult, see Swillus, "Hostienfrevellegende"; Faensen, "Zur Synthese," who sees blood hosts as an expression of clerical control; Kühne, "'Ich ging durch Feuer und Wasser . . .'," who sees hosts as a protest of the people against clerical control; and the studies of Sternberg cited in n. 94 below.

7. In the literature on Wilsnack, few scholars have taken the step of looking at what came before. German historians tend to start with 1383 and ask what happened and why; Anglophone historians study how the accounts were constructed. Köster, "Gottsbüren, das hessische 'Wilsnack'," is a partial exception, but it involves not much more than the assertion that the particular local cult it examines may be a precursor to Wilsnack.

8. A point made by Gerhard Lutz in his paper "*Salve Caput Cruentum*: The Veneration of Holy Blood in Late Medieval Germany—Art and Architecture," presented at the International Medieval Conference at Kalamazoo, April 2003. On problems with evidence for bleeding-host miracles, see Browe, "Verwandlungswunder," pp. 146–61.

9. Bauerreiss, *Pie Jesu*; Browe, *Die eucharistischen Wunder*; Heuser, "'Heilig-Blut'."

10. Kühne, "Ich ging durch Feuer und Wasser . . .'," pp. 50–51; idem, "Der Harz und sein Umland," p. 6; and see below n. 21.

11. See Rothkrug, "Popular Religion and Holy Shrines," and idem, *Religious Practices and Collective Perceptions*. Despite their characteristic energy, originality, and high intelligence, these studies were out of date in their quantitative details when they appeared; see Sargent, "A Critique."

12. Heuser, "'Heilig-Blut'." See also Kolb, *Vom Heiligen Blut*. I essayed a brief treatment of the three types of blood and their wider setting in Bynum, "The Blood of Christ."

13. There are two excellent recent treatments of blood relics: Vincent, *Holy Blood*, and Holtz, "Cults." Holtz, p. 95, distinguishes the more suffering-oriented piety of bleeding hosts from the piety of blood relics, which he sees as related to an earlier soteriology that stressed victory over Satan. Holtz's sophisticated analysis of the liturgy

at Weingarten lends weight to his argument about the spirituality of earlier relic cult, and indeed his argument draws on the standard view of differences between earlier and later piety. But I have not found a clear divide between relic and host veneration in the fragmentary evidence we have about northern cult sites, nor have I found a special emphasis on empathetic suffering in the piety associated with bleeding-host sites.

14. On miracle hosts, see Bauerreiss, *Pie Jesu*; Browe, *Die eucharistischen Wunder*; idem, "Verwandlungswunder"; and Merback, "Channels of Grace."

15. See Chapter 1 n. 55. Peter Browe's foundational work in the 1920s on eucharistic miracles did put anti-Jewish libels in the context of eucharistic devotion.

16. Scholars still generally maintain that a certain number of early medieval blood relics went back not to Golgotha but to the cross of Beirut (a crucifix supposedly made by Nicodemus and molested by Jews), but that most stories of bleeding images emerged after the fifteenth century and replaced older relics and wonders. On bleeding images—which do not come into my story except insofar as the Beirut cross is argued to be the source of blood relics—see Kolb, *Vom Heiligen Blut*, pp. 65–84 and 167–88. On the general tendency of piety to move from blood relic and bleeding host to image, see Bauerreiss, *Pie Jesu*, and Merback, "Channels of Grace."

17. In this older scholarship, explanations of blood cult range from Bauerreiss's brilliant but not widely accepted argument (in *Pie Jesu*) that in many cases cult was generated by image (in this interpretation, the Man of Sorrows surrounded by the instruments of his torture, for example, gives rise to stories of Jews attacking Christ with the same instruments) to the suggestion that it was all a misunderstanding of the natural phenomenon of the *Hostienpilz* (or *micrococcus prodigiosus*), a red fungus that appears on damp bread. The theory that it was all the result of fungus or a microbe goes back to the nineteenth century and is discussed by Bauerreiss himself on p. 20, also by Browe, "Die scholastische Theorie," p. 332, and Löffler, "Mittelalterliche Hostienwunder," p. 9. A variety of political and economic interpretations have also been proposed. See above n. 6.

18. For example, Schäfer, "Märkische Fronleichnamsverehrung"; Kolb, *Vom Heiligen Blut*; Kötzsche, "Das wiedergefundene Hostiengrab;" Kühne, "Der Harz und sein Umland"; and Faensen, "Zur Synthese."

19. The earliest western blood relics are those of Reichenau (from between 923 and 950, supposedly given by the countess Swanahild who had acquired it from Charlemagne), Weingarten (supposedly a gift from Judith of Flanders of a portion of the blood found at Mantua in the eleventh century), and Fécamp (from before 1120). See Weichenrieder, "Das Heilige Blut von Mantua," and Holtz, "Cults," pp. viii–xii. For Jerome's reference to the column of the flagellation, see Chapter 1 n. 9. Our earliest reference to a relic of the blood Christ shed at the passion may be in a letter from Braulio of Saragossa, written circa 649, which expressed concern that such veneration might overshadow the mass; see Bynum, *Resurrection*, pp. 107–8 n. 179.

20. See Paltz, *Supplementum Coelifodinae*, p. 405 n. 16. Arnold of Lübeck's *Chronica Slavorum* tells of a priest in the village of Bechstette who (supposedly in 1191) failed to clean a water cruet properly; the host particle left there turned to blood and a finger, which were allegedly translated to Erfurt, where a blood chapel was built. A later account, the *Annales Reinhardsbrunnenses*, adds that the miracle occurred because of a girl who did not believe that those who had received the last rites could recover.

21. It is not clear how we should understand references to a consecrated host ven-

erated in the Mary chapel at Buchow bei Nennhausen (in the Havelland not far from Wilsnack). Either a miracle host or ordinary eucharistic veneration could be meant. See Schäfer, "Märkische Fronleichnamsverehrung," p. 104.

22. Perles, "Geschichte der Juden in Posen"; Prümers, "Der Hostiendiebstahl zu Posen."

23. According to Breest, *Wunderblut* (1881), p. 183, the Wilsnack priest was later charged with having attempted to engineer a pilgrimage at Esefelde. Jan Hus cited cases of fraud in Bononja, Krakow, and in the dioceses of Bratislava and Prague, in "Tractatus," sect. 11, pp. 28–29, and sect. 14, p. 34. See Chapter 2 n. 51.

24. In what follows I concentrate on Mecklenburg and the Mark Brandenburg but consider also a few well-documented and recently studied cases from Middle Germany, such as Einbeck and Gottsbüren, the circle of blood relics in Lower Saxony and Holstein centered on Braunschweig, and two cases from Poland.

25. Bauerreiss, Browe, and Heuser all give charts in which cult is dated to the year attributed by legend, not to the date of the first documentation, although Heuser, in his individual summaries, carefully indicates both.

26. Supposedly a portion of a relic brought by Henry the Lion from the Holy Land in 1177. Several of the blood relics in this area were credited to the gift, direct or indirect, of Henry. See this chapter at nn. 30 and 74.

27. On Mariengarten, see Heuser, "'Heilig-Blut'," pp. 22–23 and n. 73 below. The cathedral in Brandenburg had a holy blood altar, dedicated in 1409, but nothing else is known about this; see ibid., p. 31.

28. We do not know what kind of blood relic the nuns at Wienhausen possessed, but there are stories in the surviving chronicle (seventeenth-century but based on earlier traditions) of miracles it worked. See Appuhn, ed., *Chronik des Klosters Wienhausen*, pp. 140–42. We also have records of several fourteenth-century donations to maintain an eternal light before the holy blood; see idem, "Der Auferstandene," p. 98. There has recently been lively art historical debate over Appuhn's conjecture that an extant statue of the resurrected Christ is a blood reliquary; see Hartwieg, "Drei gefasste Holzskulpturen," pp. 188, 194, and nn. 64 and 131; Hengevoss-Dürkop, *Skulptur und Frauenkloster*, pp. 139–61; Tripps, *Das handelnde Bildwerk*, pp. 140–46.

29. Heuser, "'Heilig-Blut'," p. 22; and Aufgebauer, "Einbeck im Mittelalter." According to Aufgebauer, p. 78, it "perhaps" received an indulgence from Gelasius II in 1118–19.

30. Kühne, "Der Harz und sein Umland," pp. 15–16.

31. Ibid., pp. 13–14; Heuser, "'Heilig-Blut'," pp. 23–24; and Browe, "Verwandlungswunder," p. 140.

32. Köster, "Gottsbüren, das hessische 'Wilsnack'."

33. Falckenheiner, "Der Wallfahrtsort Gottsbüren."

34. Köster, "Gottsbüren," pp. 199–200.

35. In the 1330s, a portion of the nuns under a prioress settled at Gottsbüren; in time the cloister there came to house the entire community.

36. Köster's work on the distribution of pilgrimage badges suggests that the height of the pilgrimage was circa 1340, and that its great days were over before the rise of Wilsnack at the end of the fourteenth century; see ibid., pp. 209–21.

37. See Chapter 2 n. 49.

38. See Faensen, "Zur Synthese," pp. 239–49; Schneider et al., *Die Cistercienser*,

pp. 7–26, and Ahlers, *Weibliches Zisterziensertum*, pp. 10–127. See also Bresgott and Cobbers, *Reiseziele*, which is without footnotes but nonetheless quite useful.

39. Riedel, *Codex dipl. Brandenb.*, A 7 (Berlin, 1847), p. 310. And see Schäfer, "Märkische Fronleichnamsverehrung," p. 102. Note that there is here no reference to blood.

40. Schäfer, "Märkische Fronleichnamsverehrung," pp. 100–102; Lichtenstein, "Der Vorwurf," pp. 189–90; Heuser, "'Heilig-Blut'," p. 28; *Germania Judaica*, ed. Avneri, vol. 2, pt. 1, pp. 61–63, esp. nn. 3 and 4; and Rubin, *Gentile Tales*, p. 213 n. 1. See also Riedel, *Codex dipl. Brandenb.*, A 9 (Berlin, 1849), doc. 2, pp. 470–75.

41. Jews seem to have arrived in the Mark Brandenburg in the second half of the thirteenth century. Our earliest evidence is from Stendal, Strausberg, Frankfurt (Oder), Spandau, and Berlin. See *Germania Judaica*, ed. Avneri, vol. 2, pt 1, pp. 61–63 and 102; and Heise, *Die Juden in der Mark Brandenburg*, p. 7.

42. Riedel, *Codex dipl. Brandenb.*, A 9, pp. 475–76. (The original of the document is lost, and Riedel's copy is taken from Creusing.) In a document of 1370, the event is once again referred to and still no identifiable perpetrator is mentioned; see Faensen, "Zur Synthese," p. 240 n. 7.

43. Faensen, "Zur Synthese," p. 240.

44. See Schäfer, "Märkische Fronleichnamsverehrung"; Kirchner, "Das Cisterzienser-Nonnenkloster . . . Zehdenick"; Faensen, "Zur Synthese"; and Bresgott and Cobbers, *Reiseziele*.

45. For ways in which women's houses, especially nonincorporated Cistercian houses, were subject to local episcopal authority and hence to manipulation by secular rulers as well as secular clergy, see Ahlers, *Weibliches Zisterziensertum*, pp. 126–27.

46. For the charter, see Riedel, *Codex dipl. Brandenb.*, A 1 (Berlin, 1838), pp. 243–44. On Marienfliess, see *Die Legende vom Ursprunge des Klosters Heiligengrabe*, ed. Simon, pp. 32–33; Schäfer, "Märkische Fronleichnamsverehrung," p. 104; Heuser, "'Heilig-Blut'," p. 26; and Faensen, "Zur Synthese," pp. 239–40. On Heiligengrabe, see below n. 52.

47. Riedel, *Codex dipl. Brandenb.*, A 13 (Berlin, 1857), docs. 1–3, pp. 128–30; *Germania sacra*, pp. 336–49; Heuser, "'Heilig-Blut'," p. 27; Faensen, "Zur Synthese," p. 240 n. 7; and Kirchner, "Das Cisterzienser-Nonnenkloster . . . Zehdenick."

48. Riedel, *Codex dipl. Brandenb.*, A 13, doc. 16, pp. 136–37.

49. Kirchner, "Zehdenick," pp. 157–60 and 180–83.

50. Ibid., p. 115.

51. For similar cults of holy earth (often fused with blood cult)—for example, at Bamberg, Heiligenstadt bei Altötting, and Erding in Bavaria—see Faensen, "Zur Synthese," p. 242, and below n. 121. For an English example, see Vincent, *Holy Blood*, p. 45, who reports that, after the execution of "the troublemaker" William fitz Osbern in the 1190s, his followers are said to have carried away the blood-impregnated earth from the place of his execution, claiming William was a martyr whose blood could effect miraculous healing.

52. On Heiligengrabe, see Kötzsche, "Das wiedergefundene Hostiengrab"; Plate and Plate, "Die Ergebnisse der Ausgrabungen"; Strohmaier-Wiederanders, *Geschichte*; Treue, "Schlechte und gute Christen," pp. 113–14; and Faensen, "Zur Synthese." The Low German version of the Legend with reproductions of the woodcuts (1521) is given in *Die Legende*, ed. Simon, based on G. Schmidt, "Rostocker Drucke," pp. 339–50.

53. *Die Legende*, p. 38.

54. Ibid., p. (10) of the facsimile; p. 23 of the transcription.

55. Kötzsche, "Das wiedergefundene Hostiengrab," p. 25.

56. Faensen, "Zur Synthese"; Merback, "Channels of Grace."

57. Both Erding and Assisi have churches erected near or over places of execution. For the connection of execution, blood cult, and the Man of Sorrows, see Bauerreiss, *Pie Jesu*. On the medieval sense that the blood of criminals could be salvific, see Merback, *The Thief, the Cross and the Wheel*, pp. 97–98, 220, and 271, and Edgerton, *Pictures and Punishment*, pp. 15, 47–55, 131 n. 7, 172, 183–88, and passim.

58. Reproduced in *Die Legende*, p. (4).

59. For these trials, see pp. 68–73.

60. Laabs, *Malerei und Plastik*, pp. 76, 80, 94–95, and passim. Laabs sees the *Tugendkruzifixion* as particularly bloody in its iconography; but see Chapter 9 n. 23 and Plate 30.

61. On Doberan, see Dolberg, "Die heiligen Bluts-Kapellen der . . . Doberan"; Heuser, "'Heilig-Blut'," p. 29; Fründt, *Zisterzienser-Kloster Doberan*; Erdmann, *Zisterzienser-Abtei Doberan*; Laabs, *Malerei und Plastik*.

62. Laabs, *Malerei und Plastik*, pp. 93–94.

63. Heuser, "'Heilig-Blut'," p. 31; Hoogeweg, *Die Stifter und Klöster der Provinz Pommern*, vol. 1, pp. 113–14.

64. Riedel, *Codex dipl. Brandenb.*, A 18 (Berlin, 1859), doc. 6, pp. 64–65; and Heuser, "'Heilig-Blut'," p. 31. An indulgence of 1296 (Riedel, A 18, doc. 14, p. 70) does not mention the blood miracle.

65. Heuser, "'Heilig-Blut'," p. 30. According to Donath, *Geschichte der Juden in Mecklenburg*, p. 37, the emperor Louis of Bavaria gave a letter of protection to the Krakow Jews in 1325.

66. In southern sites from the same period, such as Iphofen and Deggendorf, pogroms can be demonstrated to predate host-desecration charges by decades; thus historians have usually treated the charges as rationalizations for the pogroms. See Eder, *"Die Deggendorfer Gnad,"* and Swillus, "Hostienfrevellegende und Judenverfolgung in Iphofen." If Kirchberg can be trusted, the events at Güstrow came before the synagogue burnings at Iphofen and Deggendorf (which are documented in chronicles). I can find no independent verification that the Güstrow chapel was on a synagogue site, but it seems plausible that this detail of city space would have been correctly remembered forty years later, however much the details of the desecration story may have been invented. In connection with the events of 1492 at Sternberg, we learn that Jews lived in a number of places in fifteenth-century Mecklenburg; see Backhaus, "Die Hostienschändungsprozesse," p. 8. Avneri, in *Germania Judaica*, vol. 2, pt 2, pp. 528–29, says there were Jews in Güstrow before the mid-fourteenth-century but seems, like Donath, to use the host-desecration charge as proof of this. According to Donath, *Geschichte der Juden in Mecklenburg*, Jews settled in Mecklenburg in the second half of the thirteenth century. We have a gravestone from Parchim from 1258.

67. See Hofmeister, "Weitere Beiträge."

68. Heuser, "'Heilig-Blut'," p. 30, citing Kirchberg.

69. Hofmeister, "Weitere Beiträge," p. 197.

70. Schlager, "Geschichte des Franziskanerklosters zu Güstrow," p. 71.

71. Ibid., pp. 71–72.

72. We have, however, evidence of an actual execution of a woman for host abuse

in the fourteenth century in Lauingen, close to Margaret Ebner's monastery at Dillingen on the Danube; see Margaret Ebner, *Offenbarungen*, pp. 116–17.

73. The Cistercian women's cloister of Mariengarten in Lower Saxony, south of Göttingen, also claimed a blood relic, supposedly brought by a follower of the lords of Ziegenberg from Naples. There are documents and accounts of miracles from the fourteenth century, including the healing of one of the sisters from a hemorrhage; see Hellfaier, "Die historia de duce Hinrico," p. 387 n. 36.

74. On Cismar, see Finke, "Zur Geschichte"; Heuser, "'Heilig-Blut'," p. 25; and Ehresmann, "Iconography of the Cismar Altarpiece." On the relic donations, see esp. ibid., pp. 1–2.

75. See Weichenrieder, "Das Heilige Blut von Mantua"; Binder, "Das Heilige Blut in Weissenau"; and Jensch, "Die Weingartener Heilig-Blut- und Stiftertradition."

76. Herbst, "Literarisches Leben"; and Hellfaier, "Die historia de duce Hinrico."

77. Hellfaier, "Die historia de duce Hinrico," pp. 380–89, who essentially follows Herbst.

78. Ehresmann, "Iconography of the Cismar Altarpiece," p. 28.

79. Bansleben, *Sermo de sanguine Christi* on Isaiah 63.3, "Aspersus est sanguis eorum super vestimenta mea," Stadtbibliothek Braunschweig MS 48, fol. 233r, cited in Herbst, "Literarisches Leben," p. 162.

80. See Finke, "Zur Geschichte," pp. 167–69. On the Bursfeld reform movement, see Engelbert, "Die Bursfelder Benediktinerkongregation," and Schreiner, "Benediktinische Klosterreform."

81. Finke, "Zur Geschichte," p. 169; Ehresmann, "Iconography of the Cismar Altarpiece," pp. 29–30.

82. For examples of medieval discussions that devote much attention to the historical provenance of blood relics, see Vincent, *Holy Blood*, pp. 123–28, on William Sudbury's defense of the blood of Westminster, and Berg, ed., "Der Traktat des Gerhard von Köln."

83. Indulgence of Honorius III for Schwerin, June 29, 1220, doc. 33, p. 315, in Lisch, "Geschichte der Heiligen-Bluts-Kapelle." Thus we seem to have here a case where host veneration of some sort precedes a blood relic. It is worth noting that, at Fécamp, as at Mantua, earlier blood relics seem to have preceded later discoveries. On Fécamp, see Holtz, "Cults," pp. 36–54. At Rothenburg ob der Tauber, the reverse situation probably obtained: a blood relic preceded a corporal miracle (1442); see Heuser, "'Heilig-Blut'," p. 14. Such cases suggest that veneration of *blood* was more important than veneration of a specific kind of blood.

84. Bishop Brunward of Schwerin approved the veneration of the holy blood; Lisch, "Geschichte der Heiligen-Bluts-Kapelle," doc. 34, p. 317.

85. Ibid., pp. 317–19. See also Lisch, "Geschichte der Heiligen-Bluts-Kapelle," pp. 151–58. The traditional Maundy Thursday market was moved to the day before. As at Einbeck, there is clearly a connection of pilgrimage to market; see n. 30.

86. Lisch, "Geschichte," p. 170.

87. Ibid., pp. 183–84. The inventory of 1542 lists: "Item ein suluern verguldet salvatoris bilde, dat syne beiden hande ad gloriam resurrectionis vphelt vnde wiset eynen Jaspis in der brust gewracht hebbende, dar inne (wo men glofflick daruon schrifft vunde secht) dat blodt Christi entholden. . . ."

88. We have no details about the "cruor miraculosus" at Gotha, which Johannes

von Dorsten described, circa 1480, as "quem quondam in hostia transportavit lantgravius thuringie de partibus transmarinis" and held up as a model of proper cult. See von Dorsten quoted in Paltz, *Supplementum Coelifodinae*, p. 408, and Heuser, "'Heilig-Blut'," p. 24. Berndt Hamm, the editor of Johannes von Paltz, refers to a manuscript in Berlin that gives an account of a later legend (1487) concerning miraculous blood connected to Landgraf Balthasar (1349–1406); *Supplementum Coelifodinae*, p. 408, nn. 15, 16, and 19.

89. See this chapter at nn. 65–71.

90. Oberman, *Roots*; see also Treue, "Schlechte und gute Christen," pp. 102–3. On medieval anti-Semitism generally, see Langmuir, *History, Religion and Antisemitism*, and idem, *Toward a Definition*.

91. For an English translation of one of the early accounts, published by Hieronymus Höltzel of Nuremberg, see Oberman, *Roots*, pp. 97–99; for the German original, see ibid., pp. 147–49. See also Lichtenstein, "Der Vorwurf der Hostienschändung"; Backhaus, "Die Hostienschändungsprozesse"; and Chapter 6 at nn. 26 and 65.

92. See n. 123 below.

93. For Luther's text, see Chapter 2 n. 5.

94. Heise, *Die Juden in der Mark Brandenburg*, pp. 210–33; Honemann, "Die Sternberger Hostienschändung"; Backhaus, "Die Hostienschändungsprozesse"; Schuder and Hirsch, eds., *Der gelbe Fleck*, pp. 129–44; Maschek, ed., *Deutsche Chroniken*, pp. 134–38; K. Schmidt, *Das heilige Blut von Sternberg*; Donath, *Geschichte der Juden in Mecklenburg*, pp. 2, 50–78, and 312–17; and Lisch, "Hauptbegebenheiten in der ältern Geschichte der Stadt Sternberg." (I acquired a four-page xeroxed guide "Kirchlicher Wegweiser" [Sternberg, n.d.], in Sternberg in October 2002.) The accounts I cite here differ markedly about who profited from the pilgrim trade and about the role of the church authorities in Schwerin, but all agree in focusing on the question and in suggesting competition for revenues as a major motive in the events. Honemann, "Die Sternberger Hostienschändung," pp. 83–88 and 95, has an interesting discussion of the "material proofs" (that is, of the objects); his focus is on why they were convincing to sixteenth-century contemporaries. I have treated Sternberg in Bynum, "The Presence of Objects," and "A Matter of Matter."

95. Backhaus, "Die Hostienschändungsprozesse," p. 10.

96. Heise, *Die Juden*, pp. 210–33. Oberman, *Roots*, pp. 95–96, points out that there were about ninety expulsions of Jews from urban areas in Germany between 1388 and 1519 but very few after 1520, when a growing power vacuum in the empire seems to have led city elites and local lords to protect Jews in order to get taxes, although city guilds continued to favor expulsion to remove economic competition.

97. For the documents, see Donath, *Geschichte der Juden in Mecklenburg*, pp. 313–17.

98. K. Schmidt, *Das heilige Blut von Sternberg*, p. 18; Backhaus, "Die Hostienschändungsprozesse," pp. 12–13 and see n. 27 for editions of Marschalk; Honemann, "Die Sternberger Hostienschändung," pp. 90–92.

99. K. Schmidt, *Das heilige Blut von Sternberg*, p. 27.

100. It is worth noting that the earliest accounts, including the confession of Eleazar's wife, say the martyring was done with knives, not nails; see Honemann, "Die Sternberger Hostienschändung," p. 83 n. 10. Presumably knives metamorphosed into nails to accord more closely with accounts of Christ's crucifixion.

101. Honemann, "Die Sternberger Hostienschändung," p. 79.

102. Lisch, "Hauptbegebenheiten," p. 224. We have, however, evidence of seven pilgrims coming in 1562; see K. Schmidt, *Das heilige Blut von Sternberg*, p. 45.

103. Backhaus, "Die Hostienschändungsprozesse."

104. Ibid., pp. 20–21. See also Heise, *Die Juden*, pp. 218 n. 25 and 232–33.

105. Heise, *Die Juden*, pp. 225–26.

106. Gerhard of Cologne made this point already in the thirteenth century. Christians are lukewarm, he says; they must be stirred up to eucharistic devotion. Outrage against the Jews seems to help. See Bynum, "Blood of Christ," pp. 699–704.

107. Browe, *Die Verehrung*, p. 170; and see Honemann, "Die Sternberger Hostienschändung," p. 87 n. 27.

108. See Chapter 2 at nn. 56–60 and Chapter 4 at nn. 44–47.

109. James was concerned about false miracles encouraging Jewish critics and undermining Catholic belief; see Damerau, *Gutachten*, pp. 66–71. Damerau also transcribes an anonymous position paper on Wilsnack that sees such miracles as encouraging heretics; ibid., p. 31.

110. "Ne igitur illi totam patriam stagnalem cum marcia inficerent. . . ." The editor suggests (p. 406 n. 2) that *patria stagnalis* refers to Mecklenburg, in which both Sternberg and Güstrow are located.

111. Paltz, *Supplementum Coelifodinae*, pp. 405–7, in part quoting Johannes von Dorsten. And see Browe, "Verwandlungswunder," pp. 167–69 for earlier use of host miracles as proof and propaganda against heresy.

112. See n. 42 above.

113. On Marschalk's *Mons stellarum*, see n. 98 above. On the issue of what to do with transformed hosts, see Brückner, "Liturgie und Legende," and Chapter 4 at nn. 28–33.

114. Kühne, "Der Harz und sein Umland," p. 7.

115. There was a European-wide context to this debate that I shall consider in Chapters 4 and 6.

116. Paltz, *Supplementum Coelifodinae*, p. 410.

117. From Ägidius Faber's treatise of 1533, "Von dem falschen blut vnd Abgott jm Thum zu Schwerin," excerpt in Lisch, "Geschichte," pp. 169–70; there is another excerpt that refers to Sternberg and Güstrow as well, in Honemann, "Die Sternberger Hostienschändung," app. 3, p. 102. For Labes's attack on Sternberg, see Lisch, "Geschichte," p. 170.

118. Honemann, "Die Sternberger Hostienschändung," app. 3, p. 102. And see K. Schmidt, *Das heilige Blut von Sternberg*, p. 45.

119. Faber, cited in Lisch, "Geschichte," p. 169. For a similar argument made by Hus a century earlier, see Chapter 2 n. 79. On Waltmann, see Chapter 2 n. 95.

120. See Chapter 10, pp. 226–27, on Fisher and Luther.

121. For the survival of such objects in the south, see the cases of the Deggendorf host and its contact relics (Eder, "*Die Deggendorfer Gnad*") and of the Judenmesser of Passau. On the latter, I am grateful to Mitchell Merback, who let me read his work in progress tentatively titled "'mit ainen messer zwsnitten . . .' or the Passion Relics of Christ in the Age of their Mythological Reproducibility." A tendency to take away something (earth, oil, bits of cloth, etc.) from cult sites is found all over Germany in the fifteenth century; see Heuser, "'Heilig-Blut'," p. 38, and Faensen, "Zur Synthese,"

p. 242. At the Elisabeth church in Marburg in the fifteenth century, the public had to be forced back from the relics because they wanted to lie on the tomb and take away the earth; see Lichte, *Die Inszenierung einer Wallfahrt*, p. 39. For a survival of this sort of devotion in Catholic areas, see the case of Erding (just north of Munich), where little models of the Man of Sorrows were made of earth from the host-finding site as late as the eighteenth century. See Merback, "Channels of Grace," n. 56; and Bauer, "Eucharistische Wallfahrten." At Walldürn (in a similar conflation of object and image), the devout took away little silk replicas of the blood-stained corporal—replicas that had been touched to the original holy cloth and had presumably absorbed some of its power. See Kolb, *Vom Heiligen Blut*, pp. 163–67.

122. See *Die Legende*, ed. Simon, p. 34. At the Cistercian men's house of Lehnin, the roof supposedly contained a piece of the tree under which the founder, Otto I, from the Askanier family, had dreamed of establishing the house.

123. Oberman, *Roots*, pp. 99 and 148–49. Such an account attributes to Jews a Christian sense of contact relics.

124. Backhaus, "Die Hostienschändungsprozesse," pp. 24–25; Kolb, *Vom Heiligen Blut*, p. 147. And see Swanson, *Religion and Devotion*, pp. 158–59, on the presence of secular relics in Protestant Europe.

125. Damerau, ed., *Gutachten*, q. 9, p. 29. Waltmann charged that the faithful were blessed with this corporal.

126. Ludecus, *Historia von der erfindung*, Vorrede, [p. 24]. See also Breest, *Wunderblut* (1881), p. 279. The fact that Ellefeldt burned the blood may indicate that a sense of its sacrality had continued, making it necessary for the Protestant pastor to prove that the supposedly indestructible thing *could* be destroyed by fire. But we should remember, on the other hand, that canon law had long required that contaminated hosts and altar linen be buried in the altar or burnt.

127. See above, Chapter 2 n. 32.

128. This is a pattern we see farther south in Germany as well; see this chapter nn. 3 and 4.

129. See this chapter nn. 156–57 and Chapter 11 nn. 45–54.

130. See Chapter 1 n. 67 and Chapter 2 n. 39.

131. See Sigal, *L'homme et le miracle*; Soergel, *Wondrous in His Saints*, pp. 20–30; Merback, "Channels of Grace."

132. See my "Seeing and Seeing Beyond," and Chapter 4 nn. 13 and 14.

133. "Caro salutis est cardo," Tertullian, *De resvrrectione mortvorvm*, chap. 8, p. 931, ll 6–7. And see Bynum, *Resurrection*, pp. 34–43 on Tertullian and pp. 104–14, 156–225, and 318–29 on relic cult and soteriology. In contrast to many religions, in which place is more important than object—and to the early modern period of Christianity, when visions provide the predominant goal of pilgrimage—late medieval Christianity put holy matter squarely at the center of piety.

134. For bibliography on relics, see Chapter 4 n. 50. After 787, relics were required for consecration of churches. Donors (e.g., the house of Gans at Marienfliess) competed to give churches especially valuable ones in order to underline their own prestige and authority.

135. See Chapter 1 n. 9.

136. Dinzelbacher, "Die 'Realpräsenz' der Heiligen"; Lutterbach, "The Mass and Holy Communion"; Snoek, *Medieval Piety from Relics to the Eucharist.*

137. Rothkrug, *Religious Practices*, pp. xi–xii and 3–10, and "German Holiness and Western Sanctity," pp. 215–29.

138. For a vivid meditation on this paradox, see the often cited Middle English poem that explains: "Hyt [the host] semes quite [white], and is red / Hyt is quike, and seemes dede; / Hyt is flesche and seemes brede / Hyt is on and semes too; / Hyt is God body and no more." Robbins, "Popular Prayers," p. 344; also cited in Duffy, *Stripping*, p. 102 n. 35; another version in Gray, *Themes and Images*, p. 69.

139. The regional fragmentation of political power in Germany thus did, of course, contribute to the proliferation of bloods, in contrast to, for example, England, where Henry III failed to establish a blood cult at Westminster.

140. Comparing the true cross to blood relics, he preached: "the cross is . . . holy . . . on account of the more holy shedding of Christ's blood made upon it, not the blood-shedding holy on account of the cross." Matthew Paris, *Chronica majora*, vol. 4, pp. 640–44, and vol. 5, pp. 29, 48, and 195. And see Roberts, "The Relic of the Holy Blood," pp. 138–39; and Chapter 4 n. 64.

141. There were of course sites that claimed other bodily relics such as Christ's teeth and foreskin. But they never achieved anything like the popularity of blood relics—a fact that I attribute in part to blood's capacity to suggest life. See Chapters 6–8. Innocent III mentions the foreskin relics at the Lateran and at Charroux (which supposedly went back to Charlemagne) in *De sacro altaris mysterio*, bk 4, c. 30, PL 217, cols. 876D–877B. Gerhard of Cologne also refers to the foreskin given to Charlemagne; Gerhard, *Tractatus*, ed. Berg, in "Der Traktat des Gerhard von Köln," p. 465, ll. 324–28. Rival foreskin relics were attributed by legend to Antwerp, Reading abbey in England, and Niedermünster in the Alsace. For the devotion of some women mystics to the foreskin, see Bynum, *Holy Feast*, p. 377 n. 135.

142. According to theology, only consecrated hosts (or other objects that had been blessed or translated) could be "de-secrated." And Christ's blood could appear only in transubstantiated wafers. Both the faithful and religious authorities seem, however, to have been somewhat confused about this point; it is clear that not all host miracles involved consecrated hosts. The woman from Lauingen who is reported by Margaret Ebner to have stolen "unconsecrated" hosts for sale to Jews was executed in a particularly hideous manner; and Margaret agonizes over the incident as a dishonor to God. See above n. 72.

143. See Mitchell Merback, "'mit ainen messer zwsnitten . . .'" (work in progress). The lance at Nuremberg, known as the lance of Constantine and used in imperial coronation rites, reputedly contained a piece of one of the crucifixion nails.

144. See above at n. 114.

145. I thank Mitchell Merback for correspondence that helped me to see this point.

146. See this chapter nn. 40–43 on Beelitz.

147. On Walldürn, see Kolb, *Vom Heiligen Blut*, pp. 160–66; and Heuser, "'Heilig-Blut'," p. 17; on Erfurt, see ibid., p. 23, and n. 22 above.

148. See bibliography in Chapter 1 n. 55.

149. Langmuir, "Tortures." Ginzburg, "Representations of German Jewry," connects stories of host desecration and ritual murder not only to eucharistic theology but also to anxieties about the Jews' role in a money economy.

150. See Chapter 2 n. 104.

151. Cohen, "Who Desecrated the Host?" For what Jews actually thought about the eucharist, see Rubin, *Gentile Tales*, pp. 93–103.

152. See Herbst, "Literarisches Leben," p. 159 n. 12. James of Jüterbog worried that Jews would use false miracles to attack the veracity of Christian preaching generally; see Damerau, *Gutachten*, pp. 66–71. If one wishes to make the argument that Christians projected their own religious ambivalence onto Jews, it seems at least as likely that the projected ambivalence was about sacrifice and blood. Some of the texts analyzed in Chapters 8 and 11 show that Christians felt guilty (and were urged so to feel) about being the "new Jews," who daily killed Christ.

153. Once host-desecration libels disappeared in the Protestant north, other charges such as ritual murder (which had been current before) flooded in to replace them. See this chapter nn. 3 and 4.

154. Lotter gives an interpretation similar to mine, arguing that both ritual murder accusations (which provided martyrs) and anti-Jewish host-desecration libels (which, as he puts it, provided Corpus Christi cult) were in the early years primarily efforts to get pilgrimage going. See Lotter, "Innocens Virgo et Martyr," pp. 71–72.

155. See this chapter at n. 54. The text is titled "Van dem ortsprunghe des klosters tome hilligen graue jn der marke belegen vnde deme hilligen Sacramente dar suluest"; *Die Legende*, pp. 1 and 18.

156. The Güstrow account from 1510 is titled "Historia de venerabili sacramento in Gustrow"; see Hofmeister, "Weitere Beiträge," pp. 196–97. Of the four broadsides discussed by Backhaus that give the confession of the Jews in the Sternberg affair, three mention Jews in the title but one runs "Allen Christen mynschen sy tzo wiyssen, dat in dem land van Mecklenburg in der stat Sternenberch eyn groys myrakel geseyet is. . . ." See Backhaus, "Die Hostienschändungsprozesse," p. 11 n. 22.

157. Titled "Eyn wunderbarlich geschichte," they move immediately to the Jews, but stress the sacrament while doing so: "wye die marckiscchen Jüdenn das hochwirdigst sacrament gekaufft. . . ." See Heise, *Die Juden*, p. 210 n. 2.

158. We must also not forget the Christian tendency generally to associate Jews with blood. On this, see Bildhauer, "Blood, Jews and Monsters," and Chapter 1 n. 106.

Chapter 4. Debates About Eucharistic Transformations and Blood Relics

1. It was also used to support the Weingarten relic and the Westminster one; see Berg, "Der Traktat des Gerhard von Köln," and Vincent, *Holy Blood*, esp. pp. 123–28.

2. Jorissen, *Die Entfaltung*; McCue, "The Doctrine of Transubstantiation"; Sylla, "Autonomous and Handmaiden Science"; Stock, *The Implications of Literacy*, pp. 241–325; Burr, *Eucharistic Presence*; Macy, "The Dogma of Transubstantiation in the Middle Ages," and "Reception of the Eucharist According to the Theologians: A Case of Diversity in the Thirteenth and Fourteenth Centuries," in Macy, *Treasures*, pp. 81–120, 36–58; Fitzpatrick, "On Eucharistic Sacrifice"; and Bynum, "Seeing and Seeing Beyond."

3. This is not to argue that there was no anxiety about presence and the mode of presence. See Chapter 1 at nn. 47–51 above.

4. In this formulation, I have been greatly influenced by the essay of Pranger, "Le sacrement de l'eucharistie." We shall see, in Chapters 6 to 8, that there was something

unique about blood that seemed to the fifteenth-century devout, whether learned or not, to capture this paradox.

5. The standard scholarly line has been that eucharistic visions emerged to "prove" the doctrines of the real presence and of transubstantiation. The formulation is somewhat problematic, since "transubstantiation" continued to be debated long after 1215 (as Gary Macy and others have shown) and the "real presence" of Christ in the eucharist had been established since the patristic period. See the works cited in n. 2 above. Nonetheless it is true that polemic against the position of Berengar of Tours in the late eleventh century (Berengar held that Christ was really present but without change in the elements) led to an atmosphere in which theologians and the ordinary devout tended to think that the Christ present in consecrated bread and wine might erupt into visibility.

6. For an example, see Colette of Corbie's vision, cited in Chapter 1 n. 22. The standard work is Browe, *Die eucharistischen Wunder*.

7. Augustine, *De Genesi ad litteram libri duodecim*, bk 12, paras. 6–12, pp. 386–97; and *De cvra pro mortuis gerenda*. And see Baschet, "Âme et corps," p. 7; and Schmitt, *Ghosts*, pp. 22–24.

8. Hamburger, "Seeing and Believing," pp. 48–52; and Séjourné, "Reliques," esp. cols. 2360–65. And see Aquinas, ST 2-2, q. 103, arts. 2–3, pp. 659–60.

9. For example, Christina Ebner of Engelthal, whose visions were often to her moments of glory, responded with terror, not welcome, when she saw Christ hanging on the cross at the elevation. See Chapter 1 n. 99. On the paramystical phenomena of medieval women, see Bynum, *Holy Feast*. For the widespread distrust of visionary women in the fifteenth century and efforts to curtail their spirituality, see the works cited in Chapter 1 nn. 47–48.

10. Sigal, *L'homme et le miracle*; Soergel, *Wondrous in His Saints*, pp. 20–30.

11. Jungmann, *The Mass*, vol. 1, pp. 119–21 and vol. 2, pp. 206–12. And see Browe, *Die Verehrung*.

12. The incident is cited by Rothkrug, "Popular Religion," p. 36, and by Mayer, *Die Liturgie*, p. 45.

13. On the absence in eucharistic presence, see Pranger, "Le sacrement de l'eucharistie." On the inwardness of spiritual communion, see Caspers, "*Meum summum desiderium*"; idem, "The Western Church . . . *Augenkommunion*"; and Mitchell, *Cult and Controversy*, pp. 163–86.

14. On the veiling of presence, see Dutton, "Eat, Drink, and Be Merry," pp. 9–10; Macy, *Theologies of the Eucharist*, pp. 28–51, 72, and 108 (Macy tends to underestimate the element of sacrifice in twelfth-century eucharistic theology); Pelikan, *Growth of Medieval Theology (600–1300)*, p. 199; Rubin, *Corpus Christi*, p. 91 n. 56; Stock, *The Implications of Literacy*, pp. 290–91; and Berg, "Der Traktat des Gerhard von Köln," pp. 442, 449–50. And see Aquinas, Sentence Commentary, bk 4, d. 10, q. 1, art. 1, pp. 470–71.

15. Alger of Liège, *De sacramentis*, bk 2, chap. 3, PL 180, col. 815.

16. Bacon, *Opus majus*, vol. 2, p. 822. Fitzpatrick, "On Eucharistic Sacrifice," p. 134, thus sees the elements as a kind of "camouflage." On stercoranism see Chapter 6 n. 12.

17. Aquinas, Sentence Commentary, bk 4, dist. 10, q. 1, art. 4c, p. 473, col. 2: "Sed contra, nihil horrendum est committendum in hoc sacramento. Sed horrendum est

comedere carnem crudam. . . ." Peter Damian, who seems to have thought transformation miracles were direct and immediate revelations of Christ's flesh and blood, commented after describing a host miracle: "Ubi notandum quam sit immane periculum indignis manibus attrectare tam terribile sacramentum." Damian, *Opusculum* 34: *De variis miraculosis narrationibus*, PL 145, col. 573.

18. Some later commentators (for example, Antoninus of Florence) thought Thomas meant new accidents were overlaid. See Browe, "Die scholastische Theorie," p. 314 n. 1.

19. Aquinas, Sentence Commentary, bk 4, dist. 10, q. 1, art. 4, pp. 473–74; ST 3, q. 77, art. 1, pp. 896–97; and ibid., 3, q. 80, art. 4 ad 4, p. 905 col. 1. The best guide to all this is Browe, "Die scholastische Theorie," on which I have relied heavily. See also Hirn, *The Sacred Shrine*, pp. 124–25.

20. Aquinas, Sentence Commentary, bk 4, dist. 10, q. 1, art. 1, esp. ra 4, pp. 470–71. And for the same idea, see Alexander of Hales, *Glossa in quatuor libros Sententiarum*, bk 4, dist. 10, vol. 4, pp. 152–68; see esp. p. 156: "Respondemus quod verbum creatum, ratione virtutis divinae quam habet, habet posse super panem ut de eo fiat corpus Christi; et ita in panem et vinum extenditur sua virtus simpliciter, non in corpus Christi. Unde non est absolute dicere: corpus Christi fit, sed panis transsubstantiatur in corpus Christi iam exsistens."

21. Aquinas, Sentence Commentary, bk 4, dist. 10, q. 1, art. 4, pp. 473–74.

22. Gerhoh of Reichersberg, *Commentarium in Psalmos*, pt 2, Ps. 22, PL 193, cols. 150C–151A. Peter Damian seems to have assumed the same thing; see above, n. 17.

23. Baronius and Raynaldus, *Annales ecclesiastici 1198–1534*, vol. 19, no. 23 for 1487 [no pagination]: " . . . subito in dicto calice miraculose verus sanguis oculis corporeis visibilis apparuit, eiusque pars ex dicto calice in corporalibus super altare existentibus effusus est, atque item sanguis ita visibilis mansit, et hodie pro reliquijs reseruatus conspicitur, vt sanguis hominis vel hoedi recenter effusus, coagulatus tamen videatur." It is important that the letter describes the miracle as "olim quampluribus annis effluxis." See Browe, "Verwandlungswunder," p. 147 n. 20, and idem, "Die scholastische Theorie," p. 317 n. 2.

24. For Scotus, see Browe, "Die scholastische Theorie," pp. 309–10 n. 2; for Auriol, ibid., p. 310. For resistance to miracles of lasting transformation, see Browe, "Verwandlungswunder."

25. For Gerson, see Snoek, *Medieval Piety from Relics to the Eucharist*, p. 373. For Biel, see his *Canonis misse expositio*, lectio 51, vol. 2, pp. 287–97; Goossens, "Résonances eucharistiques," p. 177; and Browe, "Die scholastische Theorie," p. 311 n. 2.

26. See Chapter 2 n. 21.

27. Browe, "Die scholastische Theorie," pp. 319–20. This was a minority opinion, but it is important that it was held at all. Albert the Great seems to have taught it. To deal with the difficulty Thomas came up with a very complicated theory concerning the survival of dimension, into which it is not necessary to go here. For further discussion of the concern for God's immutability implied here, see Chapter 6.

28. Aquinas, Sentence Commentary, bk 4, dist. 10, q. 1, art. 4c, p. 474, col. 1: "usus sacramenti debet materiae sacramenti competere. . . ." And Browe, "Die scholastische Theorie."

29. Brückner, "Liturgie und Legende," p. 151; Browe, "Die scholastische Theorie," pp. 324–32; idem, "Verwandlungswunder," p. 157; Vincent, *Holy Blood*, p. 122.

30. On Waltmann, see Chapter 2, nn. 91–95; on the Erfurt *Gutachten*, see Chapter 2, nn. 80–83. Number 6 of the thirty articles prepared by Tocke in 1446 stated: "Si vere quis miraculose cruor apparuisset, debuisset cum reliquiis abscondi, non publice populo ostendi, ne erraret circa illum. Haec videtur intentio doctorum de eucharistia transformata." Breest, *Wunderblut* (1881), app. 2, p. 298.

31. See Snoek, *Medieval Piety from Relics to the Eucharist*, pp. 19, 68–69, and 186–97.

32. See Mansi, *Sacrorum conciliorum*, Synod of Celichyth (Chelsea), canon 2, vol. 14, col. 356; Braun, *Der christliche Altar*, vol. 1, pp. 623–29; Heuser, "'Heilig-Blut'," pp. 70 and 218; and Snoek, *Medieval Piety*, p. 187.

33. Heuser, "'Heilig-Blut'," pp. 67–72; Brückner, "Liturgie und Legende"; Snoek, *Medieval Piety*, pp. 191–97.

34. Even James of Jüterbog, who tried to support both sides in the Wilsnack controversy, argued that the fact that the Wilsnack host did decay and hence needed overlaying was a reason for rejecting it as a miracle. James of Jüterbog (or Klusa), "Tractatus de concertatione super cruore in Welsenaco," Wolfenbüttel H.A.B. Cod. Guelf. 152 Helmst., fols. 176va–186vb; the argument I refer to is on fol. 186vb.

35. Browe, "Die scholastische Theorie," pp. 325–28, and Rubin, *Gentile Tales*, pp. 65–68.

36. See Breest, *Wunderblut* (1881), pp. 186–90.

37. Wine poured over blood relics was also sometimes offered to the faithful to drink as *sanguis Christi*; see Chapter 1 n. 33.

38. Jungmann, *Mass*, vol. 2, pp. 381–85, 412–14; King, *Liturgies of the Religious Orders*, pp. 129–30, 372.

39. Aquinas, ST 3, q. 80, art. 12, reply obj. 3, p. 908 col. 1: ". . . quia sacerdos in persona omnium sanguinem offert et sumit, et sub utraque specie totus christus continetur. . . ." See also ST 3, q. 76, art. 2, pp. 894–95; Jungmann, *Mass*, vol. 2, p. 364; and Bynum, *Holy Feast*, pp. 56–58.

40. Megivern, *Concomitance*. And see Chapter 1 n. 33.

41. See Chapter 3 n. 111. For examples of bleeding-host miracles used by Bonaventure and William of Melitona to prove concomitance, see Megivern, *Concomitance*, pp. 195 and 213.

42. See Chapter 3 at n. 91 and Chapter 6 at n. 65.

43. See the case of Dorothy of Montau, discussed by Kieckhefer, *Unquiet Souls*, pp. 22–23.

44. The demand for the chalice came from Jacobellus of Stříbro (or Mies), who claimed he had received it in a revelation, not from Hus. See n. 48 below.

45. Martin V in 1425 also confirmed the denial of the cup. It was reintroduced in the Roman Catholic Church in 1963.

46. See Šmahel, *Die Hussitische Revolution*, vol. 1, pp. 479–652; Kaminsky, *The Hussite Revolution*, pp. 97–140; idem, "Hus, John," and "Hussites"; Girgensohn, *Peter von Pulkau*, pp. 82–162; Grégoire, "Sang," cols. 322–23; and Vincent, *Holy Blood*, pp. 120–23. Ties, both real and perceived, between Hussites and Waldensians are discussed by De Schweinitz, *The History of the Church Known as the Unitas Fratrum*, pp. 140, 180–81, and passim; Audisio, *The Waldensian Dissent*, pp. 844–85; and Tamar Herzig, "Witches, Saints and Heretics: Heinrich Krämer's Ties with Italian Women Mystics," paper presented at the Sixteenth-Century Studies Conference, 2005.

47. This is true of both Kaminsky and Šmahel. Scholarship on the cryptoflagellants of Thuringia has also tended to ignore the movement's obvious blood obsession: see Chapter 2, pp. 34–36.

48. Asked by Jacobellus of Stříbro about communion in both kinds, Hus approved of it but urged Jacobellus to hold back in instituting the practice and asserted that it was not necessary for salvation; see Hilsch, *Johannes Hus*, p. 254; and Werner, *Jan Hus*, pp. 99–104.

49. See Chapter 2 at nn. 69–79; and Hilsch, *Johannes Hus*, pp. 76–86.

50. Recent bibliography on relics is voluminous. For an introduction, see Séjourné, "Reliques"; Hermann-Mascard, *Les reliques*; Dinzelbacher, "Die 'Realpräsenz' der Heiligen"; Angenendt, *Heilige und Reliquien*; and Legner, *Reliquien*. On the eucharist as a kind of relic, see Snoek, *Medieval Piety*; and Lutterbach, "The Mass and Holy Communion." On the competition between eucharist and relics, see Hirn, *The Sacred Shrine*, pp. 135–36, and Pelikan, *The Growth of Medieval Theology*, pp. 181–84. Fuller treatment of some of the texts I treat in the next section and in Chapter 5 can be found in Holtz, "Cults," and Vincent, *Holy Blood*. Vincent gives very full bibliography and some major new archival evidence as well.

51. Braulio of Saragossa, *Epistola* 42, PL 80, cols. 687–90; and see Bynum, *Resurrection*, pp. 107–8, n. 179.

52. Braulio, *Epistola* 42, col. 688C: ". . . ac sic, quia sine sanguine esse non possumus, in quo virtus animae in corpore divina asseritur auctoritate [Lev. 17.14], reddendus est non superfluus, sed naturalis, id est, *non alienus, sed noster*" (my emphasis). And see Holtz, "Cults, " pp. 183–94.

53. Guibert, *De pigneribus*, esp. bks. 1 and 3, pp. 79–109 and 138–57. Guibert says, for example (bk 3, p. 139): "Si resurrexit, particulariter, queso, resurrexit an totus? Si totum surrexisse testamini, ubi quas vobis assumitis partes erunt? Si partim, quae de nobis resurrecturis edixerat promissa quid proderunt?" And again (bk 3, pp. 148–49): "Si igitur capilluli, dentes, aquae fluxus et sanguinis, quadrifidi vulneris cruor, qui indubie ad terram usque distillare potuerit, in terrenis ruderibus in finem corrumpenda desederint, resurrectionis humanae status ac nostrae promissio ex ore dominico ad sui similitudinem conformitatis non video quo modo constare sine enormi fallacia possint." On Guibert, see Holtz, "Cults," pp. 195–206; Vincent, *Holy Blood*, pp. 82–86; and Guth, *Guibert von Nogent*. For criticism of the conventional reading of Guibert as a rationalist, see Platelle, "Guibert de Nogent"; and Stock, *The Implications of Literacy*, pp. 244–53.

54. See Bynum, *Resurrection*, p. 140, where I point to Guibert's distaste for the idea that the body of the Virgin might have decayed in death and his shrill insistence that the body we eat in the eucharist remains whole. Benton, "Introduction," in Guibert, *Self and Society*, pp. 26–31, argued that Guibert's objection to corporal relics was pathological—a kind of castration complex. This seems to me to go too far; but there is, in Guibert, an obsession with decay.

55. Guibert, *De pigneribus*, bk 3, p.145.

56. Ibid., bk 3, p. 140.

57. Ibid., bk 3, p. 139 ll. 63–64; see ibid., ll. 51–52, for citation of Luke 21.18.

58. Ibid., bk 3, p. 143.

59. On identity and material continuity, see Bynum, *Resurrection*, pp. 117–225.

60. In the years around 1200, theologians were debating what the essential core,

or *veritas humanae naturae*, was. See Reynolds, *Food and the Body*. To Guibert, it was necessary that *all* particles rise; Innocent seems to say both that all must rise ("not a hair of your head" can be omitted) and that it is the *veritas*—or essential blood—that rises.

61. Innocent III, *De sacro altaris mysterio*, bk 4, chap. 30, PL 217, cols. 876D–877B. Innocent also mentions the foreskin supposedly given by an angel to Charlemagne, who placed it at Aachen; Charroux afterward claimed to have received it as a gift from Charles the Bald. According to Vincent (*Holy Blood*, p. 86 n. 19), Innocent's discussion is based on chap. 6 of Peter Comestor's *Historia scholastica*. On Charroux, see Chapeau, "Les grandes reliques de . . . Charroux," pp. 115–27. On foreskin relics generally, there is excellent bibliography in Vincent, *Holy Blood*, pp. 62 n. 107, pp. 86–87 nn. 19–20, p. 141 n. 14, and p. 170 n. 44. And see Chapter 3 n. 141.

62. Grosseteste, "De sanguine Christi." And see Vincent, *Holy Blood*, pp. 3 and 88 n. 21. On the translation, see Matthew Paris, *Chronica majora*, vol. 4, pp. 640–44, and vol. 5, pp. 29, 48, and 195.

63. Vincent, *Holy Blood*, p. 88.

64. Matthew Paris, *Chronica majora*, vol. 4, p. 642. Grosseteste makes the same argument in "De sanguine Christi," p. 143.

65. Matthew Paris, *Chronica majora*, vol. 4, pp. 643–46.

66. For the historical arguments, which do not concern me here (although they are important for a full history of relic cult), see Holtz, "Cults," pp. 212–18, and Vincent, *Holy Blood*, pp. 87–91.

67. Vincent, *Holy Blood*, p. 87.

68. Grosseteste, "De sanguine Christi," p. 143. The phrase "friend of nature" is also used by Alexander of Hales, Albert the Great, and the anonymous *De medicina animae* found in PL 176, col. 1187D (see Vincent, *Holy Blood*, p. 99 n. 40) and by Johannes von Paltz (see Chapter 7 nn. 43, 45–47). Vincent suggests it may come from Aristotle.

69. Grosseteste, "De sanguine Christi," p. 143.

70. Both Vincent, *Holy Blood*, and Holtz, "Cults," stress the inconsistency. For a good statement of the soteriological argument, see Holtz, p. 221.

71. Grosseteste stresses that the crucifixion was not particularly bloody, "De sanguine Christi," p. 143: "Et de tali sanguine Christi habemus in terra, licet sane non fuisset sanguinolentus, Deo sic volente, ut videlicet habeatur recentior memoria Dominicae Passionis."

72. Grosseteste, "De sanguine Christi," pp. 143–44: "Et nos quidem sic resurgemus, videlicet sine aliqua corporis vel mutilatione vel deformitate. Qualiscunque enim extiterit homo in hoc mundo, contractus, gibbosus, vel leprosus, vel nanus, vel abortivus, in resurrectione sibi plene restaurabitur. Re vera in corpore Christi, Suorum vulnerum stigmata post resurrectionem Suam recentium et adhuc hiantium, quod apparuerunt, et quod Se Christus post resurrectionem et corporis glorificationem Se palpabilem praebuit et ad Suum beneplacitum visibilem, vel vulneratum monstravit, miraculosum et obstupendum. Ut sic videlicet dubitantium fides roboraretur, quia tam duri et tardi fuerunt quidam discipulorum ad credendum resurrectionem, quod postquam viderant, non crediderunt, et ut benedictio non visuris et tamen credituris largius donaretur. Tertia causa fuit et potissima, ut scilicet sic sciretur quod Omnipotens fuit, ut contra consuetum usum et naturalem foret corpus Ejus, Qui fuit Dominus naturae, ad Suum nutum et beneplacitum monstrabile et palpabile et saucium cernere-

tur, Qui tamen ad discipulos intravit foribus obseratis. Et sic omnium cessare debent morsus detractorum."

73. Grosseteste, *De cessatione legalium*, pt 3, sect. 6, paras. 8–9, pp. 150–51. The argument is summarized in Dales, *Problem of the Rational Soul*, pp. 42–45, and in Holtz, "Cults," p. 219 n. 24.

74. Grosseteste, *De cessatione legalium*, pt 3, sect. 6, paras. 8–9, pp. 150–51. And see Dales, *Problem of the Rational Soul*, pp. 43–44.

75. Bonaventure, Sentence Commentary, bk 4, dist. 12, pt 1, dub. 2, vol. 4, p. 287: "Respondeo: Dicendum, quod in Christo resurrexit totum, quod fuit de veritate humanae naturae et quod spectat ad decentiam; et ideo dicitur totus esse in caelo.—Quod ergo obiicit de praeputio, dicendum, quod vel non fuit de carne *secundum speciem*, sed divina dispensatione parum de carne *secundum materiam* ibi fuit, ut daretur nobis in devotionem, sicut reliquiae—et sic dicendum est de sanguine—vel aliquid fuit de *veritate*, et illud resurrexit cum Christo et est in caelo, et residuum mansit."

76. Bonaventure, Sentence Commentary, bk 4, dist. 44, pt 1, art. 1, qq. 1–2, vol. 4, pp. 907–10. Bonaventure, following Francis, was devoted to the passion of Christ, but like Grosseteste stressed Christ's death and pain at least as much as his bleeding. He of course held, along with all thirteenth-century theologians, that the spilling [*effusio*] of blood was the price of salvation; see Bonaventure, *Sermo 2, de nostra redemptione*, in *Opera omnia*, vol. 9, sect. 5: *Sermones de diversis*, pp. 725–29, and Caggiano, "Il sangue di Cristo."

77. Terrinca, *La devozione*, p. 89, says Bonaventure does not hold separation during the *triduum* although later commentators misread him. Pius II in his commentaries, reporting Franciscan opinion, says Bonaventure held that blood was separated during the *triduum*; for only the "essential parts of man," that is soul and body, "which do not include the blood," are never laid down: ". . . nihil a verbo dimissum, quod semel assumpserit . . . principia vero naturae anima est & corpus, vel partes essentiales hominis, inter quas sanguis non continetvr, vt monstratum est: dimissus igitur fuit." See Pius II, *Commentarii*, bk 11, p. 284, and *Commentaries of Pius II*, trans. and ed. Gragg and Gabel, p. 715. Gabel in her notes comments, however, that Bonaventure does not say exactly this; see ibid., p. 715 n. 60. A. Michel, "Forme du corps," col. 585, and Cocci, "Il sangue di Cristo," p. 1288, agree with Pius's summary. They argue that Bonaventure held that blood was not informed by rational soul but only co-assumed under body; therefore they deduce that he would hold separation. It seems that Bonaventure is hard to understand on this issue exactly because he was not addressing directly the question as later posed. Richard of Middleton held that the Logos did not remain united to the spilled blood during the *triduum* because the spilled blood did not belong to the *veritas humanae naturae*; therefore the spilled blood should not be adored. See Terrinca, *La devozione*, p. 94, and Vincent, *Holy Blood*, pp. 104 and 127–28. Scotus did not treat explicitly the question of the blood during the *triduum*. He did deny that there was complete resumption of the blood scattered in the passion; therefore the Scotists, following him, held that relics could remain. See Terrinca, *La devozione*, p. 93. On the Franciscan Tostado (d. 1455) see Chapter 5 n. 40. On *Quod assumpsit* see n. 85 below.

78. Bonaventure, Sentence Commentary, bk 4, dist. 44, pt. 1, art. 1 q. 1, vol. 4, p. 908. After distinguishing between *humor* and *humiditas*, Bonaventure writes: "Sed quid de *humoribus* dicemus, cum sint *currentes* et non sint de substantia membri nec de

complexione radicali? Dicendum, quod absque dubio resurgent; cum vinum convertatur in Sacramento altaris in sanguinem, qui effusus est in *remissionem peccatorum* [Matt. 26.28], et iste est sanguis habens *speciem* sanguinis. Unde non video, quomodo vere sanguis non resurrexerit in Christo; et si hoc, pari ratione et in quolibet alio. Et *praeterea*, numquid venae remanebunt vacuae? . . ." Bonaventure is responding to the objection: " . . . in Sacramento altaris convertitur vinum in verum sanguinem; sed hoc esset impossibile, nisi sanguis resurrexisset in Christo. . . ."

79. Bonaventure, *Sermo* 2, *de nostra redemptione*. And see Terrinca, *La devozione*, p. 90.

80. Albert the Great did not expressly treat either the question of whether the blood in the *triduum* remained united to the Logos or the question of blood relics. He was interested in Christ's blood, however, and held that it was hypostatically united to the Word as a part of the *veritas humanae naturae*; hence it should be adored like all Christ's humanity. See, for example, Albert, *De sacrificio missae*, tractate 3, chap. 5, n. 1, in *Opera omnia*, vol. 38, p. 93; and Terrinca, *La devozione*, pp. 98–99.

81. Aquinas, ST 3, q. 54, art. 3, ra 3, p. 854, col. 1; and *Questiones quodlibetales* 5 q. 3 art. 1, in *Opera omnia*, vol. 3, p. 466. See Terrinca, *La devozione*, pp. 101–5; Holtz, "Cults," pp. 222–37; and Vincent, *Holy Blood*, pp. 100–103.

82. Holtz, "Cults," pp. 229–30, rightly points to the difference between this formulation, which says all blood that flowed at passion rises *because* it belongs to the *veritas humanae naturae*, and Quodlibet 5, which simply says the blood that belongs to the *veritas humanae naturae* rises.

83. Aquinas, ST 3, q. 54, art. 3, ra 3, p. 854; trans. Fathers of the English Dominican Province, *Summa theologica*, vol. 4, p. 2310. And see Bynum, *Resurrection*, pp. 263–64, esp. nn. 137–39.

84. Vincent, *Holy Blood*, p. 101.

85. *Questiones quodlibetales* 5, q. 3, art. 1, vol. 3, p. 466, col. 2. The principle of *Quod assumpsit* was widely used in thirteenth-century debates over Christology and soteriology. The idea was often attributed to John Damascene (d. between 754 and 787), *De Fide Orthodoxa*, bk 3, chap. 27, PG 94, cols. 1096–97. Pius II, *Commentarii*, bk 11, p. 280, cites Leo I (440–61) as the authority for it. For Leo's use of the idea, see *Sermo* 30 (or 31): *In nativitate Domini* 10, PL 54, cols. 233C–234B, and *Sermo* 28 (or 27): *In nativitate Domini* 8, col. 222A: "Unde utrique naturae in suis proprietatibus permanenti, tanta est unitatis facta communio, ut quidquid ibi est Dei, non sit ab humanitate disjunctum; quidquid autem est hominis non sit a Deitate divisum."

86. "Sanguis enim ille in passione effusus humanum genus sanctificavit, secundum illud Heb. 13.12: 'iesus, ut sanctificaret per suum sanguinem populum, extra portam passus est.' humanitas autem Christi salutiferam virtutem habuit ex virtute verbi sibi uniti, ut damascenus dicit . . . unde manifestum est quod sanguis in passione effusus, qui maxime fuit salubris, fuit divinitati unitus; et ideo oportuit quod in resurrectione iungeretur aliis humanitatis partibus." *Questiones quodlibetales* 5, q. 3, art. 1, vol. 3, p. 466, col. 2. Note the emphasis on the blood being united to the Logos—a point that becomes important in the *triduum mortis* controversy. See Chenu, "Sang du Christ," col. 1096; Cocci, "Il sangue di Cristo"; and idem, "Le dispute teologiche del *triduum mortis*."

87. It is worth noting that John of Capistrano, in citing Thomas's Quodlibet, takes the *alias* to mean "other things from the consecrated body of Christ" and to refer

to miracles of bloody corporals, of which he adduces two, Bolsena/Orvieto and Trani. See Capistrano, *De sanguine*, art. 13, sect. B, para. 2, ed. Terrinca, p. 23*, and ed. Cocci, pp. 1376–77: "Sanguis autem Christi, qui in quibusdam Ecclesiis ostenditur, dicitur ex quadam imagine Christi percussa miraculose fluxisse, vel etiam alias ex corpore Christi. Haec Thomas. Et intellige: cum dicit vel etiam alias ex corpore Christi, scilicet consecrato, ut patet in corporale quod servatur in ecclesia Sanctae Mariae, quae est ecclesia episcopalis in civitate Urbis Veteri, et similiter in ecclesia episcopali civitatis Tranensis."

88. Reynolds, *Food and the Body*. I have also made this argument; see Bynum, *Metamorphosis and Identity*, pp. 19–33.

89. Peter Lombard, *Sententiae*, bk 2, dist. 30, chap. 15, vol. 1, pp. 504–5; discussed in Bynum, *Resurrection*, pp. 125–26.

90. A useful statement about the reality of change to Aquinas is McInerny, "Aquinas," pp. 358–60.

91. Such a position would also, of course, present insuperable difficulties for the resurrection of Christ. Thomas in fact, as I explain below, preserved the matter of Christ's body *as his body* during the *triduum* by its continued union with the Logos.

92. Aquinas, ST 3, q. 25, art. 6, ra 3, p. 808, col. 3: ". . . corpus mortuum alicuius sancti non est idem numero quod primo fuerit dum viveret, propter diversitatem formae, quae est anima, est tamen idem identitate materiae, quae est iterum suae formae unienda." And see Bynum, *Resurrection*, pp. 263–64 and 270–71. Holtz, "Cults," pp. 226–37, is especially good on the context in piety.

93. Thomas makes a complex point about a cadaveric form or form of the corpse coming in naturally (not being "assumed") during the period of separation. Hence when it disappears it is not "laid down," and thus does not violate the principle *Quod assumpsit*. See A. Michel, "Forme du corps," cols. 569–71 and 576–78.

94. I return to this in Chapter 6. And see Terrinca, *La devozione*, pp. 141–42.

95. Aquinas, ST 3, q. 54, arts. 3–4, pp. 853–54; trans. in *Summa theologica*, vol. 5, pp. 2310–11 (with changes).

96. See, for example, Holtz, "Cults," pp. 226 and 235.

97. Aquinas, ST 3, q. 25, arts. 1–6, pp. 807–9; see also Séjourné, "Reliques," cols. 2360–65.

98. Aquinas, ST 3, q. 25, art. 4, p. 808, col. 2.

99. The need to have something to venerate in the relic contributes to Thomas's insistence that the bodies of the saints are the same because they have the same matter (if not the same form). And this position contributes to his insistence on continuity of matter between the earthly and the resurrection body. See Bynum, *Resurrection*, pp. 263–64 and 270–71, and A. Michel, "Forme du corps," col. 577.

100. Aquinas, ST 3, q. 25, art. 3, sc, p. 808, col. 1.

101. I omit here Roger Marston's Quodlibet 4.14 of circa 1285/86, in which the discussion is so unclear that Vincent and Holtz, considering it, reach rather different conclusions about what it argues. See Vincent, *Holy Blood*, pp. 103 n. 50 and 106; Holtz, "Cults," pp. 253–58. What is clear is that Marston, a Franciscan, opposes the idea that a blood relic could be any superfluity of Christ, for Christ "had nothing superfluous" (Holtz, p. 254, n. 127). But Marston holds that Christ could have left blood behind, because we see (*videmus*) relics. And he does not want to attribute all blood venerated in cult to the icon of Beirut, which he mentions explicitly (Holtz, pp. 254–57, esp. nn.

128 and 131). Gabriel Biel held that relics of Christ's blood could have been left behind on earth, but his emphasis was on the blood of Christ, into which the wine of the eucharist is transubstantiated, as living and red. See Biel, *Canonis misse expositio*, lectio 53, vol. 2, p. 318: "Modo autem etsi alique relique in ecclesia reperiantur, tamen maxima pars sanguinis christi in resurrectione fuit reassumpta et corpori reunita, et ita nunc habet rationem totius sanguinis christi."

102. On Gerhard, see Berg, "Der Traktat des Gerhard von Köln," pp. 435–57; Holtz, "Cults," pp. 237–52; and Bynum, "Blood of Christ," pp. 699–704.

103. Gerhard, *Tractatus*, pp. 465–66.

104. Holtz, "Cults," p. 247, points out quite correctly that Gerhard's point is not to denigrate philosophy but to avoid reducing theology to physiology.

105. Gerhard, *Tractatus*, p. 467. Thomas of Chobham in his treatise on preaching (ca. 1210) makes similar use of the eucharistic analogy. Discussing how Christ's foreskin can both remain on earth and be resurrected, Thomas asserts: ". . . just as by a miracle the body of Our Lord can be at one and the same time in several places, so that body can exist in several forms. . . . Christ's foreskin, glorified as part of his integral body, may exist in another place unglorified." Cited in Vincent, *Holy Blood*, p. 85.

106. Gerhard argues that the name "Weingarten" was prophetic; Christ knew there would be a blood relic there. See *Tractatus*, p. 474.

107. For fourteenth-century discussion that bears on the issue of blood relics, see Chapter 5. I have chosen to treat Mayronis (and Duns Scotus as background to him) there, because the primary focus of their discussion is the nature of Christ's body and blood, not relics.

108. See Chapter 2 n. 77.

109. Hus, "Tractatus," obj. 4, para. 12, pp. 13–14. Hus acknowledges that the blood shed in the circumcision might have been corrupted and uses Aristotle to acknowledge that once something is substantially corrupted it cannot become again materially "the same thing." But his general argument (familiar since the patristic period) is that divine power can restore anything, since it can create ex nihilo, which is even more difficult. Ibid., obj. 6, pp. 15–17.

110. Hus, "Tractatus," obj. 7, paras. 23 and 24, p. 19.

111. See Chapter 2 n. 73. For similar arguments in the *Gutachten* of 1446 (the "Super dubiis"), see Chapter 2, nn. 80–83.

112. Hus, "Questio," p. 5.

113. See Terrinca, *La devozione*, pp. 112–14; Chenu, "Sang du Christ," cols. 1094–97; Vincent, *Holy Blood*, pp. 110–11. The fullest treatment is Holtz, "Cults," pp. 290–95.

114. Account of the Paris faculty concerning the blood of Christ at La Rochelle, May 28, 1448, in Denifle, ed., *Chartularium*, vol. 4, # 2634, p. 682.

115. Ibid.

116. Ibid., # 2635, p. 683. It is worth noting that Nicholas refers to the blood as "aliquam particulam."

117. Ibid.

118. See Vincent, *Holy Blood*, p. 110 n. 80. We need to remember the Reformation tendency to exaggerate what they thought of as Catholic "superstition."

119. Vincent, *Holy Blood*, p. 111 n. 81.

120. Holtz, in his splendid discussion, makes the case for this sort of analysis

("Cults," pp. 290–95 and passim). Vincent (*Holy Blood*, pp. 110–11 and passim) takes this line as well. Much of Heuser's analysis (for example, "'Heilig-Blut'," pp. 77–84) also sees the issue as primarily disciplinary. Moreover, historians of Wilsnack from Breest to Zika have tended to argue that, by the 1440s, debate had shifted away from Hus's concern with soteriology to a rather pragmatic focus on what to do with contaminated wafers and suspicious pilgrimages. But, as I hope my summary of the Erfurt *Gutachten* of 1446 and of the arguments of Bremer and Waltmann suggests, this is a nineteenth-century Protestant interpretation projected back onto fifteenth-century material.

Chapter 5. Christ's Blood in the Triduum Mortis

1. Chenu, "Sang du Christ."

2. In putting it this way, I differ from Italian scholars such as Cocci and Terrinca, who tend to see the difference as lying in the fact that Dominicans understand the saving blood more physiologically while Franciscans treat its significance as moral and spiritual. See Terrinca, *La devozione*; Cocci, "Le dispute teologiche"; and idem, "Il sangue di Cristo."

3. The basic study is now Garceau, "Fear of a 'Public Sphere'." I am grateful to Michelle Garceau and to the Chairman of the Board of Examiners for the M.A. in Medieval Studies (UCL) for permission to cite this work. I have also consulted Wadding, *Annales minorum seu Trium Ordinum*, vol. 8, pp. 68–73; Chenu, "Sang du Christ"; Terrinca, *La devozione*; Cocci, "Il Sangue di Cristo . . . ," and "Le dispute teologiche"; Haubst, *Die Christologie*, pp. 298–304; Holtz, "Cults," pp. 295–304; Vincent, *Holy Blood*, pp. 111–17. The Franciscan account (the *Annales minorum*) places less emphasis on Baiuli and gives the impression that several people taught the contested opinion about the blood.

4. As Garceau points out ("Fear of a 'Public Sphere,'" p. 10 n. 13), MS Add 22795 appears to be the only source that records this second opinion.

5. The other sources I have looked at mention only Nicholas Roselli as inquisitor. Garceau, "Fear of a 'Public Sphere,'" p. 15 n. 23 and pp. 22–23, says that she has not been able to find any information about "Pontius de Eppli'," not even an indication of how to expand the abbreviation "Eppli'."

6. According to Garceau, "Fear of a 'Public Sphere,'" p. 16, MS Add 22795 does not give the bulls but records in full the three letters from John. In the mid-fifteenth century, Pius II does not seem to have known of such bulls, a fact that led Cocci, "Le dispute," pp. 1198–1201, to doubt their existence. Pius does report that Nicholas Eymeric, in his *Directorium inquisitorum*, compiled in 1376, said the separation of the blood during the *triduum* was preached in Barcelona and that Clement VI condemned the doctrine as "erroneous and heretical"; see Pius II, *Commentarii*, bk 11, p. 283; and *Commentaries*, trans. and ed. Gragg and Gabel, pp. 712–13 n. 53.

7. The last three concerned Christ's age at death; Garceau, "Fear of a 'Public Sphere,'" p. 17.

8. Chenu, "Sang du Christ"; and A. Michel, "Forme du corps."

9. On *forma corporeitatis* and Franciscans, see A. Michel, "Forme du corps."

10. As Vincent argues (*Holy Blood*, p. 110), Clement VI made his agreement with

the Thomistic position clear in *Unigenitus* (issued in 1343), which asserted that a single drop of Christ's blood was sufficient to redeem all humankind, and seemed to imply that it redeemed exactly owing to its union with the Logos. See Denzinger, pp. 300–301. The phrase is often attributed to Bernard of Clairvaux; see Chapter 5 at n. 58. For its use in Capistrano, see Capistrano, *De sanguine*, art. 10, sect. B, para. 4, ed. Terrinca, p. 17*, and ed. Cocci, p. 1366. Like Bonaventure, Capistrano stresses that Christ shed not one drop but waves of blood; see Chapter 4 at n. 79.

11. See above n. 6.

12. On Mayronis, see Roth, *Franz von Mayronis*, esp. p. 554; Rossmann, "Meyronnes"; and Mayronis, *Der Tractatus de transcendentibus*, ed. Möhle, pp. 70–74. Scholars differ over whether Mayronis died in 1325 or 1328, but the most recent scholarship favors 1328.

13. Mayronis, Sentence Commentary, bk 4, dist. 43, q. 1, pts. 1 and 2, pp. 216–17. In my account of Mayronis, I have also relied on Vincent, *Holy Blood*, pp. 104–10, who has consulted the sermons "In festo Pasche," "In Parasceve," and "De Sacramento in cena Domini," which I have not seen; and on John of Capistrano's summary of his resurrection sermon; see below n. 16.

14. The Franciscan Peter of Aquila (d. 1361), known as Scotellus, disagreed; see this chapter at n. 27.

15. Mayronis, Sentence Commentary, q. 1, pt. 1, p. 216: ". . . in triduo divinitas non fuit vnita cum sanguine sicut cum corpore et anima. . . . Et tamen non fuit verum dicere: deus est in cruce cum ibi esset sanguis Christi nec deus iacet effusus super terram. . . ."

16. John of Capistrano gave a somewhat different formulation when he summarized Mayronis's sermon on the resurrection in his *De sanguine*, art. 1, ed. Terrinca, pp. 1*–2*, and ed. Cocci, pp. 1343–44. Capistrano put it thus: "Magister Franciscus de Mayronis in sermone de Resurrectione Domini . . . inter alia dicit, quod in morte Christi fuerunt factae quatuor separationes, quarum prima fuit animae a corpore. . . . Secunda fuit separatio divinitatis ab humanitate, quia Christus in triduo non fuit homo. . . . Tertia fuit separatio sanguinis a carne, quando fuit effusus post mortem ex laterali vulnere. . . . Quarta separatio fuit sanguinis ab ipsa deitate, ut remanente coniuncta cum corpore, cuius separationis signum est communicatio idiomatum, quae oritur ex illa. Quia licet in triduo fuerit verum dicere: Deus est in sepulcro propter corpus unitum, Christus est in inferno propter animam, tamen non fuit verum dicere: Christus igitur iacet super faciem terrae propter sanguinem, etc. Nunc autem ad propositum, in Christi resurrectione fuerunt quatuor reuniones. Quarum prima fuit unio sanguinis ad carnem, quia anima non potest uniri corpori nisi sit humore sanguinis sufficienter dispositum. Et ideo antequam anima corpori reuniretur, oportuit effusum sanguinem reinfundi. Secunda reunio fuit sanguinis cum divinitate, quia sicut sanguis a carne separatus fuit et sic etiam a deitate, per talem separationem, ita fuit coniunctus et per reinfusionem. Tertia reunio fuit animae cum corpore. . . . Quarta reunio fuit deitatis cum humanitate, quia licet Christus in triduo non fuerit homo, tamen post triduum, sicut ante triduum, vere fuit homo." In art. 13, sect. A. (ed. Terrinca, p. 22*, ed. Cocci, p. 1374), Capistrano cites the (still unpublished) commentary of Mayronis on the pseudo-Dionysian *Ecclesiastical Hierarchy*.

17. Vincent, *Holy Blood*, pp. 106–8; and Capistrano summarizing Mayronis in *De sanguine*, art. 1, ed. Terrinca, p. 1*, and ed. Cocci, pp. 1344: "Non videtur tamen incon-

veniens, si aliqua particula in aliquibus reliquiis inveniretur, quia forte corpus immortale non indigebat tanto sanguine."

18. Mayronis, Sentence Commentary, q. 1, pt. 1, p. 216. On the *Quod assumpsit*, see Chapter 4 n. 85.

19. Mayronis, Sentence Commentary, q. 1, pt. 1, p. 217: ". . . de nouo fuit humanatus. . . ." Capistrano summarizing Mayronis in *De sanguine*, art. 1, ed. Terrinca, p. 2*, and ed. Cocci, p. 1344, says: " . . . post Christi incarnationem eius resurrectio praecellit omnia alia misteria, sicut ad eius humanitatem pertinentia; quia per incarnationem fuit factus homo Deus, ita per resurrectionem fuit iterum Deus homo factus; cum in triduo non fuisset Deus homo."

20. Garceau, "Fear of a 'Public Sphere,'" pp. 6 and 8. This dossier was in turn copied into MS Add 22795 in 1511.

21. The hitherto unnoticed fact that Capistrano later lifted the more polemical part of his treatise—the descriptions of the Daroca and Brussels miracles—into his treatise against Waltmann makes it clear that he was, however, never far from polemic. Capistrano's "Epistola responsialis," Wolfenbüttel H.H.B, Cod. Guelf 550 Helmst., fols. 204r–207r, repeats verbatim Capistrano's *De sanguine*, arts. 13.B–16; see Chapter 2 n. 24. As Breest has pointed out, Capistrano was predisposed to oppose Wilsnack's defender Döring because Döring was a Conventual Franciscan but predisposed to favor blood miracles because of his own reputation as a miracle worker. See Breest, *Wunderblut* (1881), p. 273. On James of the March, see Lioi, "S. Jacques de la Marche."

22. On Capistrano, see the works by Terrinca and Cocci, and Breest, *Wunderblut* (1881), pp. 255–61 and 272–73; Hofer, *Johannes Kapistran*, esp. vol. 1, pp. 252–53, and vol. 2, pp. 172–77; Nimmo, *Reform and Division*, pp. 583–94 and 604–14; and Petrecca, *San Giovanni da Capestrano*.

23. See Cocci, "Il Sangue di Cristo," pp. 1332–40.

24. Breest, *Wunderblut* (1881), pp. 257–61, and Terrinca, *La devozione*, pp. 95–96, 106, and 113–15. Ziesak, "'Multa habeo vobis dicere . . . '," p. 231, lists 12 manuscripts of Capistrano's "Epistola responsialis ad Everhardum Waltmann."

25. Capistrano, *De sanguine*, arts. 2–4 and 6, ed. Terrinca, pp. 2*–6* and 9*–10*, and ed. Cocci, pp. 1344–60 and 1355–56.

26. Capistrano, *De sanguine*, art. 5, sect. B, para. 1, ed. Terrinca, p. 8*, and ed. Cocci, pp. 1353–54. On the Council of Vienne's decision, see Chapter 7 n. 63.

27. Capistrano, *De sanguine*, art. 10, sect. A, ed. Terrinca, p. 16*, and ed. Cocci, p. 1364. And see Vincent, *Holy Blood*, p. 108; and Teetaert, "Scotellus di Tonnaparte."

28. Following Scotus, he argues that Christ's body—because it was a real body, subject to natural laws—would have putrefied after three days, even with the embalming, had it not been for this second miracle. Capistrano, *De sanguine*, art. 6, ed. Terrinca, pp. 9*–10*, and ed. Cocci, pp. 1354–56.

29. Capistrano, *De sanguine*, art. 7 (esp. sect. D), ed. Terrinca, pp. 10*–13*, and ed. Cocci, pp. 1356–60. Cusanus also stresses the purity of Mary's blood, from which Christ is formed; see "Quod resurgit," p. 326.

30. Capistrano, *De sanguine*, art. 6, sect. C, ed. Terrinca, p. 9*, and ed. Cocci, p. 1355.

31. Grosseteste was not himself a Franciscan but was closely associated with them.

32. In the *De sanguine*, art. 5, sect. A, para. 3, ed Terrinca, p. 7*, and ed. Cocci, p. 1352, Capistrano says he has seen the blood at Piscaria.

33. *De sanguine*, art. 13, sect. B, para. 2, ed. Terrinca, p. 23*, and ed. Cocci, p. 1377.

34. *De sanguine*, arts. 15–16, ed. Terrinca, pp. 25*-29*, and ed. Cocci, pp. 1378–84.

35. See Breest, *Wunderblut* (1881), pp. 255–74, and Chapter 2 nn. 25 and 123.

36. See n. 33 above and Chapter 4 n. 87. The passage usually cited to suggest that blood relics come from abused images not from Christ's body is here used to support the claim that what appears in host and corporal miracles is from the body of Christ.

37. Capistrano, *De sanguine*, art. 16, sect. B, ed. Terrinca, p. 28*, and ed. Cocci, p. 1383. The same passage is used in Capistrano, "Epistola responsialis ad Everhardum Waltmann," Wolfenbütttel H.A.B. Cod. Guelf. 550 Helmst., fol. 206v.

38. On Capistrano as a fomenter of anti-Semitism, see Rubin, *Gentile Tales*, pp. 120–27.

39. He did use some paragraphs from the discussion of blood miracles in his later attack on Waltmann; see above n. 21.

40. A Franciscan from the same period who took the traditional Franciscan line was Alonso Tostado (d. 1455); see Terrinca, *La devozione*, pp. 97–98. For a later example of a Dominican (the Portuguese Vincent Pons) who wavered toward the Franciscan position, perhaps because his house of St. Maximin in Provence claimed a blood relic (supposedly collected by Mary Magdalene), see Vincent, *Holy Blood*, p. 115.

41. See Benedict XIV, *Opus de servorum Dei beatificatione*, bk 2, chap. 30, vol. 2, pp. 283–88; Chenu, "Sang du Christ"; and Holtz, "Cults," p. 296.

42. See Pius II, *Commentaries*, trans. and ed. Gragg and Gabel, p. 729 n. 87; for Pius's own statement of his reasons for postponing the decision, see Pius II, *Commentarii*, p. 292.

43. Vincent, *Holy Blood*, p. 117 n. 103; Holtz, "Cults," pp. 300–304; Cocci, "Le dispute"; and Terrinca, *La devozione*. In the early modern period, theological opinion gradually moved toward a consensus that the essential blood of Christ's body was united hypostatically and immediately to the Word, remained united in the *triduum*, and was resumed in resurrection. It was therefore to be adored. Both Dominicans and Franciscans came to hold, somewhat confusedly, that nonessential bits might remain and be devotionally "useful" as reminders of Christ's sacrifice.

44. For Pius's account, see *Commentarii*, bk 11, pp. 278–92; on the work, see Gabel, "Introduction," in *Commentaries*, trans. and ed. Gragg and Gabel, pp. vii–xiii.

45. Pius II, *Commentarii*, bk 8, pp. 192–202. And see Gabel, "Introduction," *Commentaries*, pp. xxix–xxx.

46. Pius II, *Commentarii*, bk 8, pp. 208–11.

47. Ibid., p. 280.

48. Ibid.; translated in *Commentaries*, trans. and ed. Gragg and Gabel, p. 707.

49. Pius II, *Commentarii*, bk 11, pp. 288–90. It is worth noting that the Dominicans argue (p. 289) that Bonaventure never held that blood in the *triduum* was separated: " . . . sed arbitramur principia naturae apud Bonauenturam cuncta complecti, quae cum anima & corpore hominem constituunt: coassumpta vero ad accidentia trahi, quae tandem desiuerunt, nec apparet Bonauenturam de sanguine loqui."

50. Ibid., p. 290.

51. Ibid., pp. 286–87.

52. Ibid., p. 287.

53. For more on the significance of this, see Chapters 6, 7, and 8.

54. The phrase "price of redemption" is used throughout by both sides but with

a telling difference. To the Dominicans, blood is the price. For example, Pius II says (*Commentarii*, p. 280) that the Dominicans "multa sacri eloquii testimonia produxerunt, quae sanguinem Christi humanae redemptionis pretium fuisse commemorant. . . ." On p. 281, the Dominicans argue: "Cumque omnium doctorum sententia sit, sanguinem Christi tanquam nostrae redemptionis pretium non diabolo . . . sed Deo patri atque ipsi Trinitati fuisse traditum. . . . " And on p. 291, conceding in part the Franciscan argument, they assert: " . . . filius igitur Dei, Deus & homo Christus Iesus redemptor fuit & pretium, caro pretium, & sanguis pretium, & anima pretium, & vita pretium; nec tamen multa pretia, sed unum pretium, Christus Iesus, in quo continentur omnia." The Franciscans argue that passages calling blood the "price of redemption" refer to Christ's death, not to the fluid, blood. See, e.g., this chapter at n. 62.

55. Pius II, *Commentarii*, p. 281. Speaking of Old Testament sacrifice, the Dominicans assert: "Huc & figuras traxere veteris testamenti, quae per sanguinem agni fusum, & vitulorum, & hircorum fundendum Christi sanguinem praesignabant, & tum primum vim purgatiuam, conseruatiuamque inesse sanguini ostendebant cum erat sparsus: ipso enim & postes & altaria liniebant, neque sine illo audebat summus sacerdos Sancta Sanctorum ingredi, coaptanda est figurato figura, & cum Apostolo concludendum valere Christi sanguinem extra corpus, quam illorum animalium, atque adeo valere, vt ipse fuerit, qui Sancta Sanctorum purgauerit, & alia fecerit, quae animalium sanguini scriptura vetus attribuit; & tandem nos in cruce fusus ab hoste redemerit."

56. Pius II, *Commentarii*, p. 291.

57. Ibid., pp. 282–83; translated in *Commentaries*, trans. and ed. Gragg and Gabel, pp. 711–12. For more on this passage, see Chapter 7 at nn. 21 and 25.

58. Pius II, *Commentarii*, p. 283: " . . . quanto magis putatis deteriora mereri supplicia, qui filium Dei conculcauerit, & sanguinem testamenti *pollutum* dixerit? *pollutum* videtur dicere sanguinem Saluatoris, qui iacentem in terra diuinitate priuatum fuisse contendit. *Corruptus* fuisset illico sanguis diuinitate priuatus aduersus Dauiticam sententiam, quae ait: Non dabis Sanctum tuum videre corruptionem. Ac si dicat Saluator Dominus vt homo: Quid proderit humano generi sanguis meus, si postquam illum effudero reliqueris eum Deus, & *putrescere*, atque corrumpi permiseris?" (emphasis added).

59. Pius II, *Commentarii*, pp. 283–84.

60. This misrepresents Albert, who held that blood was the most excellent of the humors but also held that it was alive; Terrinca, *La devozione*, pp. 140–41.

61. Pius II, *Commentarii*, p. 284: "Ostenditur autem in Laterano, Venetiis, Mantuae, & in aliis plerisque locis incineratus atque corruptus, non ergo retinuit vnionem."

62. Ibid., p. 285; and *Commentaries*, trans. and ed. Gragg and Gabel, pp. 716–17. In replying to this point, the Dominicans go so far as to admit that Christ could even have saved humanity without dying but assert that God did not choose to do it thus. See *Commentarii*, p. 291.

63. Pius II, *Commentarii*, p. 285.

64. See Ettlinger, *Sistine Chapel*, p. 83.

65. See Chapter 2 n. 21. For the texts from Cod. Cus. 40, fols. 144r–146v and 149r–150v, edited by Haubst, see Haubst, *Die Christologie*, pp. 315–19 and 320–28 respectively. For Haubst's argument for authenticity and dating, see pp. 298–303.

66. See Haubst, *Die Christologie*, pp. 276–98, for the development of Cusa's position.

67. Ibid., p. 282.

68. For the centrality of the hypostatic union in Cusanus's Christology, see Haubst, *Die Christologie*, especially pp. 305–8. For a fuller discussion of this, see Chapter 6 at nn. 34–36.

69. "Quod resurgit . . . ," Cod. Cus. 40, fols. 149r–150v, ed. Haubst, *Die Christologie*, pp. 320–26.

70. Pius II, *Commentarii*, p. 285. The stress on will echoes that found in Grosseteste; see Chapter 4 nn. 73–74.

71. Pius II, *Commentarii*, p. 290. Note that they take here the position Aquinas dismissed in his Quodlibet; see Chapter 4, nn. 86 and 87.

72. For example, Ettlinger, *Sistine Chapel*, p. 83, says that the Dominicans, who held that Christ's blood remained united with his divinity during the *triduum*, "favored the cult of Sacred Blood preserved in a number of relics."

73. Heuser "'Heilig-Blut'," pp. 38–39; Herbst, "Literarisches Leben," p. 162.

74. For example, Gerhard of Cologne, who defended the Weingarten relic, and the Portuguese Vincent Pons; see Chapter 4 at n. 103 and this chapter n. 40.

75. On flagellation as a dissident movement, see Chapter 1 n. 26 on the fourteenth-century flagellants and Chapter 2 at nn. 61–66 on the fifteenth-century cryptoflagellants.

76. Breest hypothesized long ago (*Wunderblut* [1881], p. 200) that the Franciscan enthusiasm for blood relics and host miracles was owing to a general enthusiasm for blood going back to Francis's stigmata. A number of scholars have objected that the two sorts of blood are not really analogous; see, for example, Oliger, "Johannes Kannemann," p. 46. Moreover, in view of the greater enthusiasm among Dominicans both for shedding blood in flagellation and for revering Christ's glorified blood, Breest's explanation does not seem to hold.

77. The most famous Dominican competition to Francis, Catherine of Siena, is depicted in a fifteenth-century German manuscript as flagellating herself to a bloody pulp. See Paris, Bibliothèque Nationale, MS All. 34, fol. 4v; here Plate 11. And see Hamburger, *The Visual and the Visionary*, pp. 460–64, and idem, "Un jardin," pp. 6 and 20. On this manuscript and more generally on the High German translation of Catherine's *Vita* known as "Der geistliche Rosengarten," I have profited from Thomas Kortmann, "Körpererfahrung und Heiligkeit im 'Geistlichen Rosengarten'," paper for the German Historical Institute Transatlantic Medieval Seminar, October 2003. But it is important to note that Catherine had (according to her hagiographers) only "invisible stigmata."

78. Chenu, "Sang du Christ," Cocci, "Le dispute," Terrinca, *La devozione*, pp. 170–226. See n. 43 above.

79. On such devotion as voyeuristic, see Lewis, "Wound"; and Binski, *Medieval Death*, pp. 124–26. See also Bynum, "Violent Imagery."

Chapter 6. A Concern for Immutability

1. See Chapter 1 nn. 37–39.

2. See Belting, *Image*, pp. 32–33. John of Capistrano cited the two Italian sites as support for blood miracles. See Chapter 5 n. 33.

3. My use of northern material is *not* an argument for northern particularity. Such an interpretation could obviously not be established by using only northern material. I shall be delighted if others who explore Italian and Spanish cults, piety, and theology find parallels to what I argue here. But in light of the general scholarly agreement that the north and south are, at least to a degree, different, I find it correct scholarly procedure to try, as much as possible, to locate the particular cults and devotions I study here in the context of spiritual literature and art from the same regions.

4. Duffy's monumental work, *Stripping*, makes the argument that there was much less of a gulf between elite and popular religion than was hitherto supposed. The point has recently been made in a different way by a number of literary scholars who argue for devotional writing as "vernacular theology." See Watson, "Visions of Inclusion," who uses the term to mean something like "lay theology" (including the theology of women, some of whom wrote in Latin); and Newman, *God and the Goddesses*, pp. 292–304, who uses "visionary theology." McGinn, *Flowering*, pp. 19–30, and idem, "Introduction," in *Meister Eckhart and the Beguine Mystics*, coined the term to refer to concepts in high theology that had vernacular roots. German scholarship has preferred to use "narrative theology" or "theology of experience"; see, for example, Steer, "Der Laie als Anreger," and Acklin Zimmermann, *Gott im Denken berühren*. Mulder-Bakker in *Lives of the Anchoresses*, pp. 16, 216 n. 35, and passim, uses "common theology," which sounds slightly awkward in English. Some of this discussion is semantic quibbling, and I shall try to avoid it by simply talking about devotional theology. But, whatever term one uses, it is crucial to emphasize that religious writing of all sorts—not just the products of universities and monasteries—explores theological issues.

5. It seems to me that, in fact, the danger in scholarship at the moment is not so much a neglect of the assumptions behind devotional writing and religious practice as a failure to read university theology in any broad context or with any attempt to probe its assumptions.

6. Scholars such as Giles Constable have suggested that what we find in fifteenth-century religiosity is not so much originality of thought as the reception and creative use of older ideas by new groups, especially cloistered women and lay people of both genders. See Constable, "Twelfth-Century Spirituality and the Late Middle Ages." This is true if one looks at texts such as the *Imitation of Christ*, on which Constable focused. But the recent interpretations of McGinn, Watson, and Newman (above n. 4) seem to me quite rightly to attribute a greater theological creativity than this suggests to some texts of vernacular or devotional theology, such as Julian of Norwich's *Showings* and *Piers Plowman*. See also Van Engen, "Friar Johannes Nyder," and Elm, "Die 'Devotio moderna' und die neue Frömmigkeit."

7. See Chapter 2 at nn. 33–36, Chapter 3 at nn. 148–59.

8. See Chapter 2 n. 50. I am persuaded by Hartmut Kühne's argument, on the basis of the text, that the particular story of the bishop and the effort to reconsecrate the bleeding hosts is a textual interpolation. See Kühne "'Ich ging durch Feuer und Wasser . . .'."

9. James of Jüterbog, "Tractatus de concertatione," Wolfenbüttel H.A.B. Cod. Guelf. 152 Helmst., quoted passage at fol. 186vb. On James's treatise generally, see Breest, *Wunderblut* (1881), pp. 250–52. A portion of Alexander of Hales's *Summa theologica*, written after his death, argued that subsequent decay meant the supposed miracle had never been actually miraculous; see below n. 23.

10. It is worth noting that similar concerns were raised earlier in the case of the host-desecration charges at Korneuburg in 1305, where the priest was called upon to answer (among other things): whether the host had been consecrated? Whether the blood on it was liquid or dry? Whether what he saw in the Jew's hand was bloody or white? Whether the blood came by divine or human operation? Whether the host now venerated was the same one as that concerned in the supposed desecration? Whether he thought the blood there was Christ's blood or some other miraculous blood? The priest answered that he was convinced the blood appeared first liquid and red, only later dry, and that the blood caused the associated miracles of spontaneously lighting candles. Behind such questions, there is clearly a suspicion that fraud might be involved; but there seems also to be both the assumption that blood reveals presence and abuse, and the assumption that, for a miracle, there should be liquid blood on a consecrated host. See Rubin, *Gentile Tales*, p. 61.

11. Although he stresses the social meaning of hosts, Charles Zika agrees to some extent with this interpretation when he notes that, whereas earlier debates questioned whether the miracle hosts were consecrated, later debates over Wilsnack queried how Christ could continue to be present once the supposedly miraculous matter deteriorated; see Zika, "Hosts, Processions and Pilgrimages," p. 53.

12. Macy, *Theologies of the Eucharist*, pp. 31–35, and Gaudel, "Stercoranisme."

13. Jorissen, *Die Entfaltung*; McCue, "The Doctrine of Transubstantiation"; Sylla, "Autonomous and Handmaiden Science"; Stock, *Implications of Literacy*, pp. 241–325; Burr, *Eucharistic Presence*; Macy, "The Dogma of Transubstantiation," in *Treasures*; Fitzpatrick, "On Eucharistic Sacrifice"; Bynum, "Seeing and Seeing Beyond."

14. Innocent III, *De sacro altaris mysterio*, bk 4, chap. 20, PL 217, cols. 871B–D, and see Jorissen, *Die Entfaltung*, pp. 95–97.

15. Burr, *Eucharistic Presence*, pp. 17–18, citing Albert's Sentence commentary of 1249.

16. Macy, "The Dogma of Transubstantiation," in *Treasures*; Dutton, "Eat, Drink, and Be Merry"; Schrade, "Beiträge zur Erklärung"; and Goossens, "Résonances eucharistiques," esp. pp. 175–78. For technical questions about whether the body of Christ can bilocate, see Browe, "Die scholastische Theorie," p. 312.

17. See Hindsley, *Mystics of Engelthal*, pp. 127–28. For another example, see the passage from William of St. Thierry cited in Caspers, "*Meum summum desiderium*," p. 137.

18. Hindsley, *Mystics of Engelthal*, p. 80. Schrade, "Beiträge zur Erklärung," discusses passages and images in which the eucharistic elements are lifted up rather than Christ descending. See also Harris, "The Body as Temple," p. 241.

19. See Chapter 4 at nn. 18 and 19.

20. See Chapter 4 at n. 24.

21. Aquinas, Sentence Commentary, bk 4, dist. 10, q. 1, art. 1, esp. ra 4, pp. 470–71. And see Chapter 4 at n. 49 for Jan Hus, who made a similar argument. Lépin, *L'idée du sacrifice*, pp. 84–85, points out that the patristic emphasis on the sacrifice of the mass as "bloodless," for example in Chrysostom, was an effort to exclude not only blood and death from the eucharist but also the idea that any modification could affect Christ's body.

22. See Riedel, *Codex dipl. Brandenb.*, A 2, doc. 17, pp. 152–56, quoted in Chapter 2 n. 21.

23. Alexander of Hales, *Summa theologica* (1481–82 ed.), tractatus 4, q. 53, membrum 4, art. 3 [no pagination]. "Consequenter queritur quid sit illud, quod quandoque apparet in speciem carnis vel pueri in altari, an sit corpus christi? Quod sic: videtur, quia constat quod caro que videtur ibi non est caro animalis alicuius: nec etiam alicuius rei mortalis, quod patet per deductionem, ergo est caro christi. . . . Item corpus Christi est incorruptibile et incomputribile, sed quandoque accidit quod caro que apparet in casu proposito propter temporis diuturnitatem corrumpitur et denigratur, sicut est in marchia tervisina [the March of Treviso, near Venice], ibi enim caro que apparuit sic a multis diebus videtur corrumpi vt constat ex certitudine sensus: ergo caro illa non est caro vel corpus christi. . . . Item caro christi velatur ipso sacramento, ne evacuatur meritum fidei. . . . Responsio quod in casu proposito . . . videtur igitur insipientie mee quod quando per conversionem panis in corpus christi et vini in sanguinem opere mirabili apparet puer vel . . . frustum carnis et sanguinis in calice: quod est christus vel caro christi et sanguis. Ex quo enim huiusmodi reuelationes solent fieri in condescensione defectus fidei alicuius vt videlicet fides sacramenti huius roboraretur. Si autem caro vel sanguis sic apparens esset alicuius animalis vet subito creata, nullum argumentum veritatis induceret. . . . Si enim crederetur esse caro vel sanguis bouis: nunquam propter hoc crederetur veritas ipsius sacramenti, nec credi deberet, quia ergo ostensio ipsius sacramentalis debet fieri per indicia vera et non simulata vel ficta: videtur dicendum quod caro vel sanguis in huiusmodi apparitione quando a domino est, est ipsius domini, a domino esse dico: quia huiusmodi apparitiones quandoque accidunt humana procuratione et forte dyabolica." This material is not found in the published critical edition of Alexander's *Summa theologica*, which contains the material left unfinished at Alexander's death in 1246. See *Doctor irrefragabilis Alexandri de Hales . . . Summa theologica* (1924–48). The final version of the *Summa*, which was expanded after Alexander's death by William of Melitona and others, was imposed on the Franciscan order by two ministers general in the fourteenth century and was published at least seven times between 1475 and 1622. Browe, *Die eucharistischen Wunder*, pp. 151, 175, 185, and 200, and idem, "Die scholastische Theorie," pp. 309 and 329, quotes from this membrum as Alexander.

24. See Chapter 4 n. 27.

25. There are occasionally cases where the highest ecclesiastical authorities support bleeding-host shrines by claiming a continuing or renewed miracle. See Chapter 4 n. 23.

26. Oberman, *Wurzeln*, p. 199.

27. See Bynum, "The Presence of Objects," and Eder, "*Die Deggendorfer Gnad*".

28. On Guibert, see Chapter 4 at nn. 53–58. I thus place in a long theological tradition the same fear of fragmentation and decay that John Benton interpreted, using psychoanalytic theory, as Guibert's castration complex.

29. Capistrano, *De sanguine*, art. 4, sect. C, ed. Terrinca, pp. 5–6*, and ed. Cocci, pp. 1349–50.

30. Capistrano, *De sanguine*, art. 7, ed. Terrinca, pp. 10*–13*, and ed. Cocci, pp. 1356–60. And see Chapter 5 at n. 29.

31. Capistrano, *De sanguine*, art. 6, ed. Terrinca, pp. 9*–10*, and ed. Cocci, pp. 1354–56. And see Chapter 5 at n. 28. For the argument in Scotus, see Scotus, *Quaestiones in lib. III Sententiarum*, pt 1, dist. 21, q. 1: "Utrum corpus Christi fuisset putrefactum, si resurrectio non fuisset accelerata?" pp. 434–38.

32. See Chapter 5 n. 30.

33. See Vincent, *Holy Blood*, p. 107 n. 67, citing Mayronis, "In Parasceve II": "Dicitur quod virtute divina fuit recollectus et a corruptione servatus sicut caro et corpori infusus. . . . licet enim divinitas . . . tamen in triduo non putatur unita cum effuso sanguine immediate." William Sudbury, who is discussed at length by Vincent, seems to have held the same position; see Vincent, *Holy Blood*, p. 130 at n. 41.

34. See Chapter 5, pp. 125–27, and Haubst, *Die Christologie*, pp. 276–98.

35. Haubst, *Die Christologie*, p. 282.

36. Ibid., p. 277.

37. Nagel, "Das heilige Blut Christi," p. 201.

38. See Chapter 4, pp. 106–8.

39. See Nagel, "Das heilige Blut Christi," p. 201; and Holtz, "Cults," p. 92.

40. The bishop of Rochester denounced it as a fraud in February 1538, claiming that it was topped up each week with the blood of a freshly slaughtered duck; see Vincent, *Holy Blood*, p. 198 n. 32. A commission sent by Cromwell in October of the same year, at the abbot's request, found the relic glistening like blood when viewed from outside the crystal but only colored gum or birdlime when the jewel was opened. In November the bishop of Rochester claimed it was honey, dyed with saffron. See ibid., pp. 198–99, esp. nn. 33–36, and Baddeley, "The Holy Blood of Hayles," p. 283.

41. See Chapter 3 at n. 81.

42. For the cases of Bruges, Weingarten, and Schwerin, where *sanguis Christi* supposedly liquefied or divided as if alive, see Chapter 7 nn. 72–73. The most famous claim for liquefaction relates not to a relic of Christ but to a saint's cult, that of Januarius in Naples; see Roux, *Le sang*, pp. 202–3, and Holtz, "Cults," p. 96.

43. See Chapter 5 at n. 61.

44. To most writers, the scars are healed, but there are those who stress that they flow until the Last Judgment. See Chapter 8 n. 50.

45. "Super dubiis" (the *Gutachten* of the Erfurt theological faculty in 1446), q. 2, Wolfenbüttel H.A.B. Cod. Guelf. 152 Helmst., fols. 161rb–162rb, especially fols. 161vb–162ra. The professors argue that, even if Christ left inessential blood behind, he did not leave it *on* miracle hosts. See Chapter 2 n. 83.

46. See Chapter 4 n. 105. The Weingarten texts stress repeatedly that Christ rises whole yet leaves blood behind; see Holtz "Cults," pp. 97–150, 170–78, and passim.

47. In *Metamorphosis and Identity*, pp. 15–36, I argued, using very different material, that the issue of what constitutes change and identity was crucial in late medieval religiosity. As we shall see in Chapters 7 and 8, this is not to argue that change and identity were the only crucial issues.

48. Hus cited Aristotle as objecting that it could not be. "Tractatus," sect. 6, para. 15, p. 15: "Sexto obicitur sic ex tibi dubio: sangwis Christi, qui in eius circumcisione effluxit, fuit substancialiter corruptus, cum possibile fuit eum substancialiter corrumpi, sicud et Christum mori. Et si substancialiter corruptus est, non potest vel non poterat reverti idem materialiter secundum senteneiam Philosophi 2 'de generacione.' Igitur non omnem sangwinem, qui de corpore Christi effluxit, ipse Christus glorificauit." Hus's reply to this is basically to give the argument, familiar since the patristic period, that the God who can create *ex nihilo* can certainly re-create; "Tractatus," sect. 6, para. 18, p. 16. His specific answer to the Aristotelian theory of change seems to make use of the Thomistic principle that form accounts for numerical identity but he clearly argues

that all particles return. See "Tractatus," sect. 6, para. 19, pp. 16–17: "Ex isto dicto faciliter respondetur ad argumentum, ut posito per possibile, quod Christi sangwis, qui in circumcisione de suo corpore effluxit, fuisset substancialiter conuersus in rem alteram secundum formam, vel sangwis in cruce si exsiccatus fuisset, et sic per calorem solis aliqualiter conuersus in vaporem: per cuis [sic] potenciam sic conuertebatur in altera, per eiusdem potenciam in die resurreccionis de illis reuertetur in formam propriam et sic idem sangwis in numero, quoad formam. Et sic concessa prima parte antecedentis in argumento negatur vltima pars sc. ista 'non potest vel non poterat reuerti idem materialiter.' "

49. Herbst, "Literarisches Leben," pp. 160–61.

50. Bansleben actually cites Thomas in "Conclusio 2" to his "Questio de sanguine Christi": "Ut plebis fides firmaretur decuit quod sanguis miraculosus visibiliter in esse produceretur. . . . Sanguis qui in quibusdam ecclesiis ostenditur, ex quadam imagine dicitur percussus miraculose vel alias ex corpore Christi." Herbst, "Literarisches Leben," p. 160.

51. See Chapter 3 n. 42.

52. See Cazelles, *Le corps de sainteté*; Bynum, *Resurrection*, pp. 305–17; and Perrot, "Du sang au lait."

53. On the incorruptibility of holy cadavers, see Angenendt, "Der 'ganze' und 'unverweste' Leib"; and Bynum, *Resurrection*, pp. 200–225, 320–29. For cases in which incorruption was a sign of evil, see Bynum, *Fragmentation and Redemption*, p. 413 n. 120.

54. Bynum, *Fragmentation and Redemption*, pp. 187, 266, and 372 n. 32.

55. See the case of Elizabeth von Weiler, discussed by Hamburger in *Visual and the Visionary*, pp. 414 and 577 nn. 124–25. It was also thought to remain sweet tasting. See Bihlmeyer, ed., "Mystisches Leben," p. 68: "die es von andacht langzeit behilten rosenvarb und wolsmeckert." This is a particularly interesting case since it combines, as does *sanguis Christi*, "being shed" (that is, exuding, gushing forth) with surviving incorruptible (that is, lasting on alive).

56. Snoek, *Medieval Piety from Relics to the Eucharist*, pp. 189–90, 222, 319–22, and 328–34; and see Browe, *Die eucharistischen Wunder*, pp. 72–77, for the motif of surviving fire. For a case (ca. 1300) of holy blood coming unscathed through fire, see app. 4 in Vincent, *Holy Blood*, pp. 209–10. Thomas Head has called our attention to the practice of testing relics by burning to see whether they survived unharmed; "Saints, Heretics, and Fire."

57. Holtz, "Cults," p. 49.

58. See Chapter 3, pp. 58–59 and 63; Eder, *"Die Deggendorfer Gnad"*; Swillus, "Hostienfrevellegende"; Prümers, "Der Hostiendiebstahl zu Posen"; and (for Bamberg, Erding and Altötting) Faensen, "Zur Synthese," p. 242. See also Bauerreiss, *Pie Jesu*, pp. 28–33, for specific cases where hosts supposedly survived burial and pp. 87–91 on the motif of burial in ditches or latrines.

59. Browe, "Verwandlungswunder," p. 148.

60. Browe, "Die scholastische Theorie," p. 316.

61. Gray, "The Five Wounds," p. 50.

62. The liturgy stresses in its choice of words that the relic is a drop (*gutta*, *stilla*, *stillula*) and that it is red (*ruber*, *rutilans et apricus*)—liquid and incorrupt. See Holtz, "Cults," pp. 111, 117–20.

63. From the antiphon for the gospel canticle at First Vespers, Weingarten liturgy, cited in Holtz, "Cults," p. 120.

64. Brückner, "Liturgie und Legende," pp. 139–66. And see Browe, "Verwandlungswunder," pp. 161–64, for other examples.

65. Oberman, *Wurzeln*, pp. 198–99.

66. On this theme in saints' lives, see Delehaye, *The Legends of the Saints*, pp. 97 and 130–34; Cazelles, *Le corps de sainteté*, pp. 50–60; Elliott, *Roads to Paradise*, pp. 14–15 and 151.

67. On this quality of devotional images, see Suckale, "*Arma Christi*."

68. Not all Schmerzensmänner are bleeding; some show only wounds and appear to be dead. In general, the figure is corpselike in Mediterranean areas; in the north, it tends to be living, gesturing toward the side wound. But even the Mediterranean type stands upright—thus hinting at resurrection. And the Schmerzensmänner associated with blood cult tend to be bleeding. See Panofsky, "'Imago Pietatis'"; Belting, *Image*, pp. 29–40, 60–80, 84–90, and 131–96.

69. Bauerreiss, *Pie Jesu*.

70. I describe the blood chest from my own examination of it. To my knowledge, the only previously published pictures of the inside wings are the poor black and white plates in Cremer, *Die St. Nikolaus-Kirche zu Wilsnack*, vol. 2, plates 45a, b; see also ibid., vol. 1, pp. 185–86.

71. On Schwerin, see Chapter 3 n. 87. There has been lengthy debate over whether a small figure of the rising Christ at Wienhausen was also a blood reliquary; see Chapter 3 n. 28.

72. On Cismar, see Ehresmann, "Iconography of the Cismar Altarpiece," and Chapter 3 nn. 80–82. On Rothenburg ob der Tauber, see Heuser, "'Heilig-Blut'," pp. 14–15; and Welzel, *Abendmahlsaltäre*, pp. 24, 26, and 116–31.

73. *Die Legende*, [p. 1].

74. *Supplementum Coelifodinae*, p. 406: "Et dicit praefatus reverendus pater Dorsten: Si hostia consecrate aculeis perforaretur et exiret cruor, sicut quandoque legitur factum [at Sternberg] non est credendum, quod ille cruor esset de corpore Christi ibi contento; quia Christus, ut ibi est, non est tangibilis vel passibilis vel laesibilis. Sed esset miraculosus, de novo a deo creatus vel factus; quia ex nihilo potest facere aliquid, ubi vult et quando vult." But he also says (p. 407) that the first cause or reason for the blood is the memory of the passion of the Lord "quae clarius in sanguine repraesentatur." "Etiam memoria sanguinis vehementius imprimit memoriam passionis. Etiam sanguis est amicus naturae et sedes animae, igitur horribilius est eum fundere, Levitici 17." The second cause is that we may recognize the "pretium redemptionis nostrae."

Chapter 7. Living Blood Poured Out

1. Gemäldegalerie, Berlin, Kat.-Nr. 2156; Dok.-Nr. 02552129 in Gemäldegalerie Digitale Galerie.

2. Gemäldegalerie, Berlin, Kat.-Nr. 1662. It is important to note that the side wound here is a sort of blood rosette—a point to which I shall return in the next chapter. The image is on the Gemäldegalerie Web site as Dok.-Nr. 02558056 in Gemäldegalerie Digitale Galerie, and in SMB-PK, Gemäldegalerie Gesamtverzeichnis 1996, as

Abb. 124. The Gemäldegalerie describes the crucifixion in Plate 20 as Austrian/Bohemian circa 1400; Robert Suckale tells me he thinks it is Bohemian from about 1430. For an example of Christ laid in the tomb, where the wounds are still running with fresh blood, see Plate 13; see also *Goldgrund und Himmelslicht: Die Kunst des Mittelalters in Hamburg* (Hamburg: Kunsthalle, 2000), pp. 141–51, plate p. 146.

3. Eisler, *Masterworks in Berlin*, p. 42 and plate 14, and Boehm and Fajt, eds., *Prague*, cat. no. 1, p. 132. Gemäldegalerie, Berlin, Kat.-Nr. 1219; Dok.-Nr. 02554098 in Gemäldegalerie Digitale Galerie. In this particular painting, the way the blood drips from Christ's right hand toward the grotesquely twisted head of the good thief makes it appear as if the red bits are falling into his open mouth. Below, on the left, Longinus holds the lance and cups his hand to carry healing blood to his eyes. The painting was probably "the best-known painting of the fourteenth century in Prague" and was widely imitated (ibid.). For other examples, including southern ones, see Finaldi, ed., *The Image of Christ*, pp. 122–23, 126–27, and 144–47.

4. See Hamburger, "Un jardin," p. 20 (fol. 4v); for Catherine drinking and seeing the blood, p. 40 (fols. 43 and 43v). For a number of fifteenth-century woodcuts that emphasize blood to a remarkable extent, see Parshall et al., *Origins of European Printmaking*, pp. 141, 165, 170, 173, 177, 178, 181, 186, and 243. All are German.

5. For the Landsberger Altar, see *Gemäldegalerie Berlin*, Prestel Museum Guide, 3rd rev. ed. (Munich: Prestel, 2002), pp. 20–21; Eisler, *Masterworks in Berlin*, pp. 73 and 75. For other northern examples of the risen Christ with freshly bleeding wounds, see Schiller, *Ikonographie*, vol. 3, plates 204, 222, and 223, pp. 387 and 395. For northern examples of Christ in Judgment with bleeding wounds, see Baschet, *Les justices de l'au-delà*, plates V.2 and VI.1; and Harbison, *Last Judgment*, plate 23. See also the fascinating Last Judgment scene, now in the Dom Museum in Würzburg, that depicts an actual trial occurring below a Christ in judgment with vividly dripping wounds. The recent catalogue attributes the painting to Prague (?), circa 1435; Boehm and Fajt, eds., *Prague*, cat. no. 151, p. 316. The painting appears to be greatly overpainted or perhaps of more modern date, but the iconography is certainly fifteenth-century.

6. See Chapter 1 at nn. 67–71. In the patristic period, grapes and wine (like bread) were often also seen as symbols of ingathering or community, although even there the image usually appeared in conjunction with the image of Christ as the cluster (*botrus*), pressed in the winepress (*torcular*) of the cross. Cyprian interpreted the mingling of water and wine in the chalice as a symbol that the people (water) are mingled with Christ (wine/blood); Rohling, *Blood of Christ*, p. 14. For a Carolingian example of grapes as "seeds joined together," see Rabanus Maurus, *Enarrationes in Librum Numerorum*, bk 2, chap. 10, PL 108, cols. 668D–669A. The shift in the later Middle Ages to wine/blood as a symbol of breaching is striking. For a fifteenth-century example of bread/body as incorporation, wine/blood as spilling, see the long quotation from Gabriel Biel at n. 45.

7. On fundamental ambivalence about blood, understood in many cultures as both the cause and the cure of ill health, see Bildhauer, "Blood," pp. 45–47.

8. See Chapter 8 at nn. 23–39.

9. As I pointed out in Chapter 1, historians have often called attention to the themes of fertilizing, nourishing, enlivening, and cleansing that permeate late medieval devotion to *sanguis Christi* all across northern Europe, and I do not want merely to pile up examples here. Scholars such as Louis Gougaud, Douglas Gray, Eamon Duffy, Peter Dinzelbacher, and many others have made us vividly aware of the ways in which

blood signifies the wine of eucharist, the bath of baptism, and the bright mark of penance and absolution. See Chapter 1 nn. 30, 32, and 80 for examples.

10. To say this is not to hold that there were no differences among discourses. Medical discourse, for example, tended to locate soul or spirit (understood as life) physiologically, whereas devotional and university theology stressed the noncorporeality of soul and therefore the impossibility of its physical location. But even these discourses were not completely separate.

11. For examples in addition to those given in Chapter 3, see Heuser, "'Heilig-Blut'," pp. 71–77, and Browe, "Die Eucharistie als Zaubermittel."

12. Gerhard, *Tractatus*, pp. 474–75. As I pointed out above, Gerhard's treatise focuses not on blood as eucharist but on blood as presence more immediate than eucharist. On the ritual of "blood-drinking," in which wine or water was poured over the relic and drunk, see Jensch, "Die Weingartener Heilig-Blut- und Stiftertradition," pp. 23–24, and Nagel, "Das Heilige Blut Christi," pp. 201–3. In a parallel ritual, Edmund Rich of Abingdon (d. 1240), archbishop of Canterbury, washed the wounds of a crucifix with wine and then drank it; see Gougaud, *Dévotions et pratiques ascétiques*, pp. 77–78.

13. Holtz, "Cults," pp. 97–150.

14. Ibid., p. 121. There are some interesting examples of agricultural metaphors for Christ's breast blood in fifteenth-century Irish literature in Ryan, "'Reign of Blood'," pp. 137–49, esp. p. 141.

15. See *Le sang au moyen âge*, especially the articles by Berthelot, Fery-Hue, Van Proeyen, Voisenet, and Buschinger; Vincent, *Holy Blood*, pp. 43–45; Camporesi, *Juice of Life*, pp. 13–52 (which must be used with caution); and Bildhauer, "Blood." There are many examples of blood cures in Heuser, "'Heilig-Blut'," pp. 125–43. On the assumption in early myths that blood cures leprosy—an assumption both Jewish and Christian stories see their traditions as transcending or sublimating into symbolic eating—see Yuval, "Jews and Christians: Shared Myths," pp. 89–104.

16. Meditation on the Passion from the cloister of Mariae Pax in Ringenberg bei Wesel; see Richstätter, *Die Herz-Jesu-Verehrung*, p. 222. The Jews are said to have put the spear of blind Longinus to Christ's side. Longinus then pushed in the spear, blood ran along the shaft, and when he wiped his eyes, they were opened and he cried out. I translate Richstätter's modern German translation; the prayer he cites is unpublished. On the Longinus legend, in which the healing theme is common, see Morgan, "Longinus and the Wounded Heart"; Peebles, *The Legend of Longinus*; and n. 3 above.

17. Buschinger, "Sang versé, sang guérisseur"; McCracken, *Curse of Eve*, pp. 1–2, 47–50; Walter Michel, "Blut und Blutglaube im Mittelalter," TRE, vol. 6, pp. 737–38. Heuser, "'Heilig-Blut'," pp. 127–29, and Bildhauer, "Blood," p. 46, give examples of charms against blood flow.

18. They were also supposedly collecting Christian blood in order to wash off their guilt for shedding the blood of Christ; see Boureau, *Théologie, science et censure*, p. 253, and Bildhauer, "Blood," p. 47.

19. See Treue, "Schlechte und gute Christen," pp. 104–6.

20. See nn. 43, 45, and 47 below.

21. Teuscher, "Parenté, politique et comptabilité," p. 851, and Stahuljak, *Bloodless Genealogies*. A great deal of modern work on blood simply assumes that its primary denotation in past times is lineage or descent. See, for example, the work by Nancy Jay

referred to in Chapter 10 n. 7. McCracken, *Curse of Eve*, p. 91, makes the same assumption about patrilineal descent as dominant when she argues: "Medieval stories about unknown maternal blood-lines and forbidden birth scenes suggest that, because it challenges the rhetoric of paternal blood ties, the scene of birth is always monstrous."

22. Langland, *Piers Plowman*, B Text, Passus xviii, ll. 377–79, p. 232. As formulated, this is a move toward universalism but an ambiguous one. The poet says both that the Jews are "lost" and that Christ takes all men's souls out of hell for "we are all brothers in blood, if not all in baptism."

23. See Duffy, *Stripping*, p. 104.

24. Baldric of Bourgueil, *Historia Jerosolimitana*, in *Recueil des historiens des croisades: historiens occidentaux*, ed. L'Académie royale des inscriptions et belles-lettres, 5 vols. (Paris: Imprimerie royale, 1844–95), vol. 4, p. 101.

25. Pius II, *Commentarii*, pp. 282–83; trans. in *Commentaries*, trans. and ed. Gragg and Gabel, pp. 711–12. And see Chapter 5 at n. 57. The blood referred to here is collateral relations as well as lineage.

26. See Letter 36 in Catherine of Siena, *Epistolario*, vol. 1, pp. 148–52, esp. 150–51.

27. I have discussed this in Bynum, *Fragmentation*, pp. 206–18.

28. See Chapter 5 n. 29. According to Pius II, the Dominicans at Rome argued that all structures of the body are generated *ex sanguine menstruo*; Pius II, *Commentarii*, pp. 286–87, and see Chapter 5 at n. 51.

29. Holtz, "Cults," p. 127, citing Berthold, *Annotatio*, in Swarzenski, *The Berthold Missal*, p. 119.

30. The image of the soul pregnant with Christ is found, not surprisingly, more often in texts by and for women, but it is found in texts for and by men as well. See, for example, the prayer of Adelheid Langmann: "I ask you to give me true, perfect love to receive your Holy Body so that I may conceive you spiritually even as your mother conceived you bodily. . . ." Friedrich Sunder, chaplain to the nuns of Engelthal, claimed that the Christ child came into his soul and divinized [*vergottet*] it. He was united with the Christ child in "the cradle of his heart," nursed the baby "with his right breast," and became Christ's mother in giving birth to him. For Adelheid and Friedrich, see Hindsley, *Mystics of Engelthal*, pp. 63 and 104–7. See also Bynum, *Holy Feast*, pp. 203–4 and 268–69.

31. Pfeiffer, *Deutsche Mystiker*, vol. 1, p. 402: ". . . wie lieplîchen er uns in im selben getragen hât, noch lieplîcher danne kein muoter nie ir kint getruoc; wan diu treit ir kint under ir herzen, sô truoc uns der vater, als uns der sun erzeigete, in sînem herzen; wan er lie dar în bôren mit einem sper, daz wir saehen des vater heize minne nâch sînem kinden. Wie? Dà erkaltet unde gestêt eins ieglîchen menschen bluot daz tôt ist: dô was daz sîn heiz unde resch." And see ibid, pp. xlii–xliii, and Richstätter, *Die Herz-Jesu-Verehrung*, p. 127.

32. Bede, *In cantica canticorum*, bk 3, chap. 5, vol. 10, p. 283, ll. 485–90.

33. See Chapter 1 at n. 113. And see Dionysius the Carthusian cited in n. 80 below.

34. Although the analogy between the blood of the passion and birthing blood was widespread, it seems to have been given most graphic and extensive treatment in works by and for women. See Bynum, *Jesus as Mother*, pp. 110–262 passim. On the question of whether women are especially attracted to blood devotion, see Alexandre-Bidon, "La dévotion," who points out that about 20 percent of women's Books of Hours show a "taste for the blood of Christ beyond the ordinary" but wisely refrains

from generalizing without a comparison of male devotion. Grossel, "'Le suave calice de la passion'," cites some examples of female devotion but tends to conflate water and blood and tells us little that is new about piety.

35. Marguerite of Oingt, *Pagina meditationum*, cc. 30–39, in Marguerite, *Les oeuvres*, pp. 77–79. The passage is quite close to Bernard's Sermon 11, sect. 3 (7), in *Sermones super Cantica Canticorum*, in *Sancti Bernardi opera*, vol. 1, p. 59, but it is interesting to note that Marguerite adds the female analogy.

36. There is a great deal of recent work on Julian. I have found especially useful Baker, *Julian of Norwich's* Showings; Bauerschmidt, *Julian*; Watson, "Julian of Norwich"; Maisonneuve, "Le sang . . . chez Julienne"; and Newman, *God and the Goddesses*, pp. 193–94 and 225–34.

37. See Bynum, *Holy Feast*, pp. 266–67. Both Barbara Newman and Benedicta Ward think Julian was a widow who had probably borne children. See Ward, "Julian the Solitary," pp. 11–35, and Newman, *God and the Goddesses*, pp. 223–24.

38. See Chapter 9 at nn. 39–50. For an even more graphic example of such piety from the early modern period, see the Carmelite mystic Mary Magdalene de' Pazzi (d. 1607), who supposedly received a rain of blood on the night of May 6, 1585. Seeing an explicit parallel between the blood in God's breast and that in Mary's, Mary Magdalene wrote that both suckle and wash human beings until the soul, "transformed in blood," "comprehends, sees, tastes, feels, thinks nothing but blood." Imaging salvific blood as female birthing blood, Mary Magdalene prayed: "Oh Word, you conceived this soul in blood, you gave birth to it in blood, you washed it with blood, clothed it with blood, crowned it with blood." "Colloquio 5" in *Tutte le opere di Santa Maria Maddalena de' Pazzi*, vol. 2, pp. 97–98; and "Colloquio 35," pp. 362–80 at p. 379. Cited in Grégoire, "Sang," cols. 330–31, in a different edition.

39. Capistrano, *De sanguine*, art. 11, sect. A, ed. Terrinca, p. 18*, and ed. Cocci, p. 1367.

40. See Chapter 5 at nn. 59–64. On the Franciscan position, especially Scotus, Middleton, and Mayronis, see Terrinca, *La devozione*, p. 106; on Durandus of St. Pourçain and Biel, who held that the blood joined Christ only via his body and humanity, see ibid., p. 138, and Biel, *Canonis misse expositio*, lectio 53, vol. 2, pp. 312–34.

41. See A. Michel, "Forme du corps," at col. 584, and Aquinas, ScG, bk 2, chap. 72, p. 46, col. 1: "anima autem est actus corporis organici, 'non unius organi tantum. est igitur in toto corpore, et non in una parte tantum, secundum suam essentiam. . . ."

42. No trained theologian in the fourteenth or fifteenth century held that soul was material. Even those such as Pomponazzi (d. 1525), who came to hold that soul could not be proved not to die with body, did not base this in the idea that soul or life is corporeal.

43. The idea that blood is life or life force is found in many religions; see A. Closs, "Blut," LTK, vol. 2, cols. 537–38; Schumann, "Blut: religionsgeschichtlich," in RGG, vol. 1, cols. 1154–56; Kasper, "Der bleibende Gehalt," pp. 377–80; and Bildhauer, "Blood," pp. 45–46. Grosseteste, in his "De sanguine Christi," states this explicitly; see p. 143: "duo sunt sanguines vel genera sanguinum. Unus enim sanguis est qui ex nutrimentis generatur. . . . Est et alius sanguis, qui corpori animato substantialis. . . . qui secundum phisicos dicitur amicus naturae, et de quo dicit Moyses, quod in sanguine sedes est animae."

44. For example, Alger of Liège, *De sacramentis*, bk 2, chap. 8, PL 180, col. 826D,

and Aquinas, ST 3, q. 74, art. 1, pp. 889–90; and q. 76, art. 2, ra 1, p. 895, col. 1: ". . . corpus exhibetur pro salute corporis, sanguis pro salute animae." For other examples, among them Peter Lombard, Rupert of Deutz, Gerald of Wales, and Peter the Chanter, see Macy, *Theologies of the Eucharist*, pp. 64–70, and Dinzelbacher, "Das Blut Christi," nn. 58 and 67.

45. Biel, *Canonis misse expositio*, lectio 52, vol. 2, p. 304.

46. Aquinas, ST 3, q. 48, art. 5, p. 845, col. 2. For other uses of the phrase, which is very common in scholastic writing, see Bonaventure, Sentence Commentary, bk 4, dist. 11, pt 2, art. 1, q. 3, vol. 4, p. 257; ibid., bk 4, dist. 4, pt 2, art. 1, q. 3; ibid., vol. 4, p. 110; idem, *Sermo* 2, *de nostra redemptione*, in *Opera omnia*, vol. 9, p. 726, col. 2; and Grosseteste, *De cessatione legalium*, pt 1, sect. 2, para. 9, p. 11. Grosseteste says: "quia anima carnis in sanguine est." For the idea in Albert, see Terrinca, *La devozione*, p. 140.

47. Paltz, *Supplementum Coelifodinae*, p. 407: "Etiam sanguis est amicus naturae et sedes animae, igitur horribilius est eum fundere, Levitici 17." And see Chapter 6 n. 74.

48. See Chapter 4 n. 68. For a similar passage, see James of Milan, *Stimulus amoris*, chap. 17, Bibliotheca franciscana ascetica medii aevi 4 (Quaracchi: Collegium S. Bonaventurae, 1949), p. 104: "O quam mirabilis est tua dilectio, cum non possis ab hominibus separari? Nonne, quia ascensurus eras ad dexteram Patris tui, potestatem homini dimisisti, ut te, cum velit, habeat in altari? . . . Cur semper cum homine vis morari? Sed tuo corpore incorporare nos totaliter voluisti et tuo nos voluisti potare sanguine, ut sic tuo inebriati amore tecum unum cor et unam animam haberemus. Quid enim est aliud tuum sanguinem, qui est sedes animae, bibere, nisi nostram animam tuae inseparabiliter colligare? Hoc certe est quod vis . . . . Hoc nobis concedas qui pro nobis plenum amore sanguinem effudisti." See also ibid., chap. 14, pp. 67–76.

49. The parallel to Julian of Norwich's famous parable of the servant is clear. See Chapter 9 at n. 39.

50. Dorlandus, *Viola animae p(er) modum dyalogi* (ed. 1499), treatise seven (not paginated). The rubric reads: "Cur flagellatus christus." On Dorlandus, see Moereels, "Dorlant." Of the seven dialogues of the *Viola animae*, the first six are a resume of the *Theologia naturalis* of Raymond of Sebonde, a learned Spaniard who died in 1437. Most scholars agree that the seventh, a dialogue between Mary and Dominicus on the passion of the Lord, is original and by Dorlandus; it has been hailed as a major piece of Renaissance Latin prose.

51. Sister-Book of Adelhausen, 155.13–22, quoted in G. Lewis, *By Women, for Women*, p. 252.

52. That body carries identity also in some irreducible sense is a theme of medieval theology and devotion I have pursued elsewhere. See, most recently, Bynum, "Soul and Body."

53. Letter 31 in Catherine of Siena, *Epistolario*, pp. 126–32; trans. as Letter T273 in *Letters of Catherine*, vol. 1, pp. 85–89. And see Bynum, *Holy Feast*, pp. 165–82.

54. Letter 31 in Catherine, *Epistolario*, pp. 126–32; trans. in *Letters*, vol. 1, pp. 85–89.

55. Catherine was a Dominican tertiary. For Dominican arguments at Rome in the 1460s, see Chapter 5.

56. Letter T87 in Catherine of Siena, *Le Lettere*, vol. 2, pp. 88–93, esp. p. 90; trans. in *Letters*, vol. 2, p. 632. And see chap. 27 of her *Dialogue* for a similar image of Christ's

blood mixed into the mortar of his divinity: ". . . ciò è che 'l sangue è intriso con la calcina della deità e con la fortezza e fuoco della carità." *Il Dialogo*, p. 73.

57. Letter T87, in *Le Lettere*, vol. 2, p. 91; trans. in *Letters*, vol. 2, pp. 632–33. Noffke translates "messo a mano" as "handed over." In the context it seems clearly to mean "shed," or "left at hand." In her *Dialogue*, chap. 41, Catherine says that the faithful rejoice in the wounds of Jesus, which are always fresh; and the scars remain in his body, continually crying for mercy to God. "Dicevoti del bene che avarebbe il corpo glorificato ne l'umanità glorificata de l'unigenito mio Figliuolo la quale vi dà certezza della vostra resurrezione. Ine esultano nelle piaghe sue, le quali sono rimase fresche, riservate le cicatrici nel corpo suo, le quali gridano continuamente misericordia a me, sommo ed eterno Padre, per voi." *Il Dialogo*, pp. 104–5.

58. See Chapter 1 n. 29.

59. *Ancient Devotions to the Sacred Heart . . . by Carthusian Monks*, pp. 1–4 and passim. See also Lanspergius, pt 3, canon 19, of *Alloquiorun libri duo*, in *D. Joannis Justi Lanspergii cartusiani opera omnia*, vol. 4, *Opera minora*, p. 353. Christ supposedly writes in a letter to a group of Premonstratensian sisters that nothing shows so clearly how he loves them as his desire "in mortem pro te animam meam tradere, corpus vero meum omni ex parte sauciandum vulneribus offerre. Ad haec, quia ardenter sitiebam tuam salutem, cupiebam sanguinem meum omnem pro te effundere. Quod ita tandem effeci, ne unam quidem guttam retinens."

60. Sermon 24, *De festivitatibus Christi*, cited in Richstätter, *Die Herz-Jesu-Verehrung*, p. 163, from an edition of 1500 not available to me. See also Biel, *Canonis misse expositio*, lectio 53, vol. 2, pp. 328–30: "*Effundetur*, non dicitur secundum partem sed secundum se totum. Liquor quippe qui de vase funditur secundum partem, fundi quidem dicitur, sed non effundi. De sanguinem autem christi hic dicitur *effundetur*, id est totaliter et penitus de corpore fundetur. Quamvis autem una gutta tam preciosi sanguinis sufficiens fuisset pro totius mundi redemptione, ut vult beatus Anselmus . . . et beatus Bernardus, voluit tamen christus ipsum liberaliter et largiter fundere, ut dilectionis sue et virtutis magnitudinem demonstraret, quatenus ad se super omnia diligendum nos invitaret. Cetera quidem omnia deus fecit in pondere, numero et mensura, non sic in sui effusione sanguinis. Ibi enim nequem numerum servavit, ut centum aut mille guttulas funderet. . . . Sed totum dedit, totum fundit, ut copiosa esset apud eum redemptio. . . . Effundendus igitur erat sanguis, non de capite tantum aut tantum de manibus et pedibus sed de his et toto residuo corpore. . . . Verum quicquid sit de numero vulnerum, certum est quod totus sanguis effluxerat. . . . Neque tantum semel effusus est, sed vicibus multis. Unde preter effusionem eius in circumcisione, sex vicibus legitur effusus in passione. Prior in oratione facta in orto post cenam ultima. . . . Sexto in lateris aperitione, de qua idem IOH.: Et unus militum lancea eius aperuit. et continuo exivit sanguis et aqua."

61. For the statement in Clement VI's bull *Unigenitus* (issued 1343) that one drop of Christ's blood is enough to save the whole world, see Vincent, *Holy Blood*, p. 34 n. 8 and p. 110, and Denzinger, pp. 300–301. For Bernard on waves of blood, see sermon 22, *in Cantica Canticorum*, sect. 3 (7), in Bernard of Clairvaux, *S. Bernardi Opera*, vol. 1, p. 133: "Ad cumulum postremo pietatis *tradidit in mortem animam suam* [Isa. 53.12], et de proprio latere protulit pretium satisfactionis quo placares Patrem; per quod illum plane ad se versiculum traxit: *Apud Dominum misericordia, et copiosa apud eum redemptio* [Ps. 129.7]. Prorsus copiosa, quia non gutta, sed unda sanguinis largiter per quin-

que partes corporis emanavit." The passage is cited by Bonaventure in *Sermo* 2, *de nostra redemptione, Opera omnia*, vol. 9, p. 726, who also emphasizes "non . . . gutta sed . . . sanguinis unda." It is referred to by Biel, *Canonis misse expositio*, lectio 53, cited in n. 60 above.

62. See Catherine of Siena, Letter T163, *Le Lettere*, vol. 3, pp. 43–45, esp. p. 44: "Or vi levate su con una pazienzia e vera umiltà, a seguitare l' Agnello mansueto, col cuore liberale largo e caritativo: e abbandonare voi per lui, imparando da esso Gesù che per darci la vita della Grazia, perdè l' amore del corpo suo. E in segno di larghezza egli aperse tutto sè medesimo; e poi che fu morto in segno d' amore, del costato suo fece bagno." Letter T166, *Le Lettere*, vol. 3, pp. 59–63, esp. p. 60, asserts: ". . . solo Cristo crocifisso fu quello Agnello che coll' amore ineffabile svenò e aperse il corpo suo, dandoci sè in bagno e in medicina, e in cibo, e in vestimento, e in letto dove ci possiamo riposare." And see the quotation in n. 57 above.

63. The Council of Vienne pronounced in 1311–12 that Christ was already dead when his side was pierced—a position taken in opposition to the views of Peter Olivi. See Denzinger, pp. 283–84; A. Michel, "Forme du corps"; Burr, *Persecution of Peter Olivi*, pp. 73–80; idem, *The Spiritual Franciscans*, pp. 151–58; and Vincent, *Holy Blood*, p. 105 n. 61.

64. Gerhard, *Tractatus*, p. 467. It is also worth noting that John Peckham and Roger Marston argued in the 1270s that Christ produced bloody rather than ordinary sweat because his perfect complexion would naturally have produced the most perfect of humors: blood. Although a naturalistic rather than a supernaturalist interpretation of the production of *sanguis Christi*, such ratiocination also associates blood especially with Christ's power and perfection. Boureau, *Théologie, science et censure*, pp. 242–44.

65. Pfeiffer, *Deutsche Mystiker*, vol. 1, p. 378. On this passage, see also Richstätter, *Die Herz-Jesu-Verehrung*, p. 56.

66. Mechtild of Magdeburg, *Das fliessende Licht*, bk 6, chap. 24, vol. 1, pp. 233–34; trans. in Mechtild, *The Flowing Light*, p. 252. Note the parallel to Nicholas of Cusa's idea of Christ's humanity continuing during the *triduum*; see Chapter 5 at nn. 66–69.

67. See Chapter 8 n. 15.

68. Aquinas also stresses that Christ cries out at the moment of death to show that he succumbs by choice. Even though others slew him, violence prevails in the end because Christ wills that it should. See ST 3, q. 47, art. 1, pp. 842–43.

69. Grosseteste, *De cessatione legalium*, pt 3, sect. 6, paras. 8–9, pp. 150–51. See also Grosseteste, "De sanguine Christi." And see Dales, *Rational Soul*, pp. 43–44; Holtz, "Cults," p. 219; and Chapter 4 nn. 73 and 74.

70. See Chapter 5 at n. 52.

71. See Bonaventure's sermon *de nostra redemptione*, cited in Chapter 4 n. 79, and n. 69 above on Grosseteste.

72. See Lisch, "Geschichte der Heiligen-Bluts-Kapelle," p. 319, quoting a description from the fourteenth century.

73. On Bruges, see Toussaert, *Le sentiment religieux en Flandre*, p. 261, and Holtz, "Cults," p. 91. For a supposed liquefaction in the seventeenth century in Pairis-Lützel in the Alsace, see Kolb, *Vom Heiligen Blut*, p. 19. Such stories were also told about Weingarten; see Heuser, "'Heilig-Blut'," p. 133. And see Holtz, p. 91, for stress on blood at Weingarten, Bruges, and Weissenau as liquid. On the liquefaction of the blood of St. Januarius in Naples, see Roux, *Le sang*, pp. 202–3.

74. Process of canonization, chap. 3, para. 24, AASS March, vol. 3 (1865), p. 749.

75. J. König, ed., *Die Chronik der Anna von Munzingen*, pp. 189–90. And note the emphasis on wine/blood as liquid in Biel, *Canonis misse expositio*, lectio 52, vol. 2, p. 304: "In passione facta est redemptio nostra, effusione sanguinis, quod significatur in sacramento sanguinis sub specie vini liquentis."

76. Cited in Rhodes, "The Body of Christ," p. 393, from Durham Univ., Cosin MS V.III.8, fol. 23v. The author of the Middle English *Goad of Love* prays to be "softened" and "dipped" in Christ's precious blood; also cited in Rhodes, p. 412 n. 37. Julian of Norwich, *Showings*, Long Text, chap. 7, sees the blood that issues like pellets from Christ's bleeding head as first brown-red and thick but becoming bright red; see Chapter 8 n. 22.

77. Emphasizing the image of blood as heat, an English preaching manual admonishes: "As the nails of the cross were warmed by the blood of Christ [*sanguine Christi calefiebant clavi in cruce*], so ought sinners to be inflamed in charity to the service of Christ by the blood of Christ." In *Quinti belli sacri scriptores minores*, ed. Reinhold Röhricht (Geneva: J.-G. Fick, 1879), quoted in Vincent, *Holy Blood*, p. 37.

78. This is a prominent theme in Gerhard of Cologne, *Tractatus.*

79. Richstätter, *Die Herz-Jesu-Verehrung*, p. 225, citing Niederdeutsches Gebetbuch, Münster, Bibliothek des Vereins für Geschichte Westfalens, Handschrift 8, 151a. My trans. from Richstätter's modern German. For the continuation of this theme in Martin Luther, see Chapter 10 n. 78.

80. "Expositio passionis," in Dionysius, *Dionysii carthusiani opera omnia*, vol. 42, pp. 489–587. Kent Emery, in his prolegomena to the study of Dionysius, *Opera selecta*, vol. 1, CCCM 121 A, pp. 156–57, says that the arguments for authenticity are "fairly strong."

81. According to Stoelen, "Denys le Chartreux," col. 431, Dionysius accompanied Nicholas of Cusa on his legation to the Rhineland from August 1451 to March 1452. He may indeed have been part of the legation somewhat longer. See Emery, prolegomenon to Dionysius, *Opera selecta*, p. 19 n. 19. In any case, he would certainly have been aware of Cusa's investigation of the miraculous bloods in Brandenburg.

82. Dionysius repeats his argument about the miraculous nature of the blood in his discussion of Christ's bloody sweat in the garden, where he says that the doctors agree the sweat was "verum sanguinem et naturalem" but not shed in a natural way; "unde sanguis iste fuit miraculosus quoad modum profluentiae, sed naturalis quoad veritatem suae exsistentiae, sicut etiam oportet dicere de sanguine et aqua fusis de latere Christi jam mortui"; see "Expositio passionis," p. 494.

83. "Expositio passionis," art. 25, pp. 545–46.

84. See Chapter 1 at n. 80 for the argument that scholars have tended to overemphasize the eucharistic connotations of blood and neglect the ways in which it represents baptism and penance.

85. The Franciscan Stephen Fridolin of Nuremberg (d. 1498) argued that "all goods of belief and baptism, the manifold fruits of Corpus Christi, the power and grace of holy oil, in short all the sacraments of the New Testament that people pray for and sing of in the mass and the office, and what they show in Nuremberg [that is, the holy lance], and all we preserve of the blood and heart of Christ—all this and all our blessedness come out of the heart of Christ." See Richstätter, *Die Herz-Jesu-Verehrung*, p.

186. The close connection of the sacraments and literal vestiges of Christ—relics—is striking. For the Franciscan provincial in Cologne, Henry of Herp (d. circa 1478), who saw the side wound as the "door of the sacraments," especially baptism and eucharist, see Gougaud, *Dévotions et pratiques ascétiques*, p. 109. In letter T189, Catherine of Siena saw the blood and water from Christ's side as two kinds of baptism—the baptism of water and the baptism of martyrdom: Letter 84 in *Epistolario*, pp. 340–42. John Fisher (d. 1535) argued that the blood of Christ is "sprinkled abroad to cleanse and put away sin" wherever the sacraments are repeated. Fisher, *English Works*, p. 111.

Chapter 8. Blood as Separated and Shed

1. Aquinas, ST 3, q. 83, art. 2, ra 2, p. 912, col. 1.

2. Ibid., ST 3, q. 76, art. 2, ra 1, p. 895, col. 1; trans. *Summa theologica*, vol. 5, p. 2450. ST 3, q. 74, art. 1, pp. 889–90, also stresses the importance, in the eucharist, of the *separation* of the bread and wine as an image of the separation of blood from body in the passion; art. 8, p. 891, col. 3, stresses the special connection of wine/blood with the passion. For Alexander of Hales, and later Herveus Natalis, similarly stressing both the double institution as a sign of separation of Christ's blood and the connection of blood with the passion, see Lépin, *L'idée du sacrifice*, pp. 165–67 and 225 n. 1.

3. Biel, *Canonis misse expositio*, lectio 52, vol. 2, p. 309.

4. Ibid., lectio 53, vol. 2, pp. 332–33; see also pp. 328–29 for an emphasis on wounding and drops.

5. Holtz, "Cults," p. 35 n. 77, and Kruse, "Die historischen Heilig-Blut-Schriften," pp. 108–9. The relationship of the preface to the texts concerning Weingarten and Mantua, which follow it in the manuscript, is unclear; see Holtz, p. 28 n. 63, and Kruse, pp. 96–102. I have used Holtz's translation with modifications.

6. Gerhard, *Tractatus*, p. 467.

7. See Holtz, "Cults," pp. 52–53, and Bynum, "Blood of Christ," pp. 691–92.

8. *Thomae de Argentina . . . Commentaria*, dist. 11, q. 2, art. 3, fol. 97v, col. 2, cited in Lépin, *L'idée du sacrifice*, pp. 225 n. 2.

9. Aquinas, ST 3, q. 74, art. 1, pp. 889–90. The point is made repeatedly.

10. *Hervei Natalis . . . Commentaria*, dist. 8, q. 2, p. 342, col. 2, cited in Lépin, *L'idée du sacrifice*, p. 225 n. 1.

11. Biel, *Canonis misse expositio*, lectio 52, vol. 2, p. 304.

12. See Bynum, *Holy Feast*, pp. 48–51, and Chapter 7 at n. 6. Aquinas, ST 3, q. 74, art. 1, pp. 889–90, esp. 890, col. 1, quotes "the gloss" as saying the eucharist should be in two species because the whole church "constituitur ex diversis fidelibus, sicut panis conficitur ex diversis granis, et vinum fluit ex diversis uvis." Although the point is that the whole church is gathered together from individuals, the difference between *conficitur* and *fluit* is noticeable. (The passage comes originally from Augustine, *Tractates on the Gospel of John*, 26.17, and is found in the *Glossa ordinaria* for John 6.43; see *Biblia latina cum Glossa ordinaria: Facsimile Reprint*, vol. 4, p. 241.) By the High Middle Ages, there are thinkers such as Durandus of St. Pourçain (d. 1334) who interpret both bread and wine not as gathered but as pressed out. See Durandus, *In Sententias . . . Commentariorum*, dist. 11, q. 4, ad 2m, no. 13, fol. 276b, cited in Lépin, *L'idée du sacrifice*, p. 222 n. 1: "Per panem, qui fit ex multis granis in area excussis, deinde in mola attritus, et per vinum, quod confluit ex multis racemis in torculari compressis, sufficienter

repraesentatur amaritudo passionis Christi." Unlike Herveus, Thomas of Strasbourg, and Biel, Durandus is here stressing both bread and wine in the mass as images of the passion.

13. See Chapter 1 nn. 15, 16, and 29, and Chapter 7 at nn. 58–61. For emphasis in the Weingarten liturgy on blood as both drops (*guttae, stillae*) and living, red liquid (*ruber*), see Chapter 6 n. 62.

14. Peter Damian, *Opusculum* 19: *De abdicatione episcopatus* [Letter 72], chap. 5, PL 145, col. 432B; trans. Blum in *Letters of Peter Damian*, vol. 3, pp. 129–30; Dinzelbacher, "Das Blut Christi," p. 425, n. 147, says this is the first such vision.

15. "Visio monachi de Eynsham," chap. 2, 10–11, and 54 in *Revelation to the Monk of Evesham*, pp. 21, 31–32, and 105–6; trans. from the abbreviated version in Roger of Wendover's chronicle in "The Monk of Evesham's Vision," in Gardiner, ed., *Visions of Heaven and Hell*, pp. 198, 202–3, 214. Note the stress on "veins of a living man."

16. See the passage from the "Hundred Pater Nosters" discussed in Chapter 1 at n. 17 and at nn. 36–41 below; see also Chapter 7 n. 76 for the *Prickynge of Love*, in which blood drops into the "mouth of heart" and the "marrow of soul."

17. See Chapter 7 n. 50.

18. See Chapter 2 nn. 62–65.

19. On the general tendency, see Kaye, *Economy and Nature*; on the piety of enumeration, see Chapter 1 n. 16.

20. Tubach, *Index exemplorum*, no. 713, p. 59, and Ryan, "'Reign of Blood'," p. 146 n. 64.

21. See Chapter 7 n. 61.

22. Julian of Norwich, *Book of Showings*, Long Text, chap. 7, vol. 2, pp. 311–13; trans. in *Julian: Showings*, pp. 187–88.

23. On the Röttgen (or Bonn) pietà, see Hawel, *Die Pietà*, pp. 63–66, who dates it to circa 1300; Schiller, *Iconography*, vol. 2, p. 180, dates it to circa 1370 and describes the dripping blood as emphasized sculpturally and with color. Both the Fritzlar and the Wetzlar pietàs show blood dripping in discrete round pellets. See Passarge, *Das deutsche Vesperbild*, pp. 99 and 120; Reinhold, "Das Fritzlarer Vesperbild"; and Krönig, "Rheinische Vesperbilder," pp. 121, 138, and 157. Krönig, pp. 181–91, argues for an early date (before 1300) for the Röttgen pietà and suggests that the Fritzlar pietà is before 1350, the Wetzlar from the later fourteenth century, and the Leubus about 1400.

24. Krönig, "Rheinische Vesperbilder," pp. 117–19; there are three such pietàs now at Marienstern. On the pietà from Marienstern shown in Plate 16 (from ca. 1360–70), see the exhibition catalogue, Oexle et al., *Zeit und Ewigkeit: 128 Tage in St. Marienstern*, p. 112. There is a quite similar pietà from Burgeis in south Tirol; see Krönig, "Rheinische Vesperbilder," p. 189. Krönig's interest is in arguing for the priority of the Bonn pietà over the middle German group (Coburg, Naumburg, etc.); the depiction of blood does not figure in his analysis. For emphasis on blood in a woodcut pietà, see Parshall et al., *Origins of European Printmaking*, p. 141. I am grateful to C. Mohr of the Landesamt für Denkmalpflege-Hessen for information about the medieval condition of the Fritzlar pietà.

25. *Gemäldegalerie Berlin*, Prestel Museum Guide, 3rd rev. ed. (Munich: Prestel, 2002), p. 19, Gemäldegalerie, Berlin, Kat.-Nr. 2005.

26. See Chapter 7 at nn. 2 and 5, and Plates 21 and 22. In both the Landsberger Altar of circa 1437 (Plate 22) and the Christ on the cross in Plate 20, the wounds can

be described as blood rosettes; the blood is vividly red. On the date and provenance of the image in Plates 20–21, see Chapter 7 n. 2.

27. The side wound in the pietà from Marienmünster in Mittelzell on Reichenau island is described by Dinzelbacher as shaped like a bunch of grapes; see Dinzelbacher, "Das Blut Christi," p. 421. Reinhold, "Das Fritzlarer Vesperbild," describes the wounds on the Fritzlar pietà as "Blutstrauben." Passarge, *Das deutsche Vesperbild*, p. 99, relates the "Blutstrauben" of the wounds to the five-petaled "rosa mystica" of the Virgin and hence to her "fruit," Christ the host. Hawel, *Die Pietà*, p. 66, says Bonaventure saw red roses as a symbol of Christ's wounds and points to the roses on the sockle of the Röttgen pietà. According to Reinhold, the side wound on the Fritzlar pietà "certainly" had a relic container attached where we see the two holes; the side wound, unlike the hand wounds, is concave. See Plate 15 and Reinhold, "Das Fritzlarer Vesperbild."

28. See the Röttgen, Fritzlar, and Wetzlar pietàs.

29. Hawel, *Die Pietà*, p. 64, asserts that the grapes/wounds on the Röttgen pietà are "a deliberate reference to the mystical grapes of Christ." The latter statement seems to me to go beyond the evidence and to reflect the over-interpretation of fifteenth-century piety as eucharistic, of which I spoke in Chapter 1.

30. On the pietà from Anröchte near Soest (perhaps as late as 1400), now in the Westfälisches Landesmuseum in Münster, see Jászai, *Gotische Skulpturen*, pp. 17 and 65–66, and Krönig, "Rheinische Vesperbilder," p. 185.

31. See n. 53 below.

32. For a wonderful and complex treatment of the depiction of blood that suggests how blood can mediate between a viewer and the divine, see Peers, *Sacred Shock*, pp. 35–58.

33. Rohling, *Blood of Christ*, p. 145.

34. See Chapter 3 n. 141. Charroux provides an example of devotion to parallel bodily relics of foreskin and blood from the circumcision: see Barbier de Montault, *Oeuvres complètes*, vol. 7, p. 528.

35. There may also be a sense in which blood is a mark of special favor, as it appears to be in the case of stigmata—a mostly female phenomenon. G. Lewis, *By Women, for Women*, p. 83, says flowing blood (in this case bleeding from the mouth of a nun) is a sign of election because "blood is a life force." See also Weinstein and Bell, *Saints and Society*, p. 149. The natural bleeding of menstruation was also, however, understood as a mark of fallenness; see Blamires, "Beneath the Pulpit," p. 149; Wood, "The Doctors' Dilemma"; and L'Hermite-Leclercq, "Le lait et le sang."

36. "Hundred Pater Nosters," p. 172.

37. Ibid., p. 175.

38. Ibid., p. 177. In another example of this sort of experiential piety, Ludolf of Saxony, in his *Life of Christ*, explained how Christians should conform themselves to Christ (*actus conformationis*), not only by meditating on how Christ was slapped but also by slapping themselves. (The slap should, however, be "moderate.") See Ludolf, *Vita Jesu Christi . . .* , pt. 2, chap. 60, para. 3, vol. 4, p. 497.

39. "Hundred Pater Nosters," p. 178.

40. Ibid., p. 174.

41. Ibid., pp. 173 and 175.

42. Ibid., p. 179.

43. For the case of Margery Kempe, see n. 68 below. The theme of Christians as

murderers of Christ was not new in the fifteenth century; see pseudo-Anselm, *Meditatio* VII (addressing Christ): "Quoties armavi me contra te in alienam mortem," PL 158, col. 742C. Wilmart, *Auteurs spirituels*, p. 194, attributes this text to William of Auvergne (d. 1249).

44. See R. Naz, "Sang (effusion de)," *Dictionnaire de droit canonique*, vol. 7 (Paris: Letouzey et Ané, 1965) cols. 870–71. For a summary of the medieval canonists' position on clerical involvement in blood judgments, see Baldwin, *Masters, Princes and Merchants*, vol. 1, pp. 178–9 and 186–91, and vol. 2, pp. 118–19 and 124–30. Canonists and theologians in the thirteenth century debated whether clerics could serve as judges in any cases that might involve criminal charges since even those who relaxed cases to the secular arm could be deemed tainted by blood judgments.

45. The idea that the glance of a menstruating woman clouds glass was a trope used to illustrate the scientific principle of "action at a distance." See Boureau, *Théologie, science et censure*, p. 241, for an example of this in a quodlibet of Roger Marston, who borrows it from Peckham, along with the assertion that seeing a wolf makes men mute. As Miramon has argued ("La fin d'un tabou?" and "Déconstruction"), such throwaway lines taken from folk tradition are not really correctly described as taboos against either women or wolves. And see Buschinger, "Sang versé, sang guérisseur."

46. See Chapter 1 nn. 114–16.

47. For examples of objects that bleed to protest or accuse, see Bynum, *Holy Feast*, p. 329 nn. 135 and 138; Geary, *Furta sacra*, p. 153, and Boussel, *Des reliques*, pp. 270–71.

48. See, for example, the case of the relic of Jane Mary of Maillé; Chapter 7 n. 74. Thus various themes come together. Hosts, relics, and bodies that bleed seem both to demonstrate thereby the life within them (and their sacrality) and to accuse perpetrators.

49. Boureau, *Théologie, science et censure*, pp. 227–28 and 244–91.

50. See Sinka, "Christological Mysticism," p. 126, and on Margaret, see Barbier de Montault, *Oeuvres complètes*, vol. 7, p. 385. (The wounds, in bleeding, of course intercede as well as accuse. Mechtild of Magdeburg makes them parallel to the breasts of Mary, which also do not dry up until Judgment. See Mechtild, *Das fliessende Licht*, bk 2, chap. 3, vol. 1, pp. 39–41.)

51. London, British Library MS Add. 37049, fol. 20r; see Hogg, ed., *An Illustrated Yorkshire Carthusian Miscellany*, vol. 3, p. 22. On this manuscript, see Morgan, "Longinus," p. 515, and Hennessy, "Morbid Devotions," p. 125. Morgan points out that most wounded-heart poetry is an admonition to avoid sin.

52. Wildhaber, "Feiertagschristus." See also Berliner, "Arma Christi," p. 68, who sees the motif more broadly as "Christ attacked by the sins of the world," and Gray, *Themes and Images*, pp. 51–54, who gives examples of the theme in devotional literature. Rothkrug, *Religious Practices and Collective Perceptions*, p. 106, draws a parallel between the "Feiertagschristus" image and the idea in the *Malleus Maleficarum* that male witches crucify Christ by shooting arrows at him. Medieval writers occasionally understood unworthy reception as itself killing Christ; see, for example, Gerald of Wales, *Gemma ecclesiastica*, chap. 50, in *Opera*, vol. 2, p. 139.

53. There is much evidence for blood piety as reproach and accusation in Duffy, *Stripping*, passim, esp. pp. 102–10, 238–56; and Bennett, *Poetry of the Passion*, pp. 43–50. By the fifteenth century, we find sculpted images in which blood is depicted with red

wires; see the examples from Lübeck and Willisau discussed in Kolb, *Vom Heiligen Blut*, pp. 169–72.

54. Peebles, *The Legend of Longinus*, pp. 1–131, and Morgan, "Longinus."

55. The weapons that attacked Christ were also understood to release love. See the discussion of the iconographical motif of "Christ crucified by the virtues" in Chapter 9 at n. 23 and Plate 30.

56. James of Voragine, *Legenda aurea*, ed. Graesse, chap. 1, p. 9. And see Schiller, *Iconography*, vol. 2, p. 189, referring to Panofsky, "Imago Pietatis," p. 288.

57. *Ancient Devotions to the Sacred Heart . . . by Carthusian Monks*, pp. 185–86. On John, see Cardona, "Torralba (Jean)," DS, vol. 15, cols. 1054–55.

58. Bede, *In Lucae Euangelium Expositio*, 24.40, ed. Hurst, p. 420. The text is cited in James of Voragine, *Legenda aurea*, p. 322.

59. Schrade, "Beiträge zur Erklärung," 170–72. On the early medieval background to this sense of blood as blame and guilt, see now Fulton, *From Judgment to Passion*.

60. Bonaventure, *Sermo* 2, *de nostra redemptione*, in *Opera omnia*, vol. 9, p. 726.

61. Marguerite of Oingt, *Speculum*, chap. 1, para. 4, in *Les oeuvres*, pp. 90–91; trans. Petroff, *Medieval Women's Visionary Literature*, p. 291.

62. Schiller, *Iconography*, vol. 2, p. 197. The theme of using supposed Jewish desecrations to warn Christians of the consequences of their sins against God was an old one. See for example Gerhard of Cologne, discussed in Bynum, "Blood of Christ," pp. 699–704.

63. See Browe, "Die scholastische Theorie," p. 327. The Bergen story is parallel to Wilsnack in that a surviving-the-flood miracle vindicates itself by a later bleeding miracle.

64. I have emphasized in Chapter 3 how early visions and later *Dauerwunder* also differ in that the latter produce material for cult.

65. See Chapter 2 nn. 94–95 above for Waltmann on blood as accusatory. For the elephant analogy, see Capistrano, *De sanguine*, art. 16, sect. B, ed. Terrinca, p. 28*, and ed. Cocci, p. 1383, and the same passage used against Waltmann in Capistrano, "Epistola responsialis ad Everhardum Waltmann," Wolfenbüttel H.A.B. Cod. Guelf. 550 Helmst., fol. 206v.

66. Capistrano, *De sanguine*, arts. 15–16, ed. Terrinca, pp. 25*–29*, and ed. Cocci, pp. 1378–84. See also Browe, "Verwandlungswunder," pp. 161–62, and idem, "Die Hostienschändungen," p. 180. Jews themselves clearly understood that accusations against them had to do especially with blood, gathering it, plotting to acquire it, etc.; see Miri Rubin's discussion of the laments after the Rintfleisch massacres; *Gentile Tales*, p. 101.

67. See Fitzpatrick, "On Eucharistic Sacrifice," who notes that most discussion is not of course of the sacrifice issue at all but of the nature of presence. See also Lépin, *L'idée du sacrifice*. Heesterman, *Broken World*, p. 47, argues that once the crucifixion was understood as a sacrifice it would need to be repeated—that is, it would have to be ritualized. The conflict between a unique historical event and sacrifice, which he sees as a reenacting of the riddle of life and death, meant that "Christian liturgy and dogma wrestled to square the circle of an unrepeatable event that had to be repeated."

68. Kempe, *The Book of Margery Kempe*, ed. Meech and Allen, bk 1, chap. 60, pp. 147–48; and see Dinshaw, "Margery Kempe," p. 231. For a similar sentiment, see the excerpt from a 1522 collection cited by Wachinger, "Die Passion Christi und die Literatur," p. 1: "Es war ein Priester, der het den Passion gepredigt an dem Karfreitag, das

vil Luet weinten. Der nerrisch Priester wolt sie troesten und sprach: 'Nit weinen, lieben Kind! Es ist jetz wol 15 hundert Jar, das es geschehen sol sein; es mag wol erlogen sein. . . ." Wachinger's point is, of course, the satiric nature of the selection but the phenomenon the preacher responded to existed.

69. On the theology of bodily resurrection as a locus for discussions of change and identity, see Bynum, *Resurrection*, and Vidal, "Brains, Bodies, Selves." On the general medieval concern with change, see Bynum, *Metamorphosis and Identity*, esp. pp. 15–36.

70. See above, Chapter 1, nn. 47–50.

71. On purgatory, the basic work is Le Goff, *Birth of Purgatory*. For more recent discussion, see Newman, "On the Threshold of the Dead," and Matsuda, *Death and Purgatory*. On the penitential system, see most recently Ohst, *Pflichtbeichte*.

72. On the concern with death and decay, see Binski, *Medieval Death*, pp. 123–63; Bynum, *Resurrection*, pp. 200–225, 318–29; Swanson, *Religion and Devotion*, pp. 198–203, 212–15, and 233–34; and Rädle, "*Ars moriendi*." On partible burial, see Brown, "Death and the Human Body." On the *transi* tomb, see K. Cohen, *Metamorphosis of a Death Symbol*.

73. Gertrude, *Legatus divinae pietatis*, bk 3, chap. 17, *Oeuvres spirituelles*, vol. 3, pp. 74–76.

74. I made this point in Bynum, "Blood of Christ," pp. 705–7. And see von Staden, "Women and Dirt," p. 7: "Words are not the only bearers of meaning. Matter, too, is a matrix of meanings, and as such it invites interpretation."

75. See Dumézil, "Le sang," and Conticelli, "Sanguis suavis."

76. See Chapter 5 n. 57.

77. For Catherine, see Chapter 7 n. 57; for Pius II, see Chapter 5 n. 55. James of Milan put it explicitly: ". . . you [Christ] cannot be separated from humankind. Is it not exactly because you are ascended to the right hand of the Father that you have relinquished power to human beings that they may . . . have you here on the altar?" See Chapter 7 n. 48.

78. For Multscher, see Chapter 7 n. 5 and Plate 22; for discussion of Christ's scars, see Bede, *In Lucae Euangelium Expositio*, 24.40, p. 420; James of Voragine, *Legenda aurea*, p. 322; and n. 50 above.

79. There is, behind some of my analysis of the symbolic usefulness of blood, an anthropologically informed understanding of natural symbols; see Douglas, *Natural Symbols*. But I have deliberately declined to take the step of reading theological differences as images or expressions of social groupings. For two examples of this kind of analysis, see Gager, "Body-Symbols," and Baschet, "Âme et corps." It is possible to go a little way down this road in analyzing the Hussite demand for the cup. Such analysis also illuminates late fifteenth-century Christian arguments that Jewish desecrators spread conspiracy from town to town by carrying bits of abused eucharistic wafer. One can clearly see, in these two instances, attitudes toward the chalice as expressing power and resistance to power, fantasies of the host as expressing, in complex ways, understandings of inclusion and exclusion (not to mention paranoia). It is even possible to see in the high blood theology of the Dominicans, and in Capistrano's agreement with its ontology, a reflection of their authoritarian role as inquisitors and propagandists for ecclesiastical power. But, in general, fifteenth-century theological positions, whether dissident or orthodox, Franciscan or Dominican, learned or popular, show both such

wide variety and such deep underlying agreement as to discourage efforts to find group identity mirrored in distinctive uses of natural symbols.

80. See Chapter 6 n. 29. For ways blood symbolizes other aspects of redemption, see Chapter 9.

81. See Chapter 7 n. 58, and also nn. 36 and 37 above for references in the "Hundred Pater Nosters" to "purchace" and "raenson."

82. Catherine of Siena, Letter T87, *Le Lettere*, vol. 2, pp. 89–90; trans. in *Letters*, vol. 2, pp. 631–32. When Matthew Paris repeats the argument that the shedding of Christ's blood is greater than the cross upon which he hung, the argument stresses blood as the price of redemption; see Chapter 4 n. 64. For another example of references to blood price in an affective, even erotic text, see *Talkyng*, pp. 7–8. There is a long quotation from the *Talkyng* in Chapter 1.

83. Letter T259, *Le Lettere*, vol. 4, pp. 127–37, esp. pp. 128–29; trans. in *Letters*, vol. 2, pp. 610–11.

84. Margaret Ebner, *Offenbarungen*, p. 146; trans. in *Major Works*, p. 164.

85. Mechtild, *Das fliessende Licht*, vol. 1, bk 6, chap. 24, p. 233; trans. in *The Flowing Light*, pp. 251–52.

86. See n. 83 and Chapter 2 n. 66. In a parallel use of sacrificial language, a sister of Töss in the fourteenth century spoke of herself as a kind of sacrifice for God and the whole world: she "wanted her body to be tortured to serve the Christchild," her skin to be pulled off for his diaper, her veins to make threads for his garments, her marrow pulverized for his gruel, her blood shed for his bath, and "all her flesh [to] be used up for all sinners." See Rublack, "Female Spirituality," pp. 26–27, and G. Lewis, *By Women, for Women*, pp. 21–25, 112, and 229. On a very similar exhortation from a male adviser to a nun, see Henry of Nördlingen's letter to Margaret Ebner in *Margaretha Ebner*, p. 234, ll. 47–50; cited in Schmidt and Hindsley, "Introduction" to Margaret Ebner, *Major Works*, p. 54.

87. Poor, *Mechthild of Magdeburg*.

88. Gray, *Themes and Images*, p. 142. As another example of the ubiquity of Christ as sacrifice in late medieval devotion, one might mention the East Window in the cathedral of Christchurch, Canterbury, influentially analyzed by Norman Bryson a generation ago as an example of the supremacy of the discursive over the figural in art (a point with which I do not agree); see Bryson, *Word and Image*, pp. 1–4, 21, and 254 n. 8. Circling the square central panel of Christ on the cross are a priest sacrificing a lamb and marking the lintel, two figures carrying grapes, Moses striking water from the rock, and the sacrifice of Isaac by Abraham. The images themselves make clear not only the identification of Christ with the sacrificial lamb of the Old Testament but also God's substitution of something for earlier intended victims. The body lifted on the cross is parallel both to the lamb whose blood marks the doorway, protecting his people against passing death, and to the animal substituted by God for the child who, without this substitution, would have been offered to slaughter.

89. Dorlandus, *Viola animae*, treatise 7 (not paginated). The rubric reads: "Cur cum sanguineis vulneribus."

90. Aquinas, ST 3, q. 48, art. 3, p. 844, col. 3, and q. 46, art. 4, pp. 839–40 respectively. I return to these in Chapter 10.

91. Capistrano, *De sanguine*, art. 11, ed. Terrinca, p. 19*, and ed. Cocci, "Il Sangue di Cristo . . . ," pp. 1369–70.

92. We should not forget, of course, that to the Franciscans the stress was on the fact of death, rather than on the blood per se. See above, Chapter 5. Nonetheless, even to the Franciscans, devotion to blood as a making present of death was not a demotion of blood veneration. Quite the contrary, as we have seen. It was primarily Franciscans who supported host miracles and blood relics.

93. Dawson, *The Mongol Mission*, pp. 73–74, cited in Swanson, *Religion and Devotion*, pp. 24–25. See also the statement of faith from the preface to the legislation of the Fourth Lateran Council (1215): "having suffered and died on the wood of the cross for the salvation of the human race, he descended to the underworld, rose, . . . and ascended. . . . [And] there is indeed one universal church of the faithful . . . , in which Jesus Christ is both priest and sacrifice." Tanner, ed., *Decrees of the Ecumenical Councils*, vol. 1, p. 230; cited in Swanson, *Religion and Devotion*, p. 22.

Chapter 9. Late Medieval Soteriology

1. See Pelikan, *Growth of Medieval Theology*, pp. 106–57 and 184–214, and Fitzpatrick, "On Eucharistic Sacrifice."

2. A version of portions of this chapter has appeared in Bynum, "Power." It is reprinted by permission of Oxford University Press.

3. The classic statements are Rashdall, *Idea of Atonement*, and Rivière, *Le dogme de la rédemption*. For a quick summary of the standard textbook account, see the article "Atonement," in *The Oxford Dictionary of the Christian Church*, ed. F. L. Cross and E. A. Livingstone, 3rd ed. (Oxford: Oxford University Press, 1997), pp. 122–24. A recent effort at theological restatement is A. W. Bartlett, *Cross Purposes*. A very different effort to replace Anselm with a sort of super-exemplarist understanding of the crucifixion as reconciliation and embrace is Volf, *Exclusion and Embrace*, and idem, "Forgiveness, Reconciliation, and Justice." See also Hulmes, "Semantics of Sacrifice." For a dismissal of much of medieval (and modern) atonement theory as amoral or "nothing less than terrorism," see E. L. Peterman, "Redemption, Theology of," *New Catholic Encyclopedia* (New York: McGraw-Hill, 1967), vol. 12, pp. 144–60. On recent theological interest in, and doubts about, sacrifice, see the introduction to Gerhards and Richter, eds., *Das Opfer*, and Wohlmuth, "Opfer—Verdrängung und Wiederkehr eines schwierigen Begriffs."

4. Anselm, *Cur Deus Homo*, in *Opera omnia*, vol. 2, pp. 37–133; Southern, *St. Anselm and His Biographer*, pp. 77–121; idem, *Saint Anselm, a Portrait*, pp. 197–227. But we should note that Anselm did not locate any necessity in God. In his *Meditatio redemptionis humanae*, he says explicitly: "Non enim deus egebat ut hoc modo hominem salvum faceret. . . ." In *Opera omnia*, vol. 3, p. 86.

5. Abelard, *Commentaria in epistolam . . . ad Romanos*, bk. 2, in *Opera theologica*, vol. 1, pp. 113–18. And see Clanchy, *Abelard*, pp. 283–87.

6. A. W. Bartlett, *Cross Purposes*. See also Wallace and Smith, eds., *Curing Violence*; and Merback, "Reverberations of Guilt." For a similar reinterpretation, without the extravagance of Bartlett or the use of Girard, see Dalferth, "Christ Died for Us." On Girard, see Hamerton-Kelly, "Religion and the Thought of René Girard," and Schwager, *Must There Be Scapegoats?* In contrast to religionists, anthropologists have not been not very sympathetic to Girard or Walter Burkert recently; see Bell, *Ritual Theory, Ritual Practice*, pp. 172–75.

7. See Bynum, "Power"; the works cited in n. 12; Greshake, "Der Wandel der Erlösungsvorstellungen"; and idem, "Erlösung und Freiheit."

8. Bernard, "De gradibus," 3.6–12, in *Sancti Bernardi opera*, vol. 3, pp. 20–26. See also "Liber de diligendo Deo," in *Sancti Bernardi opera*, vol. 3, esp. pp. 123–24 and 138–44. And see Javelet, *Image et ressemblance*, and Bynum, "Monsters, Medians . . . in Bernard," in *Metamorphosis and Identity*, pp. 113–62.

9. On Julian, see nn. 47 and 48.

10. For more on this, see E. Cohen, "Animated Pain of the Body," and Bynum, "Power."

11. Abelard, "The Personal Letters," p. 92; trans. in *Letters of Abelard and Heloise*, Letter 4, pp. 152–53.

12. The most balanced account of the entire issue is Pelikan, *Growth*, pp. 106–57; and see Luscombe, "St. Anselm and Abelard."

13. Peter Lombard, *Sententiae*, bk. 3, dist. 19.1, vol. 2, p. 118. See De Clerck, "Questions de sotériologie médiévale," on the later history of Lombard's teaching.

14. Aquinas, ST 3, qq. 46–49 and 83, pp. 838–47 and 911–15. And see n. 19.

15. See epigraph to this volume from Bernard of Clairvaux and the discussion in Chapter 11, first two sections

16. See Chapter 7 n. 69. The emphasis can also be seen as an attempt to avoid any implication that God is passive victim or that destruction (*mutatio*) can touch God.

17. Pelikan, *Reformation of Church and Dogma*, pp. 22–25. On Biel, see Oberman, *Harvest*, pp. 266–75. And see Biel, *Canonis misse expositio*, lectio 53, vol. 2, p. 329, where Biel, who refers frequently to the *pretium redemptionis*, concludes that Christ poured out all his blood "ut dilectionis sue et virtutis magnitudinem *demonstraret*, quatenus ad se super omnia diligendum nos *invitaret*" (emphasis added).

18. It is sometimes even suggested that academic soteriology is satisfaction theory, whereas popular devotion is more exemplarist; a glance at the texts I quote in this book shows that this is not correct. Devotional texts are filled with references to *pretium* and *satisfactio*.

19. Aquinas, ST 3, q. 46, art. 3, p. 839, esp. col. 2. And see q. 46, art. 4, p. 839: "Respondeo dicendum quod convenientissimum fuit christus pati mortem crucis. primo quidem, propter exemplum virtutis. . . ."

20. "Visio monachi de Eynsham," in *Revelation to the Monk of Evesham*, chap. 54, pp. 105–6, citation at p. 106; trans. in Gardiner, ed., *Visions*, p. 214. For another example, see Peter Damian, Sermon 66 *De sancta Columba*, PL 144, col. 884A.

21. See Chapter 8 n. 68.

22. *Talkyng*, pp. 33 and 50. See also p. 8: "Mi sunnes haþ me fuiled. . . . what shal þenne þe pris of þi deore blood don: þat sched was on Roode. . . . a drope of þi derworþe blod miȝte wasschen a wey alle Mennes sunnes . . ."

23. Kraft, "Die Bildallegorie der Kreuzigung"; Hamburger, *Visual and the Visionary*, pp. 121–24; and Newman, *God and the Goddesses*, pp. 159–67. Laabs, *Malerei und Plastik*, p. 76, claims that the Doberan image is bloodier than others. The bloodiest of the twenty-five images reproduced by Kraft appears to be the fresco (late medieval but of uncertain specific date) from Malujowice in Poland. On *arma Christi*, see Chapter 8 at nn. 55–57.

24. O'Collins, "Redemption: Some Crucial Issues."

25. See nn. 5 and 11.

26. Fitzpatrick, "On Eucharistic Sacrifice," pp. 131–33 and 150.

27. If it conflicts with modern assumptions, it is not in science but in contemporary philosophy—which would reject Platonic participation and define "representation" very differently—that one should locate the conflict.

28. See Tierney, *Foundations.*

29. See n. 8.

30. On concomitance, see Megivern, *Concomitance*, and Bynum, "Violent Imagery," pp. 20–23. As Bauerschmidt, *Julian*, p. 220 n. 72, points out, the idea was widespread and regularly included in instruction for the laity. On the saint as synecdoche for community, see Otter, *Inventiones*, p. 34.

31. Aquinas, ST 3, q. 48, art. 2, ra 1, p. 844, col. 3.

32. For ways in which it is crucial to the doctrine of purgatory, see Bynum, "Power," pp. 191–94.

33. Anti-Judaism, misogyny, and scapegoating of the lower classes echo palpably in the litanies of those responsible for injury to God. For more on this, see Bynum, "Violent Imagery," pp. 26–32.

34. See the poem from an English commonplace book of the fourteenth century that speaks of union with Christ as the incorporation of our blood in his: "I wolde ben clad in cristes skyn / That ran so longe on blode / & gon t'is herte & taken myn In." Gray, "Five Wounds," p. 129.

35. See Life of Alice of Schaerbeke, chap. 2, para. 22–23, and chap. 3, para. 26–27, AASS June, vol. 2 (1867), pp. 475–76. For another example, see Life of Christina Mirabilis, chap. 7, 11, and 12, AASS July, vol. 5 (1868), pp. 651–62. On Catherine of Genoa, see n. 37.

36. On Hadewijch, see Bynum, *Holy Feast*, pp. 241–42. On Adelheid, see Hindsley, *Mystics of Engelthal*, p. 62. And see the words of another Adelheid, a sister of Töss, cited in Chapter 8 n. 86, which also relate a woman's bodily suffering and service to the redemption of "all sinners."

37. As reported by the redactor in *Vita*, chap. 27, in Catherine of Genoa, *S. Caterina Adorno*, vol. 2, p. 297, and in *Vita mirabile*, chap. 43, in ibid., pp. 146–47; trans. in *Life and Doctrine of Catherine of Genoa*, chap. 33, pp. 143–44, with my changes. It is impossible to know how much of the language attributed to Catherine is her own, but it is sufficient for my purposes here that the sentiment was typically associated with women.

38. On suffering for others as a theme especially characteristic of women's lives, see McNamara, "The Need to Give"; Newman, "On the Threshold"; and Sweetman, "Thomas of Cantimpré." On women's illness as a suffering with Christ that releases souls from purgatory, see Garber, *Feminine* Figurae, pp. 109–26.

39. Julian, *Book of Showings*, Long Text, chap. 51, vol. 2, pp. 513–45, esp. pp. 533–34; trans. in *Julian: Showings*, pp. 274–75.

40. Julian explains this in her theology of God as mother; *Book of Showings*, Long Text, chaps. 52–63, vol. 2, pp. 546–618. As Barbara Newman puts it (*God and the Goddesses*, p. 228), Julian "means not simply that Christ is a perfect or complete human being, but that he is the perfection and completion of humanity as such, uniting in himself both of its 'kinds' [that is, its 'substance'—its eternal being or nature—and its 'sensuality'—its empirical, fallen being in time] and all of its members."

41. Newman, "On the Threshold," pp. 124–26 and 130–33.

42. Julian, *Book of Showings*, Long Text, chap. 9, vol. 2, pp. 321–22; trans. in *Julian: Showings*, pp. 191–92. See also Long Text, chap. 37, vol. 2, p. 443: "What may

make me more to loue myn evyn cristen than to see in god that he louyth alle that shalle be savyd, as it were alle one soule?" And see Greenspan, "Autohagiography," pp. 220–22.

43. Nor is it my purpose here to tackle the philosophical and theological problems of universalism. Julian's theology runs into problems both with theodicy and with what we would today call "difference." Bauerschmidt, *Julian of Norwich*, gives a critique of the limits of her universalism. For Julian's struggling with the doctrine of damnation, see *Book of Showings*, Long Text, chaps. 32–33, vol. 2, pp. 422–29. It is possible to see deep ambivalence in Julian's remark that she did not "see" anything specified concerning the Jews but "knew in [her] faith" that they were eternally condemned (p. 428).

44. See Chapter 7 at n. 50 for Dorlandus, and Chapter 7 n. 22 for a more explicit move toward universalism in *Piers Plowman*.

45. For the first of Julian's "showings" or visions, see *Book of Showings*, Short Text, chaps. 2–5, and Long Text, chaps. 3–5, vol. 1, pp. 207–18, and vol. 2, pp. 289–303; trans. here from the Long Text in *Julian: Showings*, pp. 179–83.

46. "Wytt it wele, loue was his menyng." Julian, *Book of Showings*, Long Text, chap. 86, vol. 2, p. 733. For other examples of blood as love, see Gray, "Medieval English Mystical Lyrics," pp. 204–6.

47. Julian, *Book of Showings*, Long Text, chap. 57, vol. 2, p. 580: "oure savyoure is oure very moder, in whome we be endlessly borne and nevyr shall come out of hym."

48. Relevant here is Julian's teaching on the godly will. *Book of Showings*, Long Text, chap. 37, vol. 2, p. 443: "For in every soule that shalle be savyd is a godly wylle that nevyr assentyth to synne, nor nevyr shalle. Ryght as there is a bestely wylle in the lower party that may wylle no good, right so there is a godly wyll in the higher party, whych is so good that it may nevyr wylle evylle, but evyr good."

49. See Scott, "Mystical Death, Bodily Death," and eadem, "Urban Spaces, Women's Networks," pp. 107–11. On Catherine's later influence (in a somewhat tamed version), see Barratt, "Continental Women Mystics," pp. 251–52.

50. Julian of Norwich's text was virtually unknown; Mechtild of Magdeburg's *Flowing Light of the Godhead* circulated but mostly in anonymous excerpts. See Watson, "Julian"; Barratt, "Continental Women Mystics," p. 242; and Poor, *Mechthild of Magdeburg*. Hadewijch seems to have gotten into difficulties; Margaret Porete, whose ideas have some affinities with Julian's and Mechtild's, was burned.

51. Gen. 4.10–11; Matt. 27.4, 24–25. For patristic and Carolingian texts that cite Christ's blood crying out in parallel to Abel's, see Rohling, *Blood of Christ*, pp. 91–93. For a twelfth-century example, see pseudo-Anselm, *Meditatio IX*, PL 158, col. 756D: "Ecce vox sanguinis fratris nostri Jesu clamat ad te de cruce." (Wilmart attributes this text to Eckbert of Schönau; see Chapter 11 n. 16.) For an example from Jan Hus's "Tractatus," see Chapter 2 n. 76.

52. Of the general accounts of medieval theology, Pelikan, *Growth*, is the best for seeing the importance of sacrifice.

Chapter 10. Sacrificial Theology

1. Klawans, "Pure Violence." As most experts agree, no one theory of sacrifice fits all cases; see ibid.; Heesterman, *Broken World*, pp. 1–17 and 36–41; Thachil, *Vedic*

and Christian Sacrifice, pp. 1–12; Bourdillon, "Sacrifice"; and Hénaff, *Le prix*, pp. 145–220, esp. pp. 213–15. On the inutility of the Christian understanding of sacrifice as a model for sacrifice generally, see Detienne, "Culinary Practices and the Spirit of Sacrifice," in Detienne and Vernant, eds., *Cuisine of Sacrifice*, pp. 1–20; Bell, *Ritual, Perspectives and Dimensions*, pp. 111–14; and Scheid, *Quand faire, c'est croire*, pp. 7–10. There is no Indo-European word for sacrifice, and in most traditions, a word emerges late for the set of acts scholars understand as "sacrifice." In their classic work, Henri Hubert and Marcel Mauss argued that the essential structure involved someone who benefits, a victim (consecrated and then immolated), and a process of purification that reintegrates participants into ordinary life: Hubert and Mauss, *Sacrifice*. Heesterman sees three elements in sacrifice—killing, destruction of the offering, and a common meal—of which the second is key; Heesterman, *Broken World*, p. 9. The entry "Sacrifice," in *The Harper Collins Dictionary of Religion*, ed. Jonathan Z. Smith (San Francisco: Harper, 1995), p. 948, argues that every sacrifice has four points of focus: the sacrificer, the sacrifice, the mode of transference, and the recipient of the sacrifice. For the argument that the prominence of blood in Hebrew ritual is not typical of ancient Near Eastern and Mediterranean concepts of sacrifice, see McCarthy, "Symbolism of Blood and Sacrifice."

2. Hubert and Mauss, Heesterman, Bourdillon, and Thachil all stress the destruction aspect; see n. 1 above. Stressing the sweet odor, Klawans, "Pure Violence," sees sacrifice as an effort to attract God. Lépin, *L'idée du sacrifice*, pp. v–vi, agrees that destruction is a crucial element in ancient (Roman and Hebrew) sacrifice and points to the absence of it as a key element in the Last Supper, which was nonetheless early understood as a sacrifice. In contrast (and to my mind correctly), recent interpretation of Roman sacrifice stresses the ritual as an expression of the hierarchical relationship between gods and humans; Scheid, *Quand faire, c'est croire*, pp. 273–80.

3. Branham, "Blood in Flux," and Klawans, "Pure Violence."

4. Klawans, "Interpreting the Last Supper"; Heesterman, *Broken World*, pp. 15 and 45–48; Rainey and Rothkoff, "Sacrifice," esp. cols. 602–4; B. J. Cooke, "Sacrifice in Christian Theology," and K. Sullivan, "Burnt Offering," in *New Catholic Encyclopedia*, 2nd ed. (Detroit: Thomson Gale, 2003), vol. 12, pp. 515–18; vol. 2, pp. 709–10 respectively; and Rohling, *Blood of Christ*.

5. According to Nahmanides (d. 1270), commentary on Lev. 1.9, the sacrificer acknowledges that, were it not for God's grace, he should in justice be the victim; see Rainey and Rothkoff, "Sacrifice." Hénaff also stresses the extent to which sacrifice is an act that acknowledges the dependence of all life on God; see *Le prix*, pp. 177–213, 230–40. For general interpretations of sacrifice that stress (indeed perhaps overstress) liberation of life or reconciliation, see Thachil, *Vedic and Christian Sacrifice*; Bourdillon, "Sacrifice"; and Sykes, *Sacrifice and Redemption*.

6. Girard, *The Scapegoat*, and idem, *Violence and the Sacred*. For a similar theory applied to ancient Greek religion, see Burkert, *Homo necans*, and idem, *Anthropologie des religiösen Opfers*. Against Girard, see Heesterman, *Broken World*, pp. 8, 41–43; Hénaff, *Le prix*, pp. 260–67; Klawans, "Pure Violence"; and Bell, *Ritual Theory, Ritual Practice*, pp. 172–75. Also Chapter 9 at n. 6. For German discussion of this, see Höhn, "Spuren der Gewalt."

7. I have not dealt here with Nancy Jay's feminist and functionalist argument that sacrifice—done by Christ alone but participated in by a male priesthood—underlines

patriarchy, although I do not discount it. See Jay, *Throughout Your Generations*, pp. 112–27. As Jay acknowledges, however, Reformation understandings of the priest as nonsacrificing also underlined patriarchy, as did much else in medieval and early modern Christianity. The nexus between priesthood (religious leadership) and patriarchy (male dominance in familial and/or political leadership) is clear, but it is not necessary, for this nexus, that the priest be a sacrificer. Jay assumes that the connection lies in an understanding of blood as signifying lineage. But, as I argued in Chapter 7 at n. 21, the texts give no support to the assumption that, in the fourteenth and fifteenth centuries, blood is primarily a symbol of lineage and/or descent.

There are some parallels between Jay's sense of sacrifice as expressing both social and cosmological hierarchy and Scheid's interpretation of Roman sacrifice; see Scheid, *Quand faire, c'est croire*, pp. 275–84.

8. It is not necessary for me to go into the debates among New Testament scholars over the extent to which the early uses of sacrifice language are "spiritualizing" or "supersessionist," although I am inclined to agree with Jonathan Klawans that Paul himself is operating within a tradition of using rather than rejecting sacrifice language. See Klawans, "Interpreting the Last Supper." See also Levenson, *Death and Resurrection*, pp. 220–32. On early medieval discussion of the mass as sacrifice, see Moll, *Die Lehre von der Eucharistie als Opfer*, and Schulte, *Die Messe als Opfer der Kirche*. On the Old and New Testament background, see Willi-Plein, "Opfer," and Merklein, "Der Sühnegedanke."

9. Note the emphasis here on the incorruptibility of blood, which I emphasize in Chapter 8 above.

10. Hénaff, *Le prix*, pp. 145–81.

11. On the change in the late medieval/early modern period from sacrifice as debt to sacrifice as a gesture of moral generosity and renunciation, see the brilliant analysis of Hénaff, *Le prix*, pp. 267–68. Hulmes, "The Semantics of Sacrifice," suggests that the full range of meanings is there earlier than most other theorists would claim.

12. Rohling, *Blood of Christ*, pp. 21–22, 76, and 141–44. The account in the next few pages owes much to Rohling's magisterial study.

13. On patristic ideas, see Rohling, *Blood of Christ*; Daley, "'He Himself Is Our Peace'"; Lépin, *L'idée du sacrifice*; and Geiselmann, *Die Eucharistielehre*.

14. Rohling, *Blood of Christ*, pp. 30–77. The quotation is from Augustine, *Enarrationes in Psalmos: LXXX–CL*, sermon on Ps. 147.16, PL 37, col. 1925.

15. On the separatedness of the blood, see Rohling, *Blood of Christ*, p. 78. See Chapter 8 nn. 1–4 and 8–11, for Aquinas and later commentators stressing the two-ness of the eucharistic elements.

16. For the patristic texts most commonly cited in later discussions of the sacrifice of the mass (Augustine, Gregory the Great's *Dialogues*, Chrysostom [under the name of Ambrose], and Faustus of Riez [known as Eusebius of Emesa]), see Lépin, *L'idée du sacrifice*, pp. 37–47 and passim. I have relied much on Lépin's deeply learned account in what follows. Where I have been able to check his quotations against incunabula I have done so. But I have not always had access to early editions and have sometimes had to rely on the extensive Latin excerpts in his footnotes.

17. Gregory the Great, *Dialogorum libri IV*, bk 4, chap. 58, PL 77, cols. 425C–428A. For its later popularity, see Lépin, *L'idée du sacrifice*, pp. 39–41; and Schrade, "Beiträge zur Erklärung," p. 177.

18. See Lépin, *L'idée du sacrifice*, pp. 84 and 99–100, for the emphasis on "offer" as a synonym for "sacrifice" in patristic texts. According to Lépin, *sacrificare* and its synonym *immolare* usually, in patristic and Carolingian texts, mean "offer, " although they occasionally mean "kill" or "slaughter."

19. Heesterman, *Broken World*, p. 16. Bataille sees this less as killing and destruction than as abandonment. "Sacrifier n'est pas tuer, mais abandonner et donner. . . . Le sacrifice est l'antithèse de la production . . ."; see Bataille, *Théorie de la religion*, p. 66. Many scholars interpret the element of destruction in sacrifice as a way of ensuring that the gift is really given; see Heesterman, *Broken World*, pp. 16–18.

20. Bonnet, ed., *Passio Andreae*, pp. 13–14.

21. I return in Chapter 11 to the aporia of a sacrifice in which sacrificer, victim, and recipient are one and the same. And, on this point, see Detienne in *Cuisine of Sacrifice*, pp. 15–16.

22. Alger of Liège, *De sacramentis*, bk 1, chap. 16, PL 180, cols. 787–89.

23. Isidore, *Etymologiarvm . . . libri*, bk 6, chap. 19, para. 38, vol. 1, pp. 249–50; also PL 82, col. 255B–C. "Sacrificium dictum quasi *sacrum factum*, quia prece mystica consecratur in memoriam pro nobis Dominicae passionis; unde hoc eo iubente corpus Christi et sanguinem dicimus. Quod dum sit ex fructibus terrae, sanctificatur et fit sacramentum, operante invisibiliter Spiritu Dei; cuius panis et calicis sacramentum Graeci Eucharistian dicunt, quod Latine *bona gratia* interpretatur. Et quid melius sanguine et corpore Christi?" Aquinas uses the idea, without citation, in ST 2-2, q. 85, art. 3, ra 3, p. 636, col. 1: ". . . sacrificia proprie dicuntur quando circa res deo oblatas aliquid fit, sicut quod animalia occidebantur, quod panis frangitur et comeditur et benedicitur. et hoc ipsum nomen sonat, nam sacrificium dicitur ex hoc quod homo facit aliquid sacrum. oblatio autem directe dicitur cum deo aliquid offertur, etiam si nihil circa ipsum fiat. . . . unde omne sacrificium est oblatio, sed non convertitur. primitiae autem oblationes sunt, quia deo offerebantur, ut legitur deut. xxvi, 'non autem sunt sacrificia, quia nihil sacrum circa eas fiebat'." For the idea in Beleth, see *Svmma de ecclesiasticis officiis*, chap. 42, CCCM 41A, pp. 76–77.

24. Aquinas, ST 3, q. 48 art. 3, p. 844; trans. in *Summa theologica*, vol. 4, pp. 2278–79 (with changes).

25. ST 3, q. 48, art. 6, p. 845.

26. The emphasis stems both from the increasing voluntarism in theology from the thirteenth century on—that is, the increasing stress on will, both God's and man's—and from an anxiety about seeing Christ as object of violence and killing; the anxiety emerged even as piety made the suffering and killing ever more palpable. See Chapter 11 n. 4.

27. Albertus Magnus, *Commentarii in IV Sententiarum*, bk 4, dist. 8, A, art. 2, fig. 2, in *Opera omnia*, vol. 29, pp. 176–79, esp. p. 178. Answering those who object that the blood from the side effects salvation but the blood of communion is a drink, Albert answers that the sacramental blood is both. Hence we receive it as it flows to us (*fluens ad nos*) even if we do so by concomitance (*per unionem ad corpus*). And see Terrinca, *La devozione*, p. 100 n. 99.

28. See Terrinca, *La devozione*, pp. 100–101, esp. nn. 93 and 99–101.

29. Alexander of Hales, *Glossa in quatuor libros Sententiarum*, bk 3, dist. 19, paras. 2, 9, 21, and 27, vol. 3, pp. 209–12 and 216–17.

30. Peter Lombard, who discussed the eucharist as sacrifice, also seems to con-

flate *oblatio* and *sacrificium* or *immolatio*; see *Sententiae*, bk 4, dists. 8–13, esp. dist. 12, in vol. 2, pp. 808–18. His major concern is to treat sacrament, not sacrifice, and to deal with the problem of "once only (*tantum semel*) yet daily." Later commentators on the *Sentences* treat sacrifice only in passing; as is true for the Lombard, their attention is given primarily to the problem of "daily yet once." On this, see Lépin, *L'idée du sacrifice*, pp. 147–82, esp. 148–53, and 214–15.

31. Aquinas, ST 3, q. 48, art. 5 (citing Lev. 17.11 and 14), p. 845.

32. Basing himself on Isidore, Beleth says: "Sacrificium dicitur quasi sacrum factum." Beleth, *Svmma de ecclesiasticis officiis*, chap. 42, CCCM 41A, p. 76. Here Beleth seems to equate sacrifice with consecration and thus eclipses any implication of killing or destroying. He also uses *immolatio* in the sense of "offered up for."

33. Aquinas, ST 2-2, q. 86, art. 1, p. 636, col. 2; trans. in *Summa theologica*, vol. 3, p. 1552.

34. Ibid., q. 83, pp. 911–15, esp. art. 1, p. 911.

35. Ibid., q. 46, art. 4, p. 840, col. 1; trans. in *Summa theologica*, vol. 4, p. 2262.

36. Aquinas, ST 2-2, q. 48, art. 3, pp. 844–45; trans. in *Summa theologica*, vol. 4, p. 2279.

37. Baldwin of Canterbury, *Liber de sacramento*, PL 204, cols. 647C–D. Here Baldwin sees the animal sacrifice of the Old Testament as a substitute for our death, the price we owe. But he goes on to say, following Augustine, that the *immolatio* of the eucharist is not a killing but a mystical signification and representation. Ibid., cols. 722B–C: "De quo Augustinus: 'Semel immolatus est in seipso Christus, et tamen quotidie immolatur in sacramento, vocaturque, ipsa carnis immolatio, quae sacerdotis manibus fit, Christi passio et mors, et crucifixio, non rei veritate, sed significati mysterio.' Immolatio haec non est occisionis, sed significationis et repraesentationis." On this point, see Lépin, *L'idée du sacrifice*, pp. 160–61.

38. Robert Paululus, *De caeremoniis*, bk 2, chap. 26; PL 177, col. 428B: "Quoniam ergo in victualibus, sine quibus vita animalis non transigitur, principalia sunt panis et vinum, haec servus offerens quod animaliter vivit occidit; vitam enim occidit qui victum sibi subtrahit." But later (c. 29, cols. 430A–D) he speaks only of offering the means of life—that is, bread and wine—to God. "In hac principalia [that is, the canon of the mass] victus nostri panem, scilicet qui cor hominis confirmat et vinum, quod laetificat cor hominis [Ps. 103.15; Eccli., 40.20] offerimus Domino in sacrificium. Haec triplici vocabulo nuncupamus. Dona dicimus quia nobis a Deo sunt donata: munera, quia a nobis illi oblata. Donum enim est quod a superiore datur; munus, quod ab inferiore. Quod autem additur *haec sacrificia*, determinatio est qualiter Deus inde muneretur. Super illa fit crucis signum in memoriam Dominicae passionis, cujus nos participes facimus, dum vitae nostrae sustentamenta nobis subtrahendo Deo offerimus."

39. This is not so much a semantic difference (most theologians use *effundere*) as a stress on the state of the blood shed rather than on the act of spilling; see Lépin, *L'idée du sacrifice*, esp. p. 167 on Alexander of Hales and p. 187 on Aquinas.

40. See, for example, Guitmond of Aversa, *De corpore et sanguine Christi*, bk 2, PL 149, cols. 1455B–1456A. See also Peter the Venerable, *Contra Petrobrvsianos hereticos*, paras. 198–200, pp. 116–18.

41. Albertus Magnus, *Commentarii in IV Sententiarum*, bk 4, dist. 13, F, art. 23, in *Opera omnia*, vol. 29, pp. 370–71. In this formulation, killing is what the Jews do. On this point see Chapter 11 at nn. 27 and 49–57. On recent rejection of the "Schlachtung"

at the heart of sacrifice, see Wohlmuth, "Opfer—Verdrängung und Wiederkehr eines schwierigen Begriffs."

42. Biel, *Canonis misse expositio*, lectio 52, vol. 2, p. 309.

43. Gerson, "Collectorium super Magnificat," tractatus 9, in *Oeuvres complètes*, vol. 8, *L'oeuvre spirituelle et pastorale (399–422)*, pp. 405–6.

44. Ibid., pp. 406–7.

45. Lépin, *L'idée du sacrifice*. See also Fitzpatrick, "On Eucharistic Sacrifice." McHugh, "The Sacrifice of the Mass," p. 175, points out that the theologians at Trent tended to use *oblatio* and *immolatio* interchangeably—a conflation that tends to eclipse the killing behind the offering up.

46. See Chapter 8 n. 88.

47. Mechtild of Hackeborn, *Liber specialis gratiae*, bk 1, chap. 12–13, pp. 37–45.

48. See Chapter 1 n. 15, and Chapter 9 n. 37.

49. See Chapter 6 nn. 17 and 18.

50. William of Auvergne (or of Paris), "De legibus," chap. 24, in *Opera omnia*, vol. 1, p. 72, col. 2.

51. L. Meier, "Johannes Bremer" gives incipits of *disputationes* and *sermones* by Bremer, Witten, Bansleben, and others, as does Ziesak, "'Multa habeo vobis dicere . . .'" Meier gives crucial excerpts from Bremer's "Questio magistralis"; Herbst, "Literarisches Leben," gives a summary of the content of Witten and Bansleben, including crucial excerpts from Bansleben. I have consulted the Bremer "questio" and the two sermons in Wolfenbüttel H.A.B. Cod. 19.6. Aug. 2°, fols. 56r–84r; and the "questio" in Wolfenbüttel H.A.B. Cod. Guelf. 152 Helmst., fols. 136a–153c, and Union Theological Seminary, Cod. 13, fols. 165r–184v. I have consulted the Witten and Bansleben *determinationes* in Wolfenbüttel H.A.B. Cod. 19.6. Aug. 2°, fols. 87v–90r.

52. On the widespread influence of this passage from Isaiah, see Gray, *Themes and Images*, pp. 14–15, and Holtz, "Cults," chap. 4. I have not been able to consult Bansleben's sermon.

53. See n. 51 above. Herbst and Hellfaier date Witten's *determinatio* to circa 1445, the *determinatio* by Bansleben to 1448 and Bansleben's sermons to between 1448 and 1455 (when Bremer used them), probably closer to 1448. See Herbst, "Literarisches Leben," and Hellfaier, "Die Historia de duce Hinrico," pp. 378–80.

54. See n. 51 above. Wolfenbüttel H.A.B. Cod. 19.6. Aug. 2°, sermon 1, fol. 57r.

55. Wolfenbüttel H.A.B. Cod. 19.6. Aug. 2°, sermon 1, fol. 58r.

56. Wolfenbüttel H.A.B. Cod. 19.6. Aug. 2°, sermon 1, fol. 60r, gives conventional devotion to the seven wounds, especially that of the side.

57. Wolfenbüttel H.A.B. Cod. 19.6. Aug. 2°, sermon 2, fol. 64v, where reference is made to blood curing leprosy. For defending against enemies, see fol. 63v. For blood as defense against demons, see fol. 68v.

58. See Chapter 2 at n. 109.

59. Cusanus, "Fourteen Christological Questions," Cod. Cus. 40, fols. 144r–146v, ed. in Haubst, *Christologie*, 318; and see Haubst, p. 295.

60. Cusanus, "Quod resurgit," Cod. Cus. 40, fols. 149r–150v, ed. in Haubst, *Christologie*, pp. 325–26; "Fourteen Questions," p. 318.

61. "Fourteen Questions," p. 317; "Quod resurgit," p. 322. Cusanus is paraphrasing Leo the Great.

62. Klüppel, *Reichenauer Hagiographie*, p. 152; cited in Holtz, "Cults," p. 6 n. 13. References to Isa. 53.7 and 63.3 follow.

63. Klüppel, *Reichenauer Hagiographie*, p. 152; cited in Holtz, "Cults," p. 7 n. 18.

64. Kajava, *Études sur deux poèmes français*, p. 35; cited in Holtz, "Cults," p. 43 n. 90.

65. See Chapter 4 n. 64, and Roberts, "Relic of the Holy Blood," pp. 138–39.

66. Ehresmann, "Iconography of the Cismar Altarpiece," p. 9. The most famous example of an image focused on the sacrificial lamb is the Ghent altarpiece of Jan and Hubert van Eyck; for a reproduction, see Koerner, *Reformation of the Image*, plate 214. Another well-known example is the Isenheim altar, where the lamb standing at the feet of John the Baptist bleeds directly into a chalice from a wound in its right side; see Kolb, *Vom Heiligen Blut*, p. 168.

67. Capistrano, *De sanguine*, art. 11, ed. Terrinca, p. 19*, and ed. Cocci, p. 1369. See also Terrinca, *La devozione*, p. 86; Cocci, "Il Sangue di Cristo," p. 1309; and Chapter 5 n. 25.

68. Pius II, *Commentarii*, pp. 280–81; trans. in *Commentaries*, trans. and ed. Gragg and Gabel, pp. 708–10 (with changes).

69. Ettlinger, *Sistine Chapel*, pp. 80–84.

70. As I pointed out in Chapter 5, some Franciscans such as Capistrano took a basically Dominican position on the inseparability of Christ's blood. It is also worth remembering that the Franciscan Bremer took a basically Thomistic position on identity; see Chapter 2 at nn. 98 and 99 and Chapter 6 n. 50. I return in Chapter 11 to the significance of the Franciscan move to see *mors Christi* rather than *sanguis Christi* as the central soteriological fact.

71. Fisher, *English Works*, p. 110

72. Ibid., p. 110; see p. 111 for the idea that all sacraments are sacrifices.

73. Ibid., p. 129.

74. "If sinne were so displeasant to almighty God the father, that rather then hee would suffer it, he would giue his owne sonne vnto death for the expulsion of it. How much rather now doth it displease him, when his sonne hath suffered death therefore, and yet sinne rayneth neuerthelesse, and more generally then euer it dyd before." Yet, though the blood of Abel "cryed vengeance," the blood of Christ "cryeth mercy." Now before the face of his father, our savior "sheweth his most precious bloud, and ceaseth not to procure mercy. . . ." Ibid., p. 412.

75. Ibid., p. 413. "But you will aske me what meaneth this word reconciled? It is as much to sai, as to be made attone with the almighty God and to be at friendship with hym." On ransom and comfort, see ibid., pp. 412 and 427.

76. Ibid., p. 405.

77. See above, Chapter 3, nn. 86 and 117–19. For the survival of themes of blood and wounds in Puritanism, see Gray, *Themes and Images*, p. 225.

78. Luther, "Sermon at the Baptism of Bernhard von Anhalt," in Luther, *Werke, kritische Gesamtausgabe*, vol. 49, p. 132; cited in Clifton, "Fountain Filled with Blood," p. 250 n. 24, from an English translation.

79. A number of the Protestant images bypass clerical mediation, omitting priest or chalice. See, e.g., the Cranach altar in Weimar, reproduced in Koerner, *Reformation of the Image*, plate 135. But as my second example above suggests, not all Protestant images omit clerical mediation. Nor are all images in which blood flows directly to believers post-Reformation. In the stained glass at Rothenburg ob der Tauber, one stream flows to the chalice held by the priest, another to the baptismal basin; see Gott-

fried Frenzel, "Die mittelalterlichen Glasgemälde zu Rothenburg/Tbr: Verfall und Rettung," in *500 Jahre St. Jakob Rothenburg o. d. T., 1485–1985: Festschrift anlässlich der 500. Wiederkehr der Weihe der St.-Jakob-Kirche. . . .* (Rothenburg: Ev.-Luth. Kirchengemeinde St. Jakob Rothenburg, 1985), p. 140. In a woodcut from a Psalter of the Virgin, circa 1493, blood goes through a cask at the base of the cross and then through bungholes left to monks and right to laypeople; see Thomas, *Die Darstellung Christi in der Kelter*, plate 16, fig. 32. The famous Dürer woodcut of 1509 shows blood splashing directly on a human couple; Stump and Gillen, "Hl. Blut," col. 955, plate 6. See also the Soest Gregorymass discussed in Chapter 1.

80. Schneeberg is in the Erzgebirge, in southern Saxony. See Magirius, *Schneeberg: St. Wolfgang*, and Koerner, *Reformation of the Image*, plates 88, 94, and 133.

81. Pamphlet, "Der Cranachaltar in St. Wolfgang, Schneeberg" (Zwickau: Förster und Borries, n.d.), text by Pastor F. Meinel.

82. See Kretzenbacher, *Bild-Gedanken*, p. 89, fig. 10; and Koerner, *Reformation of the Image*, plate 211.

83. On Protestant rejection of the eucharist as sacrifice, see Cavenaugh, "Eucharistic Sacrifice"; Clark, *Eucharistic Sacrifice and the Reformation*; Shuger, *The Renaissance Bible*, passim, esp. p. 163; and Schulz, "Das Opfermotiv in . . . Reformationskirchen." Calvin, for example, objected that taking the mass as sacrifice makes God to be man's debtor. Calvin, *Institutes*, trans. Beveridge, vol. 2, p. 612. For Catholic discussion, see Fitzpatrick, "On Eucharistic Sacrifice"; McHugh, "The Sacrifice of the Mass"; and Goossens, "Résonances eucharistiques." So difficult was the question of sacrifice once and for all yet daily that, even at the Council of Trent, only the most general of formulations was able to win agreement. See Lépin, *L'idée du sacrifice*, pp. 252–331; and Jorissen, "Das Verhältnis von Kreuzesopfer und Messopfer."

84. Pelikan, *Reformation of Church and Dogma*, chaps. 3 and 5, esp. pp. 299–302 and 324, emphasizes that in the sixteenth century mainstream Protestants and Catholics agreed—and laid great stress—on the idea of the crucifixion as sacrifice. Hénaff, *Le prix*, pp. 319–80, argues that sacrifice must be a gift. Once grace is conceptualized as a gift of everything (that is, as what God gives to man, what man gives to God, and what man gives to others) as it is in Protestantism, sacrifice therefore becomes superfluous. It is, however, noticeable that sacrifice comes to new prominence in early Protestant theology.

Chapter 11. The Aporia of Sacrifice

1. Köpf, "Die Passion Christi," pp. 24–25, and idem, "Kreuz IV. Mittelalter," pp. 736–37 and 743–57. Newman, *God and the Goddesses*, p. 160, suggests that images such as the crucifixion of Christ by the virtues were disturbing and meant to disturb.

2. See Chapter 4 nn. 14–19.

3. Bernard of Clairvaux, *Epistola 190*, chap. 8, in *S. Bernardi Opera*, vol. 8, p. 34. The letter is an appeal to Pope Innocent II against heretics, especially Abelard.

4. A. Michel, "Volontarisme," and idem, "Volonté de Dieu."

5. In his Commentary on Romans, Abelard raised the question. "Quam uero crudele et iniquum uidetur, ut sanguinem innocentis in pretium aliquod quis requisierit, aut ullo modo ei placuerit innocentem interfici, nedum Deus tam acceptam Filii mor-

tem habuerit, ut per ipsam uniuerso reconciliatus sit mundo." *Opera theologica*, vol. 1, p. 117. Exactly this puzzlement about why God chose to lodge salvation in the death of Christ was a trigger for his theology of example or response.

6. Bernard concludes his paragraph with: "Numquid dicit figmentum ei qui se finxit: quid me finxisti sic?" *Epistola 190*, chap. 8, in *S. Bernardi Opera*, vol. 8, p. 34.

7. See Chapter 1 n. 99 and Chapter 8 n. 73 for Gertrude the Great's discomfort with blood. But in bk 3, chap. 51 of the *Legatus*, her hagiographer reports that she hears her Lord ask God to rejoice with him that "the price [*pretium*] of my blood was so usefully expended [*tam utiliter expendi*] for the redemption of the just. . . ." *Legatus*, bk 3, chap. 17, in *Oeuvres spirituelles*, vol. 3, p. 224. For Mechtild, see *Das fliessende Licht*, bk 6, chap. 24, cited in Chapter 7 n. 66. When asked why he suffers such distress, Christ answers that his earlier suffering is not enough. Only the pouring of his blood upon the earth after the lance prick opens heaven.

8. On the enormous popularity of the *Meditations*, see Baker, "Privity of the Passion," pp. 85–88; Köpf, "Die Passion Christi," p. 33; and Bestul, *Texts of the Passion*, pp. 7–8, 13–14, 48–50. Wrongly attributed to Bonaventure, the work is usually now dated to the mid-fourteenth century. McNamer argues for a date between 1336 and 1360. It is often attributed (doubtfully) to John of Caulibus, a Franciscan from Tuscany. It is addressed to a Franciscan nun or a community of Franciscan nuns. On the authorship question, see Elisabeth Salter, *Nicholas Love's "Myrrour of the Blessed Lyf of Jesu Christ"*, Analecta Cartusiana 10 (Salzburg: Institut für Englische Sprache und Literatur, 1974), pp. 39–41 and 44; and McNamer, "Further Evidence for . . . the Pseudo-Bonaventuran 'Meditationes'." The Latin text is edited in [pseudo-Bonaventure], *Johannis de Cavlibvs Meditaciones vite Christi*, ed. Stallings-Taney. There is an English translation made from a fourteenth-century Italian version (Paris BN MS Ital. 115) completed from the Latin in *Meditations on the Life of Christ*, trans. and ed. Ragusa and Green.

9. *Meditaciones*, chaps. 75, 76, 78, and 83, ed. Stallings-Taney, pp. 258–59, 265, 272, and 302; trans. Ragusa and Green, pp. 322–24, 328–29, 334, and 360–61. There is probably a reference to contemporary pilgrimage practice and blood relics in the reference to Mary going back into the city, kneeling at the place of the cross, and saying (with the second verb in the present tense): "Hic requieuit filius meus, et hic est sanguis suus preciosus"; *Meditaciones*, chap. 80. ed. Stallings-Taney, p. 284, ll. 110–11; trans. Ragusa and Green, chap. 83, p. 346. It is worth noting that in Lanspergius's homilies on Christ's passion from the early sixteenth century the only references to blood that are more than passing are in homily 7 (on the bloody sweat) and homily 54 (on the lance prick); see *D. Joannis Justi Lanspergii Opera omnia*, vol. 3, pp. 20–21 and 114–17.

10. *Meditaciones*, chap. 75, ed. Stallings-Taney, p. 259; trans. Ragusa and Green (with changes), p. 323.

11. *Meditaciones*, chap. 75, ed. Stallings-Taney, p. 260. The author also describes Jesus, the sacrificial lamb, led away by dogs (Jews).

12. *Meditaciones*, chap. 75, ed. Stallings-Taney, p. 263; trans. Ragusa and Green (with changes), p. 327.

13. *Meditaciones*, chap. 78, ed. Stallings-Taney, p. 271; trans. Ragusa and Green, p. 334. For a reference to "agnus mansuetissimus," which occurs often, see *Meditaciones*, chap. 77, ed. Stallings-Taney, p. 268.

14. *Meditaciones*, chap. 78, ed. Stallings-Taney, p. 273; trans. Ragusa and Green, p. 335.

15. Newman, *From Virile Woman*, p. 78. It is worth noting that the sacrifice of Seila, Jephthah's daughter, became in both Christian and Jewish texts an image of obedience. To Christians, she was a model for and symbol of the monastic vows of women. See Alexiou and Dronke, "The Lament of Jephtha's Daughter," and Elisheva Baumgarten, "'Remember That Glorious Girl': Jephthah's Daughter in Medieval Jewish Culture," *Jewish Quarterly Review* (2007), forthcoming.

16. *Meditaciones*, chap. 81, ed. Stallings-Taney, p. 299; trans. Ragusa and Green, chap. 85, p. 358. The author of the *Meditations* says he is quoting Bernard, but the passage actually comes from Meditation 9, attributed to Anselm of Canterbury but not by him; *Meditatio IX*, PL 158, cols. 758A–B. Wilmart, *Auteurs spirituels*, p. 194, attributes Meditation 9 to Eckbert of Schönau (d. 1184).

17. *Meditaciones*, chap. 81, ed. Stallings-Taney, p. 294; trans. Ragusa and Green, chap. 85, p. 353; quoted from Bernard, Sermon 22 in *Cantica Canticorum*, sect. 3 (7), in *Sancti Bernardi opera*, vol. 1, p. 133.

18. *Meditaciones*, chap. 81, ed. Stallings-Taney, pp. 293–94; trans. and ed. Ragusa and Green (with changes), chap. 85, p. 352; quoted from Bernard, Sermon 11 in *Cantica Canticorum*, sect. 3 (7), in *Sancti Bernardi opera*, vol. 1, pp. 58–59. And see *Meditaciones*, chap. 81, ed. Stallings-Taney, p. 299: "Diligendus es mihi toto corde, tota mente tota anima, tota uirtute (Luke 1.34), et tua mihi sequenda uestigia, qui pro me mori dignatus es. Et quomodo fiet illud in me, nisi per te?" Attributed to Bernard but actually from pseudo-Anselm, *Meditatio IX*, PL 158, col. 758B.

19. Pius II, *Commentarii*, p. 285.

20. Pius II, *Commentarii*, p. 285. For the point raised in Aquinas, see ST 3, q. 46, arts. 1–4, pp. 838–40; esp. art. 2, p. 839, col. 2: "simpliciter igitur et absolute loquendo, possibile fuit deo alio modo hominem liberare quam per passionem christi. . . ."

21. Pius II, *Commentarii*, p. 291.

22. Ibid.

23. See Chapter 5 n. 72.

24. See Chapter 1 nn. 80 and 113, and Chapter 7 nn. 33 and 80.

25. See Chapter 7 n. 76.

26. For Christian sacrifice as most perfect because involving human flesh, see Aquinas quoted in Chapter 10 at nn. 31 and 32. For Christian sacrifice as superior to Jewish because the blood is hidden, see Alger of Liège, cited in Chapter 4 n. 15. For Beleth, see *Svmma de ecclesiasticis officiis*, chap. 42, CCCM 41A, p. 77: "Hostia secundum Hebreos dicitur ab hostio, quia ad hostium tabernaculi offerebatur, a gentilibus uero dicitur ab hoste, quia deuictis hostibus fiebat, uictima pro uincendis. Dicitur quoque inmolatio, quia ibi Christus sacramentaliter inmolatur, qui semel in ueritate pro peccatis nostris in cruce inmolatus. Et est tractum de mola, que solebat fieri de quodam genere frumenti, quod far uel ador dicitur; unde *et adorea liba per herbas*. Et ponebatur inter cornua altaris facto ibi foramine cum cultro. Mola uero in altari dicitur pars media, sub qua reliquie sigillantur et cui in dedicatione ecclesie crux inprimitur et ubi corpus Christi consecratur." Robert Paululus stressed that Christians offer bread and wine, not animal flesh: see *De caeremoniis*, bk 2, chap. 29, PL 177, cols. 430A–D.

27. See Chapter 10 n. 38 for Paululus, and Chapter 10 n. 41 for Albert.

28. See Chapter 1 n. 15.

29. For Mechtild of Magdeburg, see Chapter 1 n. 97.

30. A sense of exchange or payment of course lasts on in all those passing references to blood as *pretium*.

31. Hindsley, *The Mystics of Engelthal*, p. 15 n. 54.

32. "Das Minnebüchlein," in Suso, *Heinrich Seuse. Deutsche Schriften*, p. 537. The attribution to Suso is not certain (see Haas and Ruh, "Seuse, Heinrich," cols. 1114 and 1124) although it was argued for by Preger, *Geschichte der deutschen Mystik*, vol. 2, pp. 344–47, and some recent scholars think it likely.

33. Nor of course should we forget the emphasis placed on religious works and on accumulating merits in fifteenth-century piety—a topic I touched on in Chapter 8 when I discussed the devotion to blood drops.

34. See Chapter 8 n. 84.

35. See Hindsley, *The Mystics of Engelthal*, pp. 143–52, referring to the *Tochter Syon*, medieval German versions of the thirteenth-century *Filia Syon* that circulated widely in the fourteenth and fifteenth centuries among German nuns, monks, and mystics.

36. For an early sixteenth-century example, see Lanspergius, *Alloquia*, pt 3, canon 33, in *Opera omnia*, vol. 4, p. 370. In a letter supposedly addressed to nuns, Christ argues that he values only gifts offered for his sake alone. "Nam si propter aliud, puta propter favorem, familiaritatem, necessitudinem, aut propter commodum et retributionem agis aliud, quamlibet magnum sit atque praeclarum, hoc ego neque recipio neque respicio. Nihil enim sacrificatur quod mei causa non sacrificatur." The classic modern formulation of sacrifice as giving up or even surrender is, of course, Kierkegaard's; see *Fear and Trembling*, p. 89.

37. König, ed., *Die Chronik der Anna von Munzingen*, quoted passage at p. 161; German from two differing manuscripts in Garber, *Feminine* Figurae, p. 206 n. 157; and see ibid., p. 90. (Garber gives the name as Mechtildis Tuschelin.) Trans. G. Lewis in *By Women, for Women*, p. 249.

38. The obedience given priority among the virtues here is both an old and a new idea. A traditional monastic vow going back to St. Benedict himself, it is at the same time a reworking of Eckhart's radical notion of *Gelassenheit* (detachment or disengagement from practices and works) into something tamer, intended to curb female enthusiasm. The Dominican adviser to holy women Eberhard Marbach (d. 1428) defined *Gelassenheit* as obedience. See Williams-Krapp, "'Dise ding'," p. 65. On the old idea, see Butler, *Benedictine Monachism*, pp. 139–41; Southern, *St. Anselm and Biographer*, pp. 103–5; and idem, *Anselm, a Portrait*, pp. 216–21.

39. See Chapter 10 nn. 23 and 24.

40. See Chapter 8 nn. 90 and 91.

41. For an example, see Chapter 9, n. 34.

42. Bynum, *Holy Feast*, pp. 56–58.

43. See Gy, "La passion du Christ," pp. 175–77; and Avril, "Une curieuse illustration."

44. Yuval, "'They tell lies'," pp. 95–96. Yuval cites Hebrew chronicles of the First Crusade that see the deaths of Jewish martyrs not only as sacrifices but even as becoming food on heavenly altars. He sees in this an influence of Christian eucharistic motifs on Jewish conceptions. For parallels in Jewish myth to Christian claims of eating blood, see idem, "Jews and Christians," pp. 102–4.

45. Hofmeister, "Weitere Beiträge," pp. 197–98.

46. Heise, *Die Juden*, p. 211 n. 2.

47. Lichtenstein, "Der Vorwurf der Hostienschändung," p. 190.

48. Backhaus, "Die Hostienschändungsprozesse," p. 11.

49. See Langmuir, "Tortures," p. 287.

50. See Lefèvre, "La valeur historique," p. 330 n. 2 and p. 343, and idem, "Le miracle eucharistique."

51. Cited in Rubin, *Gentile Tales*, p. 140.

52. Thomas of Cantimpré, *Bonum universale de apibus*, II, 29, 23, cited in Thomas of Cantimpré, *Les exemples*, exemplum 112, pp. 164–65. On the conflation of host-desecration and ritual-murder charges, see Enders, "Theatre Makes History," p. 992.

53. See above n. 11.

54. See Chapter 8 n. 60.

55. See Chapter 8 at nn. 51–62

56. Caesarius of Heisterbach, *Dialogus miraculorum*, dist. 8, chap. 19, vol. 1, p. 97.

57. Aquinas, ST 3, q. 47, arts. 3–4, p. 843, esp. q. 47, art. 4, ra 2: ". . . passio christi fuit sacrificii oblatio inquantum christus propria voluntate mortem sustinuit ex caritate. inquantum autem a persecutoribus est passus, non fuit sacrificium, sed peccatum gravissimum."

58. See Chapter 8 nn. 65–66.

59. See Chapter 1 n. 106.

60. Hsia, *Myth of Ritual Murder*. See also Lotter, "Innocens Virgo et Martyr," pp. 64–66, and Boureau, *Théologie, science et censure*, p. 253, both of whom cite the account of Thomas of Cantimpré in his *Bonum universale de apibus*, II, 29, 23. On Thomas see above n. 52.

61. See Chapter 6 n. 70 for a discussion of the Wilsnack bloodchest.

62. See Chapter 2 at nn. 94 and 95.

63. Hsia, *Myth of Ritual Murder*.

64. See Chapter 3 nn. 41 and 66.

65. Aelred, *Quand Jésu eut douze ans*, p. 76, cited in Sapir Abulafia, "The Intellectual and Spiritual Quest," p. 68.

66. See Peter the Venerable, "Sermones tres," p. 252; and idem, *Contra Petrobrvsianos*, para. 162, ed. Fearns, p. 95, cited in J. Cohen, "Christian Theology," p. 51.

67. Verse 11: "Da er das sacrament gestochen hat, / ain figure die sach er trah, / ain antliz, das was plutes varb / ander Juden haben da pei gesechen / trei plutstropfen, kunden si selber verjichen / fliehsen auf dem sacrament so clar." Verse 21: "Nu merkt, ir frumen kristen gut / das uns got ainen peispiel tut / umb unser sund und schulde/ daran gedenkt, ir frawen und ir man / lat euch das übel zo herzen gan / dahs wir erberben gotes hulde!" cited in Heuser, "'Heilig-Blut'," p. 163.

68. As I pointed out in Chapter 3 (see nn. 149–54), Langmuir, "Tortures," has argued that Christians doubted transubstantiation and projected their guilt about doubting it onto the Jews. But when Christians worried about Jewish unbelief they worried about more than eucharistic mocking and doubt. The standard work on guilt in this period is Delumeau, *Sin and Fear*.

69. As I point out below, the coming of Protestantism did nothing to solve the dilemmas I have spoken of in this section; see n. 78.

70. Lépin, *L'idée du sacrifice*, pp. 252–331. In general they concluded that the mass is a sacrifice, but Christ is not sacrificed anew in it.

71. See Chapter 2 n. 95, Chapter 3 at nn. 143–58, and Chapter 5 n. 37. And see also Barton, "An Emotional Economy."

72. See Chapter 2 n. 95 and Chapter 4 n. 30 for Waltmann commenting on Gregory's vision. The Erfurt *Gutachten* of 1446 shows a similar concern; see Chapter 2 nn. 80–83. And see Chapter 4 n. 19 for Aquinas.

73. James of Jüterbog (or Klusa), "Tractatus de concertatione super cruore in Welsenaco," Wolfenbüttel H.A.B. Cod. Guelf. 152 Helmst., fol. 186vb.

74. Oberman, *Wurzeln*, p. 199. And see Chapter 6 at n. 26.

75. See Chapter 3 at nn. 121–27.

76. See Chapter 10 nn. 83–84, for Protestant rejection of the eucharist as sacrifice and discussion of the issue at the Council of Trent. And see now Wandel, *The Eucharist and the Reformation*, and Schultz, "Das Opfermotiv in . . . Reformationskirchen," pp. 234–56, esp. p. 253.

77. See Chapter 10 at nn. 77–82 above.

78. See the brilliant treatment by Hénaff, *Le prix*, pp. 319–80. To early Protestants, as Jonathan Sheehan puts it, "the crucifixion broke the sacrificial economy of debt and replaced it with an economy of communication." See Sheehan, "Idolatry and Sacrifice: Rites of Communication and Distinction in Early Modern Europe," p. 9; paper for the conference, "The Discovery of Paganism in Early Modern Europe," Princeton University, November 13 and 14, 2004. Hence *Blut Christi* became not an element of exchange but God's gift to humankind. All reciprocal implications of sacrifice were lost. Christ's sacrifice—and by extrapolation any use of the word for human action—became simply one-way giving or giving up.

Chapter 12. Conclusion: Why Blood?

1. See Chapter 3 n. 45.

2. Matthias Döring, in his "Determinatio de sanguine Christi contra Johannem Hus," also known as the "Quoniam/Cum olim," the first major answer to Tocke's anti-Wilsnack polemic, argues that the Wilsnack pilgrimage has had a healthy effect on the region; see Döring, "Determinatio," Wolfenbüttel H.A.B. Cod. Guelf. 152 Helmst., fols. 164va–170vb, at fol. 170rb. See also Breest, *Wunderblut* (1881), p. 213. James of Jüterbog, in his "Tractatus de concertatione super cruore in Welsenaco," Wolfenbüttel H.A.B. Cod. Guelf. 152 Helmst., fol. 186va, sees the poverty of the village of Wilsnack and the devastation of the original fire as reasons behind the need for, and success of, the pilgrimage.

3. Resistance is clear in the story of the Wilsnack hosts bleeding anew to protest an episcopal effort at reconsecration, although in the story as recorded the hosts themselves indicate their consecrated (i.e., controlled) status; see Chapter 2 n. 50 and Chapter 6 nn. 6 and 8. Chapter 3 gives other examples of holy objects bleeding in protest against clerical control.

4. Hoyer, "Die thüringische Kryptoflagellantenbewegung," p. 158; for a similar confusion in a chronicle of Sangerhausen, see p. 154 n. 34.

5. See Chapter 4 nn. 44–49.

6. Carruthers, *Craft of Thought*, and Newman, "What Did It Mean to Say 'I Saw'?" See also Hamburger, "Seeing and Believing," pp. 48–52, and Chapter 1 at nn. 48–49.

7. For the complexity of late medieval attitudes toward images—which were

increasingly popular yet always in certain ways feared as possible objects of idolatry—see Hamburger, *Visual and the Visionary*, and Camille, *The Gothic Idol*. For images of visions that explore the process of depiction, see Bynum, "Seeing and Seeing Beyond," and Plate 31.

8. Kessler, *Seeing Medieval Art*, and Lentes, "So weit das Auge reicht."

9. See, for example, Hoyer, "Die thüringische Kryptoflagellantenbewegung," p. 167.

10. Particularly good on this point about medieval art, although it focuses on the east, is Peers, *Sacred Shock*; see esp. pp. 1–10 and 133–34.

11. See Binski, *Medieval Death*.

12. See epigraph to this volume from Heesterman, *Broken World*, p. 2.

13. For a Middle English meditation on such paradox, see Chapter 3 n. 138; for some lovely Italian examples, see Thompson, *Cities of God*, pp. 366–69.

14. Paradox is at the heart of all religions to which sacrifice is crucial; see Heesterman, *Broken World*, p. 2. But I am mindful of the dangers, against which many scholars have recently warned, of generalizing from particular cases of sacrifice; see Chapter 10 n. 1 above. Paradox is particularly central to Christianity, as Barbara Newman observes, because of the doctrine of the incarnation of the transcendent; see Newman, *God and the Goddesses*, p. 326. But in late medieval Christianity it is not so much the coming of the divine into matter as the death of the God-man that brings salvation.

15. See, for example, Chapter 8 n. 79.

Bibliography of Works Cited

With the exception of a few sources or short articles mentioned only once, the bibliography is a complete list of works cited. A list of the abbreviations used here is given at the beginning of the notes.

Primary Sources

Manuscripts

Union Theological Seminary, New York. Cod. 13.
Wolfenbüttel H.A.B. Cod. 19.6. Aug. 2°.
Wolfenbüttel H.A.B. Cod. Guelf. 152 Helmst.
Wolfenbüttel H.A.B. Cod. Guelf. 153 Helmst.
Wolfenbüttel H.A.B. Cod. Guelf. 550 Helmst.
Wolfenbüttel H.A.B. Cod. Guelf. 630b Helmst.

Printed Sources

Abelard, Peter. *The Letters of Abelard and Heloise.* Trans. Betty Radice. Harmondsworth: Penguin, 1974.

———. *Opera theologica.* Ed. Eligius M. Buytaert. 5 vols. CCCM 11–13, 15, 190. 1969–2004.

———. "The Personal Letters Between Abelard and Heloise." Ed. Joseph T. Muckle. *Mediaeval Studies* 15 (1953): 47–94.

Aelred of Rievaulx. *De institutione inclusarum.* Ed. Anselme Hoste and C. H. Talbot. In Aelred, *Opera omnia.* CCCM 1, pp. 635–82. 1971.

———. *Quand Jésu eut douze ans.* Ed. Anselme Hoste, trans. Joseph Dubois. SC 60. 1958.

Albertus Magnus. *Opera omnia.* Ed. August Borgnet. 38 vols. Paris: Vives, 1890–95.

Alexander of Hales. *Doctoris irrefragabilis Alexandri de Hales ordinis minorum Summa theologica.* Ed. Collegium S. Bonaventurae. 4 vols. in 5. Quaracchi: Collegium S. Bonaventurae, 1924–48.

———. *Glossa in quatuor libros Sententiarum Petri Lombardi.* Ed. Collegium S. Bonaventurae. 4 vols. Quaracchi: Collegium S. Bonaventurae, 1951–57.

———. *Summa theologica.* 4 parts. Nuremberg: Anton Koberger, 1481–82.

Alger of Liège. *De Sacramentis corporis et sanguinis dominici libri tres*. PL 180, cols. 727–856.
Ancient Devotions to the Sacred Heart of Jesus by Carthusian Monks of the XIV–XVII Centuries. 1895. 2nd ed. London: Burns Oates and Washbourne, 1920.
Anonymous. *De medicina animae*. PL 176, cols. 1183–1202.
Anselm of Canterbury. *S. Anselmi Cantuariensis Archiepiscopi Opera omnia*. Ed. Francis S. Schmitt. 6 vols. 1946. Reprint Stuttgart-Bad Cannstatt: Friedrich Frommann, 1968.
pseudo-Anselm. *Meditationes VII and IX*. PL 158, cols. 741–45 and 748–61.
Appuhn, Horst, ed. *Chronik des Klosters Wienhausen*. Celle: Bomann-Archiv, 1956.
Aquinas, Thomas. *S. Thomae Aquinatis opera omnia*. Ed. Robert Busa. 7 vols. Stuttgart-Bad Cannstatt: Frommann-Holzboog, 1980.
———. *The "Summa Theologica" of St. Thomas Aquinas*. Trans. Fathers of the English Dominican Province. 21 vols. 1911. Reprint in 5 vols Westminster, Md.: Christian Classics, 1981.
Augustine. *De cvra pro mortvis gerenda*. Ed. Joseph Zycha. In *Sancti Avrelii Avgvstini opera*. CSEL 41, sect. 5, pt 3, pp. 619–60. 1900.
———. *Enarrationes in Psalmos*. Ed. Eligius Dekkers and Iohannes Fraipont. 3 vols. In *Sancti Avgvstini opera*. CCSL 38–40, pt 10, nos. 1–3. 1956.
———. *Enarrationes in Psalmos: LXXX–CL*. PL 37.
———. *De Genesi ad litteram libri duodecim*. Ed. Joseph Zycha. In *Sancti Avrelii Avgvstini opera*. CSEL 28, pt 1, pp. 1–456. 1894.
Bacon, Roger. *The Opus majus of Roger Bacon*. Trans. Robert Belle Burke. 2 vols. Philadelphia: University of Pennsylvania Press, 1928.
Baldwin of Canterbury. *Liber de sacramento altaris seu epistola ad Bartholomeum Oxoniensem episcopum*. PL 204, cols. 641–774.
Baronius, Cesare and Ordericus Raynaldus. *Annales ecclesiastici 1198–1534*. 21 vols. Antwerp: Platiniana, 1611–77.
Bede. *In cantica canticorum libri VI*. Ed. David Hurst. In *Opera*, part 2, *Opera exegetica*, pt 2B, pp. 165–375. CCSL 119B. 1983.
———. *In Lucae Euangelium Expositio*. Ed. David Hurst. In *Opera*, part 2, *Opera exegetica*, pt 3, pp. 5–425. CCSL 120. 1960.
Beleth, John. *Svmma de ecclesiasticis officiis*. Ed. Herbert Douteil. CCCM 41, 41A. 1976.
Bernard of Clairvaux. *Sancti Bernardi opera*. Ed. Jean Leclercq, C. H. Talbot, and H. M. Rochais. 8 vols. Rome: Editiones Cistercienses, 1957–77.
———. *The Steps of Humility*. Trans. George B. Burch. Cambridge, Mass.: Harvard University Press, 1940.
Biblia latina cum Glossa ordinaria: Facsimile Reprint of the First Printed Edition of Adolph Rusch of Strassburg 1480. Intro. Karlfried Froelich and Margaret T. Gibson. 4 vols. Turnhout: Brepols, 1992.
Biel, Gabriel. *Canonis misse expositio*. Ed. Heiko A. Oberman and William J. Courtenay. 5 vols. Veröffentlichungen des Instituts für europäische Geschichte Mainz 31–34, 79: Abteilung für abendländische Religionsgeschichte. Wiesbaden: Franz Steiner, 1963–76.
Bihlmeyer, Karl, ed. "Mystisches Leben in dem Dominikanerinnenkloster Weiler bei Esslingen im 13. und 14. Jahrhundert." *Württembergische Vierteljahreshefte für Landesgeschichte* N.F. 25 (1916): 61–93.

Bonaventure. *Opera omnia*. Ed. Collegium S. Bonaventurae. 11 vols. in 10. Quaracchi: Collegium S. Bonaventurae, 1882–1902.

pseudo-Bonaventure [John of Caulibus?]. *Johannis de Cavlibvs Meditaciones vite Christi olim S. Bonauenturo attributae*. Ed. M. Stallings-Taney. CCCM 153. 1997.

———. *Meditations on the Life of Christ: An Illuminated Manuscript of the Fourteenth Century*. Trans. and ed. Isa Ragusa and Rosalie B. Green. Princeton Monographs in Art and Archaeology 35. Princeton, N.J.: Princeton University Press, 1961.

Bonnet, Maximilian, ed. *Passio Andreae*. In *Acta apostolorum apocrypha . . . .* Ed. Ricardus Adelbertus Lipsius and Maximilian Bonnet. 2 vols. in 3. Vol. 2, pt 1, pp. 1–37. 1891–1903. Reprint Hildesheim: Georg Olms, 1959.

Braulio of Saragossa. *Epistola 42*. PL 80, cols. 687–90.

Caesarius of Heisterbach. *Dialogus miraculorum*. Ed. Joseph Strange. 2 vols. Cologne: H. Lempertz, 1851.

Calvin, John. *Institutes of the Christian Religion*. Trans. Henry Beveridge. 2 vols. London: John Clark, 1953.

Capistrano, John of. *Tractatus de Christi sanguine pretioso*. Ed. in Natale da Terrinca, *La devozione al Preziosissimo Sangue di nostro Signore Gesú Cristo: Studio storico teologico a proposito di un trattato inedito di S. Giovanni da Capestrano*. Rome: Pia Unione del Preziosissimo Sangue, 1969, pp. 1*–29*; and in Natale Cocci, "Il sangue di Cristo in San Giovanni da Capestrano," *Sangue e antropologia* 3: 1342–87.

Catherine of Genoa. *Life and Doctrine of Saint Catherine of Genoa*. Trans. Mrs. G. Ripley. New York: Catholic Publication Society, 1875.

———. *S. Caterina Fieschi Adorno*. Ed. Umile Bonzi da Genova. 2 vols. Vol. 2. *Edizione critica dei manoscritti cateriniani*. Turin: Marietti, 1962.

Catherine of Siena. *Il Dialogo della divina provvidenza ovvero libro della divina dottrina*. Ed. Giuliana Cavallini. 2nd ed. Testi Cateriniani 1. Rome: Edizioni Cantagalli, 1995.

———. *Epistolario di Santa Caterina da Siena*. Ed. Eugenio Dupré Theseider. Vol. 1. Fonti per la Storia d'Italia pubblicate dal R. Istituto Storico Italiano per il Medio Evo: Epistolari Secolo XIV. Rome: Istituto Storico Italiano, 1940.

———. *Le Lettere di S. Caterina da Siena, ridotte a miglior lezione, e in ordine nuovo disposte con note di Niccolò Tommaseo*. Ed. Piero Misciattelli. 6 vols. Siena: Giuntini & Bentivóglio, 1913–22.

———. *The Letters of Catherine of Siena*. Trans. Suzanne Noffke. 2 vols. Medieval and Renaissance Texts and Studies 202–3. Tempe: Arizona Center for Medieval and Renaissance Studies, 2000–2001.

Cusanus, Nicholas [attributed to]. "Fourteen Christological Questions" and "Quod resurgit." Cod. Cus. 40, fols. 144r–146v, 149r–150v. Ed. Rudolf Haubst in *Die Christologie des Nikolaus von Kues*, pp. 315–28. Freiburg: Herder, 1956.

Damerau, Rudolf, ed. *Das Gutachten der theologischen Fakultät Erfurt 1452 über "Das heilige Blut von Wilsnak"*. Studien zu den Grundlagen der Reformation 13. Marburg: Rudolf Damerau Selbstverlag, 1976.

Denifle, Henricus, ed. *Chartularium universitatis Parisiensis*. 4 vols. Paris, 1891–99. Reprint Brussels: Culture et Civilisation, 1964.

Denzinger, H. and Adolf Schönmetzer, eds. *Enchiridion symbolorum definitionum et declarationum de rebus fidei et morum*. 36th ed. Freiburg: Herder, 1976.

Dionysius the Carthusian. *Dionysii cartvsiensis opera selecta*. Ed. Kent Emery. Vol. 1 A, B. CCCM 121. 1991.

———. *Doctoris ecstatici D. Dionysii carthusiani opera omnia in unum corpus digesta*. . . . . 42 vols. in 44. Montreuil-Tournai: Typis Cartusiae S. Mariae de Pratis, 1896–1935.

Dorlandus, Peter. *Viola animae p(er) modum dyalogi: inter Raymundu(m) Sebundiu(m) . . . et dominu(m) Dominicu(m) seminiverbium. De hominis natura . . . tractans. . . .* Cologne: H. Quentell, 1499.

Ebner, Margaret. *Major Works*. Ed. and trans. Leonard Hindsley and Margot Schmidt. New York: Paulist Press, 1993.

———. *Offenbarungen der Margaretha Ebner*. In *Margaretha Ebner und Heinrich von Nördlingen: ein Beitrag zur Geschichte der deutschen Mystik*. Ed. Philipp Strauch. Tübingen: Mohr, 1882. Reprint Amsterdam: P. Schippers, 1966.

"The Fifteen Oes." Trans. Rebecca Krug in Anne Clark Bartlett and Thomas H. Bestul, eds., *Cultures of Piety: Medieval English Devotional Literature in Translation*, pp. 107–17. Ithaca, N.Y.: Cornell University Press, 1999.

Fisher, John. *The English Works of John Fisher*. Ed. John E. B. Mayor. EETS Extra Series 27. 1876. Reprint Millwood, N.Y.: Kraus, 1987.

Gerald of Wales. *Giraldi Cambrensis Opera*. Ed. J. S. Brewer, J. F. Dimock, and G. F. Warner. 8 vols. Rerum Britannicarum medii aevi scriptores 21. London, 1861–91. Reprint Millwood, N.Y.: Kraus, 1964–66.

Gerhard of Cologne. *Tractatus de sacratissimo sanguine domini*. Ed. Klaus Berg in "Der Traktat des Gerhard von Köln." *900 Jahre Heilig-Blut-Verehrung*, vol. 1, pp. 459–76.

Gerhoh of Reichersberg. *Commentarium in Psalmos*. PL 193, cols. 619–1814, and PL 194, cols. 9–998.

Germania sacra. Ed. Kaiser-Wilhelm-Institut für deutsche Geschichte. Sect. 1, *Die Bistümer der Kirchenprovinz Magdeburg*. Vol. 1, *Das Bistum Brandenburg*, pt 1. Ed. Gustav Abb and Gottfried Wentz. Berlin: de Gruyter, 1929.

Gerson, Jean. *Oeuvres complètes*. Ed. P. Glorieux. 10 vols. Paris: Desclée, 1960–73.

Gertrude of Helfta. *Legatus divinae pietatis*. In *Oeuvres spirituelles*, vols. 2–5, *Le Héraut*. Ed. Pierre Doyère. SC 139, 143, 255, 331. 1968–86.

Giles of Rome. "Theoremata de corpore Christi." *Opera Exegetica: Opuscula I*. Rome, 1554–55. Reprint: Frankfurt: Minerva, 1968.

Gregory the Great. *Dialogorum libri IV, de vita et miraculis patrum italicorum et de aeternitate animarum*. PL 77, cols. 149–430.

Grosseteste, Robert. *De cessatione legalium*. Ed. Richard C. Dales and Edward B. King. London: Oxford University Press, 1986.

———. "De sanguine Christi." In Matthew Paris, *Chronica majora*, vol. 6, *Additamenta*, pp. 138–44.

Guibert of Nogent. *De pigneribus*. Ed. R. B. C. Huygens. In Guibert of Nogent, *Quo ordine sermo fieri debeat; De bucella iudae data et de veritate dominici corporis; De sanctis et eorum pigneribus*. CCCM 127. 1993.

———. *Self and Society in Medieval France: The Memoirs of Abbot Guibert of Nogent*. Ed. J. F. Benton, trans. C. C. S. Bland. New York: Harper Torchbook, 1970.

Guitmond of Aversa. *De corporis et sanguinis Christi veritate in Eucharistia*. PL 149, cols. 1427–94.

"Historia de venerabili sacramento in Gustrow." In Adolf Hofmeister, "Weitere Beiträge zur Geschichte der Buchdruckerkunst in Meklenburg," *Jahrbücher des Vereins für meklenburgische Geschichte und Alterthumskunde* 54 (1889): 196–97.

Hus, Jan. "Questio de sangwine Christi" and "Tractatus." In *Opera Omnia: Nach neuentdeckten Handschriften . . .*, ed. Wenzel Flajšhans. Vol. 1, fasc. 3. Prague: Jos. R. Vilímek, 1903.

Innocent III. *De miseria humanae conditionis*. Ed. Michele Maccarone. Lugano: Thesaurus mundi, 1955.

———. *De sacro altaris mysterio libri sex*. PL 217, cols. 763–916.

Isidore of Seville. *Isidori Hispalensis episcopi etymologiarvm sive originvm libri XX*. Ed. W. M. Lindsay. 2 vols. Oxford: Oxford University Press, 1911.

James of Voragine. *Legenda aurea vulgo Historia lombardica dicta*. Ed. Theodore Graesse. 3rd ed. 1890. Reprint Osnabrück: Otto Zeller 1965.

John of Damascus. *De Fide Orthodoxa*. PG 94, cols. 781–1228.

Julian of Norwich. *A Book of Showings to the Anchoress Julian of Norwich*. Ed. Edmund Colledge and James Walsh. 2 parts. Studies and Texts 35. Toronto: Pontifical Institute of Mediaeval Studies, 1978.

———. *Julian of Norwich: Showings*. Trans. Edmund Colledge and James Walsh. New York: Paulist Press, 1978.

Kempe, Margery. *The Book of Margery Kempe: A New Translation, Contexts, Criticism*. Trans. and ed. Lynn Staley. New York: W.W. Norton, 2001.

———. *The Book of Margery Kempe: The Text from the Unique MS. Owned by Colonel W. Butler-Bowdon*. Ed. S. B. Meech and Hope Emily Allen. EETS 212. London: Oxford University Press, 1940.

König, J., ed. *Die Chronik der Anna von Munzingen*. *Freiburger Diöcesan-Archiv* 13 (1880): 129–236.

Kurze, Dietrich, ed. *Quellen zur Ketzergeschichte Brandenburgs und Pommerns*. Veröffentlichungen der Historischen Kommission zu Berlin 45: Quellenwerke 6. Berlin: de Gruyter, 1975.

Langland, William. *The Vision of Piers Plowman: A Complete Edition of the B Text*. Ed. A. V. C. Schmidt. 2nd ed. London: Everyman Library, 1978.

Lanspergius, Joannes Justus [John Justus of Landsberg]. *D. Joannis Justi Lanspergii Cartusiani opera omnia*. 5 vols. Montreuil: Typis Cartusiae Sanctae Mariae de Pratis, 1888–90.

Die Legende vom Ursprunge des Klosters Heiligengrabe in der Prignitz: Nach dem Drucke von 1521 neu herausgegeben und erläutert. Ed. Johannes Simon. Heiligengrabe: Museumsverein Heiligengrabe, 1928.

Leo I. *Sermones*. PL 54, cols. 117–468.

Life of Alice of Schaerbeke. AASS, June, vol. 2 (1867), pp. 471–77.

The Life of Beatrice of Nazareth, 1200–1268. Trans. Roger De Ganck with J. B. Hasbrouck. Cistercian Fathers 50. Kalamazoo, Mich.: Cistercian Publications, 1991.

Life of Christina Mirabilis. AASS, July, vol. 5 (1868), pp. 637–60.

Life and Process of Canonization for Jane Mary of Maillé. AASS, March, vol. 3 (1865), pp. 733–62.

Ludecus, Matthaeus. *Historia von der erfindung, Wunderwercken vnd der zerstörung des vermeinten heiligen Bluts zu Wilssnagk . . . .* Wittenberg: Clemens Schleich, 1586.

Ludolf of Saxony. *Vita Jesu Christi . . . .* Ed. L.-M. Rigollot. 4 vols. Paris: Palmé, 1870.

Luther, Martin. *D. Martin Luthers Werke: kritische Gesamtausgabe.* 70 vols. Weimar: H. Böhlau, 1883–2003.

———. *Luthers Werke in Auswahl: Unter Mitwirkung von Albert Leitzmann.* Ed. Otto Clemen. 8 vols. (edition varies). Berlin: de Gruyter, 1959–66.

Mansi, J. D. *Sacrorum conciliorum nova et amplissima collectio.* 53 vols. in 60. Paris: H. Welter, 1901–27.

Marguerite of Oingt. *Les oeuvres de Marguerite d'Oingt.* Ed. and trans. Antonin Duraffour, Pierre Gardette, and Paulette Durdilly. Publications de l'Institut de Linguistique Romane de Lyon 21. Paris: Belles Lettres, 1965.

Mary Magdalene de' Pazzi. *Tutte le opere di Santa Maria Maddalena de' Pazzi: dai manoscritti originali.* Ed. Claudio Maria Catena. 7 vols. Florence: Centro Internazionale del Libro, 1960–66.

Maschek, Hermann, ed. *Deutsche Chroniken.* Deutsche Literatur: Sammlung literarischer Kunst- und Kulturdenkmäler in Entwicklungsreihen. Reihe Realistik des Spätmittelalters 5. Ed. Anton Pfalz. Leipzig: P. Reclam, 1936.

Matthew Paris. *Chronica majora.* Ed. Henry Richards Luard. 7 vols. Rerum Britannicarum medii aevi scriptores 57. London, 1872–83. Reprint New York: Kraus, 1964.

Mayronis, Franciscus de. *In Libros Sententiarum, Quodlibeta, Tractatus Formalitatum, De Primo Principio, Terminorum Theologicalium Declarationes, De Univocatione.* Venice, 1520. Reprint Frankfurt: Minerva, 1966.

———. *Der Tractatus de transcendentibus des Franciscus Mayronis.* Ed. Hannes Möhle. Recherches de théologie et philosophie médiévales: Bibliotheca 7. Louvain: Peeters, 2004.

Mechtild of Hackeborn. *Sanctae Mechtildis Liber specialis gratiae.* In *Revelationes Gertrudianae ac Mechtildianae.* Ed. monks of Solesmes. Vol. 2. Paris: Oudin, 1877.

Mechtild of Magdeburg. *The Flowing Light of the Godhead.* Trans. Frank Tobin, intro. Margot Schmidt. New York: Paulist Press, 1998.

———. *Mechthild von Magdeburg, "Das fliessende Licht der Gottheit": Nach der Einsiedler Handschrift . . .* Ed. Hans Neumann and Gisele Vollmann-Profe. 2 vols. Munich: Artemis, 1990–93.

Meuthen, Erich, and Hermann Hallauer, eds. *Acta Cusana: Quellen zur Lebensgeschichte des Nikolaus von Kues.* Hamburg: Meiner, 1996.

Mirk, John. *Mirk's Festial: A Collection of Homilies by Johannes Mirkus.* Ed. Theodor Erbe. EETS Extra Series 96. 1905. Reprint Millwood, N.Y.: Kraus, 1987.

Paltz, Johannes von. *Supplementum Coelifodinae.* Ed. Berndt Hamm with Christoph Burger and Venicio Marcolino. Johannes von Paltz, *Werke*, vol. 2. Spätmittelalter und Reformation Texte und Untersuchungen 3. Berlin: de Gruyter, 1983.

Paululus, Robert. *De caeremoniis, sacramentis, officiis et observationibus ecclesiasticis.* PL 177, cols. 381–456.

Peter Damian. *Letters.* Trans. Owen J. Blum. 5 vols. Fathers of the Church, Mediaeval Continuation. Washington, D.C.: Catholic University of America Press, 1989–98.

———. *Opuscula.* PL 145, cols. 20–858.

———. *Sermones.* PL 144, cols. 501–924.

Peter Lombard. *Sententiae in IV libris distinctae.* Ed. Collegium S. Bonaventurae. 2 vols. Grottaferrata: Collegium S. Bonaventurae ad Claras Aquas, 1971–81.

Peter the Venerable. *Contra Petrobrvsianos hereticos.* Ed. James Fearns. CCCM 10. 1968.

———. "Petri Venerabilis Sermones tres." Ed. Giles Constable. *Revue bénédictine* 64 (1954): 224–72.

Petroff, Elizabeth A. *Medieval Women's Visionary Literature*. Oxford: Oxford University Press, 1986.

Pfeiffer, Franz. *Deutsche Mystiker des vierzehnten Jahrhunderts*. 2 vols. 1845–57. Reprint Göttingen: Vandenhoeck & Ruprecht, 1906–7.

Pius II. *The Commentaries of Pius II*. Trans. Florence A. Gragg, intro. and notes by Leona C. Gabel. Smith College Studies in History 22, 25, 30, 35, 43. Northampton, Mass.: Smith College Department of History, 1936–37.

———. *Pii secvndi pontificis max. commentarii rervm memorabilivm, qvae temporibvs svis contigervnt, a r.d. ioanne gobellino . . . compositi* . . . . Frankfurt: Aubriana, 1614.

Reifferscheid, Alexander. *Neun Texte zur Geschichte der religiösen Aufklärung in Deutschland während des 14. und 15. Jahrhunderts*. Festschrift der Universität Greifswald. Greifswald: Julius Abel, 1905.

"The Revelation of the Hundred Pater Nosters." Ed. Francis Wormald, "The Revelation of the Hundred Pater Nosters: A Fifteenth-Century Meditation." *Laudate* 14 (1936): 165–82.

The Revelation to the Monk of Evesham, 1196, carefully edited from the unique copy . . . of the ed. . . . of 1482. Ed. Edward Arber. 1869. English Reprints 5. New York: AMS Press, 1966.

Riedel, Adolph Friedrich, ed. *Codex diplomaticus Brandenburgensis: Sammlung der Urkunden, Chroniken und sonstigen Quellenschriften für die Geschichte der Mark Brandenburg und ihrer Regenten*. 41 vols. in 32. Berlin: Morin, 1838–69.

Rolle, Richard. *English Writings of Richard Rolle, Hermit of Hampole*. Ed. Hope Emily Allen. Oxford: Clarendon Press, 1931.

Rupert of Deutz. *Commentaria in Joannem*. PL 169, cols. 205–826.

Schannat, Johann Friedrich and Joseph Hartzheim, eds. *Concilia Germaniae*. 11 vols. Cologne, 1759–. Reprint Aalen: Scientia-Verlag, 1970–96.

Scotus, John Duns. *Quaestiones in lib. III Sententiarum*. In *Opera omnia*, vol. 7, pts 1, 2. Lyon, 1639. Reprint Hildesheim: Georg Olms, 1968.

Sulpicius Severus. *Epistulae*. In *Svlpicii Severi opera*. Ed. Carolus Halm. CSEL 1, pp. 138–51. 1866.

Suso, Heinrich. *Heinrich Seuse: Deutsche Schriften*. Ed. Karl Bihlmeyer. Stuttgart: Kohlhammer, 1907. Reprint Frankfurt: Minerva, 1961.

A Talkyng of þe Loue of God: Edited from MS. Vernon (Bodleian 3938) and Collated with MS. Simeon (Brit. Mus. Add. 22283) . . . . Ed. and trans. M. Salvina Westra. The Hague: Nijhoff, 1950.

Tanner, Norman P., ed. *Decrees of the Ecumenical Councils*. 2 vols. London: Sheed and Ward, 1990.

Tertullian. *Apologeticvm*. Ed. E[ligius] Dekkers. In *Tertvlliani opera*, pt 1, *Opera catholica*. CCSL 1, pp. 77–171. 1954.

———. *De resvrrectione mortvorvm*. Ed. J. G. P. Borleffs. In *Tertvlliani opera*, part 2, *Opera Montanistica*. CCSL 2, pp. 921–1012. 1954.

Thomas of Cantimpré. *Les exemples du "Livre des abeilles": une vision médiévale*. Trans. with commentary by Henri Platelle. Miroir du Moyen Age. Turnhout: Brepols, 1997.

Tocke, Heinrich. "Rapularius." In *Der Wolfenbütteler "Rapularius": Auswahledition*. Ed. Hildegund Hölzel-Ruggiu. MGH: Quellen zur Geistesgeschichte des Mittelalters 17. Hannover: Hahn, 2002.

———. "Synodalrede." Trans. Ernst Breest in "Synodalrede des Domherrn Dr. Heinrich Tocke von Magdeburg . . . Nach einem Manuscripte der herzoglichen Behörden-Bibliothek zu Dessau." *Blätter für Handel, Gewerbe und sociales Leben (Beiblatt zur Magdeburgischen Zeitung)* 23 (Monday, June 5, 1882): 167–68, 174–76, 177–80.

Vincent of Beauvais. *Vincentius Bellovacensis. Speculum quadruplex: sive Speculum maius: naturale, doctrinale, morale, historiale.* 4 vols. 1624. Reprint Graz: Akademische Druck- und Verlagsanstalt, 1964–65.

"Les 'Vitae Sororum' d'Unterlinden. Edition critique du Manuscrit 508 de la Bibliothèque de Colmar." Ed. Jeanne Ancelet-Hustache. *Archives d'histoire doctrinale et littéraire du moyen âge* 5 (1930): 317–509.

William of Auvergne (or of Paris). *Guilielmi Alverni opera omnia.* 2 vols. in 1. 1674. Reprint Frankfurt: Minerva, 1963.

Das Wunderblut zu Wilsnack: niederdeutscher Einblattdruck mit 15 Holzschnitten aus der Zeit von 1510–1520. Nach mehreren in der königlichen Universitätsbibliothek in Greifswald aufbewahrten Fragmenten. Ed. Paul Heitz. Drucke und Holzschnitte des XV. und XVI. Jahrhunderts in getreuer Nachbildung 10. Strasbourg: J.H. Ed. Heitz, 1904.

Secondary Sources

Acklin Zimmermann, Béatrice W. *Gott im Denken berühren: die theologischen Implikationen der Nonnenviten.* Freiburg: Universitätsverlag, 1993.

Ahlers, Gerd. *Weibliches Zisterziensertum im Mittelalter und seine Klöster in Niedersachsen.* Berlin: Lukas, 2002.

Alberigo, G. "Flagellants." DHGE, vol. 17, cols. 327–37.

Albert, Peter P. *Mattias Döring, ein Minorit des 15. Jahrhunderts.* Stuttgart: Süddeutsche Verlagsbuchhandlung (D. Ochs), 1892.

Alexandre-Bidon, Danièle. "La dévotion au sang du Christ chez les femmes médiévales: Des mystiques aux laïques (XIIIe–XVIe siècle)." In *Le sang au moyen âge*, pp. 405–13.

Alexiou, Margaret and Peter Dronke. "The Lament of Jephtha's Daughter: Themes, Traditions, Originality." *Studi Medievali* 12 (1971): 819–69.

Angenendt, Arnold. "Der 'ganze' und 'unverweste' Leib: Eine Leitidee der Reliquienverehrung bei Gregor von Tours und Beda Venerabilis." In *Aus Archiven und Bibliotheken: Festschrift für Raymund Kottje zum 65. Geburtstag*, ed. Hubert Mordek, pp. 33–50. Frankfurt: Peter Lang, 1992.

———. *Heilige und Reliquien: die Geschichte ihres Kultes vom frühen Christentum bis zum Gegenwart.* Munich: C.H. Beck, 1994.

Appuhn, Horst. "Der Auferstandene und das Heilige Blut zu Wienhausen: über Kult und Kunst im späten Mittelalter." *Niederdeutsche Beiträge zur Kunstgeschichte* 1 (1961): 73–138.

———. "Sankt Thomas." *Kunst in Hessen und am Mittelrhein* 5 (1965): 7–9.

Areford, David. "The Passion Measured: A Late-Medieval Diagram of the Body of Christ." In MacDonald et al., eds., *Broken Body*, pp. 211–38.

Audisio, Gabriel. *The Waldensian Dissent: Persecution and Survival, c. 1170–c. 1570.* Trans. Claire Davison. Cambridge: Cambridge University Press, 1999.

Aufgebauer, Peter. "Einbeck im Mittelalter." In *Geschichte der Stadt Einbeck*, vol. 1, *Von den Anfängen bis zum Ende des 18. Jahrhunderts*, ed. Horst Hülse and Claus Spörer, pp. 73–124. 2nd ed. Einbeck: Einbecker Geschichtsverein, 1991.

Avril, François. "Une curieuse illustration de la Fête-Dieu: l'iconographie du Christ prêtre élévant l'hostie et sa diffusion." In *Rituels: Mélanges offerts à Pierre-Marie Gy*, ed. Paul De Clerck and Eric Palazzo, pp. 39–54. Paris: Éditions du Cerf, 1990.

Backhaus, Fritz. "Die Hostienschändungsprozesse von Sternberg (1492) und Berlin (1510) und die Ausweisung der Juden aus Mecklenburg und der Mark Brandenburg." *Jahrbuch für Brandenburgische Landesgeschichte* 39 (1988): 7–26.

Backmund, Norbert. *Monasticon Praemonstratense: id est, historia circariarum atque canoniarum candidi et canonici.* 2nd ed. 1 vol. in 2 parts. Berlin: de Gruyter, 1983.

Baddeley, St. Clair. "The Holy Blood of Hayles." *Transactions of the Bristol and Gloucestershire Archeological Society* 23 (1900): 276–84.

Baix, François and C[yrille] Lambot. *La dévotion à la eucharistie et le VIIe centenaire de la Fête-Dieu.* Gembloux: Duculot, 1964.

Baker, Denise Nowakowski. *Julian of Norwich's* Showings*: From Vision to Book.* Princeton, N.J.: Princeton University Press, 1994.

———. "The Privity of the Passion." In Bartlett and Bestul, eds., *Cultures of Piety*, pp. 85–106.

Baldwin, John. *Masters, Princes and Merchants: The Social Views of Peter the Chanter and His Circle.* 2 vols. Princeton, N.J.: Princeton University Press, 1970.

Baraz, Daniel. *Medieval Cruelty: Changing Perceptions, Late Antiquity to the Early Modern Period.* Conjunctions of Religion and Power in the Medieval Past. Ithaca, N.Y.: Cornell University Press, 2003.

Barbier de Montault, Xavier. *Oeuvres complètes.* 16 vols. Poitiers: Blais, Roy, 1889–1902.

Barnay, Sylvie. "Le coeur de la Vierge Marie et l'épiphanie du sang de Dieu: visions et apparitions mariales à coeur et à corps du Christ (XIIIe siècle)." In *Le sang au moyen âge*, pp. 361–75.

Barratt, Alexandra. "Continental Women Mystics and English Readers." In *The Cambridge Companion to Medieval Women's Writing*, ed. Carolyn Dinshaw and David Wallace, pp. 240–55. Cambridge: Cambridge University Press, 2003.

Bartlett, Anne Clark and Thomas H. Bestul, eds. *Cultures of Piety: Medieval English Devotional Literature in Translation.* Ithaca, N.Y.: Cornell University Press, 1999.

Bartlett, Anthony W. *Cross Purposes: The Violent Grammar of Christian Atonement.* Harrisburg, Pa.: Trinity Press International, 2001.

Barton, Carlin A. "An Emotional Economy of Sacrifice and Execution in Ancient Rome." *Historical Reflections/Reflexions historiques* 29, 2 (2003): 341–60.

Baschet, Jérôme. "Âme et corps dans l'occident médiéval: une dualité dynamique, entre pluralité et dualisme." *Archives de sciences sociales des religions* 112 (2000): 5–30.

———. *Les justices de l'au-delà: les représentations de l'enfer en France et en Italie (XIIe–XVe siècle).* Bibliothèque des Écoles Françaises d'Athènes et de Rome 279. Rome: École Française de Rome, 1993.

Bataille, Georges. *Théorie de la religion.* Paris: Gallimard, 1973.

Bauer, Anton. "Eucharistische Wallfahrten zu 'Unserm Herrn,' zum 'Hl. Blut,' und zum 'St. Salvator,' im alten Bistum Freising." *Beiträge zur altbayerischen Kirchengeschichte* 21, 3 (1960): 37–71.

Bauerreiss, Romuald. "Der 'gregorianische' Schmerzensmann und das 'Sacramentum S. Gregorii' in Andechs." *Studien und Mitteilungen zur Geschichte des Benediktiner-Ordens und seiner Zweige* N.F. 13, 44 (1926): 57–78.

———. *Pie Jesu: Das Schmerzensmann-Bild und sein Einfluss auf die mittelalterliche Frömmigkeit*. Munich: Karl Widmann, 1931.

Bauerschmidt, Frederick C. *Julian of Norwich and the Mystical Body Politic of Christ*. Studies in Spirituality and Theology 5. Notre Dame, Ind.: University of Notre Dame, 1999.

Baumgarten, Elisheva. *Mothers and Children: Jewish Family Life in Medieval Europe*. Princeton, N.J.: Princeton University Press, 2004.

Bell, Catherine. *Ritual: Perspectives and Dimensions*. New York: Oxford University Press, 1997.

———. *Ritual Theory, Ritual Practice*. New York: Oxford University Press, 1992.

Belting, Hans. *The Image and Its Public in the Middle Ages: Form and Function of Early Paintings of the Passion*. Trans. Mark Bartusis and Raymond Meyer. New Rochelle, N.Y.: Caratzas, 1990.

Benedict XIV. *Opus de servorum Dei beatificatione et beatorum canonizatione*. Vols. 1–7 of *Opera omnia*. 18 vols. Prato: Aldina, 1839–47.

Bennett, J. A. W. *Poetry of the Passion: Studies in Twelve Centuries of English Verse*. Oxford: Oxford University Press, 1982.

Berg, Klaus. "Der Traktat des Gerhard von Köln über das kostbarste Blut Christi aus dem Jahre 1280." *900 Jahre Heilig-Blut-Verehrung*, vol. 1, pp. 435–76.

Berliner, Rudolf. "Arma Christi." *Münchner Jahrbuch der Bildenden Kunst* 3rd ser. 6 (1955): 35–152.

Berthelot, Anne. "Sang et lèpre, sang et feu." In *Le sang au moyen âge*, pp. 25–37.

Bestul, Thomas H. *Texts of the Passion: Latin Devotional Literature and Medieval Society*. Philadelphia: University of Pennsylvania Press, 1996.

Bildhauer, Bettina. "Blood." In *Medieval Folklore: A Guide to Myths, Legends, Tales, Beliefs and Customs*, ed. Carl Lindahl, John McNamara, and John Lindow, pp. 45–47. Oxford: Oxford University Press, 2004.

———. "Blood, Jews and Monsters in Medieval Culture." In *The Monstrous Middle Ages*, ed. Bettina Bildhauer and Robert Mills, pp. 75–96. Toronto: University of Toronto Press, 2003.

Biller, Peter. "Views of Jews from Paris Around 1300." *Studies in Church History* 29 (1992): 187–207.

Binder, Helmut. "Das Heilige Blut in Weissenau." In *900 Jahre Heilig-Blut-Verehrung*, vol. 1, pp. 348–58.

Binski, Paul. "The English Parish Church and Its Art in the Later Middle Ages: A Review of the Problem." *Studies in Iconography* 20 (1999): 1–25.

———. *Medieval Death: Ritual and Representation*. Ithaca, N.Y.: Cornell University Press, 1996.

Binterim, Anton Joseph. *Pragmatische Geschichte der deutschen National-, Provinzial- und vorzüglichsten Diöcesanconcilien vom vierten Jahrhundert bis auf das Concilium zu Trient*. 7 vols. Mainz: Kirchheim, Schott und Thielmann, 1835–48.

Blamires, Alcuin. "Beneath the Pulpit." In *The Cambridge Companion to Medieval Women's Writing*, ed. Carolyn Dinshaw and David Wallace, pp. 141–58. Cambridge: Cambridge University Press, 2003.

Boehm, Barbara Drake and Jiří Fajt, eds. *Prague: The Crown of Bohemia, 1347–1437*. New York and New Haven, Conn.: Metropolitan Museum of Art and Yale University Press, 2005.

Boockmann, Hartmut. "Der Streit um das Wilsnacker Blut: zur Situation des deutschen Klerus in der Mitte des 15. Jahrhunderts." *Zeitschrift für historische Forschung* 9 (1982): 385–408.

Bourdillon, M. F. C. "Sacrifice." In *Dictionary of Ethics, Theology and Society*, ed. Paul Barry Clarke and Andrew Linzey, pp. 734–37. London: Routledge, 1996.

Boureau, Alain. *Théologie, science et censure au XIIIe siècle: le cas de Jean Peckham*. Paris: Belles Lettres, 1999.

Boussel, Patrice. *Des reliques et de leur bon usage*. Paris: Balland, 1971.

Brackmann, Albert. *Die Entstehung der Andechser Wallfahrt*. Abhandlungen der Preussischen Akademie der Wissenschaften, philosophisch-historische Klasse 5. Berlin: de Gruyter, 1929.

Bradburne, James M., ed. *Blood: Art, Power, Politics and Pathology*. Munich: Prestel, 2002.

Branham, Joan R. "Blood in Flux, Sanctity at Issue." *Res* 31 (1997): 53–70.

Braun, Joseph. *Der christliche Altar in seiner geschichtlichen Entwicklung*. 2 vols. Munich: Guenther Koch, 1924.

———. *Die liturgische Gewandung im Occident und Orient nach Ursprung und Entwicklung, Verwendung und Symbolik*. Darmstadt: Wissenschaftliche Buchgesellschaft, 1964.

Braun, Manuel and Cornelia Herberichs, eds. *Gewalt im Mittelalter: Realitäten—Imaginationen*. Munich: Wilhelm Fink, 2005.

Breest, Ernst. *Das Wilsnacker Wunderblut*. Für die Feste und Freunde des Gustav-Adolf-Vereins 77. Barmen: Hugo Klein, 1888.

———. *Das Wunderblut von Wilsnack (1383–1552): Quellenmässige Darstellungen seiner Geschichte. Märkische Forschungen* 16 (1881): 131–301.

Breeze, Andrew. "The Number of Christ's Wounds." *Bulletin of the Board of Celtic Studies* 32 (1985): 84–91.

Bresgott, Klaus-Martin and Arnt Cobbers. *Reiseziele einer Region: die Zisterzienserklöster im Land Brandenburg*. Berlin: Kai Homilius Verlag, 1999.

Browe, Peter. "Die Eucharistie als Zaubermittel im Mittelalter." *Archiv für Kulturgeschichte* 20 (1930): 134–54.

———. "Die eucharistischen Verwandlungswunder des Mittelalters." *Römische Quartalschrift* 37 (1929): 137–69.

———. *Die eucharistischen Wunder des Mittelalters*. Breslauer Studien zur historischen Theologie N.F. 4. Breslau: Müller & Seiffert, 1938.

———. "Die Hostienschändungen der Juden im Mittelalter." *Römische Quartalschrift* 34, 4 (1926): 167–97.

———."Die scholastische Theorie der eucharistischen Verwandlungswunder." *Theologische Quartalschrift* 110 (1929): 305–32.

———. *Die Verehrung der Eucharistie im Mittelalter*. Munich: M. Hueber, 1933.

Brown, Elizabeth A. R. "Death and the Human Body in the Later Middle Ages: The Legislation of Boniface VIII on the Division of the Corpse." *Viator* 12 (1981): 221–70.

Brückner, Wolfgang. "Liturgie und Legende: zur theologischen Theorienbildung und zum historischen Verständnis von Eucharistie-Mirakeln." *Jahrbuch für Volkskunde* 19 (1996): 139–66.

Bryson, Norman. *Word and Image: French Painting of the Ancien Régime*. Cambridge: Cambridge University Press, 1981.

Buchholz, Rita and Klaus-Dieter Gralow. *Zur Geschichte der Wilsnacker Wallfahrt unter besonderer Berücksichtigung der Pilgerzeichen*. Kleine Schriftenreihe zur Geschichte von Bad Wilsnack 2. Bad Wilsnack: Evangelische Kirchengemeinde Bad Wilsnack, 1992.

Burkert, Walter. *Anthropologie des religiösen Opfers: die Sakralisierung der Gewalt*. Munich: Siemens Stiftung, 1987.

———. *Homo necans: Interpretationen altgriechischer Opferriten und Mythen*. Berlin: de Gruyter, 1972.

Burkitt, F. C. "Ubertino da Casale and a Variant Reading." *Journal of Theological Studies* 23 (1922): 186–88.

Bürkle, Susanne. *Literatur im Kloster: historische Funktion und rhetorische Legitimation frauenmystischer Texte des 14. Jahrhunderts*. Tübingen: Francke, 1999.

Burr, David. *Eucharistic Presence and Conversion in Late Thirteenth-Century Franciscan Thought*. Transactions of the American Philosophical Society 74, 3. Philadelphia: American Philosophical Society, 1984.

———. *The Persecution of Peter Olivi*. Transactions of the American Philosophical Society 66, 5. Philadelphia: American Philosophical Society, 1976.

———. *The Spiritual Franciscans: From Protest to Persecution in the Century After Saint Francis*. University Park: Pennsylvania State University Press, 2001.

Buschinger, Danielle. "Sang versé, sang guérisseur, sang aliment et sang du Christ dans la littérature médiévale allemande." In *Le sang au moyen âge*, pp. 257–66.

Butler, Edward Cuthbert. *Benedictine Monachism: Studies in Benedictine Life and Rule*. 1924. Reprint: New York: Barnes and Noble, 1961.

Bynum, Caroline Walker. "The Blood of Christ in the Later Middle Ages." *Church History* 71, 4 (2002): 685–715.

———."Das Blut und die Körper Christi im späten Mittelalter: eine Asymmetrie." *Vorträge aus dem Warburg-Haus* 5 (2001): 77–119.

———. *Fragmentation and Redemption: Essays on Gender and the Human Body in Medieval Religion*. New York: Zone Books, 1991.

———. *Holy Feast and Holy Fast: The Religious Significance of Food to Medieval Women*. Berkeley: University of California Press, 1987.

———. *Jesus as Mother: Studies in the Spirituality of the High Middle Ages*. Berkeley: University of California Press, 1982.

———. "A Matter of Matter: Two Cases of Blood Cult in the North of Germany in the Later Middle Ages." In *Medieval Paradigms: Essays in Honor of Jeremy duQuesnay Adams*, ed. Stephanie Hayes. 2 vols. Vol. 2, pp. 181–210. New York: Palgrave, 2005.

———. *Metamorphosis and Identity*. New York: Zone Books, 2001.

———. "The Power in the Blood: Sacrifice, Satisfaction and Substitution in Late Medieval Soteriology." In Davis et al., eds., *The Redemption*, pp. 177–204.

———. "The Presence of Objects: Medieval Anti-Judaism in Modern Germany." *Common Knowledge* 4 (2003): 1–32.

———. *The Resurrection of the Body in Western Christianity, 200–1336*. New York: Columbia University Press, 1995.

———. "Seeing and Seeing Beyond: The Mass of St. Gregory in the Fifteenth Century." In *The Mind's Eye: Art and Theology in the Middle Ages*, ed. Anne-Marie Bouché and Jeffrey F. Hamburger, pp. 208–40. Princeton, N.J.: Department of Art History, Princeton University, 2005.

———. "Soul and Body." DMA, supplement, pp. 588–94.

———. "Violent Imagery in Late Medieval Piety." *Bulletin of the German Historical Institute* 30 (Spring 2002): 1–36.

Bynum, Caroline Walker and Paula Gerson, eds. *Body-Part Reliquaries. Gesta* (special issue) 36, 1 (1997).

Caciola, Nancy. *Discerning Spirits: Divine and Demonic Possession in the Middle Ages.* Ithaca, N.Y.: Cornell University Press, 2003.

Caggiano, E. "Il sangue di Cristo in S. Bonaventura." In Vattioni, ed., *Sangue e antropologia*, vol. 2, pp. 1165–84.

Camille, Michael. *The Gothic Idol: Ideology and Image-Making in Medieval Art.* Cambridge: Cambridge University Press, 1989.

Camporesi, Piero. *Juice of Life: The Symbolic and Magic Significance of Blood.* Trans. Robert R. Barr. New York: Continuum, 1995.

Carruthers, Mary. *The Craft of Thought: Meditation, Rhetoric and the Making of Images, 400–1200.* Cambridge Studies in Medieval Literature 34. Cambridge: Cambridge University Press, 1998.

Caspers, Charles M. A. "*Meum summum desiderium est te habere*: l'eucharistie comme sacrement de la rencontre avec Dieu pour tous les croyants (ca. 1200–ca. 1500)." In Haquin, ed., *Fête-Dieu*, vol. 1, pp. 127–51.

———. "The Western Church During the Late Middle Ages: *Augenkommunion* or Popular Mysticism." In Caspers et al., eds., *Bread of Heaven*, pp. 83–97.

Caspers, Charles M. A., Gerard Lukken, and Gerard Rouwhorst, eds. *Bread of Heaven: Customs and Practices Surrounding Holy Communion: Essays in the History of Liturgy and Culture.* Kampen, the Netherlands: Kok Pharos, 1995.

Cavenaugh, William T. "Eucharistic Sacrifice and the Social Imagination in Early Modern Europe." *Journal of Medieval and Early Modern Studies* 31 (2001): 585–605.

Cazelles, Brigitte. *Le corps de sainteté d'après Jehan Bouche d'Or, Jehan Paulus, et quelques vies des XIIe et XIIIe siècles.* Geneva: Droz, 1982.

Chapeau, G. "Les grandes reliques de l'Abbaye de Charroux." *Bulletin de la Société des Antiquaires de l'Ouest* 3rd ser. (1928): 101–28.

Chenu, Marie-Dominique. "Sang du Christ." DTC, vol. 14, cols. 1094–97.

———. *La théologie au douzième siècle.* Paris: Vrin, 1957.

Clanchy, M. T. *Abelard: A Medieval Life.* Oxford: Blackwell, 1997.

Clark, Francis. *Eucharistic Sacrifice and the Reformation.* Oxford: Blackwell, 1967.

Clifton, James. "A Fountain Filled with Blood: Representations of Christ's Blood from the Middle Ages to the Eighteenth Century." In Bradburne, ed., *Blood*, pp. 65–87.

Cocci, Natale. "Le dispute teologiche del 'triduum mortis' nei secoli xiv–xv: aspetto storico e dommatico." In Vattioni, ed., *Sangue e antropologia*, vol. 2, pp. 1185–233.

———. "Il sangue di Cristo in San Giovanni da Capestrano. Problema storico-teologico." In Vattioni, ed., *Sangue e antropologia*, vol. 3, pp. 1287–1387.

Cohen, Esther. "The Animated Pain of the Body." *American Historical Review* 105, 5 (2000): 36–68.

———. "Who Desecrated the Host?" In *De Sion exibit lex et verbum domini de Hieru-*

salem: Essays on Medieval Law, Liturgy, and Literature in Honour of Amnon Linder, ed. Yitzhak Hen, pp. 197–210. Cultural Encounters in Late Antiquity and the Middle Ages 1. Turnhout: Brepols, 2001.

Cohen, Jeremy. "Christian Theology and Anti-Jewish Violence in the Middle Ages: Connections and Disjunctions." In Sapir Abulafia, ed., *Religious Violence*, pp. 44–60.

Cohen, Kathleen. *Metamorphosis of a Death Symbol: The Transi Tomb in the Late Middle Ages and the Renaissance*. California Studies in the History of Art 15. Berkeley: University of California Press, 1973.

Cohen, Mark. "Anti-Jewish Violence and the Place of the Jews in Christendom and in Islam: A Paradigm." In Sapir Abulafia, ed., *Religious Violence*, pp. 107–37.

Constable, Giles. "Twelfth-Century Spirituality and the Late Middle Ages." *Medieval and Renaissance Studies* 5 (1971): 27–60. Reprinted in Constable, *Religious Life and Thought (11th–12th Centuries)*. London: Variorum, 1979.

Conticelli, Valentina. "Sanguis suavis: Blood Between Microcosm and Macrocosm." In Bradburne, ed., *Blood*, pp. 55–63.

Cors, August. *Chronik der Stadt Bad Wilsnack*. Berlin: Berliner Stimmen Verlag, 1930.

Cremer, Folkhard. *Die St. Nikolaus- und Heiligblut-Kirche zu Wilsnack (1383–1552)*. 2 vols. Beiträge zur Kunstwissenschaft 63. Munich: Scaneg, 1996.

Cressy, David. "Purification, Thanksgiving and the Churching of Women in Post-Reformation England." *Past and Present* 141 (1993): 106–46.

Dales, Richard C. *The Problem of the Rational Soul in the Thirteenth Century*. Leiden: Brill, 1995.

Daley, Brian. "'He Himself Is Our Peace' (Eph. 2.14): Early Christian Views of Redemption in Christ." In Davis et al., eds., *The Redemption*, pp. 149–76.

Dalferth, Ingolf U. "Christ Died for Us: Reflections on the Sacrificial Language of Salvation." In Sykes, ed., *Sacrifice and Redemption*, pp. 299–325.

Davis, Stephen T., Daniel Kendall, and Gerald O'Collins, eds. *The Redemption: An Interdisciplinary Symposium on Christ as Redeemer*. Oxford: Oxford University Press, 2004.

Dawson, Christopher. *The Mongol Mission: Narratives and Letters of the Franciscan Missionaries in Mongolia and China in the Thirteenth and Fourteenth Centuries: Translated by a Nun of Stanbrook Abbey*. London: Sheed and Ward, 1955.

De Clerck, D. E. "Questions de sotériologie médiévale." *Recherches de théologie ancienne et médiévale* 13 (1946): 150–84; 14 (1947): 32–64.

Dehio, Georg. *Handbuch der deutschen Kunstdenkmäler, Brandenburg*. Ed. Gerhard Vinken et al. Munich: Deutscher Kunstverlag, 2000.

Delehaye, Hippolyte. *The Legends of the Saints*. Trans. V. M. Crawford. Westminster Library. London: Longmans, Green, 1907.

Delumeau, Jean. *Sin and Fear: The Emergence of a Western Guilt Culture*. Trans. Eric Nicholson. New York: St. Martin's Press, 1990.

De Schweinitz, Edmund Alexander. *The History of the Church Known as the Unitas Fratrum, or the Unity of the Brethren, Founded by the Followers of John Hus, the Bohemian Reformer and Martyr*. Bethlehem, Pa.: Moravian Publications Office, 1885.

Detienne, Marcel and Jean-Pierre Vernant, eds. *The Cuisine of Sacrifice Among the Greeks*. Trans. Paula Wissing. Chicago: University of Chicago Press, 1989.

Die deutsche Literatur des Mittelalters: Verfasserlexikon. Ed. Kurt Ruh et al. 2nd ed. 10 vols. Berlin: de Gruyter, 1978–99.

Dinshaw, Carolyn. "Margery Kempe." In *The Cambridge Companion to Medieval Women's Writing*, ed. Carolyn Dinshaw and David Wallace, pp. 222–39. Cambridge: Cambridge University Press, 2003.

Dinzelbacher, Peter. "Das Blut Christi in der Religiosität des Mittelalters." In *900 Jahre Heilig-Blut-Verehrung*, vol. 1, pp. 415–34.

———. "Die 'Realpräsenz' der Heiligen in ihren Reliquiaren und Gräbern nach mittelalterlichen Quellen." In *Heiligenverehrung in Geschichte und Gegenwart*, ed. Peter Dinzelbacher and Dieter Bauer, pp. 115–74. Ostfildern: Schwabenverlag, 1990.

Dolberg, L[udwig]. "Die heiligen Bluts-Kapellen der Cistercienser-Abtei Doberan." *Anzeiger für Kunde der deutschen Vorzeit* N.F. 30 (1883): cols. 259–63, 281–86.

Donath, Leopold. *Geschichte der Juden in Mecklenburg von den ältesten Zeiten (1266) bis auf die Gegenwart (1874)*. Leipzig, 1874. Reprint Walluf bei Wiesbaden: Martin Sändig, 1974.

Dor, Juliette, Lesley Johnson, and Jocelyn Wogan-Browne, eds. *New Trends in Feminine Spirituality: The Holy Women of Liège and Their Impact*. Medieval Women: Texts and Contexts 2. Turnhout: Brepols, 1999.

Douglas, Mary. *Natural Symbols: Explorations in Cosmology*. 1970. Reprint with new introduction. London: Routledge, 1982.

Duffy, Eamon. *The Stripping of the Altars: Traditional Religion in England, 1400–1580*. New Haven, Conn.: Yale University Press, 1992.

Dumézil, Georges. "Le sang dans les langues classiques." *Nouvelle revue française d'hématologie* 25 (1983): 401–4.

Dumouchel, Paul. *Violence and Truth: On the Work of René Girard*. Stanford, Calif.: Stanford University Press, 1988.

Dumoutet, Édouard. *Le désir de voir l'hostie et les origines de la dévotion au Saint-Sacrement*. Paris: Beauchesne, 1926.

Dutton, Marsha. "Eat, Drink, and Be Merry: The Eucharistic Spirituality of the Cistercian Fathers." In *Erudition at God's Service*, ed. John R. Sommerfeldt, pp. 1–31. Studies in Medieval Cistercian History 11. Kalamazoo, Mich.: Cistercian Publications, 1987.

Eder, Manfred. *"Die Deggendorfer Gnad": Entstehung und Entwicklung einer Hostienwallfahrt im Kontext von Theologie und Geschichte*. Deggendorf Archäologie und Stadtgeschichte 3. Deggendorf/Passau: Passavia Universität-Verlag, 1992.

Edgerton, Samuel Y., Jr. *Pictures and Punishment: Art and Criminal Prosecution During the Florentine Renaissance*. Ithaca, N.Y.: Cornell University Press, 1985.

Ehresmann, Donald L. "The Iconography of the Cismar Altarpiece and the Role of Relics in an Early Winged Altarpiece." *Zeitschrift für Kunstgeschichte* 64 (2001): 1–36.

Einbinder, Susan. *Beautiful Death: Jewish Poetry and Martyrdom in Medieval France*. Princeton, N.J.: Princeton University Press, 2002.

Eisler, Colin. "The Golden Christ of Cortona and the Man of Sorrows in Italy." *Art Bulletin* 51, 2 (1969): 107–18, 233–46.

———. *Masterworks in Berlin: A City's Paintings Reunited*. Boston: Little, Brown, 1996.

Elliott, Alison Goddard. *Roads to Paradise: Reading the Lives of the Early Saints*. Hanover, N.H.: University Press of New England, 1987.

Elliott, Dyan. *Fallen Bodies: Pollution, Sexuality, and Demonology in the Middle Ages.* Philadelphia: University of Pennsylvania Press, 1999.

———. *Proving Women: Female Spirituality and Inquisitional Culture in the Later Middle Ages.* Princeton, N.J.: Princeton University Press, 2004.

———. "Seeing Double: John Gerson, the Discernment of Spirits and Joan of Arc." *American Historical Review* 197, 1 (2002): 26–54.

Elm, Kasper. "Die 'Devotio moderna' und die neue Frömmigkeit zwischen Spätmittelalter und früher Neuzeit." In *Die "Neue Frömmigkeit" in Europa im Spätmittelalter*, ed. Marek Derwich and Martial Staub, pp. 15–29. Göttingen: Vandenhoeck & Ruprecht, 2004.

Enders, Jody. "Theatre Makes History: Ritual Murder by Proxy in the *Mistere de la Sainte Hostie*." *Speculum* 79 (2004): 991–1016.

Engelbert, Pius. "Die Bursfelder Benediktinerkongregation und die spätmittelalterlichen Reformbewegungen." *Historisches Jahrbuch* 103 (1983): 35–55.

Erdmann, Wolfgang. *Zisterzienser-Abtei Doberan: Kult und Kunst.* Königstein: Langewiesche, 1995.

Escher, Felix. "Brandenburgische Wallfahrten und Wallfahrtsorte im Mittelalter." *Jahrbuch für die Geschichte Mittel- und Ostdeutschlands* 27 (1978): 116–37.

Ettlinger, Leopold D. *The Sistine Chapel Before Michelangelo: Religious Imagery and Papal Primacy.* Oxford: Clarendon Press, 1965.

Faensen, Hubert. "Zur Synthese von Bluthostien- und Heiliggrab-Kult: Überlegungen zu dem Vorgängerbau der Gnadenkapelle des märkischen Klosters Heiligengrabe." In *Festschrift für Ernst Schubert*, pp. 237–55. Jahrbuch der Historischen Kommission für Sachsen-Anhalt 19. Weimar: Böhlau, 1997.

Falckenheiner, Carl Bernhard Nicolaus. "Der Wallfahrsort Gottsbüren, nach grösstentheils ungedruckten Quellen." *Zeitschrift des Vereins für hessische Geschichte und Landeskunde* 1 (1837): 14–33.

Fery-Hue, Françoise. "Des pierres et du sang." In *Le sang au moyen âge*, pp. 39–68.

Festschrift zur 900-Jahr-Feier des Klosters: 1056–1956. Ed. Gebhard Spahr. Weingarten: Weingarten Abtei, 1956.

Finaldi, Gabriele. *The Image of Christ.* London: National Gallery, 2000.

Finke, H. "Zur Geschichte der holsteinischen Klöster im 15. und 16. Jahrhundert." *Zeitschrift der Gesellschaft für Schleswig-Holstein-Lauenburgische Geschichte* 13 (1883): 145–248.

Fitzpatrick, P. J. "On Eucharistic Sacrifice in the Middle Ages." In Sykes, ed., *Sacrifice and Redemption*, pp. 129–56.

Fliege, J. "Nikolaus von Kues und der Kampf gegen das Wilsnacker Wunderblut." In *Das Buch als Quelle historischer Forschung: Fritz Juntke anlässlich seines 90. Geburtstages gewidmet*, pp. 62–70. Beiheft zum Zentralblatt für Bibliothekswesen 89. Leipzig: Bibliographisches Institut, 1977.

Fründt, Edith. *Zisterzienser-Kloster Doberan.* Das christliche Denkmal 12. Berlin: Union Verlag, 1967.

Fulton, Rachel. *From Judgment to Passion: An Intellectual History of Devotion to Christ and the Virgin Mary.* New York: Columbia University Press, 2002.

Gager, John G. "Body-Symbols and Social Reality: Resurrection, Incarnation, and Asceticism in Early Christianity." *Religion* 12, 4 (1982): 345–64.

Gallagher, Catherine and Stephen Greenblatt. *Practicing New Historicism.* Chicago: University of Chicago Press, 2000.

Gandert, Otto-Friedrich. "Das Heilige Blut von Wilsnack und seine Pilgerzeichen." In *Brandenburgische Jahrhunderte, Festgabe für Johannes Schultze zum 90. Geburtstag*, pp. 73–90. Berlin: Duncker & Humblot, 1971.

Garber, Rebecca L. R. *Feminine* Figurae*: Representations of Gender in Religious Texts by Medieval German Women Writers, 1100–1375*. Studies in Medieval History and Culture 10. New York: Routledge, 2003.

Garceau, Michelle E. "Fear of a 'Public Sphere': The Trial Records of Francis Baiuli in MS Add 22795." M.A. thesis, University of London, 2003.

Gardiner, Eileen, ed. *Visions of Heaven and Hell Before Dante*. New York: Italica Press, 1989.

Gaudel, A. "Stercoranisme." DTC, vol. 14, cols. 2590–2612.

Geary, Patrick J. *Furta sacra: Thefts of Relics in the Central Middle Ages*. Rev. ed. Princeton, N.J.: Princeton University Press, 1990.

Geiselmann, Josef. *Die Eucharistielehre der Vorscholastik*. Paderborn: Ferdinand Schöningh, 1926.

Gerhards, Albert and Klemens Richter, eds. *Das Opfer: Biblischer Anspruch und liturgische Gestalt*. Quaestiones disputatae 186. Freiburg: Herder, 2000.

Gerl-Falkovitz, Hanna-Barbara. "'Die Braut auf dem Bett von Blut und Feuer': Zur Bluttheologie der Caterina von Siena (1347–1380)." In *900 Jahre Heilig-Blut-Verehrung*, vol. 1, pp. 494–500.

Germania Judaica. Ed. Zvi Avneri et al. 2 vols. in 3. Tübingen: Mohr [Siebeck], 1963–68.

Ginzburg, Carlo. "Representations of German Jewry: Images, Prejudices, Ideas—A Comment." In Hsia and Lehmann, eds., *In and Out of the Ghetto*, pp. 209–12.

Girard, René. *The Scapegoat*. Trans. Yvonne Freccero. Baltimore: Johns Hopkins University Press, 1986.

———. *Violence and the Sacred*. Trans. Patrick Gregory. Baltimore: Johns Hopkins University Press, 1977.

Girgensohn, Dieter. *Peter von Pulkau und die Wiedereinführung des Laienkelches: Leben und Wirken eines Wiener Theologen in der Zeit des grossen Schismas*. Veröffentlichungen des Max-Planck-Instituts für Geschichte 12. Göttingen: Vandenhoeck & Ruprecht, 1964.

Goossens, André. "Résonances eucharistiques à la fin du moyen âge." In Haquin, ed., *Fête-Dieu*, vol. 1, pp. 173–91.

Gougaud, Louis. *Dévotions et pratiques ascétiques du moyen âge*. Collection Pax 21. Paris: Desclée de Brouwer, 1925.

Gray, Douglas. "The Five Wounds of Our Lord." *Notes and Queries* (1963): 50–51, 82–89, 127–34, 163–68.

———. "Medieval English Mystical Lyrics." In *Mysticism and Spirituality in Medieval England*, ed. William Pollard and Robert Boenig, pp. 203–18. Cambridge: D.S. Brewer, 1997.

———. *Themes and Images in the Medieval English Religious Lyric*. London: Routledge and Kegan Paul, 1972.

Greenspan, Kate. "Autohagiography and Medieval Women's Spiritual Autobiography." In *Gender and Text in the Later Middle Ages*, ed. Jane Chance, pp. 216–34. Gainesville: University Press of Florida, 1996.

Grégoire, Réginald. "Sang." DS, vol. 14, cols. 319–33.

Greshake, Gilbert. "Erlösung und Freiheit: Zur Neuinterpretation der Erlösungslehre Anselms von Canterbury." *Theologische Quartalschrift* 153 (1973): 325–45.

———. "Der Wandel der Erlösungsvorstellungen in der Theologie." In *Erlösung und Emanzipation*, ed. Leo Scheffcyzk, pp. 63–101. Freiburg: Herder, 1973.

Groebner, Valentin. *Defaced: The Visual Culture of Violence in the Later Middle Ages*. Trans. Pamela Selwyn. New York: Zone Books, 2004.

———."Der verletzte Körper und die Stadt: Gewalttätigkeit und Gewalt in Nürnberg am Ende des 15. Jahrhunderts." In *Physische Gewalt: Studien zur Geschichte der Neuzeit*, ed. Thomas Lindenberger and Alf Lüdkte, pp. 162–89. Frankfurt: Suhrkamp, 1995.

Grossel, Marie-Geneviève. "'Le suave calice de la passion': images et appréhension de l'Eucharistie chez quelques mystiques médiévales." In *Le sang au moyen âge*, pp. 415–32.

Guth, Klaus. *Guibert von Nogent und die hochmittelalterliche Kritik an der Reliquienverehrung*. Studien und Mitteilungen zur Geschichte des Benediktiner-Ordens und seiner Zweige, Supplement 21. Augsburg: Winfried, 1970.

Gy, Pierre-Marie. "La passion du Christ dans la piété et théologie aux XIVe et XVe siècles." In *Le mal et le diable: leurs figures à la fin du moyen âge*, ed. Nathalie Nabert, pp. 173–85. Cultures et christianisme 4. Paris: Beauchesne, 1996.

Haas, Alois and Kurt Ruh. "Seuse, Heinrich." *Verfasserlexikon*, vol. 8, cols. 1109–29.

Hahn, Cynthia. "The Voices of the Saints: Speaking Reliquaries." *Gesta* 36, 1 (1997): 20–31.

Hamburger, Jeffrey F. "Un jardin de roses spirituel: une vie enluminée de Catherine de Sienne." *Art de l'enluminure* 11 (Dec. 2004–Jan./Feb. 2005): 1–75.

———. *Nuns as Artists: The Visual Culture of a Medieval Convent*. Berkeley: University of California Press, 1997.

———."Seeing and Believing: The Suspicion of Sight and the Authentication of Vision in Late Medieval Art." In *Imagination und Wirklichkeit: Zum Verhältnis von mentalen und realen Bildern in der Kunst der frühen Neuzeit*, ed. Alessandro Nova and Klaus Krüger, pp. 47–70. Mainz: Philipp von Zabern, 2000.

———. *The Visual and the Visionary: Art and Female Spirituality in Late Medieval Germany*. New York: Zone Books, 1998.

Hamerton-Kelly, Robert G. "Religion and the Thought of René Girard: An Introduction." In *Curing Violence*, ed. Mark I. Wallace and Theophus H. Smith, pp. 3–24. Sonoma, Calif.: Polebridge, 1994.

———, ed. *Violent Origins: Walter Burkert, René Girard and Jonathan Z. Smith on Ritual Killing and Cultural Formation*. Stanford, Calif.: Stanford University Press, 1987.

Hamm, Berndt. *Frömmigkeitstheologie am Anfang des 16. Jahrhunderts: Studien zu Johannes von Paltz und seinem Umkreis*. Tübingen: Mohr, 1982.

Haquin, André, ed. *Fête-Dieu, 1246–1996*. Vol. 1, *Actes du Colloque de Liège, 12–14 Septembre 1996*. Publications de l'Institut d'Études Médiévales 19. Louvain-la-Neuve: Institut d'Études Médiévales de l'Université Catholique de Louvain, 1999.

Harbison, Craig. *The Last Judgment in Sixteenth Century Northern Europe: A Study of the Relation Between Art and Reformation*. New York: Garland, 1976.

Harris, Jennifer. "The Body as Temple in the High Middle Ages." In *Sacrifice in Religious Experience*, ed. Albert I. Baumgarten, pp. 237–56. Leiden: Brill, 2002.

Hartwieg, Babette. "Drei gefasste Holzskulpturen vom Ende des 13. Jahrhunderts im Kloster Wienhausen." *Zeitschrift für Kunsttechnologie und Konservierung* 2 (1988): 187–262.

Haubst, Rudolf. *Die Christologie des Nikolaus von Kues*. Freiburg: Herder, 1956.

Haug, Walter and Burghart Wachinger, eds. *Die Passion Christi in Literatur und Kunst des Spätmittelalters*. Tübingen: Niemeyer, 1993.

Hawel, Peter. *Die Pietà: eine Blüte der Kunst*. Würzburg: Echter, 1985.

Head, Thomas. "Relics." DMA, vol. 10, pp. 296–99.

———. "Saints, Heretics, and Fire: Finding Meaning Through the Ordeal." In *Monks and Nuns, Saints and Outcasts: Religious Expression and Social Meaning in the Middle Ages*, ed. Barbara Rosenwein and Sharon Farmer, pp. 220–38. Ithaca, N.Y.: Cornell University Press, 1999.

Heesterman, J. C. *The Broken World of Sacrifice: An Essay in Ancient Indian Ritual*. Chicago: University of Chicago Press, 1993.

Heise, Brigitte and Hildegard Vogeler. *Die Altäre des St. Annen-Museums: Erläuterung der Bildprogramme*. Lübeck: Museum für Kunst und Kulturgeschichte, 1993.

Heise, Werner. *Die Juden in der Mark Brandenburg bis zum Jahre 1571*. Historische Studien 220. Berlin: Emil Ebering, 1932.

Hellfaier, Detlev. "Die historia de duce Hinrico—Quelle der Heiligblutverehrung in St. Ägidien zu Braunschweig." In *Heinrich der Löwe*, ed. Wolf-Dieter Mohrmann, pp. 377–406. Göttingen: Vandenhoeck & Ruprecht, 1980.

Hénaff, Marcel. *Le prix de la vérité: le don, l'argent, la philosophie*. Paris: Éditions du Seuil, 2002.

Hengevoss-Dürkop, Kerstin. *Skulptur und Frauenkloster: Studien zu Bildwerken der Zeit um 1300 aus Frauenklöstern des ehemaligen Fürstentums Lüneburg*. Berlin: Akademie Verlag, 1994.

Hennessy, Marlene Villalobos. "Morbid Devotions: Reading the Passion of Christ in a Late Medieval Miscellany, London, British Library, Additional MS 37049." Ph.D. dissertation, Columbia University, 2001.

Hennig, Bruno. "Kurfürst Friedrich II. und das Wunderblut zu Wilsnack." *Forschungen zur brandenburgischen und preussischen Geschichte* 19 (1906): 73–104.

Herbst, H. "Literarisches Leben im Benediktiner-Kloster St. Ägidien zu Braunschweig: Nebst einem Versuch der Rekonstruktion der Bibliothek dieses Klosters." *Niedersächsisches Jahrbuch für Landesgeschichte* 13 (1936): 131–89.

Hermann-Mascard, Nicole. *Les reliques des saints: formation coutumière d'un droit*. Paris: Klincksieck, 1975.

Herrmann, Erwin. "*Veniet aquila, de cuius volatu delebitur leo*: zur Gamaleon-Predigt des Johann von Wünschelburg." In *Festiva Lanx: Studien zum mittelalterlichen Geistesleben. Johannes Spörl dargebracht aus Anlass seines sechzigsten Geburtstages*, ed. Karl Schnith, pp. 95–117. Munich: Verlag Salesianische Offizin, 1966.

Heuser, Johannes. "'Heilig-Blut' in Kult und Brauchtum des deutschen Kulturraumes. Ein Beitrag zur religiösen Volkskunde." Dissertation, Bonn, 1948.

Hilsch, Peter. *Johannes Hus (um 1370–1415): Prediger Gottes und Ketzer*. Regensburg: Friedrich Pustet, 1999.

Hindsley, Leonard P. *The Mystics of Engelthal: Writings from a Medieval Monastery*. New York: St. Martin's Press, 1998.

Hirn, Yrjö. *The Sacred Shrine: A Study of the Poetry and Art of the Catholic Church*. London: Macmillan, 1912.

Hirsh, John C. *The Boundaries of Faith: The Development and Transmission of Medieval Spirituality*. Studies in the History of Christian Thought 67. Leiden: Brill, 1996.

Hofer, Johannes. *Johannes Kapistran: Ein Leben im Kampf um die Reform der Kirche.* Bibliotheca franciscana. 2 vols. New ed. Rome: Editiones franciscanae, 1964–65.

Hofmeister, Adolf. "Weitere Beiträge zur Geschichte der Buchdruckerkunst in Meklenburg." *Jahrbücher des Vereins für meklenburgische Geschichte und Alterthumskunde* 54 (1889): 181–224.

Hogg, James, ed. *An Illustrated Yorkshire Carthusian Religious Miscellany: British Library London Additional MS. 37049.* 3 vols. Analecta Cartusiana 95. Salzburg: Institut für Anglistik und Amerikanistik, Universität Salzburg, 1981.

Höhn, Hans-Joachim. "Spuren der Gewalt: Kultursoziologische Annäherungen an die Kategorie des Opfers." In Gerhards and Richter, eds., *Das Opfer*, pp. 11–29.

Holtorf, Christian. "My Blood for Thee." In Bradburne, ed., *Blood*, pp. 21–31.

Holtz, Mark Daniel. "Cults of the Precious Blood in the Medieval Latin West." Ph.D. dissertation, University of Notre Dame, 1997.

Hölzel, Hildegund. "Toke, Heinrich." *Verfasserlexikon*, vol. 9, cols. 964–71.

Honemann, Volker. "Die Sternberger Hostienschändung und ihre Quellen." In *Kirche und Gesellschaft im Heiligen Römischen Reich des 15. und 16. Jahrhunderts*, ed. Hartmut Boockmann, pp. 75–102. Abhandlungen der Akademie der Wissenschaften in Göttingen, Phil.-Hist. Kl. 3 Folge, Nr. 206. Göttingen: Vandenhoeck & Ruprecht, 1994.

Hoogeweg, H. *Die Stifter und Klöster der Provinz Pommern.* 2 vols. Stettin: Leon Saunier, 1924–25.

Hoyer, Siegfried. "Die thüringische Kryptoflagellantenbewegung im 15. Jahrhundert." *Jahrbuch für Regionalgeschichte* 2 (1967): 148–74.

Hsia, R. Po-Chia. *The Myth of Ritual Murder: Jews and Magic in Reformation Germany.* New Haven, Conn.: Yale University Press, 1988.

Hsia, R. Po-Chia and Hartmut Lehmann, eds. *In and Out of the Ghetto: Jewish-Gentile Relations in Late Medieval and Early Modern Germany.* Washington, D.C.: German Historical Institute, 1995.

Hubert, Henri and Marcel Mauss. *Sacrifice: Its Nature and Function.* 1898. Trans. W. D. Halls. Chicago: University of Chicago Press, 1964.

Huizinga, Johan. *The Autumn of the Middle Ages.* Trans. Rodney J. Paynton and Ulrich Mammitzsch. Chicago: University of Chicago Press, 1996.

Hulmes, Edward. "The Semantics of Sacrifice." In Sykes, ed., *Sacrifice and Redemption*, pp. 265–81.

James, Mervyn. "Ritual, Drama and Social Body in the Late Medieval English Town." *Past and Present* 98 (February 1983): 3–29.

Jászai, Géza. *Gotische Skulpturen, 1300–1450.* Bildhefte des Westfälischen Landesmuseums für Kunst und Kulturgeschichte Münster 29. Münster: Westfälisches Landesmuseum, 1990.

Javelet, Robert. *Image et ressemblance au douzième siècle de saint Anselme à Alain de Lille.* 2 vols. Paris: Letouzey et Ané, 1967.

Jay, Nancy. *Throughout Your Generations Forever: Sacrifice, Religion and Paternity.* Chicago: University of Chicago Press, 1992.

Jensch, Rainier. "Die Weingartener Heilig-Blut- und Stiftertradition: ein Bilderkreis klösterlicher Selbstdarstellung." Dissertation, Tübingen, 1996.

Johnson, Willis. "The Myth of Jewish Male Menses." *Journal of Medieval History* 24, 3 (1998): 273–95.

Jorissen, Hans. *Die Entfaltung der Transsubstantiationslehre bis zum Beginn der Hochscholastik*. Münster: Aschendorff, 1965.

———. "Das Verhältnis von Kreuzesopfer und Messopfer auf dem Konzil von Trent." In Gerhard and Richter, eds., *Das Opfer*, pp. 92–99.

Jungmann, Josef. *The Mass of the Roman Rite: Its Origins and Development (Missarum Sollemnia)*. Trans. F. A. Brunner. 2 vols. New York: Benziger, 1951, 1955.

Kajava, Oskari. *Études sur deux poèmes français relatifs à l'abbaye de Fécamp*. Helsinki: Société de Littérature Finnoise, 1928.

Kaminsky, Howard. *A History of the Hussite Revolution*. Berkeley: University of California Press, 1967.

———. "Hus, John," and "Hussites." DMA, vol. 6, pp. 364–69, 371–78.

Karant-Nunn, Susan. *Reformation of Ritual*. London: Routledge, 1997.

Kasper, Walter. "Der bleibende Gehalt der Heilig-Blut-Verehrung aus theologischer Sicht." In *900 Jahre Heilig-Blut-Verehrung*, vol. 1, pp. 377–90.

Kaye, Joel. *Economy and Nature in the Fourteenth Century: Money, Market Economy and the Emergence of Scientific Thought*. Cambridge: Cambridge University Press, 1998.

Kessler, Herbert. *Seeing Medieval Art*. Rethinking the Middle Ages 1. Peterborough, Ont.: Broadview Press, 2004.

Kieckhefer, Richard. *Unquiet Souls: Fourteenth-Century Saints and Their Religious Milieu*. Chicago: University of Chicago Press, 1984.

Kierkegaard, Søren. *Fear and Trembling: Dialectical Lyric by Johannes de silentio*. Trans. Alastair Hannay. London: Penguin, 1985.

King, Archdale. *Liturgies of the Religious Orders*. London: Longmans, 1955.

Kirchner. "Das Cisterzienser-Nonnenkloster zum heiligen Kreuz in Zehdenick." *Märkische Forschung* 5 (1857): 109–83.

Klawans, Jonathan. "Interpreting the Last Supper: Sacrifice, Spiritualization, and Anti-Sacrifice." *New Testament Studies* 48, 1 (2002): 1–17.

———. "Pure Violence: Sacrifice and Defilement in Ancient Israel." *Harvard Theological Review* 94, 2 (2001): 133–57.

Kleineidam, Erich. *Universitas Studii Erffordensis: Überblick über die Geschichte der Universität Erfurt im Mittelalter 1392–1521*. Vol. 1, *1392–1460*. Leipzig: St. Benno-Verlag, 1964.

Klinck, Roswitha. *Die lateinische Etymologie des Mittelalters*. Munich: Wilhelm Fink, 1970.

Klüppel, Theodor. *Reichenauer Hagiographie zwischen Walahfrid und Berno*. Sigmaringen: J. Thorbecke, 1980.

Koerner, Joseph Leo. *The Reformation of the Image*. Chicago: University of Chicago Press, 2004.

Kolb, Karl. *Vom Heiligen Blut: Eine Bilddokumentation der Wallfahrt und Verehrung*. Würzburg: Echter, 1980.

Köpf, Ulrich. "Kreuz IV. Mittelalter." TRE, vol. 19, pp. 732–61.

———. "Die Passion Christi in der lateinischen religiösen und theologischen Literatur des Spätmittelalters." In Haug and Wachinger, eds., *Die Passion Christi*, pp. 21–41.

Köster, Kurt. "Gottsbüren, das hessische 'Wilsnack.' Geschichte und Kultgeschichte einer mittelalterlichen Heiligblut-Wallfahrt im Spiegel ihrer Pilgerzeichen." In *Festgabe für Paul Kirn. Zum 70. Geburtstag . . .* , ed. Ekkehard Kaufmann, pp. 198–222. Berlin: Schmidt, 1961.

Kötzsche, Lieselotte. "Das wiedergefundene Hostiengrab im Kloster Heiligengrabe/Prignitz." *Berliner Theologische Zeitschrift* 4, 1 (1987): 19–32.

Kraft, Heike. "Die Bildallegorie der Kreuzigung Christi durch die Tugenden." Dissertation, Freie Universität, 1976.

Kretzenbacher, Leopold. *Bild-Gedanken der spätmittelalterlichen Hl. Blut-Mystik und ihr Fortleben in mittel- und südosteuropäischen Volksüberlieferungen.* Munich: Verlag der Bayerischen Akademie der Wissenschaften, 1997.

Krönig, Wolfgang. "Rheinische Vesperbilder aus Leder und ihr Umkreis." *Wallraf-Richartz-Jahrbuch: Westdeutsches Jahrbuch für Kunstgeschichte* 24 (1962): 97–192.

Krüger, Renate. *Die Nikolauskirche zu Wilsnack.* Das christliche Denkmal 92. 2nd ed. Berlin: Union Verlag, 1979.

Kruger, Steven F. "The Bodies of the Jews in the Middle Ages." In *The Idea of Medieval Literature: New Essays on Chaucer and Medieval Culture in Honor of Donald R. Howard*, ed. James M. Dean and Christian K. Zacher, pp. 301–23. Newark: University of Delaware Press, 1992.

Kruse, Norbert. "Die historischen Heilig-Blut-Schriften der Weingartener Klostertradition." In *900 Jahre Heilig-Blut-Verehrung*, vol. 1, pp. 77–123.

Kühne, Hartmut. "Der Harz und sein Umland: eine spätmittelalterliche Wallfahrtslandschaft?" In *Spätmittelalterliche Wallfahrt im mitteldeutschen Raum: Beiträge einer interdisziplinären Arbeitstagung (Eisleben 7./8. June 2002)*, ed. Hartmut Kühne, Wolfgang Radtke, and Gerlinde Strohmaier-Wiederanders. 2002. http://dochost.rz.hu-berlin.de//conferences/conf2/Kuehne-Hartmut-2002-09-08/HTML/.

———. "'Ich ging durch Feuer und Wasser . . .': Bemerkungen zur Wilnacker Heilig-Blut-Legende." In *Theologie und Kultur: Geschichten einer Wechselbeziehung: Festschrift zum einhundertfünfzigjährigen Bestehen des Lehrstuhls für Christliche Archäologie und Kirchliche Kunst an der Humboldt-Universität zu Berlin*, ed. Gerlinde Strohmaier-Wiederanders, pp. 51–84. Halle: Andre Gursky, 1999.

Die Kunstdenkmäler der Provinz Brandenburg. Ed. Paul Eichholz et al. 4 vols. Berlin: Deutscher Kunstverlag, 1907–39.

Laabs, Annegret. *Malerei und Plastik im Zisterzienserorden: Zum Bildgebrauch zwischen sakralem Zeremoniell und Stiftermemoria, 1250–1430.* Studien zur internationalen Architektur- und Kunstgeschichte 8. Petersberg: Michael Imhof, 2000.

Ladner, Gerhard B. "Der Ursprung und die mittelalterliche Entwicklung der päpstlichen Tiara." In *Tainia: Roland Hampe zum 70. Geburtstag*, 2 vols., ed. Herbert A. Cahn and Erika Simon, vol. 1, pp. 449–81; vol. 2, plates. 86–93. Mainz: Philipp von Zabern, 1980.

Langer, Otto. *Mystische Erfahrung und spirituelle Theologie: zu Meister Eckharts Auseinandersetzung mit der Frauenfrömmigkeit seiner Zeit.* Munich: Artemis, 1987.

Langmuir, Gavin. "At the Frontiers of Faith." In Sapir Abulafia, ed., *Religious Violence*, pp. 138–56.

———. *History, Religion and Antisemitism.* Berkeley: University of California Press, 1990.

———. "The Tortures of the Body of Christ." In *Christendom and Its Discontents: Exclusion, Persecution, and Rebellion, 1000–1500*, ed. Scott Waugh and Peter Diehl, pp. 287–309. Cambridge: Cambridge University Press, 1996.

———. *Toward a Definition of Antisemitism.* Berkeley: University of California Press, 1990.

Largier, Niklaus. *Lob der Peitsche: eine Kulturgeschichte der Erregung.* Munich: C.H. Beck, 2001.

Larrington, Carolyne. "The Candlemas Vision and Marie D'Oignies' Role in Its Dissemination." In Dor et al., eds., *New Trends,* pp. 195–214.

Lefèvre, Placide. "Le miracle eucharistique de Bruxelles en 1370." *Analecta Bollandiana* 51 (1933): 325–36.

———. "La valeur historique d'une enquête épiscopale sur le miracle eucharistique de Bruxelles en 1370." *Revue d'histoire ecclésiastique* 28 (1932): 329–46.

Legner, Anton. *Reliquien in Kunst und Kult zwischen Antike und Aufklärung.* Darmstadt: Wissenschaftliche Buchgesellschaft, 1995.

Le Goff, Jacques. *The Birth of Purgatory.* Trans. Arthur Goldhammer. Chicago: University of Chicago Press, 1984.

Lehmann, Paul. "Aus dem Rapularius des Hinricus Token." In Lehmann, *Erforschung des Mittelalters: ausgewählte Abhandlungen und Aufsätze.* 5 vols. Vol. 4, pp. 187–205. Stuttgart: A. Hiersemann, 1959–62.

Lentes, Thomas. "'Andacht' und 'Gebärde': das religiöse Ausdrucksverhalten." In *Kulturelle Reformation: Sinnformationen im Umbruch, 1400–1600,* ed. Bernhard Jussen and Craig Koslofsky, pp. 26–67. Göttingen: Vandenhoeck & Ruprecht, 1999.

———. "Gezählte Frömmigkeit im späten Mittelalter." *Frühmittelalterliche Studien* 20 (1995): 40–71.

———. "So weit das Auge reicht: Sehrituale im Spätmittelalter." In Welzel et al., eds., *Das "Goldene Wunder",* pp. 241–58.

Lépin, Marius. *L'idée du sacrifice de la messe d'après les théologiens depuis l'origine jusqu'à nos jours.* Paris: Beauchesne, 1926.

Levenson, Jon D. *The Death and Resurrection of the Beloved Son: The Transformation of Child Sacrifice in Judaism and Christianity.* New Haven, Conn.: Yale University Press, 1993.

Lewis, Flora. "The Wound in Christ's Side and the Instruments of the Passion: Gendered Experience and Response." In *Women and the Book: Assessing the Visual Experience,* ed. Lesley Smith and Jane H. M. Taylor, pp. 204–29. London: British Library, 1996.

Lewis, Gertrud Jaron. *By Women, for Women, About Women: The Sister-Books of Fourteenth-Century Germany.* Studies and Texts 125. Toronto: Pontifical Institute of Mediaeval Studies, 1996.

L'Hermite-Leclercq, Paulette. "Le lait et le sang de la Vierge." In *Le sang au moyen âge,* pp. 145–62.

Lichte, Claudia. *Die Inszenierung einer Wallfahrt: der Lettner im Havelberger Dom und das Wilsnacker Wunderblut.* Worms: Werner, 1990.

Lichtenstein, Hans. "Der Vorwurf der Hostienschändung und das erste Auftreten der Juden in der Mark Brandenburg." *Zeitschrift für die Geschichte der Juden in Deutschland* 4 (1932): 189–97.

Lioi, Renato. "S. Jacques de la Marche." DS, vol. 8, cols. 41–45.

Lisch, G. C. F. "Geschichte der Heiligen-Bluts-Kapelle im Dome zu Schwerin." *Jahrbücher des Vereins für meklenburgische Geschichte und Alterthumskunde* 30 (1848): 143–87, 311–25.

———. "Hauptbegebenheiten in der ältern Geschichte der Stadt Sternberg." *Jahr-*

bücher des Vereins für meklenburgische Geschichte und Alterthumskunde aus den Arbeiten des Vereins 12 (1848): 187–307.

Lochrie, Karma. "Mystical Acts, Queer Tendencies." In *Constructing Medieval Sexuality*, ed. Karma Lochrie, Peggy McCracken, and James A. Schultz, pp. 180–200. Minneapolis: University of Minnesota Press, 1997.

Löffler, K. "Mittelalterliche Hostienwunder und Wunderhostien in Westfalen und Niedersachsen." *Auf Roter Erde: Beiträge zur Geschichte des Münsterlandes und der Nachbargebiete* 6 (1931): 9–22.

Lotter, Friedrich. "Innocens Virgo et Martyr: Thomas von Monmouth und die Verbreitung der Ritualmordlegende im Hochmittelalter." In *Die Legende vom Ritualmord: Zur Geschichte der Blutbeschuldigung gegen Juden*, ed. Rainer Erb, pp. 25–72. Berlin: Metropol, 1993.

Luscombe, D. E. "St. Anselm and Abelard." *Anselm Studies: An Occasional Journal* 1 (1983): 207–29.

Lutterbach, Hubertus. "The Mass and Holy Communion in the Medieval Penitentials (600–1200): Liturgical and Religio-Historical Perspectives." In Caspers et al., eds., *Bread of Heaven*, pp. 61–81.

MacDonald, A. A., H. N. B. Ridderbos, and R. M. Schlusemann, eds. *The Broken Body: Passion Devotion in Late-Medieval Culture.* Groningen: Egbert Forsten, 1998.

Macy, Gary. *The Theologies of the Eucharist in the Early Scholastic Period: A Study of the Salvific Function of the Sacrament According to the Theologians, c. 1080–c. 1220.* Oxford: Clarendon Press, 1984.

———. *Treasures from the Storeroom: Medieval Religion and the Eucharist.* Collegeville, Minn.: Liturgical Press, 1999.

Magirius, Heinrich. *Schneeberg: St. Wolfgang.* Passau: Kunstverlag Wieck, 1996.

Maisonneuve, Roland. "Le sang rédempteur chez Julienne de Norwich." In *Le sang au moyen âge*, pp. 433–50.

Mâle, Emile. *L'art religieux de la fin du moyen âge en France.* 7th ed. Paris: Armand Colin, 1995.

Marrow, James H. *Passion Iconography in Northern European Art of the Late Middle Ages and Early Renaissance: A Study of the Transformation of Sacred Metaphor into Descriptive Narrative.* Kortrijk, Belgium: Van Ghemmet, 1979.

Marti, Susan. "Der Papst in der Klausur: Gregorsmessen aus Klöstern." In Welzel et al., eds., *Das "Goldene Wunder"*, pp. 223–40.

Matsuda, Takami. *Death and Purgatory in Middle English Didactic Poetry.* Woodbridge: D.S. Brewer, 1997.

Mayer, Anton. "Die heilbringende Schau in Sitte und Kult." In *Heilige Überlieferung: Ausschnitte aus der Geschichte des Mönchtums und des heiligen Kultes. Festschrift für Ildefons Herwegen*, ed. Odo Casel, pp. 234–62. Münster: Aschendorff, 1938.

———. *Die Liturgie in der europäischen Geistesgeschichte: gesammelte Aufsätze.* Ed. E. von Severus. Darmstadt: Wissenschaftliche Buchgesellschaft, 1971.

McCarthy, Dennis J. "The Symbolism of Blood and Sacrifice." *Journal of Biblical Literature* 88 (1969): 166–76.

McCracken, Peggy. *The Curse of Eve, the Wound of the Hero: Blood, Gender, and Medieval Literature.* Philadelphia: University of Pennsylvania Press, 2003.

McCue, James F. "The Doctrine of Transubstantiation from Berengar Through the Council of Trent." *Harvard Theological Review* 61 (1968): 385–430.

McCulloh, John. "Jewish Ritual Murder: William of Norwich, Thomas of Monmouth, and the Early Dissemination of the Myth." *Speculum* 72, 3 (1997): 698–740.

McGinn, Bernard. *The Flowering of Mysticism: Men and Women in the New Mysticism (1200–1350)*. Vol. 3 of McGinn, *The Presence of God: A History of Western Christian Mysticism*. New York: Crossroad, 1998.

———. "Introduction: Meister Eckhart and the Beguines in the Context of Vernacular Theology." In *Meister Eckhart and the Beguine Mystics: Hadewijch of Brabant, Mechthild of Magdeburg, and Marguerite Porete*, ed. McGinn, pp. 1–14. New York: Continuum, 1994.

McHugh, J. F. "The Sacrifice of the Mass at the Council of Trent." In Sykes, ed., *Sacrifice and Redemption*, pp. 157–81.

McInerny, Ralph. "Aquinas, St. Thomas." DMA, vol. 1, pp. 353–66.

McNamara, Jo Ann. "The Need to Give: Suffering and Female Sanctity in the Middle Ages." In *Images of Sainthood in Medieval Europe*, ed. Renata Blumenfeld-Kosinski and Timea Szell, pp. 199–221. Ithaca, N.Y.: Cornell University Press, 1991.

McNamer, Sarah. "Further Evidence for the Date of the Pseudo-Bonaventuran 'Meditationes vitae Christi'." *Franciscan Studies* 50 (1990): 235–61.

Megivern, James J. *Concomitance and Communion: A Study in Eucharistic Doctrine and Practice*. Studia Friburgensia n.s. 33. Fribourg: University Press, 1963.

Meier, Esther. "Die Gregorsmesse im Bildprogramm der Antwerper Schnitzretabel." In Welzel et al., eds., *Das "Goldene Wunder"*, pp. 183–199.

Meier, Ludger. "Christianus de Hiddestorf OFM Scholae Erfordiensis columna." *Antonianum* 14 (1939): 43–76.

———."Der Erfurter Franziskanertheologe Johannes Bremer und der Streit um das Wilsnacker Wunderblut." In *Aus der Geisteswelt des Mittelalters (Festschrift Grabmann)*, ed. Albert Lang, Josef Lechner, and Michael Schmaus, pp. 1247–64. Beiträge zur Geschichte der Philosophie und Theologie des Mittelalters: Texte und Untersuchungen, Supplementband 3. Münster: Aschendorff, 1935.

———. *Die Werke des Erfurter Kartäusers Jakob von Jüterbog in ihrer handschriftlichen Überlieferung*. Beiträge zur Geschichte der Philosophie und Theologie des Mittelalters: Texte und Untersuchungen 37, 5. Münster: Aschendorff, 1955.

———. "Wilsnack als Spiegel Deutscher Vorreformation." *Zeitschrift für Religions- und Geistesgeschichte* 3, 1 (1951): 53–69.

Merback, Mitchell B. "Channels of Grace: Eucharistic Imagery, Architecture and Purgatory Cult at the Host-Miracle Pilgrimages of Late Medieval Bavaria." In *Art and Architecture of Medieval Pilgrimage in Northern Europe*, ed. Sarah Blick and Rita Tekippe, pp. 587–646. Leiden: Brill, 2004.

———. "Reverberations of Guilt and Violence, Resonances of Peace: A Comment on Caroline Walker Bynum's Lecture." *Bulletin of the German Historical Institute* 30 (Spring 2002): 37–50.

———. *The Thief, the Cross, and the Wheel: Pain and the Spectacle of Punishment in Medieval and Renaissance Europe*. Chicago: University of Chicago Press, 1999.

Merklein, Helmut. "Der Sühnegedanke in der Jesustradition und bei Paulus." In Gerhards and Richter, eds., *Das Opfer*, pp. 59–91.

Mertens, Dieter. "Jacques de Paradiso." DS, vol. 8, cols. 52–55.

———. "Jakob von Paradies." *Verfasserlexikon*, vol. 4, cols. 478–87.

Meuthen, Erich. "Die deutsche Legationsreise des Nikolaus von Kues, 1451/1452." In

Lebenslehren und Weltentwürfe im Übergang vom Mittelalter zur Neuzeit: Politik, Bildung, Naturkunde, Theologie: Bericht über Kolloquien der Kommission zur Erforschung der Kultur des Spätmittelalters 1983 bis 1987, ed. Hartmut Boockmann, Bernd Moeller, and Karl Stackmann, pp. 421–99. Göttingen: Vandenhoeck & Ruprecht, 1989.

———. "Das Itinerar der deutschen Legationsreise des Nikolaus von Kues 1451/52." In *Papstgeschichte und Landesgeschichte: Festschrift für Hermann Jacobs zum 65. Geburtstag*, ed. Joachim Dalhaus et al., pp. 484–85. Cologne: Böhlau, 1995.

———. *Nikolaus von Kues, 1401–1464: Skizze einer Biographie*. Münster: Aschendorff, 1982.

Meyerson, Mark D., Daniel Thiery, and Oren Falk, eds. *"A Great Effusion of Blood"? Interpreting Medieval Violence*. Toronto: University of Toronto Press, 2004.

Michel, Albert. "Forme du corps humain." DTC, vol. 6, cols. 546–88.

———. "Volontarisme." DTC, vol. 15, cols. 3309–22.

———. "Volonté de Dieu." DTC, vol. 15, cols. 3322–74.

Miramon, Charles. "Déconstruction et reconstruction du tabou de la femme menstruée (XIIe–XIIIe siècle)." In *Kontinuitäten und Zäsuren in der europäischen Rechtsgeschichte: europäisches Forum junger Rechtshistorikerinnen und Rechtshistoriker, München 22.–24. Juli 1998*, ed. Andreas Thier, Guido Pfeifer, and Philipp Grzimek, pp. 79–107. Rechtshistorische Reihe 196. Frankfurt: Peter Lang, 1999.

———. "La fin d'un tabou? L'interdiction de communier pour la femme menstruée au moyen âge: le cas du XIIe siècle." In *Le sang au moyen âge*, pp. 163–81.

Mitchell, Nathan. *Cult and Controversy: The Worship of the Eucharist Outside Mass*. New York: Pueblo, 1982.

Moereels, Louis. "Dorlant . . . Chartreux, 1454–1507." DS, vol. 3, cols. 1646–51.

Molls, Helmut. *Die Lehre von der Eucharistie als Opfer*. Theophaneia: Beiträge zur Religions- und Kirchengeschichte des Altertums 26. Cologne: Peter Hanstein, 1975.

Morgan, Nigel. "Longinus and the Wounded Heart." *Wiener Jahrbuch für Kunstgeschichte* 46–47: *Beiträge zur mittelalterlichen Kunst* 2 (1933/34): 507–18.

Most, Glenn W. *Doubting Thomas*. Cambridge, Mass.: Harvard University Press, 2005.

Mulder-Bakker, Anneke. *Lives of the Anchoresses: The Rise of the Urban Recluse in Medieval Europe*. Trans. Myra Heerspink Scholz. Philadelphia: University of Pennsylvania Press, 2005.

900 Jahre Heilig-Blut-Verehrung in Weingarten 1094–1994: Festschrift zum Heilig-Blut-Jubiläum am 12. März 1994. Ed. Norbert Kruse and Hans Ulrich Rudolf. 3 vols. Sigmaringen: J. Thorbecke, 1994.

Nagel, Adalbert. "Das Heilige Blut Christi." In *Festschrift zur 900-Jahr-Feier*, pp. 188–229.

Newman, Barbara. *From Virile Woman to WomanChrist: Studies in Medieval Religion and Literature*. Philadelphia: University of Philadelphia Press, 1995.

———. *God and the Goddesses: Vision, Poetry and Belief in the Middle Ages*. Philadelphia: University of Pennsylvania Press, 2003.

———. "On the Threshold of the Dead: Purgatory, Hell, and Religious Women." In Newman, *From Virile Woman to WomanChrist*, pp. 108–36.

———. "What Did It Mean to Say 'I Saw'? The Clash Between Theory and Practice in Medieval Visionary Culture." *Speculum* 80, 1 (January 2005): 1–43.

Nimmo, Duncan. *Reform and Division in the Medieval Franciscan Order: From St. Fran-*

cis to the Foundation of the Capuchins. Bibliotheca seraphico-capuccina 33. Rome: Capuchin Historical Institute, 1987.

Oberman, Heiko A. *The Harvest of Medieval Theology: Gabriel Biel and Late Medieval Nominalism*. Cambridge, Mass.: Harvard University Press, 1963.

———. *The Roots of Anti-Semitism in the Age of Renaissance and Reformation*. Trans. J. I. Porter. Philadelphia: Fortress Press, 1984.

———. *Wurzeln des Antisemitismus: Christenangst und Judenplage im Zeitalter von Humanismus und Reformation*. Berlin: Severin und Siedler, 1981.

O'Collins, Gerald. "Redemption: Some Crucial Issues." In Davis et al., eds., *The Redemption*, pp. 1–22.

Oexle, Judith, Markus Bauer, and Marius Winzeler, eds. *Zeit und Ewigkeit: 128 Tage in St. Marienstern: Ausstellungskatalog*. Halle: Stekovics, 1998.

Ohst, Martin. *Pflichtbeichte: Untersuchungen zum Busswesen im Hohen und Späten Mittelalter*. Beiträge zur historischen Theologie 89. Tübingen: Mohr [Siebeck], 1995.

Oliger, Livarius. "Johannes Kannemann, ein deutscher Franziskaner aus dem 15. Jahrhundert." *Franziskanische Studien* 5 (1918): 44–50.

Oliver, Judith. "Image et dévotion: le rôle de l'art dans l'institution de la Fête-Dieu." In Haquin, ed., *Fête-Dieu*, vol. 1, pp. 153–72.

Otter, Monika. *Inventiones: Fiction and Referentiality in Twelfth-Century English Historical Writing*. Chapel Hill: University of North Carolina Press, 1996.

Panofsky, Erwin. "'Imago Pietatis': ein Beitrag zur Typengeschichte des 'Schmerzensmanns' und der 'Maria Mediatrix'." In *Festschrift für Max J. Friedländer zum 60. Geburtstage*, pp. 261–308. Leipzig: Seemann, 1927.

Parshall, Peter and Rainier Schoch, with David S. Areford, Richard S. Field, and Peter Schmidt. *Origins of European Printmaking: Fifteenth-Century Woodcuts and Their Public*. Washington, D.C.: National Gallery of Art with Yale University Press, 2005.

Passarge, Walter. *Das deutsche Vesperbild im Mittelalter mit 40 Abbildungen*. Cologne: F.J. Marcan, 1924.

Peacock, Edward. "Extracts from Lincoln Episcopal Visitations in the 15th, 16th, and 17th Centuries." *Archaeologia: or Miscellaneous Tracts Relating to Antiquity* 48 (1885): 251–53.

Pedersen, Else Marie Wiberg. "The In-Carnation of Beatrice of Nazareth's Theology." In Dor et al., eds., *New Trends*, pp. 61–80.

Peebles, Rose J. *The Legend of Longinus in Ecclesiastical Tradition and in English Literature, and Its Connection with the Grail*. Baltimore: J.H. Furst, 1911.

Peers, Glenn. *Sacred Shock: Framing Visual Experience in Byzantium*. University Park: Pennsylvania State University Press, 2004.

Pelikan, Jaroslav. *The Growth of Medieval Theology (600–1300)*. Vol. 3 of Pelikan, *The Christian Tradition: A History of the Development of Doctrine*. Chicago: University of Chicago Press, 1978.

———. *Reformation of Church and Dogma (1300–1700)*. Vol. 4 of Pelikan, *The Christian Tradition: A History of the Development of Doctrine*. Chicago: University of Chicago Press, 1983.

Perles, J. "Geschichte der Juden in Posen." *Monatsschrift für Geschichte und Wissenschaft des Judenthums* 13 (1864): 281–95, 321–34, 361–73, 409–20, 449–61.

Perrot, Jean-Pierre. "Du sang au lait: l'imaginaire du sang et ses logiques dans les passions de martyrs." In *Le sang au moyen âge*, pp. 459–70.

Peters, Ursula. "Vita religiosa und spirituelles Erleben: Frauenmystik und frauenmystische Literatur im 15. und 16. Jahrhundert." In *Deutsche Literatur von Frauen*, ed. Gisela Brinker-Gabler, vol. 1, pp. 88–112. Munich: Beck, 1988.

Petrecca, Paolo. *San Giovanni da Capestrano*. Florence: Atheneum, 1992.

Plate, Christa and Friedrich Plate. "Die Ergebnisse der Ausgrabungen in der Wunderblutkapelle des Klosters Heiligengrabe, Krs. Wittstock." *Ausgrabungen und Funde: Archäologische Berichte und Informationen* 32 (1987): 94–99.

Platelle, Henri. "Guibert de Nogent et le 'De pignoribus sanctorum.' Richesses et limites d'une critique médiévale des reliques." In *Les reliques: objets, cultes, symboles: Actes du colloque international de l'Université du Littoral-Côte d'Opale (Boulogne-sur-Mer) 4–5 septembre 1997*, ed. E. Buzóky and A.-M. Helvétius, pp. 109–21. Turnhout: Brepols, 1999.

Pollard, William and Robert Boenig, eds. *Mysticism and Spirituality in Medieval England*. Cambridge: D.S. Brewer, 1997.

Poor, Sara S. *Mechthild of Magdeburg and Her Book: Gender and the Making of Textual Authority*. Philadelphia: University of Pennsylvania Press, 2004.

Pranger, Burcht. "Le sacrement de l'eucharistie et la prolifération de l'imaginaire aux XIe et XIIe siècles." In Haquin, ed., *Fête-Dieu*, vol. 1, pp. 97–116.

Preger, Wilhelm. *Geschichte der deutschen Mystik im Mittelalter*. 3 vols. Leipzig: Dörffling und Franke, 1874–93.

Prümers, Rodgero. "Der Hostiendiebstahl zu Posen im Jahr 1399." *Zeitschrift der historischen Gesellschaft für die Provinz Posen* 20 (1905): 293–317.

Puppi, Lionello. *Torment in Art: Paint, Violence and Martyrdom*. New York: Rizzoli, 1991.

Rädle, Fidel. "*Ars moriendi*: Sterben und Sterbebeistand im späten Mittelalter und im Humanismus." *Jahrbuch der Akademie der Wissenschaften zu Göttingen* (2003): 177–88.

Rainey, Anson and Aaron Rothkoff. "Sacrifice." In *Encyclopaedia Judaica*. 16 vols. Vol. 14, cols. 519–616. New York: Macmillan, 1971–72.

Rashdall, Hastings. *The Idea of Atonement in Christian Theology*. London: Macmillan, 1919.

Raynaud, Christiane. *Images et pouvoirs au moyen âge*. Paris: Léopard d'Or, 1993.

———. *La violence au moyen âge: XIIIe–XVe siècle: d'après les livres d'histoire en français*. Paris: Léopard d'Or, 1990.

Reinhold, Uta. "Das Fritzlarer Vesperbild: ein Meisterwerk mittelalterlicher Schnitz- und Fasskunst." *Denkmale und Kulturgeschichte* 2 (2000): 33–38.

Resnick, Irven M. "Medieval Roots of the Myth of Jewish Male Menses." *Harvard Theological Review* 93 (2000): 241–63.

Reynolds, Philip Lyndon. *Food and the Body: Some Peculiar Questions in High Medieval Theology*. Leiden: Brill, 1999.

Rhodes, J. T. "The Body of Christ in English Eucharistic Devotion, c. 1500–c. 1620." In *New Science Out of Old Books: Studies in Manuscripts and Early Printed Books in Honour of A. I. Doyle*, ed. Richard Beadle and A. J. Piper, pp. 388–419. Aldershot: Scolar Press, 1995.

Richstätter, Karl. *Die Herz-Jesu-Verehrung des deutschen Mittelalters*. 2nd ed. Munich and Regensburg: Kösel & Pustet, 1924.

Ridderbos, Bernhard. "The Man of Sorrows: Pictorial Images and Metaphorical Statements." In MacDonald et al., eds., *Broken Body*, pp. 145–81.

Rigaux, Dominique. "Autour de la dispute *De Sanguine Christi*: une relecture de quelques peintures italiennes de la seconde moitié du XVe siècle." In *Le sang au moyen âge*, pp. 393–404.

Rivière, Jean. *Le dogme de la rédemption: essai d'étude historique*. Paris: V. Lecoffre, 1905.

Robbins, R. H. "Popular Prayers in Middle English Verse." *Modern Philology* 36 (1939): 337–50.

Roberts, M. E. "The Relic of the Holy Blood and the Iconography of the Thirteenth-Century North Transept Portal of Westminster Abbey." In *England in the Thirteenth Century: Proceedings of the 1984 Harlaxton Symposium*, ed. W. M. Ormrod, pp. 129–42. Woodbridge: Boydell, 1986.

Rohling, Joseph Henry. *The Blood of Christ in Christian Latin Literature Before the Year 1000*. Washington, D.C.: Catholic University of America, 1932.

Rossmann, Heribert. "Meyronnes." DS, vol. 10, cols. 1155–61.

Roth, Bartholomäus. *Franz von Mayronis O.F.M.: sein Leben, seine Werke, seine Lehre vom Formalunterschied in Gott*. Franziskanische Forschungen 3. Werl: Franziskus-Druckerei, 1936.

Rothkrug, Lionel. "German Holiness and Western Sanctity in Medieval and Modern History." *Historical Reflections/Réflexions historiques* 15, 1 (1988): 161–249.

———. "Popular Religion and Holy Shrines: Their Influence on the Origins of the German Reformation and Their Role in German Cultural Development." In *Religion and the People, 800–1700*, ed. J. Obelkevich, pp. 20–86. Chapel Hill: University of North Carolina Press, 1979.

———. *Religious Practices and Collective Perceptions: Hidden Homologies in the Renaissance and Reformation. Historical Reflections/Réflexions historiques* 7, 1 (1980).

Roux, Jean-Paul. *Le sang: mythes, symboles et réalités*. Paris: Fayard, 1988.

Rubin, Miri. *Corpus Christi: The Eucharist in Late Medieval Culture*. Cambridge: Cambridge University Press, 1991.

———. *Gentile Tales: The Narrative Assault on Late Medieval Jews*. New Haven, Conn.: Yale University Press, 1999. Reprint Philadelphia: University of Pennsyvania Press, 2004.

———. "Imagining the Jew: The Late Medieval Eucharistic Discourse." In Hsia and Lehmann, eds., *In and Out of the Ghetto*, pp. 177–208.

Rublack, Ulinka. "Female Spirituality and the Infant Jesus in Late Medieval Dominican Convents." In Scribner and Johnson, eds., *Popular Religion in Germany*, pp. 16–37.

Rudolf, Hans Ulrich. "Heilig-Blut-Brauchtum im Überblick." In *900 Jahre Heilig-Blut-Verehrung*, vol. 2, pp. 553–74.

Ryan, Salvador. "'Reign of Blood': Aspects of Devotion to the Wounds of Christ in Late Medieval Gaelic Ireland." In *Irish History: A Research Yearbook*, ed. Joost Augusteijn and Mary Ann Lyons, vol. 1, pp. 137–49. Dublin: Four Courts Press, 2002.

Salisbury, Joyce E. *The Blood of the Martyrs: Unintended Consequences of Ancient Violence*. New York: Routledge, 2004.

Le sang au moyen âge: Actes du quatrième colloque international de Montpellier, Université de Paul Valéry (27–29 novembre 1997). Ed. Marcel Faure. Cahiers du C.R.I.S. I.M.A. 4. Montpellier: Université Paul Valéry, 1999.

Sapir Abulafia, Anna. "The Intellectual and Spiritual Quest for Christ and Central Medieval Persecution of Jews." In Sapir Abulafia, ed., *Religious Violence*, pp. 61–85.

———, ed. *Religious Violence Between Christians and Jews: Medieval Roots, Modern Perspectives*. Hampshire: Palgrave, 2002.

Sargent, Stephen D. "A Critique of Lionel Rothkrug's List of Bavarian Pilgrimage Sites." *Archive for Reformation History/Archiv für Reformationsgeschichte* 78 (1987): 351–58.

Schäfer, Karl H. "Märkische Fronleichnamsverehrung und ihre kulturelle Auswirkung vor Luther." *Wichmann Jahrbuch* 2/3 (1931/32): 99–107.

Scheid, John. *Quand faire, c'est croire: les rites sacrificiels des Romains*. Aubier: Flammarion, 2005.

Schiller, Gertrud. *Iconography of Christian Art*. Trans. Janet Seligman. 2 vols. Greenwich, Conn.: New York Graphic Society, 1972.

———. *Ikonographie der christlichen Kunst*. 4 vols. Gütersloh: Mohn, 1966–80.

Schlager, Patricius. "Geschichte des Franziskanerklosters zu Güstrow in Mecklenburg." *Franziskanische Studien* 5 (1918): 68–82.

Schmidt, G. "Rostocker Drucke zu Halberstadt." *Jahrbücher des Vereins für meklenburgische Geschichte und Alterthumskunde* 53 (1888): 339–50.

Schmidt, K. *Das heilige Blut von Sternberg*. Halle: Verein für Reformationsgeschichte (Max Niemeyer), 1892.

Schmitt, Jean-Claude. *Ghosts in the Middle Ages: The Living and the Dead in Medieval Society*. Trans. Teresa L. Fagan. Chicago: University of Chicago Press, 1998.

Schneider, Ambrosius et al. *Die Cistercienser: Geschichte, Geist, Kunst*. 3rd ed. Cologne: Wienand, 1986.

Schrade, Hubert. "Beiträge zur Erklärung des Schmerzensmannbildes." In *Deutschkundliches: Friedrich Panzer zum 60. Geburtstage überreicht von heidelberger Fachgenossen*, ed. Hans Teske, pp. 164–82. Heidelberg: C. Winter, 1930.

Schreiner, Klaus. "Benediktinische Klosterreform als zeitgebundene Auslegung der Regel: geistige, religiöse und soziale Erneuerung in spätmittelalterlichen Klöstern Süddeutschlands im Zeichen der Kastler, Melker und Bursfelder Reform." *Beiträge zur westfälischen Kirchengeschichte* 86 (1986): 105–95.

Schuder, Rosemary and Rudolf Hirsch, eds. *Der gelbe Fleck: Wurzeln und Wirkungen des Judenhasses in der deutschen Geschichte: Essays*. Cologne: Pahl-Rugenstein, 1988.

Schulte, P. Raphael. *Die Messe als Opfer der Kirche: die Lehre frühmittelalterlicher Autoren über das eucharistische Opfer*. Liturgiewissenschaftliche Quellen und Forschungen 35. Münster: Aschendorff, 1958.

Schulz, Frieder. "Das Opfermotiv in der liturgischen Tradition der Reformationskirchen bis heute." In Gerhards and Richter, eds., *Das Opfer*, pp. 234–56.

Schwager, Raymund. *Must There Be Scapegoats? Violence and Redemption in the Bible*. 2nd ed. Leominster: Gracewing, 2000.

Scott, Karen. "Mystical Death, Bodily Death: Catherine of Siena and Raymond of Capua on the Mystic's Encounter with God." In *Gendered Voices: Medieval Saints and Their Interpreters*, ed. Catherine M. Mooney, pp. 136–67. Philadelphia: University of Pennsylvania Press, 1999.

———. "Urban Spaces, Women's Networks, and the Lay Apostolate in the Siena of

Catherine Benincasa." In *Creative Women in Medieval and Early Modern Italy: A Religious and Artistic Renaissance*, ed. E. Ann Matter and John Coakley, pp. 105–19. Philadelphia: University of Pennsylvania Press, 1999.

Scribner, Bob [Robert]. "Popular Piety and Modes of Visual Perception in Late-Medieval and Reformation Germany." *Journal of Religious History* 15 (1989): 448–69.

———. "Vom Sakralbild zur sinnlichen Schau." In *Gepeinigt, begehrt, vergessen: Symbolik und Sozialbezug des Körpers im späten Mittelalter und der frühen Neuzeit*, ed. Klaus Schreiner and Norbert Schnitzler, pp. 309–36. Munich: Fink, 1992.

Scribner, Bob [Robert] and Trevor Johnson, eds. *Popular Religion in Germany and Central Europe, 1400–1800*. New York: St. Martin's Press, 1996.

Séjourné, P. "Reliques." DTC, vol. 13, pt. 2, cols. 2330–65.

Shuger, Debora Kuller. *The Renaissance Bible: Scholarship, Sacrifice, and Subjectivity*. Berkeley: University of California Press, 1995.

Sigal, Pierre-André. *L'homme et le miracle dans la France médiévale (XIe–XIIe siècle)*. Paris: Éditions du Cerf, 1985.

Sinka, Margit M. "Christological Mysticism in Mechtild von Magdeburg's *Das fliessende Licht der Gottheit*: A Journey of Wounds." *Germanic Review* 60, 4 (1985): 123–28.

Šmahel, František. *Die Hussitische Revolution*. Trans. Thomas Krzenck. 3 vols. MGH Schriften 43. Hannover: Hahn, 2002.

Snoek, Godefridus J. C. *Medieval Piety from Relics to the Eucharist: A Process of Mutual Interaction*. Studies in the History of Christian Thought 63. Leiden: Brill, 1995.

Soergel, Philip M. *Wondrous in His Saints: Counter-Reformation Propaganda in Bavaria*. Berkeley: University of California Press, 1993.

Southern, R. W. *Saint Anselm, a Portrait in a Landscape*. Cambridge: Cambridge University Press, 1990.

———. *St. Anselm and His Biographer: A Study of Monastic Life and Thought, 1059–c. 1130*. Cambridge: Cambridge University Press, 1966.

Spinka, Matthew. *John Hus: A Biography*. Princeton, N.J.: Princeton University Press, 1968.

Stacey, Robert C. "From Ritual Crucifixion to Host Desecration: Jews and the Body of Christ." *Jewish History* 12, 1 (1998): 11–28.

Stahuljak, Zrinka. *Bloodless Genealogies of the French Middle Ages:* Translatio, *Kinship, and Metaphor*. Gainesville: University Press of Florida, 2005.

Steer, Georg. "Der Laie als Anreger und Adressat deutscher Prosaliteratur im 14. Jahrhundert." In *Zur deutschen Literatur und Sprache des 14. Jahrhunderts: Dubliner Colloquium 1981*, ed. Walter Haug, T. R. Jackson, and J. Janota, pp. 354–67. Heidelberg: S. Winter, 1983.

Stock, Brian. *The Implications of Literacy: Written Language and Models of Interpretation in the Eleventh and Twelfth Centuries*. Princeton, N.J.: Princeton University Press, 1983.

Stoelen, Anselme. "Denys le Chartreux." DS, vol. 3, cols. 430–49.

Strohmaier-Wiederanders, Gerlinde. *Geschichte vom Kloster Stift zum Heiligengrabe*. Berlin: Nicolai, 1995.

Stump, Thomas and Otto Gillen. "Hl. Blut." RDK, vol. 2, cols. 947–58.

Suckale, Robert. "*Arma Christi*: Überlegungen zur Zeichenhaftigkeit mittelalterlicher Andachtsbilder." *Städel-Jahrbuch* N.F. 6 (1977): 177–208.

Sullivan, Donald. "Nicolas of Cusa as Reformer: The Papal Legation to the Germanies, 1451–52." *Mediaeval Studies* 36 (1974): 382–428.

Sumption, Jonathan. *Pilgrimage: An Image of Medieval Religion*. Totowa, N.J.: Rowman and Littlefield, 1975.

Swanson, R. N. "Passion and Practice: The Social and Ecclesiastical Implications of Passion Devotions in the Late Middle Ages." In MacDonald et al., eds., *Broken Body*, pp. 1–30.

———. *Religion and Devotion in Europe, c. 1215–c. 1515*. Cambridge: Cambridge University Press, 1995.

Swarzenski, Hanns. *The Berthold Missal: The Pierpont Morgan Library MS 710 and the Scriptorium of Weingarten Abbey*. New York: Pierpont Morgan Library, 1943.

Sweetman, Robert. "Thomas of Cantimpré, *Mulieres Religiosae*, and Purgatorial Piety: Hagiographical *Vitae* and the Beguine 'Voice.'" In *A Distinct Voice: Medieval Studies in Honor of Leonard E. Boyle, O.P.*, ed. Jacqueline Brown and W. P. Stoneman, pp. 606–28. Notre Dame, Ind.: University of Notre Dame Press, 1997.

Swillus, Harald. "Hostienfrevellegende und Judenverfolgung in Iphofen: Ein Beitrag zur Entstehungsgeschichte der Kirche zum hl. Blut im Gräbenviertel." *Würzburger Diözesan-Geschichtsblätter* 58 (1996): 87–107.

Sykes, S. W., ed. *Sacrifice and Redemption: Durham Essays in Theology*. Cambridge: Cambridge University Press, 1991.

Sylla, Edith Dudley. "Autonomous and Handmaiden Science: St. Thomas Aquinas and William of Ockham on the Physics of the Eucharist." In *The Cultural Context of Medieval Learning: Proceedings of the First International Colloquium on Philosophy, Science and Theology in the Middle Ages, September 1973*, ed. John E. Murdoch and Edith D. Sylla, pp. 349–91. Boston Studies in the Philosophy of Science 36. Dordrecht: Reidel, 1974.

Tarayre, Michel. "Le sang dans le *Speculum majus* de Vincent de Beauvais: de la science aux *Miracula*." In *Le sang au moyen âge*, pp. 343–59.

Teetaert, A. "Scotellus di Tonnaparte." DTC, vol. 14, pt. 2, cols. 1730–33.

Terrinca, Natale da. *La devozione al Preziosissimo Sangue di nostro Signore Gesú Cristo: Studio storico teologico a proposito di un trattato inedito di S. Giovanni da Capestrano*. Rome: Pia Unione del Preziosissimo Sangue, 1969.

Teuscher, Simon. "Parenté, politique et comptabilité: chroniques familiales autour de 1500 (Suisse et Allemagne du sud)." *Annales. Histoire, sciences sociales* 59, 4 (2004): 847–58.

Thachil, Jose. *The Vedic and the Christian Concept of Sacrifice*. Kerala, India: Pontifical Institute of Theology and Philosophy, 1985.

Thomas, Alois. *Die Darstellung Christi in der Kelter: eine theologische und kulturhistorische Studie, zugleich ein Beitrag zur Geschichte und Volkskunde des Weinbaus*. Forschungen zur Volkskunde 20/21. Düsseldorf: L. Schwann, 1936.

Thompson, Augustine. *Cities of God: The Religion of the Italian Communes, 1125–1325*. University Park: Pennsylvania State University Press, 2005.

Tierney, Brian. *Foundations of the Conciliar Theory: The Contribution of the Medieval Canonists from Gratian to the Great Schism*. Cambridge: Cambridge University Press, 1955.

Tixier, René. "Richard Rolle: la mémoire des plaies." In *Le sang au moyen âge*, pp. 377–90.

Tönsing, Michael. *Johannes Malkaw aus Preussen (ca. 1360–1416): Ein Kleriker im Spannungsfeld von Kanzel, Ketzerprozess und Kirchenspaltung.* Warendorf: Fahlbusch, 2004.

Torsy, Jakob. "Eucharistische Frömmigkeit im späten Mittelalter." *Archiv für mittelrheinische Kirchengeschichte* 23 (1971): 89–102.

Toussaert, Jacques. *Le sentiment religieux en Flandre à la fin du moyen âge.* Paris: Librairie Plon, 1963.

Trachtenberg, Joshua. *The Devil and the Jews: The Medieval Conception of the Jew and Its Relation to Modern Anti-Semitism.* New Haven, Conn.: Yale University Press, 1943.

Treue, Wolfgang. "Schlechte und gute Christen: zur Rolle von Christen in antijüdischen Ritualmord- und Hostienschändungslegenden." *Aschkenas: Zeitschrift für Geschichte und Kultur der Juden* 2 (1992): 95–116.

Tripps, Johannes. *Das handelnde Bildwerk in der Gotik: Forschungen zu den Bedeutungsschichten und der Funktion des Kirchengebäudes und seiner Ausstattung in der Hoch- und Spätgotik.* Berlin: Gebrüder Mann, 1998.

Tubach, Frederic C. *Index exemplorum: A Handbook of Medieval Religious Tales.* FF Communications 204. Helsinki: Suomalainen Tiedeakatemia, 1969.

Tüskés, Gábor and Éva Knapp. "Die Verehrung des Heiligen Blutes in Ungarn: ein Überblick." *Jahrbuch für Volkskunde* 10 (1987): 179–202.

Van Engen, John. "Friar Johannes Nyder on Laypeople Living as Religious in the World." In *Vita Religiosa im Mittelalter: Festschrift für Kaspar Elm zum 70. Geburtstag*, ed. Franz Felten and Nikolas Jaspert, pp. 583–615. Berliner historische Studien 31, Ordensstudien 13. Berlin: Duncker & Humblot, 1999.

Van Proeyen, Michel. "Sang et hérédité: À la croisée des imaginaires médicaux et sociaux des XIIIe et XIVe siècles." In *Le sang au moyen âge*, pp. 69–75.

Vansteenberghe, Edmond. *Le cardinal Nicolas de Cues (1401–1464): l'Action—la pensée.* Paris: H. Champion, 1920.

Vattioni, Francesco, ed. *Sangue e antropologia nella teologia. Atti della VI settimana, Roma 23 al 28 novembre 1987.* Vol. 2. Rome: Pia Unione del Preziosissimo Sangue, 1989.

———, ed. *Sangue e antropologia nella teologia. Atti della VII settimana, Roma 27 novembre–2 dicembre 1989.* Vol. 3. Rome: Pia Unione del Preziosissimo Sangue, 1991.

Vidal, Fernando. "Brains, Bodies, Selves, and Science: Anthropologies of Identity and the Resurrection of the Body." *Critical Inquiry* 28 (2002): 930–74.

Viljamaa, Toivo, Asko Timonen, and Christian Krötzel, eds. *Crudelitas: The Politics of Cruelty in the Ancient and Medieval World: Proceedings of the International Conference, Turku (Finland), May, 1991.* Medium Aevum Quotidianum, Sonderband 2. Krems, Austria: Medium Aevum Quotidianum, 1992.

Vincent, Nicholas. *The Holy Blood: King Henry III and the Westminster Blood Relic.* Cambridge: Cambridge University Press, 2001.

Voaden, Rosalynn. *God's Words, Women's Voices: The Discernment of Spirits in the Writing of Late-Medieval Women Visionaries.* York: York Medieval Press, 1999.

Voisenet, Jacques. "Le tabou du sang dans les pénitentiels du haut moyen âge." In *Le sang au moyen âge*, pp. 111–25.

Volf, Miroslav. *Exclusion and Embrace: A Theological Exploration of Identity, Otherness, and Reconciliation.* Nashville, Tenn.: Abingdon Press, 1996.

———. "Forgiveness, Reconciliation, and Justice: A Theological Contribution to a More Peaceful Social Environment." *Millennium: Journal of International Studies* 29, 3 (2000): 861–77.

von Staden, Heinrich. "Women and Dirt." *Helios* 19, 1–2 (1992): 7–30.

Wachinger, Burghart. "Die Passion Christi und die Literatur." In Haug and Wachinger, eds., *Die Passion Christi*, pp. 1–20.

Wadding, Luke. *Annales minorum seu Trium Ordinum a S. Francisco Institutorum*. 32 vols. 3rd ed. Quaracchi: Tipografia Barbera, Alfani e Venturi proprietari, 1931–64.

Wallace, Mark I. and Theophus H. Smith, eds. *Curing Violence*. Sonoma, Calif.: Polebridge, 1994.

Wandel, Lee Palmer. *The Eucharist in the Reformation: Incarnation and Liturgy*. Cambridge: Cambridge University Press, 2006.

Ward, Benedicta. "Julian the Solitary." In *Julian Reconsidered*, ed. Kenneth Leech and Sister Benedicta Ward, pp. 11–35. Fairacres, Oxford: Sisters of the Love of God, 1988.

Watanabe, Morimichi. "The German Church Shortly Before the Reformation: Nicolaus Cusanus and the Veneration of the Bleeding Hosts at Wilsnack." In *Reform and Renewal in the Middle Ages and the Renaissance: Studies in Honor of Louis Pascoe, S.J.*, ed. Thomas M. Izbicki and Christopher M. Bellitto, pp. 210–23. Leiden: Brill, 2000.

Watson, Nicholas. "Julian of Norwich." In *The Cambridge Companion to Medieval Women's Writing*, ed. Carolyn Dinshaw and David Wallace, pp. 210–21. Cambridge: Cambridge University Press, 2003.

———. "Visions of Inclusion: Universal Salvation and Vernacular Theology in Pre-Reformation England." *Journal of Medieval and Early Modern Studies* 27, 2 (1997): 145–87.

Wattenbach, Wilhelm. "Beiträge zur Geschichte der Mark Brandenburg aus Handschriften der Königlichen Bibliothek." In Wilhelm Wattenbach, *Kleine Abhandlungen zur mittelalterlichen Geschichte: Gesammelte Berliner Akademieschriften*. 1882. Reprint Leipzig: Zentralantiquariat der DDR in cooperation with Hakkert [Amsterdam], 1970.

Weichenrieder, Lukas. "Das Heilige Blut von Mantua." In *900 Jahre Heilig-Blut-Verehrung* vol. 1, pp. 331–36.

Weinstein, Donald and Rudolph Bell. *Saints and Society: The Two Worlds of Western Christendom, 1000–1700*. Chicago: University of Chicago Press, 1982.

Welzel, Barbara. *Abendmahlsaltäre vor der Reformation*. Berlin: Gebr. Mann Verlag, 1991.

Welzel, Barbara, Thomas Lentes, and Heike Schlie, eds. *Das "Goldene Wunder" in der Dortmunder Petrikirche: Bildgebrauch und Bildproduktion im Mittelalter*. Dortmunder Mittelalter-Forschungen 2. 2nd ed. Bielefeld: Verlag für Regionalgeschichte, 2004.

Werner, Ernst. *Jan Hus: Welt und Umwelt eines Prager Frühreformators*. Weimar: Böhlau, 1991.

Wildhaber, Robert. "Feiertagschristus." RDK, vol. 7, cols. 1002–10.

Williams-Krapp, Werner. "'Dise ding sint dennoch nit ware zeichen der heiligkeit': Zur Bewertung mystischer Erfahrung im 15. Jahrhundert." *Lili* 20 (1990): 61–71.

Willi-Plein, Ina. "Opfer in Alten Testament." In Gerhards and Richter, eds., *Das Opfer*, pp. 48–58.

Wilmart, André. *Auteurs spirituels et textes dévots du moyen âge latin: Études d'histoire littéraire*. Paris: Bloud et Gay, 1932.

Wilson, Adrian. "The Ceremony of Childbirth and Its Interpretation." In *Women as Mothers in Pre-Industrial England: Essays in Memory of Dorothy McLaren*, ed. Valerie Fildes, pp. 68–107. London: Routledge, 1990.

Wochnik, Fritz. *Brandenburg: St. Katharinenkirche*. Schnell Kunstführer 2280. 2nd ed. Regensburg: Schnell and Steiner, 2000.

Wohlmuth, Josef. "Opfer—Verdrängung und Wiederkehr eines schwierigen Begriffs." In Gerhards and Richter, eds. *Das Opfer*, pp. 100–127.

Wood, Charles T. "The Doctors' Dilemma: Sin, Salvation and the Menstrual Cycle in Medieval Thought." *Speculum* 56, 4 (1981): 701–27.

Yuval, Israel J. "Jews and Christians in the Middle Ages: Shared Myths, Common Language." In *Demonizing the Other: Antisemitism, Racism, and Xenophobia*, ed. Robert S. Wistrich, pp. 88–107. Studies in Antisemitism 4. Amsterdam: Harwood Academic, 1999.

———. "'They tell lies: you ate the man': Jewish Reactions to Ritual Murder Accusations." In Sapir Abulafia, ed., *Religious Violence*, pp. 86–106.

Ziesak, Anne-Katrin. "'Multa habeo vobis dicere . . . '—eine Bestandsaufnahme zur publizistischen Auseinandersetzung um das Heilige Blut von Wilsnack." *Jahrbuch für Berlin-Brandenburgische Kirchengeschichte* 59 (1993): 208–48.

Zika, Charles. "Hosts, Processions and Pilgrimages: Controlling the Sacred in Fifteenth-Century Germany." *Past and Present* 118 (1988): 25–64.

Index

Notes are indexed only where they contain significant substantive information. Biblical citations are indexed under "Bible" in the order used in the Vulgate. Iconographical motifs and subjects are indexed as a group under "Iconographic motifs." Sites of supposed miracles or relic cult are indexed separately under place names; for classification of sites, see the tables on p. 51.

Acknowledgments

Several invitations were crucial in the genesis of this book. When Paul Freedman asked me to speak at the meeting of the New England Medievalists at Yale University in the fall of 2000—a conference titled "Blood, Sweat, and Tears"—he started me off on years of research, although he is hardly to blame for the fact that I became obsessed with a fifteenth-century obsession. The opportunity to spend the spring of 2000, when I was beginning to draft my essay for Freedman's conference, as a visiting professor at the Aby Warburg Haus in Hamburg, contributed to the art historical turn my early work on the topic took. The firstfruits of that research appeared as "Das Blut und die Körper Christi im späten Mittelalter: Eine Asymmetrie," *Vorträge aus dem Warburg-Haus* 5 (2001) and "The Blood of Christ in the Later Middle Ages," *Church History* 71, 4 (2002). It was the Ellen Maria Gorrissen Fellowship from the American Academy in Berlin and the research I did while at the Hans Arnhold Center in the fall of 2002 that embedded my topic in the local history of Mecklenburg and the Mark Brandenburg. Without the assistance of Yolande Korb, library researcher for the Arnhold Center, I could never have tracked down all those obscure nineteenth-century periodicals. At a later stage in working on this project, I profited from the opportunity to spend a week at that scholarly haven (one is tempted to write heaven), the Herzog August Bibliothek in Wolfenbüttel; I am grateful to its director, Helwig Schmidt-Glinzer; Gillian Bepler; and their staff for a warm welcome.

Beyond these debts to conferences and research centers, I have others to individuals, accumulated over many years of thinking about religious practices, images, and texts. For advice about art history, I thank Jeffrey Hamburger, David Stone, Mitchell Merback, Irving Lavin, Jane Rosenthal, and Jacqueline Jung. Without the friendship and advice of Gerhard Lutz, who accompanied me to Heiligengrabe and Bad Doberan, I would not have learned as much as I did about specific sites and liturgical furnishings in northern Germany. For conversations about the power of objects, I thank Josh Fogel, Joan Scott, Oleg Grabar, Mika Natif, Heinrich von Staden, Thomas Walter Laqueur, Ronald Surtz, Eli Friedländer, Michal Grover-Friedländer, and Debora Silverman. On the topic of sacrifice, I have benefited from discussions with Carlin

Barton, Richard Kieckhefer, Susan Einbinder, Madeline Kochen and Rachel Neis. Roberta Bondi, Indrani Chatterjee, Vittorio Hösle, and Shira Wolosky have guided and inspired me in conversations about the power of theological ideas. Peter Brown's penetrating questions have several times put me back on track when I had quite lost the train of my own argument. For research help, I am grateful to Patricia Decker, Jane Sykora, and Jelena Trkulja, to Consuelo Dutschke and Karen Green of the Columbia University libraries, to the entire library staff at the Institute for Advanced Study in Princeton, and above all to Susan Kramer. Hubert Treiber, Karen Margolis, Anne-Marie Bouché, Robert Suckale, Jeffrey Hamburger, and Jiří Fajt generously tracked down art historical references and acquired (or even made) photographs for me. Tsering Wangyal Shawa, with the assistance of Jelena Trkulja, made the map. Jane Sykora helped with the index. Sara Poor advised on some difficult bits of fifteenth-century German. Carmela Vircillo Franklin and Erik Hamer helped with problematic passages in both Italian and Latin, and Franklin gave assistance also with paleography. Gert Melville located inaccessible German material; a visit to his research group in Dresden encouraged me at the very beginning of this project, when I needed it most. Two readers for the University of Pennsylvania Press, Robert Lerner and John van Engen, gave attentive and gracious advice, providing suggestions both on overall argument and on dozens of specific matters of fifteenth-century history. Jerome Singerman, Alison Anderson, and Marie Deer provided many hours of editorial assistance. As always, Joel Kaye, Dorothea von Mücke, Guenther Roth, and Stephen D. White have given critical readings to more drafts than I can keep track of. Without their insistent questions and supportive friendship, I might have drowned between the Scylla of particularity and the Charybdis of generalization.

My greatest debt is to other scholars who have worked on the many topics I explore here, both giants of the past—such as Romuald Bauerreiss, Peter Browe, Louis Gougaud, and Douglas Gray—and others—such as Rachel Fulton, Michelle Garceau, Marlene Villalobos Hennessy, and Mark Daniel Holtz—who are at the beginning of their careers. I am grateful to all those on whose shoulders I have stood.